Investing in Property

Abroad

A Survival Handbook

by
Anne Hall

SURVIVAL BOOKS • LONDON • ENGLAND

First Edition 2007

Copyright © Survival Books 2007
Illustrations & cartoons © Jim Watson
Cover photograph © JakezC (🖥 www.istockphoto.com)

Survival Books Limited
26 York Street, London W1U 6PZ, United Kingdom
☎ +44 (0)20-7788 7644, 🖨 +44 (0)870-762 3212
✉ info@survivalbooks.net
🖥 www.survivalbooks.net

British Library Cataloguing in Publication Data.
A CIP record for this book is available
from the British Library.
ISBN-10: 1-905303-08-4
ISBN-13: 978-1-905303-08-3

Printed and bound in India by Ajanta Offset.

ACKNOWLEDGEMENTS

I would like to thank all those who contributed to the publication of this book, including my long-suffering family and friends and in particular Joanna Styles (friend and fellow Survival Books writer) for her support, advice and encouragement, David Hampshire for his guidance, Graeme Chesters (editing), Joe Laredo (sub-editing and proofreading) and Kerry Laredo (page design, layout and index). Finally, special thanks are due to Jim Watson for the superb illustrations, cartoons, maps and cover design.

TITLES BY SURVIVAL BOOKS

The Best Places To Buy A Home
France; Spain

Buying a Home
Australia & New Zealand; Bulgaria,
Cyprus; France; Greece; Italy;
Portugal; South Africa; Spain;
Buying, Selling & Letting Property (UK)

Buying and Renting a Home
London; New York

Culture Wise
Australia; Canada; England; France;
New Zealand; Spain

**Foreigners Abroad: Triumphs
& Disasters**
France; Spain

Living and Working
America; Australia; Britain
Canada; France; Germany

The Gulf States & Saudi Arabia;
Ireland; Italy; London; New Zealand;
Spain; Switzerland

Earning Money from Your Home
France; Spain

Making a Living
France; Spain

Retiring Abroad
France; Spain

Other Titles
Investing in Property Abroad;
Renovating & Maintaining
Your French Home;
Running Gîtes and B&Bs
in France;
Rural Living in France;
Shooting Caterpillars in Spain;
Wild Thyme in Ibiza

WHAT READERS & REVIEWERS

'If you need to find out how France works then this book is indispensable. Native French people probably have a less thorough understanding of how their country functions.'

LIVING FRANCE MAGAZINE

'The ultimate reference book. Every subject imaginable is exhaustively explained in simple terms. An excellent introduction to fully enjoy all that this fine country has to offer and save time and money in the process.'

AMERICAN CLUB OF ZURICH

'Let's say it at once. David Hampshire's Living and Working in France is the best handbook ever produced for visitors and foreign residents in this country. It is Hampshire's meticulous detail which lifts his work way beyond the range of other books with similar titles. This book is absolutely indispensable.'

RIVIERA REPORTER MAGAZINE

'A must for all future expats. I invested in several books but this is the only one you need. Every issue and concern is covered, every daft question you have but are frightened to ask is answered honestly without pulling any punches. Highly recommended.'

READER

'In answer to the desert island question about the one how-to book on France, this book would be it.'

THE RECORDER NEWSPAPER

'It's everything you always wanted to ask but didn't for fear of the contemptuous put down. Its pages are stuffed with practical information on everyday subjects.'

SWISS NEWS MAGAZINE

'A must for all future ex-pats. Deals with every aspect of moving to Spain. I invested in several books but this is the only one you need. Every issue and concern is covered, every daft question you have on Spain but are frightened to ask is answered honestly without pulling any punches. Highly recommended!'

READER

'If I were to move to France, I would like David Hampshire to be with me, holding my hand every step of the way. This being impractical, I would have to settle for second best and take his books with me instead!'

LIVING FRANCE MAGAZINE

Have Said About Survival Books

'The amount of information covered is not short of incredible. I thought I knew enough about my birth country. This book has proved me wrong. Don't go to France without it. Big mistake if you do. Absolutely priceless!'

Reader

'A mine of information. I might have avoided some embarrassments and frights if I had read it prior to my first Swiss encounters. Deserves an honoured place on any newcomer's bookshelf.'

English Teachers Association, Switzerland

'A thoroughly interesting and useful read, it crams in almost every conceivable bit of information that a newly-arrived immigrant could need. A great book to read and have close at hand when you arrive in Canada to begin your new life. The best all-round handbook on Canada.'

Reader

'A concise, thorough account of the DO's and DON'Ts for a foreigner in Switzerland. Crammed with useful information and lightened with humorous quips which make the facts more readable.'

American Citizens Abroad

'Covers every conceivable question that might be asked concerning everyday life — I know of no other book that could take the place of this one.'

France in Print

'I found this a wonderful book crammed with facts and figures, with a straightforward approach to the problems and pitfalls you are likely to encounter. The whole laced with humour and a thorough understanding of what's involved. Gets my vote!'

Reader

'We would like to congratulate you on this work: it is really super! We hand it out to our expatriates and they read it with great interest and pleasure.'

ICI Switzerland, AG

'If you are thinking of moving to New Zealand this is the book for you. Of all the books about New Zealand I've bought, this is the only one I still refer to.'

Reader

'A vital tool in the war against real estate sharks; don't even think of buying without reading this book first!'

Everything Spain magazine

THE AUTHOR

Anne Hall was born in the UK and began her working life at the BBC in London, where she worked chiefly in broadcasting and television production, both for the BBC and for independent production companies. She studied English literature as a mature student at the University of London and began her freelance writing career after a family move to the Costa del Sol, Spain in 2002. She writes for both UK publications and English-language publications in Spain. She has written *Making a Living in Spain* and *Buying a Home in Cyprus*, both for Survival Books. Anne is married with two children.

CONTENTS

Part 1

IMPORTANT NOTE

Readers should note that the rules and regulations for buying property usually vary considerably from country to country, and in some countries they even vary by region or are open to local interpretation or even 'formulated' on the spot. I therefore cannot recommend too strongly that you check with an official and reliable source (not always the same) before making major decisions, or undertaking an irreversible course of action. **Don't believe everything you're told or read – even, dare I say it, herein!**

To help you obtain further information and verify data with official sources, useful addresses, references and websites have been included throughout the book. Important points have been emphasised in bold print, some of which it would be expensive or even dangerous to disregard. **Ignore them at your cost or peril!** Unless specifically stated, the reference to any company, organisation, product or publication in this book doesn't constitute an endorsement or recommendation and you should always check the credentials of an individual, company or organisation before using its services.

Author's Notes

- Frequent references are made in this book to the European Union (EU), which comprises Austria, Belgium, Bulgaria, Cyprus, the Czech Republic, Denmark, Estonia, Finland, France, Germany, Greece, Hungary, Ireland, Italy, Latvia, Lithuania, Luxembourg, Malta, the Netherlands, Poland, Portugal, Romania, Slovakia, Slovenia, Spain, Sweden and the United Kingdom; and to the European Economic Area (EEA), which includes the EU countries plus Iceland, Liechtenstein and Norway.

- Times are shown using the abbreviations am (Latin: *ante meridiem*) for before noon and pm (*post meridiem*) for after noon.

- Property prices quoted should be taken as estimates only, although they were correct when going to print. Prices vary considerably according to the local property market and the world economy, and are increasing rapidly in many countries.

- In Chapters 1-8 prices are given in sterling (£), while in the country profiles prices are given in local currency with sterling, euro or US dollar equivalents as appropriate.

- His/he/him/man/men (etc.) also mean her/she/her/woman/women. This is done simply to make life easier for the reader and, in particular, the author, and isn't intended to be sexist.

- British English is used throughout, but American English equivalents are given where applicable.

- Warnings and important points are shown in **bold** type.

- The following symbols are used in this book: ☎ (telephone), 🖷 (fax), 🖳 (internet) and ✉ (e-mail).

ON SECOND THOUGHTS,
I'D PREFER IT OVER THERE

INTRODUCTION

If you're planning to buy property abroad or even just thinking about it, this is **THE BOOK** for you. Whether you want a villa, farmhouse, townhouse or apartment, a holiday or permanent home or 'simply' a good investment, *Investing in Property Abroad* will help you make the right decision.

The main aim of this book is to provide you with the information necessary to help you choose, not only the best investment, but also the most suitable country, the most favourable location, and the most appropriate home **to satisfy your particular requirements.** Most importantly, *Investing in Property Abroad* will help you avoid the risks and pitfalls often associated with buying property abroad – and there are still many lying in wait for the unwary – which could be one of the biggest financial transactions you'll ever make.

As is evident from the ever-increasing number of TV programmes, magazines, internet sites and exhibitions devoted to overseas property buying, more and more people are purchasing holiday homes or upping sticks to live abroad – but this doesn't make doing it any easier. If anything, it has become more difficult in recent years to find a good investment or the home of your dreams, as prices rise and eager buyers snap up the few remaining bargains in popular countries and areas, leaving others to explore unfamiliar territory in search of their property idyll.

You may already own a property in your home country, but buying a home abroad is a different matter altogether. One of the most common mistakes people make when buying a home in a foreign country is to assume that the laws and purchase procedures are the same as in their home country. **This is rarely, if ever, the case.** The procedures for buying property can vary considerably from country to country and in some countries even vary with the region or state. The risk of buying property in a foreign country ranges from low to ... watch out! Unless you're aware of the latest regulations and potential hazards – and take legal advice – a purchase can result in serious financial loss, as many people have discovered to their cost.

Before investing a penny in property abroad you need to ask yourself numerous questions, not least **exactly** why you want to buy property. Is your primary concern a good long-term investment or do you want a holiday home or plan to work or retire abroad? What sort of property do you want – and, more importantly, where and what can you afford to buy? How will property taxes, capital gains tax and inheritance tax affect your investment? *Investing in Property Abroad* will help you answer these and many other questions. It won't, however, tell you where or what to buy, or whether having made your decision you will be happy with it; that part is up to you.

Investing in property abroad is usually an excellent investment and can also be a wonderful way to make new friends, broaden your horizons and revitalise your life. I trust this book will help you avoid the pitfalls and smooth your way to many happy years of ownership of a home abroad, secure in the knowledge that you've made a good investment.

Good luck!

Anne Hall
September 2007

1

WHY INVEST IN PROPERTY ABROAD?

Investing in property abroad is no longer the unattainable dream that it used to be for many people. As global interest rates have fallen, pension funds collapsed and property prices regularly outstripped inflation, property has become an increasingly attractive investment proposition – particularly for the British. According to the UK Office for National Statistics (ONS), between 1999 and 2004, the number of homes abroad owned by British citizens increased by 45 per cent to almost 257,000, almost half of these being in Spain. According to consumer research specialists Mintel, however, the current figure is much higher: almost 800,000 – and forecast to rise to 2m by 2027. The Institute for Public Policy Research (IPPR) reported in 2006 that the number of British citizens emigrating each year has increased by around 50,000 a year over the last ten years, more than 1m leaving in the last six years; in 2005, the figure was 198,000 (almost 4,000 per week). Of these, 20 per cent went to Australia, France and Spain being the second and third most popular countries respectively. Many northern European and US citizens are just as enthusiastic about finding a holiday home or investment property abroad.

All property is an investment, whether it's your family home in your own country, a pied-à-terre in Paris, a holiday home in Hungary or a buy-to-let in Bulgaria. So it's important to establish at the outset exactly why you want to buy property abroad. Many people begin by purchasing second homes abroad to use as holiday homes. Some of these people, tempted by the sunny climate and lower cost of living, decide to live in their holiday home permanently, or semi-permanently, when they retire. Some prefer their property to be nothing more than another source of income, a temporary or permanent investment, depending on their requirements.

Growing numbers of ordinary people have realised that investing in property abroad, for whatever reason, can be an affordable and enjoyable way to ensure their future financial security. Secure pensions seem to be a thing of the past, and stocks and shares are complicated and risky, but most people agree that there will always be a demand for property. While this is probably true, you cannot assume that bricks and mortar will always make you money. It's important to ensure that your property abroad turns out to be the kind of investment that you intended it to be by planning your purchase carefully and doing meticulous research.

IMPORTANT CONSIDERATIONS

Your decision to buy a property abroad can have a huge influence not just on your finances but on other aspects of your life, including your health, security and safety; your family relationships and friendships; your lifestyle and well-being; your opinions and view of the world; and, not least, on your cost of living and net worth. Before making any decisions, try to be clear about what you're looking for by asking yourself the following questions:

- How do you plan to use your home abroad?

- If you're thinking of a permanent home abroad, do you plan to work or start a business abroad?

- Are you seeking a second home for holidays or eventual retirement?

- Will it be used for short breaks or for longer stays?

- Do you plan to let it to offset the mortgage and running costs? If so, how important is the property income?

- Are you looking purely for an investment property which you plan to let long or short term and have no plans to use yourself?

- Are you interested in a short-term investment, i.e. a property or land which you plan to sell on quickly for a profit?

Whatever your reasons for investing in property abroad, it's a major financial commitment, so before you make any rash commitments, think carefully about whether you'll be able to afford the kind of home (and lifestyle) that you want. Can you really afford to buy property abroad? What are your prospects? Is your income secure and protected from inflation and currency fluctuations? In the '80s, many people purchased second homes overseas by taking out second mortgages on their family homes, stretching their financial resources to the limit. When the recession struck in the '90s, many of these people had their homes repossessed or were forced to sell at a huge loss when they couldn't meet the mortgage payments.

Once you've decided you can afford to invest in a property abroad and how you want your property to work for you, there are a host of further considerations before you think about the most appropriate country, region or city. These considerations are explored briefly below and in more detail in later chapters of this book, and are dependent on the type of investment you wish to make.

Types of Investment

Whether you're considering a rustic *gîte* in France, a seafront villa in Spain or a buy-to-let apartment in Eastern Europe, your decision should be guided by how the property will work for you, both long and short term.

Permanent Home

Buying a permanent home is a big step but it's one that a growing number of people, young and not so young, are taking. Some have secured a job abroad or want to start a business. Others are simply looking for a better quality of life for themselves and their families or want to experience a different culture. Many have dreams of retiring to the sun. If you plan to use a property as a permanent home, you need to take into consideration any restrictions that might affect your choice of location and type of property. Do you plan to work or start a business abroad? If the answer is yes, you're faced with a completely different set of criteria from those of people who want to retire or semi-retire.

1

Consider whether you'll need (or be able) to learn another language and adapt to a different culture, and whether you'll be able (or allowed) to find work. Will you need to find schools for your children? How good are the transport connections within and to and from the country you're thinking of buying in? Will you enjoy the climate all year? And will you be able to take your pets with you?

If you're thinking of investing in a permanent home abroad, one of the golden rules is to start by renting a property in the area that you're interested in, for at least six months, possibly longer.

Renting helps you familiarise yourself with the area you're considering and its property market before you buy, which is difficult to do from a distance. It also gives you a more realistic view of a place you may have visited only on holiday. A mountain retreat, for example, may be idyllic for short breaks, but if you have to drive a long distance through snow and ice to work or school every day, the idyll could soon turn into a nightmare. Consider all the routine conveniences that you take for granted in your home country; how accessible are shops, local facilities and medical care? What would you do in an emergency?

An investment in a permanent home abroad is principally an investment in your future happiness and security; any financial gain should be considered a bonus.

Holiday or Second Home

A holiday or second home can give a return in many ways, not all of them financial. It can provide you, your family and friends with rent-free accommodation for holidays, while (hopefully) maintaining its value and possibly producing a capital gain, if property values rise faster than inflation. You may also be able to let the property while you aren't using it, either long or short term, which will generate income. Many people buy property and let it until they decide to move abroad permanently when they retire. This can provide a regular income or ensure that maintenance costs and mortgage payments are covered until retirement, at which point the mortgage is paid off and the home is yours to enjoy. If you plan eventually to retire to the property, you also need to consider residence issues for retirees, banking and pensions and taxation laws.

Buy-to-let & Capital Investment

The popularity of buy-to-let and capital investment in property abroad has increased significantly over the last decade or so. This type of investment is no longer solely the domain of the rich but is also open to 'ordinary' people, who choose property investment over other types of investment for optimum capital return. The increase in value of the worldwide property market makes it a tempting prospect, but you should consider disadvantages as well as advantages before you decide to proceed. It's a risky business, so if you aren't a natural risk taker, think again. When buying to let, you should ensure that the rent will cover the mortgage (if applicable) and running costs, taking into account periods when the property isn't let. If the property isn't even paying for itself, let alone providing an income, it its value as an investment is diminished.

Bear in mind that rental rates and competition vary according to the country and region, and an area with high rents and occupancy rates today may not be so popular next year.

There are many different types of capital investment, one of the most popular being to buy one or more properties off-plan to sell before completion. This is known as flipping and is explained in detail in **Chapter 4** (see page 92). Alternatively, you might prefer to buy a property in need of renovation or restoration, which you plan to do up and sell at a profit, or to buy land on which to build a single home or several homes (property development). This kind of investment requires intensive research into the political and economic stability, purchase procedures and mortgage market in your chosen country. You must also consider likely short- and long-term capital appreciation, rental prospects, local building laws, taxation of property assets for non-residents and currency exchange rates. There are also often a host of extra costs to consider, such as maintenance and management fees if you have an agent in the country handling your property for you.

All of these issues are considered in detail in the following chapters. **Unless you're a seasoned investor with plenty of available funds, you shouldn't regard buying property abroad merely as a financial investment, but also as an investment in your family's future happiness.**

2

HOLIDAY & SECOND HOMES

Growing numbers of people have decided that investing in a holiday or second home is now within their reach. By using their savings or equity in their main home, or taking out a foreign currency mortgage (perhaps all three), they are able to buy their little piece of holiday heaven. If this is what you're considering, careful planning will ensure that your second home is an investment rather than a liability.

It's difficult to be precise about the number of people investing in a holiday or second home abroad, but those from the UK and northern Europe seem to have the most voracious appetites for a stake in the overseas property market. The UK's Office of National Statistics (ONS) estimates that in the last ten years the number of Britons who own property abroad has almost doubled. Investing in a home abroad can be an excellent long-term investment, although in recent years many people have had their fingers burnt in the volatile property market, particularly in European countries such as France and Spain. In many countries, local people don't buy domestic property as an investment, but as a home for life, so you shouldn't expect to make a quick profit (although it's possible). In most countries, you must usually own a home for at least three years simply to recover the costs associated with buying, and in many, capital gains tax (see page 137) can wipe out much of the profit on the sale of a second home. Check the costs and taxes associated with property purchase and sale in your chosen country in the **Country Profiles**.

There are a variety of ways to get the most from your holiday or second home, but before you commit yourself to a purchase, it's important to decide on your priorities. Will your second home be used solely for holidays by you, your friends and family and, if so, what kind of holidays do you enjoy? Do you want to let the property for all or part of the year? Do you plan eventually to retire to the property? There are often several reasons behind the purchase of a holiday home. Some people decide to let their property, so that running costs are covered until they're ready to retire. Naturally, if you're planning on eventual retirement to your holiday home, there are many more factors to take into account than if you're 'simply' buying a home to holiday in (see **Chapter 2**).

LOCATION

Whatever your reasons for investing in a holiday or second home, location is of prime importance. It's even more imperative if you plan to let your property for part of the year (see **Letting** on page 45). A property in a reasonable condition in a popular area is likely to be a better investment than an outstanding property in an out-of-the-way location. **The wrong decision regarding location is one of the main causes of disenchantment among foreigners who have invested in property abroad.**

If your home will be used only by you and your family and friends, the world is your oyster. Your principal criteria are your own holiday preferences (beach, sightseeing, activities, etc.) and your financial resources. However, you should also consider how easy a property might be to sell at a later date, should that become necessary. For example, while you might delight in a remote country property, it will limit the number of prospective buyers and probably take longer to sell than a more accessible home. If you have no specific idea about where you want to invest your money, do as much research as possible. See **Chapter 5** for details of useful publications and foreign property exhibitions, and refer to the **Country Profiles** at the end of this book. Draw up a shortlist of countries or areas of interest and, most importantly, make a list of what you want and don't want from a property. This will help you avoid feeling overwhelmed.

Once you've made a shortlist, try to visit the countries and regions you're interested in several times and at different times of the year, to help you get a feel for the neighbourhood (it's often better to walk than to drive around). Take into account the immediate surroundings as well as the general area or region. If you're planning to holiday out of the traditional tourist season, remember that somewhere that's wonderful in summer can be forbidding and inhospitable in winter (or vice versa if you don't like extreme heat and crowds). In any case, you should view a property a number of times before deciding to buy it.

Accessibility

Whatever use you want to make of your holiday or second home, one of the major considerations should be transport connections (e.g. air, sea, road and rail links) with your home country. Think about when and how often you're likely to want to travel to your second home. If you intend to make frequent trips back and forth, it obviously makes sense to choose somewhere that involves a relatively short journey **and** isn't too expensive. If a long journey is involved, you should bear in mind that it takes most people a day or two fully to recover from a long journey, particularly when a long flight (and possibly jet-lag) is involved.

Is the property close to an international airport or port and with reasonably easy access to a main road? Are there frequent air, sea and road connections and what's transport like both at the height of summer (when roads may be impossibly clogged) and out of season (when public transport may be curtailed or non-existent)? Don't believe all you're told about the distance or travelling times to the nearest airport, main road, beach or town, but check yourself. Journey times to and from airports in resort areas are always longer in the summer months. Once you arrive at your destination, you may want to stay put, especially if you're on holiday. However, if you want to explore your surroundings, it's useful to find out about the reliability of public transport or whether you need to hire a car to get the most out of your stay.

Airlines

Many people base their property-buying decisions on budget airline routes, which offer cheap and frequent flights to convenient airports. The availability of cheap flights is one of the main factors influencing the steep rise in the number of people investing in property abroad. However, it's worth remembering that budget routes can change or be withdrawn at short notice, so it's wise to look at countries and areas which are also served by 'major' airlines.

Popular locations have plenty of flights to choose from and many airlines offer discounts for shareholders and special deals for frequent fliers. Check the airlines that fly to your chosen destination (see **Country Profiles** starting on page 175), including the national airline, budget airlines and charter flights, although some charter flight companies can be unreliable, especially during the busy summer season. Don't forget to take into account journey times to and from the airport and how easy the journey is.

Airlines usually offer lower prices for flights booked via the internet and for some destinations it may even be cheaper to fly via another country than to take a direct flight from your home country. Take the time to shop around for the lowest fares available. British readers can compare the fares listed in newspapers such as *The Sunday Times*, the *Observer* and London's *Time Out* entertainment magazine.

Sea, Road & Rail Links

It may be possible to drive to your home abroad, using cross-channel ferry services or the Channel Tunnel. One of the main advantages of being able to drive is that you can take much more luggage with you (including provisions unavailable locally) and the cost for a family may be significantly lower than using public transport. If you plan to take a pet with you, it's usually less stressful for the pet to travel by car, although you must ensure you have all the correct paperwork to hand for inspection (see **Pets** on page 148). Those travelling between the UK and the continent by ferry can make substantial savings (around one-third) by joining a 'property owners' club' such as those operated by Brittany Ferries for homeowners in France and Spain. P&O shareholders owning a certain amount of stock receive discounts of up to 50 per cent on most routes. Long-distance ferries (e.g. from Ireland to France or from the UK to Spain) may be another transport option, though they can be expensive and tedious. Check if it's possible to travel by rail, e.g. via Eurostar from the UK to France? What does it cost? How frequent are trains at the time(s) of year when you plan to travel.

Communications

If your second home is a retreat from the hustle and bustle of normal life, you may not care if you cannot get a telephone for months or that mobile phone reception is variable to non-existent. On the other hand, if you're planning to spend longer periods in your home or eventually to retire there, communications will be important to you. Before you commit to a property, check how long it takes to get a land line connection (in many countries it can be months!) and, if you think it necessary, a high-speed internet connection. Check whether your mobile phone will work (you may have difficulty getting a signal in a remote location). Communications are considered in more detail in **Chapter 3** and in the **Country Profiles**.

Facilities

Assess the local facilities and amenities, taking into account the present and future needs of all members of your family. How far is it to the nearest town with reasonable shopping facilities, e.g. a supermarket? How would you get there if your car was out of action? Rural villages often have few if any shops or facilities, which may be your idea of heaven while on holiday, but if you require regular supplies for day-to-day living it may not be practical to be miles from places where you can buy them. What about the proximity of leisure activities and medical facilities in case of an emergency? These are points which can easily be overlooked when you fall in love with a holiday home, but you ignore them at your peril!

2

TYPE OF PROPERTY

If you're buying a holiday home that will be occupied for only a few weeks a year, you may be satisfied with a studio or a one-bedroom apartment. On the other hand, if you're looking for a home that you may want to spend longer periods in or retire to, your priorities will be different. Before committing yourself to any property, you should have a clear idea of your long-term plans and goals. What sort of home will best suit these? An apartment or a detached house? New or old – perhaps something in need of renovation? In the country or in a town, on the coast or inland? Do you want a mature garden or prefer to create one from scratch? How much land do you want?

Often investing in a home abroad provides the opportunity to buy a home of a size and style that you couldn't afford in your home country. However, it's important to be realistic when it comes to the size of a property. Many people buy a bigger house and more land than they need simply because prices are relatively low and their dream has suddenly become feasible. Bear in mind that a large property, particularly an older property, requires a lot of work to maintain it and keep it clean, particularly when it has a large garden and a swimming pool. If it's a holiday home, you're unlikely to want to start running repairs and overdue maintenance as soon as you arrive for your annual break, and if you're retired you may be unable to maintain the property yourself. Can you afford to employ someone to do it for you?

When you're considering what kind of property to buy, you must also consider how easy it may be to sell. Depending on your budget, most experts recommend investing in a two-bedroom apartment as a minimum. This gives you a wider range of prospective buyers than, for example, a studio flat or an expensive villa. Buying a huge house with acres of land may seem like a good investment but, should you wish to sell, buyers may be thin on the ground, particularly if the price has doubled or trebled after the cost of renovation. Buyers naturally become scarcer as prices go up, unless a property is outstandingly attractive, in a popular area **and** in a superb location.

Resale Properties

Resale (or second-hand) properties are often good value abroad, particularly in resort areas, where many apartments and townhouses are sold fully furnished, although the quality of furnishings varies considerably (from beautiful to junk) and may not be to your taste. Luxury apartments and villas, however, are rarely sold furnished. With a resale property you can see exactly what you get for your money (unlike when buying off plan), most problems will have been resolved, and previous owners may have made improvements or added a swimming pool, which may not be fully reflected in the price. You also save on the cost of installing water and electricity meters and telephone lines, or the cost of extending these services to a property.

When buying a resale property in a development, you should ask neighbours about any problems, community fees, planned developments and anything else that may affect your enjoyment of the property. Most residents are usually happy to tell you, unless of course they're trying to sell you their own home! You should consider having a survey done on a resale property even though in many countries this isn't common practice or part of the purchase procedure. If it's an old house, it may have been built with inferior materials. Common problems include rusting water pipes, poor wiring, humidity and rising damp, uneven flooring, collapsing façades, subsidence, and cracked internal and external walls. Some of these problems are even evident in developments less than five years old. The cost of a survey is a small price to pay for the peace of mind it provides.

Owners often advertise their properties directly in the local expatriate press or simply by putting a 'for sale' sign in the window. Note, however, that although it may be cheaper buying directly from an owner, particularly when he's forced to sell, you should still employ a lawyer to carry out the necessary checks. If you're unsure of the value of a property, you should obtain an independent valuation from an experienced local valuer.

Old Properties

If you want a property with abundant charm and character, a building for renovation or conversion or one with outbuildings and/or a large plot, you must usually buy an 'old' property. In many countries it's still possible to buy a 'derelict' property for a relatively small amount of money, although you usually need to carry out major renovation and restoration, which can double or even treble the price. Because the purchase cost of unrestored buildings is usually low, many foreign buyers are lulled into a false sense of security and believe they're getting a bargain, without investigating the renovation costs. **Bear in mind that renovation or conversion costs are invariably more than you imagined or planned!**

Derelict properties seem to set some hearts racing, but romantic dreams about restoring a property to its former glory should be firmly resisted. Don't even go and look at this kind of property unless you have the courage, determination and money to overcome the many problems you will certainly face (it isn't for the faint-hearted!). Unless you're prepared to rent another property or live in a caravan for a long time, it's better to spend a bit more and buy something habitable but untidy than a property that needs gutting and rebuilding before it can be lived in. In some countries you also need to do battle with obstructive local bureaucrats and negotiate arcane planning laws. **Taking on too large a restoration task is a common mistake made by foreign buyers in some countries, e.g. France and Italy.** Bear in mind that if you buy and restore a property with the intention of selling it for a profit, you must take into account not only the initial price and restoration costs, but also the fees and taxes included in the purchase cost, plus capital gains if it's a second home. It's often more difficult to sell a renovated property at an above average market price (irrespective of its added value) than it is a modern property. The local inhabitants in many countries have little interest in restored properties, which may be an important point if you need to sell in a hurry. If you want to make a profit, you're often better off buying or building a new house.

Even old houses that are in good condition often require extensive modernisation. Some lack basic services such as electricity, gas, a reliable water supply and sanitation. If you're planning to buy a property that needs restoration or renovation, always obtain an **accurate** estimate of the cost **before** signing the contract. As a rough guide, a property in need of total restoration is likely to cost **at least** as much to restore as it does to buy, and it isn't unusual for restoration costs to be two or three times the purchase price. Unless you're a serious do-it-yourself enthusiast, you may be far better off to buy a new or recently built property or one that has already been partly or wholly restored. If you need to pay for total restoration, the cost may be prohibitive and is rarely recovered when you sell.

As with most things in life, you generally get what you pay for with property, so don't expect to secure an exquisitely restored cottage for a song. In some countries, there's a wealth of beautiful castles, spacious manor houses and luxurious country houses costing no more than an average three- or four-bedroom townhouse in northern Europe. However, if this kind of property catches your eye, remember that the reason many are on the market and appear to be so reasonably priced is that the cost of restoration and upkeep is **astronomical!**

New Properties

New properties are widely available in most countries and include coastal and city apartment and townhouse complexes, golf, marina and winter sports developments, and a wide range of individually designed, detached and semi-detached houses, chalets and villas.

Advantages

Although new properties may lack the charm and character of older buildings, they often offer attractive financial and other advantages. These may include a smaller deposit, lower conveyancing fees, lower property taxes, a builder's guarantee, no costs or problems associated with renovation or modernisation and a wide range of fixtures and fittings. Many new properties are part of purpose-built leisure developments, particularly in southern Europe and on Mediterranean islands. These are often on the coast and encompass a golf course, swimming pool, tennis courts, a gym or fitness club and a restaurant. If you prefer this type of property and facilities, check the annual fees (which may be included in the cost of the property), as they can be very high. When buying a new apartment or house off plan, you may be able to choose your bathroom suite, kitchen, fireplace, wall and floor tiles, and carpets, which may be included in the price. You can also choose the decoration and may

2

even be able to alter the interior room layout of the property, although this will increase the price. New homes also usually contain a high level of 'luxury' features.

In most countries new properties are covered by a builder's warranty, e.g. for 10 or 15 years, against structural defects, and it's usually against the law to sell a new house without a guarantee. Other systems and equipment, e.g. the electrical, plumbing and ventilation systems, are usually covered by a minimum two-year guarantee. In some countries, an architect is also responsible for ten years for defects due to instructions given to the builder or problems relating to the land on which it stands, e.g. subsidence. In most countries, a developer, builder and architect must have financial bank guarantees, and stage payments and completion times are strictly monitored.

When you have a limited warranty, such as the first two years of a builder's warranty, you should ensure that any claims for defects are made during the relevant period, e.g. a claim for poor workmanship may need to be made in the first year. If necessary (and to support a claim), have a professional inspection carried out before the warranty expires. **Whether you have a warranty or not, the most important consideration when buying a new home is the reputation and integrity of the builder or developer.** Ask the builder or developer what other homes and developments he has built and ask owners about any problems they've had and whether they're satisfied.

Disadvantages

There are some disadvantages to a new property, especially one in a development. Many are planned as summer holiday homes, which is fine if that's what you want. However, they may not be as attractive if you plan to spend longer periods, holiday out of season or eventually retire there. Such developments can be full of noisy holidaymakers in the summer and deserted and disheartening in the winter. The quality of new homes in many countries is extremely variable and it's often poorer in southern European and Mediterranean countries than in northern Europe and North America. The quality of the materials used is usually reflected in the price, so when comparing prices make sure that you're comparing similar quality. The golden rule is that you get what you pay for, and less expensive properties aren't usually the best built, although there are exceptions.

In some countries, there are no guarantees for buyers against faults in workmanship or materials, such as exist in northern Europe and North America. A small minority of builders and developers in some countries deliberately cut corners, and use inferior or illegal building materials and methods to save time and money. Problems may not come to light for many years, if at all, and when they do the perpetrators know that they can usually avoid responsibility (unless a building collapses). If you do have problems you must usually be extremely patient and persistent to obtain satisfaction.

The problems experienced by people buying off-plan or unfinished properties in some countries have prompted some experts to advise not to buy a property that isn't finished, in a completed development. In some countries, almost half of all new properties have construction defects or deficiencies and in one third of cases the contract conditions aren't met, particularly regarding the completion date and the quality of materials used. See also **Avoiding Problems** on page 33.

COST OF PROPERTY

A factor which attracts many property buyers to foreign countries is the low cost of homes compared with their own countries. However, you should bear in mind that there are high property purchase fees in some countries (see **Country Profiles**), which can add as much as 20 per cent to the purchase price. When investing in a home abroad you should also bear in mind the cost of maintenance and upkeep.

Agents often declare that there has never been a better time to invest in a home abroad, but whether or not this is true depends largely on where you buy. In established markets such as France and Spain, the mid-'90s was the best time to buy, when homes in resort areas were severely under-valued because of the recession in the early '90s. There was a huge surge in the sale of holiday and permanent homes in popular resort and rural areas, e.g. in France and Italy, in the late '90s. This resulted in spiralling prices, which doubled in just a few years in many popular areas. Many established markets have stabilised over the last few years (since around 2001), which is why there's so much interest in emerging markets, such as eastern Europe.

Local inhabitants in many countries are often astonished at the high prices foreigners are prepared to pay for nondescript homes in uninspiring areas. The French think that the British are particularly insane for buying their tumbled-down farmhouses and crumbling *châteaux* (few foreigners share the British passion for spending their holidays and weekends up to their elbows in bricks and mortar).

Apart from obvious points such as size, quality and land area, the most important factor influencing the price of a property is its location. A home in an area popular with local and foreign buyers can cost two or three times as much as a similar property in a remote location. Similarly, the closer to the coast, the higher the cost of property, properties on a fashionable coastline (such as the French or Italian Riviera) costing up to £7,000 per square metre. You also usually pay a hefty premium for properties in ski resorts in all countries because of the high cost of land and infrastructure and the year-round letting potential.

Sellers generally expect buyers to haggle and rarely expect to receive the asking price for a property. **In popular areas, asking prices may be unrealistically high, particularly to snare the unsuspecting and ignorant foreign buyer.** Always do your research, compare prices and try to obtain a reduction, even if you think a property is a bargain. Find out how long a property has been on the market, as the longer it has been for sale, the more likely a lower offer will be accepted. The state of a property and its surrounds is usually a good indication of how long it has been empty. Generally the older the property, the more likely you are to get the price reduced (unless it's a period property in excellent condition).

If you're dealing with an agent, you should always discuss an offer with him. If you make a lower offer, you should indicate to the owner a few points of weakness (without being too critical) which merit a price reduction. In some countries, however, if you make too low an offer, an owner may feel insulted and refuse to do business with you. If a property has been realistically priced, you shouldn't expect to get more than a 5 or 10 per cent reduction. Cash buyers in some countries may be able to negotiate a considerable price reduction, e.g. 20 or 25 per cent, for a quick sale, depending on the state of the local property market. An offer should always be made in writing, as it's likely to be taken more seriously than an oral offer.

To get an idea of property prices in different regions of a country, check the prices of properties advertised in magazines, newspapers, and property journals and websites. **Before deciding on the price to offer, make sure you know** *exactly* **what's included in the sale, as it isn't unusual for sellers in some countries to strip a house bare and take everything that isn't part of the structure.** Ensure that fixtures and fittings which are included in a purchase are listed in the contract and check that they're still there before signing the final contract.

2

Fees

A variety of fees (also called closing or settlement costs) is payable when you buy a home abroad, but they vary considerably by country, e.g. around 2 per cent in the UK, 5 per cent in the US, 10 per cent in Spain, 12 per cent in Italy and some 15 per cent in France. Most fees are payable by the buyer and may include a lender's appraisal or valuation fee, title search and insurance, mortgage tax and insurance, notary's fees, value added tax (VAT) or transfer tax, land tax, property registration fees, legal fees, surveyor's or architect's fees, and utility connection and registration fees. **Before signing a purchase contract (even a preliminary contract) or paying any money, always check exactly what fees are payable and how much they are, and have them confirmed in writing.**

In many countries, a public official called a notary handles all property sales, irrespective of whether you use an agent or lawyer. He represents the government (not the seller or buyer) and his main task is to ensure that the documentation is in order and that all state taxes and fees are paid on completion of a sale. The notary is also required to withhold capital gains tax in some countries, e.g. France. All fees are payable on completion of a sale.

Land tax is payable in some countries, e.g. Spain. This is a municipal tax on the deemed increase in the value of the land since the last change of ownership. It's usually payable by the vendor, as he's the one who has made the profit, although the purchase agreement may stipulate that the buyer pays. VAT is payable on new properties in many countries and is usually included in the purchase price when they're sold for the first time. In some countries, e.g. France, the fees payable when buying a new property are much lower than when buying an old property (see **Country Profiles**).

Property prices may be quoted inclusive or exclusive of agency fees, which may be paid by the vendor or by the buyer or they may be shared, depending on the country, although it's usual for the vendor to pay in most countries. Always check in advance who pays the agent's fees and whether **all** agents' fees are included in the price quoted; if you negotiate a price reduction, check that the agent or vendor hasn't merely excluded some fees which you must pay separately.

Declared Price

Most property fees are based on the 'declared' selling price and both purchasers and vendors are therefore often tempted to declare a lower price than was actually paid – i.e. to evade tax by making an 'under the table' payment. When buying a property direct from the vendor, you may find that he suggests this, particularly if he's selling a second home and must pay capital gains tax on the profit. (Obviously if the vendor can show a smaller profit, he pays less tax.) **You should steer well clear of this practice, which is strictly illegal (although widespread in some countries).** If you're selling a property, you should also bear in mind that if the buyer refuses to make the illicit payment after a contract has been signed, there's (legally) nothing you can do about it. In many countries the declared price is compared with tables of official or fiscal values maintained by local authorities, and in some, e.g. Spain, reviews of declared values are common and severe penalties have been introduced for gross under-declaration. If you grossly under-declare a purchase, the authorities may have the right to buy it within a specified period, e.g. two years, at the declared price.

Running Costs

In addition to the fees associated with buying a property you must also take into account the running costs. These may include local property taxes (rates) and other fees (e.g. refuse collection tax), community fees, building insurance, utilities (electricity, water, gas, etc.), garden and pool maintenance, telephone, wealth tax, 'letting' tax, and a local fiscal representative's or tax consultant's fees. In most countries, annual running costs average around 2 to 3 per cent of the cost of a property.

AVOIDING PROBLEMS

The problems associated with investing in property abroad have been highlighted in the last 15 years or so and it should go without saying that it pays to exercise extreme caution, especially if you're considering previously unheard-of locations. Think about the precautions you or your legal representative might take when buying property in your home country, such as researching local infrastructure plans, checking title and having a survey carried out. Investing in a property abroad requires at least double the vigilance you might exercise at home. In most countries, the purchase procedure differs from what you're used to (see **Country Profiles**) and in some, the laws regarding the purchase and sale of property are full of holes and an open invitation for dishonest sellers to exploit a foreign buyer's ignorance. For example, professionals operating in many countries aren't required to have liability insurance, and developers are sometimes grossly under-funded. These countries attract more than their fair share of crooks and fraudsters.

On the other hand, a little common sense is also needed and buyers must take full responsibility for their actions. Some buyers do things they'd never dream of doing at home, such as handing over 'bags of cash' to agents and owners without

2

any security whatsoever. While the possible pitfalls shouldn't be exaggerated (there are millions of foreign property owners in a large number of countries, the vast majority of whom encountered few or no problems when buying their homes), nor should they be ignored (they're sometimes difficult to avoid), and your chance of a successful purchase is higher if you follow a few simple rules (see below).

Among the many problems experienced by buyers are properties purchased without legal title, properties built (or extended) illegally, e.g. without planning permission, properties sold that are subject to mortgages or embargoes, properties with missing infrastructure, properties sold to more than one buyer, and even properties sold that don't exist! Checks must be made both before signing a contract **and** before signing the deed of sale. If you get into a dispute over a property deal, it can take many years to have it resolved via the courts, and even then there's no guarantee that you'll receive satisfaction.

In many countries, e.g. Spain, there's a law of subrogation, whereby property debts, including mortgages, local taxes and community charges, remain with a property and are inherited by a buyer. This is an open invitation to dishonest sellers to 'cut and run'. It's possible, of course, to check whether there are any outstanding debts on a property and this should be done by your legal adviser. However, it may be impossible to prevent a seller fraudulently taking out a loan on a property after you've made a check. In some countries, problems arise when people buy unfinished properties (i.e. off plan) or properties on unfinished developments. In most countries there are excellent legal safeguards for people buying off plan and it's a common practice – in fact it's often the only way to buy in a popular development. **However, you should *always* ensure that payments are secured by a cast-iron guarantee.** Common mistakes made by buyers include:

- buying a house in the wrong area (rent first);

- buying a home that's difficult to resell;

- not using professional advice from the start, especially that of a local lawyer;

- buying a home for renovation and not researching the practicalities and the costs;

- not having a proper survey done.

Many people have had their fingers burnt by rushing into property deals without proper care and consideration. It's all too easy to fall in love with the attractions of a property abroad and to sign a contract without giving it sufficient thought. If you aren't absolutely certain, don't allow yourself to be rushed into making a hasty decision, e.g. by fears of an imminent price rise or of losing the property to another buyer. Although many people successfully invest in and enjoy holiday or retirement homes abroad, it's vital to do your homework thoroughly.

Legal Advice

It cannot be emphasised too strongly that the best way to avoid problems if you're planning to invest in (or sell) property abroad, is to take expert, independent legal advice. **Never** sign anything or pay any money until you've sought legal advice in a language in which you're fluent from an experienced lawyer. There are a surprising number of people who invest in a property abroad without obtaining independent legal advice. Those who experience problems have often not taken any precautions whatsoever when purchasing property. Of those that do take legal advice, many do so only after having paid a deposit and signed a contract or, more commonly, after they've run into problems. You'll find the relatively small cost (in comparison to the cost of a property) of obtaining legal advice to be excellent value, if only for the peace of mind it affords. It really isn't worth trying to cut corners to save a few hundred pounds on legal costs when several thousands are at stake. See **Chapter 5** for information about choosing a lawyer abroad.

Inspections & Surveys

Surveys aren't usually performed before purchase in most countries, particularly on a property built in the last 10 or 20 years, often because the vendor must usually certify that a property is free from 'hidden defects'. However, whether it's usual or not, it's always wise to have a survey done before committing yourself to a purchase, especially if you're buying an older property. Many older properties were built with inferior materials, and common problems include rusting water pipes, poor wiring, defective plumbing and drains, rising damp, dry and wet rot, uneven flooring, collapsing façades, subsidence, infestation, bulging walls, and cracked internal and external walls. In fact, in some countries serious problems can often be found in properties built in the boom years of the '70s and '80s, and even in properties less than five years old. **If you would have a survey carried out if you were buying the same property in your home country, you should have one done abroad.**

You can make a satisfactory survey a condition of the preliminary contract, although the vendor may refuse or insist that you carry out a survey before signing the contract. Some lenders insist on a 'survey' before approving a loan, although this usually consists of a perfunctory valuation to ensure that a property is worth the agreed price. Always discuss with a surveyor exactly what will be included in the survey, and most importantly, what will be excluded (you may need to pay extra to include certain checks and tests).

You may prefer to employ a foreign surveyor practising in the country where the property is located (who will write a report in English) rather than a local surveyor. On the other hand, a local surveyor may have a more intimate knowledge of local properties and building methods. Whoever you employ, you should ensure that he's experienced in the idiosyncrasies of local properties and has professional indemnity insurance (which means you can blithely sue him if he does a bad job!).

When you've found a property you like, you should start by making a close inspection of its condition yourself. Obviously the extent of this will depend on whether it's a shell in need of complete restoration, has been partly or totally modernised or restored, or is a new building. A common problem with restored properties is that you don't know how well the work has been done, particularly if the previous owner did it himself. If work has been carried out by professional builders, you should ask to see the bills, as building work in many countries is guaranteed, e.g. for ten years.

Some simple checks you can do yourself include testing the electrical system, central heating and air-conditioning, and checking the plumbing (plus the septic tank, if applicable), mains water and hot water boiler. Don't assume that these are functional, but check them yourself. If a property doesn't have electricity, mains gas, mains water or a telephone line, check the nearest connection point and the cost of extending the service to the property, which can be **very** high. An older building may show signs of damage and decay, such as bulging or cracked walls, damp, missing roof slates and rotten woodwork. In some countries, certain areas are liable to subsidence, radiation (which can cause cancer) and wood-boring insects such as termites. In hot climates, infestations of cockroaches, ants, termites and other insects are common in many areas, even in fairly new buildings. If you find or suspect problems, you should have the property checked by a builder or have a full structural survey carried out by a technical architect, engineer or surveyor.

Expatriate Professionals

You can find professionals who speak English and other foreign languages in all countries, and many expatriate professionals also practise abroad. However, when dealing with a fellow countryman you should never assume that he will offer you a better deal or do a better job than a local person. In fact, the opposite is sometimes true and, sadly, many frauds are perpetrated by foreigners on their fellow countrymen. Deal only with reputable and registered estate agents and other professionals. It isn't unknown for bogus agents or owners to sell the same house to a number of people and disappear with the money.

ESTATE AGENTS

In most countries, the vast majority of property sales are handled by estate agents, particularly those where non-resident foreign buyers are involved. It's common for foreigners in many countries, particularly the UK, to use an agent in their own country who works in conjunction with local agents and developers. When two agents are involved in a sale, the commission is shared, so buyers usually pay no more by using a foreign agent. **However, always check in advance whether this is the case and how much you're required to pay.** Many agents advertise abroad, as well as in local expatriate magazines and newspapers, and many have extensive websites. If your chosen location is popular with foreign buyers, you may find that estate agents have staff who speak English and other foreign languages.

Qualifications

Estate agents in most countries (but not all) are regulated by law and must be professionally qualified and licensed, and hold indemnity insurance. The rules for local estate agents also apply to foreign-based agents, who cannot usually sell property abroad without a local associate. You should choose an agent who's a member of a professional association, most of which insist that members have indemnity insurance and adhere to a code of ethics. The Federation of Overseas Property Developers, Agents and Consultants (FOPDAC, 💻 www.fopdac.com) was established in 1973 and now covers around 50 countries. FOPDAC members must meet the strict criteria of its Code of Ethics. Contact them for a list of their members and for general information about investing in property abroad.

2

Before paying a deposit to an agent, you should ensure that he's licensed (bonded) and that all clients' money is deposited in a bonded (escrow) account. There are unlicensed ('cowboy') agents operating in many countries (particularly in resort areas), who should be avoided like the proverbial plague. Ask to see an agent's registration number and check it if you aren't convinced that it's genuine.

Fees

In most countries there are no controls on agents' fees, although they may be obliged to display them in their offices. An agent's fees may be paid by the vendor, by the buyer, or by a combination of both. Although in most countries it's normal for the vendor to pay, the buyer usually pays in effect, as agents' fees are generally included in the asking price. Note also that if you view a property with one agent, you aren't permitted to buy the property through another agent or direct from the vendor without paying the commission of the first agent.

Viewing

It's wise to do some research and decide the area where you want to live, what sort of property you want (and can afford) **before** visiting agents abroad. Before travelling, obtain details of as many properties as possible in your chosen area and price range, and make a shortlist of those you wish to view. Agents vary enormously in their efficiency, enthusiasm and professionalism, and the best ones provide an abundance of associated information and guidance. If an agent shows little interest in finding out exactly what you want, you should look elsewhere. Many estate agents, especially those in popular countries, have websites, on which you can check what's on offer from the comfort of your home, although sites won't show all properties for sale or the latest properties on their books. Agents' websites have improved considerably in the last few years and many provide not only information about the properties and their areas, but also information about the country, especially for those thinking of relocating there. Some are better than others, so always double-check any information and **never** rely solely on an agent's website for legal or financial information, although they often give good basic advice. It's common in some countries (e.g. France) for agents to send you details of properties that have been sold or were never even available in order to lure you. **Always check that a property (or properties) is still for sale and re-confirm the price before making**

a trip abroad to view it and don't be surprised if it has 'just been sold' when you get there.

2

In many countries, you're usually shown properties personally by agents and won't be given the keys (especially to furnished properties) or be expected to deal with tenants or vendors directly. One reason for this is that many properties are difficult to find if you don't know the area. Many rural properties have no numbers, and street name signs are often virtually non-existent. You should always make an appointment to see properties, as agents need to ensure that the property is available for viewing and they have an agent free to show you around. If you're on holiday, it's fine to drop in unannounced to have a look at what's on offer, but don't expect an agent to show you properties without an appointment. If you view properties during a holiday, it's better to do so at the start of it so that you can return later to inspect any you particularly like a second or third time.

You should try to view as many properties as possible during the time available, but allow sufficient time to view each property thoroughly, to travel between properties and for breaks for sustenance. Don't try to see too many properties in one day (around four to six is usually a manageable number), as it's easy to become confused over the merits of each property. If you're shown properties that don't meet your specifications, tell the agent immediately. You can also help an agent narrow the field by telling him exactly what's wrong with the properties you reject. It's recommended to make notes of both the good **and** bad features and take lots of photographs of the properties you like, so that you're able to compare them later at your leisure. It's also wise to mark each property on a map so that should you wish to return later on your own, you can find them without getting lost. The more a property appeals to you, the more you should look for faults and negative points – if you still like it after stressing the negative points, it must have special appeal.

Viewing Trips

Some agents and developers arrange viewing trips with inexpensive accommodation for prospective buyers and sometimes refund the cost if you buy a property. Some agents advertise 'free' inspection flights, which you then have to pay for if you don't buy anything. Check the small print and conditions of inspection flights as well as the reputation of the estate agent offering them before you sign up. Reputable estate agents will probably vet you and how serious you are about buying before accepting you on an inspection trip, which is expensive to lay on. Most agents offer after sales services and help you arrange legal advice, insurance, utilities, and interior decorators and builders, and may offer a full management and rental service on behalf of non-resident owners. Note, however, that agents may receive commissions for referrals and therefore you may not receive independent advice.

By all means take advantage of such offers, but don't allow yourself to be pressured by a company into buying on a viewing trip. **Some agents expect you to sign up for a property after just a day or two of viewings and may try to pressurise you into a decision.** Tell the agent in advance that you want to see other properties for yourself too; if they're unhappy about this, it may be better to invest a little extra in a 'no-strings attached' trip. Bear in mind that there's always more to an area than what you can see on an inspection trip, which in any case may be designed to give you a favourable impression of an area. Always allow yourself sufficient time to view and compare properties offered by a number of agents and developers. A long weekend isn't long enough to have a good look around, unless you already know exactly what you want to buy and where, or are coming to view just one or two specific properties.

2

Buyer Beware

Remember that an agent usually represents the seller and is trying to get the highest possible price for a property (and the highest possible commission for himself) and not necessarily the best deal for you, the buyer. A reputable estate agent knows that it's in his interest that everyone goes away satisfied, but some agents leave the buyer in no doubt about where their loyalties lie. Be particularly wary of agents who try to sell you something outside your price range or properties that don't match your specifications. If an agent tries to dictate to you or argue about an offer, go elsewhere.

PURCHASE PROCEDURE

This section contains general information and guidance on conveyancing (or conveyance), the role of the notary, legal advice, types of purchase contract and deposits. Details of country-specific purchase procedures, including taxes payable on purchase, can be found in the **Country Profiles**.

Conveyancing

Conveyancing (or conveyance) is the legal term for processing the paperwork involved in buying and selling a property and transferring the deeds of ownership (a conveyance is a deed or legal document which conveys a house from the seller to the buyer, thereby transferring ownership). Conveyancing is carried out by a lawyer (or solicitor), a public notary and, in some countries, e.g. the UK, a licensed conveyancer. It usually includes the following tasks:

- verifying that a property belongs to the vendor or that he has legal authority from the owner to sell it;

- checking that there are no pre-emption rights or restrictive covenants over a property (such as rights of way) and that there are no plans to construct anything which would adversely affect the value, enjoyment or use of the property, e.g. roads, railway lines, airports, shops or factories. In some countries, many people have had the enjoyment of their property (not to mention its value) reduced by unsightly and/or noisy developments. Check whether there's a zoning plan for the surrounding area and what (if anything) can be built there.

2

- checking whether the land has been registered at the land registry, and ensuring that a new property has the necessary building permits and planning permission (and that they're genuine), and that a building was constructed in accordance with the plans. A newly completed building must usually have a 'habitation certificate', which confirms that it may be lived in. If any alterations or improvements have been made to a building, either internally or externally, they should also have the necessary planning permission.

- checking that there are no encumbrances, e.g. mortgages or loans, against a property or any outstanding debts such as local taxes (rates), community charges, water, electricity, telephone or any other debts. **Note that in many countries all unpaid debts on a property are inherited by the buyer. If there's an outstanding loan or taxes on a property, the lender or local authority has first claim on the property and has the right to take possession and sell it to repay the debt.** It's particularly important to check whether there's an outstanding loan against a property when buying from a builder or developer.

- ensuring that proper title is obtained and arranging the necessary registration of ownership. In some countries, e.g. the US, it's essential (and often mandatory) to have title insurance to protect against a future claim on the title by a third party. In some countries, it's very difficult to get legal title for political and historical reasons, or alternatively, legal title may not be transferred to you until months (or years!) after completion.

Lawyers

There are two main stages in a property purchase when a lawyer or notary usually becomes involved. The first is the signing of a preliminary contract, the second is the completion of the sale at the signing of the deed of sale. **It's important to note that even when a notary is involved, it's often beneficial to use the services of a lawyer, as a notary won't necessarily protect your interests.**

In many countries, hiring an experienced lawyer for a property transaction is standard practice. Before hiring a lawyer, compare the fees charged by a number of practices and obtain quotations in writing. Always check what's included in the fees and whether the fee is 'full and binding' or just an estimate (a low basic rate may be supplemented by much more expensive 'extras'). A lawyer's fees may be calculated as an hourly rate or a percentage of the purchase price of a property, e.g. 1 to 2 per cent, and there may be a minimum fee of £500 or £1,000. **Note that complaints about high lawyers' fees and overcharging on property transactions involving foreigners are common in some countries (see above).**

The cost of conveyancing for a home abroad depends on whether you employ a local or overseas lawyer, or both. If you employ a foreign-based lawyer, i.e. one who isn't based in the country where you're buying a home, you can expect to pay heavily for his services, e.g. around £150 per hour in the UK. It may be worth engaging a lawyer in your home country, to give you added peace of mind. However, many experts believe that when buying property abroad you should employ the services of an experienced local lawyer who speaks English or a language that you speak fluently.

Anyone buying (or selling) a home abroad shouldn't even think about doing it without obtaining expert, experienced, independent legal advice. Your lawyer should also check that the notary does his job correctly, thereby providing an extra safeguard. In some countries, estate agents carry out the conveyancing checks (listed above) for you and pass the information to your lawyer, but it's wise to have your lawyer double-check. See also **Avoiding Problems** on page 33.

2

Notaries

In many countries, conveyancing is performed by a public notary, who must follow a strict code of conduct and sign a personal insurance covering his professional responsibility and guaranteeing clients against any errors he may make. He also usually has a financial guarantee covering money temporarily held in his care.

A notary, however, represents neither the seller nor the buyer, but the government, and his main task is to ensure that the documents are in order and that all state taxes are paid on the completion of a sale. A notary may check only planned developments directly affecting the property itself and not those that might affect its value, such as a new railway line or motorway in the vicinity. (A new motorway or railway that disturbs the peace of your home will severely affect its value, although a new motorway junction or railway station a few kilometres away may increase a property's value considerably.)

Where applicable, a notary is responsible for ensuring that a sales contract is drawn up correctly and that the purchase price is paid to the vendor. He also witnesses the signing of the deed, arranges for its registration (in the name of the new owner) in the local property register and collects any fees or taxes due. **He doesn't verify or guarantee the accuracy of statements made in a contract or protect you against fraud.** Don't expect a notary to speak English or any language other than the local language (although some do) or to explain the intricacies of local property law. Even when a notary is involved in a purchase, it's wise to employ a lawyer specialising in local property law to safeguard your rights and oversee the notary's work. When the services of a notary are obligatory, you must pay a set fee for his services, irrespective of whether you employ your own lawyer.

Purchase Contracts

The first stage when buying a home abroad is usually the signing of a preliminary contract. Although it isn't always necessary to employ a lawyer before signing a preliminary contract, it's recommended, even when you're protected by local law. **Most experts believe that you should *always* have a preliminary contract checked by a legal adviser before signing it.** If necessary, obtain a translation of a contract before signing it, but bear in mind that translations are often so poor as to be misleading or meaningless (and they aren't usually legally binding).

Types of Contract

2

Property sales contracts vary greatly in different countries and you should always be guided by your legal adviser. In most countries, there are different types of preliminary contract, depending on whether you're buying a resale property or a property 'off plan', which is yet to be built or is under construction. When buying off plan it's common to sign a reservation or option 'contract' (subject to satisfactory completion) and care should be taken that you aren't asked to sign a binding purchase contract. However, you may not be able to dictate or influence the type of contract used and it may vary with the country, the area or even the individual agent or developer.

Conditional Clauses

In some countries, preliminary contracts – whether for resale or new properties – may contain conditional clauses detailing conditions that must be met to ensure the validity of the contract. Conditions usually apply to events beyond the control of the vendor or buyer. If any of the conditions aren't met, the contract can be suspended or declared null and void and the deposit returned. If you fail to see through a purchase and aren't covered by a clause in the contract, you usually forfeit your deposit. On the other hand, if the vendor withdraws from the sale, he must reimburse your deposit and in many countries pay a penalty equal to the amount of the deposit. Note, however, that with some contracts the buyer can be legally compelled to go through with a sale (as can the vendor). A deposit paid on an option or reservation contract on an un-built property should be returnable if you don't proceed. **Always ensure that you know the terms regarding the forfeiture or reimbursement of a deposit.**

The most common conditional clause states that the buyer is released from the contract if he's unable to obtain a mortgage (this condition is compulsory for property purchase in some countries). You should ensure that this clause is included even if you don't need a mortgage; if you change your mind and fail to obtain a mortgage, you will lose your deposit. You must usually make an application for a loan within a certain period after signing a contract and you have a limited time in which to secure it.

There are many other possible conditional clauses, concerning matters such as obtaining government or local planning permission, proposed public works (road, railway, etc.), third-party rights of way or state pre-emption (compulsory purchase), dependence on the sale of another property, and fixtures and fittings being included in the price. In some countries, if you don't ensure the inclusion of the bathroom suite, fitted kitchen or even the light fittings in the contract, you may find them missing when you take possession. Generally, anything that you agree with the vendor should be included as a condition in the preliminary contract. You should discuss whether conditional clauses are necessary with your legal adviser. **Note that in some countries the vendor remains responsible for any major hidden defects in a property for six months from the date of signing the deed of sale (although this is no consolation if he has 'disappeared').**

Deposits

When you sign a preliminary contract, you must pay a deposit. Although the amount varies with the country and the type of property being purchased, it's usually 5 or 10 per cent of the purchase price or a fixed sum (e.g. £1,000). The sum may be negotiable, particularly on expensive properties. Once you've paid the deposit, there's a legally binding agreement between you and the vendor. **If you fail to complete the sale within the specified time, e.g. 60 to 90 days, you lose your deposit.**

The safest and quickest method of paying a deposit is usually to make a direct transfer from your bank to that of the agent or notary who's handling the sale. However, in some countries, estate agents don't have the legal authority to hold money on behalf of clients. All deposits should be held in a separate bonded (escrow) account. Always ensure that you comply with any fiscal rules regarding the importation of money into a country, as this may be essential if you want to re-export the proceeds when you sell the property. A deposit is usually refundable only under strict conditions, notably relating to the conditional clauses mentioned above. **Make sure you know** *exactly* **what the conditions are regarding the return or forfeiture of a deposit.**

Buying off Plan

When buying a new property off plan, it's usual to pay a reservation fee, which is normally forfeited if you back out of the purchase. Before paying any money, you should ensure that a developer, builder or architect has the necessary financial bank guarantees (obligatory in many countries). If a property is still to be built or completed, payment is made in stages. The contract should include the purchase price, the payment of a deposit, the schedule for payment of the balance or stage payments, any extras that you've agreed to purchase, and the intended date of completion. Stage payments vary with the country but are typically 10 per cent on signing the contract, 30 per cent within the next 30 days, 30 per cent on completion of the roof and the final 30 per cent on completion. With off-plan purchases in some eastern European countries (such as the Baltic States), you simply pay an initial deposit and nothing more until completion.

If possible, you should have a clause inserted in the contract allowing you to withhold 5 or 10 per cent of the purchase price for up to six months as a 'guarantee' against the builder not correcting any faults in the property. The completion of each stage should be verified by an architect or other professional representing you abroad. Note that it's important to ensure that money is paid on time; if it isn't, you could lose your deposit or even lose the property to another buyer. See also **Avoiding Problems** on page 33.

Completion

Completion (or closing) is the name for the signing of the final deed, the date of which varies from country to country but is usually one to three months after signing the preliminary contract. Completion involves the signing of the deed of sale, transferring legal ownership of a property from vendor to purchaser, and the payment of the balance of the purchase price, plus other payments such as the notary's fees and any taxes that are due. When all the necessary documents regarding a purchase have been acquired by the official handling a sale, he contacts you directly and requests the balance of the purchase price (less the deposit). He also sends you a bill for his fees and all taxes, which must be paid on completion. At the same time, you should receive a draft deed of sale, which should be complete (without any spaces to be filled later). If you don't understand the deed of sale, you should have it checked by your legal adviser.

Final Checks

When you sign the deed of sale (see below), irrespective of any clauses in the purchase contract, it's usually assumed that you accept the property in its current condition, so you should be aware of anything that occurs between signing the preliminary contract and completion. **Before signing the deed of sale, you should check that the property hasn't fallen down or been damaged in any way, e.g. by a storm or a fallen tree, and that the vendor hasn't absconded with anything that was included in the price (which should be listed in the contract).** In some countries, e.g. the US, it's common to do a final check or inventory when buying a property, usually one or two days before completion. You should list the fixtures and fittings and anything that was included in the contract or paid for separately, e.g. carpets, light fittings, curtains or kitchen appliances. This is particularly important if the furniture and furnishings (and major appliances) were included in the price.

Signing

The final act of a property purchase is the signing of the deed of sale, transferring legal ownership of the property, and the payment of the balance due. Non-resident buyers in some countries must obtain a certificate from a local bank stating that the amount to be paid has been imported in a foreign currency, a copy of which is attached to the title deed. Before the deed of sale is signed, the notary checks that all the conditions contained in the preliminary contract have been fulfilled. It's usual for both parties to be present when the deed of sale is read, signed and witnessed, although you can give a representative abroad power of attorney. This is common among foreign buyers and should be arranged by your lawyer, who may himself have power of attorney. If you don't understand the local language, you can have an interpreter present, although this shouldn't be necessary, as a copy of the deed of sale should have been scrutinised by your legal adviser beforehand.

In some countries, there are no title deeds and ownership is proved and guaranteed by registration of the property at the land registry. The land registry's stamp is placed on the deed of sale, a copy of which is usually sent to the buyer a few months after completion of a sale. If you require evidence of ownership, for example to import furniture and personal effects, ask your lawyer for an attestation.

Registration

When the contract is signed by the official in charge, e.g. a notary, he gives you a certified copy of the deed. A notarised copy is lodged at the property registry office and the new owner's name is entered in the registry. As noted above, you should ensure that the deed is registered **immediately** after signing it, if necessary by registering it yourself. **Registering ownership of a property is the most important act of buying property in most countries.** Until the property is registered in your name, even after you've signed the deed before a notary, charges can be registered against it or someone else can register ownership in his own name. **Only when the deed is registered do you become the legal owner of the property.** Following registration, the original deeds may be returned to you, usually after a number of months. See also **Avoiding Problems** on page 33 and **Conveyancing** on page 39.

Inheritance & Capital Gains Tax

Before registering the title deed, you should carefully consider the tax and inheritance consequences of the person or people in whose name the deed will be registered. Property can usually be registered in one name, both names of a couple, joint buyers' names, the name or names of children (giving a surviving parent sole use during his or her lifetime), or in the name of a local or offshore company. In most countries it's no longer possible to avoid capital gains and inheritance tax by registering a property in the name of an offshore company, although there are exceptions, e.g. Portugal. Whatever you decide, it should be done at the time of purchase, as it can be difficult, expensive or even impossible to make changes later. Consult a lawyer who's experienced in local inheritance law before signing a contract. See the **Country Profiles** for details about inheritance and capital gains tax in your chosen country.

LETTING

A popular option for many people investing in property abroad is letting their holiday or second home for a few weeks or months in the summer or when they aren't using it themselves. If you do this, you can often more than recoup the running costs and pay for a holiday. Much depends on the location of your property and the climate (see below). However, before you consider where to buy a property with a view to letting it, you should consider the financial and legal implications of letting your holiday home.

The first and most important thing to ascertain (even before buying) is whether you're entitled to let a property, as in some countries you aren't (see **Restrictions** below). The next most important thing is not to overestimate the income, particularly if you're relying on letting income to help pay the mortgage and running costs. Remember that you may be unable to cover all your costs from rental income, even if a property is available to let year-round. Buyers who over-stretch their financial resources often find themselves on the rental treadmill, constantly struggling to earn enough money to cover their running costs and mortgage payments. **Most experts recommend that you don't purchase a home in any country if you will be relying on rental income to pay for it.**

Restrictions

2

You should check the local laws about letting before committing yourself to a property. In some countries, short-term holiday letting is restricted or prohibited, especially if you're a foreigner and a non-resident. In Cyprus, for example, short-term holiday letting is, in theory, allowed only if your property is inspected and passed by the country's tourist board. Malta's restrictions have been eased recently, particularly for EU citizens, but your property must still be inspected by the Malta Tourism Authority and the appropriate licence granted. In some states in the US, short-term rentals (generally less than 30 days, but possibly less than six months) are prohibited. Rules vary from state to state and even from area to area within a state (e.g. in Florida), so it's vital to ensure that the kind of letting you're intending is permitted before buying a property. Rentals are restricted in some places in order to protect local hotels (and other businesses offering permanent tourist accommodation) and also because many permanent residents don't wish to live in a community or development where short-term rentals are commonplace. If you're planning to buy a community property, you must check whether there are any local rules that prohibit or restrict short-term letting. You may also be required to notify your insurance company.

Although many people flout letting laws, you should be aware of the correct procedure and the implications of contravening regulations. Details of letting laws in specific countries can be found in the **Country Profiles**.

Tax

In most countries, you have to pay tax on letting income, either in your home country or in the country where the property is located. Get professional advice on your liabilities from a qualified tax adviser and see **Chapter 7**.

Climate

Climate is obviously one of the most important factors governing the 'lettability' of your property. Is it good for most of the year, thereby extending your letting period, or only in the summer? Are there local attractions which can compensate for poor weather out of season?

Location

If you're considering letting your holiday or second home for part of the year, its location is, naturally, of prime importance. While it's important to consider what you and your family want from a property, you should also think about how attractive and practical it might be for other visitors, who may have different priorities (see **Chapter 4**). Related considerations include transport connections, to the property itself and to local attractions such as water parks and beaches. Some locations appeal to various types of holidaymakers, others only to a particular type. For example, your income won't be as high if you choose a location which appeals only to beach-lovers, or skiers or hikers. Some traditional beach locations in southern Spain, for example, also have good walking and hiking country nearby. Cyprus offers skiing on Mount Olympus (depending on the season) as well as beaches and warm, clear waters.

2

Income

There are a number of factors which affect letting income and you should be realistic about them. If your property is a holiday home, for example, you will want to use it for part of the year yourself, when you'll obviously earn no income. Work out the maximum number of weeks that are available for letting. Your income obviously depends on your letting season, which in turn depends on where your property is and what type of holidaymaker you're trying to attract. If you choose one of the more popular holiday locations, which boast plenty of sunshine for most of the year, your letting season will be fairly long, although you won't be able to charge the highest rates all year (see below). If you buy in a ski resort, your season is almost certainly shorter, but you can usually charge higher rates and there may also be a summer hiking season.

Rates

Letting rates vary enormously and depend on many different factors. To get an idea of what you could or should charge, contact a few agents and pose as a prospective tenant, but bear in mind that agents usually quote the highest possible rate. You can also get information about holiday letting rates by contacting holiday rental companies or visiting their websites. Holiday Rentals (💻 www.holiday-rentals.co.uk) and Owners Direct (💻 www.ownersdirect.co.uk) are the two biggest companies in the UK. Both have a wide range of properties from all over the world, making it easy to compare rents and to see the most popular locations at a glance.

Set a realistic rent, especially if there's lots of competition in the area. Add a returnable deposit as security against loss (e.g. of keys) and breakages. Many people have a minimum two-week rental period in the high season. Details of low, mid- and high season variations are provided in **Chapter 4**.

Running Costs

Various maintenance or running costs will reduce your profit. In order to try to identify likely costs, think through all the facilities you would expect to find in a holiday home and the logistics of cleaning and maintenance, as well as factoring in a percentage of annual insurance and utility bills. Your costs will also depend on whether you're using an agent to manage the property (see **Chapter 4**) or doing your own letting (see below).

2 Doing Your Own Letting

Some owners prefer to let a property to family, friends, colleagues and acquaintances, which allows them more control – and **hopefully** the property will also be better looked after. In fact, the best way to get a high volume of lets is usually to do it yourself, although many owners use a letting agency in addition to doing their own marketing in their home country. You need to decide whether you want to let to smokers or accept pets and young children – some owners won't let to families with children under five due to the risk of bed-wetting, and some prefer not to let to groups of young, single people, who may be rowdy and destructive. However, such restrictions naturally reduce your letting prospects.

Contracts

Most people who do their own holiday letting have only a simple agreement form that includes a property description, the names of the clients, and the dates of arrival and departure. However, if you let your property regularly, you may wish to check with a lawyer that your agreement is legal and contains all necessary safeguards.

Marketing

If you wish to let a property yourself, you'll need to spend time and money on marketing. Most of your marketing budget will probably go on advertising, but this should be carefully controlled, as it's easy to spend a lot of money and get little return.

There's a wide range of newspapers and magazines in which you can advertise, e.g. *Dalton's Weekly* (UK ☎ 020-7955 3760, 🖳 www.daltonsholidays.com) and newspapers such as the *Sunday Times* in the UK, though most owners find it's prohibitively expensive to advertise a single property in a national newspaper or magazine. You need to experiment to find the best publications and days of the week or months to advertise.

A cheaper and more targeted method is to advertise in property directories such as *Private Villas* (☎ 020-7955 3768, 🖳 www.privatevillas.co.uk) or on websites such as Owners Direct (☎ 01372-722708, 🖳 www.ownersdirect.co.uk) and Holiday Rentals (☎ 020-8740 3865, 🖳 www.holiday-rentals.co.uk), where you pay for the advertisement and handle the bookings yourself. Another option is to let through a company such as Brittany Ferries Holidays (☎ 0870-9000 259, 🖳 www.brittany-ferries.com), which provides a bond and includes a discount on ferries. **Advertising in printed directories and brochures needs to be arranged the previous year.**

You can advertise among friends and colleagues, in company and club magazines (the advertising may be free), and on notice boards in companies, shops and other public places. The more marketing you do, the more income you're likely to earn, although you should also ensure that you provide a quick and efficient response to any enquiries. Note that it's usually necessary to have an answering machine and preferably also a fax machine.

In addition to advertising locally and in your home country, you can also extend your marketing abroad (or advertise on the internet).

Internet: Advertising on the internet is an increasingly popular option for property owners, particularly a personal website, which is an excellent advertisement and can include photographs, booking forms and maps, as well as comprehensive information about your property. You can also provide information about flights, ferries, car hire, local attractions and sports facilities and links to other websites. A personal website should be easy to navigate (avoid complicated page links or indexes) and must include contact details, ideally an email address.

Brochures & leaflets: If you don't have a website containing photographs and information, you should ideally produce a coloured brochure or leaflet. This should contain external and internal photographs, comprehensive details of the property, the exact location, information about local attractions and details of how to get there (including a map). You should enclose a stamped addressed envelope when sending out details and follow up within a week if you don't hear anything.

Handling Enquiries

If you plan to let a home yourself, you need to decide how to handle enquiries about flights and car hire. It's easier to let clients make such arrangements themselves, but you should be able to offer advice and put them in touch with airlines, ferry companies, travel agents and car rental companies.

Information Packs

After accepting a booking, you should provide guests with a pre-arrival information pack containing the following:

● a map of the local area and instructions how to find the property;

● information about the local area and nearby attractions (available free from tourist offices);

● emergency contact numbers in your home country and the country the property is in;

● the keys or instructions about where to collect them on arrival.

It's ideal if someone can welcome your guests when they arrive, explain how things work, and deal with any special requests or problems.

You should also provide an information pack in your home for guests explaining the following:

- how things work, e.g. kitchen appliances, TV/video, heating and air-conditioning;

- security measures to be observed (see page 51);

- what not to do and possible dangers (e.g. if you rent to families with young children and pets, you should emphasise dangers such as falling into the pool);

- local emergency numbers and health services such as a doctor, dentist and hospital;

- contact details for assistance such as a general repairman, plumber, electrician and pool maintenance person (you may prefer to leave the telephone number of a local caretaker who can contact the relevant person);

- recommended shops, bars, restaurants and attractions, etc.

Many people provide a visitors' book for guests to write comments and suggestions, and some send out questionnaires. If you want to impress your guests, you can arrange for fresh flowers, fruit, a bottle of wine and a grocery pack to greet them on their arrival. Personal touches ensure repeat business and recommendations; you may even find after the first year or two that you rarely need to advertise, as many people return to the same property year after year; simply do an annual mail-shot to previous clients. **Word-of-mouth advertising is the cheapest and most effective.**

Maintenance & Cleaning

If you do your own letting, you'll need to arrange for cleaning and maintenance, including pool cleaning and gardening if applicable. Is there someone reliable nearby who can organise cleaning and regular maintenance of the property for you and, ideally, will meet and greet new tenants and hand over and collect keys? What about those urgent problems that often seem to happen late at night or at the weekend and are impossible to sort out from a distance (e.g. if a tenant arrives and there's no electricity or water)? If you have a professional agent managing the property, all this is taken care of – for a price, of course. However, it may be worth the cost for the peace of mind it affords, and if you have a formal agreement with an agent and things go wrong, you have some comeback.

Ideally you should have someone on call seven days a week. A property should always be spotlessly clean when holidaymakers arrive and you should provide basic cleaning equipment. You need to arrange for cleaning between lets and also at regular intervals, e.g. weekly or twice-weekly, for lets of more than one week. If you use a local agent, they usually arrange cleaning, at your expense.

Caretaker: If you own a holiday or second home, it's beneficial or even essential to employ a local caretaker, irrespective of whether you let it. The caretaker can prepare the house for your family and guests, as well as looking after it when it isn't in use. Ask your caretaker to check it periodically (e.g. weekly) and allow him to authorise minor repairs. If you let a property yourself, your caretaker can arrange for (or do) cleaning, linen changes, maintenance, repairs and gardening and pay bills.

Closing a property for winter: Before closing a property for the winter, you should turn off the water at the mains (required by insurance companies), remove or 'trip' off fuses (except ones for a dehumidifier or air-conditioner if you leave them on), empty food cupboards and the fridge/freezer, disconnect gas cylinders and turn off mains gas, and empty bins. You should leave interior doors and a few small windows (with grilles or secure shutters) open, as well as wardrobes, to provide ventilation. Lock main doors, windows and shutters, and secure anything of value or leave it with a neighbour or friend. Check whether any work needs to be done before you leave and, if necessary, arrange for it to be done in your absence. Most importantly, leave a set of keys with a neighbour or friend and arrange for them (or a caretaker) to check your property periodically.

Security

Most people aren't security conscious when on holiday and you should therefore provide detailed instructions for guests regarding security measures and emphasise the need to secure the property when they're out. It's also important for them to be security conscious when in the property, particularly when they're in the garden, as it isn't unusual for valuables to be stolen while guests are outside.

Ideally you should install a safe for your guests (and for yourself when you're there) and leave the key for it in the property. When you or your guests leave the property unattended, it's important to employ all security measures available, including the following:

- storing valuables in a safe (if applicable) – hiding them isn't a good idea, as thieves know **all** the hiding places;

- closing and locking all doors and windows;

- locking grilles on patio and other doors;

- closing shutters and securing any bolts or locks;

- setting the alarm (if there is one) and notifying the alarm company when you're absent for an extended period;

- making it appear the property is occupied, by using of timers and leaving lights and a TV/radio on.

Bear in mind that prevention is always better than cure, as stolen possessions are rarely recovered. If you suffer a robbery, you should report it to your local police station, where you must make a statement. You will receive a copy, which is required by your insurance company if you make a claim.

Furnishings

When furnishing a property that you plan to let, you should choose hard-wearing carpets and/or rugs that won't show stains (although many properties have tiled or marble floors rather than carpets) and buy durable furniture and furnishings. Simple, inexpensive furniture is best in a modest home, as it will need to stand up to hard wear. Small, two-bedroom properties usually have a sofa bed in the living room. Properties should be well equipped with cooking utensils, crockery and cutlery, and it's also usual to provide bed linen and towels (some agents provide a linen hire service). Make sure the bed linen and towels are of good quality and replace them before they wear out.

Appliances should include a washing machine and microwave, and possibly a dishwasher and tumble dryer. Depending on the rent and quality of a property, your guests may also expect central heating, air-conditioning, covered parking, a barbecue and garden furniture (including loungers). Heating is essential if you want winter lets, while air-conditioning is an advantage when letting property in summer, although it's only considered mandatory when letting a luxury villa. Electricity is usually included in the rent, with the possible exception of long winter lets.

Some owners provide bicycles and badminton and table tennis equipment. It isn't usual to have a telephone, although you could install a credit card telephone or one that only receives incoming calls.

Keys

You will need several sets of spare keys (plus spare remote controls for electric gates, etc.), as some will probably get lost. If you employ a management company, their address should be on the key fob (rather than the address of the house). If you lose keys or they can easily be copied, you should change the lock barrels regularly (at least annually). You don't have to provide guests with keys to all the external doors, only the front door (the others can be left in the property). If you arrange your own lets, you can send keys to guests or install a security key-pad entry system, the code of which can be changed after each let.

2

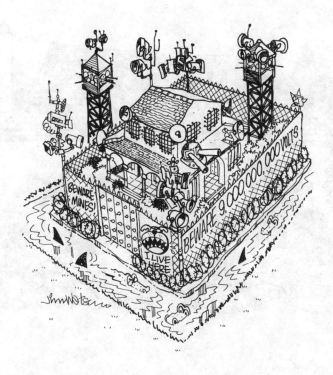

3

A PERMANENT HOME ABROAD

I t's almost impossible to pick up a newspaper or magazine without reading about yet another happy couple or family who have realised their dream of living abroad. If you believe everything you read, record numbers of people (especially in northern Europe) are fleeing their home countries in search of warmer climes. In 2005, a survey by ICM Research in the UK found that over half the British population would move abroad if they could – and an increasing number of them can and do. But if you're thinking of investing in a permanent home abroad, it's crucial to realise that this will have a dramatic effect on you and your family and essential to be realistic about your needs and those of your family. If you aren't, dreams can rapidly turn into nightmares. This chapter looks in detail at the crucial things to consider before you make any irreversible decisions. Information about the type and cost of property and purchase procedures is included in **Chapter 2**, about taking pets abroad in **Chapter 7** and about specific countries is in the **Country Profiles** starting on page 175.

3

WHY LIVE ABROAD?

It isn't just the prospect of better weather that makes people consider living abroad, although many northern Europeans are influenced by the search for a warmer climate. Some people are also keen to escape the 'rat race', experience a different culture and, hopefully, enjoy a more relaxed lifestyle.

Many popular locations for homes abroad (especially in Europe) are no longer a trying journey from family and friends thanks to the budget airlines' ever-growing list of destinations. Even if you choose to live in a country on the other side of the world, an inexpensive internet connection makes the distance from your home country seem less significant, and 'webcam' technology can bring family and friends into your home at any time. The internet also allows many people to work 'remotely', while in any case few people these days are tied to jobs for life, which makes it seem less daunting to move abroad permanently.

If you're thinking of taking the plunge, you should consider **exactly** why you want to move abroad and what kind of lifestyle you want – and, more importantly, can reasonably expect – there. This is particularly important if you're buying a permanent home. Do you, for example, want to work or start a business; do you have children of school age or are you planning to retire, with no need to make a living? Once you've thought through such issues, it will be easier to decide which countries are the most suitable for you to investigate further. A period of reflection is extremely valuable, as it will influence your research and many decisions about your purchase and help you make the right move.

As with any major decision in life, it pays to be cautious: do as much research as possible (see **Chapter 5**) and consider renting for a period before buying (see below).

PERMITS & VISAS

Before making any plans to buy a home abroad, you must ensure that you'll be permitted to use the property for whatever purpose you have in mind and, if necessary, obtain a residence or work permit. A national of a European Union (EU) country, for example, can live and work in any other EU country, although retirees must usually meet minimum income or asset levels. In the US, non-resident foreigners are permitted to buy property, but most aren't permitted to remain longer than six months per year without an appropriate permit (green card) or visa.

If you or a family member wishes to work or start a business in a country where you're planning to buy a permanent home, you should enquire whether it's permitted before making any plans. Details of residence permits, work permits and visa regulations for 34 countries are included in the **Country Profiles** at the end of this book, but in some countries regulations governing permits and visas change frequently, so it's important to obtain up-to-date information from the relevant embassy or consulate in your home country.

Permit infringements are taken seriously by the authorities in most countries and there are penalties for breaches of regulations, including fines and even deportation for flagrant abuses.

3

Working Abroad

If you have plans to make a living in your chosen country, you **must** ensure that it will be possible before making any commitments. If you don't qualify to live and work in a country by birthright or treaty (e.g. among European Union countries), obtaining a work permit may be impossible. For example, Americans and others wishing to work in the EU must normally have their employment approved by a country's Ministry of Labour and obtain an employment visa **before** arrival. Most Europeans find it equally difficult to obtain a permit to work in the US or Canada (unless they buy a business).

Even if you don't require a work permit, you should take a hard look at yourself from a foreign employer's point of view. What are your qualifications and experience? Are they recognised abroad? (The embassy or consulate of your chosen country should be able to help with advice about acceptable qualifications – see **Country Profiles**.) What kind of work can you realistically expect to do? How much can you expect to earn and will it be enough to support you and your family?

You shouldn't assume that you'll secure employment in a particular country unless you have a firm job offer or special qualifications and/or experience for which there's a strong demand. One of the most important factors to consider is how good is your local language ability (see **Language** below). Speaking the lingo will help you to integrate with the local community and put you way ahead of the competition when it comes to finding a suitable job (or any job). Unless you're fluent, you won't be competing on equal terms with the locals and most employers aren't interested in hiring anyone without, at the very least, an adequate working knowledge of the local language.

If you plan to arrive without a job you should have a detailed plan for finding employment and try to make some contacts before you arrive. If you're an EU citizen, you can find out about living and working in any EU member state on the European Union website (🖳 http://ec.europa.eu/eures). It contains general and country specific information.

Self-employment & Starting a Business

Many people turn to self-employment or try to start their own business when they move abroad. It's tempting to throw off the shackles of employment and imagine that you'll be in a position to work as and when you want to. It's all part of the idyllic dream – the beautiful house with wonderful views and the successful business that needs little or no input from you. However, if you need to make a living abroad, you must stop dreaming and be realistic: as anyone who has run his own business will tell you, it's anything but easy, even in your own country where you're doing business in your native language and a familiar culture and have plenty of local contacts. In many foreign countries, you must do battle with often obstructive local bureaucracies, in an unfamiliar language, and come to terms with alien business practices – all with few or no contacts. Although many foreigners do run successful businesses abroad, there are many failures for every success story in most countries. Those who make it do so as a result of extensive market research, wise investment, excellent customer relations, a degree of luck and, most importantly, a lot of hard work.

Most people don't do enough research about business possibilities before moving abroad. If you aren't prepared thoroughly to research the market and obtain expert business and legal advice, you shouldn't even think about starting a business abroad.

RENTING BEFORE BUYING

It's wise to rent a property for a reasonable time before you commit to investing in a permanent home abroad. You may have spent many happy holidays in a country, but living there permanently is a very different matter and, depending on your circumstances, your priorities are likely to be different. If you're uncertain about exactly what kind of property you want, how much you wish to pay or even where you want to live, renting a furnished property for six months or a year reduces the chances of making a costly error.

If possible, you should rent a similar property to that which you're planning to buy and live there for a full year so that you can experience the advantages and disadvantages of your chosen location. An area that's quiet and relaxing between November and March can become noisy, congested and stressful between April and October, particularly in popular holiday regions. Conversely, a place that's attractive in the summer can 'close' in the winter. If you cannot rent for as long as a year, try to visit for two-week periods in each of the four seasons.

Renting allows you to become familiar with an area's weather and amenities and the local people, and to meet other foreigners who have made their homes there, share their experiences, and, not least, to discover the cost of living at first hand. Renting also 'buys' you time to find your permanent home at your leisure. You may even wish to consider renting a home long term (or even 'permanently') as an alternative to buying, as it saves tying up your capital and can be surprisingly inexpensive in many regions. Some people let their family homes and rent one abroad, covering their costs without any commitment.

Rental Properties

There's usually a wide selection of properties for rent in every price range in most countries, particularly during winter, when rates for long lets are often relatively low. Standards vary considerably, from dilapidated, ill-equipped cottages in rural areas to luxurious, beach-side villas with every modern convenience. Most properties are equipped with at least essential facilities, but check that a property has everything you consider necessary, for example central heating if you're planning to rent in winter. Property rental costs vary considerably, depending on the size (number of bedrooms) and quality of a property, its age and the facilities provided, as well as the time of year. However, the most significant factor affecting rentals is location, e.g. whether a property is by the sea or in a village, town or city.

Long-term rentals are hard to find in most popular holiday destinations because it's more lucrative for owners to take short-term holiday lets than long-term residential lets. However, many companies offer long-term holiday lets during the winter months (November to Easter). Elderly people and retirees have traditionally taken advantage of these reduced price breaks to seek out winter sun and save on heating bills, but they're available to anyone. They're a good way to stay in a self-catering apartment or hotel for several months at an extremely reasonable cost while you get to know the surrounding area. But they don't suit all prospective buyers, especially those with young families, who may need more space and prefer to be more settled.

Rental properties are advertised in local newspapers and magazines, particularly expatriate publications, and can be found through property publications in countries such as France, Spain and the US. Many estate agents offer rentals, and developers in many countries rent properties to potential buyers.

Home Exchange

An alternative to renting is to exchange your home for one in your chosen destination for a period of six months to a year. It's a good way to experience 'home living' in a new country for a relatively small cost and save yourself the expense of a long-term rental. Although there's always an element of risk involved in exchanging your home with another family, most agencies thoroughly vet clients and have a track record of successful swaps. Home exchange companies in the UK include Homelink International, 7 St. Nicholas Rise, Headbourne Worthy, Winchester, SO23 7SY (☎ 01962-886882, 🖳 www.homelink.org.uk), which publishes a directory of homes and holiday homes for exchange and Home Base Holidays, 7 Park Avenue, London N13 5PG (☎ 020-8886 8752, 🖳 www.homebase-hols.com). Other companies include Home Swap International (🖳 www.singleshomeexchange.com) and Home Exchange.com (🖳 www.homeexchange.com). *The Home Exchange Guide* by M.

Simon and T.Baker (Poyeen Publishing) gives comprehensive information and advice as well as a list of home exchange companies.

LANGUAGE

If you're thinking of buying a permanent home abroad, it's essential to consider learning the local language, especially if you want to work or do business in your chosen country. Try to learn at least the basics before you arrive and put aside time and money for plenty of lessons once you're settled. Even if you aren't working, a knowledge of the language will help you fully integrate into the local community and way of life. If you're unable to speak the local language, you'll be excluded from everyday situations and may feel uncomfortable and isolated. **The most common reason for negative experiences among foreigners abroad, both visitors and residents, is an inability or unwillingness to speak the local language.** Some foreign residents (particularly British retirees) make little or no effort to learn the local tongue, beyond the few words necessary to buy groceries and order a cup of coffee or a beer, and they often live as if they were on holiday.

Even if you're living in a country or area where English (or your native language) is widely spoken, it's worth making an effort to learn at least the rudiments of the local language, as it will make your daily life far easier. Think about simple, but nonetheless important, benefits such as being able to understand and query bills, use the telephone, deal with tradesmen and communicate with your town hall. If you don't learn the language, you'll be continually frustrated in your attempts to communicate and will be constantly calling on friends and acquaintances to assist you, or even paying people to do jobs that you could easily do yourself.

The most important reason for learning at least a little of the language, especially when you're living permanently in or retiring to a foreign country, is that you may need it to help a loved one in an emergency. Hospital and local welfare services staff don't usually speak English and even in areas where English (and other languages) are commonly spoken, you may find that an English speaker isn't available when your emergency happens. Find out the procedure for contacting emergency services (in many countries there's more than one emergency number, depending on which service you require). Learn basic phrases by heart, such as your address and instructions to find your house in case you need to call an ambulance. Think through the kind of information you might have to tell medical staff and work out how to say it. You must usually learn the language if you wish to make friends among the local inhabitants. It will also help you to appreciate the local way of life and make the most of your time abroad, and will open many doors that remain closed to resident 'tourists'.

Although it isn't easy, making the effort is well worth the 'pain'. Some people claim they aren't very good at languages or are too old to learn anything new, let alone a language. But if you're imaginative and motivated enough to buy a home abroad, you can almost certainly learn the rudiments of a new language. Even if languages aren't your strong point and you're of retirement age, you can usually acquire a working knowledge of most foreign tongues. All that's required is hard work, perseverance and some help. You won't just 'pick it up' (apart from a few words), but must make a real effort to learn.

Remember also that, however terrible your language ability, your efforts in the local language (even including bad grammar, limited vocabulary and a foreign accent) will be far better appreciated than if you make no effort at all and simply speak English (or your native tongue) loudly. The locals may wince as you torture their beloved tongue, but they cannot say you haven't tried!

Language Courses

Many people can teach themselves a great deal by using books, DVDs, tapes, videos and CD- and computer-based courses. However, even the best students require some 'live' help and you may find that the support of a language school and learning alongside others will keep you motivated. Many language schools offer free tests to help you find your level and a free introductory lesson, so take advantage of this before you make a decision. Everyone learns at a different pace, so try not to commit to a very long course to begin with; your language needs will change and you may not want to be tied to a particular language school.

Don't expect too much of yourself: you won't become fluent quickly unless you have a particular flair for languages or already have a good command of the local lingo. A new language comes slowly to most people, but perseverance and practice always pay off. Try to listen to the language as much as possible, for example on television and radio and by paying attention to other people in the street and in shops, etc. If you have difficulty learning languages in the traditional way, you could try the 'suggestological' method, where the structure is assimilated while you're under deep relaxation – apparently it works! Gradually you'll begin to feel comfortable with the language and begin to speak it yourself. **For most people, the key to mastering a language is total immersion in it.**

Language teaching is big business in most countries, with classes offered by language schools, colleges and universities, private and international schools, foreign and international organisations, local associations and clubs, and private teachers. Courses range from those for complete beginners through business- or culture-oriented courses to university-level courses leading to recognised diplomas. Universities in most countries organise summer language courses, and myriad organisations offer holiday courses all year, particularly for children and young adults. If you already speak a language but just need conversational practice, you may wish to enrol in an art or craft course at a local institute or club.

Private Lessons

You may prefer to have private lessons, which are a quicker, although more expensive way of learning a language. The main advantage of private lessons is that you learn at your own speed and aren't held back by slow learners or left floundering in the wake of the class genius. You can advertise for a teacher in local newspapers, on shopping centre/supermarket bulletin boards and university notice boards, and through your and your spouse's employers. Don't forget to ask friends, neighbours and colleagues if they can recommend a private teacher, as personal recommendations are invariably the best.

Further Information

If you're serious about learning the language of your chosen country, a good place to start and a resource you can continue to use once you've made the move, is the impressive languages section on the BBC website (⌨ www.bbc.co.uk/languages). You can gauge your level, do a beginner's online course and get interactive practice on a range of popular topics. The site includes the six most common European languages and Mandarin Chinese.

HEALTH

One of the most important aspects of living abroad – or anywhere for that matter – is maintaining good health. The quality of healthcare and healthcare facilities varies considerably from country to country, although most countries provide good to excellent healthcare for those who can afford to pay for private treatment (many Americans may not agree). This chapter covers some common health problems encountered abroad and your possible entitlement to public health services. Private health insurance abroad is covered in **Chapter 6** (see **Insurance** on page 123).

Health Problems Abroad

Common health problems experienced by expatriates include sunburn and sunstroke, stomach and bowel problems (mostly due to the change of diet and, especially, water, but they can also be caused by poor hygiene), and various problems related to excess alcohol consumption, including a high incidence of alcoholism in some countries. The dangers of disease and infection are considerably greater in some countries. Other health problems are caused by the high level of airborne pollen in spring in many countries, which affects asthma and hay fever sufferers, and noise and traffic pollution (particularly in major cities).

Climate

If you aren't used to hot sun, you should limit your exposure to it and avoid it altogether during the hottest part of the day, by wearing protective clothing and using sun block (or staying in the shade). The climate and lifestyle in any country has a noticeable effect on your mental health, and those who live in hot climates are generally happier and more relaxed than people who live in cold, wet climates (such as parts of North America and northern Europe). The generally slower pace of life in most southern countries is beneficial for those susceptible to stress, although it takes some people a while to adjust.

Pre-departure Check

It's wise to have a full health check before going to live abroad, particularly if you have a record of poor health. The only immunisation that's mandatory is yellow fever for parts of Africa and South America, although a number of others are recommended for some countries, as are anti-malaria tablets.

If you're already taking regular medication, you should note that the brand names of medicines vary from country to country, and you should ask your doctor for the generic name. If you wish to match medication prescribed abroad, you need a current prescription with the medication's trade name, the manufacturer's name, the chemical name and the dosage. Most medicines have an equivalent in other countries, although particular brands may be difficult or impossible to obtain.

It's possible to have medication sent from abroad and no import duty or tax is usually payable. In an emergency a local doctor will write a prescription that can be made up at a local chemist's (pharmacy), or a hospital may refill a prescription from its own pharmacy. It's wise to take some of your favourite non-prescription medicines, e.g. aspirins, cold and flu remedies and ointments with you, as they may be difficult or impossible to obtain abroad or may be much more expensive. If applicable, take a spare pair of glasses or contact lenses with you.

Public Health Services

The majority of residents in European countries are covered for health treatment under a national health service or compulsory health insurance schemes. These provide free or subsidised healthcare for those who make social security contributions, including their families. If you're an EU citizen living abroad permanently, you may be able to take advantage of the public health schemes in other EU countries, but only if you're contributing to the local social security scheme, or if you're a retired pensioner who has paid into a social security scheme in your home country (see **Retirement Abroad** below). If you've been claiming benefits in your home country, check with the relevant government department; many benefits aren't transferable, even within the EU. In the UK, contact the Department of Work and Pensions (DWP), which can advise you on your particular situation. There's extensive information on the DWP website (🖥 www.dwp.gov.uk) about specific countries and particular benefits. Click on the area you need information about and look for the 'Visiting or Living Abroad' section.

If you'll be working or running a business, make it a priority to find out which social security contributions you must or can make, how to register for them and which services you'll be entitled to; you usually have to pay social security contributions for a specific number of years to be able to claim a pension, for example. If you don't qualify for healthcare under a public health service, it's essential to have private health insurance (see **Chapter 6**); in fact it may be impossible to obtain a residence permit without it. Private health insurance is often recommended in any case, because of the shortcomings of public health services and long waiting lists in some countries.

It's vitally important to find out local emergency numbers for police, fire and ambulance as soon as possible after arrival, as well as for a local doctor and the nearest hospital with a casualty unit. Unlike the UK and the US, many countries have a variety of numbers for different emergency services, which can be difficult to remember in an emergency. Keep the numbers close to the telephone, as they could save a life!

3

RETIREMENT ABROAD

If you wish to invest in a retirement home abroad or are planning to buy a holiday home with a view to living abroad permanently when you retire, you must ensure that this is (or will be) possible **and** that you'll be able to afford to live abroad permanently. If you aren't a national of a country that's a member of a treaty zone such as the EU, it's very difficult – often impossible – to obtain a residence permit. Americans may find it difficult to retire in a European country and the US doesn't permit foreigners without a green card to retire in America, irrespective of their income or whether they own a home there.

However, despite the red tape encountered in some countries, an increasing number of people are retiring abroad and the number is expected to rise sharply in the future as more people choose early retirement and are fit and active in their later years. Many retirees seeking a home abroad are northern Europeans, who can often buy a retirement home abroad for much less than the value of their family home. The difference between the money raised on the sale of your family home and the cost of a home abroad can be invested to supplement your pension, allowing you to live comfortably in retirement, particularly when the often lower cost of living abroad is taken into consideration.

However, before planning to retire abroad permanently you must take into account many factors, including the cost of living, pension payments (some countries, such as the UK, automatically freeze state pensions when retirees move to certain countries), eligibility for and the cost of healthcare, investment income and local taxes. In most countries, it's necessary for retirees to have a minimum income and sometimes private healthcare to qualify for a residence permit, and in some countries residents must also own a property (a long-term lease on a property may be insufficient). There are advantages and disadvantages to retiring abroad, although for most people the benefits far outweigh the drawbacks.

Advantages

The advantages of retiring abroad may include a more favourable climate, lower taxation, lower cost of living, increased standard of living, and the availability of a wider range of leisure and sports activities at an affordable cost. For most people, one of the principal benefits is the improved health that results from living in a warmer climate and a more relaxing environment (provided you don't expect things to be done the same way as at 'home'). Those who suffer from arthritis and other illnesses exacerbated by cold and damp weather may enjoy longer and more agreeable lives in a warm climate, while those who suffer from stress are often advised to live in a country with a more relaxed way of life. (If you're planning to retire abroad for health reasons, you should ask your doctor for his advice regarding suitable countries and locations.) For retirees (and many others) the advantages of living abroad add up to an improved quality of life and an increased life expectancy.

Disadvantages

3

The main disadvantages of retiring abroad include separation from family and loved ones; language problems; boredom (what are you going to do all day?); the dangers of too much sun and alcohol, overeating and too little exercise; poor social services, e.g. less state support for the elderly and infirm; danger of disease and infection and inferior health facilities (in some countries); financial problems (resulting from a higher-than-expected cost of living and taxation, exchange rate fluctuations and poor investment); possible loss of pension indexation; homesickness and culture shock.

Before investing in a home that you plan to use for your retirement, you should also consider how you would cope if your mobility was restricted. For example, how would you get to your home if you had to rely on public transport? A house in a remote location may be your dream, but it becomes totally impractical if you suddenly find that you're unable to drive.

Obtaining Information

Retiring abroad is a big step and the most important thing is to be reliably informed, but often this is easier said than done. Many of those offering 'advice' have other agendas, such as selling you property, insurance or other services. If you're a UK citizen, the UK Foreign and Commonwealth Office (or your nearest British embassy or consulate) is an excellent source of reliable information and has downloadable guides about moving abroad and other information for retirees on its website (🖳 www.fco.gov.uk). Click on 'Travel Checklists' in the left-hand menu where you'll find a 'Retiring Abroad' section.

Specialist organisations dedicated to the care of retired and elderly people also offer advice about retiring abroad. For example, Age Concern has a downloadable fact sheet on its website (🖳 www.ageconcern.org.uk). Go to the 'How Can we Help You?/Income and Pensions' section. Age Concern also has branches abroad; contact the information line (UK ☎ 0800-009966) to find details.

US citizens can get reliable information from The Department of State's Bureau of Consular Affairs website (🖳 http://travel.state.gov), which has a section called

'Residing Abroad'. The Department also produces *Background Notes* (💻 www. state.gov/travelandbusiness), which contain useful information on various countries around the world.

Financial Planning & Tax

It pays dividends for your peace of mind if you plan your retirement abroad well in advance and thoroughly research all the financial implications. Your first step is to obtain professional advice on your financial and tax position in your home country and in your intended destination country. You need to look at all your available assets on retirement, whether your future income is likely to be sufficient for your needs, bearing in mind the cost of living, and any income tax and property-related taxes you will have to pay if you become resident in another country.

Financial Advisers

It's wise to consult a reputable independent financial adviser **before** you make any irrevocable decisions. It's the best way to organise your affairs and make the most of your income, as well as ensure that your move abroad is as tax efficient as possible. Financial services in your home country may be regulated by the government but this isn't always the case abroad. Information about financial service providers abroad can usually be found via the regulatory body (if there is one) in your chosen country. Alternatively, the country's central bank, which regulates and supervises the national banking system, usually has this kind of information. Many people believe there's no substitute for a word of mouth recommendation, but always make sure that your chosen adviser is a member of a recognised regulatory body, which ensures that its members abide by a code of conduct.

Assets

A good financial adviser can help you decide how to make the best use of your financial assets, such as your principal home and any savings plans or capital that you may have. You may want to sell up completely to release as much capital as possible to buy your new home or you may wish to retain a property in your home country. It's often wise to keep a small property at home so that you can return easily if things don't work out. Even if you stay abroad, your property at home will hopefully increase in value and can be used for short stays. Check also whether you'll be able to access your savings abroad quickly and easily should you need to.

Income

Work out how much money you think you'll need to live on – then double it! However low the cost of living is in your chosen country, there will always be unexpected running costs for your property and the unforeseen emergencies which always seem to arise when funds are low.

Open a resident's bank account as soon as possible. Rates for residents are often more favourable than those for non-residents, and in any case you'll need a local bank account so that your pension can be paid directly to you. Some other important considerations for your current and future income are:

- whether you can continue to receive your current income abroad. Some government benefits aren't exportable, and some private occupational pensions may not be paid abroad;

- whether your chosen destination is one where your pension is adjusted for cost of living rises;

- whether it's worth 'insuring' against fluctuations in exchange rates, e.g. by taking out a 'forward option';

- how you would cope if your partner died or became ill or infirm. Would that affect your income? Does your health insurance cover professional nursing care or can you afford to pay?

- whether it would be beneficial to open an offshore bank account, which may include an estate planning and asset protection service. An offshore bank can provide increased security and the benefit of dealing with English-speaking professionals who understand the needs of expatriates; it can also help to minimise your tax liability but you must take professional advice before making a decision.

Expenses

Financial planning must also take into account your expenses, the majority of which are likely to be in your chosen retirement location, but some of which may be in your home country.

You may still have a property at home, which will have to be maintained and, if necessary, let to tenants. This isn't easy to do at a distance, so allow for the cost of a managing agent and any repairs in your calculations. Most people retain a bank account in their home country for this purpose as well as having an account abroad.

You may still need to pay tax on income received in your home country, but if you retire to a country which is party to a double-taxation agreement, you should pay tax only in the country where you're considered a tax resident (normally the one where you spend more than 183 days per year). In the British Inland Revenue publishes several free leaflets which provide all the necessary information about your tax liability in its 'International Series'. They can be obtained from any UK tax office or from the Inland Revenue's 'orderline' (☎ 0845-900 0404) or website (🖳 www. inlandrevenue.gov.uk/lealets). The Revenue can also advise you about your situation if you contact the Centre for Non-Residents in Newcastle-Upon-Tyne (☎ 0191-225 4811, 'helpline' ☎ 0845-915 4811). For further information about tax, see **Chapter 6**.

Apart from the initial cost of your property abroad and the fees involved in the purchase procedure, you must consider what your annual running costs will be. If you buy a property in a development, there will be service changes and renovation costs which may not be under your control. Don't forget insurance premiums and allow for emergency repairs. In your cost of living calculations, you should include the cost of running a car (including depreciation), if relevant, and journeys home a couple of times a year. You may miss family and friends to begin with and it's comforting to know that you can afford to see them at least every six months.

Location

3

If you're investing in a home for your retirement, you'll have specific considerations that may not concern people buying a family home, for example. The best way to find out about your chosen location is by renting a property there first (see **Renting Before Buying** on page 58). In particular, what are the leisure facilities in your chosen area like? When you retire, you'll have 'nothing' to do all day and can easily become bored. Transport and communications are also important issues, as is the availability of good medical facilities. How far is the nearest hospital with an emergency department? You're recommended to check these and other local facilities, such as businesses and shops in the area. Many are closed outside the main tourist season, and in some areas even 'essential' services such as public transport and postal collections may be severely curtailed.

Consider also the terrain of your chosen home, as a location with lots of hills or steps could become an insurmountable problem if you have mobility problems or become disabled in later years.

Retirement Developments

Purpose-built retirement developments, which vary from communities for fit and active retirees to sheltered housing for those who require everyday assistance, are well established in the US and UK but less widespread in some other countries, e.g. France and Spain, although generally they're becoming increasingly common. In southern European countries, most developments are built and managed by foreign companies for foreigners, as the local inhabitants prefer to live among their family and friends in their 'twilight' years.

Elderly Accommodation Counsel (EAC) is a registered charity based in the UK which offers independent, free advice to elderly people to help them meet their housing and care needs, including information about housing care for the elderly abroad. You can contact the EAC at 89 Albert Embankment, London SE11 7TP (☎ 020-7820 1343). Its excellent website (🖳 www.eac.org.uk – also available in Dutch, French, German, Italian and Spanish) has general information for those wishing to retire abroad and lists 13 countries which have existing or planned retirement accommodation, with relevant links and useful translations of key words and phrases in all the above languages.

Retirement developments usually consist of one- and two-bedroom apartments or a combination of apartments, townhouses and villas, which can be purchased freehold or leasehold. Properties usually have central heating, air-conditioning, fully-fitted kitchens and satellite television. A wide range of communal facilities and services are usually provided and may include medical and dental clinics (possibly with a resident doctor and dentist), nursing facilities, lounges, laundry, housekeeping, restaurant, bar, meal delivery, handyman, mini-supermarket, post and banking services, guest apartments, free local transport, 24-hour security with closed-circuit television, intercoms, alarm system and a 24-hour multi-lingual reception. Sports and leisure facilities may include swimming pools, tennis courts, sauna, jacuzzi, lawn bowling, gymnasium, video/DVD room, library and a social club.

All sheltered housing developments levy monthly service charges, which can run into hundreds or even thousands of pounds a month. It's important to ensure that you can afford (and will continue to be able to afford) the fees, which may increase annually. The fees may include a number of weeks' (e.g. six) nursing care a year (usually per illness) in a residents' nursing home or even unlimited nursing care in some communities. Note, however, that sheltered housing and retirement communities aren't nursing homes, which can be prohibitively expensive in most countries.

3

Local Community & Neighbours

Find out as much as possible about your prospective neighbours and others living close by. **Good neighbours are invaluable, particularly when investing in a retirement home in a village.** If you'll be living in your property for long periods or permanently, neighbours can have a huge effect on your everyday life. For example, are they noisy, sociable or absent for long periods? Do you think you'll get on with them? If you plan to retire to a development, check whether other owners live there all year or just come for short holidays. Some areas can be like ghost towns for long periods out of season, which can be dispiriting. Are any properties on the development let to tourists during the summer? If they are, the summer could be noisy and disruptive, with holidaymakers partying into the early hours.

The other important factor is whether you want to live in an area with many other expatriates from your home country or as far away from them as possible (practically impossible in some popular locations). You may be happy only mixing with your own countrymen, indeed many expatriate retirees find great comfort in this. However, if you wish to integrate with the local community, avoid foreign 'ghettos' and choose an area or development with mainly local inhabitants. Generally, if you take the time and trouble to integrate into the local community and learn a little of the language, you'll invariably be warmly welcomed.

Transport

General transport considerations are covered under **Getting Around** on page 74, including information about importing a car and driving abroad. If you're retiring abroad, you'll have specific transport considerations, which should include present and future requirements. Make a point of checking local public transport systems, which may be unreliable or non-existent in isolated areas, especially outside the tourist season, as you may not always be able (or wish) to drive. Ask yourself whether you would cope without a car. There's little point in choosing an isolated spot or somewhere with a limited public transport system when in a few years' time you may have to rely on local bus, taxi or train services to get about.

Health & Welfare Benefits

3

Health (and health insurance) is an important issue for anyone retiring abroad. Even if you're entitled to use the public health service (see below), provision for the elderly, sick and the terminally ill may be unavailable or at least not up to the standard of your home country. Foreigners who can no longer care for themselves are often forced to return to their home countries. Welfare provisions, such as old people's homes, community care and district nursing are often non-existent. **It's important to check on facilities available, even if you think (or hope!) you'll never have to use them.** The UK Foreign Office has a downloadable guide for citizens moving abroad on its website (🖳 www.fco.gov.uk/travel). The US State Department has similar information for US citizens (🖳 http://travel.state.gov/travel, which has an extensive 'Living Abroad' section).

The good news for EU pensioners is that they're entitled to use the public health system in other EU countries, either free or at considerably reduced cost. You need to obtain the necessary forms from your home country and submit them to the health authorities in your destination country. In the UK, you can contact the Department of Work and Pensions (DWP), Medical Benefits Section (☎ 0191-218 7547, 🖳 www. dwp.gov.uk) for more information. You can download form SA29, which includes information about social security insurance, benefits and healthcare rights in the European Economic Area (EEA) and must obtain form E121, which should be submitted along with any other paperwork that's required to qualify for free or subsidised healthcare in the destination country. If you're moving to a country outside the EEA, you should contact the International Pension Centre (IPC), run by the Pension Service (part of the DWP), which deals with queries about UK benefits payable overseas (☎ 0191-218 7777).

Foreign Pensions

British Pensions: You can claim a British state pension if you're living abroad, but whether it's indexed (i.e. increases with inflation) depends on which country you're living in. Your pension is usually indexed when you live in an EEA country, but outside the EEA your pension stays 'frozen' at the rate paid when you moved abroad. Before you move, you should ask for a pension forecast, which will tell you how much you've got in your pension fund and how much you'll receive when you reach pensionable age. Contact the DWP's Retirement Pension and Forecasting Advice Unit (RPFA,

☎ 0845-300 0168). If you're already living abroad, you should contact the UK Inland Revenue Centre for Non-Residents in Newcastle-Upon-Tyne (☎ 0191-225 4811, 'helpline' ☎ 0845-915 4811).

You can find out how all social security benefits are affected when you move abroad (including your pension) in leaflet GL29, which is available from any UK social security office. The Pension Service has extensive information on claiming a British pension in more than 30 countries on its website (💻 www.thepensionservice.gov.uk). Alternatively you can call the IPC (see above), which has a Telephone Liaison Unit to deal with calls from overseas about retirement pensions and other benefits.

American Pensions: US citizens are also entitled to receive benefits when they're living abroad, although there are a small number of countries where benefits cannot be paid. Visit US Social Security Online (💻 www.socialsecurity.gov), which has booklets to download that detail procedures for claiming benefits outside the US.

Payments: You should open a foreign bank account as soon as possible after you arrive. In many countries your pension can be paid directly into your account. The DWP (see above) also has information on its website about the practicalities of receiving pension payments abroad. If you're moving to an EU country, you may have to open a non-resident account to begin with, but once you receive a residence permit you can open a resident account. Remember to allow for currency fluctuations and bank charges, which can considerably reduce your pension income.

Other Benefits

If you were receiving any other state benefits in your home country, you'll need to find out whether you can still claim them from abroad. Each benefit has different qualifying rules and some cannot be claimed from outside your home country. If you're planning to retire to a country in the EEA or with a reciprocal social security agreement with your home country, you may still be able to claim them but you must check with the relevant government department. In the UK, this is the Department for Work and Pensions (DWP – see above).

Making a Will

It's important to make a will as soon as possible after arrival in your new home abroad. It may be the last thing you want to consider, but if you die abroad without a will, it can generate distressing difficulties for your heirs. You should have two wills, one for your assets in your home country (if relevant) and a second for any in your destination country, such as your home. Take professional advice to ensure that neither will invalidates the other. You can ask for an addendum to be attached to each will with information about the other. The embassy or consulate of your home country can usually provide a list of local lawyers who can help you in your own language. They will draw up the will and ensure that it's written, signed and witnessed in accordance with local regulations.

Property Rights for Surviving Spouses

Make sure you fully understand the rights of the surviving spouse or partner, should one of you die. In addition, check carefully your responsibilities under local inheritance tax laws (see page 138). **In some countries, the surviving partner doesn't have automatic right of inheritance in the event of death.** You must check the laws in your chosen country of residence very carefully before purchasing a property, and take advice on the method of ownership and the preparation of a local will. It's vital to ensure that the names of all joint owners are entered on the title deeds.

3

SCHOOLS

If you have children of school age, it's imperative to research the schooling options as far as possible in advance of your move abroad. This can be difficult from a distance but it's wise to try to do the ground work from your home country and then take several trips to visit the schools you're interested in – or those your children would have to attend, if you have no choice of schools.

There are a number of considerations to be made before you do anything. The first and most important is whether you want your child to attend a local school, where teaching is naturally in the local language, or an international school, where the teaching is in English and the curriculum and examinations are usually similar to those followed in the UK or US, often with some local adaptation. There are advantages and disadvantages to each option and you (and your children, if they're old enough to decide) should carefully weigh these up.

Local Schools

First you should find out about the education system in your chosen country and, if applicable, region. For EU countries, you can make use of an information network, established by the European Commission, called Euridyce (🖥 www.eurydice.org).

Language

The most obvious advantage (or disadvantage, depending on your view) of a local school – apart from the fact that the teaching is free – is that all teaching is in the local language and young children usually pick it up very quickly because they're immersed in it and using it naturally with other children. Many children respond positively to this immersion and become fluent in a short time, easily making friends and becoming integrated into the school community. This, in turn, is helpful for parents, as they're able to make friends through their children, practise their language skills and become more easily integrated. For some children, however, the experience is a nightmare, as they're forced to sink or swim, are unable to learn at their usual pace and may suffer additional learning difficulties as a result of failing to master the language.

Whether your child responds well or not depends on many factors: the character and attitude of the child, his age, the school and the co-operation of the teaching staff, and even the country in question. Generally, the younger the child, the more easily he will adapt, learn the new language and start making friends. Older children, particularly teenagers, often find it a stressful experience.

Many expatriate children who attend local schools find that, a few years later, they have difficulty with the mechanics of their native language. If children are working hard to master a new language, the old one sometimes gets ignored! As a parent, you may need to ensure that your children have ample opportunity to speak and understand the grammar of their native language. You can give them plenty of support yourself, just by speaking your native language at home, but also by making sure they practise their reading and writing skills regularly.

Long-term Considerations

It may seem a long way off, especially if you have a younger child, but when you consider your child's schooling abroad, you should also consider where you would like him to undergo higher education (e.g. university). For example, if your child follows a local education system, he or she will be prepared for higher education in that country. If you would like your child to attend an institution in your home country, you must ensure that you know what qualifications are required and whether your child's country-specific qualifications can be adapted to meet the requirements.

International Schools

International schools, which provide a UK- or US-style education in English, are the other option if you're taking children abroad, but, of course, they're fee-paying and can be very expensive.

The main advantage of an international school for English-speakers is that children are taught in their native language and can generally follow the same or a similar curriculum, sit the same exams and apply for university in the same way as in their home country. On the other hand, if you send your children to an international school, you run the risk of their not learning the local language fluently and not integrating with children from the local community. The extent of the risk depends on the school in question and you should ask detailed questions about how much time is spent learning the local language and how many local children attend the school. If there's a reasonably high percentage, the chances are that your children will have the chance to integrate with them and practise their foreign language skills both inside and outside the classroom.

The number of international schools across the world is growing steadily and students aren't just expatriate children but also local children (usually those of wealthy families) who want a British or American education. This means that usually your child will be integrating with local children as well as expatriate children from many countries, which encourages tolerance and understanding of other cultures. However, not all international schools are created equal and you must make sure you visit the schools of your choice and ask questions about the accreditation system, the curriculum, the academic level and expectations of your child's age group, the target qualifications, and extra-curricular facilities.

The Council of British Independent Schools in the European Community (COBISEC – 🖳 www.cobisec.org) can help with information about schools in the EU. Details of American international schools all over the world can be found on the website of the International Schools Service (ISS, 🖳 www.iss.edu), a non-profit organisation dedicated to helping children who are attending overseas schools. Information is also available from your country's embassy or consulate and local expatriate organisations.

GETTING THERE

One of your principal considerations when investing in a permanent home abroad, whether you intend to retire or live and work there with a young family, is the quality and frequency of transport connections between your chosen country and your home country. You may need to travel frequently on business and family and friends will want to visit you and vice versa. If you intend to make frequent trips back and forth, it obviously makes sense to choose somewhere that involves a relatively short journey **and** isn't too expensive (see **Accessibility** on page 25).

GETTING AROUND

For many people, an important aspect of owning a home abroad is being able to get around the local area easily and cheaply. For most people this means importing, hiring or buying a car, which gives them independence and flexibility. Having your own transport also allows you a much wider choice of where you can buy a home abroad. If you'll be working or have a young family, a car is usually essential, especially if you'll be living some distance from the nearest town. If you plan to retire abroad, think about whether you'll want (or be able) to drive as you get older. Many retirees on a limited budget decide to live in towns, where they can make use of all the local amenities without having to drive.

Whatever your age, bear in mind that driving abroad can be a nerve-wracking and even dangerous experience in some countries. It's particularly difficult to begin with, when it's easy to get lost in an unfamiliar area and you may have to adapt to driving on the opposite side of the road; some people never get used to it. A car can be a liability in towns if you don't have private parking and you'll save a lot of money if you can manage without one.

Public Transport

If you don't drive or aren't planning to own a car abroad, you usually need to buy a home in a city or large town where there's adequate public transport. Check this carefully before you commit to a property. In some countries, public transport is poor, there's no rail service and only an infrequent and unreliable local bus service. Remember that services which are fairly frequent during the summer, when there are plenty of tourists, may be non-existent during the winter months. If you've decided that a rural idyll is for you, it's usually essential to have your own transport. Think carefully about your everyday needs (such as shopping) and how you would cope in an emergency.

3

Importing a Car

Many people buy an inexpensive car in their home country and drive it to their home abroad. Before planning to do this, you should check whether it's permitted (it may need to be modified to meet local regulations) and the costs involved (import duty and local insurance, road tax, etc.), and compare them with the cost of hiring a car. Check the regulations of any country you're planning to pass through to reach your destination. If you're travelling outside western Europe, you may need a *Carnet de Passages en Douane* (*CPD*), which is a customs document that identifies your car. The number of countries that require this is diminishing, but check with the motoring association in your home country before making any plans.

If you're an EU national moving permanently to another EU country, you can import duty-free and use a vehicle that has been registered in your home country, **but only for a limited period**. This is the same as the time that a non-resident is permitted to remain in another EU country without becoming a resident, which is a maximum of six months (183 days) in a calendar year. After that period you must register and insure your car, have it inspected (for roadworthiness) and pay local road and vehicle taxes. If you plan to live abroad permanently, it's usually easier to buy an inexpensive car locally because once the six-month period has elapsed, you must find a way to dispose of your imported vehicle or drive it back to your home country.

Hiring a Car

If you don't import a car, you may decide to hire (rent) one for a short period until you find a suitable car to buy. Plan this in advance because hiring a car can be prohibitively expensive in some countries, particularly during the high season. You can usually get better rates for longer periods and out of season. **There are inexpensive car hire companies in some countries, but exercise extreme caution if you hire from one of them, as cars can be unroadworthy or even dangerous.** One way to reduce the cost is to hire a car through the American office of an international car rental company such as Alamo, Avis, Budget and Hertz, and pay by credit card. This is a legitimate practice and can save 50 per cent or more on local European rates. The US freephone (800) numbers of other international hire companies can be obtained from international directory enquiries. (Note that when dialling freephone numbers from abroad, you're charged at international rates.)

Driving Abroad

An International Driving Permit (IDP) is recognised around the world and identifies you as a legal driver when accompanied by a driving licence from your home country. You don't need an IDP when driving within the European Union (although it's often useful to have one), but in some countries outside the EU they're compulsory. Contact the recognised motoring organisation in your home country for information about which countries require them.

In most countries, foreign residents can exchange their driving licence for a local licence without taking a test (although a test is necessary in some countries, depending on your nationality). If you have a driving licence issued by an EU country, it's no longer necessary to exchange it for a local licence when you're resident in another EU country (unless you're caught for infringing the rules), but you may be required to register with the local motoring licensing authorities.

You may be unfamiliar with the road rules and regulations in the country where you're planning to buy a home, which may differ considerably from those in your home country. The following tips are designed to help you survive driving abroad:

- If you're planning a long journey, a mechanical inspection for your car is recommended, particularly if it's some time since your car's last service or inspection.

- Don't forget your car registration and insurance papers, passports, identity cards, visas and vaccination certificates (also for pets). Make sure you have sufficient local currency (for petrol, tolls, food, fines, etc.) for the countries you'll pass through.

- Note that the procedure following an accident isn't the same in all European countries, although most western European countries use a standard accident report form provided by insurance companies. As a general rule, you should call the police to the scene of anything other than a minor accident.

- Ensure that your car complies with local laws and that you have the necessary equipment. For example, spare tyre, spare bulbs and fuses, warning triangle (in some countries, e.g. Spain, you need two), first-aid kit, fire extinguisher, petrol can (note that carrying cans of petrol or keeping petrol in plastic containers is forbidden in some countries) and headlight beam deflectors. Check the latest regulations with a motoring organisation in your home country.

- Seat belts must be worn in all European countries and in North America. In some countries dipped headlights (low beam) must be used at all times.

- If you're moving to a country where traffic drives on the opposite side of the road from your home country, take extra care until you're accustomed to it. Be particularly alert when leaving lay-bys, T-junctions, one-way streets and petrol stations, as it's easy to lapse into driving on your usual side of the road. It's helpful to display a notice, e.g. 'Keep right!' or 'Keep left!' as a constant reminder on your car's dashboard.

● In continental Europe, where all traffic drives on the right, most main roads are designated priority roads, as indicated by a sign, the most common of which is a yellow diamond on a white background (the end of priority is shown by the same sign with a black diagonal line through it). On roads **without** priority signs and in built-up areas, you must give way to all vehicles coming from your RIGHT. **Failure to observe this rule is the cause of many accidents.** If you're ever in doubt about who has priority, always give way to trams, buses and all traffic coming from your RIGHT (particularly large trucks!). Emergency (ambulance, fire, police) and public utility (electricity, gas, telephone, water) vehicles attending an emergency also have priority on all roads in most countries. Note that at roundabouts (traffic circles) vehicles on the roundabout normally have priority and not those entering it, usually indicated by a 'give way' sign.

● Drivers of foreign-registered cars must have the appropriate nationality plate or sticker affixed to the rear of their car when motoring abroad. (If your nationality plate has been incorporated into the registration plate, a separate nationality plate isn't required.) In many countries you can be fined on the spot for not displaying it, although this seldom happens. Cars must show the correct nationality plate only and not an assortment.

● The legal blood alcohol level when driving varies with the country: it's 80mg per 100ml of blood in Mexico, New Zealand, the UK, the US and Canada; in most European countries the level is lower (50mg per 100ml) and a few countries have a zero level. Note also that the strength of alcoholic beverages (and the size of drinks) varies considerably from country to country.

Never carry anything across an international border unless you're absolutely sure what it contains, as it could contain drugs or other prohibited goods. The same applies to any passengers (and their baggage) that you pick up on your journey.

COMMUNICATIONS

The availability of good communications makes the decision to buy a permanent home abroad less daunting. The world seems to get smaller every day, thanks to improved technology and the growth of the internet. Wherever you choose to live abroad, if you have a high-speed internet link, anything is possible – or so it seems. Business correspondence, photographs and videos of your friends and family can all be sent at the touch of a button. Internet telephone services (see below) allow you to talk freely to people thousands of miles away for a fraction of the cost of a similar call on a standard telephone line.

On the other hand, the range of services and reliability of postal services and telephone systems vary considerably all over the world. You won't be able immediately to enjoy all the benefits of the internet if it takes weeks or months (or years!) to have the necessary lines and cables installed.

Telephones

Most developed countries provide an excellent telephone service, although there's a long wait to have a telephone line installed in some countries (you can sometimes pay a surcharge to have a phone installed quicker). Telephone services in specific countries are detailed in the **Country Profiles**. There are public call boxes in many countries which allow you to make inexpensive international calls and use a pre-paid phone card or credit card.

International Calls

The cost of international telephone calls varies widely from country to country and can be prohibitively expensive. However, competition in most countries has increased considerably in recent years and it's now possible to make international calls at a fraction of the cost of even just a few years ago. Shop around and compare call rates from a number of companies. There's a confusing array of cheap call plans, and you should consult individual companies to find the cheapest rate for particular countries. The most dramatic development in this sector in recent years is the growth of internet telephone services (see below).You must have a high-speed internet connection, but once you've downloaded the relevant service, calls are significantly cheaper and the traditional telephone providers are struggling to compete.

Internet Telephone Services

Technology has improved considerably over the last few years and it's now possible to chat to friends and family on the other side of the world for little or no cost, via the internet. Calls are usually excellent quality. Costs and services vary. With all services you must initially download software from the provider's website. Some companies then allow free calls to other users of the same service and charge a small fee for calls outside the system. Some services require a headset, which you must plug into your computer, while others offer a 'callback' system and you simply use your standard telephone handset. In some countries you can use internet telephone services from call boxes, by dialling a short prefix.

Mobile Phones

Most countries provide a mobile phone service in densely populated areas, many nationwide. A mobile phone is particularly useful in countries where there's a long wait for the installation of a fixed telephone line. In some countries there are more mobile phone users than landline users. Note, however, that in some countries mobile phones are expensive to buy and operate, and have high connection fees, standing charges and call rates. You can use a mobile purchased in your home country abroad if your phone and the country in question operate on the Global System for Mobile (GSM) communications system. Ensure that your phone will operate in the country you're planning to visit, e.g. in North America you normally need a tri-band phone that operates across three frequencies. However, so-called 'roaming agreements' are invariably expensive and it's usually cheaper to buy a local SIM card, which allows you to take advantage of local rates, although you should check that your phone is 'unlocked' or 'open' (i.e. can take a SIM card).

Digital mobile phones that subscribe to the GSM communications system can be used to make and receive calls in over 160 countries (called international roaming). For information about individual countries, contact the GSM Association, 6-8 Old Bond Street, London, UK (☎ 020-7518 0530, 🖳 www.gsmworld.com/gsminfo/gsminfo.htm). Before using a GSM phone abroad, you must contact your service provider to make sure that your tariff allows this and check the roaming charges, which can be high. Remember that, as well as any calls you make, you'll be charged for receiving calls on your GSM phone when you're abroad. If you're going to be living abroad permanently or for long periods, it's therefore cheaper to buy a mobile phone locally once you arrive.

International tariffs can vary by hundreds of per cent according to your network provider and your contract. It's a complicated business checking out all the tariffs and special rates, but each company has a list of its rates on its website. Check the country specific information in the **Country Profiles**, which gives details of the websites of the main mobile telephone providers in each country.

Fax Services

Fax machines are available in all countries, although the cost varies considerably. It may be possible to take a fax machine abroad, but you must check that it's compatible or that it can be modified at a reasonable cost. Most fax machines made for use in a European country will operate in most other European countries, although getting a fax machine repaired abroad may be difficult unless the same model is sold locally. Public fax services are provided by main post offices in many countries, although they may only send faxes, not receive them. It's possible to send and receive faxes via a computer. Telexes can also be sent via post offices, and telexes and faxes can be sent and received via major hotels, business services offices and newsagents in many countries.

4

BUY TO LET &
CAPITAL INVESTMENT

There has been an enormous increase in the number of people investing in buy-to-let properties and making capital investments abroad, not just in traditional holiday hotspots, but in many other parts of the world. According to the UK Office of National Statistics, Britons invested over £23bn in property abroad during the years 2000-04. Those who let their properties for all or part of the year earned around £190m in rental income. This chapter provides information for people whose plans to buy abroad are purely investment driven, whether they're looking for a buy-to-let property or wish to make a short- or long-term capital investment.

Thanks in part to a global property boom, which has been gathering pace over the last ten years, increasing numbers of people are investing in property abroad. Some are seasoned investors who might normally have restricted their portfolios to stocks and shares, but have begun to view property as a more stable or profitable investment. Others are new to investment but, thanks to rising property prices in their home countries, have benefited from increased equity in their principal homes, which has made mortgages are easier to obtain (in the UK and elsewhere) and foreign investment feasible.

A 2006 survey by UK research analyst Mintel found that many people are disillusioned with the return they're receiving (or will probably receive in the future) from their pension plans. Buy-to-let or capital investment mean that they can generate an income or a lump sum to supplement their pension. While it must be remembered that, like stocks and shares, the value of property can go down as well as up, many people feel it's a more tangible and realistic investment. And it has suddenly become within the reach of many people for a variety of reasons, which has 'democratised' property investment.

The growth of information technology has played a part, as it has revolutionised the research capabilities of anyone with a high-speed internet connection. An enormous amount of information about the property market in almost any country can be accessed quickly, while budget airlines have made international travel easier and cheaper. There are very few countries (especially in Europe) not served by budget airlines and these airlines' lists of new destinations are very similar to the roster of emerging property investment hotspots. Many of these places were physically inaccessible to foreigners until recently, good examples being those countries once under the control of the former Soviet Union.

PRINCIPAL CONSIDERATIONS

While this kind of investment is easier to make than it was a few years ago, it still requires careful research and a business-like approach if you're going to give yourself the best chance of getting a worthwhile return on your investment. Before deciding if property investment is suitable for you, ask yourself the following questions:

- Am I a risk-taker or do I prefer security?

- Am I aware of all the risks involved and how comfortable am I with taking those risks?

- Can I afford to tie up capital in the medium to long term?

- How much can I afford to invest?

- How likely is the value of the property to rise during this period?

- Can I rely on a regular income from my investment? How easy will it be to generate that income, e.g. to find tenants?

- Will there be extra costs, e.g. management fees and maintenance charges?

- Will I be able to pay the mortgage (if relevant) if the property is empty, and if so, for how long?

- Do I have enough information to make a rational decision?

Once you've answered these questions, you can begin to think about whether you want a buy-to-let investment or a capital investment. **Whichever you decide on, you must be clear from the start about the kind of gain you want from your investment. It's only a good investment if it achieves that aim.**

4

Exit Strategy

Before investing in a property, you must have an 'exit strategy'; in other words, a plan as to when and how to sell in order to make the best return on your investment – which is an art (or science) in itself. If you've done all the research you can into the country's economy, the property market, and the mortgage and rental market – i.e. if you avoid countries and regions where there is, or could be, an oversupply of similar properties (which is usually the case in established markets such as popular holiday destinations) – you should already know what your exit strategy is. An experienced investor will always be looking for the next emerging market, buying into it as early as possible and selling before it becomes too popular. If you want to do the same, the key is professional advice and research, more research and continuing research to keep one step ahead of developments in the global property market. For information about selling, see **Chapter 8**.

BUY-TO-LET

Traditionally, people wanting to buy to let follow the sun to popular holiday home destinations such as France and Spain, but some are discovering a wealth of other locations around the world, where their money goes further. A new generation of property buyers is realising (and estate agents everywhere aren't slow to point out) that their investment can give them a regular return if they let all year or put the property in the hands of an agent or developer who will manage it for them. This type of buy-to-let property should be considered solely as an investment and it's important to distinguish it from letting a holiday or second home which you use yourself for part of the year, which is discussed in **Chapter 2**. If you're looking at buy-to-let as an investment, you'll be interested in more than just covering the running costs and reducing the mortgage payments. If so, when choosing a property, you should focus less on your own preferences and more on letting potential, both to tourists and to the local market.

Maximising your investment means choosing the right property in the right location, but that's often easier said than done. Newspapers and magazines, television and radio programmes and the internet all offer views – not always convergent – on where the emerging markets are. There are promises of booming economies and flourishing housing markets, but the promises are usually made by those with an interest in your buying there. You must research the rental market carefully, looking at how it has developed historically and any economic or political factors that may affect it in the future. If you're prepared to make a financial commitment, you must also commit to seek out expert, independent information (see below for sources) and not be swayed by 'promises' of high rental returns or yields, which vary with the country, the city and the property. When comparing yields, take into consideration the difference between gross yield (the annual rent as a percentage of a property's value) and net yield (after expenses have been deducted), the latter usually being around 2 to 3 per cent lower.

Research

If you're new to buy-to-let investment, researching the market can be a daunting prospect, not least because of the wealth of information available. Property exhibitions (see page 106) are useful for potential investors because they give an overall perspective of the property and lettings markets in several different countries. Try to banish preconceived ideas about a country or area: just because you've enjoyed holidaying in a particular location, it isn't necessarily a good place to invest. Conversely, you should look at markets in countries you've never even considered. Make a short list of those that seem to be the best investment prospect, bearing in mind the considerations below, and then research each in more detail. You can do this by looking at the **Country Profiles** at the end of this book or by using other research tools, which are also detailed in **Chapter 5**.

Your research should cover the following:

- **Climate** – Is this important in your chosen location (i.e. will your market be predominantly holidaymakers or local people)? If so, how many weeks per year can you expect good weather (or snowfall)?

- **Transport links** – If you plan to let to holidaymakers, it's important that the property be within easy reach of an international airport served by a range of airlines, ideally offering established scheduled services as well as budget flights. Ensure that there's also easy access to major road and rail networks.

- **Economy** – A strong economy means the likelihood of increased wealth in the country or region and hence a high demand for property, to buy and rent. Signs of a healthy economy include low inflation, low unemployment and high foreign investment. If you're considering letting (or buying) property as an investment, the best way to benefit is to buy when a country's economy is at the start of a period of growth. Such countries or locations are usually known as emerging markets (see below), but you need to be well informed to see one coming.

● **Political stability** – While it's obvious that investing in a war zone isn't a wise move, what isn't so obvious is whether a foreign government (and its laws regarding foreign property ownership) could change to your detriment. Look at the country's recent political history: does the government have a majority, has it been in power for a while and has it achieved a reasonable amount of economic growth during its term of office?

● **Cost & type of property** – Research what's available and at what price but, more importantly, what is (and is likely to be) in demand by tourists in the short-term and by locals for long-term rentals. While tourists may prefer to rent a romantic, rambling, older property for a couple of weeks, local people are more likely to choose newer properties with low maintenance costs. If you plan to let your property as an investment, it's important to calculate (or at least estimate) which type of property is likely to have the highest rental yield. This will obviously differ depending on what type of tenants you're trying to attract (e.g. whether you'll be letting short term at a high rent for part of the year or long term at a lower rent all year round) and where the property is. For example, if you're investing in a popular holiday location, such as Spain or France, your choice of property could be anything from a two-bedroom apartment to a large family villa, appealing to a range of holidaymakers. If your property is in a city, you may prefer to invest in a new or resale apartment, which should appeal to tourists on a short-break or locals and foreigners who live and work there. Modern properties generally more popular for long-term lets.

● **Purchase & letting restrictions** – Are there any restrictions imposed on foreigners who buy property and land? Will you be permitted to let your property (long or short term)? Some countries restrict letting by non-resident foreigners.

● **Rental market** – It's important that you're clear about which type of tenant you want to attract and that you research the rental market accordingly before you commit to a property. In some countries, it may be more profitable to offer short-term lets to tourists and in others to offer long-term lets either to foreign businessmen or the local population. Get advice about the market from a range of agents, preferably those who are well established in the country, but remember that they may inflate potential letting income, so check that they can substantiate figures and occupancy rates (see **Using an Agent** below). Is the property rental market in your chosen destination well established with reasonable demand from tenants for the type of property you're considering? Or are you looking at a country with an emerging economy and property market, which may – or may not – result in increased demand in the future? Always be cautious about promises of big financial gains and be wary of areas which already seem popular with investors, as there may be a risk of oversupply.

- **Mortgage market** – The local mortgage market is an important consideration and can have a positive or negative effect on your letting potential. A liberal mortgage market for foreigners and locals means that it may be relatively easy for you to get a mortgage to help pay for your property, but it could also mean that it's easier for locals to buy a property than rent one, therefore limiting your letting potential. This applies to several of the ex-Soviet Bloc countries. A more restricted mortgage market may mean you have to obtain a mortgage in your home country, but property to rent will be in demand from locals who are struggling to get a mortgage.

- **Purchase procedure** – How long is the purchase procedure for resale and new properties? How much deposit are you expected to pay and at what point are you legally committed to a property? Most importantly, check that you can have legal title transferred to your name. In some countries (such as Croatia), this can be a serious problem for historical and political reasons, while in others legal title isn't transferred to you until months after you've paid for the property.

- **Taxation** – Look carefully at your tax liabilities as a property owner at the time of purchase and sale and any annual taxes payable. You must also pay tax on the letting income from your property, sometimes in the country in which you choose to be a tax resident, sometimes in the country where the property is.

4

Using an Agent

If you're letting a property abroad in order to earn a regular return on your investment, it's usually wise to use a local agent. Your investment should be regarded as a business and you should allow for the cost of a managing agent in your calculations. It will be very difficult to organise letting remotely yourself. A good local agent will save you the time and expense of advertising and finding clients. What's more, he is (or should be) on the spot and can organise regular cleaning and maintenance, and sort out any problems at short notice. Make sure that an agent has staff dedicated to dealing with lettings who are familiar with the local market. If you're buying a new or off-plan property, the developer or estate agent will often have a letting department or an associate who handles letting.

One of the main advantages of using an agent is their greater marketing power than you as an individual lessor. The larger companies market homes via newspapers, magazines, the internet, overseas agents and coloured brochures, and have representatives in a number of countries.

Agents' commission varies from country to country, so check carefully before you commit yourself. If you want your property to appear in an agent's catalogue or website, you must usually contact him some months before you wish to let it.

Important Questions

It's absolutely essential to find a reliable and honest agent, which means obtaining disinterested recommendations. Always ask him to substantiate rental income and occupancy rate claims by showing you examples of actual income and occupancy on other properties. Request the names of satisfied customers and contact them.

Other things to ask a letting agent include:

● Will the letting income be paid into an escrow account?

● Does he have a bonding scheme which pays you the rent **before** the arrival of guests (some do)?

● If not, when is the letting income is paid?

● What additional charges are made and what are they for?

● Does he provide detailed accounts of income and expenses (ask to see samples)?

● Who does he let to (e.g. what nationalities and whether families, children or singles)?

● How does he market properties?

● Are you expected to contribute towards marketing costs?

● Are you free to let the property yourself?

4

Management Contracts

Management contracts usually run for a year and the services provided depend on the type of property, e.g. whether it's a budget apartment or an expensive villa. A good agent will provide a standard contract, in your native language and the local language, and take care of many other things that you would struggle to deal with from your home country, such as emergency repairs; routine maintenance of the property and garden, including lawn cutting and pool cleaning; cleaning and linen changes between lets; advising guests on the use of equipment and providing them with information and help (24 hours a day in the case of emergencies). Agents may also provide someone to meet and greet guests, hand over the keys and check that everything is in order. A letting agent's representative should also make periodic checks when a property is empty to ensure that it's secure and everything is in order. (You may wish to check whether a property is actually let when the agent tells you it's empty, as it isn't unknown for some agents to let a property and pocket the rent.)

Long- or Short-term Lets?

Long- and short-term lets each have advantages and disadvantages if you're letting purely as an investment. Much depends on the letting market in your chosen location. Are you planning to invest in a property which will be attractive to tourists in a traditional holiday location (which may limit the number of weeks you're able to let it) or would you prefer to buy in a city and offer long-term lets to locals or foreign businessmen? While you can charge more for short-term holiday lets, especially in the high season, you won't have a year-round income. A long-term let gives you a lower weekly rental income but one which is assured throughout the year. A city apartment can be one of the best investments, as lettings aren't dependent on the weather and your property may be popular for long lets and short breaks. You may even be able to let short term all year round.

Long-term Lets

Long-term lets are usually easier in terms of logistics. You don't have to organise frequent changeovers (or pay an agent to do it) and if you choose the right tenant he may stay for several years, assuring you of a relatively hassle-free, regular income. And climatic considerations become irrelevant, as do the provision of facilities such as a swimming pool and the availability of local attractions. A property's letting potential will be determined by the state of the local housing and mortgage market and whether renting property long-term is popular there.

Long-term Letting Locations

In some countries, locals prefer to buy their own property (especially if it's relatively affordable and easy to do) and will rent only as a temporary option. In other countries, renting for long periods, sometimes permanently, is the norm. Large cities (especially capital cities) around the world are usually excellent locations for long-term lets because there's a wide range of potential tenants to choose from. Local workers, expatriate businessmen, diplomats and their families always need accommodation. They (or their employers) pay good rates for high quality properties. A property on the outskirts of a city may be attractive to foreigners and locals as long as it's within easy commuting distance of the city centre. Consider transport links very carefully, including air, road and rail connections. In addition, proximity to shops and amenities, parking facilities and public transport is important.

Short-term Lets

Short-term letting can be lucrative, not only in a seaside location during high season, but also in popular cities that are easy and cheap to travel to for short breaks. You should consider how long your letting season will realistically be in a particular location. It depends on a number of factors:

Climate: This is obviously important in a popular holiday location, where many visitors want to soak up the sun. Properties in areas with a pleasant year-round climate have greater rental potential, particularly outside the high season. If you want to buy in a ski resort, research snow records and the availability of snow-making machines. For city locations, the climate is less important, although good weather is an attraction.

Proximity to an Airport: A property should be within easy reach of a major airport, as most tourists won't consider travelling more than 45 minutes to their destination after arriving at an airport, especially if they're on a short break. Choose an airport with frequent flights from your home country and a range of scheduled and charter flights. It isn't wise to rely on an airport served only by budget airlines, as they may alter or cancel routes at short notice.

Public transport & access: It's an advantage if a property is served by public transport or is situated in a town where a car is unnecessary. If the property is difficult to find, consider how easy it will be to let, and if you buy it, you must ensure that you or the agent provides a detailed map and instructions for finding the property. Holidaymakers who have to spend hours trying to find a place are unlikely to return or recommend it!

Attractions: The property should ideally be close to attractions and a good beach (if relevant). If you want to let to families, a property should be within easy distance of leisure activities such as theme parks, water parks, sports activities and nightlife. If you're planning to let a property in a rural area, it should have leisure, sporting or scenic attractions. Proximity to golf courses is an advantage to many holidaymakers and can be an attraction outside the high season. Properties in city locations should be close to the main tourist attractions such as galleries, museums and places of historical interest.

Swimming Pool: If your property is in a traditional holiday location, a swimming pool is usually obligatory – properties with pools are much easier to let than those without, unless the property is on a beach, lake or river. It's usually necessary to have a private pool with a single-family home (e.g. a detached villa), although a shared pool is adequate for an apartment or townhouse. If you plan to let mainly to families, it's wise to choose an apartment or townhouse with a 'child-friendly' communal pool, e.g. with a separate paddling pool or a pool with a shallow area. Country properties should also have a private pool (some private letting agencies won't handle properties without a pool). You can charge a higher rent for a property with a private pool and it may be possible to extend the letting season by installing a heated or indoor pool, although the cost of heating a pool may be higher than the rental return.

You should have third-party insurance covering accidents and injuries for guests (or anyone) using your pool (and your property in general).

Short-term Letting Locations

If you're intending to buy a property in a traditional holiday location, choose one which will attract a wide range of holidaymakers (see **Chapter 3**). City locations, especially capital cities, are becoming more popular for weekend and short breaks. The capitals of several eastern European countries, for example, have recently begun to claim their share of the short break market, competing with the capitals of western Europe, e.g. Paris, Madrid and Rome.

The eastern European countries that have recently become members of the European Union (EU) – the Czech Republic, Estonia, Hungary, Latvia, Lithuania, Poland, Slovakia and Slovenia – are usually referred to as 'emerging markets' or 'emerging Europe' or the Eastern European Eight. See the **Country Profiles** for detailed information about these countries. Since their independence from the Soviet Union, their economies have grown rapidly, although this is partly because they started from a very low level. Their housing markets are healthy and, partly because they're served by budget airlines, they've become increasingly popular for short breaks, which make them a good letting prospect.

Unfortunately, many of these short break travellers are large groups of young people on boisterous, drunken weekends, making the countries unattractive to other travellers. Local authorities in the countries concerned are trying to control this kind of tourism, but it's still a problem and something you need to be aware of. Travel to a potential location by budget airline on a Friday evening to see whether it's popular with stag and hen parties.

Letting Rates

4

Ask several different agents about letting rates and take an average to discover what's realistic. Rates vary greatly with the season (there are low, medium and high season rates), the region, and the size and quality of a property. Depending on which part of the world your property is in, the high season usually includes the months of July and August and possibly the first two weeks of September. Mid-season usually comprises June, late September and October, plus the Easter and Christmas/New Year periods, when rents are around 25 per cent lower than in high season. The rest of the year is classed as the low season. During the low season, which may extend from October to May, rates are usually up to 50 per cent lower than the high season.

Rentals usually include linen, gas and electricity, although electricity and heating are usually charged separately for long lets in winter. Rates for longer lets are naturally lower and fixed for a longer period, but income is assured and it's less likely that you'll have any void periods (when the property isn't let).

Costs

Ensure that you allow for the various costs that inevitably reduce the profit you'll make. As with letting rates, obtain quotes for management fees from a variety of agents and be clear exactly what services their 'management' includes. Management should include: marketing your property, vetting clients, organising contracts and all maintenance services, i.e. cleaning between and during lets, laundry of household linen, garden and pool maintenance, maintenance of appliances, replacement of damaged or soiled items, and paying insurance and utility bills (note that electricity bills can be high if your property has air-conditioning or electric heating). Some property owners find that their costs can be as much as half the amount received in rent.

Guaranteed Rental Returns

Estate agents and developers in many countries offer guaranteed rental returns, especially on properties bought off plan. This can be a very attractive prospect to an investor and some developers also allow owners to use the property for certain weeks of the year. Under a guaranteed rental return system, you effectively hand the property back to the agent or developer for an agreed period (usually one or two years) and they take care of the letting and guarantee you a certain rent. These offers usually apply only to properties in popular locations, where they can be let easily (and at a profit to the agent or developer). A variation on this principle is 'leaseback', a common letting arrangement in France (see page 212).

Before you commit to this type of agreement, make sure the developer is a well established, reputable company. Check that you really will have ownership of the property at the end of the rental period (some agreements are self-perpetuating and almost impossible to terminate). And ask yourself how easy it will be to let the property once the guaranteed rental period is over. You may find yourself competing with many other similar properties and find it difficult to let your property for a reasonable return. If you're tempted to go for this option, ensure that the property and the location meet all the requirements that make it a good rental prospect (see above).

CAPITAL INVESTMENT

Capital investment in property abroad differs from buy-to-let in that there's no income from the property and it's usually a relatively short-term investment, although it doesn't have to be. Capital appreciation (or capital growth) is the profit on your investment after expenses. To achieve a substantial profit, you must usually buy and sell relatively quickly, and it's an option which has proved attractive to many people. However, some experienced investors recommend that relying on capital appreciation alone isn't wise and suggest combining it with buy-to-let, so that you generate an income as well as achieving a capital gain when you sell. If you decide to opt for capital appreciation alone, be absolutely sure you can afford it before you commit yourself. Your money will be tied up, the property won't be earning you an income, and its value could fall rather than rise. If you aren't an experienced investor, you should take professional advice and be clear about what you want to achieve from your investment and over what period. Ask yourself the following questions:

- How much you can afford to invest?

- What kind of profit do you want to make?

- Do you want a short-, medium-, or long-term investment?

- Can you afford to tie up the money for the required period?

- Are you prepared to research new, unfamiliar markets or do you prefer more established markets? The former are usually more risky but likely to give a better (and faster) return on your investment. The latter are less of a risk but the returns aren't usually as high.

- Can you afford to buy a 'portfolio' of properties in different markets, which will offset risky investments with more stable ones?

● Do you want to invest in one or more properties, using the profit from one to make further investments?

Short-, Medium- or Long-term Investment?

One of the first things to decide is whether you want a short-, medium- or long-term investment. Much depends on how much capital you have and how long you're able or willing to tie it up. The basic requirement for a good property investment – a desirable location in which demand exceeds supply – applies whichever type of investment you choose, but the type of property you buy is often determined by whether it's to be a short-, medium- or long-term investment.

A short-term investment (18-24 months) often involves buying off plan and selling before completion. This is known in the property investment world as 'flipping' and is explained in detail below.

A medium-term investment (e.g. between two and five years) may involve off-plan or resale property. The investor holds onto the property for up to five years (possibly longer), until the price rises sufficiently to sell for a good profit. During this period, the investor may let the property to generate income.

A long-term investment might be a buy-to-let property (see above) or involve buying land to build a new home (or homes) or buying one or more older properties cheaply in order to renovate them.

Short-term Investment & Flipping

This type of investment is high risk but you reap large returns if it's successful. If you opt for it, you should take professional advice, be well informed and put in place as many safeguards as possible to protect your investment (see below). The most common type of short-term investment is often called flipping, which means buying an off-plan property either before construction has started or during construction and selling it after a short period, always before completion.

You pay the builder or developer a booking deposit and, depending on the circumstances, a number of stage payments, following the same procedure as any off-plan purchase, but you sell before completion – when you decide you've made a satisfactory profit. In some eastern European countries (such as the Baltic States), there are no stage payments and you simply pay a booking deposit, which ensures the minimum outlay for this kind of investment. You're in effect funding the developer to continue with construction and the earlier you buy into a project, the cheaper the property usually is, as most developers offer discounts for early commitment. If demand is sufficient, you can sell for a higher price than you committed to the developer for even before completion, when you then pay the developer the agreed balance and pocket the profit – and the new owner incurs the completion costs. It's possible to sell after completion, but then you will have incurred completion costs, which will eat into your profit, though you may be able to sell at a correspondingly higher price to offset these extra costs. Timing is everything.

The key to success with this type of investment, as well as buying as early as possible in the construction process and selling at the critical moment, is to buy as early as possible in the 'emergence' of a new market, when prices can escalate rapidly in a short time. In a stable market, prices won't usually be rising fast enough to make flipping worthwhile. **Governments in some countries have made flipping illegal because it results in an overheated property market, which in turn affects the country's economy. They encourage, or sometimes require, developers to add a clause to the purchase contract which prevents flipping. If you want to invest in this way, you must ensure that your contract allows it.**

Protecting Your Investment

Although short-term capital investment, which might accurately be called 'speculation', is high risk, there are measures you can take to protect your money.
Developer: Check that the developer is reputable and well established in the country concerned. Look at previous projects it has been involved in. Are they high quality, and do they sell quickly and easily? This is relatively easy to check in an established market, but more difficult in an emerging one, where you must be especially careful. Make sure your lawyer checks the contract to ensure that your interests are catered for. The developer should have an insurance policy or bank guarantee to protect your investment in case he goes out of business before the project is completed. **In some countries, bank guarantees and insurances aren't a legal requirement and developers don't offer them so that they can keep their prices as low as possible. If this is the case, check if there are other safeguards.**

The developer should also have any required building licences before construction, although this often doesn't happen and building (and selling) begins before licences are issued. The best safeguard in this situation is to ensure that any money is held in a bonded (escrow) account until the required licences are issued and have been checked.

Finally, make sure that the developer has legal title to the land it plans to build on. It isn't unknown for some developers to sell property on land they don't own! A good lawyer should check this, thereby ensuring that separate title for any property built on the land can be transferred to the new owner on completion.

Supply & Demand: The other important thing to check – as far as possible – is whether you'll be able to sell your property (or the option to buy it) when you want to. Some countries and regions have a glut of off-plan property and too few buyers to go round. Demand needs to equal or exceed supply for you to stand a realistic chance of selling. If your property is just one of hundreds of similar properties, you could be stuck with it. You should research this kind of investment in the same way as any other. Is the property in a good position and what's being built close by – yet more similar properties or facilities that might enhance the area? When the property and development are finished, will anyone want to buy or rent it? If you're realistic about these factors – rather than being seduced by the promise of a quick profit – you reduce the risk of losing money (as much as is possible).

Medium-term Investment

A medium-term investment continues past completion; you keep the property until you're able to sell at a profit (usually between two and five years, but it could be longer). During this time, you can let short-term, allowing you an income to cover running costs and the flexibility to sell quickly should the market take a significant upturn. Both off-plan and resale properties are suitable for this type of investment. Once you complete the purchase and become the legal owner, you're liable for paying the balance, taxes associated with the purchase, any annual property taxes and capital gains tax if you sell the property. You have to offset these costs, which means your return on investment won't be as high.

You should protect your investment in the same way as with a short-term investment (see above), checking the developer's credentials, obtaining guarantees and trying to ensure that demand outstrips supply and will continue to do so for some time after purchase.

4

Long-term Investment

For those who can afford to wait, long-term investments can yield significant capital appreciation, but your best bet is to find an emerging market. Emerging markets are covered briefly above (page 89) and specific countries are detailed in the **Country Profiles**. Once you've made your investment, you must be prepared to watch the market carefully, regularly review your position and be ready to sell quickly if necessary. As with a medium-term investment, it may be wise to let the property short-term to offset running costs and expenses.

Buying Land

If you're considering land as an investment, your first consideration should be whether, as a foreigner, you're permitted to buy land. Some countries impose restrictions on the purchase of property or land (or both) by foreigners. A reputable local lawyer can advise you on the matter. Sometimes you can avoid restrictions by forming a local company, which buys the land on your behalf, but you must take professional advice. Employ the services of a local lawyer and architect to check important issues such as ownership, boundaries and planning permission.

In some countries, large areas of land often have several owners (usually from the same family) and each owner **must** sign the contract to transfer their portion of the land.

Identify the boundaries of the plot with the help of a land surveyor, especially on unfenced rural properties. Check that there are no disputes over boundaries and, if there are trees on the land, that they're included in the sale. It isn't unknown for fruit trees, for example, to belong to someone else! Check rights of way over the land and whether neighbours may have rights to water from any streams or underground springs on the land.

Check that you (or anyone you might want to sell the land to) will be permitted to use it to build the type of property you or they want to. Many countries have a land classification system which prohibits building at all in certain areas and restricts it in others (e.g. to a certain size or height according to the size or location of the plot). **Always ensure that you can obtain planning permission.** Your lawyer or an architect should check the position carefully before you sign anything. In some countries, speculators buy land cheaply in an area where building isn't allowed and then try to have the classification changed. If they're successful, they can sell at a hefty profit; if not, they're unlikely to be able to sell at all!

Building Houses

You may decide to invest in land to build your own home or several homes (in effect becoming a property developer). This often requires deep pockets and a keen eye for an emerging market. It isn't usually the type of investment you can manage from a distance because you need to monitor changes in the local property market and move quickly. You need reliable advisers and agents in the country concerned or must be prepared to spend considerable amounts of time there yourself. If you decide to buy land and build a home and won't be there yourself, you must ensure adequate supervision of the building work by someone you trust. When buying land to build on, take into account the considerations considered above (under **Buying Land**) and hire a reputable local architect to guide you through the procedures before building and during building, including:

- **Permits** – Your architect should secure the necessary building permits, which will determine how much of the land you can build on and the maximum height of the property or properties and may also include matters such as access to utilities and a main road. If utilities such as water and electricity cannot be connected or there's no main road access, a permit may not be granted.

- **Costs** – It's essential to obtain an accurate estimate of the construction costs. You should obtain written estimates from at least two reputable builders before employing anyone. Make sure that a quotation includes everything you want done and that you fully understand it (if you don't, have it translated). You should fix a date for the start and completion of work, and if you can get a builder to agree, include a penalty clause for failing to finish on time.

- **Supervision** – Even if you're able to supervise the work yourself, you should employ a project manager to work alongside the architect and oversee the job, especially if it's a complicated or large project. This will add around 10 per cent to your overall bill, but it's usually worth it. Be extremely careful who you employ if you have work done in your absence and ensure that your instructions are accurate and unambiguous in every detail. Always ensure that you understand exactly what has been agreed and, if necessary, put it in writing (with drawings).

Renovation & Restoration

Many people are attracted by the low price of properties that are little but ruins. However, if your sole aim is capital appreciation, it's probably one of the worst investments you can make. This is because it's all too easy to spend more on restoration than you could ever hope to recoup when you sell, which means no return on your investment whatsoever! As a rough guide, you should expect the cost of totally renovating an old 'habitable' building to be at least equal to its purchase price; in the case of a ruin, the cost is likely to be two or three times.

If you do decide to buy this type of property, you should check it yourself for obvious faults, obtain an appraisal and quotation for rebuilding from a qualified builder, and arrange for a surveyor to do a more detailed check before you commit yourself. The most important factor is that the building must have sound walls. Almost any other problem can be fixed or overcome (at a price). A sound roof that doesn't leak is desirable, as is ensuring that a building is waterproof. Sound roof timbers are also important as they can be expensive to replace. Old buildings often need a damp-proof course, timber treatment, new windows and doors, a new roof or extensive repairs, a modern kitchen and bathroom, re-wiring and central heating.

While it's possible to renovate an old property using cheap modern materials, this often destroys its character and charm and makes it more difficult, rather than easier, to sell. **Proper restoration is a highly skilled, time-consuming and expensive job.**

Electricity and mains water should preferably already be connected, as they can be expensive to extend to a property if it's in a remote area. If a house doesn't have electricity or mains water, it's important to check the cost of extending these services.

FINANCING YOUR INVESTMENT

The financial aspects of investing in all types of property abroad are discussed in detail in **Chapter 6**. However, when you make a capital investment, you may want your money to 'work' for you in a different way than if you were buying, say, a holiday home. This section outlines various financial options which may enhance your investment, by using your own or other people's money.

You should always get professional advice about the best way to finance your investment and how to make it as tax-efficient as possible. Apart from an English-speaking lawyer, you'll need to consult specialist tax and financial advisers and possibly also a currency 'expert' (see **Chapter 5**), as currency fluctuations can make a big difference to your profit (or loss). **Transferring large sums of money abroad at the wrong time and in the wrong way can considerably reduce the return on your investment!**

Some people pay for their capital investment with their available financial resources and have no wish or need to borrow money, either in their home country or abroad. In some countries (see **Country Profiles**), there are no alternatives because mortgages aren't available to foreigners. Experienced investors, however, usually prefer to use other people's money if possible, so that they make the highest possible gain with the minimum amount of risk. This is often called 'gearing', which is financial-speak for borrowing money to finance your investment. You can 'gear' in a number of ways, as described briefly below and in detail in **Chapter 6**.

Equity Release

Mortgaging or re-mortgaging your principal home is known as equity release and is becoming an increasingly popular method of financing property purchase abroad, especially for buyers from Ireland and the UK, who have recently seen huge rises in the value of property in their home countries. These rises and a reduction in the size of their mortgages after a number of years mean that they've accumulated considerable equity (the profit they would make if they sold the house and paid off the mortgage), which lenders can use as security for another loan.

The advantage of equity release is that you're already known to the lender, who is therefore likely to look favourably on your request. In addition, your repayments will be in your own currency, the paperwork is all in your own language and your lender and its practices are familiar. If you have a good credit record and accumulated equity, the lender cannot lose and will sometimes advance as much as 100 per cent of the cost of your investment property. In some countries, you may not be able to obtain a local mortgage, so this method is your only option.

The disadvantages are that you're working in different currencies and may lose out on exchange rates at the point of purchase and, of course, you're putting your principal home at risk, which you may feel uncomfortable about.

4

Local Mortgages

Many investors prefer to deal in local currency because it eliminates the risk of fluctuating exchange rates, which can considerably reduce your capital appreciation (although they can equally well increase it). In addition, if you have a buy-to-let property, your rental income will be in the same currency as your mortgage repayments, again eliminating currency fluctuation risk. Some people simply prefer to keep loans for investments unconnected with their principal residence, to limit the risk to their own home.

If you decide to take out a local mortgage, you must research the mortgage market carefully. In some countries foreigners aren't entitled to mortgages and in others the mortgage market may not be as sophisticated as you're used to. Lenders abroad often have less flexible lending policies, such as advancing only a small percentage of the purchase price, and the repayment period might be far shorter (10 or 15 years). In some countries, lenders won't take buy-to-let income into account when advancing you a mortgage; you must present documentation to prove that you have sufficient income to make the repayments.

Finally, check interest rates carefully, especially if you're buying outside Europe. Within the euro zone (those countries which have adopted the euro currency), rates are generally lower than in the UK, as lenders must offer the current European Central Bank (ECB) rate plus an extra 1 or 1.5 per cent. In other countries, rates may be considerably higher, which will increase your running costs and reduce rental income. You or your financial adviser should research the local mortgage market carefully before you make a decision about mortgage facilities.

Offshore Loans

Depending on your country of residence and financial status, you may be able to take advantage of a mortgage from a financial institution within an offshore banking centre. This is explored in more detail in **Chapter 6**.

Developer Finance

4

In some countries where mortgages are difficult to obtain, a developer may offer a financial package to entice would-be buyers. Many developers already offer a kind of financing package when you buy an off-plan property, in the form of stage payments until completion. This suits both parties because it reduces the buyer's costs and gives the developer regular injections of cash throughout the project. If a developer offers further finance, it's usually in the form of deferred payments which continue after completion. If you're offered this type of finance, make sure you or your financial adviser checks the terms carefully. How long will you have to pay? When will you have full ownership of the property (which is important if you wish to sell it to realise your capital gain)? Is the developer charging interest on the loan and at what rate?

Shared Investments

If you have a limited amount of money to invest, there are a number of shared investment schemes which allow you to increase your purchasing power by pooling your financial resources with those of other small investors. These range from simply buying with a group of friends, family or colleagues (part-ownership) to collective investment schemes which you can be part of through a property investment club or 'real estate investment trust' (REIT), as outlined below.

If you decide to invest this way, exercise extreme caution, take professional advice and ensure that your interests are protected by having a contract drawn up. This ensures that all investors are clear about the terms and conditions of the agreement.

Part-ownership

Part-ownership (also called co-ownership and joint ownership) includes schemes such as a consortium of buyers owning shares in a property-owning company. The number of part owners should be determined by the amount each has to invest.

Obviously, the more owners there are, the smaller your share of the investment profit when you sell.

As with any property purchase, always take legal advice and ensure that a legal contract or agreement is drawn up between the group of buyers and (if applicable) the developer of the property. Even if part-ownership is between family and friends, you should have the agreement in writing and ensure that there's provision to transfer ownership to another friend or family member if required. A separate agreement should be drawn up covering the maintenance of the property, repairs, renovation, insurance, taxes and utilities bills.

Investment Funds

Putting your money into an investment fund means that, for a relatively small outlay (and less research), you can be part of a large investment that would otherwise be beyond your reach. Your money is pooled with that of other investors in a collective investment scheme and professionally managed for you by fund managers. You spread the risk because the fund spreads the total investment in a way you wouldn't have been able to do with a single, modest investment. You don't have to worry about research because it's done for you and the fund managers decide when to buy and sell. However, you must look carefully at the investment objectives of the fund and the scope of its investments.

4

Property Investment Clubs

These work on the same principle as investment funds, by pooling single investments and sharing the profits. To join one of these clubs, you usually have to pay a reasonably large sum up front (between around £2,000 and £6,000), as well as a monthly subscription. You may need to prove that you're a 'serious' investor, with a minimum net worth. Becoming a member means you have access to properties at supposedly discount prices and will usually be invited to attend property seminars with expert speakers on a range of different subjects. **Investors should be aware that property investment clubs are unregulated, unlike other financial services. Exercise extreme caution before parting with your money.**

Real Estate Investment Trusts

A real estate investment trust (REIT) is an investment fund operated by a large financial institution which owns and manages commercial or residential property producing an income from rentals. Most of this income (90-95 per cent) is distributed annually to shareholders. As a result, companies with REIT status are exempt from corporation tax and capital gains tax; governments allow REITs in order to encourage property investment in their countries. Investing in an REIT means being part of an enormous investment fund alongside big investors such as pension funds.

An REIT trades on the stock market and anyone can buy shares in it. They've been popular for many years in the US and Australia, and were launched in the UK on 1st January 2007.

The advantage of investing in an REIT is that the rental income is passed to the shareholders and you're fairly certain of a regular income because the REIT normally has long-term lease agreements with tenants; at the same time, you can buy and sell shares in an REIT quickly, giving you the perfect 'exit strategy' (see **Selling** below), which isn't always possible with other property investments.

You must take professional advice from a stockbroker or an independent financial adviser about whether this kind of investment is right for you. If you decide to invest, you should check how investments are managed and where the most recent funding has come from. It's usually a positive sign if there are significant investments from well known sources. You should also ensure that the investment is in a range of sectors and geographical areas. REITs often concentrate on a particular type of commercial development, such as apartments or office buildings, which may leave them exposed if that particular market weakens.

4

4

5
RESEARCH

The secret of making the right kind of property investment, in whatever location you choose, is research, research and more research. A successful investment is much more likely if you thoroughly investigate all possible countries and regions, the types of property available, their prices and (where applicable) letting rates, and the local procedures for buying and selling property (see **Country Profiles**). Once you've developed your knowledge of the international property market and of those countries you're especially interested in, you can ask more informed questions of professional advisers.

This chapter guides you through the research sources available and outlines the kind of professional advice you should seek to get the most from your investment.

It can be difficult to find unbiased advice and information about the best locations and types of property to invest in. The international property market is big business, not just for property professionals, but also for the print and broadcast and internet media, which provide limitless amounts of easily accessible information. (Simply type 'property' and a country name into an internet search engine and you hundreds of thousands of sites will be listed.) Yet behind every glossy article or impressive website, there's usually someone with an interest in selling or promoting a country, region or development. There are, however, independent sources of unbiased information and you should seek them out when doing your research.

Some people find themselves overwhelmed by the sheer amount of available information, so start by making a comprehensive list of what you want (and don't want) from your property, so that you can narrow the field and save time and bewilderment.

It's usually easiest to start with the print media, progress to the internet as you refine your search and then tackle some overseas property exhibitions. The final step is visiting your chosen location, preferably several times and at different times of the year, for some all-important research before making a decision. You should be absolutely sure how much you wish to spend and where before making a commitment.

Bear in mind that the cost of a few weekends at property exhibitions and the price of some books or magazines (and other research) is tiny compared to the expense of making a big mistake!

BOOKS, MAGAZINES & NEWSPAPERS

Read as many books as you can about buying property and living abroad. Survival Books has an extensive range of country-specific books, which offer advice about buying a home abroad, living and working abroad, making a living abroad and many other related matters (🖳 www.survivalbooks.net).

Specialist overseas property magazines – including *A Place in the Sun*, *International Homes*, *Homes Overseas* and *World of Property* – offer information about a range of countries and properties, useful country-specific information and a wealth of related articles. Remember that these magazines, although excellent, are all 'selling the dream', so they rarely discuss the disadvantages of investing in property abroad or the pitfalls that lie in wait for investors.

Once you've read a few of them, take a look at the overseas property sections of the national newspapers. Most have useful articles about popular locations and emerging markets which will help you get a feel for the global property market. Their websites often have more detailed overseas property sections, such as those of *The Times* (💻 www.timesonline.com), *The Telegraph* (💻 www.telegraph.co.uk) and *The Daily Mail* (💻 www.dailymail.co.uk).

If you want further specialist comment and analysis of the global property market, news magazines are an excellent source of information. *The Economist* (💻 www.economist.com) and *The Financial Times* (💻 www.ft.com) are two of the best, and their websites are comprehensive. *The Economist* produces an annual house price index which gives a useful overview of the world housing market, although, increasingly, much of the information on its website is available only on subscription.

INTERNET

Once you've done your initial research, make a short list of the countries and areas that interest you and begin your internet research. The internet is one of the most powerful research tools available, but you should always be cautious about who is behind a website and their motives for setting it up. Information is often biased, out-of-date or even incorrect. Try to find reliable, independent sources which don't have an interest in selling you anything. These include the following.

5

Banks & Financial Institutions

The website of the national bank of the country you're interested in usually has links to information and statistics about the currency, economy and business information and details of monetary policy. Almost all national banks (especially those in Europe) have websites in English. The World Bank (💻 www.worldbank.org) has extensive information about countries around the world, as does the International Monetary Fund (💻 www.imf.org).

Banks and building societies in your own country, especially those keen to help with property purchase abroad, are likely to have comprehensive websites, which will include financial information and details of their lending policies for foreign property. Barclays in the UK launched a new website in September 2006 aimed at helping UK citizens buy abroad in four European countries: France, Italy, Portugal and Spain (💻 www.barclays.co.uk/buying abroad).

Business & Industry Websites

Most international accountancy firms produce regular, up-to-date country guides, which are an invaluable source of information (in English and other languages) for investors. These guides are principally intended for companies who wish to do business abroad, but they contain useful country-specific information about such things as property ownership by foreigners, banking, finance and taxation. Ernst & Young (💻 www.ey.com/global), PricewaterhouseCoopers (💻 www.pwcglobal.com)

and Deloitte Touche (💻 www.deloitte.com) are the leading providers of this sort of information. You may have to subscribe to them to access all of it, but there's a considerable amount of information available free. The websites list the countries they cover and you simply click on the country (or countries) which interest you. Sometimes information is contained in a 'Publications' section and you can download anything of interest.

Two other useful annual profiles of the global property market are *The European Housing Review*, published by The Royal Institute of Chartered Surveyors (RICS, 💻 www.rics.org) and *The International Residential Review*, published by Knight Frank Global (💻 www.knightfrank.com).

Government Websites

The quality of government websites varies. Some are easy to navigate, have an English version and offer detailed, up-to-date information about various aspects of the country: history, political system, economy, local culture and much more. Others are less accessible, with few, if any, pages in English, and have out-of-date statistics buried in unlikely areas. This is changing, as more and more governments realise the importance of a strong internet presence, but if your chosen country's administration has yet to arrive in the internet age, you must look for alternative sources of information. You may find that your own government can help, especially those departments whose job it is to promote trade and industry abroad. In the UK, the department which supports British companies doing business overseas, UK Trade and Investment, has extensive and detailed country-specific information. Although it's geared towards overseas trade and industry, it's also useful for an overall picture of a country's economy, communications, politics and trade opportunities (💻 www.uktrade invest.gov.uk). The UK Foreign Office has excellent advice pages, including country-specific information, for those considering going to live abroad, particularly retirees (💻 www.fco.gov.uk). The US government has similar websites, including the CIA's World Factbook (💻 www.cia.gov/cia/publications/factbook), which has country profiles and maps along with information about the country's population, economy and politics and a brief history. The US Commercial Service also has country-specific information for US citizens wishing to set up business or invest abroad (💻 www.buyusa.gov).

PROPERTY EXHIBITIONS

Property exhibitions are useful because they provide an overall picture of the type and cost of property in a number of countries. They often have a relaxed (or even party) atmosphere, but remember that everyone present has an interest in selling you something, so don't allow yourself to be pressured or be tempted to do anything beyond gathering information to help with your own research. **Most importantly, don't sign anything on the spot. Despite what agents may tell you, the property (or a similar one) will still be there once you've had time to think things through carefully.**

The UK has a lot of property exhibitions every year, often in London but also in other large cities. Most cover a range of countries, but some are country-specific. Exhibitions are also common in Ireland, some European cities, the US and Dubai. You can find details of exhibitions in specialist property magazines, many of which organise their own. Leading exhibitions include:

- **A Place in the Sun** – organised by Brooklands Media, Westgate, 12-128 Station Road, Redhills, Surrey RH1 1ET (☎ 01737-786800, 🖥 www.aplacein thesunlive.com);

- **Homes Overseas** – which takes place several times a year, run by Blendon Communications, 1 East Poultry Ave, West Smithfield, London EC1A 9PT (☎ 020-7002 8300, 🖥 www.blendoncommunications.co.uk);

- **World of Property** – organised by Outbound Publishing, 1 Commercial Road, Eastbourne, East Sussex BN1 3XQ (☎ 01323-726040, 🖥 www.outbound publishing.com).

The Outbound Publishing website also has a wealth of useful contacts and information aimed at people thinking of emigrating and the company stages another exhibition, called *Emigrate*, at which you can find out everything about living overseas.

5

LOCAL RESEARCH

Once you've identified the country or area that interests you, it's vital to do some local research, especially if you've decided to invest in a permanent home abroad. **Don't be tempted to commit yourself without visiting the area.** You need to have a close look at your chosen region(s) and obtain an accurate picture of the types and cost of properties. Your research should include seeking advice from property professionals (see below) and, if possible, people who own a home in your chosen area. They can often give you invaluable information (sometimes based on their own mistakes). Local expatriate organisations can usually put you in touch with such people.

Try to visit your chosen location at different times of the year, in different weather conditions. Think about how you want to use your investment. If you want a buy-to-let property, look at the property and the area through the eyes of prospective tenants. If you're planning to live there permanently, it's vitally important that you think through every aspect of your life and how it would fit with the location and property.

Although it's common practice, mixing a holiday with property purchase isn't wise, as most people are inclined to make poor decisions when their mind is fixed on play rather than business. Some people make expensive (even catastrophic) errors when investing in property abroad, often because they don't do sufficient research and are simply in too much of a hurry – often setting themselves impossible deadlines such as choosing and buying a property during a long weekend.

Embassies & Consulates

Your home country's embassy or consulate can usually offer unbiased advice about living and working in a particular country. They can also provide you with lists of English-speaking lawyers and details of expatriate organisations and clubs, where you can contact and gather useful information from others who have lived in the country. Countries which are popular with expatriates usually have a wide variety of expatriate organisations and support groups that you can draw on.

Local Newspapers

Many countries and regions have a local English-language newspaper, which may be helpful for your research – many have a property supplement. Local newspapers are also useful for finding out what's going on in the area and what services and facilities are available.

Professional Advice

5

Financial institutions in your own country can advise you about tax planning and investments, and are often a good first point of contact. Many have international offices or representatives abroad and are experienced in advising expatriates, but check that your adviser is fully informed about local tax laws and investment matters. International accountants (see **Business & Industry Websites** above) have local offices and English-speaking staff who are familiar with procedures and tax regulations for foreign property buyers. The national bank of the country concerned (which may also have branches in your home country) often has information about local financial services and the country's financial services regulatory body. **Chapter 6** has more detailed information about financial services.

In addition to professional advice in your home country, you should seek professional advice in the country of your choice.

Estate Agents

Many people are wary of estate agents, but a good local agent can save you time and money (see **Chapter 3**). Remember that if you're in an unfamiliar country and don't speak the language, it can be virtually impossible to visit properties on your own and, even if you can, you'll be limited to properties that are being sold 'direct', which is often fraught with problems. Not only do estate agents have dozens or hundreds of properties on their books but a good agent's familiarity with an area can help you find that romantic cottage in the middle of nowhere or the site of the new development that hasn't had a brick laid yet. Agents are usually the first to hear about properties and developments that are soon to come onto the market.

Needless to say, agents' advice will be geared towards your buying a property from them, so always double check any claims they make about likely profits and ease of selling. They should offer you a variety of property within your price range – if they seem overly keen on a particular house or development, question their motives. Most agents offer an excellent service, but try to visit a range of reputable agents to get a comprehensive view of the market.

Legal & Financial Advice

Part of your research should be to find local English-speaking legal and financial advisers. It would be foolish to rely solely on advice or recommendations given by those with a financial interest in selling you a property, such as a developer or agent, although their advice may be excellent and totally unbiased. Engage professionals who have been highly recommended by someone you can trust. This is often easier said than done in a foreign country where you don't speak the language, but there are a number of international property lawyers and organisations who can point you in the right direction.

A growing number of organisations have responded to the need for English-speaking lawyers abroad. One is the Property Lawyers Abroad Network (PLAN), which is a group of experienced international property lawyers who can provide independent legal advice to those thinking of investing in property abroad. PLAN has member lawyers in 30 countries, all of whom are English-speaking and have knowledge of the local property market. You can find more information on PLAN's website (🖥 www.plani.net).

The Law Society in the UK (🖥 www.lawsociety.org.uk) has a directory of English-speaking, qualified lawyers abroad on its website (go to 'Finding Legal Help Abroad'), as well as links to European and worldwide Bar Associations and Law Societies. Members of a Bar Association have to work to a strict code of conduct and you have some redress if you're unhappy with the service you receive. Bar Associations around the world have websites (often with an English version) and members are listed with contact details. Finally, your embassy or consulate in the country concerned will also have a list of lawyers who speak your language.

You may find it useful to employ a lawyer in your own country who specialises in foreign property conveyancing and usually works with a local associate in the country concerned. Although this can be expensive, it's usually worth paying the extra because you'll receive advice about how the law compares in the two different countries and what you can expect from the local property purchase. You can find details of these companies in the specialist property and lifestyle magazines, and they're often represented at property exhibitions (see above).

Familiarise yourself with the local purchase procedure and never sign anything or pay any money until you've sought legal advice in your own language from an independent lawyer who's experienced in local property law.

6
MONEY MATTERS

One of the most important aspects of investing in property and living abroad (even for brief periods) is finance, which includes everything from transferring and changing money to mortgages and local taxes. This chapter provides general information on exchange rates and foreign money transfers, banks and bank accounts (including offshore bank accounts), mortgages – in your home country and abroad – insurance, taxation and the cost of living. Country-specific details can be found in the **Country Profiles** starting on page 175.

Before you start to search for property abroad, it's important to work out how you'll finance the purchase and cover regular expenses. Proper research and preparation can save you significant amounts of money. You'll want to find the most efficient (and cheapest) method of sending money abroad, the best way to borrow money for your purchase (if necessary), the most efficient banking option and the taxes that will be payable on the property – on purchase and sale and annually.

TRANSFERRING MONEY

During the last few decades, exchange controls have been abolished in most countries, particularly within the European Union (EU), and countries that allow property sales to foreigners generally impose few or no restrictions on the import and export of funds. If you're planning to invest in a property or business abroad financed with funds imported from another country, it's important to take into account the fluctuation of exchange rates (see below). In addition, if you plan to live and work abroad and earn your income in the local currency, you should consider how this may affect your financial commitments in your home country (particularly if the local currency is devalued).

Transferring large sums of money in another currency for a property purchase or making regular transfers to and from your home country can prove expensive, as you're at the mercy of exchange rates and sometimes high bank charges. You should also be aware that many countries require you to declare the import or export of funds above a certain amount (see **Restrictions** below).

International Money Transfers

Transferring money between countries is, in theory, more reliable now that banks across the world have Bank Identifier Codes (BIC). This is a universal method of identifying banks and other financial institutions. The Society for Worldwide Interbank Financial Telecommunications (SWIFT) registers the BIC codes, and its network enables the automated processing of telecommunications messages within the banking system. Using the correct BIC code or SWIFT number helps avoid payment delays but it isn't a foolproof system and transfers can still 'to astray'; nor does it speed up the process, which can still take several days.

Before you decide on the best method of transferring funds, check the charges and how soon your money will be available to use.

Restrictions

Although few exchange controls remain, many countries have laws which dictate that 'substantial' sums (the amount varies from country to country) must be declared on entering the country. These regulations are designed to curb criminal activities, e.g. money laundering and tax evasion. The central bank of the country concerned can advise you about specific limits and regulations. **If you don't declare the funds, they may be subject to confiscation.** Anti-money laundering measures mean that banks are usually required to obtain comprehensive confirmation of the identification of their account holders, track their account movements and report any amounts deposited in excess of approved limits. If you plan to export money to another country to buy property or set up a business, you must check the regulations and obtain professional legal and financial advice.

International Bank Account Number

Transferring funds within Europe has been made simpler since July 2003 with the introduction of the International Bank Account Number (IBAN), which identifies an account held anywhere in Europe and standardises the procedure. Payments made using IBAN and within the EU are considered domestic payments (and therefore cheaper), as long as the euro currency is used. If you don't quote an IBAN, the payment is considered a foreign transfer and you're charged more.

Despite its name, the IBAN isn't a separate bank account number but precedes your own account number and contains the country code under the IBAN system, certain check digits and the bank branch reference number. This number identifies financial institutions and enables the automated processing of SWIFT transfers (see below).

6

Despite the fact that the IBAN is an international standard for numbering bank accounts, it isn't widely used outside Europe and isn't expected to be for several years. If you wish to transfer money outside the EU, you must use the SWIFT method (see below). Although it's usually fast and efficient, it's charged as a foreign transfer.

SWIFT Transfers

SWIFT (short for the Society of Worldwide Interbank Financial Telecommunications) is an electronic service used by banks to transfer funds. You need to find out your bank's SWIFT code and that of the receiving bank. If this isn't possible, you need the IBAN (see above), the account number, the name and address of the receiving bank and the name of the beneficiary. SWIFT is probably the fastest and most efficient method of transferring money to and from another country, taking as little as two or three hours. However, the bank that initiates the transfer charges you a fee and it may be several working days before you actually gain access to your money.

Telegraphic Transfers

One of the quickest (it takes around ten minutes) and safest methods of transferring cash is via a telegraphic transfer, e.g. Moneygram or E-Moneygram, allowing you to transfer via the internet (UK ☎ 0800-666 3947, 🖳 www.moneygram.com) and Western Union (🖳 www.westernunion.com). Western Union's website has an 'agent locator' section which you can use to help you find an agent in more than 200 countries. Note that this method is one of the most expensive, e.g. commission of 7 to 10 per cent of the amount sent!

Bank Drafts & Personal Cheques

Check with your bank abroad to find out how long it takes to clear bank drafts or foreign cheques. Note that the clearance of personal cheques can take a long time (currently more than **20 working days**). Some banks may offer a shorter clearance service to established customers.

Bank Mandates

This is a standing instruction to allow a bank to transfer funds to a specific account on a specific date or dates. You should set it up well in advance and check that everything is in order before the date of the transfer. Some banks offer preferential rates for regular transfers set up with a mandate, but check costs carefully.

6

Banknotes

Banknotes can be imported into other countries, although it obviously isn't wise to carry very large sums, especially in view of the extensive anti-money laundering regulations (see above) that exist in most countries.

Exchange Rates & Charges

If you're transferring large sums overseas, you must ensure that you get the best possible exchange rate and that the transfer of funds is done in the most economical way. Many people don't realise the impact that exchange rate fluctuations can have on their funds. Some lose substantial amounts simply through lack of preparation and professional advice. Foreign exchange has become a more competitive market during the last few years and other businesses are challenging the banks and offering better exchange rates and lower charges. Shop around and compare your bank's rate with that of at least one foreign exchange broker which specialises in sending money abroad (particularly large sums). If you're well informed you can save a considerable amount of money.

To begin with, if you intend to send a large amount of money abroad for a business transaction such as buying a property, you should ensure that you receive the commercial rate of exchange rather than the tourist rate, which can be considerably higher. The minimum amount you must transfer to qualify for the commercial rate varies from bank to bank but is usually around £25,000.

Secondly, you should investigate whether it's cheaper for the sending bank to make all charges or the receiving bank or for charges to be shared between them (there's usually little or no difference).

Banks

Banks have traditionally had, if not a monopoly, certainly the lion's share of foreign currency transfers and their customers seem to assume they offer the best available rates. Although banks are sometimes willing to negotiate about fees and exchange rates when you're transferring large amounts, they charge a transfer fee each time you transfer money. If you're making regular transfers, this can prove expensive. Keep records of transactions and check your account regularly for unexpected foreign exchange charges.

Foreign Exchange Brokers

Foreign exchange brokers deal directly with the currency markets and can often offer better exchange rates than banks and/or lower charges, although there may be other 'catches'. Certain companies allow you to fix or guarantee the exchange rate for an agreed period, or set upper limits on the rate that you're prepared to accept. Fixed exchange rates can save you considerable amounts of money and allow you to calculate your costs in advance. On the other hand, of course, you can fix a rate and then find that you'd have been better off if you hadn't. Needless to say, there's a charge for fixing a rate: the further in advance you do so, the higher the charge.

6

The leading foreign exchange companies include Currencies Direct (UK ☎ 020-7813 0332, 🖳 www.currenciesdirect.com), Foreign Currency Direct (UK ☎ 01494-725353, 🖳 www.currencies.co.uk) and Moneycorp (UK ☎ 020-7808 0500, 🖳 www.moneycorp.com).

BANKING

If you're investing in property abroad, you'll want banking that will make your life as easy and tax efficient as possible. Although it's possible to own and use a home abroad without having a local bank account, e.g. by making use of debit and credit cards from your home country, this can be an expensive option. Another alternative is an offshore bank account (see below). General information about the banking system in a particular country can be found on the website of the relevant central bank.

Bank Accounts

Your banking requirements will depend on your circumstances, the country you're buying in and how you intend to use your property. For example, people who intend to live abroad permanently have different requirements from those who are buying a holiday home or investing in a buy-to-let property.

Permanent Home Owners

If you plan to live abroad permanently or for long periods each year, the most flexible arrangement is to retain your bank account at home and open a local one. That way you can cover any existing financial commitments in your home country, such as direct debits, but also have a local bank account to pay utility and tax bills on your home abroad. Many utility companies accept payment by direct debit only from a local bank. In addition, if you're being paid a salary in a foreign country, most employers expect to pay you via a local bank account. If you're receiving a pension from your home country, it can usually be paid directly into your foreign bank account, thereby saving you transfer charges.

Buy-to-Let & Holiday Home Owners

If you plan to invest in a buy-to-let property or holiday home abroad, having a local bank account is necessary so that bills can be paid by direct debit and any income, e.g. from letting, can be paid in local currency into your account. You can usually have all documentation, e.g. cheque books and statements, sent to your permanent address in your home country.

Opening an Account

Within the European Economic Area (EEA), you can apply to open a non-resident foreigner's account immediately upon (or before) your arrival. If the country you're in requires a residence permit, you must wait until residence is granted before transferring money to a resident's account, which is usually cheap and flexible to operate. With increasing numbers of foreigners investing in property abroad, banking staff often speak English and other languages, and banks are modern and equipped with the latest technology, especially within the EU. A few banks in some countries are still lagging behind, but most go out of their way to attract foreign customers.

It's wise to open a bank account in person rather than by correspondence from abroad, although many foreign banks have branches abroad, where you can open a bank account before arriving in the country. Obtain details from as many banks as you can as early as possible so that you have plenty of time to compare their services. **Before choosing a bank, you should compare the fees charged for personal accounts, overdrafts, international money transfers and other**

services. Ask friends, neighbours or colleagues for their recommendations and visit the bank to introduce yourself. You must be over 18 years old and provide proof of identity, e.g. a passport and your local address.

Banking policies may not be as liberal as you're used to in your home country. Overdrawing a bank account is prohibited in many countries (in some it's a criminal offence!) and offenders can be barred from holding a bank account; it will also severely damage your credit rating.

Obtaining Cash

An easy way to obtain cash abroad is to use your existing debit, credit or charge card in an automatic teller machine (ATM). You key in your 'personal identification number' (PIN) just as you would in your home country – check with your bank at home whether this is possible. You must usually pay a small fee for this service (e.g. £1 per withdrawal), and some credit card companies don't offer the best exchange rate on withdrawals. Many foreigners living abroad (particularly retirees) keep the bulk of their money in a foreign account (perhaps an offshore bank) and draw on it locally with a cash card. This is an ideal solution for holidaymakers and holiday-homeowners, although homeowners will still need a local bank account to pay their bills. Visa and MasterCard cards are commonly accepted in major cities and tourist areas, although in the remote rural areas of most countries, cash is usual and sometimes the only accepted form of payment.

Offshore Banking

6

If wish to invest in more than one country, it may be worthwhile considering the accounts and services (e.g. pensions and trusts) provided by offshore banking centres in 'tax havens' such as the Channel Islands (Guernsey and Jersey), Gibraltar and the Isle of Man (some 50 locations worldwide are officially classified as tax havens, though they're no longer able to shield you from the tax man!). The big attraction of offshore banking is that money can be deposited in a wide range of currencies, there are no double-taxation agreements to negotiate, no withholding tax is payable and you can deal with English-speaking staff familiar with the needs of expatriates.

A large number of American, British and European banks, as well as various other international financial institutions, provide offshore banking facilities in one or more locations. Most institutions offer high-interest deposit accounts for long-term savings and investment portfolios, in which funds can be deposited in any major currency. Many people living abroad keep a local account for everyday business and maintain an offshore account for international transactions and investment purposes. However, most financial experts advise investors not to rush to invest their life savings in an offshore tax haven until they know their long-term plans. **Always seek independent financial advice before making a decision.**

Offshore accounts have minimum deposit amounts, which start as low as £500 but are usually higher. In addition to minimum balances, accounts may have stringent terms and conditions, such as restrictions on withdrawals or high early withdrawal penalties. You can deposit funds on call (instant access) or for a fixed period, e.g. from 90 days to a year (usually for large sums). Interest is usually paid monthly or annually, with monthly interest payments slightly lower than annual payments, although monthly payments have the advantage of providing a regular income. There are usually no charges if a specified minimum balance is maintained. Many accounts offer a cash card or a credit card, e.g. MasterCard or Visa, which can be used to obtain cash from ATMs worldwide. Some offshore banks also offer telephone banking (usually seven days a week) and internet banking.

When selecting an offshore banking centre and a particular financial institution, your first priority should be the safety of your money. In some offshore banking centres, bank deposits are covered by a deposit protection scheme, whereby a maximum sum is guaranteed should a financial institution go out of business (the Isle of Man, Guernsey and Jersey all have such schemes). Unless you're planning to bank with a major international bank (which is unlikely to fold until the day after the end of the world), you should check the credit rating of a financial institution before depositing any money, particularly if it doesn't provide deposit insurance. All banks have a credit rating (the highest is 'AAA') and a bank with a high rating will be happy to tell you this (but get it in writing). You can also check the rating of an international bank or financial organisation with Moody's Investor Service. You should be wary of institutions offering higher than average interest rates: if it looks too good to be true, it probably is! The magazine *Investment International*, which can be accessed online (⌨ www.investmentinternational.com), contains useful, easy-to-understand information about offshore accounts.

6

MORGAGES

MORTGAGES

With the recent explosion of the overseas property market has come increased competition for your business (i.e. money) and consequently you can obtain better mortgage deals – indeed mortgages in countries where mortgages had never been heard of until recently. The amount that can be borrowed, however, varies according to the country where the property is situated, the country where the loan will be raised, the lender, and, not least, the financial standing of the borrower. It's recommended to consult an international mortgage adviser before deciding what's best for you. There are several ways you can raise money to buy property abroad: via your current lender in your home country, with an overseas mortgage from a local bank, or from a financial institution within an offshore banking centre. Each has its advantages and disadvantages, which are detailed below.

Current Mortgage Provider

UK lenders cannot grant a mortgage directly on an overseas property because they're unable to secure a charge on foreign property or have it valued to their standards. However, if you have equity in a British home, you can mortgage or re-mortgage it rather than take out an overseas mortgage. The advantages include the following:

- Your credit history with your current lender eases the process.

- Familiar practices and transactions are carried out in your native language.

- It's a relatively straightforward process, with less paperwork and therefore lower legal fees.

- Mortgage plans can be tailored to your requirements.

- The mortgage market in your home country is likely to be more sophisticated than in some foreign countries, allowing you more flexibility and a larger range of products.

- Depending on the equity in your existing property and the cost of the property abroad, you may be able to pay cash, putting you in a stronger position as a buyer.

There are also possible disadvantages, including the following:

- higher mortgage repayments and the possibility that you will have to continue to pay after retirement;

- a negative interest rate change;

- a reduction in the amount of equity in your home property, limiting your ability to raise money in an emergency;

- putting your principal home at risk if you cannot keep up the repayments or sell your overseas property.

Foreign Currency Mortgages

Foreign currency mortgages are available for established foreign property markets, such as Spain, France and the US, and, more recently, they've become possible in less developed markets, such as some eastern European countries. (See the **Country Profiles** for information about mortgage availability in your chosen country.) Mortgages can be obtained in a variety of major currencies, e.g. sterling, US dollars, Swiss francs and euros. It's generally regarded as wise to take out a mortgage in the currency in which your income is paid or in the currency of the country where a property is situated. If the local currency becomes devalued, your income is worth less in other currencies and you may face problems making mortgage repayments in another currency. However, if your mortgage is also in the local currency, repayments should remain manageable relative to your income.

When choosing a currency, you should take into account the costs, fees, interest rates and possible currency fluctuations. Some of the advantages of an overseas mortgage are:

- potentially lower interest rates than in your home country, especially in EU countries – but this isn't always the case, so always check and compare rates;

- If you plan to let the property, you'll receive rent in the same currency as your mortgage repayments, making it easier to offset your rental income against your mortgage repayments.

- Repayments are unaffected by fluctuating exchange rates and you avoid the cost of international transfers.

The disadvantages can include:

- lack of regulation of the local mortgage market (unlike, for example, the UK's, which is regulated by the Financial Services Authority);

- unfamiliar procedures and possible language problems;

- possibly a less sophisticated mortgage market, often with lower loan-to-value (LTV) ratios, repayment-only mortgages and no consideration of possible letting income (see **Foreign Lenders' Terms** below);

- If the mortgage is in a different currency from your earnings, currency fluctuations can dramatically affect your repayments.

6

Foreign Lenders' Terms

These differ from country to country, but they may be more stringent and less flexible than in your home country. The established markets may lend as much as 90 per cent of a property's value, but in general the loan-to-value (LTV) ratio is around 70 per cent, although it can be as low as 50 per cent for non-residents and buyers of second homes. Banks may also offer 'non-status' loans of around 50 per cent, where no proof of income is required. Loans may be repaid over as few as 5 or as many as 30 years, depending on the lender and country, although the usual term in most countries is 10 to 20 years for residents (possibly less for non-residents).

Repayment mortgages are the most common type of mortgage in most countries (the only type in some), although endowment and pension-linked mortgages are also available in some countries. Some overseas lenders apply strict rules regarding income, employment and the type of property on which they will lend. They generally offer around a third of your disposable income, which doesn't usually include anticipated rental income. Joint incomes and liabilities are included when assessing a couple's borrowing limit (usually a bank will lend to up to four joint borrowers).

Most banks require proof of your monthly income and all outgoings such as mortgage payments, rent and other loans and commitments. Proof of income includes three months' pay slips for employees, confirmation of income from your employer and tax returns. If you're self-employed, you usually require an audited copy of your balance sheets and trading accounts for the past three years, plus your last tax return.

Fees

There are various fees associated with mortgages, e.g. all lenders charge an 'arrangement' fee and although it's unusual to have a survey in most countries, lenders usually insist on a 'valuation survey' before they grant a loan. The fees on an overseas mortgage can be high, amounting to up to 20 per cent of the purchase price (depending on the country), although high set-up costs may be balanced by low interest rates. **Always shop around for the best interest rate** *and* **ask the effective rate including** *all* **commissions and fees.**

Interest Rates

In August 2007, the European Central Bank (ECB) raised the interest rate to 4 per cent. This influences the rate at which banks within Europe offer funds to other banks, known as the Euro Interbank Offered Rate (EURIBOR), which in turn is the benchmark for mortgage interest rates. (Mortgage lenders typically charge around 1.5 per cent over the EURIBOR.) However, rates vary from bank to bank. UK and US interest rates are currently around 5 per cent but are also rising.

Payment Problems

6

If you're unable to meet your mortgage payments, it's essential to talk to your lender. The worst thing you can do is simply to stop paying the mortgage, because the lender can embargo the property and eventually forcibly sell it at auction. Some lenders will happily renegotiate mortgages so that payments are made over a longer period, thereby allowing you to reduce your monthly payments. Although interest rates have fallen dramatically in recent years, many lenders have been slow to reduce their interest rates for existing borrowers and some try to prevent existing mortgage holders from transferring to another lender offering a lower rate by imposing prohibitive cancellation fees. However, some countries have introduced legislation to enable borrowers with fixed rate mortgages to change their mortgage lender or re-negotiate a mortgage with their existing lender for a small penalty. In some countries, a mortgage can be taken over (assumed) by the new owner when a property is sold, which can be advantageous for a buyer.

Tax Relief

Residents in many countries receive tax relief on mortgages, which may include capital and interest repayments, so it might be beneficial to have a mortgage when living abroad, even when you can afford to pay cash for a property. Some countries, e.g. the UK, allow taxpayers to deduct the interest on a mortgage taken out on an overseas home.

Foreign Mortgage Providers

There's a variety of possible providers: local banks and financial institutions, lenders from your home country which have foreign subsidiaries, and offshore financial institutions.

Local Lenders: The central bank of the country concerned can give you information about the main clearing banks and those which offer mortgages to foreigners. You may get a favourable interest rate with a local lender, but do shop around. In addition, if you want a country-specific loan (such as the leaseback scheme in France), it's wise to use a local lender who has specific knowledge of the scheme. You can approach a local lender directly about a loan or, alternatively, a good mortgage broker will be familiar with the market and can arrange the best deal for you. Look for brokers who are specialists in the overseas mortgage market, familiar with the country in question and fluent in its language, and be clear about the charges you're expected to pay.

Banks Operating Abroad: Several banks based in the UK (and other countries) operate in the most popular foreign property locations, e.g. Spain, France, Portugal and Italy. While it may be comforting to go with a familiar name from home, remember that domestic banks abroad must operate under the jurisdiction of the country concerned. Hence, for example, the Spanish arm of the UK bank, the Halifax, is a Spanish company (Banco Halifax Hispania), which comes under the supervision of the Bank of Spain. This is true of all banks operating abroad: they don't work in the same way as in your home country.

Other UK banks operating abroad are Abbey National and Lloyds TSB. Abbey National (🖳 www.abbeynational.co.uk) is part of Spain's Banco Santander Group and offers euro mortgages on Spanish properties at fixed and variable rates. Barclays (🖳 www.barclays.co.uk/buying abroad) offers euro mortgages – and will re-mortgage your foreign home – through subsidiaries in France, Spain, Portugal and Italy, which, though claimed to be 'familiar', adhere to local and not British banking practices. The website details the terms available in each country and includes downloadable guides to living there. Lloyds TSB, which offers mortgages only on Spanish properties through its subsidiary company, Own Overseas, operates slightly differently (see page 304).

Foreign Banks with Branches in the UK: In 2006, two foreign banks opened branches in London specifically to offer loans to UK citizens who want to buy abroad. Crédit Foncier, one of France's leading mortgage providers (owned by Caisse d'Epargne, a French bank) offers favourable interest rates on euro mortgages for French properties. The (Greek) Piraeus Bank (🖳 www.piraeusbank.co.uk) offers mortgages to British and Irish residents buying property in Greece and Bulgaria, countries where local mortgages are difficult to obtain.

Mortgages from Offshore Banks

If you're living and working abroad and have an offshore bank account, you may be able to obtain a mortgage from that bank. Banks from a variety of countries have offshore services and, depending on your circumstances, they can offer more flexibility than a local bank. UK banks operating offshore include Abbey (formerly Abbey National), HSBC and Lloyds TSB. Abbey's international arm, Abbey International (🖳 www.abbeyinternational.com), offers a vast range of offshore services. The HSBC (🖳 www.offshore.hsbc.com) offers buy-to-let mortgages and local mortgages in a variety of currencies via members of the HSBC group in Canada, France, India, Taiwan, the United Arab Emirates (UAE) and the US. Lloyds TSB International (🖳 www.lloydstsb-offshore.com) has an international mortgage service for people who wish to buy property in Dubai, France, New Zealand, Portugal, Spain, the UK and other locations.

BUYING THROUGH AN OFFSHORE COMPANY

Buying property through an offshore company has traditionally been popular among non-resident property buyers in many countries, as it has meant that they could legally avoid paying wealth tax, inheritance tax and capital gains tax. Buyers could also avoid transfer tax or stamp duty when buying a property owned by an offshore company. However, buying through an offshore company isn't possible in many countries and the owners of properties purchased through offshore companies in some countries, e.g. Spain, have been required to register their ownership with the authorities in recent years or face punitive taxes. In general, offshore banking legislation has been seriously tightened since 2003 in an effort to combat tax avoidance, money laundering and terrorist financing. (The terrifying-sounding Financial Action Task Force on Money Laundering (FATF) has been given the unenviable task of 'persuading' countries to put regulatory legislation into place. You should obtain expert advice from an experienced lawyer before buying through an offshore company.

6

INSURANCE

An important aspect of investing in a home abroad is insurance, not only for your home and its contents, but also for you and your family when travelling and staying abroad. If you live abroad permanently, you may require or want additional insurance. It's unnecessary to spend half your income insuring yourself against every eventuality, but it's important to insure against any event that could precipitate a major financial disaster, such as a serious accident or your house falling down. The cost of being uninsured or under-insured can be astronomical, not just in financial terms but also in terms of the distress it can cause you and your family. This chapter deals with health insurance, holiday and travel insurance, buildings and contents insurance for your overseas property, including third-party liability insurance, car and breakdown insurance.

As with anything connected with finance, it's important to shop around when buying insurance. Collecting a few brochures from insurance agents or making a few telephone calls can save you a lot of money.

You're responsible for ensuring that you and your family and your possessions are legally insured in the country concerned. The law in your chosen country may differ considerably from that in your home country or your previous country of residence and you should never assume that it's the same. Always read insurance contracts carefully. If a policy is written in a language you don't understand, get someone to check it and don't sign it unless you understand the terms and the cover provided. Policies often contain traps in the small print, and you should obtain professional advice and have contracts checked before signing them. If you're uncertain of your rights, you're advised to obtain legal advice for anything other than a minor claim.

Not all insurance companies are equally reliable or have the same financial stability and it may be better to insure with a large international company with a good reputation (see below) than with a small company, even if this means paying higher premiums.

Some insurance companies do almost anything to avoid paying claims and will use any available legal loophole, so it pays to deal with reputable companies, although this doesn't provide you with a guarantee of prompt payment.

Health Insurance

6

If you're visiting, living or working abroad, it's imperative that you have sufficient health insurance for you and your family; if you're uninsured or under-insured you could be faced with some very high bills. Many countries provide free emergency treatment and some medical care under reciprocal agreements (see below), although these don't apply to citizens of some countries and won't cover all associated costs. Visitors spending short periods abroad should have travel insurance (see page 126) even if they're covered by a reciprocal agreement or an international health policy (see below).

Residents

If you're living abroad permanently and don't qualify for free or subsidised medical treatment under the local public health service (usually you need to pay into the national social security scheme to qualify, e.g. by earning a salary and paying taxes), you're strongly advised to have private health insurance, which is compulsory in some countries. A health insurance policy should, if possible, cover you for **all** essential healthcare whatever the reason for needing it, including accidents, whether they occur at your home, in your place of work or while travelling. Make sure you're fully covered abroad before you receive a large bill.

It's foolhardy for anyone living abroad (or even visiting) not to have comprehensive health insurance.

Even in countries with a public health service, those who can afford it often take out private health insurance, which provides a wider choice of medical practitioners and hospitals, and frees you from the inadequacies of the public health service, e.g. waiting lists and other restrictions. Private insurance may also allow you to choose an English-speaking doctor or a hospital where staff speak English or other languages. When changing employers or moving abroad, you should ensure that you have uninterrupted health insurance. If you're planning to change your health insurance company, make sure that important benefits aren't lost. Policies offered in different countries vary considerably in the extent of cover, limitations and restrictions, premiums, and the choice of doctors, specialists and hospitals. **Don't take anything for granted, but check in advance.**

UK citizens should contact their insurance provider or the UK's Department of Health (🖥 www.dh.gov.uk) for advice. The UK Foreign and Commonwealth Office (🖥 www.fco.gov.uk) also has some excellent advice about travel and medical insurance. US citizens should contact the US Department of State (🖥 www.state.gov/travelandbusiness) to find out what their health insurance will cover overseas. Most standard US healthcare policies cover only routine hospital expenses and not medical emergencies or a stay in hospital.

Cost: It's impossible to give guide prices because premiums and conditions vary enormously according to your circumstances and the level of cover you require, and are constantly changing in a highly competitive market. Due to the enormous diversity of cover, it's essential that you research the market thoroughly before you choose a policy. Most policies have an excess on each claim and a discount may be available if you accept a larger excess value; conversely, you must pay (sometimes much) more to have the excess waived. There may be an annual surcharge for those over 60, which increases with age, and supplements for certain services, such as basic dental or pregnancy treatment. Generally, the higher the premium, the more choice you have regarding doctors, specialists and hospitals. If you already have private health insurance in another country, you may be able to extend it to cover you for living abroad.

6

Long-stay Visitors

If you plan to spend up to six months abroad you should take out a travel, long-stay or international health policy, which should cover you in your home country and when travelling in other countries. Policies offered by local and international companies may differ considerably in the extent of cover, limitations and restrictions, premiums, and the choice of doctors, specialists and hospitals. Most international health policies include repatriation or evacuation (although it may be optional), sometimes including shipment by air of the body of a person who dies abroad to his home country for burial. An international policy also allows you to have non-urgent medical treatment in the country of your choice.

When travelling, you should always have proof of health insurance with you.

Holiday & Travel Insurance

Holiday and travel insurance is recommended for anyone who doesn't wish to risk having a holiday or travel spoilt by financial problems. As you probably know, anything can go wrong with a holiday, sometimes before you even reach the airport or port (particularly when you **don't** have insurance). Travel insurance is available from many sources, including travel and insurance agents, motoring organisations, transport companies and insurance companies. Package holiday companies also offer insurance polices, most of which are compulsory and expensive and often don't provide adequate cover. **Don't rely on credit card insurance cover or home insurance, which often falls far short of what's required.**

Before taking out travel insurance, carefully consider the level of cover you require and compare policies. Most good travel insurance policies include cover for medical expenses and accidents (including repatriation if necessary), money, personal liability, legal expenses, loss of deposit or holiday cancellation, missed flights, departure delay at both the start and end of a holiday, delayed, lost or stolen baggage and personal effects, and protection against a tour operator or airline going bust.

Medical & Health Insurance Cover

You must ensure that any holiday or travel insurance cover includes unexpected medical problems and emergencies. Even if you're taken ill in a country which has a reciprocal health agreement with your home country (see below), you may find that you have to pay some expenses. Reciprocal agreements don't cover the cost of a relative to fly out to bring you back to your home country, which a good travel policy would. You should ensure that you have the minimum insurance cover of £1m for within Europe and £2m for the rest of the world. If applicable, check whether pregnancy-related claims are covered and whether there are any restrictions for those over a certain age, e.g. 65 or 70. If you have an existing health problem which means you aren't covered under a standard policy, ask advice from your insurer, as there are some specialist policies available, although they're more expensive. Always check any exclusion clauses in contracts by obtaining a copy of the full policy document (all relevant information won't be included in the insurance leaflet). Skiing and other high risk sports and pursuits should be specifically covered and **listed** in a policy. Winter sports policies are available but are usually more expensive than normal holiday insurance.

24-hour Emergency Assistance: Ensure that your policy includes 24-hour emergency assistance. This means that in the case of a serious accident or illness, an assistance company will make all arrangements to get you emergency treatment (including repatriation if necessary) and offer help and advice when you most need it. This can save you a small fortune not just in medical treatment, but also in repatriation costs. The UK Foreign Office quotes £30,000 as a typical repatriation cost from the East Coast of the US to the UK and around £10,000 from European destinations to the UK.

Cost

The cost of travel insurance varies considerably according to your destination and the duration of the trip. In general, the longer the period of cover, the cheaper the daily or weekly rate, although the maximum period is usually six months. In Europe you should expect to pay from around £20 to £30 for up to four weeks' insurance. Premiums can be around double these amounts for travel to North America and the Caribbean, where medical treatment costs are sky high. Premiums may be higher for those aged over 65.

Annual Policies

For people who travel abroad frequently or spend long periods abroad, an annual travel policy usually provides the best value. As with all policies, always carefully check exactly what it includes. Many insurance companies offer annual travel policies for a premium of around £100 to £150 for an individual (the equivalent of around three months' insurance with a standard travel insurance policy), which are excellent value for frequent travellers. Some insurance companies offer an 'emergency travel policy' for holiday homeowners who need to travel abroad at short notice to inspect a property, e.g. after a severe storm. The cost of an annual policy may depend on the area covered, e.g. Europe, the world excluding North America, and the world including North America, although it doesn't usually cover travel within your country of residence. There's also a limit on the number of trips per year and the duration of each trip, e.g. 90 or 120 days. **Always check exactly what's covered (or omitted), as an annual policy may not provide adequate cover.**

6

Claims

Although travel insurance companies gladly take your money, they aren't always so keen to honour claims and you may have to persevere before they pay up. Always be persistent and make a claim **irrespective** of any small print, as this may be unreasonable and therefore invalid in law. Insurance companies usually require you to report a loss (or any incident for which you intend to make a claim) to the local police within 24 hours and obtain a written report. Failure to do this may mean that a claim won't be considered. Many policies have an excess (deductible) of £25 to £50.

Reciprocal Health Agreements

If you're entitled to social security health benefits in a European country, you can take advantage of reciprocal healthcare agreements in most other European countries, **but not if you're a permanent resident.** For example, anyone insured under social security in an EU country is covered for medical expenses while **travelling** for short periods (e.g. holidays and business trips) in other EU countries, provided you can obtain a European Health Insurance Card (EHIC) from your government health department in advance. In the UK, where the new card has replaced form E111, you can obtain a card online by visiting 💻 www.dh.gov.uk. The UK Department of Health website (💻 www.dh.gov.uk) also has a list of countries where you can receive free or low cost medical care.

Note that the EHIC cannot be used by those living abroad permanently. To take advantage of state health care as a permanent resident you must either be contributing to the country's social security system or be an EU pensioner who has contributed to a social security scheme in your home country (see Chapter 2).

International Health Insurance

If you plan to travel frequently for business or pleasure, it's best to have an international health policy. These generally offer wider cover than local policies, although if local medical facilities are adequate and you rarely travel abroad, they can be a waste of money. Most international health policies include repatriation or evacuation (although it may be optional), which can be an important consideration if you need treatment that's unavailable locally but is available in your home (or another) country. Repatriation may also include repatriation (by air) of the body of someone who dies abroad to their home country for burial.

Some companies offer policies for different areas, e.g. Europe, worldwide excluding North America, and worldwide including North America. A policy may offer full cover anywhere within Europe and limited cover in North America and certain other countries, e.g. Japan. Some policies offer the same cover worldwide for a fixed premium, which may be an important consideration for globetrotters. Note that an international policy allows you to have non-urgent medical treatment in another country. Most companies offer different levels of cover, for example 'basic', 'standard', 'comprehensive' and 'prestige'.

There's often a limit on the total annual medical costs, which should be at least £750,000, and some companies limit costs for specific treatment or costs such as specialists' fees, surgery and hospital accommodation. Some policies include permanent disability cover, e.g. £300,000, for those in full-time employment.

A medical isn't usually required for health policies, although existing health problems are usually excluded for a period, e.g. one or two years, and sometimes permanently. Always check carefully before you sign up for anything.

Cost

The cost of international heath insurance varies considerably according to your age and the extent of cover. Note that with most international insurance policies, you must enrol before you reach a certain age, e.g. between 60 and 80, to be guaranteed continuous cover in your old age. Premiums can sometimes be paid monthly, quarterly or annually, although some companies insist on payment annually in advance. When comparing policies, always carefully check the extent of cover and

© Courtesy Tourism New South Wales

© Marek Slusarczyk (www.123rf.com)

© Peter Farmer

© Hbak (www.123rf.com)

© South Africa Tourism (www.southafrica.net)

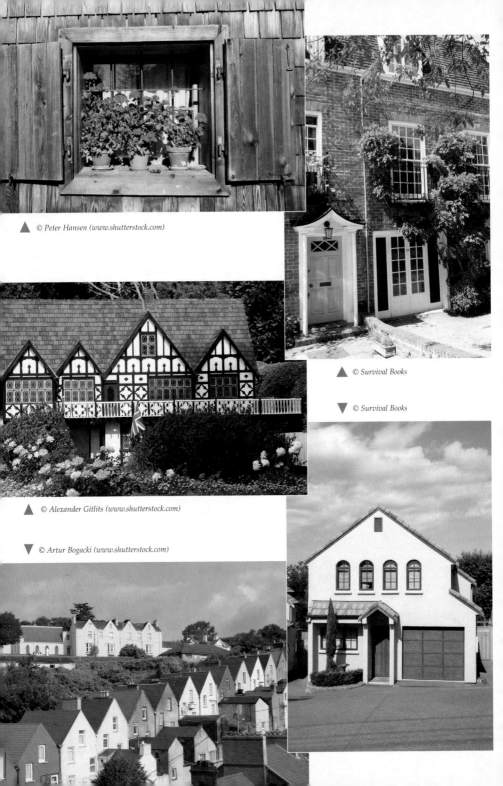

© Peter Hansen (www.shutterstock.com)

© Survival Books

© Survival Books

© Alexander Gitlits (www.shutterstock.com)

© Artur Bogacki (www.shutterstock.com)

exactly what's included **and** excluded from a policy (which may be noted only in the **very** small print), in addition to premiums and excess charges.

Although there may be significant differences in premiums, generally you get what you pay for. The most important questions to ask yourself are whether the policy provides the cover required and whether it's good value? If you're in reasonable health and are able to pay for your own out-patient treatment, such as visits to your family doctor and prescriptions, the best value policy may be one limited to specialist visits and hospital treatment.

Claims

Claims are usually settled in all major currencies and large claims are usually settled directly by insurance companies (although your choice of hospitals may be limited). Always check whether an insurance company will settle large medical bills directly. If you're required to pay bills and claim reimbursement from the insurance company, it may take several months to receive your money (some companies are slow to pay). It isn't usually necessary to translate bills into English or another language, although you should check a company's policy. Most international health insurance companies provide 24-hour emergency telephone assistance.

Household Insurance

In most countries, household insurance includes third-party liability, building and contents insurance, all of which are usually contained in a multi-risk or homeowner's insurance policy (although in some countries these risks must be covered separately – see below). When investing in a home abroad, you're usually responsible for insuring it from the moment you become the owner, e.g. for third-party risks. **Don't be tempted not to have full cover for your property. In some countries it isn't unusual for buildings to be severely damaged by floods and storms.**

Policies are usually offered by local and international insurance companies.

Building

Although it isn't usually compulsory for property owners, it's always wise to take out building insurance. If you have a mortgage, your lender will usually insist that your home, including most permanent structures on your land, is insured. It may be mandatory to take out building insurance with a lender for the whole of the mortgage term.

Building insurance generally covers damage caused by fire, lightning, water, explosion, storm, smoke, freezing, snow, theft, riot or civil commotion, vandalism or malicious damage, acts of terrorism, impact (e.g. by aircraft or vehicles), broken glass (constituting part of the building) and natural catastrophes (such as falling trees). Insurance should include glass, external buildings, aerials and satellite dishes, and gardens and garden ornaments. Note that if a claim is made as a result of a defect in the building or design, e.g. the roof is too heavy and collapses, the insurance company won't pay (yet another reason to have a survey before buying).

The amount for which you should insure your home isn't the current market value, but its replacement value, i.e. the cost of rebuilding it should it be destroyed. This should be increased each year in line with inflation. **Make sure that you insure your property for the true cost of rebuilding.**

In some countries, e.g. the US, many people lose their homes each year as a result of natural disasters such as earthquakes, fires, floods, hurricanes and tornadoes. In high risk areas, owners must usually pay an extra premium to cover risks such as subsidence (e.g. where homes are built on clay), floods or earthquakes, although the cost may be extremely high (only some 15 per cent of Californians have earthquake insurance, as it's simply too expensive). Read the small print carefully, e.g. some policies don't include water coming in from ground level, e.g. flood water, but only water seeping through the roof. **You should investigate the occurrence of natural disasters in the area where you're planning to buy and the cost of insurance before committing yourself, as premiums can be prohibitive.** In certain cases, claims for damage caused by storms aren't considered by insurance companies unless the situation is declared a natural catastrophe or an 'act of God' by the government.

Community Developments: If you own an apartment or townhouse that's part of a development, building insurance should be included in your service charges, although you should check exactly what's covered. You must, however, still be insured for third-party risks in the event that you cause damage to neighbouring properties, e.g. through flood or fire.

Rented Property: A rental contract normally requires you to insure against 'tenant risks' (i.e. to have third-party liability insurance), including damage you may cause to the property and to neighbouring properties if you live in an apartment, e.g. due to a flood, fire or explosion. You can choose your own insurance company and aren't required to use one recommended by your landlord.

Third-party Liability: It's common practice in many countries to have third-party liability insurance. This is often combined with household insurance (see above) and covers all members of a family and includes damage caused by you, your children and pets. Third-party liability insurance also protects you against claims from anyone who injures himself or suffers loss while on your property. Where damage is due to negligence, compensation may be reduced. In some countries, if your children attend school they're automatically covered by third-party liability insurance. Check whether third-party liability insurance covers you against accidental damage to your home's fixtures and fittings (which may in any case be covered by your household insurance).

Contents

Your home contents are usually insured for the same risks as the building (see above) and in most countries for their replacement value (new for old), with a reduction for wear and tear for clothes and linen. However, in some countries, e.g. the US, possessions are insured for their 'actual cash value' (cost minus depreciation). You can, however, buy replacement value insurance, although policies often include limits and are more expensive. Valuable items are covered for their authenticated value. Most policies include automatic indexation of the insured sum in line with inflation.

Contents insurance may include accidental damage to sanitary installations, theft or loss of money, replacement of locks following damage or loss of keys, frozen food following a power cut or freezer breakdown, alternative accommodation in the event that the property becomes uninhabitable, and property belonging to third parties stored in your home. Some items are usually excluded but may be included for an extra premium, e.g. credit cards, emergency assistance (plumber, glazier, electrician, etc.), redecoration, garaged cars, replacement pipes and loss of rent. Most contents policies don't include third-party liability, although this may be an option.

Items of high value must usually be itemised and documentation (e.g. a valuation) and photographs provided. Some companies even recommend or insist on a video film of belongings. When claiming for contents, you should produce the original bills if possible (always keep bills for expensive items) and bear in mind that replacing any imported items abroad may be more expensive than buying them in your home country. Contents policies usually contain security clauses and if you don't adhere to them a claim won't be considered, e.g. that ground-floor windows and patio doors must be locked or protected by grilles. Most companies give a discount if properties have high -ecurity locks and alarms (particularly alarms connected to a monitoring station). Policies pay for theft only when there are signs of forcible entry.

Premiums

The cost of household insurance varies considerably according to the country, the type of property, its location and the local crime rate. Premiums are usually calculated on the size of the property – either the habitable (constructed) area in m^2 or the number of rooms, rather than its value. The sum insured may be unlimited, provided the property doesn't exceed a certain size and is under a certain age, e.g. 200 years, although some companies restrict home insurance to properties with a maximum number of rooms or a maximum value of contents. In general, detached, older and more remote properties cost more to insure than apartments and new properties (particularly when located in towns), because of the higher risk of theft. Premiums are also higher in certain areas, and some policies impose a small excess (deductible) for each claim.

Security

In some countries, a building must have iron bars on the ground-floor windows and patio doors, window shutters and secure locks. In countries and areas with a high risk of theft, e.g. major cities and resort areas, an insurance company may insist on extra security measures, e.g. two locks on all external doors (one of a mortise type) and shutters or security gratings on windows. A policy may specify that all forms of protection on doors must be employed whenever a property is unoccupied and that

6

all other forms (e.g. shutters) must also be used at night (e.g. after 10pm) and when a property is left empty for more than a few days. It's unwise to leave valuable or irreplaceable items in a holiday home or in a property that's vacant for long periods.

Some companies offer a discount if properties have steel reinforced doors, security locks and alarms (particularly alarms connected to a 24-hour security centre). An insurance company may send someone to inspect your property and to advise on security measures. Policies usually pay out for theft only when there are signs of forced entry and don't include thefts by a tenant (but may include thefts by domestic staff). All-risks cover is available from some insurance companies, offering a worldwide extension to a household policy and including items such as jewellery and cameras.

Inventory

To calculate the amount of insurance you need, make a complete list of your possessions containing a description, purchase price and date, and their location in your home. Some insurance companies use a formula based on your buildings insurance value (i.e. the value of your home), although this is no more than a 'guesstimate'. Keep the list and all receipts in a safe place (such as a safety deposit box), and add new purchases and make adjustments to your insurance cover when necessary.

Claims

6

If you wish to make a claim, you must usually inform your insurance company in writing (by registered letter) within two to seven days of an incident or 24 hours in the case of theft. Thefts should also be reported to the local police within 24 hours, as the police report, of which you receive a copy for your insurance company, constitutes irrefutable evidence of your claim. Check whether you're covered for damage or thefts that occur while you're away from your property and are therefore unable to inform the insurance company immediately.

Take care that you don't under-insure your house contents and that you periodically reassess their value and adjust your insurance premium accordingly. You can arrange to have your insurance cover automatically increased annually by a fixed percentage or amount. If you make a claim and the assessor discovers that you're under-insured, the amount due is reduced by the percentage by which you're under-insured.

Settlement: Bear in mind that if you make a claim you may need to wait months for it to be settled. Generally the larger the claim, the longer you'll have to wait for your money, although in an emergency some companies make an interim payment. If you aren't satisfied with the amount offered, don't accept it, but try to negotiate a higher figure. If you still cannot reach agreement on the amount or the time taken to settle a claim, you may be able to take your claim to an ombudsman or an independent industry organisation for arbitration. **Note that some insurance**

companies do their utmost to find a loophole which makes you negligent and relieves them of liability.

Holiday Homes

Premiums are generally higher for holiday homes, because they're usually left unattended for long periods, which makes them more vulnerable, particularly to burglaries. Premiums are usually based on the number of days a year a property is inhabited and the interval between periods of occupancy. Cover for theft, storm, flood and malicious damage may be suspended when a property is left empty for an extended period. Note that you're required to turn off the water supply at the mains when vacating a building for more than 72 hours. It's possible to negotiate cover for periods of absence for a hefty surcharge, although valuable items are usually excluded (unless you have a safe). If you're absent from your property for long periods, e.g. longer than 30 days a year, you may be required to pay an excess on a claim arising from an occurrence that takes place during your absence (and theft may be excluded). You should ensure that the details listed on a policy are correct; otherwise your policy could be void. Where applicable, it's important to ensure that a policy specifies that a property is a holiday home and not a principal home. If you're planning to let a property, you may be required to inform your insurer.

It's unwise to leave valuable or irreplaceable items in a holiday home or a property that will be vacant for long periods.

Insuring in Your Home Country

6

It's possible and legal to take out building and contents insurance in your home country for a property abroad (some insurance companies offer policies designed for holiday homeowners), although you must ensure that a policy is valid under local laws. For example, EU residents with a home in another EU country can buy insurance in their home country, but the insurance company must be licensed to underwrite insurance in the country where the property is located, and any taxes or charges that apply in that country must be paid.

The advantage of insuring in your home country is that you have a policy you can understand and you can handle claims in your own language. Insuring in your home country may seem like a good option for a holiday home abroad, although it can sometimes be more expensive than insuring with a local company and can lead to conflicts if, for example, the building is insured with a locally registered company and the contents with a foreign-based company. Most experts advise that you insure with a local insurance company.

Car Insurance

Some insurance companies insure foreign-registered cars, although there may be a limit on the period (e.g. six months or a year). If you drive a UK-registered car and spend over six months a year abroad, you may need to take out a European insurance policy or (more likely) obtain insurance with a foreign insurance company.

Green Card

An international insurance certificate (green card) isn't required to cross borders within the EU. This is because motorists insured in EU member states and Andorra, Croatia, Iceland, Liechtenstein, Norway, and Switzerland are automatically covered for basic third-party liability in these countries. However, a green card is automatically recognisable in all countries as proof of third-party insurance and it's a good idea to carry one in case of an accident. Some European countries aren't part of the above European Directive and so a green card is compulsory and in others it's mandatory to buy car insurance at the border. Your insurer can advise you about a particular country.

A green card is available at no extra cost when you're insured in most western European countries and extends your normal insurance (e.g. comprehensive) to other countries covered by the green card agreement. Without a green card, your insurance may be restricted to third-party liability. However, you must always check with your insurance company whether there are any restrictions and whether you need to arrange extra cover. For cars insured in the UK, insurance companies charge a fee or provide a free green card for a limited period of 30 or 45 days a year, and usually cover motorists for a maximum period of around three months a year. However, some companies allow motorists a green card for up to six months a year or longer.

6

Breakdown Insurance

In most European countries, motor breakdown insurance is provided by local motor insurance companies. Many companies providing European breakdown insurance operate multilingual, 24-hour emergency centres where assistance is available for motoring, medical, legal and travel problems.

TAXES

Before investing in a property abroad, you should investigate the taxes levied on resident and non-resident property owners, such as property taxes (rates), residential tax, tax on rental income, capital gains tax, wealth tax and inheritance tax. If you plan to live abroad permanently, you also need to compare income tax, social security contributions and other taxes incurred by residents. For many people, moving abroad is an opportunity to reduce their overall tax burden, particularly when moving from a high- to a low-tax country, when the timing of a move can be decisive. Some countries encourage foreigners, e.g. retirees, to take up residence by offering tax incentives. Note that in most countries, taxes are payable on property transactions, which can increase the cost of buying a property considerably.

Property Taxes

Property taxes (also called real estate taxes or rates) are levied by local authorities in most countries and are payable by all property owners, irrespective of whether they're residents or non-residents. In some countries, an additional 'residential' or local income tax is paid by residents. Property taxes pay for local services, which may include rubbish (garbage) collection, street lighting, sanitary services (e.g. street and beach cleaning), local schools and other community services, local council administration, social assistance, cultural and sports amenities, and possibly mains water. Before buying a property, check the tax rate with the local town hall, as rates usually vary from area to area.

Property tax is usually payable irrespective of whether a property is occupied, provided it's furnished and habitable. It may be split into two amounts, one for the building and another for the land, with tax on the land payable irrespective of whether it's built on. Before buying a property you should check that there are no outstanding property taxes for the current or previous years; in many countries the new owner assumes all unpaid property-related taxes and debts. When you buy a property in any country, your ownership must be registered at the local land registry, which is usually done by the public notary officiating at the completion of the sale.

Property taxes are normally based on the fiscal or notional letting value of a property, which is usually lower than the actual purchase price or a property's market value. If the fiscal value of your property increases greatly, check that it has been correctly calculated. You can appeal against the valuation of your property if you believe it's too high (e.g. higher than that of similar properties in the same area). **It's important to check that the fiscal value of your property is correct, as in some countries (e.g. Spain) a number of taxes are linked to this value, such as property letting tax, wealth tax, transfer tax on property sales and inheritance tax.**

6

Property values are calculated according to a variety of measurements and evaluations which usually include the area of the property (i.e. the built or living area, terraces, outbuildings, garage and land areas), building and zoning restrictions in the area, the quality and date of construction, the proximity to services, e.g. mains water, electricity and gas, and roads, and the location. You can check that your property is correctly specified at the local town hall or land registration office, where a dossier is maintained for all properties. This usually contains official papers, plans, and photographs relating to a property. Carefully check that all the information recorded is correct, as errors are fairly common in some countries. Note that property valuations may be adjusted periodically to account for inflation.

Tax Rates

Tax rates may depend on the population of the municipality and the level of public services provided, and can vary considerably for similar properties in different areas. Therefore a high property tax may be a good rather than a bad sign, although it may also indicate that the local council is dishonest or profligate.

Payment

Town halls in some countries don't send out bills and it's the property owner's responsibility to discover the amount due and when it's payable. If you're a non-resident, you should pay your property tax (and other local taxes and utility bills) by direct debit from a local bank account. You can also employ a local property management company or representative to pay your property tax and other bills relating to your property. If property tax isn't paid on time, a surcharge may be levied in addition to interest, plus possible collection costs. If you get into debt and are unable to pay your property tax, you should talk to your local tax office. They will be pleased to know that you haven't absconded and will usually be willing to agree a payment schedule.

If you don't pay your property taxes, your property can (after a certain period) be seized and sold at auction, often for a fraction of its market value.

Other Local Taxes

Local authorities in some countries may also levy fees for services such as beach cleaning or sewerage. Extra taxes are levied in some popular tourist areas, where local authorities must pay for the upkeep of gardens, parks and other 'attractions'. In France (and some other countries), there's an additional property-based 'residential' tax (*taxe d'habitation*), which is payable by anyone who lives in a property, whether as an owner or tenant or rent free.

6 Tax on Rental Income

Rental income earned by non-residents is taxable in most countries, often at a fixed rate, e.g. 25 or 30 per cent, rather than on a sliding scale. In some countries, e.g. Spain, non-resident home owners must pay an imputed 'letting' tax based on the value of their property, irrespective of whether or not it's let. Other taxes may also be payable on property that is let or on rental income, such as value added tax (VAT), or (e.g. in Florida) sales and 'tourist development' taxes; see **Country Profiles** for details.

Non-residents with property-related income must usually file an annual tax return (joint property owners may need to file separately). **If you fail to declare rental income to the local tax authorities, you could be liable for a large assessment and possibly a fine, and your future declarations will be under scrutiny.**

Generally all property-related expenses such as repairs and maintenance, cleaning costs, mortgage interest, management expenses, business trips abroad in connection with property ownership, and possibly an allowance to cover depreciation and insurance, can be deducted from your property income for tax purposes. It's possible for owners in some countries, e.g. the UK, to offset the interest paid on a mortgage secured on an overseas property against the income received from that property.

The taxation of rental income is a complicated subject and you should obtain professional advice from an experienced accountant or tax specialist. If possible, this should be done before buying in order to determine the best method of ownership (which may be through a trust or offshore company).

Wealth Tax

Some countries levy a wealth tax, although this is usually applicable only to residents. Spain is a notable exception, where wealth tax also applies to non-resident property owners. Your wealth is generally calculated by totalling your assets and deducting your liabilities. When calculating your wealth tax, you must include the value of all assets including property (real estate), vehicles, boats, aircraft, business ownership, cash (e.g. in bank accounts), life insurance, gold bars, jewellery, stocks, shares and bonds. If you fail to declare your total assets you can be fined.

Assets that are exempt from wealth tax usually include *objets d'art* and antiques (provided their value doesn't exceed certain limits), the vested rights of participants in pension plans and funds, copyrights (so long as they remain part of your net worth), assets forming part of a country's historical heritage, and 'professional assets' in a business. Deductions are usually made for mortgages, business and other debts, and wealth tax paid in another country.

The level at which wealth tax is applicable varies greatly according to the country and, in the case of Spain, whether you're a resident or non-resident. Check the **Country Profiles** for details of tax in your chosen country.

Wealth tax may depend on your domicile, e.g. if you're domiciled in France, the value of your estate is based on your worldwide assets, whereas if you're resident in France but not domiciled there, the value of your estate is based only on your assets in France.

6

Capital Gains Tax

Capital gains tax can be a complicated subject and you should always obtain legal advice before buying a property abroad. **Note that the tax authorities in many countries co-operate to track down those attempting to avoid capital gains tax.**

Capital gains tax is payable on the profit from the sale of certain assets in most countries, which usually includes property. International tax treaties usually decree that capital gains on property are taxable in the country where the property is located. In most countries, capital gains are treated as ordinary income for residents and there's an exemption if gains are within a certain limit. In most countries, capital gains are treated as ordinary income for residents.

If you move abroad permanently and retain a property in your home country, this may affect your position regarding capital gains there. If you sell your property in your home country before moving abroad, you're exempt from CGT because it's your principal residence. However, if you then establish your principal residence abroad and keep your property at home, this then becomes your second home and thus liable to CGT when it's sold. In some countries, you're exempt from CGT on a second home if you don't own your main residence, i.e. if you're a tenant or leaseholder, although this may apply only to the **first** sale of a second home.

Calculation & Exemptions

Certain gains are exempt and these may include gains resulting from the death of a taxpayer, gifts to government entities, donations of assets in lieu of tax payments, and the exchange of assets for a life annuity for those aged over 65.

Otherwise, a property capital gain is based on the difference between the purchase price and the sale price. However, in most countries there are reductions to take inflation into account (known as 'indexation relief'), which usually depend on the number of years a property has been owned and whether it's your principal residence. The amount of CGT payable is usually reduced the longer you've owned a property until it's no longer applicable (e.g. after 15 years in France).

If an asset has been owned for less than a certain period, e.g. two years in France and Spain, capital gains are taxed in full. Most countries (including the UK and France) allow an exemption on the sale of your principal residence, although some (such as Spain and the US) do so only if you buy another home within two years, and levy tax on any profits that aren't re-invested. In the US, you can make a one-time, tax-free profit of $250,000 ($500,000 for a married couple who file jointly) on the sale of your principal residence if it was used for two of the five years before the date of sale.

6 Offsetting CGT

You should keep all bills for the fees associated with buying a property, e.g. from a lawyer, estate agent and surveyor, plus any bills for renovation, restoration, modernisation and improvements of a second home, as these can usually be offset against CGT and may be index-linked. If you work on a house yourself, you should keep a copy of all bills for materials and tools, as these may also be offset against CGT (although not in France). Losses on rentals may also be able to be carried forward and offset against a capital gain when a property is sold. Costs relating to a sale can also usually be offset against any gain, as can interest paid on a loan taken out to purchase or restore a property. In some countries you can protect yourself and your survivors from capital gains tax by bequeathing appreciated property in your will, rather than giving it away while you're alive.

Inheritance & Gift Tax

Dying doesn't free you entirely from the clutches of the tax man in most countries, which impose an inheritance (also called estate tax or death duty) and gift tax on the estate of a deceased person. Usually both residents and non-residents are subject to inheritance tax if they own property abroad. The country where you pay inheritance and gift tax is usually decided by your domicile. If you're living permanently abroad at the time of your death, you're deemed to be domiciled there by the local tax authorities. If you're domiciled abroad, inheritance and gift tax payable there will apply to your worldwide estate (excluding property); otherwise it applies only to assets held abroad, such as a holiday home. It's important to make your domicile clear so that there's no misunderstanding on your death.

In many countries, e.g. France and Spain, inheritance tax is paid by the beneficiaries and not by the deceased's estate. This may mean that if you inherit a home abroad, you'll need to sell it to pay tax. The rate of inheritance tax payable usually depends upon the relationship between the donor and the recipient, the amount inherited, and (in some countries) the current wealth of the recipient. Direct descendants and close relatives of the deceased usually receive an allowance before they become liable for inheritance tax. To take advantage of lower tax rates, you should leave property to your spouse, children or parents, rather than someone who's unrelated.

In many countries, there are a number of ways to avoid or reduce inheritance tax, including buying property through an offshore company or trust. Some bequests are exempt from inheritance tax, including certain types of property and legacies to charities and government bodies.

Some countries have strict succession laws, which may also apply to foreigners (e.g. in France). Note also that most countries don't recognise the rights to inheritance of a non-married partner, although there are a number of solutions to this problem, e.g. a life insurance policy. There are many ways to limit or delay the impact of succession laws, including inserting a clause in a property purchase contract allowing a property to be left in its entirety to a surviving spouse without being shared among the children. In some countries, a surviving spouse can be given a life interest (usufruct) in an estate in preference to children or parents, through a 'gift between spouses'.

Inheritance law is a complicated subject and professional advice should be sought from an experienced lawyer who's familiar with the inheritance laws of the country where you plan to buy a home and any other countries involved. Your will is a vital component in ensuring that inheritance and gift tax is kept to a minimum or delaying its payment.

Gift tax is calculated in the same way as inheritance tax, according to the relationship between the donor and the recipient and the size of the gift. A reduction is usually granted according to the age of the donor (generally the younger the donor the larger the reduction).

It's important for both residents and non-residents owning a home abroad to decide in advance how they wish to dispose of it. If possible, this should be decided *before* buying a home or other property abroad, as it can be complicated and expensive to change later.

Income Tax

Income tax is mainly of interest (or concern!) to those planning to live or work abroad, as non-residents are usually liable to pay income tax only in a country when they receive income from a local source. However, most countries levy income tax on income earned by non-residents from letting a home (see above). If you're planning to live or work abroad permanently you should also take into account social security contributions, which are very high in some countries, particularly for the self-employed.

If you're planning to work or start a business abroad, you should seek expert tax advice, both in your present country of residence (regarding your tax liability there) and in the country where you plan to work. Note that the combined burden of income tax, social security and other taxes can make a considerable hole in your income in some countries.

Liability

Your liability to pay income tax in a country where you own property depends on whether you earn any income from your property or have income arising in that country and how long you're resident there each year, although in some countries, e.g. Spain, **all** home owners must pay an imputed 'letting' tax based on the value of their property, irrespective of whether they receive any income from it.

Under the law of most countries you become a fiscal resident (liable to income tax) if you spend 183 days there during a calendar year or your main centre of economic interest, e.g. investments or business, is there. Temporary absences are usually included in the calculation of the period spent abroad, unless residence is shown to have been in another country for 183 days in a calendar year. If your spouse and any dependent minor children normally reside in a country where you have a home, you may also be considered to be a tax resident in that country (unless you can prove otherwise). Some countries restrict the visits of non-residents over a certain period, e.g. the UK limits visits by non-residents to 182 days in any tax year or an average of 91 days per tax year over four consecutive tax years.

Dual Residence

It's possible to have 'dual residence' and be tax resident in two countries simultaneously, in which case your 'tax home' may be resolved under the rules of international treaties. Under such treaties you're considered to be resident in the country where you have a permanent home. If you have a permanent home in both countries, you're deemed to be resident in the country where you have the closest personal and economic ties. If your residence cannot be determined under the above rules, you're deemed to be resident in the country where you have your habitual abode. If you have your habitual abode in both or in neither country, you're deemed to be resident in the country of which you're a citizen. Finally, if you're a citizen of both or neither country, the authorities of the countries concerned decide your tax residence between them.

Double Taxation

Many countries have double-taxation treaties with other countries that are designed to ensure that income that has been taxed in one treaty country isn't taxed again in another. The treaty establishes a tax credit or exemption on certain kinds of income, either in the country of residence or the country where the income is earned.

Double-taxation treaties vary with the country, for example the UK has treaties with most of the countries featured in this book (see **Country Profiles**). Where applicable, a double-taxation treaty prevails over domestic law. However, even when there's no double-taxation agreement between two countries, you can still obtain relief from double taxation: tax relief is provided through direct deduction of any foreign tax paid or through a 'foreign compensation' formula. Note that if your tax liability in one country is less than in another, you may be required to pay the tax authorities the difference in the country where you're resident.

If you're in doubt about your tax liability in your home country or a country where you own property, contact your nearest embassy or consulate for information. The US is the only country that taxes its non-resident citizens on income earned abroad (US citizens can obtain a copy of a brochure, *Tax Guide for Americans Abroad*, from American consulates).

Moving Abroad

Before leaving a country for good, you must usually pay any tax due for the previous year and the year of departure, and you may also need to apply for a tax clearance. A tax return must usually be filed before departure and must include your income and deductions for the current tax year up to the date of departure. The local tax office will calculate the taxes due and provide a written statement. In some countries a tax clearance certificate is necessary to obtain a 'sailing or departure permit' or an exit visa. A shipping or removal company may also need official authorisation from the tax authorities before they can ship your effects abroad.

6

Tax Havens

If you're looking for a 'tax haven' or a low tax country, you should investigate buying a home in Andorra, certain Caribbean islands (e.g. the Bahamas, Bermuda or the Cayman Islands), the Channel Islands, Cyprus, the Isle of Man, Gibraltar, Liechtenstein, Malta, Monaco or Switzerland. Note, however, that you need a **very** large bank balance to purchase a property and become a resident in some low-tax countries, e.g. the Caribbean, the Channel Islands, Monaco and Switzerland. You should also be aware that owning a home in a particular country won't necessarily qualify you for a residence permit and that to qualify as a resident you must usually spend at least 183 days a year in a country.

Tax Planning

If you're intending to move abroad permanently, you should plan well in advance, as the timing of a move can make a big difference to your tax liabilities, both in your present and in your new country of residence. Investigate beforehand what you need to do to become a non-resident in your current country of residence and how long you need to be resident in your new home to qualify as a resident for tax purposes. In most countries, you automatically become liable for income tax if you spend longer than six months (183 days) there during a calendar year but it may be advantageous for you to 'declare yourself' as a resident before that period has elapsed or even on arrival.

If you intend to live abroad permanently, you should notify the tax authorities in your previous country of residence well in advance. You may be entitled to a tax refund if you leave during the tax year, which usually requires the completion of a tax return. The authorities may require evidence that you're leaving the country, e.g. evidence of a job abroad or of having purchased or rented a property abroad. If you move abroad to take up a job or start a business, you must register with the local tax authorities soon after your arrival.

COST OF LIVING

If you're planning to buy a property abroad, and especially if you intend to live abroad permanently, you need to estimate how far your money will stretch and how much you'll have left after paying your bills. The cost of living has risen considerably in most countries in the last decade or so, and some Mediterranean countries that previously enjoyed a relatively low cost of living are no longer so inexpensive, particularly for retirees. On the other hand, foreigners whose income is paid in 'hard' currencies, such as those of most northern European countries and North America, have seen their incomes (when converted to local currencies) in many countries rise sharply in recent years. If anything, the difference in the cost of living between 'rich' North American and northern European countries (where most holiday home buyers and retirees come from) has remained the same or has widened in favour of the richer countries.

If you spend only a few weeks abroad each year, you won't be too concerned about the local cost of living, although you'll need to investigate the cost of maintaining your home year round. However, if you plan to live abroad permanently you should ensure that your income is, and will remain, sufficient to live on, bearing in mind possible devaluations (if your income isn't paid in local currency), inflation and expenses such as medical bills or anything else that may drastically reduce your income (such as stock market crashes and recessions). If your pension is paid in a currency that's devalued, this could have a catastrophic affect on your standard of living. Some countries, e.g. the UK, freeze the pensions of state pensioners living in certain countries.

It's difficult to calculate an average cost of living for any country, as costs depend on each individual's circumstances and lifestyle. It's generally cheaper to live in a rural area than in a large city or a popular resort area (and homes are also much cheaper). Your food bill will naturally depend on what you eat and whether you eat mostly at home or in restaurants. Food in most southern European and Mediterranean countries is cheaper than in most northern European countries, although North Americans will find it costs around the same or more. The equivalent of around £250 should feed two adults for a month, including inexpensive local wine, but excluding luxuries and expensive imported foods.

A couple owning their home (with no mortgage) in many popular retirement countries can 'survive' on a net income of around £500 per month (some pensioners live on less) and most people can live comfortably on an income of £800 per month. In fact, many northern Europeans (particularly Scandinavians) and North Americans find that if they live modestly without overdoing the luxuries, their cost of living is around half that in their home country.

6

7

MISCELLANEOUS MATTERS

This chapter contains miscellaneous – but nevertheless important – information for homeowners the world over, including (in alphabetical order) advice about heating and air-conditioning, utilities, television and radio and taking pets abroad. Relevant country-specific information is included in the **Country Profiles**.

HEATING & AIR-CONDITIONING

When investing in a home abroad you need to consider whether heating and air-conditioning are necessary, which may depend on whether it's to be a permanent or a holiday home, and on the time(s) of the year when you'll be resident. Even in southern parts of southern European countries, some form of heating is usually necessary in winter, and air-conditioning is a blessed relief in summer, while in the US's sunbelt states (particularly Florida) air-conditioning is considered mandatory (by lessees, at least) at all times of the year. In some countries, the weather fluctuates between boiling hot and freezing cold, when both central heating and air-conditioning are essential.

In some countries, apartment blocks may have a centrally-controlled heating system which provides heating (and possibly air-conditioning) to a whole block, with the cost included in community fees. Heating is turned on in the autumn and off in the spring and you may have no control over room temperatures, apart from turning individual radiators on or off (although radiators may have a gauge with low, medium and high settings). If you're a non-resident or absent for long periods, you should choose an apartment with its own heating (and cooling) system rather than a central system, otherwise you'll be contributing towards your neighbours' bills.

Heating

7

Central heating, double glazing and good insulation are common in new houses in northern Europe, where they're considered essential. In the US, most modern homes have a combined heating and cooling (air-conditioning) system which is thermostatically controlled. In southern Europe, where winter temperatures are higher, central heating is usually found only in 'luxury' apartments and villas, and heating is usually provided by open fires and portable gas and electric heaters. If you're used to central heating and like a warm house, however, you'll almost certainly miss it in winter, even in many 'hot' countries. Note that in hot countries, homes are designed to exclude the heat and stay cool in summer, and most have marble, tile or stone floors. This means they can seem much cooler in winter than a home with fitted carpets. If your home has stone floors, you'll usually need carpets, rugs and some form of heating in winter.

Central heating systems may be powered by oil, gas, electricity, solid fuel (usually wood) or even solar power. **Whatever form of heating you use, it's essential to have good insulation, without which up to 60 per cent of heating is lost through walls and roof.** In rural areas in many countries, many homes have wood-burning fireplaces and stoves, which may be combined with a central heating system and also provide hot water. In most countries people burn wood rather than coal, which is a relatively cheap fuel, particularly if you buy it in 'raw' cut logs (it's sold by the cubic metre in most European countries).

Electric Heating

Electric central heating isn't common in many countries because it's too expensive and requires good insulation and a permanent system of ventilation. Most stand-alone electric heaters are also expensive to run and are best suited to holiday homes, although night-storage heaters operating on a reduced night tariff can be economical. Note that if you have electric central heating (or air-conditioning), you may need to uprate your electricity supply (see **Power Supply** on page 157). Many people find that electric fan heaters suffice in the south of Spain.

Gas Heating

Stand-alone gas heaters using standard gas bottles are an economical way to provide heating in areas with mild winters but rooms **must** be well ventilated. **Gas poisoning due to faulty ventilation ducts for water gas heaters isn't uncommon in some countries.** The filters of gas heaters must be cleaned regularly and heaters must be periodically serviced and checked for leaks.

Solar Heating

If you own a house in a hot country, solar heating may be a viable option and the local authority may provide a grant for its installation. Although it's most commonly used to provide hot water, combined solar hot water and heating systems (with a hot-air solar radiator) are available. These are usually combined with an electric or gas heating system, as solar energy cannot be relied upon year-round for hot water and heating requirements (although advances in solar cell technology are expected to increase the efficiency and reduce the cost dramatically in the next few decades).

Air-conditioning

Air-conditioning is rare in European and Mediterranean countries, even in the hottest areas, and it's usually confined to luxury properties. However, you won't consider it a luxury when the temperature soars above 40C (104F)! You can choose between a huge variety of air-conditioners, fixed or moveable, indoor or outdoor, high or low power. **Some air-conditioners are noisy, so always check before buying one.**

Most window-mounted air-conditioning units have a choice of fan speeds and the fan can usually be switched on separately from the cooling system. The cooling system can be adjusted for temperature and units often have a vent that can be opened to allow air into the room when they aren't in use. An air-conditioning system with a heat pump provides cooling in summer and economical heating in winter. In many countries, homes have ceiling fans for extra cooling in the summer.

When using air-conditioning, all windows and outside doors should obviously be closed. **If you suffer from asthma or respiratory problems, air-conditioning can cause negative health effects.**

PETS

If you have pets and want to take them abroad with you, there are many considerations to be made, not only regarding importing them into your new country but also regarding regulations and dangers for pets in that country.

Importing Pets

Taking your pet abroad is far easier now that the EU has adopted new regulations (from 2003) for the non-commercial movement of pets from what are known as 'qualifying countries'. If you're travelling within the EU and your pet meets the criteria to obtain a European Pet Passport (formerly the PETS certificate) you should be allowed to import it into another EU country without quarantine. The Pet Travel Scheme (PETS), introduced in 2000, replaced quarantine for qualifying cats and dogs, and that scheme was replaced by the European Pet Passport in July 2004. To qualify for a passport, pets must be microchipped (a microchip is painlessly inserted in their neck), vaccinated against rabies and undergo a blood test to check that they have sufficient antibodies against the disease. Once you get the all-clear, there's a wait of six months before your European Pet Passport can be issued and your pet can travel.

Additionally, 24 to 48 hours before your departure for another EU country, your pet must be checked for parasites by a government-authorised vet and a certificate issued. This certificate, along with your pet's European Pet Passport and copies of the rabies vaccination certificate and the blood test results to prove your dog is protected, are the required documentation. Some countries have minor additional requirements and you should always check with the relevant veterinary authority. You must also be able to prove where your pet started its journey and that it's a domestic pet and not intended for sale.

This arrangement is only for animals imported from rabies-free countries and countries where rabies is under control, which includes most EU countries plus Bahrain, Canada and the US. The current quarantine law remains applicable for pets coming from Eastern Europe, Africa, Asia and South America.

Particular consideration must be given before exporting a pet from a country with strict quarantine regulations, such as the UK. All of the above procedures ensure that you'll be able to return to the UK with your dog or cat at short notice, provided it's checked again for parasites 24 to 48 hours before the return journey. Additional information is available from the Department for Environment, Food and Rural Affairs

(DEFRA, UK ☎ 020-7904 6000 or ☎ 020-7238 6951, 🖳 www.defra.gov.uk/animalh/ quarantine). The cost to pet owners is around £200 (for a microchip, rabies vaccination and blood test), plus £60 a year for annual booster vaccinations. Shop around and compare fees from a number of veterinary surgeons, but all the above procedures must be carried out by a government authorised vet. Only certain routes and carriers are licensed to carry animals; DEFRA has details.

If you're transporting a pet by sea, you should notify the shipping company. Some companies insist that pets are left in vehicles (if applicable), while others allow pets to be kept in cabins. If your pet is of a nervous disposition or unused to travelling, it may be wise to tranquilise it on a long sea crossing, but always seek the advice of your vet.

Pets can also be transported by air, but only on certain routes. Check your airline for more information about the cost and method of transport. Pets must usually travel in an IATA approved container and you're usually charged per kilo. Animals may be examined at the port of entry by a veterinary officer in the country of destination, so ensure that you have the relevant paperwork to hand on arrival.

Pets Abroad

In many countries, pets must be registered and may be issued with a disc to be worn on a collar around their neck, while others require dogs to be tattooed on their body or in an ear as a means of registration. In recent years, some countries have introduced a microchip identification system for dogs (which has replaced tattooing), whereby a microchip is inserted under the skin. Irrespective of whether your dog is tattooed or microchipped, you should have it fitted with a collar and tag with your name and telephone number on it and the magic word 'reward'. Registration can be expensive.

Dogs

7

Most countries have rules regarding the keeping of dogs, which may require a health card or collar disc if they're older than three months. In public areas, a dog may need to be kept on a lead (and muzzled if it's considered dangerous). Dogs are usually prohibited from entering places where food is manufactured, stored or sold (France is a notable exception, where dogs are commonly admitted to bars and restaurants), and may also be barred from sports and cultural events and beaches. In some countries the keeping of dogs is restricted or banned from long-term rental or holiday accommodation (so check when renting an apartment). Some countries also have strict laws regarding cleaning up after pets in public places and you can be heavily fined for not doing so.

Take extra care when walking your dog in country areas, as hunters sometimes put down poisoned food to control natural predators. Don't let your dog far out of your sight or let it roam free, as dogs may be stolen or mistakenly shot by hunters.

Vaccinations & Diseases

If you intend to live abroad permanently, dogs should be vaccinated against certain diseases (in addition to rabies, which is usually required for import – see above), which may include hepatitis, distemper and kennel cough. Cats should be immunised against feline gastro-enteritis and typhus. Pets should also be checked frequently for fleas and tapeworm. Note that there are a number of diseases and other dangers for pets in some countries, e.g. Spain, that aren't found in North America and northern Europe. These include the fatal leishmaniasis (also called Mediterranean or sandfly disease and which can be prevented by using a spray such as DefendDog), processionary caterpillars, leeches, heartworm, ticks (a tick collar can lessen the effects of these), feline leukaemia and feline enteritis. Obtain advice about these and other diseases from a veterinary surgeon in your home country or on arrival abroad.

Veterinary surgeons are well trained in most countries, where there are also kennels, catteries and animal hospitals and clinics, which may provide a 24-hour emergency service, and even pet ambulances and cemeteries (not to mention 'pooch parlours'). There are also animal welfare organisations in many countries which operate shelters for stray and abused animals, although few are as effective as the UK's RSPCA, and inexpensive pet hospitals. Health insurance for pets is available in most countries (vets' fees can be astronomical) and it's wise to have third-party insurance in case your pet bites someone or causes an accident.

TELEVISION & RADIO

Many of those who move abroad permanently or for long periods find they soon begin to miss television programmes from their home country. Fortunately, the growth of satellite television (TV) over the last few decades has enabled people to enjoy TV programmes in English and a variety of other languages almost anywhere in the world, and recent developments mean that more channels are free-to-view (FTV). Cable TV is also available in many countries and often includes foreign-language stations.

Check whether a TV or radio licence is required in your chosen country and how it should be paid. The quality of local radio (including expatriate stations in some countries) is generally excellent, and if you have a high-quality receiver (or a satellite TV system) it's possible to receive radio broadcasts from around the globe. More recently, broadband internet access has allowed many people to access their favourite radio stations from anywhere in the world via their personal computer; no doubt TV programmes will soon follow.

Television

Over the last decade, the technology associated with broadcasting and telecommunications systems has moved forward in leaps and bounds. The most notable development is the move to digital television (DTV) and the projected global 'switching off' of analogue television over the next few years.

Analogue Television

The lack of compatibility of analogue television standards around the world has long been a problem for those who want to take TVs and video cassette recorders (VCRs) abroad. With the advent of digital television, this is less of a problem, but there are still some differences (see below). Analogue television has three main systems: PAL, SECAM and NTSC. To add to the confusion, there are quite a few variations on these systems.

● **PAL** – Most European countries use the PAL system (PAL B, G, D or K). The UK, however, uses a modified PAL-I system that's incompatible with other European countries.

● **SECAM** – There are several SECAM systems; France and its former colonies use a standard called SECAM-L, which is different from the SECAM standard used elsewhere in the world, e.g. SECAM B/G in the Middle East, former East Germany and Greece, and SECAM D/K in some eastern European and many African countries.

● **NTSC** – This system (the NTSC III version is the latest) is used in Canada, the Caribbean countries, Japan, Mexico, the Philippines, South and Central America, most Asian countries and the US. NTSC isn't compatible with any other system.

If you want a TV that will operate in France and other European countries, and a VCR that will play PAL and SECAM videos, you must buy a multi-standard TV and VCR. These are widely available in some countries and contain automatic circuitry that switches from PAL-I (UK), to PAL-B/G (rest of Europe) to SECAM-L (France). Some multi-standard TVs also incorporate the North American NTSC standard and have an NTSC-in jack plug connection allowing you to play back American videos. If you have a PAL TV, it's also possible to buy a 'transcoder' that converts SECAM signals to PAL. Some people opt for two TVs, one to receive local programmes or satellite TV and another to play back videos. A British or US video recorder won't work with a French TV unless it's dual-standard (with SECAM), and although you can play a SECAM video on a PAL VCR, the picture will be in black and white.

7

Digital Television

Television broadcasts are usually made simultaneously in analogue and digital format. Analogue television is gradually being 'switched off' in countries around the world, starting with the Netherlands (in 2006) and continuing elsewhere until around 2012. The switch to DTV has made compatibility easier but the world still cannot agree on a single standard. There are currently three main standards: the European

Digital Video Broadcasting (DVB) system, the American Advanced Television Systems Committee (ATSC) system and the Japanese Integrated Services Digital Broadcasting (ISDB) system. Most countries have adopted DVB, but a few have taken up the ATSC system (Canada, Mexico and South Korea), while Brazil has gone for the Japanese (IDSB) system.

To receive digital TV, you'll require a 'digi-box' and a (digital) satellite dish. Digital satellite equipment is offered by a number of satellite companies throughout Europe.

Satellite Television

Wherever you live in the world it's likely that you'll be able to receive satellite TV, although the signal strength and number of stations available depends on your equipment and location.

The continent best served by satellite TV is Europe, where a number of geo-stationary satellites, e.g. Astra and Hotbird, which is operated by Eutelsat, carry hundreds of analogue and digital channels broadcasting in a variety of languages. Satellite TV has increased in popularity in Europe in recent years, particularly in countries and regions where there's no cable TV. TV addicts are offered a huge choice of English and foreign-language stations, which can be received throughout most of Europe (the dish size required varies). A bonus is the availability of radio stations via satellite, including the major BBC stations (see **Cable & Satellite Radio** on page 154).

The signal from many stations is scrambled (the decoder is usually built into the receiver) and viewers must pay a monthly subscription to receive programmes. You can buy pirate decoders for some channels. Those best served by clear (unscrambled) stations are German-speakers (most German stations on Astra are clear).

Sky Television: You must buy a receiver with a Videocrypt decoder and pay a monthly subscription to receive Sky stations, except Sky News (which isn't scrambled). Various packages are available costing from around £15 to around £43 per month for the premium package offering all movie channels plus Sky Sports. To receive any of the packages, you need an address in the UK. Subscribers are sent a coded 'smart' card (similar to a credit card), which must be inserted in the decoder to activate it (cards are periodically updated to thwart counterfeiters). Sky won't send smart cards to overseas viewers, as they have the copyright only for a UK-based audience. However, many expatriates obtain a card through a friend or relative in the UK and use their UK address. Satellite installation companies in many countries offer Sky cards, although you must pay a premium.

Eutelsat: Eutelsat was the first company to introduce satellite TV to Europe (in 1983) and it now runs a fleet of communications satellites carrying TV stations to over 120m homes, not just in Europe but also in the Americas, Africa and Asia, although only a small number of its channels are broadcast in English. The English-language stations transmitted by Eutelsat's Hotbird satellite include Eurosport, BBC World, CNBC and, recently, Al-Jazeera in English. Other stations broadcast in Arabic, French, German, Hungarian, Italian, Polish, Portuguese, Spanish and Turkish.

BBC Worldwide: The BBC's commercial subsidiary, BBC Worldwide, broadcasts around the world, including BBC Prime (general entertainment), transmitted in

Europe, Africa, the Middle East and Asia, and the 24-hour news channel, BBC World. Analogue transmission on BBC World ended in April 2006 and it's now fully digital via the Eutelsat Hotbird 6 satellite (13° east) as well as the Astra1 satellite (19.2° east). It remains unencrypted (clear), although you now require a DVB-compliant digital receiver following the switch to digital. Full details of requirements and specific country information is available on the websites (see below).

BBC Prime is encrypted using the Viaccess system. To view programmes, your set-top box must have the Viaccess software (details are on the BBC Prime website – see below) and a smart card, which is available on subscription from BBC Prime, PO Box 5054, London W12 0ZY, UK (☎ 020-8433 2221).

The BBC website has a page dedicated to its international commercial TV channels, with full scheduling and content information (🖳 www.bbc.co.uk/tv). BBC World and BBC Prime have their own websites (🖳 www.bbcworld.com and 🖳 www.bbcprime.com). When accessing them, you need to enter the name of your country of residence so that schedules are displayed in local time.

Equipment: For analogue broadcasts, a satellite receiver should have a built-in Videocrypt decoder (and others such as Eurocrypt, Syster or SECAM if required) and be capable of receiving satellite stereo radio. A system with an 85cm (33in) dish (to receive Astra and Hotbird stations) costs from around £300, plus installation, which may be included in the price. A digital system is more expensive: e.g. a Sky system costs around £800 in most European countries (excluding the UK and Ireland). Shop around, as prices vary considerably. With a 1.2 or 1.5m (47 or 59in) motorised dish, you can receive hundreds of stations in a multitude of languages from around the world. If you wish to receive satellite TV on two or more TVs, you can buy a satellite system with two or more receivers. To receive stations from two or more satellites simultaneously, you need a motorised dish or a dish with a double feed antenna (dual LNBs).

There are satellite sales and installation companies in most countries, some of which advertise in the expatriate press. Shop around and compare prices. Alternatively, you can import your own satellite dish and receiver and install it yourself. **Before buying a system, ensure that it can receive programmes from all existing and planned satellites.**

Location: There must be no obstacles, e.g. trees, buildings or mountains, between the satellite and your dish, so check before renting or buying a home. Before buying or erecting a satellite dish, check whether you need permission from your landlord, development or municipality. Some towns and buildings (such as apartment blocks) have regulations regarding the positioning of antennae, although in some countries owners may mount a dish almost anywhere. Dishes can usually be mounted in a variety of unobtrusive positions and can also be painted or patterned to blend in with the background. Note, however, that in some countries, private dishes in apartment blocks are prohibited and have been replaced by a single communal antenna with a cable connection to individual apartments.

Sky satellite and digital TV programme listings are provided in the British publication *What Satellite and Digital TV*, which is available on subscription and from newsagents in some countries. Satellite TV programmes are also listed in expatriate newspapers and magazines in most countries. The annual *World Radio TV Handbook*, edited by Nicholas Hardyman and published in the UK by Windsor Books

International and in the US by Watson-Guptill Publications, contains over 600 pages of information and the frequencies of all radio and TV stations worldwide.

Radio

Radio flourishes in most countries, where it's often more popular than TV. Numerous public and private, local, regional, national and foreign radio stations can be received in most countries, though programme standards vary from excellent to amateurish. There's a wealth of excellent FM (VHF stereo) and AM (medium waveband) stations in the major cities and resort areas in most countries, although in remote rural areas (particularly mountainous areas) you may be unable to receive any FM stations clearly. The long wave (LW) band is little used in most countries, although LW stations are common in the UK and Ireland. A short wave (SW) radio is useful for receiving foreign stations.

Cable & Satellite Radio

If you have cable or satellite TV, you can also receive many radio stations via your cable or satellite link. For example, BBC Radio 1, 2, 3, 4 and 5, BBC World Service, Sky Radio, Virgin 1215 and many foreign-language stations are broadcast via the Astra satellites. Satellite radio stations are listed in British satellite TV magazines such as *What Satellite and Digital TV*. If you're interested in receiving radio stations from further afield, you should obtain a copy of the *World Radio TV Handbook* edited by Nicholas Hardyman and published annually in the UK by Windsor Books International and in the US by Watson-Guptill Publications.

Expatriate Stations

There are English and foreign-language commercial radio stations aimed at expatriates in the major cities and resort areas in many countries, where the emphasis is usually on music and chat, with some news. Some expatriate stations broadcast in a variety of languages at different times of the day, including English, Dutch, German and various Scandinavian languages. Inevitably, expatriate radio tries to be all things to all men (and women) and usually falls short, particularly with regard to music, as it's impossible to cater for all tastes. But the main drawback of expatriate radio (and most commercial radio) is its amateurish advertisements, which are obtrusive and repetitive, and make listening a chore. Expatriate radio programme schedules are published in the expatriate press in many countries.

BBC & Other Foreign Stations

The BBC World Service is broadcast on short wave on several frequencies (e.g. 12095, 9760, 9410, 7325, 6195, 5975 and 3955kHz) simultaneously and you can usually receive a good signal on one of them. The signal strength varies according to where you live, the time of day and year, the power and position of your receiver, and atmospheric conditions. The BBC World Service plus BBC Radio 1, 2, 3, 4 and 5 are also available via the Astra (Sky) satellite.

For a free BBC World Service programme guide and frequency information, write to BBC World Service (BBC Worldwide, PO Box 76, Bush House, Strand, London WC2B 4PH, UK, ☎ 020-8752 5040). Alternatively, the BBC World Service website (🖳 www.bbc.co.uk/worldservice) has full details of all its programmes, as well as those of BBC World, BBC Prime and BBC America. On the site you can also listen to your favourite programmes (in a variety of languages) via your computer and register for a weekly 'e-guide' to programmes.

Many other foreign stations, including Radio Australia, Radio Canada, Denmark Radio, Radio Nederland, Radio Sweden International and the Voice of America, publish programme guides and frequency information on their websites, where you can download and hear broadcast material as well as view schedules.

UTILITIES

Electricity, gas and water supplies, collectively referred to as 'utilities' in most countries, may be owned and operated by private companies, local municipalities, or the state or federal government (there are also co-operatives in some countries). In some countries, utility companies are monopolies and therefore services and prices are regulated by local and state governments. You may be billed for two or three utilities by the same company or by your municipality, although electricity and gas bills are always itemised separately.

If you buy an old property without mains utilities (or build a new property), check whether there are public guarantees of essential services such as electricity, water, sewerage, roads and telephone and whether you're obliged to pay for the installation of electricity lines or transformers, or only the connection to your property. Even connection can be expensive for remote properties. Obtain a quotation in advance from the relevant local companies. If you build your own home or refit an old home, your builder (or electrician, plumber, etc.) must provide a certificate stating that installations meet the required standard.

7

Registration

Immediately after buying a property abroad you should apply to utility companies to have the electricity, gas and water services switched on or transferred to your name. You may need to apply in person and show proof of ownership and identification such as your passport or residence permit (take a good book, as queues can be long). If applicable, you should also take bills paid by the previous owner. Make sure that all previous bills have been paid and that the contract is registered in your name from the day you take over, or you may be liable for debts left by the previous owner. When registering, non-resident owners should also give their foreign address in case there are any problems requiring your attention, such as your bank refusing to pay a bill while you're out of the country. If you wish to pay your bill by direct debit from a bank account (which is recommended), don't forget to provide your account details.

You may be required to pay a security deposit, depending on the country, your nationality and whether you're a non-resident. This should be paid into an interest-earning account and is usually refunded after a period or offset against future bills. A registration fee is usually payable to be connected to the service and have the meter read, which is included in your first bill. In most European countries, you need to sign a contract for electricity specifying the power supply installed and the tariff required (see below). You must contact your electricity, gas and water companies (well in advance in some countries) to obtain a final meter reading and bill when vacating a property.

Meters

In most countries all homes, whether apartments or detached houses, have electricity, gas and water meters. They're usually located in the basement, in a meter 'cupboard' (particularly in apartment blocks or townhouse developments) or in a box on an outside wall of a detached house, where they can be read by utility company employees when you aren't at home. You should have free access to your meter and should be able read it, though some meters don't have windows to allow you to read the consumption. **A property, whether detached or part of a development, should always have its own meters (if it doesn't, this may indicate serious problems, such as the building not having a 'habitation' or other official certificate).**

To ensure that your electricity, gas and water supply is connected and that you don't pay the previous owner's bills, you should contact your local utility office and ask them to read the meter before taking over a property. Meters are read periodically, e.g. bi-monthly or quarterly, although this varies with the country. If the meter reader is unable to read your meter, you receive an estimated bill (which is indicated on the bill). In some countries, a utility company will send out a revised bill based on a meter reading provided by the householder, although a utility company is usually required to make a number of actual readings a year, e.g. two.

Bills & Payment

You're billed by your utility company periodically, e.g. monthly or bi-annually, depending on the country and the company. Electricity and gas bills are usually payable every two or three months, while water bills may be payable bi-annually. The billing period is shown on bills. A number of bills received throughout the year, e.g. alternate bills, are usually estimated (see above). Bills include a standing (service) charge, sales or value added tax, and possibly local taxes. If you're a non-resident, you may be able to have your bills sent to an address abroad or have a copy of your bill sent to a local relative, friend or organisation.

All utility bills (plus telephone) can be paid by direct debit from a bank or post office account. It's also possible in many countries to pay a fixed amount each month by standing order based on your estimated usage (sometimes called a budget account). At the end of the year, you receive a bill for the amount owing or a rebate of the amount overpaid. These methods of payment are preferable, particularly if you spend a lot of time away from your home or you own a holiday home. If you employ a management company or agent, they should pay all bills for you, but you should check.

You're usually given around 14 days to pay a bill before it becomes overdue. If your payment arrives after the due date, you may be charged a late payment penalty. If you don't pay a utility bill, you eventually receive a 'notice of discontinuation of service', when you should pay the bill within the period stated, even if you dispute the amount. In most countries, utility companies are required by law to give adequate notice and a hearing before they can terminate the service. If your electricity, gas or water supply is cut off because of non-payment of a bill, you must pay the outstanding bill, a reconnection fee and possibly a deposit before it will be reconnected.

Most utility companies publish useful booklets explaining their services and tariffs and how to conserve energy or water (and thus reduce your bills). In some countries, utility and private companies perform a home energy conservation survey of your home. Always check the identity of anyone claiming to be a utility employee (or any kind of 'serviceman') by asking to see a photo identity card.

Electricity

All properties except those in the most remote locations have a mains electricity supply, though the reliability of this varies greatly with the country, region and age of property. **If you buy an old property, you should ensure that the electricity system is in good order well in advance of moving house, as it can take some time to get a new meter installed or obtain a reconnection, uprate or new wiring system.**

7

Power Supply

Power cuts are fairly frequent in some countries, particularly during thunderstorms, and it's wise to keep torches, candles or a gas or oil lamp handy. Power fluctuations and momentary drops are common in many countries (indicated by flickering lights) and often last just long enough to crash a computer! If you live in an area with an unstable electricity supply, you can buy a power stabiliser or an uninterrupted power supply (UPS) with a battery backup, which allows you time to save your work and shut down your computer after a power failure. **Even more important than a battery backup is a power surge protector for appliances such as TVs, computers and fax machines, without which you risk having your equipment damaged or destroyed.** In remote areas of some countries, cuts are more frequent and if you rely on electricity for your livelihood, e.g. for operating a computer, fax machine and other equipment, you may need to install a backup generator. In some remote rural areas you **must** install a generator if you want electricity, as there's no mains electricity, although many people make do with gas and oil lamps (and without television and modern conveniences). If your gas rings are sparked by electricity, keep some matches handy for use during power cuts.

If the power keeps tripping off when you attempt to use a number of high-power appliances simultaneously, it probably means that the power supply of your property is too low to operate all the appliances simultaneously. This is a common problem in many countries, particularly in holiday homes, where a low-rated power supply is installed to reduce construction costs. If this is the case, you must contact your electricity company and ask them to uprate the power supply to your property, which is usually shown on your meter (and on your bill). It can also be downgraded if the power supply is more than you require. **In some countries it can take weeks or months to get your power supply changed, so check the power supply when buying a home and if required apply to have it uprated as soon as possible.**

A power supply usually increases in increments of 3 kilowatts (KW), and you usually need a power supply of at least 12KW to operate an electrical heating system. If you have appliances such as a washing machine, dishwasher, water heater and electric heating in an average size house, e.g. two to three bedrooms, you may need an 18KW supply. To calculate the power supply required, list all the electrical appliances you have (plus any you intend installing, such as an electric shower or dishwasher) and the power consumption of each item. Add the power consumption of all the appliances you're likely to operate simultaneously to obtain the total supply required. Your standing (service) charge depends on the power rating of your supply, which is why most owners tend to keep it as low as possible.

Tariffs

In most countries, electricity companies have several tariffs, which usually apply at different times of the day and different seasons (usually summer and winter). There may be a choice of tariff 'plans', with larger or smaller standing (i.e. fixed monthly) charges combined with higher or lower consumption charges. In order to use certain plans, you must have a special meter installed.

With a standard plan, all electricity consumed is charged at the same rate, with no difference between day and night rates. This is the most expensive rate, the standing charge being low, and is for those who use only a small amount of electricity. To take advantage of a reduced tariff, which usually applies overnight but may also be valid for a limited period during the day, you must pay a higher standing charge. The reduced tariff is generally used to heat hot water and charge night storage heaters but can also be used to run a washing machine, drier or dishwasher (using a timer) and some companies install relays to automatically switch on appliances during the cheap period. In some countries, e.g. France, there's a third plan designed to encourage users to conserve electricity during severe cold weather when demand is at its highest. It allows you to use electricity at a reduced tariff throughout the year with the exception of peak demand days. This is the best choice for anyone owning a holiday home that will be unoccupied most of the time.

Wiring

In most countries, modern properties (i.e. less than around 20 years old) have adequate or good electrical installations, though they may be very different from what you're used to and may seem 'primitive' in comparison. However, if you buy an old property, you should ensure that the electricity system is in good order well in advance of moving house. If a property has inadequate electrical installations, an electricity company can refuse to connect the supply until it's rewired to conform to the latest safety regulations (standards change periodically and become ever more stringent). Bear in mind that the cost of completely rewiring a property can be high, e.g. £5,000 or more.

If you're having a property rewired, or built, make sure that you have sufficient power points installed, as even in new properties in some countries it's common for builders not to fit enough. You should use a qualified electrician for all electrical work. Apart from the danger of electrocuting yourself, wiring methods often vary from country to country and your installation could be illegal if not carried out according to local regulations and standards. In any case, in most countries, only a qualified electrician is permitted to install electrical wiring and fittings, particularly connections to fuse boxes. In some countries, electricity companies service your major electrical appliances, e.g. heating or air-conditioning systems, and some provide service contracts.

Plugs & Sockets

Depending the countries you're moving from and to, you may need new plugs or a lot of adapters. Most countries use a different system (there are over 20 plug configurations in Europe alone) and even in individual homes there may be different types of plugs and sockets. Plug adapters for imported lamps and other electrical apparatus may be difficult to obtain in some countries, so it's wise to bring some with you, plus extension cords and multi-plug extensions that can be fitted with a local plug. Electrical appliances in most countries are fitted with a moulded plug.

In many countries, small low-power electrical appliances (up to six amps), such as table lamps, small TVs and computers, don't require an earth. However, plugs with an earth must always be used for high-wattage appliances such as fires, kettles, washing machines, refrigerators and cookers. In some countries, not all sockets are earthed and many electrical appliances are operated without an earth, with the notable exception of washing machines, dishwashers and dryers. Plugs in most countries aren't fitted with fuses (the UK is one of the few exceptions). Electrical appliances that are earthed have a three-core wire and must **never** be used with a two-pin plug without an earth connection.

The colour codes for wires aren't the same in all countries. For example, in most European countries the code is blue (neutral), brown (live) and green and yellow (earth), while in the US it's usually white (neutral), black (live) and green (earth). **Always make sure that a plug is correctly and securely wired, as bad wiring can prove fatal.**

Fuses

Most apartments and all houses have their own fuse boxes. Fuses can be of various types. In some countries, the electrical system in old houses may still use fuse wire, which has different ratings (before replacing the fuse wire, turn off the mains switch!), while in others fuses have a coloured disk, which **when not displayed**, indicates that the fuse has blown. These fuses, which have different amp ratings, can be purchased in most electrical stores and supermarkets. In modern homes, fuses are of the resetting or 'trip' type. The fuse usually consists of a simple switch, which when a circuit is overloaded, trips to the OFF position. It may be necessary to switch off the main switch before opening the circuit breaker box. Before switching the fuse back to the ON position, locate and remedy the cause of the overload (if possible).

Make sure that you know where fuses or trip switches are located and keep a torch handy so that you can find them in the dark.

Bulbs

Electric light bulbs in most countries are of the Edison type with a screw fitting, although in some countries, e.g. France, there are screw **and** bayonet fittings, both of which come in different sizes. Bulbs with a bayonet fitting are unavailable in some countries, although you can buy adapters to convert from bayonet to screw or vice versa. Bulbs for non-standard electrical appliances (i.e. appliances not made for the local market), such as refrigerators, sewing machines and lamps, may not be available abroad, so you should take some spares with you.

7

Converters & Transformers

The electricity supply in most of Europe is 220/240 volts AC, while in the US and some other countries (including some older buildings in some European countries) it's 110/120 volts AC. Electrical equipment rated at 110 volts (for example from the US) requires a converter or a transformer to convert it to 240 volts, although some electrical appliances, e.g. electric razors and hair dryers, are fitted with a 110/240 volt switch. Check for the switch, which may be inside the casing, and make sure it's switched to the correct voltage **before** connecting it to the power supply. Converters can be used for heating appliances, but transformers are required for motorised appliances. Total the wattage of the devices you intend to connect to a transformer and make sure that its power rating **exceeds** this sum. Generally, all small, high-wattage, electrical appliances (e.g. kettles, toasters, heaters and irons) need large transformers. Motors in large appliances such as cookers, refrigerators, washing machines, dryers and dishwashers, will need replacing or fitting with a large transformer.

In most cases it's simpler to buy new appliances locally, which in most countries are of good quality and reasonably priced. If you buy a home in the US (or another country) with a 110 volt system, it's possible to operate electrical equipment rated at 240 volts with a converter or a step-up transformer to convert it to 110 volts, although generally it isn't worthwhile taking electrical appliances that aren't rated at 110 (or 110/220) volts.

Note also that the dimensions of imported cookers, microwave ovens, refrigerators, washing machines, dryers and dishwashers may differ from those sold locally, and **imported appliances won't fit into a standard kitchen in many countries**.

Frequency

An additional problem with some electrical equipment is the frequency rating, which in some countries, e.g. the US, is designed to run at 60 Hertz (Hz) and not Europe's 50Hz. Electrical equipment without a motor is generally unaffected by the drop in frequency to 50Hz (except TVs). Equipment with a motor may run but with a 20 per cent drop in speed, but automatic washing machines, cookers, electric clocks, record players and tape recorders are unusable if they aren't designed for 50Hz operation. To find out, check the label on the back of the equipment. If it says 50/60Hz, it should be okay. If it says 60Hz, you might try it anyway, **but first ensure that the voltage is correct as described above**. Bear in mind that the transformers and motors of electrical equipment designed to run at 60Hz will run hotter at 50Hz, so ensure that equipment has sufficient space for cooling.

Gas

Mains gas is available in cities and large towns in most countries, although modern houses are often all electric and mains gas is rarely available in rural and remote areas. If you buy a property without a mains gas supply, you may be able to have it connected, but it could be prohibitively expensive. As with electricity, you can choose the gas tariff plan that best suits your requirements.

The quantity of gas consumed may be converted to kilowatt hours for invoicing, although in the US you're charged by the cubic calorific foot or therm (which is equal to 100 cubic feet). In apartment buildings where gas is used for cooking only, a standard charge for gas may be included in your community fees. As with heating and hot water charges, this isn't ideal if you own a holiday home.

In many countries, homes use bottled gas for cooking, hot water and heating, particularly in rural areas. You can have a combined gas hot water and heating system (providing background heat) installed, which is relatively inexpensive to install and cheap to run. In many countries, cookers often have a combination of electric and (bottled) gas rings (you can choose the mix). Check when moving into a property that the gas bottle isn't empty. Keep a spare bottle or two handy and make sure you know where to buy refills and how to change bottles (get the previous owner or the estate agent to show you). A bottle used only for cooking lasts an average family six to eight weeks. Note that the rubber cover over the gas outlet may turn in the opposite direction to most other threaded devices.

The cost of bottled gas varies considerably: in some countries it's much cheaper than mains gas, while in others it's more expensive. In some countries, e.g. Spain, gas bottles are delivered to homes by the gas company, for which a contract is required (which may be approved only after a safety inspection has been made of the property where the gas appliance is to be used). In some countries, you can also buy bottled gas at petrol stations, supermarkets and hypermarkets, but you should always trade in an empty bottle for a new one; otherwise it's much more expensive. If you need to buy new gas bottles, a retailer will ask you to register and pay a bottle deposit. Some village shops also sell bottled gas. Some houses keep their gas bottles outside, often under a lean-to. If this is the case, you must buy propane gas rather than butane, as it can withstand a greater range of temperatures than butane, which is for internal use only. **Bear in mind that gas bottles are very heavy and inconvenient to use.**

Gas central heating is common in some countries, although in rural areas the gas supply comes from a gas tank installed on the property, rather than a mains supply. Some gas suppliers install a tank free of charge in return for a contract to provide gas for a fixed period. **Note that having a gas tank on your property may increase your insurance premiums.**

You should have gas appliances serviced periodically and checked for leaks, particularly in the rubber tubing. Gas leaks are extremely rare and explosions caused by leaks even rarer (although spectacular and therefore widely reported). You can install an electrically operated gas detector that activates an alarm when a gas leak is detected.

Water

7

The quality and reliability of the water supply is a **very** important consideration when buying a home in some countries, and should always be thoroughly investigated in advance. In some countries, the quality of tap water is poor and drinking and cooking water may need to be filtered, while in others (particularly some areas of Italy and Spain) there are severe water shortages – exacerbated in resort areas in summer, when the local population may swell tenfold at the hottest and driest period of the year – and mains supply cuts are frequent (see **Supply** below).

Supply

One of the most important tasks before buying a home abroad is to investigate the reliability of the local water supply and the cost. Ask your prospective neighbours and other local residents for information. In most countries supplies are adequate, although there may be cuts in summer in some areas.

During water shortages, municipalities restrict water consumption or cut off supplies altogether for hours or even days at a time. Restrictions can be severe and householders may be limited to as little as 3 cubic metres per month, which is sufficient for around ten baths or 20 showers. During severe droughts, cuts are usually scheduled to take place at the same time each day. In some areas, water shortages create low water pressure, resulting in insufficient water to take a shower. If a water company needs to cut your supply, e.g. to carry out maintenance work on pipes and other installations, they usually notify you in advance so that you can store water for cooking.

In countries and regions where water shortages are common, water tankers may deliver water to homes. Some properties don't have a mains water supply, but a storage tank that's filled from a tanker (customers are charged by the litre plus a delivery charge).

Some properties have their own well, spring or water channel, particularly in rural areas. However, a well containing water in winter may be bone dry in summer and you may have no rights to extract water from a water channel running alongside your land. If a property takes its water from a well or spring (possibly on a neighbour's land), make sure that there's no dispute about its ownership and your rights to use it, e.g. that it cannot be stopped or drained away by your neighbours. In some countries, people in remote areas need to spend a small fortune to ensure a reliable, year-round, water supply, which may need to be piped from many kilometres away – although this is rare. You don't pay water charges for well water or for water from a stream or river running through your property.

It's unwise to buy a community property where the water supply is controlled by the developer, as some developers charge many times the actual cost or charge owners for a minimum daily quantity, even when they aren't there.

Before moving into a new home, you should enquire where the main stop-valve or stopcock is, so that you can turn off the water supply in an emergency. If the water stops flowing for any reason you should ensure that all the taps are turned off to prevent flooding when the supply starts again. In community properties, the stopcock is usually located outside the building. If your water goes off suddenly, check that someone hasn't switched it off by mistake.

Quality

7

The water is (supposedly) safe to drink in most countries, although it's often of poor quality, sometimes brown or rust-coloured, full of chemicals and tastes awful. In some countries, people fit cold water taps with filters or simply drink bottled water. In rural areas, water may be extracted from mountain springs and taste excellent, although the quality standards applied in cities may be absent and water may in fact be of poor quality.

You shouldn't drink water from rivers, wells and streams, as it may be polluted. In rural areas, water may be contaminated by fertilisers used in farming and in some coastal areas drinking water is contaminated by salt water.

If you're in any doubt about the quality of your water you should have it analysed. You can install filtering or 'purifying' equipment to improve its quality. Obtain expert advice before installing a system, as not all equipment is equally effective. **Note that while boiling water kills any bacteria, it won't remove any toxic substances contained in it.**

In many countries, water is hard (i.e. has a high lime content) and it's common for homeowners to install a filter or 'softener' to prevent the furring of pipes, radiators and appliances and make the water more pleasant to use. Note, however that 'softened' water shouldn't be drunk.

Connection Costs & Standing Charges

If you buy or build a property without mains water, you may be able to have it connected to the mains water system. Water is a local matter in many countries and is controlled by municipalities, many of which have their own springs or wells. However, connection can be expensive because you must usually pay for the installation of pipes. Obtain a quotation from the local water company for the connection of the supply and the installation of a water meter.

In most areas there's a standing quarterly charge or a monthly charge for a minimum consumption, even if you don't use any water during the billing period (water shortages don't stop municipalities from levying high standing charges for water consumption that's sometimes non-existent!).

Rates

The price of water varies considerably according to the country and its availability. In most countries, homes are metered and you pay only for the water you use, plus a rental charge for the meter if it's owned by the water company. The cost of water has risen dramatically in many countries in recent years, particularly in areas where water is in short supply, e.g. in most resort areas in Spain and in parts of Italy. In some areas, tariffs start with a low basic charge per cubic metre, but become prohibitively expensive after you reach a certain consumption level.

In some countries, the cost of water in apartment blocks may be divided among apartments according to their size. Hot water may be charged by adding an amount per cubic metre consumed by each apartment to cover the cost of heating water or may be shared among apartments in proportion to their size. It's even possible (although rare) in some countries that you won't receive a water bill at all, as the cost is included in local property taxes.

Storage Tanks

If you own a detached house or villa, you can reduce your water costs by installing a storage tank for rain water. A tank can be roof-mounted or installed underground, the latter option being preferable as the tank can be any size, although it requires an electric pump. Check whether a property has a water storage tank or whether you can install one. If stored water is to be used for washing, it must be filtered; it shouldn't be used for cooking or drinking, though there are (expensive) installations that can produce drinking water. Many modern properties have storage tanks of 500 litres or so, large enough to last a family of four for around a week or even longer with careful use. It's also possible to use recycled water from baths, showers and apparatus such as washing machines and dish washers to flush toilets, wash cars or water a garden.

Hot Water

Water heating in apartments may be provided by a central heating source for the whole building, although in most countries apartments have their own water heaters. If you need to install a boiler or a tank with an immersion heater, make sure it's large enough for the size of the property. Many holiday homes have quite small water boilers, which are often inadequate for more than two people. If you need to install a water heater (or a larger water heater), you should consider the merits of both electric and bottled gas heaters. An electric water boiler with a capacity of 75 litres (sufficient for two people) usually takes between 75 and 125 minutes (in winter) to heat water to 40C.

A gas flow-through water heater is more expensive to purchase and install than an electric boiler, but you get unlimited hot water immediately whenever you want it and there are no standing charges. A gas heater should have a capacity of 10 to 16 litres per minute if it's to be used for a shower. There's usually little difference in quality between the cheaper and more expensive heaters, although a gas water heater with a permanent flame may use up to 50 per cent more gas than one without.

A resident family with a constant consumption is usually better off with an electric heater operating on a reduced tariff, while non-residents using a property for short periods will find a self-igniting gas heater more economical.

If you own a home in a hot country, solar energy, for hot water and heating is a viable option and the local authorities may provide a grant for its installation (see **Solar Heating** on page 147).

7

8

SELLING

Afinancial investment becomes worthwhile only when you redeem it; in the case of property, that means selling. Your selling priorities will depend on the purpose of your purchase, but in all cases you'll want to obtain the highest possible price and minimise your costs – as well as the hassle involved in selling. The first step is to familiarise yourself with the selling procedures in the country concerned and the taxes that may be due (e.g. on capital gains) when you sell. This chapter covers selling the property through a local or international agent, selling it yourself through traditional channels and selling via the internet.

MAIN CONSIDERATIONS

Before offering a property for sale, whether in your home country or abroad, you should investigate the state of the local property market. Is it booming or are prices depressed? Are there lots of similar properties on the market, from which yours doesn't stand out? Unless you're forced to sell, it may be wiser to let your home long-term and wait until the market has recovered. If you do decide to go ahead and sell, start by researching prices of similar properties in your area and price yours accordingly. In most countries, the vast majority of homes are sold through estate agents, although in some countries it's common for owners to sell their own homes. Whichever option you choose, there are ways of improving your chances of selling your property and maximising the profit on it.

Price

Like all other goods, property has a market price and the best way of ensuring a quick sale (or any sale) is to ask a realistic price. Overpricing by owners and agents is one of the main reasons why properties don't sell as quickly as they might. During market slumps when prices go down and buyers are thin on the ground, properties can remain on the market for years largely because owners are asking 'out-of-date' prices. If you have little or no interest from prospective buyers during the first month your property is on the market, re-think the price.

If your home is fairly standard for the area, you can find out its value by comparing the prices of other homes on the market or those that have recently been sold. Approach a few estate agents and ask for a valuation, but be aware that some agents inflate prices with an eye to their own commission! Most agents provide a free appraisal of a home's value in the hope that you'll sell it through them, but simply asking for a valuation doesn't mean you have to market through that agent. You should be prepared to drop the price slightly (e.g. 5 or 10 per cent) and should set it accordingly.

Bear in mind that it's usually easier to sell a cheaper property than an expensive property. However, in holiday locations there's a strong and constant demand for exceptional villas in the upper price bracket, particularly if they're especially attractive and in a popular area or a superb location.

When selling a second home abroad, you may wish to include the furnishings (plus major appliances) in the sale, which is a common practice in resorts when selling a relatively inexpensive second home with modest furnishings. Add an appropriate amount to the price to cover the value of the furnishings.

Presentation

The secret to selling a home quickly is presentation (assuming that it's well priced). First impressions (external and internal) are crucial and it's essential to present a property in its best light. If you're using an agent, you can ask him what you should (or need to) do to help sell your home. It may pay to invest in new furniture, new carpets, exterior paint and landscaping, but a even few plants and flowers can do wonders. If you decorate a home for resale, it's important to be conservative and not to do anything radical. Use neutral colours such as white or cream for walls and woodwork. It may also pay to modernise, e.g. install a new kitchen or bathroom, as these are vital (particularly kitchens) when selling a home, but don't overdo it, as it's easy to spend more than you can ever hope to recoup on the sale price.

If a home's in poor repair, this must be reflected in the asking price and if major work is needed that you cannot afford, you should obtain a quotation (or two) and offer to knock this off the price.

Caution

When selling your property abroad, be extremely careful whom you deal with. Sales should always be conducted through a lawyer, even if a notary must by law be involved. Make sure that you're paid with a certified banker's draft before signing over your property to a buyer, as once the deed of sale has been signed the property belongs to the buyer, whether you've been paid or not. Sellers in some countries occasionally end up with no property **and** no money!

Note that when selling a second home abroad, you must usually pay capital gains tax, and a percentage of the price may need to be retained (by law) by the buyer in lieu of tax. See the **Country Profiles** starting on page 175 for the purchase procedure in your chosen country.

8

USING AN AGENT

You may want to use the services of an estate agent, either in the country where the property is situated or in your home country. If you purchased the property through an agent, it's often wise to use the same agent when selling, as he will already be familiar with it and have the details on file. You should take particular care when selecting an agent as they vary considerably in their professionalism, expertise and experience (the best way to investigate an agent is to pose as a buyer). In many countries, agents cover only a small area, so you should choose an agent who regularly sells properties in your area and price range. If you own a property in an area popular with foreign buyers, your best course of action may be to use an overseas agent or advertise in foreign newspapers and magazines and any English-language property publications.

Contracts

Before offering a property for sale, an agent must have a signed authorisation from the owner or his legal representative. There are usually two types of contract: an ordinary or non-exclusive contract (also called a 'multiple listing'), which means that you reserve the right to deal with other agents and to negotiate directly with private individuals; and an exclusive contract, which gives a single agent the exclusive right to sell a property, although you can reserve the right to find a private buyer. **If you sign an exclusive contract without the right to find your own buyer, you must still pay the agent's commission even if you sell your home yourself.**

The main advantage of using a single agent is that he's more likely to put maximum effort into selling your home; on the other hand, his commission will be higher than for a multiple listing. Most people find that it's best to place a property with a number of agents, i.e. non-exclusive, where the agent who sells the property receives the commission.

Contracts are always for a limited period, e.g. three to six months, and state the agent's commission, what it includes and, most importantly, who must pay it. With an exclusive contract, an agent may provide a 'for sale' board, photographs and information leaflets, and may also include some advertising other than in his office window, although advertising is usually charged separately. **Generally you shouldn't pay any fees (other than the normal agent's fees) unless you require extra services, and you should never pay any fees before a sale is completed.** Check the contract and make sure you understand what you're signing.

8 Fees

Agents' fees vary considerably according to the country, the area, the local property market, the price of the property and the agency arrangement, and can be anywhere between 1 and 10 per cent of the sale price. Shop around for the best deal as there's fierce competition among agents in some countries. Fees are a percentage of the sale price and are generally higher the cheaper the property is. On more expensive properties, an agent's fee may be negotiable.

An agent usually receives a lower commission when he's acting as the sole or exclusive agent. In some countries, an agent will sell your home for a fixed fee, although this is unusual; the fee is usually non-returnable and must be paid irrespective of whether the agent sells your property.

Fees are usually paid by the vendor, although in some countries an agent's fee may be paid by the buyer or shared between the vendor and buyer. Sometimes the sale price will have been marked up to include the agent's fee, so that, in effect, the buyer is paying the agent's fees.

SELLING YOUR HOME YOURSELF

While certainly not for everyone, selling a home yourself is a viable option for many people and is particularly recommended when you're selling an attractive home at a realistic price in a favourable market. The main advantage is that it saves you an agent's fees, which may allow you to offer it at a more appealing price – an important factor if you're seeking a quick sale. How you market your home will depend on the type of home, the price and the country or area you expect your buyer to come from.

Marketing

Marketing is the key to selling your home. The first step is to get a professional 'for sale' sign made (showing your telephone number) and erect it in the garden or place it in a window. Research the best newspapers and magazines for advertising your property and place advertisements in them. (It's a good idea to add the words 'no agents' at the end of your advertisement, or most of the calls you receive will be from agents keen to sell your home!) You could also have a leaflet printed (with pictures) extolling the virtues of the property, which you could drop into local letter boxes or have distributed with a local newspaper (many people buy a new home in the vicinity of their present one). You may also need to draw up a 'fact sheet' (if your home's vital statistics aren't included in the leaflet mentioned above). Don't forget to market your home around local companies, schools and organisations, particularly if they have employees who may be looking for homes in the area. Finally, it may help to provide information about local financing sources for potential buyers.

If you have an unusual property such as a period building or a converted barn or mill, you could try selling it at auction, which may increase the price (although you must pay the auctioneer's commission). Unless you're in a hurry to sell, set yourself a realistic time limit for success, after which you can approach an agent. When selling a home yourself, you must provide a contract or engage a lawyer to do it for you.

Using the Internet

There's an enormous number of websites where you can advertise your home for a small fee. You need to research the best sites for your property – look for country-specific websites and those in your home country which you know are popular with people searching for a property abroad. Try websites that sell property in your home country and abroad, such as *Dalton's Weekly* (🖳 www.daltonsproperty.com). Excellent photographs are vital to show your home at its best, along with as many details as possible to appeal to your target buyers. For example, if it's a family home, stress local schools, amenities and transport connections.

8

8

Part 2

9

COUNTRY PROFILES

EUROPE: AUSTRIA

Background Information

Capital: Vienna.
Population: 8.2m.
Foreign Community: The population is over 90 per cent Austrian, with a few Croatians, Serbs, Slovenes and Turks, mostly living in the Austrian federal states of Carinthia and Styria. There are very few American or British residents.
Area: 83,870km^2 (32,382mi^2).
Geography: Austria is a landlocked, mountainous country in central Europe. Some two-thirds of its territory and around a third of its population are in the eastern Alps, which extend on a series of longitudinal ridges from the Swiss border in the west almost to Vienna in the east. The valleys between the ridges are home to most of the area's population. Austria is even more mountainous than neighbouring Switzerland and has a wide range of vegetation, with over 35 per cent of its landscape forested.
Climate: Austria has a moderate central European climate, with an Atlantic influence in the west and a continental influence in the east. Temperatures vary considerably according to altitude, area and geographical situation. In general, winter temperature range from a maximum of 2C (36F) to a minimum of -6C (20F), while summer temperatures vary between 13C (55F) and 25C (77F). The winter sports season generally extends from December to March (May in the higher resorts).
Language: The national language is German, spoken by some 90 per cent of the population. Turkish, Serbian, Croatian, Hungarian and Bosnian are spoken by their native communities. English is widely spoken in Austria, particularly in the major cities and resorts.
Political Situation: Austria is a federal republic and since 1945 has been one of the most stable countries in Europe. Austria is neutral (this has been enshrined in the constitution since 1955), although this doesn't prevent it from taking sides on certain international issues. Formerly a member of the European Free Trade Association (EFTA), Austria joined the European Union on 1st January 1995. The general election of 2000 saw a majority for the extreme right, advocating racist and xenophobic policies, which resulted in diplomatic sanctions by the EU. These sanctions were lifted after reassurances of moderation from the Austrian government. In October 2006, the People's Party was narrowly defeated by the Social Democrats, ending a six-year coalition between the People's Party and far-right Freedom Party. In January 2007, Social Democrat leader Alfred Gusenbauer became Chancellor, heading a coalition government with the conservative People's Party.

Finance

Currency

Austria's currency is the euro (€).
Exchange Rate: £1 = €1.52.
Exchange Controls: None.

Cost & Standard of Living

Austria's cost of living is high, but Austrians enjoy a high standard of living. Membership of the EU has reduced the country's traditional economic dependence on Germany and brought closer ties with other European economies. Economic growth in 2006 was around 3 per cent, thanks to an influx of foreign investment; this looks set to reduce the cost of many imported goods and lower the cost of living.

Taxation

Following tax reforms in 2005, corporate income tax was reduced to 25 per cent and provisions were made for the acquisition of Austrian companies to become more efficient under a group taxation system. In addition, the government introduced a variety of family tax concessions.

Personal Effects: Personal effects can be imported duty free, although an inventory is required.

Income Tax: Austria has a PAYE income tax system with four tax bands, ranging from 23 to 50 per cent. Tax exempt income for employees is €15,780 (for the self-employed, €10,000).

Capital Gains Tax (CGT): Capital gains tax is payable only on property owned by companies (at 25 per cent). Gains made by individuals from the sale of property are tax free provided the property has been owned for ten years or used as a principal residence for at least two years; otherwise they must pay CGT at income tax rates.

Wealth Tax: None.

Inheritance & Gift Tax: Inheritance tax is levied at between 2 and 60 per cent, depending on the relationship between the donor and beneficiary and the amount involved.

Value Added Tax (VAT): The standard rate of VAT is 20 per cent, with a reduced rate of 10 per cent on food, agricultural products, rents, tourism and entertainment. There's no VAT on exports.

Property

Restrictions on Foreign Ownership & Letting

Non-EU citizens require permission from the relevant provincial government office (*Amt der Landesregierung*) in order to buy property. EU citizens must still obtain a 'negative certificate', which proves their equal status with Austrian citizens and confirms they don't require approval to purchase from the provincial government. To get one, you must show your purchase contract (or a draft), proof of EU citizenship (e.g. a passport) and a current abstract from the land registry. There are no restrictions on letting.

Market

Austria has a stable property market, which is largely unaffected by outside influences such as international recessions. Property is expensive, although cheaper than in Switzerland, and the market is poor; there's a strong demand for high quality homes in decent locations. Rents are low compared with purchase prices, offering a yield of only 2 to 3 per cent. There used to be strict regulations in all Austrian provinces regarding the purchase of property by non-Austrians, but EU membership has seen these relaxed and property laws are now the same for Austrians and EU citizens. Non-EU citizens must still obtain permission to purchase from the local authority, although this is fairly straightforward.

9

Areas

Vienna and other cities have become very expensive, prices for refurbished apartments having risen by around 50 per cent over the past decade.

Salzburg has recently become increasingly popular with foreign buyers, offering older properties as well as modern housing, and good transport connections. The main residential area is north of the city.

The most popular places with foreign buyers are mainly ski areas, especially in and around Innsbruck, the only major city in the Alps, and the Sportwelt Amade region, which comprises eight holiday resorts. Property is generally expensive in these regions, although if you're prepared to buy a property a short distance from the ski slopes, prices drop. Austria is also an excellent choice for a summer holiday home, particularly for people who are keen on outdoor pursuits such as hiking and horse riding.

Building Standards

Building standards are generally high.

Cost

Prices vary in different areas, but you must generally pay at least €60,000 for a studio apartment, from €90,000 for a one-bedroom apartment, from €125,000 for a two-bedroom apartment and from €320,000 for a large, luxurious apartment. Detached four- or five-bedroom chalets cost from €800,000.

Local Mortgages

Austrian banks offer mortgages only in euros and the loan mustn't exceed 60 per cent of the purchase price. Mortgages are for a maximum of 25 years, up to the age of 65, and are repayment only; proof of income is required, including bank statements and pay slips. Non-status mortgages aren't available. There's a notary's fee of 1 per cent to cover legal costs.

Property Taxes

An annual property tax of 1 per cent is payable on the assessed value of a property, plus an additional 1 per cent for land without buildings.

Purchase Procedure

Property sales are handled by a lawyer or notary, who usually acts for both parties. Preliminary contracts aren't usual, but in most cases the buyer signs an offer document, which is given to the seller. The lawyer or notary then set the purchase in motion, with petitions to the Land Registry. A deposit of 10 per cent may be payable (this isn't always the case) but it's refunded if a sale falls through due to 'defective' title or failure to obtain registration. The purchase agreement is drafted by the lawyer or notary and is written in German (a translation is provided if required). All signatures must be notarised. The funds are payable when the deed is signed and they're deposited in a trustee (escrow) account until completion. Although you may take possession of the property once you've paid the purchase price and signed the deed, you aren't the lawful owner until you're registered at the Austrian Land Registry (*Grundbuch*) as the new owner. This usually takes between four and six months, after which taxes and fees are paid by the lawyer or notary on your behalf.

9

Fees

Fees are around 10 per cent of the purchase price. Title registration at the Land Registry is 1 per cent, property transfer tax is 3.5 per cent (2 per cent when transfers are made between spouses or parents and children) and notary's fees are usually between 3 to 4 per cent. Stamp duty is between 0.5 and 1 per cent, while an estate agent's fees are between 3 and 5 per cent, and are usually split between seller and buyer.

General Information

Getting There

Vienna airport, Austria's largest and busiest international airport, is 18km (11mi) south-east of the city. It's currently (2007) being enlarged and refurbished, with a new terminal and runway under construction to cope with increasing passenger numbers. Over 60 airlines (mainly European) operate from the airport, including the national airline, Austrian Air, and British Airways (from London Heathrow). British Airways also operates a flight from London Gatwick to Innsbruck during the ski season.

Communications

Austria has a highly a developed and efficient communications network, for fixed line telephones, mobile phones and the internet. Despite liberalisation in 2003, the main provider of fixed-line, mobile and internet services is still the state telecommunications company, Telekom Austria, which has around 60 per cent of the market. Its biggest rival is the merged Tele2/UTA Telekom, which claims around 30 per cent of the market. The country code is 43.

Fixed-line Telephones: International direct dialling (IDD) is available and public telephone boxes can be used to direct dial within Austria and abroad. Telephone boxes accept pre-paid phone cards (*Telefonwertkarte*), which are cheaper for international calls and are available from post offices and tobacconists' in a variety of denominations.

Mobile Telephones: The mobile phone network covers all but remote areas, and the main providers are T-Mobile, Mobilkom and ONE. They use the GSM standard.

Internet: Internet use is high in Austria and Vienna has free wireless internet access at various 'hotspots' throughout the city. However, broadband access is limited (Austria lags behind other western European countries in this respect) and while most companies have broadband most private users don't.

Postal Services: Postal services are run by the state-owned company Österreichische Post AG, which provides an efficient nationwide service.

Crime Rate

9

Austria's crime rate is very low and it's one of the safest countries in the world.

Medical Facilities

Austria boasts an excellent national health service, which is administered by the provinces and is available to all who make social security contributions. The country has reciprocal health agreements with all EEA countries and Switzerland, whose citizens are eligible for free or low-cost emergency medical treatment on production of a European Health Insurance Card (EHIC). Note that the EHIC can be used only by visitors. Retired EU citizens who have paid into their own country's social security system are entitled to free healthcare.

Pets

Austria has no quarantine requirement, but pets must be identifiable by a microchip or tattoo, be vaccinated against rabies and have an EU Pet Passport.

Visas & Permits

Visas: Visas (and work permits) must be obtained by non-EU nationals before arriving in Austria, although nationals of many countries, including the US and Canada, are allowed to stay for up to 90 days without a visa. You're looked upon more favourably if you plan to invest in the country and employ Austrian nationals.

Residence Permits: Residence permits are a formality for EU nationals, although you must register with the local police station after three days (if you intend to stay longer than three months). You must apply for an identity card (which includes a residence permit) and this is usually granted for six months if you don't have a job or five years if you can show evidence of permanent employment. Non-working EU residents must be able to prove sufficient income to support themselves.

Work Permits: Work permits aren't required by EU nationals. For non-EU nationals they're difficult to obtain. Your prospective employer must confirm to the authorities that you have relevant skills or specific expertise in a particular area and that an Austrian citizen isn't able to fill the position.

Reference

Useful Addresses

Austrian Embassy (US), 3524 International Court, NW, Washington, DC 20008, US (☎ 202-895 6700, 💻 www.austria.org).

Austrian Embassy (UK), 18 Belgrave Mews West, London SW1X 8HU, UK (☎ 020-7235 3731).

Austrian National Tourist Office (UK and Ireland), 3rd Floor, 9-11 Richmond Buildings, London W1D 3HF, UK (☎ 020-7440 3830, 💻 www.austriatourism.com).

9 EUROPE: BULGARIA

Background Information

Capital: Sofia.
Population: 7.7m.

Foreign Community: The population is over 80 per cent Bulgarian, around 10 per cent Turk and 5 per cent Roma. There are relatively few American or British residents, but the last few years have seen a gradual, though small, increase in the number of British residents.

Area: 110,910km^2 (42,822mi^2).

Geography: Bulgaria is in south-east Europe, with the Black Sea to the east, Greece and Turkey to the south, Serbia and Macedonia to the west and Romania to the north, strategically located between northern and southern Europe and between Europe and Asia. One of Bulgaria's attractions is that it combines beautiful coastal areas on the Black Sea with fertile plains and mountain ranges covering approximately half the country and making it a popular destination for skiers.

Climate: Bulgaria's climate is broadly continental, with cold (sometimes severe), damp winters and hot, dry summers, but along the Black Sea coast the climate is more Mediterranean, with milder weather all year. The country is divided into north and south climatic regions by the Stara Planina mountain range (also known as the Balkan range), which runs through the centre of Bulgaria and into eastern Serbia. In the north of the country, winters are typically cold – the coldest regions are on the Danube Plain and in the high valleys. Temperatures range from -30C (-22F) in winter to between 20C (68F) and 30C (86F) in summer. The coldest month is January, with an average temperature of -2C (28F) and the warmest is July with temperatures of 25C (77F). Average rainfall is 63cm per year,, coastal areas receiving less than 5.5cm but the high mountains around 120cm.

Language: The official language is Bulgarian, spoken by around 85 per cent of the population, followed by Turkish and Romany. English is quite widely spoken in popular resort areas.

Political Situation: Bulgaria's government is a parliamentary republic headed by a President. The country was under Soviet control from 1946 until it gained independence in 1990, when it held its first multiparty free elections. The current government is a coalition, headed by Prime Minister Sergei Stanishev of the Bulgarian Socialist Party (BSP). The coalition consists of the BSP, the National Movement Simeon II and the Movement for Rights and Freedoms, which mainly represents the country's Turkish minority. The President, Georgi Parvanov, has been in power since 2002 and was re-elected for a second term in October 2006. Bulgaria joined the EU on 1st January 2007 after meeting strict economic targets and partly addressing EU concerns about corruption and organised crime. The country joined NATO along with Romania and other former communist countries in 2004.

Finance

Currency

Bulgaria's currency is the lev (abbreviated to BGN), which was adopted in 1999 and pegged to the Deutschmark until Germany adopted the euro. The lev is now pegged to the euro at a rate of €1 = BGN1.955. It's expected that Bulgaria will adopt the euro in 2010.

Exchange Rate: £1 = BGN2.96.

Exchange Controls: There are some exchange controls. Export of the lev is prohibited, but foreign businesses can repatriate profits and capital in foreign currency. Individuals importing or exporting the equivalent of more than BGN5,000 (£1,680) in Bulgarian or foreign currency are required to notify customs and additional requirements apply if the amount is over BGN25,000(£8,400). Any direct investment abroad must be declared to the Bulgarian National Bank within 15 days; supporting documentation is required for outward investments over BGN25,000.

9

Cost & Standard of Living

Bulgaria's economy has grown over the last five years and unemployment and high inflation rates have been brought under control. Incomes and living standards are still low when compared with western European countries. Some of the poorest areas are in the north-west of the country, while the south-west and the area around the capital, Sofia, are the wealthiest. In 2006, a civil servant in Bulgaria earned an average of BGN350 (£120) per month and a teacher slightly less. People earning western European salaries will find the cost of living in Bulgaria low.

Taxation

Personal Effects: Personal effects can be imported duty free, as long as you intend to settle permanently in Bulgaria.

Income Tax: Bulgaria has a PAYE income tax system with three bands: 20, 22 and 24 per cent. Income gained from all sources, including rental income, is taxed at these rates.

Capital Gains Tax (CGT): If you've formed a company to buy your property or land (see below, you're charged capital gains tax at the corporate flat tax rate of 15 per cent on any profits from the sale of immovable property. If you're an individual, any profits are taxed as ordinary income (see above). You're exempt from this tax if the property has been your principal residence for at least three years or you've owned the property for at least five.

Wealth Tax: None.

Inheritance & Gift Tax: Bulgarian residents pay inheritance tax on property in Bulgaria and abroad, while non-residents are liable only for property in Bulgaria. From 2005, a surviving spouse and direct relatives are exempt. Rates vary from 0.7 per cent to 20 per cent according to the relationship between donor and beneficiary.

Value Added Tax (VAT): The VAT rate is 20 per cent on almost all goods and services. There are exemptions on the letting of residential property to individuals and the transfer of land ownership, as well as financial and insurance services, education and health services, and exports.

Property

Restrictions on Foreign Ownership & Letting

Foreigners (including EU citizens) aren't permitted to buy land in Bulgaria, although now that the country is a full member of the EU, that will change. At present (mid-2007), foreigners who want to buy land or property with land (but not apartments), must purchase it through a Bulgarian-registered limited company. This is a fairly straightforward process and usually takes three to four weeks and costs around £1,000. The lawyer dealing with your purchase can do this on your behalf. In addition to the cost of setting up a company, you must open a company bank account and deposit BGN5,000 (£1,700), although you can withdraw this money once the formalities have been completed. Buying through a company isn't necessary if you're buying an apartment or off plan, but only if you're buying land or a house with land. There are no restrictions on letting.

Market

Bulgaria has been heralded (by estate agents!) as 'the new Spain'. The Bulgarian property market was sluggish until around 2003, when it began to see frenetic activity from international

9

buyers, particularly the British. The market is now booming, although some experts think that the growth rate cannot be sustained, especially in the popular Black Sea areas (see below). Bulgaria's prices compare favourably with those of more popular European destinations, and in 2004 average prices increased by almost 50 per cent, although since then annual rises have been around 20 per cent. These huge increases stem from the fact that prices began at a very low point. Bulgaria's economy only started to recover from the effects of Soviet rule in 1997, when its currency was pegged to the Deutschmark and, subsequently, to the euro. This, combined with Bulgaria's entry into the EU on 1st January 2007, has given the country the kind of economic stability which is attractive to international investors. Initial demand for property was high, particularly along the Black Sea coast, but now investors are finding that supply is threatening to outstrip demand in coastal areas.

Areas

Many people who have flocked to buy cheap property in Bulgaria over the last few years have chosen to do so in Black Sea coastal resorts, e.g. Sunny Beach and Golden Sands, or coastal cities such as Varna and Burgas. Properties there are popular because of their coastal location, low prices and letting potential. However, Bulgaria's climate doesn't offer anything like the 300 days of sunshine per year that parts of Spain enjoy. The letting season is only around four months and because it's considered a budget location for holidaymakers, you cannot charge high rents to compensate. In addition, many areas are suffering from overdevelopment. Unless a property in this area is of exceptional quality with good additional facilities, such as a golf course, you may find that your property is competing with many other similar ones when you try to sell or let it.

Bulgaria's property market is diverse and extends beyond coastal areas to include ski resorts in the mountains, beautiful countryside and an increasingly thriving market in the capital, Sofia. In the ski resorts, prices are low compared with those in traditional European ski destinations. Resorts include Bankso, Borovets and Pamprovo, which are increasingly popular with buyers looking for holiday homes and buy-to-let investment properties. Bansko is the most popular ski resort and has recently had £165m invested in its runs as part of Bulgaria's bid for the 2014 Winter Olympics. Bansko is a UNESCO World Heritage site and parts of the picturesque town date back to the tenth century.

Bulgaria's capital, Sofia, is the other main area of interest to buyers, especially since Bulgaria joined the EU. Closer trade links with the EU will mean more foreign investment, resulting in foreign business people requiring short- and long-term lets. The city council has announced massive redevelopment plans over the coming decade, partly in the hope of securing the 2014 Winter Olympics, and this will have a positive long-term effect on the city's letting potential.

Building Standards

These can be poor, especially in buildings constructed during the Soviet era. New properties are generally of better quality, mainly due to competition among developers.

9

Cost

Coastal resort properties start at as little as £25,000 for a one-bedroom apartment but rise to as much as £150,000 for a luxury two-bedroom apartment with excellent views. Properties in the Sunny Beach area are mostly apartments. Ski resort prices start at around £35,000 and rise to around £120,000 for a two-bedroom chalet. Most properties close to the ski resorts are apartments. Prices in central Sofia are around £25,000 for a one-bedroom apartment and £80,000 for a two-bedroom apartment.

Local Mortgages

Local mortgages are available, to residents and non-residents, in euros only. The minimum amount is 40 per cent of the value of the property, with no official maximum, although it's usually around 75 per cent of the purchase price. Mortgages are repayment only and the mortgage term is a maximum of 25 years, up to age 70. Proof of income is required, both earned and unearned, and potential rental income may be included, although this depends on the lender. Non-status loans aren't available.

Property Taxes

There's an annual property tax, which varies with the area and according to whether the property is used for residential or commercial purposes. The rate is fixed by the local authority but is usually 0.15 per cent of the value of the property and is payable at the beginning of the year. There are also municipal taxes which are set locally and are usually around 1 per cent of value, but check with your lawyer or the local authority.

Purchase Procedure

A deposit of 10 per cent is required when you sign a reservation agreement and the property is taken off the market. This is refundable only if the vendor withdraws from the sale. The lawyer then makes all the legal checks to ensure that the property is free from any debts or mortgages and that all the paperwork is in order. **Ensure that your lawyer also checks the financial stability of any developer you deal with. Unlike many other countries, Bulgaria doesn't have a system of bank guarantees to ensure that you're covered if the developer doesn't deliver.**

If you're buying land, a survey will be carried out to ascertain its measurements and boundaries and to ensure that it has the correct building classification, and detailed plans will be included in the deed. These procedures usually take around three weeks. You then sign the deed in front of a notary, at which point the balance is paid along with the notary's fees (around 5 per cent of the declared value of the property). The notary registers the transfer in the Real Estate Registry.

Fees

9

Fees total around 10 per cent of the purchase price. Estate agents' commission is around 3 per cent of the purchase price and is usually paid at the time you sign the reservation document. Title registration at the Land Registry is a mere 0.1 per cent. The government, via the local authority, charges a property transfer tax of 2 per cent, and notary's fees are approximately 5 per cent. Legal fees are around 1 per cent in most cases. Make sure you agree in detail what you're expected to pay. Traditionally, these costs were split equally between the vendor and the purchaser, although these days they agree on the division of costs before the sale.

General Information

Getting There

Bulgaria has three main airports: Bourgas, in the south-east, which is used by the majority of tourists holidaying at Black Sea resorts, Sofia airport, which is 10km (6mi) east of the capital, and Varna airport, on the north Black Sea coast, 8km (5mi) west of the city of Varna.

Bourgas Airport: The national airline, Bulgarian Air, operates flights to Bourgas from London Gatwick and Dublin, and budget airline Wizz Air operates flights between London Luton and Bourgas. There are also a number of charter flights to Bourgas.

Sofia Airport: Sofia is the hub for Bulgaria Air and Hemus Air. In December 2006, a second terminal was opened to deal with increasing passenger numbers. Transport connections between the airport and the city are efficient. Bulgarian Air operates flights to Sofia from London Gatwick and Manchester. British Airways and Hemus Air fly from London Heathrow and Wizz Air flies from London Luton to Sofia.

Varna Airport: Like Bourgas, Varna is a popular airport for tourists. Previously only used by charter flights, it's now also served by scheduled flights by Bulgarian Air from London Gatwick (summer only).

Communications

Bulgaria has an extensive but somewhat antiquated telephone system, run by the state-owned Bulgarian Telecommunications Company (BTC). Despite liberalisation of the market in 2003, BTC continues to be the sole provider. The telephone system is in the process of extensive modernisation and BTC has entered into a number of joint ventures to speed up the development and efficiency of various services, such as public payphones, direct-dialling services and mobile phone transmission.

The country dialling code is 359; the main area codes are: Bourgas (56), Plovdiv (32), Sofia (2) and Varna (52).

Fixed-line Telephones: International direct dialling (IDD) isn't available to all countries, but you can dial most European countries from hotels, post offices and public telephones by inserting a pre-paid card in Betkom phones, which can be found in all major centres across the country. International calls and enquiries can be made through the operator by dialling 0123.

Mobile Telephones: There are more than 6m mobile telephones in use in Bulgaria and coverage is widespread, excluding only a few remote areas. The main mobile phone network providers are analogue and digital, the analogue system operated by Mobicom, digital GSM networks by Mobitel and Globul.

Internet: Internet usage is still in its early stages but is developing fast. There are around 200 internet service providers (ISPs) with national high-speed (broadband) coverage and there are internet cafes in all the main towns.

Postal Services: Postal services are run by the state-owned Bulgarian Posts, which offers a wide range of services from main post offices. Opening hours are from 7am to 7pm, but the General Post Office in Sofia is open 24 hours a day. Airmail to Europe can take as little as four days or as long as two weeks.

9

Crime Rate

Bulgarian crime and corruption are a cause for EU concern and threatened to delay the country's accession in 2007. Organised crime has been a problem in Bulgaria for some time, despite government initiatives to address it. The judicial system has a reputation for corruption and the general level of corruption in Bulgaria is higher than average, according to a 2005 Corruption Perception Index. In addition, the country suffers from petty street crime and a variety of scams operated in tourist areas, usually directed at foreigners. Car theft is particularly common.

Medical Facilities

Although medical staff in Bulgaria are usually trained to a high standard, medical facilities and equipment are generally of a lower level than those available in most European countries. The Bulgarian health service has been undergoing reform since 1991, following independence from Soviet rule. The country operates a system of mandatory health insurance contributions for employees, and private medical insurance is also available. Doctors in clinics and hospitals often expect immediate payment in cash for any treatment. However, as a result of EU entry in January 2007, Bulgaria has reciprocal health agreements with all EEA and Swiss nationals, who are eligible for free or low-cost emergency medical treatment on production of a European Health Insurance Card (EHIC). However, this arrangement may take some time to become operational at local level and private health insurance is recommended. Note that the EHIC can be used only by visitors. Residents must have private health insurance or contribute to the social security system. Retired EU citizens who have paid into their own country's social security system are entitled to free or low-cost healthcare.

Pets

As a member of the EU, Bulgaria has no quarantine system, but pets must be identifiable by a microchip or tattoo, be vaccinated against rabies and have an EU Pet Passport.

Visas & Permits

Visas: EU citizens don't require a visa but do require a residence permit (see below). Visas (and work permits) must be obtained by non-EU nationals before arriving in Bulgaria; do so via the Bulgarian embassy in your home country. You'll be looked upon more favourably if you plan to invest in the country and employ Bulgarian nationals. All non-EU citizens must contact their local police station within 48 hours of arrival in Bulgaria and give written details of the purpose of their visit, length of stay and where they're staying. If you're booked into a hotel or guest house, this is usually done on your behalf. You're given a dated registration slip which you must keep safely. **Failure to produce this on request can result in a large fine!**

Residence Permits: Non-EU citizens are granted permission for temporary residence (usually for a year) only under certain circumstances, including that they're doing work than no EU citizen can do. There are two types of residence permit for EU citizens: long-stay (up to five years) and permanent residence. For a long-stay permit, they must have work in Bulgaria, be enrolled in a school or a university or have sufficient funds to support themselves. For permanent residence, EU citizens must have been living in the country for five years and be legally employed. Since October 2006, in preparation for the country's EU entry, new residence permit cards (known as certificates) have been issued to EU citizens to replace the previously required identity cards. There's concern that the new certificates don't contain a photograph or the national identification number, allowing the possibility of easy forgery. In addition, the national identification number (EGN) is essential for dealing with the authorities in Bulgaria.

9

Work Permits: In theory, work permits have been unnecessary for EU nationals since the country's EU accession in January 2007. However, it remains to be seen how quickly this is adopted at local level. Check with the Bulgarian embassy or consulate. For non-EU nationals, work permits are difficult to obtain. Your prospective employer must confirm to the authorities that you have relevant skills or specific expertise and that a Bulgarian citizen isn't able to fill the position.

Reference

Useful Addresses

Bulgarian Embassy (US), 1621 22nd Street, NW, Washington DC 20008, US (☎ 202-387 0174, 🖳 www.bulgaria-embassy.org).
   Bulgarian Embassy (UK), 186-188 Queen's Gate, London SW7 5HL, UK (☎ 020-7584 9433, 🖳 www.bulgarianembassy.org.uk).
   Bulgarian State Agency for Tourism, 1 Sveta Nedelya Sq., 1040 Sofia (🖳 www.bulgariatravel.org).

Europe: **CROATIA**

Background Information

Capital: Zagreb.
Population: 4.5m.
   Foreign Community: The population is around 90 per cent Croatian and 5 per cent Serb, most of the remainder being Bosnian, Hungarian, Slovene, Czech and Roma. There's also a significant German/Austrian minority and a growing Chinese population in Zagreb and some other big cities. There are very few British and American residents.
   Area: 56,542km^2 (21,830mi^2).
   Geography: Croatia is in south-east Europe, with the Adriatic Sea to the south-west (it borders Italy), Slovenia and Hungary to the north and Bosnia and Herzegovina to the south-east. It has lowland plains in the east and north-west (known as the Pannonian plain), densely wooded mountains and rocky coastlines, with over 1,000 islands off the Adriatic Coast. The country boasts many national parks.
   Climate: Croatia has two distinct climates. The north, east and south-central interior have a continental climate, with hot summers and cold winters, average temperatures ranging from 0C (32F) in January to 23C (73F) in August. The Adriatic (Dalmatian) coast has a Mediterranean climate, average temperatures ranging from 6C (43F) in January to 27C (81F) in August.
   Language: The official language is Croatian, spoken by over 96 per cent of the population, followed by Serbian (1 per cent). English and German are spoken in popular resorts.
   Political Situation: Croatia is one of the six countries which made up the former Yugoslavia, a country that was broken up by a series of civil wars during the '90s. Croatia declared its independence from Yugoslavia in 1991, causing Serbia to declare war, and it took until 1998 for the country to regain complete control of its territory from Serbia. Needless to say, these upheavals took their toll both socially and economically. Presidential and parliamentary elections in 2000 saw the beginning of an improvement in the country's economy and a commitment to European integration. Croatia is now a parliamentary democracy and its most

9

recent election, in 2003, saw the Croatian Democratic Union (HDZ) return to power, with a new leader, Ivo Sanader, as Prime Minister. The HDZ's policies are centre-right and it has sought to distance itself from the old-style HDZ, which was considered corrupt and ineffectual. Government policy is dominated by the need for economic reform and Croatia's bid for EU accession. The country has developed quickly over the last few years, with tourism booming again (Yugoslavia was a popular holiday destination in the '80s) and increased business confidence with EU membership in sight. Croatia was given EU applicant status in 2004 and hopes to become a member between 2009 and 2010. The country is a member of the World Trade Organisation and hopes to join NATO in 2008.

Finance

Currency

Croatia's currency is the kuna (HRK), which is divided into 100 lipas. The kuna was introduced in 1994 to replace the Yugoslav dinar. It isn't pegged to any major currency, although the Croatian National Bank intervenes periodically to ensure its stability against the euro.

Exchange Rate: UK£1 = 10.13 HRK2.

Exchange Controls: There are no exchange controls on the transfer of funds to or from Croatia. Foreign investors theoretically have the same rights as Croatian investors, but some unofficial barriers remain. Foreigners (resident and non-resident) may hold foreign exchange accounts, but they're subject to limitations.

Cost & Standard of Living

Croatia experienced a recession from the late '90s into the new millennium and the government introduced a series of economic and structural reforms to combat it. Inflation is currently low (around 2 per cent) but unemployment is high (around 16 per cent), although the latter has reduced considerably from its level of a few years ago. The tourist industry has recovered after the civil war and is now a major economic contributor: the country welcomes over 8m tourists per year. Croatia's cost of living is high for the region but lower than that of neighbouring Austria or Italy.

Taxation

Personal Effects: Personal effects can be imported duty free if they've been owned and used by you for six months or longer.

Income Tax: If you're resident in Croatia, you're taxed on your worldwide income, while non-residents pay tax only on income earned in Croatia. There are four bands, from 15 to 45 per cent. Amounts earned up to HRK36,000 (£3,256) are taxed at 15 per cent, and you pay 45 per cent for amounts over HRK252,000 (£22,790). These rates can be increased by local government surcharges.

Capital Gains Tax (CGT): Capital gains from the sale of immovable property are charged at a flat rate of 25 per cent unless the property has been owned for more than three years or the owner was living in the property before the sale. Individuals aren't liable for any other CGT, although companies are subject to a profit tax on sales of over HRK2m (£180,868).

Wealth Tax: None.

Inheritance & Gift Tax: 5 per cent.

9

Value Added Tax (VAT): The rate of VAT (known as *PDV* in Croatia) is 22 per cent on most goods and services. The following are VAT exempt: basic food items, exports, rents, financial and insurance services, and medical services. VAT registration is compulsory for businesses with a turnover in excess of HRK85,000 (£7,700).

Property

Restrictions on Foreign Ownership & Letting

Buying as an individual requires permission from the Ministry of Foreign Affairs. Alternatively, you can buy through a Croatian company (see **Purchase Procedure** below). Before buying land, ensure that you take advice about local zoning restrictions and obtain confirmation that you're entitled to build on the land and that planning permission will easy to obtain. A building plot must be a minimum of 500m^2.

If you wish to let your property as an individual, you must obtain a rental licence and register your property as available for letting with the Croatian Tourist Board. Regulations vary according to the administrative area your property is in; in some you must also obtain a business licence. You must set up a business account at a local bank to hold any rental deposits.

Obtaining legal title in Croatia can be complicated and time consuming, and it's vital to ensure that you obtain independent legal advice from a lawyer experienced in Croatian property transfers and fluent in Croat and English (see Purchase Procedure below).

Market

Croatia's property market took off only in 2003, as a result of renewed confidence in the country, thanks largely to its EU application and the government's determination to meet EU criteria. Tourism is booming, not just in coastal resorts, but also in Dubrovnik and the capital, Zagreb, and this makes Croatia a good location for a buy-to-let investment, both for short-term letting to holidaymakers and for long-term letting to foreign and local businessmen, although currently the country attracts mainly those looking for a capital investment. Restrictions on building development mean that the country also appeals to those looking for a secluded second home or retirement location. Property prices are still low in comparison with western Europe, although 2004 saw growth of around 40 per cent and that rate is set to continue, or even increase, as the country approaches its anticipated EU accession (2009/2010).

Areas

The most popular areas with tourists and investors are the Adriatic Islands, the Dalmatian Coast and Istria, which is sometimes called the Croatian Tuscany.

The Adriatic Islands – especially the larger ones, such as Brac and Hvar – are becoming increasingly popular with tourists and investors because of their dramatic scenery, unspoiled environment and easy access to the mainland. There are over 1,000 islands, although only around 60 are inhabited and some have virtually no infrastructure.

The Dalmatian Coast, which includes the popular cities of Split and Dubrovnik, has all the ingredients of a popular tourist location: sunshine, beautiful scenery and an interesting cultural history. Split and Dubrovnik are popular with investors thanks to year-round rental potential, good transport links and the several golf courses which are being built close to Dubrovnik. In 2005, a motorway was opened between Zagreb and Split, reducing the journey time to three hours.

9

Istria, which borders Slovenia in the north-west, has the most established property market in Croatia, thanks to its tourist appeal and easy access to the rest of Europe. It boasts an attractive coastline, beautiful countryside and Venetian architecture. The area was once part of Italy and retains an Italian feel, with dual place names and a strong Italian influence on the language and cuisine. Although Istria is very popular during the summer, especially with Italian tourists, it doesn't have the year-round rental letting potential of Split and Dubrovnik.

Building Standards

New properties are generally of better quality than older buildings, partly as a result of increased competition among developers. The quality of older properties varies widely. Surveys aren't usual in Croatia, but it's wise to have one, especially if considering buying an older property.

Cost

The most expensive property is along the Dalmatian Coast, particularly on the islands of Brac and Hvar and in Split – known as Croatia's second city – and Dubrovnik. On the islands, you can still buy an old, two-bedroom stone house in need of restoration for around £20,000; a restored house costs only twice as much. But prices for new three- and four-bedroom villas are from around £240,000 up to several million euros, while new apartments and villas in the area cost from £70,000 to £300,000. In Split, a new one-bedroom apartment costs around £95,000, but a larger apartment in the historic old town costs £170,000. Dubrovnik's prices are even higher, two-bedroom flats costing around £200,000 (€300,000) and larger properties from £650,000.

Istria's prices are lower, a renovated two-bedroom stone house costing around £100,000 and a newly-built villa around £170,000.

Local Mortgages

A local mortgage is difficult to obtain if you're a non-resident foreigner, and domestic lenders often aren't willing to lend on a Croatian property due to uncertainty of title (see **Purchase Procedure** below). This is gradually changing but how quick or radical the change will be is at present uncertain. One bank, the Hypo Alpe Adria, offers finance in euros (up to 70 per cent of a property's value) for a period of 15 years, but the property must be purchased through a Croatian company (see **Purchase Procedure** below).

Property Taxes

There's an annual holiday home tax payable by all owners of second homes. The rate is set by the local authority and depends on location, age and local infrastructure but is usually between HRK5 and HRK15 (£0.50 and £1.50) per m^2 of the habitable area of the property.

Purchase Procedure

For non-resident foreigners in Croatia, there are two methods of buying property: as an individual or through a Croatian company. As an individual, you must obtain approval from the Ministry of Foreign Affairs. Many estate agents (*nekretnine*) will tell you that you can buy under a reciprocal agreement between Croatia and your home country and, although this is true, it doesn't make much difference in practice and doesn't speed up the process. (**Estate agents in Croatia are unregulated, so you should exercise extreme caution when dealing with them.**) Reciprocity, in brief, means that if a Croatian is entitled to buy property in your country, you can buy in Croatia. However, you must obtain **proof** of reciprocity from the Ministry of Foreign Affairs (effectively the same as approval to buy) and this can take between several months and a year. Although the procedure is usually a formality, you cannot transfer the property to your name until you've obtained approval.

The alternative is to buy through a company, which is much faster (around six weeks) and approval isn't required because a Croatian company is regarded as a Croatian legal entity, even if the company is foreign-owned. The process costs around €1,000. As buying through a company may have tax implications in Croatia and your home country, however, you should take independent legal advice before doing so.

Once approval has been obtained or a company set up, a reservation contract is signed and initial checks are made before the preliminary contract is signed. A deposit of around 10 per cent is then payable, which you lose if you don't go ahead with the purchase. Once all checks have been made and your lawyer has verified that there is clean title (see below) on the property, the balance is payable and the deed of sale is signed and certified by a notary. Ownership is then transferred to your name and registered at the Land Registry.

Off-plan purchases: When the preliminary contract is signed, a deposit of around 30 per cent is payable, with the remainder paid in three stages. When construction has finished, the deed of sale is signed and the final instalment paid. **Croatia doesn't have a system of bank guarantees in case the developer goes out of business, so ensure that your lawyer checks the financial status of the developer you're buying from and puts in place alternative safeguards to protect your investment.**

IMPORTANT NOTE

Securing clean title in Croatia is very difficult because of the country's complicated political history and less than efficient Land Registry system. A combination of more than 50 years of Soviet control and the Balkan wars (when many records were destroyed) means that some titles are simply not available. In addition, in the past, properties in Croatia were handed down through families without transfers being recorded in the Land Registry. Even if a title does exist, you may find that it lists several joint owners, who must all be tracked down and agree to the sale. All of these factors mean that obtaining legal title in Croatia can be complicated and time consuming, and it's vital to ensure that you obtain independent legal advice from a lawyer experienced in Croatian property transfers and fluent in Croat and your language.

Fees

9

Fees usually amount to 9 or 10 per cent of the purchase price. An estate agent's commission is between 2.5 and 3 per cent, a lawyer's around 1.5 per cent. Permission to buy from the Ministry of Foreign Affairs costs around HRK70 (£7). It's mandatory to engage the services of a translator, which costs around HRK500 (£50), and there's a Land Registry fee of around HRK400 (£40), which is sometimes included in the lawyer's fee. Property transfer tax is 5 per cent, and the property must be registered within 30 days. VAT (*PDV*) is payable at 22 per cent on new properties.

General Information

Getting There

Croatia's main airports are Dubrovnik, Pula on the Istrian peninsula, Split and Zagreb. Istria can also be reached via a number of Italian airports, including Trieste, Venice Treviso and Venice Marco Polo.

Dubrovnik: Situated 20km (12.5mi) south of the city, the airport is served by Aer Lingus (from Dublin), British Airways (London Gatwick and Manchester), Croatia Airlines (London Gatwick, Manchester, Nottingham and many other European destinations), Flybe (Birmingham) and Thomsonfly (London Gatwick, London Luton and Manchester).

Pula: The most convenient airport for those visiting Istria, served by Croatia Airlines (London Gatwick and Manchester), Flyglobespan (Edinburgh, Durham Tees Valley and Glasgow), Ryanair (Dublin and London Stansted) and Thomsonfly (Bristol, Doncaster, London Gatwick and Manchester).

Split: The main airport for those visiting the Dalmatian Coast and the third-largest airport in Croatia, Split is served by British Airways (London Gatwick), Croatia Airlines (London Gatwick and Heathrow, Manchester and other European destinations), Easyjet (London Gatwick) and Flybe (Birmingham).

Zagreb International Airport: Situated 14km (8.5mi) south of the capital, Zagreb is the hub for the national carrier, Croatia Airlines (London Heathrow and London Gatwick and Manchester), and is also served by Wizz Air (London Luton).

Communications

The state-owned Croatian Telecommunications (Hrvatski Telekom – HT) was privatised in 1999, but the government retained majority control. In 2001, in controversial circumstances, the German former state monopoly, Deutsche Telekom, became the major shareholder in HT and imposed high prices on fixed and mobile phones and internet services (although the service is good). Mobile phone use is widespread in Croatia's cities and towns, although coverage can be unreliable in remote regions. The country dialling code is 385, the main area codes as follows: Zagreb (1), Split (21), Dubrovnik (20) and the Istrian Peninsula (52). International direct dialling (IDD) is available but can be expensive, particularly in hotels.

Fixed-line Telephones: You can make national and international calls from public phone booths using a pre-paid phone card (*telefonske kartice*). These can be bought from post offices, kiosks and newspaper stands. Alternatively, you can make calls from phone booths in the nearest post office, using a phone card, credit cards or cash.

Mobile Telephones: The (GSM) mobile phone network covers all but a few remote areas. The main mobile phone service providers are VipNet and T-Mobile, with over 90 per cent of the market between them. A third operator, Tele-2, entered the market in 2005. All operators sell SIM cards, which you can transfer to your mobile phone.

Internet: Internet use isn't as widespread as in some other countries: 35 per cent of the population are users, the majority via dial-up connections (only just over 2 per cent have access to ADSL). There are nine internet service providers (ISPs) and the government is looking to increase internet use. There are internet cafes in Dubrovnik, Zagreb and other major towns, most of them with high-speed connections.

Postal Services: Postal services are run by the state-owned Croatian Post (Hrvatska posta), which offers a wide range of services from main post offices in the cities and large towns. Airmail to Europe takes between two and five days, surface mail up to ten.

9

Crime Rate

Croatia has a low crime rate and violent crime is rare. Foreigners aren't usually targeted and Croatians generally welcome foreign visitors.

Medical Facilities

Although medical facilities in Croatia are of a good standard, they're severely under-funded and some medicines and equipment are in short supply. The government is in the process of privatising the health service, but this has resulted in a two-tier system and a noticeable drop in preventative treatment. Medical staff may expect cash payment for treatment in public hospitals. Comprehensive private health insurance is recommended for both EU and non-EU citizens.

Pets

Although not yet a member of the EU, Croatia became part of the Pet Passport scheme in 2004. The country has no quarantine system but imported pets must be identifiable by a microchip or tattoo, be vaccinated against rabies and have an EU Pet Passport.

Visas & Permits

Visas: Although Croatia isn't yet a full member of the EU, visas aren't required for EEA citizens, who may stay in Croatia for up to 90 days within a six-month period (although you must have a return ticket). If you intend to stay for over 90 days, you must apply to the Ministry of the Interior for a temporary residence permit (see below). Citizens of Australia, Canada, Japan, the US and some other countries (check with your embassy or consulate) don't require visas for stays of up to 90 days and can apply for temporary residence permits in the same way as EU citizens (see below).

Residence Permits: If you're intending to stay for over 90 days for the purpose of working, studying or joining a member of your family in Croatia, you must apply to the Ministry of the Interior for a temporary residence permit, which is issued initially for one year and then extended if necessary. If you require an extension, you must apply at least one month before the expiry date. Permanent residence permits can be obtained only if you've had a temporary residence permit for more than five years or have been married to a Croatian citizen for at least three years.

Work Permits: Both EU and non-EU nationals must obtain work (or business) permits before undertaking any kind of paid employment or running a business of any kind. Permits are issued to those who have a registered trade or activity in the country or who have a firm job offer from a Croatian company. It may be possible to obtain a work or business permit from the Croatian embassy in your home country, although this depends on your circumstances.

Reference

9

Useful Addresses

Embassy of Croatia (UK), 21 Conway Street, London W1P 5HL, UK (☎ 020-7387 2022, ▭ www.croatia.embassyhomepage.com).

Embassy of Croatia (US), 2343 Massachusetts Avenue, NW, Washington DC 2008, US (☎ 202-588 5899, 🖳 www.croatiaemb.org).

Croatian National Tourist Office (UK and Ireland), 162-164 Fulham Palace Road, London W6 9ER, UK (☎ 020-8563 7979, 🖳 http://gb.croatia.hr).

Croatian National Tourist Office (US), 350 Fifth Avenue, Suite 4003, New York, New York 10118, US (☎ 212-279 8672, 🖳 http://us.croatia.hr).

EUROPE: CYPRUS

Background Information

Capital: Nicosia (Lefkosia).

Population: 784,000.

Foreign Community: The population of Cyprus is 78 per cent Greek, 18 per cent Turkish and 4 per cent other nationalities. The foreign community includes some 60,000 British residents, concentrated in resort areas.

Area: 9,250km^2 (3,572mi^2), of which 3,355km^2 (1,295mi^2) is in Northern Cyprus.

Geography: Cyprus lies at the eastern end of the Mediterranean, 64km (40mi) from Turkey and 122km (76mi) from Syria. It's 240km (149mi) long and 96km (60mi) wide, with a coastline of 782km (486mi). Cyprus is the third-largest island in the Mediterranean and although it's politically and culturally part of Europe, geographically it's in the Near East, strategically situated between Europe, Asia and Africa. The north coast is backed by the long limestone mountain range of Kyrenia. The central plain between Morphou and Famagusta is fertile and well irrigated, and produces fruit, flowers and early vegetables.

Climate: Cyprus is the sunniest island in the Mediterranean, with over 300 days of sunshine a year, long, hot, dry summers and mild winters. Most of the island's rain falls between November and March. August is the hottest month, when temperatures are between 21 and 40C (70-104F), and January is the coldest, with temperatures between 6 and 13C (43-55F). Sea temperatures range from 16C (61F) in January to 32C (90F) in August. In winter, it's possible to ski on Mount Olympus in the Troodos mountains. Cyprus suffered an earthquake in 1996 measuring 6.8 on the Richter scale, which damaged around 700 homes in 50 villages. Less serious earth tremors are common but modern homes are generally built to withstand them.

Language: The national languages are Greek and Turkish, although most Turkish Cypriots now live in the self-declared Turkish Republic of Northern Cyprus. English is spoken by some 90 per cent of Greek Cypriots.

Political Situation: Cyprus has had a turbulent history since the 1950s and was partitioned in 1974, when Turkish forces invaded the north. The northern part of Cyprus (40 per cent of the island) remains under the jurisdiction of the Turkish Cypriots, backed by the Turkish army, the country's capital Nicosia being partitioned. The Turkish Cypriots have declared a Turkish Republic of Northern Cyprus, a pariah 'state' recognised only by Turkey. There's little communication between the Greek and Turkish Cypriot communities. For most foreigners, Cyprus is confined to the southern region, governed by the Greek Cypriots, and the information in this section refers exclusively to that area. (For information about buying property in Northern Cyprus, refer to this book's sister-publication *Buying a Home in Cyprus*.) It should be noted that partition is of little or no consequence to foreigners living in the southern part of Cyprus.

The Republic of Cyprus is a presidential democracy and the current President is Tassos Papadopoulos, leader of the centre right Democratic Party, supported by a coalition of other parties from a broad political spectrum. The President exercises executive power through his Council of Ministers. In May 2004, the whole island legally became part of the EU, although EU

9

legislation doesn't apply in the Turkish-occupied north of the island. The next presidential election is in early 2008. Cyprus is a member of the British Commonwealth and joined the European Union (EU) in 2004.

Finance

Currency

Cyprus' currency is the Cypriot pound (CYP), which has been pegged to the euro at €1 = CYP0.58 since 1999. Cyprus will adopt the euro on 1st January 2008.

Exchange Rate: UK£1 = CYP0.86.

Exchange Controls: None.

Cost & Standard of Living

The Cypriot economy is healthy, with low inflation and low unemployment and a high standard of living. Tourism accounts for a large part of this economic success, while tough fiscal policies to meet EU criteria for adoption of the euro have also had a positive effect on the economy. The cost of living is low by European standards (around 25 per cent cheaper than in most northern European countries), but it has increased considerably in recent years. Some imported items are expensive, although car prices are as much as 50 per cent lower than in some northern European countries: residents can import a new car free of tax and duty under certain conditions. According to the Cypriot government's Household Budget Survey, a couple owning their home outright can live fairly comfortably on an income of around UK£9,200 per year.

Taxation

Cyprus' tax legislation underwent major reform in 2003 to bring it in line with other EU countries and prepare the country for EU entry in 2004. It's considered a favourable tax location, especially for retirees, who're taxed at a rate of only 5 per cent and, if they're tax resident in Cyprus, their heirs don't have to pay inheritance tax.

Personal Effects: Personal effects can be imported duty free, including vehicles (retirees are permitted to import two duty-free cars). Non-residents are allowed to import a car and use it for three months before re-exporting it or registering it in Cyprus. Household effects must have been owned and used for 12 months, and must be imported within 12 months of taking up residence.

Income Tax: Income tax on worldwide income is payable by people resident in Cyprus for more than 183 days per year. Non-residents pay tax only on income earned in Cyprus, which includes rental income. For residents, the first CYP10,000 (£11,700) of income is exempt; you pay 20 per cent tax on earnings over that amount, 25 per cent on earnings over CYP15,000 (£17,500) and 30 per cent on earnings over CYP20,000 (£23,000). Foreign pensions are taxed at 5 per cent, with a CYP2,000 (£2,300) exemption. Resident employees pay tax via a PAYE system.

Capital Gains Tax (CGT): Gains from the sale of property in Cyprus are taxed at 20 per cent, although if the property is a principal residence, there's a lifetime exemption (i.e. once only) of CYP50,000 (£59,000) – CYP10,000 if it's a holiday home. Other exemptions include transfers due to a death or gifts to close relatives or charities.

Wealth Tax: None.

Inheritance & Gift Tax: None (abolished in January 2000), as long as you're a tax resident in Cyprus and have a valid Cypriot will.

9

Special Contribution for Defence: Residents are liable for this and it's imposed on dividends and interest (but not if arising from a normal business) and on a proportion of rental income. Rental income is charged at 3 per cent, after a 25 per cent deduction.

Value Added Tax (VAT): VAT is levied at a standard rate of 15 per cent and a reduced rate of 5 per cent, which applies to hotel and restaurant bills, and alcohol. Certain essential goods and services are zero rated or exempt (including most food, medicines and financial transactions).

Property

Restrictions on Foreign Ownership & Letting

EU nationals resident in Cyprus can buy as much property or land as they wish without obtaining approval from the Council of Ministers. EU nationals not resident in Cyprus can buy as much land as they like but are permitted to buy only one property (a husband and wife may buy only one property between them) and require permission from the Council of Ministers. Approval is a formality (and may be abolished in around 2009) and can be arranged by your lawyer during the purchase procedure. Non-EU nationals may buy only 3 donums of land (4,000m^2 or around one acre) and only one house or apartment. If you wish to buy land, your lawyer should check the latest zoning regulations, which changed in 2003, and that planning permission has been obtained or will be forthcoming.

In theory, non-resident foreign property owners aren't permitted to let on a short-term basis (they may let long term to residents), unless an application has been made to the Cyprus Tourism Organisation (CTO) and the property is certified for holiday lets. This is partly to protect the holiday industry and partly linked to the fact that non-resident foreigners must still obtain permission to buy property in Cyprus. In practice, however, the law isn't strictly enforced and many foreigners let their properties short term without notifying the CTO.

Market

Cyprus has long been a popular location for holiday and retirement homes. After a period of rapid price rises ahead of the country's EU accession in 2004 – there were three or four years of annual growth of around 10 to 15 per cent – the Cypriot property market has experienced stable but healthy growth. Prices may increase more quickly again ahead of the adoption of the euro in 2008.

A wide range of properties is available, new and old, including restored and unrestored village houses. New developments abound, and although some are uninspiring, there has been a strong push by the government to attract more upmarket buyers and tourists. To this end, new developments usually have swimming pools, tennis courts and gyms. More golf courses are being built, some as part of luxury developments, including spas, shops, restaurants and hotels. Over-development and mass tourism have spoiled some coastal areas, although efforts are being made to reverse this trend, following the example of Paphos, in the south-west of the island, which for years has had strict building regulations to control the height of apartment blocks and hotels. Many inland villages are unspoiled and full of character.

Areas

Some of the most popular areas with tourists and homebuyers are in the Famagusta district (notably Ayia Napa, Paralimni and Protaras), Larnaca, Limassol, parts of Nicosia, and Paphos and the surrounding area, though many foreign homebuyers opt for the tranquillity of villages in the foothills of the Troodos Mountains.

Famagusta: Only a small part of Famagusta district, in the south-east of the island, lies within the Republic of Cyprus, the remainder being in the occupied north of the island. Several areas in Famagusta are popular with tourists and homebuyers, notably Ayia Napa, Protaras and Paralimni. The government is taking measures to improve the image of Ayia Napa, which has attracted unfavourable publicity regarding its hedonistic nightlife and binge-drinking holidaymakers (mainly young Britons). The rather more sedate Protaras and Paralimni have some of Cyprus's best beaches.

Larnaca: For many years, Larnaca, in the south-east of the island and a short drive from Larnaca International Airport, wasn't popular with foreign buyers. It doesn't have the dramatic scenery of, for example, Paphos, but it's gradually becoming more popular and property is cheaper than in Paphos. The area is currently undergoing a facelift to make it more attractive to tourists and there's a new tourist zone, better road access and improvements to the town's marina.

Limassol: Lying in the south of the island and with 18 miles of coastline, Limassol is Cyprus's second-largest city and a thriving business centre (second only to Nicosia). The surrounding coast is a popular tourist location, with a large marina and several golf courses within a short distance. Moving inland gives buyers a choice of several tranquil villages, notably Laneia and Souni.

Nicosia: The only divided capital in Europe, Nicosia isn't generally favoured by tourists and foreign property buyers. Its central location makes it very hot and dusty in the summer.

Paphos: Those looking for a holiday or retirement home have often chosen the Paphos area (in the south-west of the island), which has an international airport and a large British community. It offers a dramatic coastline, beautiful countryside and a mild climate. Some of the most popular parts of Paphos are in Peyia village, which is hugely popular with British buyers and is now classed as a Paphos suburb. Just outside Paphos lie two unspoiled resorts, Polis and Latchi, which are becoming increasingly popular with buyers.

Building Standards

The construction quality of new properties is generally high, but the quality of older properties varies widely and a survey is recommended, although this isn't common practice in Cyprus.

Cost

Property prices on Cyprus vary according to location, size and quality.

In Famagusta, apartments begin at around CYP55,000 (£65,000), villas and bungalows costing around CYP200,000 (£234,000).

Prices in Larnaca are rising, thanks to recently improved tourist facilities (see **Areas** above). They begin at CYP50,000 (£58,000) for a one-bedroom apartment, rising to around CYP400,000 (£470,000) for a luxury five-bedroom, beach-front villa.

Prices in Limassol are similar, starting at around CYP50,000 (£58,000) for a one-bedroom apartment and rising to around CYP350,000 (£410,000) for a three-bedroom, beach-front villa.

In Nicosia and its environs, one-bedroom apartments begin at around CYP55,000 (£65,000), while detached houses on large plots cost around CYP300,000 (£350,000). There are some potentially very attractive properties in the Old Town which are in need of renovation and are therefore significantly cheaper than average. Most of them are government-protected (requiring permission for renovation) but it's possible to obtain financial help to renovate them.

Paphos is Cyprus's most expensive area, especially on the Aphrodite Hills golf development. Elsewhere in Paphos, prices begin at around CYP77,000 (£90,000) for a two-

9

bedroom apartment, while three-bedroom villas can still be bought relatively cheaply, for around CYP250,000 (£290,000), although there are an increasing number of custom-built luxury villas which sell for several million euros each!

Local Mortgages

Local mortgages are reasonably easy to secure but there's a mortgage registration fee of at least 1 per cent of the amount borrowed. All are of the repayment type and available in Cypriot pounds or foreign currency. Mortgages are usually up to around 70 per cent of the purchase price, but mortgages in foreign currencies are available only for a short period (e.g. ten years) – those in Cypriot pounds usually have a longer repayment term. Some new properties are sold on 'hire purchase' terms by developers, e.g. a 25 per cent deposit with the balance payable in monthly instalments over two to five years. Other schemes require one third on signing, one third during construction and the remaining third to be paid in monthly instalments over two or three years.

Property Taxes

A local authority tax of around CYP100 (£115) per year is payable for services such as refuse collection and street lighting. There's also an annual immovable property tax based on a property's value on 1st January 1980 (*sic*) but the first CYP100,000 is exempt so in most cases no tax is due. After that, the rates are 0.25 per cent on properties valued up to CYP250,000, 0.35 per cent between CYP250,000 and CYP500,000, and 0.4 per cent over CYP500,000.

Purchase Procedure

Estate agents in Cyprus must be registered with the government, and you're advised to use an agent who is a member of the Cyprus Real Estate Agents' Association (CREAA). The purchase procedure is similar to the British system, although not entirely the same. Once you make an offer, you usually pay a small holding deposit of around CYP1,000 (£1,200). The deposit **isn't** held in a bonded account but paid directly to the vendor. This is normal practice in Cyprus and your lawyer should draw up a simple document to be signed by the vendor confirming receipt of the deposit and agreeing that its retention is subject to satisfactory searches.

Once satisfactory checks have been made, a 10 per cent deposit is normally payable, although the amount can vary according to what has been agreed. At this point your lawyer will apply for permission to buy from the Council of Ministers (see above). The balance is usually paid within one month, when your sale contract should be lodged with the Land Registry. This is to protect your rights until the property can be transferred to your name, which can take months owing to delays with the Land Registry system. If you've arranged a mortgage, this must be declared and registered at the same time that you lodge your sale contract.

With all types of purchase, the final act is the transfer of the property (which can be months, sometimes years, later!). All parties must be present, although foreign buyers can authorise power of attorney.

Off-plan Purchases: Within a month of paying the holding deposit and once satisfactory checks have been made, you pay 30 per cent of the purchase price and the other payments (usually two) are made according to the progress of the building work. After the first 30 per cent is paid, an application must be made to the Council of Ministers for permission to buy the property. This is a formality and is likely to be phased out for EU citizens by 2009. Your lawyer usually does this on your behalf and includes it in his fee.

9

It's often a difficult and long-winded process securing separate title to an off-plan property on a development in Cyprus, as the developer usually has title on the whole plot. Make sure your sale contract is deposited with the Land Registry to protect your rights and put a charge on the property until title is satisfactorily transferred to you.

Fees

Fees total at least 10 per cent of the purchase price. A lawyer's fees are around CYP1,000 (£1,200) and an estate agent's 5 per cent of the value of the property. Stamp duty is CYP1.50 per CYP1,000 of value up to CYP100,000 and CYP2 per CYP1,000 above this amount. This is payable within 30 days of signing the contract. The application to the Council of Ministers costs around CYP200 but is often included in the lawyer's fee. A Land Registry fee or transfer tax is payable at between 3 and 8 per cent, depending on the value of the property, on the transfer of the property. Where there are joint owners, the transfer tax can be split between them. VAT is payable on all new properties.

General Information

Getting There

Cyprus has certain entry restrictions (due to the Turkish invasion of the country in 1974). Some of these were relaxed in 2003, when the border between the Republic of Cyprus and the Turkish-occupied north of the island was opened. However, some restrictions remain when travelling north to south, notably that you may not enter the Republic of Cyprus via any airport or port in the north of the island, which are considered illegal ports of entry.

There are numerous flights to Larnaca and Paphos airports. Both airports are being refurbished and extended to deal with increased numbers of tourists and second home owners.

Larnaca: Larnaca International Airport, in the south-east of the island, is Cyprus's largest airport. The major airlines operating to it are British Airways (a daily, year-round service from London Heathrow) and Cyprus Airways, the national carrier, which offers twice-daily flights from London Heathrow (March to October) and a number of less frequent flights from other UK airports. Excel Airways and Eurocypria Airlines, Thomas Cook Airlines and Thomsonfly offer a number of flights from London Gatwick and other UK airports. Monarch Airlines was the first budget airline to fly to Larnaca, from London Luton, starting in March 2007.

Paphos: Paphos International Airport, in the south-west of the island, 16km from the town of Paphos, is the island's main tourist airport. British Airways franchise operator GB Airways operates flights from London Gatwick and Manchester, and Cyprus Airways flies from Birmingham, London Heathrow and Manchester. Eurocypria Airlines, Excel Airways, First Choice Airways, Flyglobespan (Aberdeen and Glasgow), Thomas Cook Airlines and Thomsonfly operate flights from London Gatwick and other UK airports.

Communications

9

Telecommunications in Cyprus are excellent and are mainly provided by the state-owned Cyprus Telecommunications Authority (CYTA). Although the market was liberalised in 2003 and some other companies offer basic services, CYTA is the only provider offering a complete service. The country dialling code is 357, relevant area codes as follows: Ayia Napa (23),

Larnaca (24), Limassol (25), Nicosia (22) and Paphos (26). International direct dialling (IDD) is available from private and public telephones.

Fixed-line Telephones: You can make national and international calls from public telephones in central locations and at airports and harbours. They take either coins or phone cards (Telecards), which can be bought from banks, post offices and CYTA offices.

Mobile Telephones: Mobile phone use is widespread, although in remote areas reception can be poor. The main (GSM 900) mobile phone network providers are CytaMobile/Vodaphone and Areeba Cyprus, which is owned by a South African company; a third operator, Tele-2, entered the market in 2005.

Internet: Internet use is widespread in Cyprus, but broadband still isn't available in some areas. There are around 15 internet service providers (ISPs) in the country and a growing number of internet cafes in the main towns and cities, most with high-speed connections.

Postal Services: Postal services are run by the state-owned Cyprus Postal Services, and the four district post offices (in Larnaca, Limassol, Nicosia and Paphos) offer a wide range of services. Airmail to Europe takes three to four days and around a week to other destinations.

Crime Rate

Cyprus has one of the world's lowest crime rates, and serious crime and crimes against property are rare. There has been a small increase in petty theft from hotels and cars in recent years, but crimes against the person are rare, and respect for women, children and the elderly is a feature of Cypriot life.

Medical Facilities

Medical facilities are excellent and government hospitals provide free or low cost healthcare. Many doctors have trained in the UK or US and therefore speak good English. Since the country's accession to the EU, citizens of EEA countries and Switzerland can use their European Health Insurance Card (EHIC), but only while visiting Cyprus. Residents of Cyprus must be paying into the Cyprus Social Insurance scheme to receive state healthcare. Retired EU citizens are able to use the health service free or at a very low cost (depending on their income). Private health insurance is necessary for anyone who doesn't fall into any of these categories. Private doctors are inexpensive and the quality of their care is generally good.

Pets

As Cyprus is a full member of the EU, there's no quarantine for pets, but they must be identifiable by microchip or tattoo, have an EU Pet Passport and be vaccinated against rabies. Dogs aren't permitted to roam freely and must be kept in an enclosed area (e.g. with a fence) or on a lead.

9 Visas & Permits

You may be refused entry to the Republic of Cyprus if you hold a passport issued by the self-proclaimed Turkish Republic of Northern Cyprus (TRNC, which is recognised only by Turkey) or if you've entered Cyprus via a port or airport in the northern (occupied) part of the island. You may also have problems entering the Republic of Cyprus if your passport is stamped by the TRNC authorities.

Visas: Visas aren't required by EU citizens (or those of several other countries, including Australia, Canada and the US). A full list of qualifying countries is available on the website of the government of Cyprus (🖳 www.cyprus.gov.cy) and citizens of countries listed may enter Cyprus with their passport or national identity card and stay for up to 90 days. Citizens of any country **not** listed must obtain a visa.

Residence Permits: If an EU citizen wishes to stay longer than 90 days, he must apply for a temporary residence permit at the nearest Immigration Office. There are various categories of residence permit, depending on whether you have a job, are self-employed or are retired. If you don't qualify for public healthcare, you must be able to prove that you have private health insurance. If you apply for a residence permit as a retired person, you aren't permitted to do paid work of any kind and must be able to show evidence that you can support yourself financially. After five years, you're able to apply for a permanent residence permit.

The requirements for non-EU citizens are more stringent and usually linked to whether they have a job offer in Cyprus. A new immigration bill was put to the Cypriot parliament in 2006, which may give non-EU nationals similar rights to EU citizens, although this isn't yet in force.

Work Permits: EU citizens don't require a work permit and have the same rights as Cypriot nationals to apply for jobs and work. Non-EU citizens require work permits from the Ministry of Labour, which they must obtain **before** arriving in Cyprus.

Further Reading

Buying a Home in Cyprus, Anne Hall (Survival Books). Everything you need to know about buying a home in Cyprus.

Cyprus Mail, PO Box 21144, 1502 Nicosia, Cyprus (☎ 22-818 585, 🖳 www.cyprus-mail.com). Daily newspaper which includes a property supplement. Available online.

Property & Home Cyprus, Catalan Ltd, 124, Makarios III Ave., Office 11, 1st floor, CY-3021 Limassol, Cyprus (☎ 25-730 203, 🖳 www.cypah.com). Bi-monthly magazine.

Useful Addresses

Cyprus High Commission (UK), 93 Park Street, London W1Y 4ET, UK (☎ 020-7499 8272).

Cyprus Embassy (US), 2211 R. Street, NW, Washington DC 20008, US (☎ 202-462 5772, 🖳 www.cyprusembassy.net).

Cyprus Tourism Organisation (US), 13 East 40th Street, New York, NY 10016, US (☎ 212-683 5280, ✉ gocyprus@aol.com).

Cyprus Tourist Office (UK), 17 Hanover Street, London W1S 1YP, UK (☎ 020-7569 8800, ✉ informationcto@btconnect.com).

Cyprus Tourism Organisation (Cyprus), Leoforos Lemesou 19, PO Box 1390, Nicosia (☎ 22-691 100, ✉ cytour@cto.org.cy).

Cyprus Real Estate Agents' Association (CREAA), PO Box 50563, 3041 Limassol, Cyprus (☎ 25-367 467).

Ministry of the Interior, Migration Officer, Department of Aliens and Immigration, D. Severis Ave, 1453 Nicosia, Cyprus (☎ 22-867 625, 🖳 www.moi.gov.cy).

EUROPE: ESTONIA

9

Background Information

Capital: Tallinn.
Population: 1.3m.

Foreign Community: The population is around 70 per cent Estonian, 25 per cent Russian and there are very small numbers of Ukranian, Belarusian and Finnish nationals. There are very few UK or US residents.

Area: 45,226km^2 (17,462 mi^2).

Geography: Estonia is the smallest and most northerly of the three Baltic States, bordered to the north and west by the Baltic Sea, to the south by Latvia and to the east Russia. Finland lies to the north across the Gulf of Finland. More than half of the country is covered by forest and it has over 1,400 lakes and 1,500 islands in the Baltic.

Climate: Estonia has a temperate climate, with warm summers and cold winters. Average rainfall is 4.7cm, with much of the rainfall in the summer. Winter lasts from November to mid-March and the coldest month is usually February, when average temperatures range from -3.5C (26F) to -7C (19F), the mercury sometimes falling to -20C (-4F). Heavy snowfall is common in winter. Spring and autumn bring mild weather and the hottest month is July, with average temperatures between 16C (61F) and 20C (68F), the temperature sometimes rising to 30C (86F).

Language: The official language is Estonian. Many people also speak Russian, which is the mother tongue of around 30 per cent of the population (mainly older people), although since the country's independence from Russia, its use has become less common. English is widely spoken and understood in the capital, Tallinn, while Finnish and German are understood by some people.

Political Situation: Good. Estonia was under Russian rule from 1940 until it gained independence in 1991, when the Soviet Union collapsed. Since then, it has been able to promote economic and political ties with western Europe and Estonia joined NATO and the EU in 2004. It has strong trading links with Finland, Sweden, Russia and Germany. The country is a Republic and since April 2005 has had a tripartite coalition government, led by Prime Minister Andrus Ansip, leader of the Reform Party.

Finance

Currency

Estonia's national currency is the kroon (EEK), which was introduced in June 1992. The kroon is divided into 100 sents and is pegged to the euro at the rate of approximately €1 = EEK15.65. Estonia plans to adopt the euro as its official currency on 1st January 2008. Property in Estonia can be purchased only in kroons but, because the kroon is pegged to the euro, currency fluctuations are usually limited.

Exchange Rate: UK£1 = EEK23.18.

Exchange Controls: None.

Cost & Standard of Living

Estonia has been experiencing strong economic growth (wages increased by 12 per cent in 2005) and its low inflation makes it a favourable investment location, resulting in high levels of foreign investment and an improving standard of living. The country's ready acceptance of modern technology will help this to continue. The cost of living is lower than the western European average.

Taxation

In its 1994 tax reforms, Estonia became the first European country to introduce a so-called 'flat tax', replacing the previous three tax rates on personal income. Its current economic success is due in part to these tax reforms. Businesses enjoy a liberal tax scheme introduced in 2000,

9

whereby the government doesn't tax profits at all until they're distributed to shareholders as dividends. This gives companies an incentive to retain and reinvest their earnings.

Personal Effects: These can be imported without restriction, provided there's no intention to resell.

Income Tax: Estonia has a flat rate of 23 per cent (which will be reduced to 20 per cent in 2009). However, this is counterbalanced by the fact that taxpayers are entitled to only modest deductions.

Capital Gains Tax (CGT): Considered as income and charged at the flat rate of 23 per cent.

Wealth Tax: None.

Inheritance & Gift Tax: None.

Value Added Tax (VAT): The standard rate of VAT is 18 per cent, there's a reduced rate of 5 per cent on some books, medicines and certain supplies of heating and energy, and there's no VAT on exports. The 18 per cent rate must be applied by businesses whose annual turnover exceeds EEK250,000 (around £11,000).

Property

Restrictions on Foreign Ownership & Letting

There are no restrictions on either, but rental income must be included on your annual tax declaration.

Market

According to the Royal Institution of Chartered Surveyors (RICS) in the UK, average house prices in Estonia rose by 28 per cent in 2005, the highest rate of increase in Europe. (The Statistical Office of Estonia's figure for 2006 is a massive 53 per cent, though it may not be reliable.) The country's EU accession, rapid economic growth and low interest rates have seen it attract significant foreign investment since 2003, and Estonia is the biggest per capita beneficiary of foreign direct investment in the EU. As a result, there has been a surge in the construction of new properties, which, coupled with the introduction of inexpensive mortgages, has allowed more Estonians to buy homes, pushing up prices. There's a healthy letting market in Tallinn, both long and short term.

Areas

Estonia's capital, Tallinn, and its suburbs are the main area of interest for foreign buyers, especially since the introduction of budget flights there in 2004. Tallinn is an attractive medieval city, popular with tourists, international businessmen and an emerging Estonian middle class. The majority of foreign buyers who purchase property in the capital do so to take advantage of high rental yields.

There's also interest from foreign buyers in the Baltic coast in the south-west of the country, particularly Parnu, a beach and health resort. Some investors are buying land in the countryside inland from Parnu.

9

Building Standards

Standards are high for new buildings, but there are plenty of buildings in a bad state of repair due to underinvestment during the Communist era. These properties require a substantial amount of work and are costly to maintain (especially to heat in the winter).

Cost

The majority of new developments in Tallinn are one- and two-bedroom apartments. Prices range from EEK1.16m (£50,000) for a small one-bedroom apartment to EEK5.8m (£250,000) for a large two-bedroom apartment in the heart of the city or an upmarket suburb. Prices in Parnu start at a mere EEK235,000 (£10,000) for a one-bedroom apartment, houses costing around EEK400,000 (£16,000).

Local Mortgages

Foreigners can secure mortgages from the large European and some Estonian banks. Loans can be in kroons, euros or US dollars, up to 70 per cent of the value of a property. Interest rates are between 3.5 and 4.5 per cent, depending on your circumstances, and you must be able to show evidence of a regular income in your home country.

Property Taxes

There's an annual land tax of between 0.2 and 2.5 per cent (of the value of the land only), depending on where the land is and what it's used for. The tax is paid in three equal instalments, in April, July and October.

Purchase Procedure

The buyer signs a preliminary sale contract and pays a deposit of between 5 and 10 per cent. This is a binding contract and there's no opt-out period; nor can property purchase contracts contain conditions (i.e. that you obtain the necessary finance). Contracts need to be in Estonian, so you must arrange a translation, which usually costs around EEK1,500 (£70). A notary must oversee the sale contract and the ownership transfer. There are no title deeds in Estonia, but a notarised application is made to the Land Registry to transfer the ownership of the property to the buyer. This cannot be done until stamp duty is paid (see below). Once this has been done, the title is legally valid.

Off-plan Purchases: The buyer signs a reservation contract and pays a non-refundable deposit (usually between 10 and 15 per cent), which is held in an escrow account at a local bank until the purchase is completed, which can take anything from 6 to 12 months. The balance is paid on completion. There are usually no stage payments during construction, as in many other countries, although some developers are beginning to ask for small stage payments.

Fees

Stamp duty is payable at between 0.3 and 0.5 per cent, depending on the value of the property (i.e. the VAT-inclusive purchase price). Notaries' fees are fixed by the state and range from 0.4 to 1 per cent of the purchase price (plus VAT at 18 per cent) and there's a fee of 0.25 per cent to register the property at the Land Registry. An estate agent's fees are between 3 and 10 per cent of the purchase price – generally, the more expensive the property the lower the percentage.

General Information

Getting There

Tallinn airport is approximately 4km (2.5mi) from the city centre and handles domestic and international flights, including flights from London Stansted (Easyjet), London Gatwick and Dublin (Estonian Air), as well as a range of flights from other European destinations.

Communications

Estonia has efficient telephone and postal services and widespread public internet use. The country dialling code is 372. International direct dialling (IDD) is available by dialling 8 followed by 00 and the country code.

Fixed-line Telephones: There's an English directory enquiries service (☎ 8-1182). Public telephones are operated by phone cards, available at tourist offices and kiosks.

Mobile Telephones: There are three main mobile telephone operators: EMT, Radiolinja Eesti and TELE2. All use the GSM 900/1800 system.

Internet: Estonia has acquired a reputation for its rapid adoption of internet technology, and public wi-fi access is widely available.

Postal Services: Domestic postal services are good, though letters to western European countries usually take around six days.

Crime Rate

Estonia is fairly safe, although there's a certain amount of petty crime such as pick-pocketing. Gangs target tourists in the capital, especially in the Old City, and car theft is also common in Tallinn. Estonia has some drug-related organised crime.

Medical Facilities

Medical care is generally good, with highly trained doctors. Facilities, however, aren't the equal of those in western European countries, hospitals and clinics generally suffering from a lack of equipment and resources. The main hospital is the East Tallinn Central Hospital, in the capital, where many of the medical staff speak English. EU citizens visiting Estonia are entitled to free healthcare with a European Health Insurance Card (EHIC), while residents must be registered with and contributing to the Health Insurance Fund. There's a growing number of excellent private clinics, and private health insurance is recommended in Estonia.

Pets

9

Now that Estonia is part of the EU, there's no quarantine for pets, but they must be identifiable by microchip or tattoo, have an EU Pet Passport and be vaccinated against rabies.

Visas & Permits

Visas: Nationals of EEA countries don't need a visa and can stay in Estonia for a maximum of 90 days at a time. Citizens of some non-EU countries, including Canada and the US, don't require a visa, although many nationalities do and it's vital that you check with the Estonian embassy or consulate in your home country **before** travelling.

Residence Permits: EU citizens have the right to live in Estonia for up to three months if they have a return travel ticket and a passport or national identity card. For longer periods, residence permits are required. You should apply to the local government authority for a temporary residence permit (within the three-month period). Within one month of your temporary residence permit being granted, you must apply for an identity card. Temporary residence is granted for five years, after which you have the right of permanent residence.

Non-EU citizens are granted a temporary residence permit for up to two years (which may be extended to five years) if they're offered a job in Estonia, are a sole proprietor or own a company that has invested at least EEK1m (£50,000) in Estonia.

Work Permits: EU citizens don't require work permits but must have a residence permit for stays longer than three months (see above); non-EU citizens must obtain a work permit, which is linked to their residence permission (see above).

Reference

Useful Addresses

Estonian Embassy (UK), 16 Hyde Park Gate, London SW7 5DG, UK (☎ 020-7589 3248, 🖥 www.estonia.gov.uk).

Estonian Embassy (US), 2131 Massachusetts Avenue, NW 20008, Washington DC, US (☎ 202-588 0101, 🖥 www.estemb.org).

Tallinn Tourist Information, Niguliste 2, Kullassepa 4, 10146 Tallinn (☎ 64 57777, 🖥 www.tourism.tallinn.ee).

Useful Websites

Estonian Investment Agency (🖥 www.investinestonia.com). Available in English.
Estonia Tourist Information (🖥 www.visitestonia.com). Available in English.

EUROPE: FRANCE

9 Background Information

Capital: Paris.
Population: 62.8m.
Foreign Community: France has large foreign communities in its major cities and some rural areas (e.g. the Dordogne) have a large number of British and other foreign residents.
Area: 643,427km^2 (248,428m^2).

Geography: France is the largest country in Europe (excluding Russia), stretching 1,050km (650mi) from north to south and almost as far from west to east (from the tip of Brittany to Strasbourg). Its land and sea border extends for 4,800km (3,000mi) and includes 2,700km (2,175mi) of coastline. Metropolitan France also incorporates the Mediterranean island of Corsica (*Corse*), situated 160km (100mi) from France and 80km (50mi) from Italy, covering 8,721km^2 (3,367mi^2) and with a coastline of 1,000km (620mi). France is bordered by Andorra, Belgium, Germany, Italy, Luxembourg, Spain and Switzerland, and the opening of the Channel Tunnel in 1994 connected it with the UK (by rail only).

Climate: France has three distinct climates, continental, maritime and Mediterranean, plus an Alpine climate in mountainous areas. It isn't easy to generalise about the French climate, as many regions have micro-climates influenced by mountains, forests and other geographical features. Generally, the Loire river is considered to be the divide between the cooler northern European climate and the warmer southern climate. Spring and autumn are usually fine throughout France, although the length of the seasons varies according to the region and altitude.

In Paris and the north, it's rare for the temperature to fall below -5C (24F) in winter or to rise above 30C (86F) in summer. The west and north-west of France (including Brittany and Normandy) have a maritime climate tempered by the Atlantic and the Gulf Stream, with mild winters and warm summers, and most rainfall in spring and autumn. Many people consider the western Atlantic coast to have the best summer climate in France, the heat tempered by cool sea breezes. The Massif Central (which acts as a weather barrier between north and south) and eastern France have a moderate continental climate, with cold winters and hot and stormy summers. However, the centre and eastern upland areas have an extreme continental climate, with freezing winters and sweltering summers.

The Midi, stretching from the Pyrenees to the Alps, is hot and dry, except in early spring, when there's usually heavy rainfall. The Cévennes region is the wettest in France, with some 200cm of rain per year, though it tends to fall in short, sharp bursts. Languedoc has hot, dry summers and much colder winters than the Côte d'Azur, snow often remaining until May in the mountainous inland areas. The Mediterranean coast, not surprisingly, enjoys a Mediterranean climate of mild winters (daytime temperatures rarely drop below 10C/50F) and hot summers, with the temperature often above 30C (86F).

Language: French. France also has a number of rapidly declining regional dialects and regional languages, including Alsatian (spoken in the Alsace), Basque (Pyrenees), Breton (Brittany), Catalan (Roussillon), Corsican (Corsica), Flemish (near the Belgian border) and Occitan (Languedoc). English is spoken by some people in most areas but generally not well.

Political Situation: Stable. France is a democratic republic which operates a semi-presidential system, where the President and Prime Minister share executive power even though they may be from different political parties. Both President and government are elected for five-year terms. Unusually, the majority of power lies with the President. After many years of Socialist rule, a conservative coalition won the general election in 1993. Although the Socialists were returned to power in 1997, by the 2002 presidential and parliamentary elections the party was in disarray, leaving the way open for the conservative President, Jacques Chirac to be re-elected. In 2007, France elected a new President, the conservative Nicolas Sarkozy, who appointed François Fillon as Prime Minister. France is a founder member of the European Union and the United Nations, as well as one of five permanent members of the United Nations Security Council.

Finance

9

Currency

France's currency is the euro (€).
Exchange Rate: £1 = €1.48.
Exchange Controls: None.

Cost & Standard of Living

Salaries in France are around the same as in the US but generally lower than in the UK. Social security contributions and taxes are high, but employees often enjoy a range of company benefits on top of their salaries. In general, the French enjoy a high standard of living with long holidays. The price of property is generally much lower than in the UK, but the cost of living has increased considerably in the last decade, although it's still lower than the EU average, particularly in rural areas.

Taxation

In 2006, the top rate of income tax was reduced from 48.9 per cent to 40 per cent and a 60 per cent ceiling was placed on the total annual taxes paid (including income tax, wealth tax and local taxes).

Personal Effects: Goods purchased within the European Union (EU) can be imported duty free and don't need to be retained for a minimum period. An inventory must be provided. If you're a non-EU resident planning to take up permanent or temporary residence in France, you're permitted to import your furniture and personal effects free of duty.

Income Tax: Residents (those with their principal home or business interests in France) are taxed on worldwide income as follows: earnings up to €5,515 are exempt, then income up to €10,847 is taxed at 5.5 per cent, up to €24,443 at 14 per cent, up to €65,559 at 30 per cent and over €65,559 at 40 per cent. There's a wide range of deductions and exemptions which reduce your taxable income and these include generous benefits for families with children. Non-residents are charged only on income in France, with a new minimum rate of 20 per cent.

Capital Gains Tax (CGT): Gains on profits made from the sale of assets (including property) are taxed at 16 per cent for residents and non-resident EU citizens. However, CGT isn't payable on a profit made on the sale of a principal residence, and the proviso that you must live in it for a minimum of five years has now been removed. Major renovation of a second home is deductible, but the regulations are strict. All work must be carried out by a registered French builder or craftsman and an official invoice, including VAT, must be produced. You may not deduct the cost of materials you've purchased yourself. Residents must pay additional CGT of 11 per cent (which is a kind of National Insurance contribution), making the effective rate for residents 27 per cent. Once you've owned the property for five years, this rate is reduced by 10 per cent and then gradually thereafter, until it's been owned for 15 years, at which point it's exempt from CGT. Those who are neither resident nor EU citizens must pay CGT at 33 per cent.

Wealth Tax: A tax of between 0.5 and 1.8 per cent is levied on French residents with worldwide assets valued at over €732,000. To gauge this amount, you may reduce the value of your principal residence by 20 per cent and you may deduct liabilities such as outstanding loans. Non-residents are liable for wealth tax only on their French property assets.

Inheritance & Gift Tax: Inheritance tax in France is paid by individual beneficiaries if the donor was resident in France (either at death or when the gift was made), if the recipient is resident in France or if the assets given or inherited are located in France. The tax is calculated on the net value of the asset after deductions and rates vary according to the relationship between the beneficiary and the deceased. Since 2005, there has been a general allowance of €50,000, divided between beneficiaries. In addition, there are allowances for close relatives, after which inheritance tax is levied on a sliding scale between 5 and 40 per cent. Other family members are permitted smaller allowances and must pay higher tax rates, between 35 and 60 per cent.

Value Added Tax (VAT): The standard rate of VAT in France is 19.6 per cent, which is included in the purchase price of properties less than five years old when sold for the first time.

9

So, in effect, the seller pays the VAT. Any subsequent sale, even if it's still within the five years, is VAT free. On the sale of leaseback properties (see below), the government refunds the 19.6 per cent, as it's keen to encourage the sale of these properties.

There's a reduced VAT rate of 5.5 per cent on wholesale food, water supplies, medical equipment, medical and dental treatment, public transport, hotel accommodation and books, and a super-reduced rate of 2.2 per cent on some pharmaceuticals, newspapers and periodicals and the TV licence.

Property

Restrictions on Foreign Ownership & Letting

There are no restrictions on either, although tax is payable on letting income. Tax is payable on the profits after deductions for renovation or repairs and mortgage interest. If you let a furnished property, you're taxed as if you're operating a commercial business.

Market

The French property market is well established and France is one of the most popular locations for second home owners and British expatriates (especially retirees) keen to enjoy a relaxed lifestyle and some of the world's best food and wine. The property market is strong and is continuing to grow, prices rising on average by around 10 per cent annually, in some areas by up to 20 per cent. These rises are thanks largely to the country's appeal as a tourist and expatriate destination. In most areas, rural property remains good value, particularly if you're after a large plot, and some bargains are available. However, coastal and city properties are at a premium and cost up to double the price of similar rural properties. Property on the French Riviera remains among the most expensive in the world, and Paris is one of Europe's most expensive cities, although property in the capital remains a good long-term investment. New properties are widely available and include coastal and city apartments, ski and golf developments, and a wide range of individually designed houses and chalets. Many new properties are part of purpose-built developments, often located along the coasts or in mountain areas, encompassing a golf course, swimming pool, tennis and squash courts, a gym or fitness club, and a restaurant.

Areas

The most popular areas for foreign buyers include Paris, the Loire Valley (famous for its *châteaux*), the South of France (particularly the French Riviera or Côte d'Azur and Provence), south-west France (including Dordogne), and Brittany and Normandy, which are particularly popular with the British. Winter holiday homes in French alpine ski resorts are also popular, especially in fashionable resorts such as Chamonix, Courchevel, Megève, Méribel, Val d'Isère and Val Thorens. Properties in French ski resorts are usually an excellent investment and also make fine summer holiday homes, especially if you're a keen hiker. In 2007, foreign buyers are showing an interest in new areas, e.g. Languedoc-Roussillon in the south (which is also favoured by French buyers), as well as in central regions such as Limousin and Auvergne, and regional towns such as Montpellier and Bordeaux.

9

Building Standards

Building quality is generally excellent. Building in France is strictly regulated and most homes are built to official quality standards that are higher than in many other countries. Older homes were invariably solidly built, but many are now in poor repair and the quality of renovation and restoration varies considerably with the builder (or previous owner).

Cost

Apart from obvious factors such as size, quality and land area, the most important factor influencing the price of a house in France is location.

Alpine Ski Resorts: Property in ski resorts varies considerably in price, according to the resort and the location of the property. A one-bedroom apartment in a purpose-built resort costs between €75,000 and €100,000, while apartments close to the ski lifts in mid-range resorts such as Courchevel, Méribel and Tignes cost from €250,000, rising to several million in Chamonix or Val d'Isère.

Dordogne: Lying in the south-west of the country, the Dordogne enjoys beautiful countryside and a timeless feel. The area has long been popular with buyers (especially the British) who want to renovate property, including barns, cottages, farmhouses and chateaux, often with land. Even if the purchase prices seem reasonable, however, check carefully how much renovation will cost. Large houses and barns in need of renovation (which may have no bedrooms at all, just space for them!) cost around €200,000. Renovated properties are obviously more expensive but could save you a lot of hard work and heartache. A renovated three-bedroom house costs from around €250,000, while a five-bedroom property is around €850,000.

French Riviera: This area has some of the highest property prices in France (apart from Paris), but if you have deep pockets and can afford to invest there, you can expect high returns on rentals, especially in the summer season. A small, one-bedroom apartment starts at around €150,000, while a two-bedroom apartment in Nice is around €350,000, although sea views can add at least €100,000 to the price. A four-bedroom villa costs around €900,000, but prices rise to several million in the most prestigious locations.

Languedoc-Roussillon: This area has increasingly been seen as an affordable alternative to the Riviera. As a result, prices have risen by around 45 per cent over the last few years, but there's still growth potential, as well as cheaper properties in need of renovation. Many properties are old stone houses, priced at around €300,000 for a small, three-bedroom cottage in an attractive village. A similar property in need of extensive renovation costs around €100,000, but budget for almost twice as much as again to make it habitable. Modern properties are available on the outskirts of some villages.

Limousin: This area of central France has become more popular with buyers over the last few years, especially as several budget airlines now fly to Limoges. Prices are low and properties for renovation can cost as little as €30,000. A renovated two-bedroom village house costs around €120,000, while a more substantial four bedroom house costs between €250,000 and €400,000.

Normandy: Normandy has long been popular with buyers looking for a second home, particularly the British. It's easy to reach from the UK, it enjoys beautiful countryside and there's a wide selection of property. These range from town apartments to small stone cottages, farmhouses, *gîtes* and enormous chateaux. A two-bedroom apartment in the tourist resort of Honfleur costs around €195,000, while a small, detached stone house in the countryside costs around €115,000. Three-bedroom farmhouses cost around €300,000, while larger properties cost upwards of €450,000. Prices for chateaux are in the region of €1.5m.

Paris: Prices in Paris have been rising steadily since around 1998. They're among the highest in France, although still considerably lower than London's. Paris is a good buy-to-let

9

location, as there are always more potential tenants than rental property, but you should buy fairly centrally if you want to let long term to local or foreign businessmen, or in a tourist area, such as Montmartre, for short-term lets. Prices vary with the district (*arrondissement*), but one-bedroom flats near popular tourist areas cost around €350,000. Homes in the most fashionable areas cost over €1.5m.

Local Mortgages

Mortgages are available from all major French banks (for residents and non-residents) and many foreign banks, including Barclays Bank and Abbey in the UK. A variety of mortgages is available, including repayment (with variable or fixed interest), interest only or a mixture of both. French mortgages used to be short term only, but that's changing as more lenders enter the market and prices rise. Mortgages are usually for between 5 and 20 years, although in recent years some lenders have begun offering mortgages over 40 and even 50 years – in most cases, however, you're required to repay the mortgage by the age of 75. Mortgages are usually limited to 70 or 80 per cent of a property's value and banks demand detailed information about earnings, typically offering one third of your gross income. Lenders won't take into account any proposed rental income. Mortgages incur an arrangement fee of 1 per cent and you're normally obliged to take out life insurance for mortgages over €150,000.

Property Taxes

There are two property-based taxes in France. Property tax (*taxe foncière*) is similar to the property tax (or rates) levied in most countries and is paid by property owners based on the average (notional) rental value of the property in the previous year, adjusted for inflation, as calculated by the Land Registry. Rates vary considerably, according to the region and even within a region. Residential tax (*taxe d'habitation*) is payable by whoever resides in a property on 1st January, whether as an owner or tenant or rent free, and is calculated according to income, number of children, etc. It's normally around half the amount of the property tax. Both taxes were substantially increased in a number of regions in 2003, so check the tax in your chosen region before committing to a purchase.

Purchase Procedure

The purchase of property in France is strictly controlled and regulated but not necessarily in the buyer's (or vendor's) interest. Property sales are conducted by a notary (*notaire*), who is a government official representing neither the vendor nor the buyer. It's therefore wise to hire a local lawyer to protect your interests and carry out the usual checks concerning title, outstanding debts, etc. A good estate agent is invaluable when buying in France, but he shouldn't be relied upon with regard to legal matters.

There are various types of purchase contract, the most common being a bilateral agreement (*compromis de vente*), which is signed by both parties. The buyer then has a seven-day cooling off period, during which time he may withdraw from the sale without penalty, although the vendor may not. Once the seven-day period is over, the contract is binding on both parties and a deposit is payable, usually 10 per cent. An agent must be bonded to hold this money and must display the sum of his financial guarantee (*pièce de garantie*). The deposit isn't returnable unless you're unable to obtain a mortgage or there are serious legal problems involved in the purchase. The balance of the purchase price and all fees are due on completion of the sale, which is a fixed time after the signing of the purchase contract (normally six weeks), when the deed of sale (*acte de vente*) is signed.

9

Arrange to view the property on the day of signing, as the final contract says that the property is sold as seen on the day of signing. Ensure that the balance is transferred to the notary's account in advance of the signing date, so that you don't miss the payment deadline and lose your property and deposit. You should be present for the final signing, but it's possible to arrange power of attorney if you aren't able to be there.

France's legal procedure regarding the purchase of property is very safe. However, any conditions of purchase **must** be included as conditional clauses in the preliminary contract. It's wise to have a survey on an older habitable dwelling or, at the very least, have it checked by a building expert, as a property is purchased 'as seen' and the vendor isn't liable for any defects unless he knowingly withheld information at the time of sale.

Buyers should be particularly cautious when buying old properties requiring extensive restoration, as the cost can escalate wildly. Before going ahead with a purchase, you should obtain detailed written quotations (*devis*) from at least two local builders. You should **always** expect the final cost of restoration to be higher than the highest estimate you receive! If a property has already been renovated, you should check who did it, how it was done (i.e. professionally or by cutting corners) and whether there's a guarantee.

Off-plan Purchases: You sign a reservation contract and pay a deposit of 5 per cent. The contract specifies the construction schedule and when each of the stage payments is to be made. Normally your first payment is around 25 per cent, with the remainder to be agreed. You should check that all is in order before paying the final 5 per cent. Buyers are well protected with bank guarantees in case the developer should fail to complete a project.

Leaseback Properties: For around 20 years, the French government has been operating a leaseback scheme to help the country's tourism industry. They offer generous incentives to buyers of this type of property, thereby encouraging the building of more developments. Under the scheme, you buy a property (often a new build, but not always) and lease it back to a rental company, which takes charge of letting it on your behalf, usually for a minimum of nine years. Your VAT is refunded on the purchase (19.6 per cent) and you can typically expect returns of between 3 and 6 per cent.

Fees

The total fees payable when buying a property in France are between 10 and 15 per cent of the price for a small to medium-size property over five years old. Fees for properties less than five years old are 3 or 4 per cent, but VAT at 19.6 per cent is included in the purchase price. The fees comprise the notary's fee, which is non-negotiable and fixed by the state (around 3.5 per cent of the price), registration taxes (0.6 per cent on new homes, 4.9 per cent on old homes) and a Land Registry fee (around €500). These taxes and legal fees are paid as a single sum to the notary, along with the balance of the purchase price. Prices may be quoted inclusive or exclusive of an estate agent's fees, so you should check whether these are included in the price quoted and who is to pay them. Their charges are normally between 4 and 10 per cent.

General Information

9

Getting There

One of the reasons for France's popularity as a second home location is the ease with which you can reach most regions from the UK and Ireland, as well as from other many European countries.

Airlines: There are plenty of airlines operating to all the major cities in France. British Airways and Air France are the major operators, and there are plenty of low cost operators, including Easyjet, Ryanair, bmibaby and GB Airways. Routes are too numerous to list here, but the main airport in Paris, Roissy-Charles de Gaulle (CDG), is the base for the national airline,

Air France. There's a wide range of worldwide flights to CDG and the airport has high-speed rail connections to all parts of the country. There are also direct flights from a range of destinations to cities such as Bordeaux, Lyon, Marseille, Nice and Toulouse, and many of the budget airlines serve smaller airports across France. Before you commit yourself to a property, check where the nearest airport is and which airlines fly there. French Entrée (🖳 www.frenchentree.com) has comprehensive details of flights to all French airports, as well as other transport options, such as ferry and train services to all parts of France.

Ferries: There's a wide range of cross-Channel ferry services between the UK and Ireland and French ports. Brittany Ferries operates services from Plymouth, Poole and Portsmouth to Caen, Cherbourg, Roscoff and Saint-Malo; P&O Ferries and SeaFrance operate frequent Dover to Calais services; and smaller operators such as Condor Ferries, LD Lines, Norfolk Line, Speed Ferries and Transmanche sail from the UK to a variety of French ports, including Dieppe, Dunkerque and Le Havre. The Irish low-cost ferry company, Irish Ferries, operates a service between Rosslare and Cherbourg and Roscoff.

Trains: The Eurostar service operates from London St Pancras and Ashford in Kent to Paris, Lille, Dijon and Toulouse. There's a summer service to Avignon and during the ski season a Eurostar 'Direct Ski Train' takes you into the Alps to within easy reach of popular ski resorts such as Val d'Isère, Méribel and Tignes (🖳 www.eurostar.com)

Communications

Communications in France are highly developed, with a large number of telephone landlines and high levels of mobile phone and internet use. The country dialling code is 33. International direct dialling (IDD) is available.

Fixed-line Telephones: Fixed-line telephone services are still mainly provided by France Telecom, the former state-owned monopoly. Although there are ten other providers, France Telecom must still install lines, but other providers offer good deals, especially when combined with internet services. Standard international and national call charges are high compared with other European countries but various low-cost service providers are available to residents. Most public telephones are operated by phone cards, available at post offices, tobacconists' and railway stations. Credit cards may also be used.

Mobile Telephones: There's wide use of mobile phones, which operate on a GSM network. There are three main mobile phone providers, Bouygues Telecom, Orange (part of France Telecom) and SFR (partly owned by Vodafone and Cegetel). SFR provides the best information for foreigners, including a website in six languages.

Internet: Internet services in France are sophisticated, with a wide range of dial-up and high speed ADSL internet providers. There's plenty of competition among providers, who offer a range of packages. There are internet cafes in all major towns and cities.

Postal Services: The French postal service, La Poste, also offers banking services. Main post offices are usually open from 9am to 7pm, Mondays to Fridays, and on Saturday mornings. The central post office in Paris is open 24 hours a day but with limited services at night. Letters within France usually reach their destination the following day and letters to European destinations usually take around three days.

Crime

9

France has a similar crime rate to other major European countries and, in common with them, has seen a considerable increase in recent years as unemployment has soared. Inner-city violence is now a particular problem, especially in poor areas with high immigrant populations. Burglary are common in some areas – holiday homes are a popular target. Theft of and from cars are also rife in Paris and other cities. The crime rate is low in rural areas, however, and it's common for people in many villages and small towns not to lock their homes and cars.

Medical Facilities

French medical facilities and services are widely considered to be the best in the world – and not without reason. French doctors are highly trained and hospitals are superbly equipped, although they're few and far between in some rural areas. There are foreign-run hospitals in Paris, principally the American and British hospitals. France has an excellent national health scheme for those paying social security contributions and retirees. However, social security payments are around 20 per cent of income, even more if you're self-employed, and it's now mandatory for all residents to pay into the social security scheme, irrespective of their nationality. You don't have to do so if you're an EU pensioner, as you're covered by reciprocal health agreements, but you must complete the correct forms and submit them to the health authorities in France. If you aren't covered by the national health scheme, private health insurance is essential and often obligatory. Whether you use public or private healthcare services, you're sometimes expected to pay when you receive the treatment and are reimbursed around two weeks later. If you contribute to the social security scheme, you're usually reimbursed for around 70 per cent of the cost. In some cases, you're reimbursed the whole amount, in others nothing.

Pets

France, as part of the EU, doesn't operate quarantine for pets, but they must be identifiable by a microchip or tattoo, have an EU Pet Passport and be vaccinated against rabies. All official paperwork must be issued by a government-authorised vet. Pets under three months old and not vaccinated against rabies aren't permitted to enter France. Treatment for tapeworm and ticks isn't compulsory but is advisable.

Visas & Permits

Visas: Nationals of EEA countries don't need a visa and can stay in France for a maximum of 90 days at a time and then different types of permit are issued, depending on your status (employed, self-employed, retired, etc.) – see **Residence Permits** below. Citizens of some non-EU countries, including Canada and the US, don't require a visa, although many nationalities do and it's vital that you check with the French embassy or consulate in your home country **before** travelling to France.

Residence Permits: Nationals of EEA countries don't need a residence permit (*titre de séjour*) , although if you intend to live permanently in France, you must still meet the criteria for a residence permit and it's recommended that you obtain one. Non-working residents must have sufficient income or financial resources to live in France without working. Normally you obtain a *carte de séjour*, which is a temporary residence permit and after three years of continuous residence in France, you may apply for permanent residence (*carte de résident*), although a *carte de séjour* is valid for up to ten years and is renewable. Non-EU nationals require a long-stay visa (*visa de long séjour*) to live in France for longer than three months.

Work Permits: EU citizens don't require a work permit. Non-EU citizens require a combined residence and work permit (*carte unique de séjour et de travail*). They're difficult to obtain unless you're coming to France to take up permanent employment.

9

Reference

Further Reading

Buying a Home in France, David Hampshire (Survival Books). Everything you need to know about buying a home in France.

France Magazine & Living France Magazine, Archant Life Publishing, Archant House, Oriel Road, Cheltenham, Gloucestershire GL50 1BB, UK (☎ 01242-216050, ▭ www.francemag.com). Monthly lifestyle magazines.

French News (formerly The News), 5 Chemin de la Monzie, BP 4042, 24004, Périgueux Cedex, France (☎ 05 53 06 84 40, ▭ www.french-news.com). Monthly English-language newspaper, also available online.

French Property News, Archant Life Publishing, F3 Battersea Studios, 80 Silverthorne Road, London, SW8 3HE, UK (☎ 020-7978 3493, ▭ www.french-property-news.com).

French Real Property and Succession Law, Henry Dyson (Robert Hale).

Living and Working in France, David Hampshire (Survival Books). Everything you need to know about living and working in France.

Making a Living in France, Joe Laredo (Survival Books). Everything you need to know about working, being self-employed and starting a business in France

Property France (incorporating Focus on France), Outbound Publishing, 1 Commercial Road, Eastbourne, East Sussex BN21 3XQ, UK (☎ 01323-726040, ▭ www.outbound publishing.com). Monthly property magazine.

Useful Addresses

French Embassy (UK), 58 Knightsbridge, London SW1X 7JT, UK (☎ 020-7073 1000, ▭ www.ambafrance-uk.org).

French Embassy (US), 4101 Reservoir Rd, NW, Washington, DC 20007, US (☎ 202-944 6195, ▭ www.ambafrance-us.org).

French Government Tourist Office (UK), 178 Piccadilly, London W1J 9AL, UK (☎ 090-6824 4123, ▭ www.franceguide.com).

French Government Tourist Office (US), 444 Madison Avenue, NY 10022, New York, US (☎ 514-288 1904, ▭ www.franceguide.com).

Useful Websites

Expatica (▭ www.expatica.com/france). Information for expatriates about living and working in a number of countries, including France.

Just Landed (▭ www.justlanded.com/English/france). Information about living and working in France.

French Entrée (▭ www.frenchentree.com). Excellent site with extensive property and tax information and useful articles about living and working in France.

Europe: GERMANY

Background Information

9

Capital: Berlin.

Population: 82.5m.

Foreign Community: Germany has over 4m immigrant workers, mostly Croats, Italians, Greeks, Poles, Russians, Serbs and Turks. A considerable number of Americans and Britons also work there.

Area: 356,844km^2 (137,777mi^2).

Geography: Germany is situated in the heart of Europe and has borders with Austria, Belgium, the Czech Republic, Denmark, France, Luxembourg, the Netherlands, Poland and Switzerland. It extends from the North Sea and Baltic coasts in the north to the foothills of the Alps in the south. Germany is characterised by three topographical features: lowlands (in the north and centre); medium-altitude mountains; and high mountains (in the south), including the Alps.

Climate: Germany is the link between maritime western Europe and continental eastern Europe, and between the cooler north and the warmer south. It has a predominantly mild, temperate climate, with occasional continental influences from the south creating periods of extreme heat or cold. Oceanic airstreams have a cooling effect in summer, although 'Indian' summers (in September/October) created by high pressure systems are common. Rainfall is evenly distributed throughout the year, April and October being the driest months. Summers are usually warm, with average temperatures of 17C (63F), although temperatures of around 22 to 23C (72 to 74F) are common in many regions and the mercury can rise to over 30C (86F) in Berlin. Winters are cold throughout the country and can be severe in mountainous regions. The average winter temperature is 0C (32F), although it can drop to -10C (14F) in the Bavarian Alps.

Language: German (with regional dialects). English is widely spoken, although less so in the former East Germany.

Political Situation: Germany (particularly the former West Germany) has been one of the most politically stable countries in Europe since the Second World War. It's a federal parliamentary republic and the Chancellor is head of government. The country is divided into 16 self-governing states, which have a large degree of autonomy and which are further sub-divided into 439 separate districts. The reunification of Germany in 1990 created enormous economic and social problems, which the country has taken a considerable time to recover from. In 2005, Angela Merkel of the conservative Christian Democratic Union (CDU) was elected as the first woman Chancellor of Germany and the country is governed by what's called a grand coalition, between the CDU, the Christian Social Union (CSU) and the centre left Social Democratic Party of Germany (SPD), which had been in power for the previous seven years. Merkel's reforms have begun to yield results and Germany is showing a slow but sure economic recovery. Germany, like France, is a founder member of the European Union.

Finance

Currency

Germany's currency is the euro (€).
Exchange Rate: £1 = €1.48.
Exchange Controls: None.

9 Cost & Standard of Living

Despite Germany's major economic problems since the reunification of the country, its people enjoy a high standard of living. The government tries to maintain a balance between growth, low unemployment and low inflation on the one hand and good working conditions and social welfare on the other. Recently this has been difficult, with slow growth and high levels of unemployment, but the country is beginning a slow recovery. The cost of living is slightly higher than in the UK and France.

Taxation

Residents are taxed on worldwide income if they live in Germany for more than 183 days during the tax year. Non-residents are taxed only on income from German sources. Taxes increased substantially in the '90s to finance the cost of reunification and the regeneration of eastern Germany. There remains a 'solidarity charge' (see **Income Tax** below).

Personal Effects: Goods purchased within the EU can be imported duty free and don't need to be retained for a minimum period. However, goods (including cars) purchased outside the EU must have been owned for at least six months and cannot be sold for one year after import in order to be exempt from import duty.

Income Tax: Germany has a PAYE system with tax rates from 19.9 to 45 per cent (the highest rate on incomes above €250,000 for a single person and €500,000 for a couple). In addition, all taxpayers must pay a 'solidarity charge' (*Solidaritätszuschlag*) of 5.5 per cent of income tax, which is levied to offset the costs of reunification.

Capital Gains Tax (CGT): Gains made from the sale of property by individuals are exempt if the property has been held for more than ten years or if the profits are used to buy another property. Rates are the same as income tax, although moves are under way to change CGT rates to between 20 and 30 per cent in 2008/09.

Wealth Tax: None.

Inheritance & Gift Tax: Inheritance tax is paid by the beneficiary, and gift tax is paid by both the donor and the recipient. For non-residents, tax is limited to property located in Germany. Exemptions and tax rates vary according to the relationship of the donor and recipient and the value of the property inherited or received as a gift. Inheritance tax ranges from 7 to 30 per cent for relatives of the first degree and from 17 to 50 per cent for non-related beneficiaries.

Value Added Tax (VAT): The standard rate of VAT is 19 per cent, which applies to most goods and services. There's a reduced rate of 7 per cent on food, public transport, books and newspapers. Some items are VAT-exempt, such as financial transactions and services, and medical and education services.

Other Taxes: Members of the Roman Catholic and Lutheran (Protestant) churches pay around 9 per cent of their income tax liability as church tax (pensioners are exempt). This is payable only if you list a religion on your tax declaration.

Property

Restrictions on Foreign Ownership & Letting

There are no restrictions on foreign ownership or letting, but Germany isn't a traditional holiday location, so the potential for short-term letting is limited. Long-term lets in the cities usually generate a regular income. Tax must be paid on any income earned in Germany.

Market

9

Germany's property market is stagnant compared with many other European markets, prices having actually fallen over the last decade, although since 2004 there has been a small, gradual recovery. There are various reasons for this: Germany's economic problems since reunification, along with high unemployment, have affected the housing market. In addition, the majority of Germans rent their homes and home ownership – at around 42 per cent – is one of the lowest in western Europe (it's higher in rural areas of Germany). Most Germans live in apartments in the cities and their suburbs, where interest in property is increasing, particularly for buy-to-let properties, but investors should take a long-term view and not expect quick returns.

Some 75 per cent of German housing has been built since the Second World War, although there are still many villages and rural areas with beautiful traditional houses. Best buys are often older properties in need of restoration, particularly in eastern Germany, although the ownership of a large number of dwellings there is in dispute.

Areas

The most popular areas among those who don't need to be close to a major city are the Rhine and Mosel valleys, Franconia, the Swabian Jura, the Black Forest and Bavaria. There's excellent skiing in the German Alps in Upper Bavaria and Allgäu (Garmisch-Partenkirchen is the most famous German ski resort). There's also potential for profit with properties in need of modernisation in the former East Germany, while Berlin, Cologne, Düsseldorf, Frankfurt and their satellite towns have properties with good rental potential, both for tourists on short breaks and for locals long term. Frankfurt is a popular buy-to-let location, as it's the financial centre of Germany, with a high standard of living and plenty of professionals looking for property to rent.

Building Standards

Building standards in the former Federal Republic (West Germany) are among the highest in the world, but in former East German (DDR) states standards are low, particularly those of the ubiquitous high-rise apartment blocks. Most pre-war housing in eastern Germany is dilapidated and hasn't been modernised or renovated since the Second World War.

Cost

German property prices have been depressed for a number of years and fell between 1994 and 2004. Although prices are now rising, growth is modest – nothing like the emerging markets in Eastern Europe. Prices vary considerably according to the city and region. Rural property and property in the former East German states is still inexpensive, apartments costing from around €20,000 and houses starting at around €100,000. However, many are in a poor state of repair and need extensive renovation. Prices in the cities are higher but still good value. A large four-bedroom apartment in Frankfurt city centre costs around €300,000, with prices in central Berlin around the same or slightly cheaper.

Local Mortgages

Local mortgages are available, although the mortgage market – like the housing market – is far less 'developed' than in many other countries. Most German banks and building societies (*Bausparkasse*) are conservative with their lending and expect borrowers to make regular savings for a number of years before they will make a home loan. A loan will usually be granted only you've paid a fixed monthly amount into a building society for five or six years (virtually no interest is paid!). Even then, the maximum mortgage (*Hypothek*) available is 60 or 70 per cent of a property's value. Bank mortgages are usually for 30 years, with a low fixed rate of interest for the whole period. Many buyers have a combination of a building society loan and a mortgage from a bank.

9

Property Taxes

A land tax (*Grundsteuer*) is levied by local communities and is calculated on the rentable value (which is below the market value) of land and buildings. The amount payable is between 1 and 1.5 per cent of a property's rentable value (depending on the location of the property).

Purchase Procedure

All contracts must be certified by a public notary (*Notar*) or a lawyer (*Rechtsanwalt*) specialising in property transactions, whose job it is to ensure that property is free of liabilities. When a buyer and seller have agreed a price, a sale contract must be signed in the presence of a notary, who then carries out all the legal formalities of the sale and checks the property's status at the Land Registry (*Grundbuchamt/Katasteramt*). Make sure you check the sale contract carefully before signing, as this is the buyer's responsibility. When the sale is completed, the final signing takes place, again in the presence of a notary, who reads the contract through verbatim in German (you'll need to hire the services of a translator to ensure you fully understand what you're signing). Buyers and sellers must be present at the signing. The title deed (*Eigentumsrecht verbriefende Urkunde*) is then registered at the local Land Registry, after which title passes to the buyer.

Fees

You should allow between 10 and 12 per cent of the purchase price to cover fees associated with the sale. An estate agent's fees are around 6 per cent (usually split between buyer and seller), but this varies with the area. Notaries' fees are around 1.5 per cent, plus any translation fees. Transfer tax (*Grundwerbsteuer*) on land and buildings is 3.5 per cent of the purchase price, and there's a registration fee of just over 1 per cent.

General Information

Getting There

Germany's main airports are at Berlin, Düsseldorf, Frankfurt and Munich.

Berlin: The capital has three airports. Berlin-Schönfeld, which is outside the city, close to Berlin's southern border, handles the majority of international flights. It will become the country's main international airport in 2011, from when it will be known as Berlin-Brandenburg International Airport. In early 2007, there were the following flights from UK and Irish airports: Aer Lingus (Cork and Dublin), Easyjet (Belfast, Bristol, Liverpool, London Gatwick and London Luton), Jet2 (Manchester) and Ryanair (Dublin, London Stansted and Nottingham).

Berlin's two other airports (Tegel International and Templehof International) will eventually close. In early 2007, there were the following flights to Tegel from UK and Irish airports: Air Berlin (London Stansted) and British Airways (Birmingham, London Heathrow and Manchester). Templehof is a commuter airport, with no international flights.

Düsseldorf: This is Germany's third-largest airport, situated in the west of the country, and serves as a secondary hub for the national airline, Lufthansa. The following airlines fly from the UK and Ireland to Düssseldorf: Aer Lingus (Dublin), Air Berlin (London Stansted), British

9

Airways (Birmingham, Bristol, London Heathrow and Manchester), Lufthansa (Birmingham, London City, London Heathrow, Manchester and Newcastle) and Jet2 (Leeds Bradford).

Frankfurt: Known as Flughafen-am-Main, this is the largest airport in Germany and the main hub for Lufthansa. The following airlines fly from the UK and Ireland to Frankfurt: Aer Lingus (Dublin), British Airways (Birmingham, Bristol, Glasgow, London City, London Heathrow and Manchester – some flights are operated by BA Connect) and Lufthansa (Birmingham, Dublin, Edinburgh, London City, London Heathrow and Manchester).

Munich: Munich International Airport (also known as Franz Josef Strauss International Airport) is Germany's second airport, 28km (17.5m) north-east of Munich. Airlines flying from the UK and Ireland to Munich are currently Aer Lingus (Dublin), British Airways (Bristol, Glasgow and London Heathrow), Easyjet (Edinburgh and London Stansted) and Lufthansa (London Heathrow).

Communications

Germany has one of the most sophisticated telecommunications systems in the world. This is because of major expenditure since reunification to upgrade and integrate the formerly backward telecommunications systems in the east with the west. Germany has a wide selection of telephone and internet services, and mobile phone use is widespread. The country dialling code is 49 and International direct dialling (IDD) is available across the country.

Fixed-line Telephones: The state communications company, Deutsche Telekom, dominated the market until 1998, when deregulation began. There are now several alternative providers and this has reduced call charges, although the majority of fixed lines are still operated by Deutsche Telekom. Germany has analogue and digital telephone systems, although most home installations are analogue. There's a directory enquiries operator service in English (☎ 11837 for domestic calls or 11834 for international calls). International call rates (particularly from mobiles) are high in Germany, but using a pre-paid calling card reduces the cost considerably. There are public telephones all over the country, although the majority operate only with phone cards, available from post offices, supermarkets and petrol stations.

Mobile Telephones: Mobile phones (called, regrettably, *Handys*) are widely used. There are four main providers: E-Plus, O2, T-Mobil and Vodafone. Like other European countries, Germany operates on the GSM network.

Internet: Internet use is widespread, with a lot of internet providers offering a choice of dial-up and ADSL connections, and plenty of internet cafes in all the main cities.

Postal Services: Postal services are operated by Deutsche Post World Net, the new name for the old government monopoly, Deutsche Bundespost. The service has been extensively modernised with 'retail outlets', rather than post offices, offering a wide range of services and more convenient opening hours. Delivery times within Europe are usually around two to three days, while outside Europe deliveries take a week to ten days.

Crime Rate

9

Germany's crime rate is low by western European standards, although it has increased significantly since unification. In particular, there has recently been a worrying increase in racially motivated violence, especially in the former East Germany. Burglaries and car crime are particularly high in Germany's major cities, but violent crime is low, although muggings have increased over the last five years.

Medical Facilities

Medical facilities and healthcare are excellent. German hospitals and clinics are among the best equipped and staffed in the world (Germany has the highest number of hospital beds per capita in the EU). Germany has a national health scheme and employers and employees share the cost of social security contributions, which are around 14 per cent of gross income. Membership of a government-regulated insurance plan is compulsory and almost all medical treatment and medicines are provided free (unless you count the cost of the contributions!). Pensioners must continue to pay health contributions. If you aren't covered by social security, private health insurance is essential.

Pets

As a full member of the EU, Germany doesn't operate a quarantine system for pets, but they must be identifiable by microchip or tattoo, have an EU Pet Passport and be vaccinated against rabies. All official paperwork must be issued by a government-authorised vet and be translated into German. An import licence is required for certain animals or when more than three animals are imported.

Visas & Permits

Visas: Non-EU citizens may need a visa from their home country (check with an embassy or consulate in your home country), though US nationals may visit Germany without one.

Residence Permits: The Immigration Law passed on 1st January 2005 allows EU citizens the right to live and work freely in Germany without any kind of residence permit (although citizens of the EU member states which joined in 2007 may have restrictions placed on them), but they do need to register their presence in the country and, if they don't have a source of income, prove they're able to support themselves and have sufficient healthcare cover. Non-EU citizens must have a temporary or permanent residence permit, which includes permission to work (see below).

Work Permits: Not required for EU citizens but required by non-EU citizens as part of a residence permit (see above). These can be difficult to obtain.

Reference

Further Reading

Living and Working in Germany, edited by Pamela Wilson (Survival Books). Everything you need to know about living and working in Germany.
Germany and the Germans, John Ardagh (Penguin).
The Germans: Who Are They Now?, Alan Watson (Mandarin).
Live & Work in Germany, Victoria Pybus (Vacation Work).
In the Know in Germany – the Indispensable Guide to Working and Living in Germany, Jennifer Phillips (Living Language).

9

Useful Addresses

German Embassy (UK), 23 Belgrave Square, SW1X 8PZ, UK (☎ 020-7824 1300, 💻 www.london.diplo.de).

German Embassy (US), 4645 Reservoir Rd, NW, Washington, DC 20007, US (☎ 202-298 4000, 💻 www.germany.info).

German National Tourist Office (UK), PO Box 2695, London W1A 3TN, UK (☎ 020-7317 0908, 💻 www.germany-tourism.co.uk).

German National Tourist Office (US), Chanin Building, 122 East 42nd Street, 52nd Floor, New York, NY 1068-0072, US (☎ 212-661 7200, 💻 www.cometogermany.com).

EUROPE: GREECE

Background Information

Capital: Athens.

Population: 10.7m.

Foreign Community: Although it's becoming more popular with north Europeans, particularly retirees, Greece as a whole doesn't have a large foreign community, although increasing numbers of Britons and other EU nationals are coming to live on some of the islands, especially Corfu and Crete.

Area: 131,990km^2 (50,965mi^2).

Geography: Mainland Greece consists of a mountainous peninsula extending some 500km (310mi) into the Mediterranean from the south-west corner of the Balkans, with the Aegean Sea to the east, the Ionian Sea to the west and the Mediterranean Sea to the south. Greece has some 3,000 islands, around 150 of which are inhabited, comprising around 20 per cent of Greek territory. The mainland and islands have a combined coastline of some 13,350km (8,300mi). The principal structural feature of Greece is the Pindus Mountains, which extend south-east from the Albanian border and cover most of the peninsula. Some 80 per cent of the mainland is mountainous, with 20 mountains over 2,000m (6,560ft) – the highest peak is Mount Olympus, at 2,900m (9,500ft) – and permanently covered in snow. Greece has little flat or cultivated land, and woodland covers around half the country (almost 90m hectares). Greece has borders with Albania, Bulgaria, Macedonia and Turkey.

Climate: Greece has a Mediterranean climate, with long, hot, dry summers and mild, sunny winters in the south, although winters can be cold in the north. It has some 3,000 hours of sunshine a year and average summer temperatures are above 25C (77F), although the heat is often tempered by a cooling breeze. Spring and autumn are the most pleasant seasons – sunny but not too hot. Annual rainfall varies from around 1.5m (59in) in the north to under 50cm (20in) in the south and is rare in summer. Athens has the worst air pollution in western Europe and often suffers from smog, particularly in summer.

Language: Greek. English and German are widely spoken in tourist areas.

Political Situation: The political situation in Greece has been reasonably stable over the last few years, following a long period of volatility, shaky coalition governments and political and financial scandals. Membership of the EU (since 1981) and tough economic measures have brought much-needed political and economic stability, although Greece's economic performance was sluggish until the country adopted the euro in 2001. By 2004, Greece's economy was growing at the fastest rate in the EU. The country is an enthusiastic member of the EU, although it has historically poor relations with its neighbour Turkey, which are exacerbated by Turkey's continuing military occupation of northern Cyprus (see **Cyprus** Country Profile). Despite the efforts of diplomats from both countries and intervention from the

9

United Nations, the dispute between the two countries remains unresolved, although there's hope that Turkey's bid for EU membership may lead to a resolution.

When democracy returned to Greece in 1975, after seven years of military dictatorship, it became a presidential parliamentary republic. The President, as Head of State, has some authority but the majority of power lies with the Prime Minister and his parliament. The current President is Karolos Papoulias (elected March 2005) and the Prime Minister is Kostas Karamanlis of the centre right New Democracy party (also elected March 2005). He took over from Kostas Simitis, whose party, the Panhellenic Socialist Movement (PASOK), had governed Greece for the previous 11 years.

Finance

Currency

Greece's currency is the euro (€).
Exchange Rate: £1 = €1.48.
Exchange Controls: None, but if you export funds as a result of selling your home, you must have the sale documentation to show to the bank.

Cost & Standard of Living

Greeks enjoy a high standard of living, despite the fact that salaries are low when compared with the EU average. Taxation and social security costs are high, and the cost of living, although still low by northern European standards, has increased significantly in the last decade. Greece is around a third cheaper than northern European countries, except in Athens and on some of the islands.

Taxation

Residents are taxed on their worldwide income and non-residents only on income earned in Greece. You qualify as a tax resident if you stay in the country for more than 183 days per year and are in possession of a residence permit.

Personal Effects: No duty is payable on personal effects imported from another EU country. A car can be imported duty free but can be kept in Greece for only six months unless you plan to become a permanent resident (and can produce a residence permit). Within a month of importing a car, you must report to the customs authorities to claim a tax exemption and buy Greek registration plates.

Income Tax: Greece has a PAYE system of income tax. Tax rates range from 15 per cent (on earnings over €12,000) to 40 per cent (over €75,000). The middle income tax rates of 29 and 39 per cent are expected to be reduced in 2008/09.

Capital Gains Tax (CGT): From 1st January 2006, individual buyers and sellers became liable for real estate capital gains tax (RECGT). Rates depend on how long you've owned a property, as follows: nil (if the property has been owned for more than 25 years), 5 per cent (owned between 15 and 25 years), 10 per cent (between 5 and 15 years) and 20 per cent (less than five years). Companies are liable for CGT at 20 per cent on gains from the transfer of an entire company or of shares in a limited liability company.

Wealth Tax: A 'large property or estate tax' is payable on certain assets, including property (see **Property Taxes** below).

9

Inheritance & Gift Tax: Inheritance and gift tax are based on the value of the bequest and the relationship between the donor and recipient. Rates are between 5 and 20 per cent.

Value Added Tax (VAT): The standard rate of VAT is 19 per cent. There are reduced rates of 9 per cent (food, medicines, water and transport services) and 4.5 per cent rate for 'cultural goods' (books, magazines, newspapers and theatre tickets). VAT also applies to the first sale of buildings whose construction permits were issued after 1st January 2006. However, in these cases, the real estate transfer tax (see **Fees** below) doesn't apply. Fees for lawyers, notaries, land registrars and bailiffs are exempt from VAT. Different VAT rates apply on some Greek islands.

Property

Restrictions on Foreign Ownership & Letting

EU citizens generally have the same property rights as Greeks, though foreign ownership of property is restricted in some border areas and islands close to Turkey, for security reasons. If the property is near a national border, you may be required to have a residence permit (Blue Card) – this applies to EU and non-EU citizens.

There are no restrictions on letting, although tax is payable on rental income at a rate of 3 per cent. All foreign property owners must submit a tax return, even if their rental income is below the tax threshold.

Market

Greece's property market is nowhere near as buoyant as the markets in Spain and France, despite the fact that it's a popular tourist destination. Greece is relatively undeveloped, with many areas as unspoiled as Portugal and Spain were several decades ago – before the concrete mixers arrived. Foreign interest in the property market has traditionally been limited to holiday and second homes, and Greece hasn't been considered attractive for investment. There were a number of reasons for this: poor infrastructure, even in the main cities; inefficient transport connections to some of the islands, especially out of season; high purchase costs; and competition from more investor-friendly nearby alternatives, such as Cyprus and Turkey. However, since 2004, things have begun to change in the Greek property market. The country's economy has made a remarkable recovery, and city infrastructure – particularly in the capital, Athens (where the 2004 Olympic Games were held) – has received a considerable amount of investment. There was further activity towards the end of 2005, as developers and private buyers tried to get their building permits secured before 1st January 2006, when VAT became applicable to all new properties (see above). Nevertheless, Greece still has a largely untapped holiday-home market and prices are still far lower than in Spain and France.

Strict controls over development and renovation ensure that local character is preserved, particularly in coastal and country areas. Old village houses are reasonably priced and plentiful in most areas, although they usually require extensive renovation and you should be particularly careful about obtaining legal title (see **Purchase Procedure** below).

Areas

Traditionally, foreign property buyers (and tourists) have been attracted to the Greek islands. That's still the case, but there's also increased investor interest in the capital, Athens, as a buy-to-let location, and in other parts of the mainland, where prices are lower and access to properties easier than on some of the islands.

The Peloponnese is the most popular mainland area for foreign property buyers, while the most popular islands are Crete, the Cyclades (especially Ios, Mykonos, Naxos and Paros), the Dodecanese (Rhodes, Kos and Kalymnos), the Ionian Islands (Corfu, Paxos and Zakynthos), the Sporades (Skiathos, Skopelos, Alonissos and Skyros), the Saronic Gulf Islands and the Peloponnese Islands. Crete is the most favoured location for winter sunshine.

Athens: Investors have only recently begun seriously to consider Athens, following the enormous financial boost to its infrastructure ahead of the 2004 Olympic Games. The city has a newly upgraded airport, served by scheduled and budget airlines (see **Getting There** below), and there's an efficient transport network within the city. Athens has a number of older, character properties suitable for renovation, as well as modern properties. The city is becoming increasingly attractive for buy-to-let – both short term for tourists and long term for locals and foreign businessmen.

Corfu: This is the second-largest Greek Ionian island and attracts large numbers of tourists from all over Europe. It therefore has plenty of potential for holiday lets. Corfu is also popular with second home owners and has retained much of its character despite being a popular holiday destination.

Crete: Crete is the largest of the Greek islands and the most popular with tourists and foreign property buyers, especially from the UK. The most popular area of western Crete is near the town Chania. The eastern part of the island is more developed and popular with tourists, so rental returns are potentially higher.

Rhodes: Rhodes, one of the Dodecanese Islands, is a popular tourist destination, as it's Greece's sunniest place. A lot of new property comes with a rental guarantee from the developer. Many older properties need extensive renovation.

Building Standards

New homes are generally well built, but the quality of old properties and restored buildings is variable, so always have them surveyed.

Cost

Costs vary considerably, according to location and the age of the property.

Athens: An average one-bedroom apartment in the city costs around €80,000, a two-bedroom apartment around €190,000. Property in fashionable areas is considerably more expensive. There are plenty of available properties on the outskirts of the city and near the sea, but a three-bedroom coastal villa with easy access to the city costs from around €600,000 to up to several million euros.

Corfu: You can buy a two-bedroom apartment for around €150,000, while a three- or four-bedroom house costs around €300,000. Larger villas will set you back around €500,000.

Crete: In Chania, a two-bedroom apartment costs around €80,000 and a three-bedroom house around €130,000, depending on the location. In the eastern part of the island, prices start at around €100,000 for a one-bedroom apartment, while an old village house typically costs around €150,000, depending on location and how much renovation it needs.

Rhodes: Property is more expensive than in much of the country, although it's possible to buy a two-bedroom house for around €180,000. A large four-bedroom house close to the beach and with a pool costs around €450,000. An old property requiring extensive renovation can be picked up for well under €100,000.

9

Local Mortgages

It has recently become easier for foreigners to obtain mortgages from Greek banks. Mortgages are repayment only (some offer an interest-only repayment scheme for the first two years) and repayments are over a maximum 25 years, subject to an age limit of 70. Depending on the lender, there may be a minimum loan, but the maximum cannot generally exceed 80 per cent of the value of the property. Detailed proof of income over the last two years (possibly more) is required and potential rental income isn't taken into account. Loans can be obtained in sterling, US dollars or euros.

Property Taxes

Property taxes in Greece were revamped on 1st January 2006 in a bid to simplify their application (before, there were around 30 different property taxes), help the economy by taxing on values closer to actual market values and make the Greek market more attractive to foreign buyers (despite the fact that they will have to pay more tax!). However, the legislation is complicated and property taxes are still in a state of flux. They're currently based on the 'objective' value of a property, rather than the market value. Objective values are usually around 30 per cent lower than market values but the government has begun to increase them to bring them more into line with real market values. In spring 2007, property taxes consisted of:

- **'large property or estate tax'** – at between 0.3 and 0.9 per cent, payable on properties valued at over €243,600 (€487,200 for a couple), although there are generous personal allowances, particularly if you have young children or loans on the property.

- **municipal tax** – currently between 0.25 and 0.35 per cent of the 'objective' value of the property. Buildings under construction are exempt from this tax.

Purchase Procedure

Before you can begin the purchase procedure, you need a tax registration number (*AFM*), which is mandatory for all buyers, as is a Greek bank account. The purchase procedure itself involves signing a pre-contract, which details the terms of the sale and, if relevant, a payment schedule. At this point, you pay a 10 per cent deposit to remove the property from the market. A lawyer and notary must be appointed to deal with the legalities of the sale. You should hire an independent, English-speaking lawyer experienced in the complexities of Greek property transfers. His responsibilities should include arranging a survey and checking the title of the property over the last 20 years. A national Land Registry system was put in place only in 1995 (amended in 2003), although some of the islands have long had their own system. Elsewhere, there was a Registry of Mortgages, which was widely believed to be unreliable. This means that it's sometimes still difficult to ascertain the legal owner (or owners) of a property and you're advised to make the securing of satisfactory title a condition of purchase. (In fact, a notary won't proceed with the sale unless title is 'full and unencumbered'.)

The legal process usually takes around six to eight weeks, at which point you sign the final contract and all fees and taxes must be paid. The notary, as the government agent who certifies all property transactions, draws up the official documents and arranges the legal transfer of the property.

9

Fees

The fees associated with buying a home in Greece are high: usually around 15 per cent of the purchase price. A lawyer's fees are around 1 per cent and a notary's between 1 and 2 per cent of the value of the property. Real estate transfer tàx (RETT) is payable by the buyer on property that was acquired by the seller before 1st January 2006. The rates are 9 per cent on the first €15,000 and 11 per cent on the balance. Certain exemptions are available if the property is a principal residence (or you're buying land on which to build a primary residence). Certain exemptions apply to first-time buyers of a primary residence. The local authority also applies a charge, which is around 3 per cent of the RETT. In addition, there's a real estate transfer duty, which is 1 per cent of the value. An estate agent's fees are usually between 2 and 5 per cent (plus VAT) and shared between the buyer and seller. If it's a new property, VAT at 19 per cent is added.

General Information

Getting There

Greece has more than its fair share of airports, 16 in total, although many are served only by charter flights. The country's main international airport is near the capital, Athens, and it was upgraded ahead of the 2004 Olympic Games. It handles more than 15m passengers per year. Other main airports are Corfu, Heraklion (Crete), Rhodes and Thessaloniki, which are served mainly by charter airlines during the summer, although some scheduled airlines also use them (principally British Airways and Olympic Airlines, the national carrier). Many other European airlines fly to the islands via Athens. In addition, there are plenty of ferry services between the islands and from Athens.

Athens (Elefthérios Venizélos) International Airport: Situated 20km (12mi) east of the city but easily accessible by the efficient Athens metro service, Athens airport is the hub of Olympic Airlines. The following airlines operate from the UK and Ireland to Athens: Aer Lingus (Dublin), British Airways (London Heathrow), Easyjet (London Gatwick and London Luton), Excel Airways (London Gatwick) and Olympic Airlines (London Gatwick and London Heathrow).

Corfu: Situated around 3km (1.8mi) from Corfu town, the airport is served mainly by charter flights, during the summer months only, e.g. GB Airways' services from Bristol, East Midlands, London Gatwick, London Heathrow and Manchester. Out of season, you must fly via Athens, e.g. with Olympic Airlines from London Heathrow.

Heraklion (Nikos Kazantzákis) International Airport: This is Crete's main airport and is served by a number of airlines, most of them charter. The exception is the British Airways subsidiary, GB Airways (London Gatwick and Manchester), although it operates only between March and October. First Choice Airways, a Manchester-based airline, flies to Heraklion from airports across the UK, but only from April to October. You can also fly to Heraklion via Athens with a wide choice of airlines, the most popular being Aegean Air.

Rhodes: Located 14km (9mi) south-west of the city of Rhodes, this is Greece's third-busiest airport. A number of charter flights operate during the summer – GB Airways, for example, flies from London Gatwick from April to October. Olympic Airlines flies to Rhodes from London Gatwick and Manchester via Athens.

Thessaloniki (Makedonia) International: The airport is 15km (9mi) south-east of the city and is served by a number of charter airlines during the summer and scheduled flights by British Airways and Olympic Airlines (London Gatwick) all year round. A number of other airlines fly via Athens.

9

Communications

Communications in Greece are generally reasonable, with modern telephone services provided primarily by the former state monopoly, Organismos Telepikinonion Ellados (OTE), but increasingly by other operators. Mobile phones are commonly used and internet use is fairly widespread, although take-up is low compared with many other EU countries. The country dialling code is 30, followed by area codes. International direct dialling (IDD) is available throughout the mainland and the islands.

Fixed-line Telephones: OTE is the main provider of fixed-line telephone services in Greece, although the market was liberalised in 1998, and still controls lines and connection. Its main competitors are Forthnet, Q-Telecom, Tellas and Vivodi.

Mobile Telephones: Mobile coverage and quality is exceptionally good in Greece, where GSM 900 and 1800 networks operate. The main mobile providers are Cosmote, Q-Telecom, Stet Hellas and Vodafone.

Internet: Private internet use in Greece is relatively low by EU standards, although more than 80 per cent of Greek businesses use the internet regularly. High-speed connection (via ADSL) is available in most urban areas, although most home users still have dial-up connections.

Postal Services: Postal services are provided by the state-owned postal service, ELTA. Post offices are open Mondays to Fridays from 7.30am to 2pm and on Saturday mornings, although central post offices may be open longer hours. Letters normally take around five days to reach Europe, six days to the US and around a week to distant destinations such as Australia.

Crime

Greece has one of the lowest crime rates in the EU. Violent and serious crime are rare, although 'petty' crime such as burglary is more common.

Medical Facilities

Local medical facilities vary considerably and you should check the location of the nearest general hospital with emergency facilities, which, if you live on an island, may be on the mainland or another island. Patients are often transferred to Athens for treatment. Although Greek medical professionals are trained to a high standard, due to severe under-funding the public health service is one of the worst in Europe. It provides free or low-cost healthcare for those making social security contributions, and Greece has reciprocal health agreements with many countries, so that retirees from EU countries enjoy free medical treatment (provided they've made social security contributions in their home country), but there are long waiting lists for non-essential treatment. The government is currently working to improve the service and upgrade facilities, but private health insurance is recommended, even for those covered by social security.

9

Pets

As a member of the EU, Greece doesn't operate a quarantine system for pets, but they must be identifiable by microchip or tattoo, have an EU Pet Passport and be vaccinated against rabies. Pets entering or leaving Greece must have a health certificate confirming that they're in good health and free from infectious diseases. All official paperwork must be issued by a government-authorised vet.

Visas & Permits

Visas: No visa is required for visitors to Greece from EEA countries and certain non-EEA countries, including Australia, Canada, Japan, some South American countries and the US (check with the Greek embassy in your home country). Other nationalities usually require a visa before travelling to Greece.

Residence Permits: EU citizens may remain in Greece for up to 90 days without a residence permit, but if you plan to stay longer or work in Greece, you must obtain a residence permit from the local police station or the Alien's Bureau – offices can be found in all large towns and cities. A residence permit is valid for five years and is usually renewable on application.

Non-EU citizens also require residence permits, but these are usually valid only for a year, though they may be renewed for a further five years (usually subject to your employment situation – see **Work Permits** below). After five years, you must apply for an 'extension', which is a more complicated process, involving approval from the Minister of Public Order and the consent of the Ministry of Labour.

Work Permits: EU citizens don't require work permits, as they're permitted to work freely in Greece. Non-EU citizens must obtain a permit, which is linked to your residence status. Your Greek employer must apply on your behalf and prove that no EU national is available to fill the post.

Reference

Further Reading

Buying a Home in Greece, Joanna Styles (Survival Books). Everything you need to know about buying a home in Greece.

Useful Addresses

Greek Embassy (UK), 1A Holland Park, London W11 3TP, UK (☎ 020-7229 3850, 🖳 www.greekembassy.org.uk).

Greek Embassy (US), 2217 Massachusetts Ave., NW, Washington, DC 20008, US (☎ 202-939 1300, 🖳 www.greekembassy.org).

Greek National Tourism Organisation (UK), 4 Conduit Regent Street, London W1S 0DJ, UK (☎ 020-7495 9300, 🖳 www.visitgreece.gr).

Greek National Tourism Organisation (US), Olympic Tower, 645 Fifth Avenue, New York, NY 10022, US (☎ 212-421 5777, 🖳 www.greektourism.com).

Europe: HUNGARY

9

Background Information

Capital: Budapest.
Population: 9.9m.

Foreign Community: Over 90 per cent Hungarian, around 2 per cent Roma, with very few UK and US residents.

Area: 93,030km^2 (35,919 mi^2).

Geography: Hungary is a land-locked country in central Europe, divided by the River Danube. It's bordered by Austria to the west, Slovakia to the north, Ukraine and Romania to the east and Croatia, Serbia and Slovenia to the south. It's mainly flat and divided into three main regions: the Great Hungarian Plain in the east, made up of rich agricultural land; the Transdanube in the west, with varied terrain including low mountains and the largest lake in Europe, Lake Balaton; and the northern, mountainous region, which borders Slovakia and forms part of the Carpathian mountain chain.

Climate: Hungary has a continental climate typical of central Europe, characterised by cold winters and hot summers. Winter temperatures range from -3C (27F) to 15C (59F) and summer temperatures are usually between 27C (81F) and 35C (95F), although temperatures as low as -29C (-20F) have been recorded in winter and as high as 42C (110F) in summer. Average annual rainfall is around 60cm.

Language: The official language is Hungarian (*Magyar*), spoken by over 90 per cent of the population.

Political Situation: Good. Hungary was controlled by a communist regime (though one of the region's most liberal) until the fall of the Berlin Wall in 1989. It has since made a successful transition from autocracy and state control to multiparty democratic parliamentary republicanism. Since 1990, all governments have completed their term in office. The country has a President, elected every five years, who holds a largely ceremonial role, and a Prime Minister, who is head of the government. The most recent elections were in 2006 and were won by the Hungarian Socialist Party (MSZP), led by Ferenc Gyurcsány, who formed a coalition with the Alliance of Free Democrats (SZDSZ). Hungary is a committed EU member – one of the first of the so-called emerging countries to join, in May 2004 – and joined NATO in 1999.

Finance

Currency

Hungary's national currency is the forint, introduced in 1946 and abbreviated as HUF. The forint is divided into 100 fillér. Hungary hopes to adopt the euro as its currency between 2010 and 2012, although financial analysts believe 2014 is more realistic. High inflation since 1990 has been partially controlled but the government and the Central Bank are struggling to meet EU criteria for adopting the euro.

Exchange Rate: £1 = HUF375.

Exchange Controls: Abolished in 2001.

Cost & Standard of Living

9

Hungary's economy has recovered from the rampant inflation which marked the early years of democracy, and the government is working hard to sustain economic growth. By 2001, the country was beginning to see annual economic growth of around 4 per cent and inflation in single figures. Foreign investment and ownership are encouraged, but financial analysts believe that government spending needs to be more tightly controlled. It's thought that the country won't meet the criteria for adoption of the euro until around 2014. The cost of living is lower than the average in western European countries. Average monthly wages for a blue collar worker are less than HUF100,000 (£275), while office workers earn around HUF175,000 (£480).

Taxation

Personal Effects: Can be imported without any restrictions, provided there's no intention to resell.

Income Tax: Residents, including foreigners with a Hungarian settlement permit or with a permanent home or business interests in Hungary, pay tax on their worldwide income. Non-residents pay tax only on income earned in Hungary. There are just two tax rates: 18 per cent for amounts up to HUF1,550,000 (£4,000) and 36 per cent for anything over that amount. A range of deductions from gross earnings is available.

Capital Gains Tax (CGT): Capital gains are considered as ordinary income and CGT is charged at 25 per cent, but CGT on property is reduced, depending on how long you've owned it. After 15 years, you're exempt from CGT. Some buyers purchase through a Hungarian company (see **Purchase Procedure** below), which reduces the tax payable on profits to 16 per cent.

Wealth Tax: None.

Inheritance & Gift Tax: Rates range from 2.5 per cent to 21 per cent, depending on the relationship to the deceased, with generous allowances and exemptions for close family members.

Value Added Tax (VAT): VAT applies to most transactions, at the rate of 20 per cent. There's a reduced rate of 15 per cent on food and some other goods, and a 5 per cent rate for textbooks and some medical supplies. Financial, health and education services and leases on accommodation are VAT-exempt, as are property sales and rents.

Property

Restrictions on Foreign Ownership & Letting

You must obtain a permit from the relevant local authority (see **Purchase Procedure** below). Permission is rarely refused but it's a long (up to two months) and complicated business.

There are no restrictions on letting. Income tax on rental income must be paid at the tax office (at a rate of 25 per cent) or the income declared in your annual tax declaration, although this may take you into the higher tax bracket. If you've bought property through a company, you pay 16 per cent on any profit from letting.

Market

The growth of Hungary's economy, increased international business confidence and increasing numbers of tourists have all contributed to the development of the property market. In addition, budget airlines have begun to fly to the capital, Budapest, boosting tourism and interest in the property market. There were significant price rises and a surge in construction in the run-up to EU entry in 2004, but since then the market has slowed considerably. New properties and older properties in need of renovation are available, but some areas have an oversupply of property, making it difficult for buy-to-let investors to charge high rents.

9

Areas

Hungary's capital, Budapest, and its suburbs are the main area of interest to foreigner buyers, especially since the introduction of budget flights to the city in 2004, which have made the city popular for short breaks. The city comprises two distinct areas: the Castle Hill district of Buda west of the Danube, and Pest, below it and making up two-thirds of the city, east of the river. The more popular area for foreign buyers has so far been Pest, where the majority of properties have been built since around 2000. Pest is divided into 17 districts, and a number of the undeveloped districts have been interesting investors, including the 'Jewish Quarter' and the university districts. Budapest was partly destroyed at the end of the Second World War but rebuilt during the '50s and '60s. It retains many attractive historic buildings and its Castle Hill district and River Danube embankments are classified as UNESCO World Heritage Sites. The majority of property in Budapest and its suburbs is over 70 years old and, if you're prepared to renovate, there's an opportunity to make money.

There's also increasing interest in Hungary's rural areas, particularly around Lake Balaton in the west. This has always been a favourite holiday location with central Europeans, but it's now attracting tourists and second home buyers from all over Europe.

Building Standards

New building standards are usually high, but a large number of older buildings are in a bad state of repair due to shoddy construction practices and underinvestment during the communist era. These properties require a substantial amount of renovation.

Cost

Prices in Budapest vary according to location and whether a property is new or old. Most properties are apartments.

In Pest, a new one-bedroom apartment can cost as little as £30,000 (although average prices are around £70,000) and a three-bedroom apartment around £150,000. If you plan to buy to let, look carefully at rental rates, as there has been an oversupply of property in some areas. Prices rise as you move up to Castle Hill, as it's considered more prestigious. It's popular with the expatriate community and property is easy to let to foreign businessmen. Prices are around £230,000 for a two-bedroom apartment and around £440,000 for a four-bedroom villa.

In the rural area around Lake Balaton in the west of the country, prices (for a 'ruin') start as low as £20,000, but a three-bedroom house on the shores of the lake costs around £80,000.

Local Mortgages

Mortgages aren't easily available in Hungary, especially if you're a non-resident. This is beginning to change, but even if a mortgage is granted, it's unlikely to be more than 50 per cent of a property's cost.

9 Property Taxes

Annual taxes are imposed by local authorities on land and buildings. The charge for buildings is 1.5 per cent of the market value of the property, but there's an upper limit of HUF900 (£2.50) per m^2 per annum. Land tax is also charged at 1.5 per cent of the market value, with an upper limit of HUF200 (£0.53) per m^2 per annum.

Purchase Procedure

There are two ways of buying property in Hungary: as a private individual or through a company.

- **Private individual** – You must apply to the local authority for a permit to buy in that district, where you're permitted to buy only one property. You must appoint a lawyer, as the permit application must be accompanied by lawyer's letters and detailed search documents for the property. You must pay an initial deposit for a lawyer's services of between £750 and £1,300 and go to a notary with your passport to have your identity certified, so that you can begin the permit approval process. Permission is rarely refused but it's a long (up to two months) and complicated business and costs around £170.

- **Company** – Many people buy through a Hungarian company because it's easier and quicker and can save you capital gains tax (see below). In addition, you don't need to apply for a permit to buy and can buy more than one property. On the other hand, you may have to pay more transfer tax (see **Fees** below) there are costs involved in setting up a company. You'll need a Hungarian lawyer to do so, for a fee of around £400, plus £230 per year for company administration. You need to deposit start-up capital of around £8,000, which you can withdraw once the company is set up, and you must employ an accountant and submit annual reports. However, almost all your transaction costs and overheads, including repairs and mortgage interest, can be offset against your rental income, thereby cutting your tax bill. When you sell the property (and therefore the company), any profit is taxed at only 16 per cent (as opposed to 25 per cent if you're selling as a private individual – see **Capital Gains Tax** above).

Whichever option you choose, you must pay a deposit of around 10 per cent and ensure that you have clear title before proceeding. **As in all former communist states, the Land Registry system isn't as efficient as it should be. Problems often occur with title deeds and it's important that your lawyer carries out detailed searches to ascertain who has legal title and that they're authorised to sell the property**.

Once this is done, the purchase/sale agreement can be drawn up and signed by both parties, and the balance is transferred. The agreement must be sent to the Land Registry within a month of signing, but it can take up to six months for the transfer of title to the new owner's name.

Off-plan Purchases: If you're buying a property off plan, you normally pay a deposit of 20 per cent, with three further stage payments until completion.

Fees

Stamp duty is payable at between 2 and 6 per cent according to whether you buy as an individual or a company (see **Purchase Procedure** above) and the cost of the property. If you're buying a property for less than HUF15m (£40,000) as an individual, you pay no stamp duty. Transfer tax is payable whether you buy as an individual or a company, although rates vary according to whether it's a new or resale property: resale properties bought by an individual or a company are taxed at 2 per cent of the market value below HUF4m (£11,000) and 6 per cent above that amount; new properties up to a value of HUF15m (£40,000) are exempt for individuals, but companies must pay 2 per cent, while on properties worth over HUF15m (£40,000), the tax is 6 per cent for individuals but 2 per cent for companies. A lawyer's fees are around 1.5 per cent of the purchase price (irrespective of whether you buy as an individual or through a company), notaries charge a fixed fee, which depends on the value of the property, and an estate agent's commission, around 4 per cent, is usually included in the price.

9

General Information

Getting There

Budapest (Ferihegy) International Airport, one of five international airports in the country, is 16km (10mi) south-east of the city, to which it's connected by fast roads. It's the hub of the national airline, Malév Hungarian Airlines, and handles scheduled (including budget) and charter flights. The following airlines fly from the UK and Ireland to Budapest: Aer Lingus (Dublin), British Airways (London Heathrow), Easyjet (London Gatwick and London Luton), Jet2 (Manchester), Hungarian Airlines (Dublin and London Gatwick) and Wizz Air (London Luton).

The nearest airport to Lake Balaton is Sármellék International Airport, to which Ryanair flies from London Stansted.

Communications

Hungary's telecommunications have recently been modernised and are now highly automated. The country's telephone service was opened to competition in 2002, when state-operated Magyar Telekom (previously known as Mátav) lost its monopoly. However, Magyar Telekom (now owned by Deutsche Telekom) still dominates the market, particularly in fixed-line services. In 2007, the Hungarian Telephone and Cable Corporation became the second-largest service provider, with a 20 per cent share of the market. There's wide use of mobile phones in Hungary (almost 100 per cent) and internet usage has begun to increase. The country dialling code is 36, and international direct dialling (IDD) is available.

Fixed-line Telephones: There are public phones in all main centres, which work with coins or phone cards, available at post offices, petrol stations and newsagents.

Mobile Telephones: Mobile phones are widely used and operate on the GSM network. There are currently three main providers: T-Mobile (Hungary), owned by Magyar Telekom, which dominates the market, Pannon GSM and Vodafone.

Internet: Hungary still has a comparatively low percentage of home internet use, although most schools and universities are connected and public use is rising fast (there were reckoned to be 1m users in 2007). The main internet service providers (ISPs) are Emitel, Hungarotel, Invitel, Magyar Telekom and Monortel. Internet cafes are becoming increasingly popular in urban areas, particularly in Budapest.

Postal Services: Services are generally reliable, letters to western Europe taking around three days by airmail and around six by surface mail.

Crime Rate

Hungary has a low rate of violent crime, but street crime occasionally involves violence, especially in popular tourist areas. There are various tourist scams and the theft of passports, currency and credit cards from tourists is prevalent, especially at airports and railway stations.

9

Medical Facilities

Medical care is generally good, although emergency services are lacking and nursing care and facilities aren't up to western European standards. Hungary has been striving to improve its healthcare services since the end of communist rule. Funding comes from social security contributions, although all citizens are covered, even if they're unable to pay contributions. Not all healthcare is free, however; there's a co-payment system for certain treatments and medicines. Some medical staff speak English, especially in Budapest. EU visitors are entitled to free care with a European Health Insurance Card. Retired EU residents are entitled to free or low-cost treatment under EU reciprocal health agreements. Working residents must be registered and contributing to the Health Insurance Fund. Others must have comprehensive private health insurance. Private hospitals and dentists have modern facilities, but even in the private sector there are waiting lists for 'elective' surgery for all treatment you must pay up front and claim from your insurance company afterwards.

Pets

Hungary is a full member of the EU and hence there's no quarantine system for pets, but they must be identifiable by microchip or tattoo, have an EU Pet Passport and be vaccinated against rabies. They must also be accompanied by a certificate (issued by a government-authorised vet) stating that they're free from disease and have received the required vaccinations.

Visas & Permits

Visas: As Hungary is a member of the EU, EU nationals don't need visas, but they must apply for a residence permit (see below) if they wish to stay in the country for over 90 days. Citizens of some countries (check with a Hungarian embassy or consulate) may stay in Hungary for up to 90 days without a visa, as long as they're not planning to work. However, if they plan to take up employment or earn an income in any way, they must apply for a visa and work permit before arriving in Hungary.

Residence Permits: EU citizens intending to stay for more than 90 days should apply to the Hungarian Immigration and Nationality Office at least two weeks before the end of the 90-day period and will be issued with a five-year residence permit, which is renewable on request.

Work Permits: Not required by EU citizens, but you must have a residence permit for stays longer than 90 days. Required by non-EU citizens (see **Visas** above).

Reference

Useful Addresses

Hungarian Embassy (UK), 35 Eaton Place, London   SW1 8BY, UK (☎ 020-7235 5218, 🖳 www.huemblon.org.uk).

Hungarian Embassy (US), 3910 Shoemaker St., NW Washington, DC 20008, US (☎ 202-362 6730, 🖳 www.huembwas.org).

Hungarian National Tourist Office (UK), 46 Eaton Place London SW1X 8AL, UK (☎ 0800-3600 0000, 🖳 www.gotohungary.co.uk).

Hungarian National Tourist Office (US), 350 Fifth Avenue, Suite 7107, New York, NY 10118, US (☎ 212-695 1221, 🖳 www.gotohungary.com).

9

Europe: IRELAND

Background Information

Capital: Dublin.
Population: 4.2m.
   Foreign Community: Britons constitute the largest expatriate community in Ireland (around 112,000) and there's also a sizeable American community (60,000), concentrated in Dublin.
   Area: 70,280km² (27,137m²).
   Geography: Ireland is a large island west of Wales in the North Atlantic and is part of the British Isles, separated from the main part of the UK by the Irish Sea. The Republic of Ireland – which this section deals with – accounts for some 80 per cent of the island (26 of its 32 counties) and excludes the six most north-easterly counties, which remained part of the UK when the Republic of Ireland was formed in 1921 and are referred to as Northern Ireland. The Irish landscape consists of rich farmland interspersed with rolling hills, bleak moors and lakes, surrounded by a rocky coastline. The country is largely unspoiled and has little industry and no large cities apart from Dublin.
   Climate: Ireland is wet for much of the year, particularly in the west, hence its green countryside and popular name, the 'Emerald Isle'. It has cool winters and warm summers, but the weather is changeable and the seasons not clearly defined.
   Language: Ireland has two official languages: Irish (or Gaelic) and English. It's mandatory for many government employees to speak Irish, but few people speak it fluently or use it on a day-to-day basis (mainly in the north-west). The everyday language is English, which is spoken by virtually everybody.
   Political Situation: Ireland is a very stable parliamentary democracy. Even at the height of the 'troubles' in Northern Ireland, there was rarely much political unrest in the Republic. Ireland's President is Head of State (elected for a seven-year term) and is mainly a figurehead, although the position does carry some powers. The Prime Minister (*Taoiseach*) is also elected for a seven-year term and since 1989 all governments have been coalitions. The current President is Mary McAleese and the Prime Minister is Bertie Ahern of the centre party Fianna Fáil, Ireland's largest and most successful political party. The current government is a coalition between Fianna Fáil and the liberal Progressive Democrats. Ireland is a member of the European Union (EU), which it joined with the UK and Denmark in 1973, but it chose to remain outside the Schengen Treaty. Relations with the UK government have improved in recent years and both countries have worked hard towards peace in Northern Ireland.

Finance

9 Currency

Ireland's currency is the euro (€).
Exchange Rate: £1 = €1.48.
Exchange Controls: None.

Cost & Standard of Living

Ireland's cost of living is high and, although salaries in some areas (especially Dublin) are high too, in rural areas they're relatively low. In 2006, the Mercer Cost of Living Survey reported that Dublin was the 18th most expensive city in the world – cars, petrol and luxury goods are particularly costly. The Irish minimum wage is €7.65 per hour but most companies pay well over this rate. An increasing number of Britons retire to Ireland, often to take advantage of the generous benefits given to pensioners, which include free public transport and TV licences, free phone rental and a number of free calls, free healthcare, and allowances for clothing, electricity and gas. The UK and the US are Ireland's largest trading partners and the country enjoys low inflation and low unemployment. The economy is buoyant; it has been growing steadily since 2003 and the general standard of living is also rising.

Taxation

Personal Effects: Personal effects (including a motor vehicle) can be imported duty free from other EU countries provided they've been owned and used for six months. VAT is payable on vehicles imported into Ireland from outside the EU.

Income Tax: Irish residents (people who remain in the country for 183 days or more per year) are taxed on their worldwide income, but non-residents are taxed only on income from Irish sources. Ireland has a PAYE system of income tax, with a rate of 20 per cent on amounts up to €32,000 and 42 per cent on amounts over €32,000 (for individuals). Single-income couples and dual-income couples have different thresholds and those in all categories with dependent children are given higher thresholds. There are large tax allowances for people with a mortgage and dependants.

Capital Gains Tax (CGT): CGT is levied at 20 per cent on gains from the sale fo property and development land. Gains made on the sale of a principal residence are exempt.

Wealth Tax: None.

Inheritance & Gift Tax: Inheritance and gift tax is called capital acquisition tax (CAT) and is payable, by the recipient, on gifts or inheritances made by or to an Irish tax resident. The tax is levied at 20 per cent above certain thresholds. The wife and children of a donor are granted exemptions of up to €496,824 and then exemptions drop dramatically to around €50,000 for less immediate relations and are around €25,000 for non-family members.

Value Added Tax (VAT): The standard rate of VAT is 21 per cent. There's a reduced rate of 13.5 per cent on certain goods and services. Most food, children's clothing, medicines and books are zero-rated and services such as insurance, health, education and finance are exempt.

Property

Restrictions on Foreign Ownership & Letting

There are no restrictions on foreign ownership or letting, but tax must be paid on rental income received by individuals at 42 per cent. Rental income received by a company is charged at the corporation tax rate of 25 per cent.

9

Market

Ireland has a flourishing property market, with home ownership of around 80 per cent, the highest rate in Europe. Some analysts and the Irish government feel that the market is flourishing rather too much, with continually soaring prices, and in 2006 there was widespread consternation that the bubble was about to burst. Currently (mid-2007) that hasn't happened and property continues to be snapped up by Irish and foreign buyers, many of them taking out huge mortgages. The country has always been popular with the British for holiday homes and an increasing number of Britons retire there. It's particularly popular with outdoor sports enthusiasts (e.g. the hunting, shooting and fishing fraternity) and it has become popular with continental Europeans seeking holiday homes (e.g. the Dutch and Germans). For those with deep pockets, there are 'stately' homes and large estates in all parts of Ireland. For those of more modest means, there are plenty of picturesque cottages and farmhouses. Modern bungalows are popular in all parts of the country. Irish property has been an excellent investment over the past few years, with apparently unstoppable growth. However, this is a market where it pays to exercise caution. Unless you buy property in Dublin, where demand for rented property always outstrips supply, you may find that although you've made a capital gain on paper, oversupply means that you cannot let your property or charge the rent you need to make to profit and it may be difficult to sell.

Areas

Dublin has Ireland's highest prices (and the salaries to afford them), particularly in fashionable areas such as Dublin 4, which has many of the country's most expensive properties. Other popular areas are almost anywhere on the south and west coasts, and most places only a short journey from a regional or international airport. The southern counties are especially popular with foreign buyers, particularly Cork, Kerry and Waterford.

Building Standards

Building standards are generally high but modern homes tend to be of a uniform and uninspiring bungalow design. Character properties are few and far between.

Cost

Average prices have been growing at tremendous annual rates since around 1997, but at the end of 2006, they finally began to slow. However, annual growth was still 10.6 per cent, a drop of 1.2 per cent from 2005. The average property price in early 2007 was €311,078.

The most expensive property is in Dublin, where the average price is around €428,000 and ordinary suburban family homes sell for around €800,000. Even a small two-bedroom terrace house in Dublin 4 costs around €550,000. As the cost of houses rises, apartments are becoming more popular, particularly in Dublin, where a one-bedroom apartment costs from €250,000 and two-bedroom apartments from €320,000. In the commuter counties of Louth, Meath, Kildare and Wicklow, the average price is €343,500. A two-bedroom terrace house in these areas costs around €450,000 and a three- or four-bedroom house from €700,000.

Property in rural areas, however, is still good value and a modern semi-detached two-bedroom house costs from as little as €130,000, a detached three-bedroom house from €165,000 and a four-bedroom bungalow from around €200,000. Smaller rural properties in need of extensive renovation can be bought from around €75,000 and renovated cottages from around €150,000. Many old rural properties have a large plot. However, in fashionable rural regions, such as the south-west, prices have risen considerably in recent years, as a result of high demand from foreign buyers and you may pay a premium of up to 100 per cent. Ireland

9

also has many fine country houses and estates, priced at €1m or more, some of which have been converted into expensive apartments, often with golf and country clubs attached.

Local Mortgages

Mortgages are easily available from Irish banks – indeed, some experts worry that they're **too** easy to obtain and that some people have been borrowing beyond their means. The Irish mortgage market is sophisticated and there's a wide variety of mortgages and repayment schemes. The maximum loan is usually 90 per cent of the purchase price, although some banks lend up to 100 per cent. The usual loan period is 25 years, sometimes longer. Loans for non-residents are usually around 75 per cent of the purchase price and may have a shorter repayment period. You must provide evidence of your ability to repay the loan, including any other financial commitments. You may be able to claim mortgage interest relief at a rate of 20 per cent.

Property Taxes

There are no annual property taxes in Ireland. Usually, the only charge is for refuse collection, which ranges from very little to €800 a year or more, depending on the location of a property. In some areas, such as Dublin, you pay a flat rate and then pay per collection (you control the collections).

Purchase Procedure

The purchase procedure is similar to that in the UK (see page 329), where contracts are prepared by the vendor's solicitor and sent to the buyer's solicitor after an offer has been accepted. Title is checked and an initial deposit taken to secure the property. If the buyer needs to obtain a mortgage, the contract is subject to a satisfactory valuation. Once the purchase deed is drafted by the buyer's solicitor and he has made his searches, he sends the deposit (10 per cent) and the purchase deed and any queries back to the vendor's solicitor. At this stage, the buyer is committed, although the vendor still isn't and can withdraw from the sale 'at the drop of a hat' – or, worse, accept a higher offer from another would-be buyer (a practice known as gazumping) and leave you to find another property or engage in a bidding war! **As in the UK, prospective buyers make an offer subject to survey and contract. Either side can amend the conditions of or withdraw from a sale without penalty at any time before the 'exchange' of contracts, when the sale becomes legally binding – which makes buying a property in Ireland something of a lottery.** Completion of the sale can take place when the buyer's solicitor is happy that all the necessary checks have been made and are satisfactory. This is usually six to eight weeks after signing the initial purchase deed.

Fees

9

The fees associated with buying a property in Ireland amount to around 12 per cent of the price but vary considerably according to whether you're a first-time buyer or not. Legal fees are 1 to 1.5 per cent of the purchase price plus VAT (21 per cent) and there are fees for land registration (between €125 and €650) and a surveyor (if necessary). VAT is included in the price of new properties and doesn't apply to resales. The main fee is stamp duty, which ranges from zero per cent on properties costing up to €126,582 to 9 per cent on properties costing over €632,911 and all properties purchased for investment. Stamp duty is waived for first-time buyers up to a property value of €317,500 and then increases in a progressive scale at rates of 3, 6 and 9 per cent (the highest rate on properties over €635,000). Second-time buyers and investors are exempt only on the first €127,000 and then the rate increases progressively (in several increments) up to 9 per cent. Stamp duty isn't payable on new properties, provided the buyer is a first-time buyer. An estate agent (called an auctioneer in Ireland) charges between 1.5 and 2 per cent, payable by the vendor but normally included by him in the selling price.

General Information

Getting There

Ireland is easily accessible from the UK and Europe by air and from the UK and France by sea. There's a wide selection of scheduled, budget and charter flights to airports across the country and ferry services to various ports. There are three major Irish airports: Cork International Airport, Dublin Airport and Shannon International Airport. There are also regional airports in the west, in Counties Galway, Kerry, Mayo, Sligo and Waterford.

Cork International Airport: The third-busiest airport in the country is south of Cork city and operates scheduled and charter flights to domestic and European destinations. Airlines that fly to Cork from the UK and Ireland are Aer Arann (Belfast, Bristol, Cardiff, Dublin, Edinburgh, Jersey, Leeds Bradford, Newquay and Southampton), Aer Lingus (Birmingham, London Heathrow and Manchester), Air Southwest (Newquay), Bmibaby (Birmingham and Manchester), Jet2 (Newcastle) and Ryanair (Dublin, Liverpool, London Gatwick and London Stansted).

Dublin Airport: The largest airport in Ireland, 10km (6mi) north of the city. It's the headquarters of Ireland's national airline, Aer Lingus, and budget airline, Ryanair. Airlines that fly to Dublin from the UK are Aer Arann (Cardiff, Isle of Man), Aer Lingus (a wide range of destinations, including Birmingham, Edinburgh, Glasgow, Jersey, London Heathrow, Manchester and Newcastle), BMI (London Heathrow), British Airways (London Gatwick), Flybe (Exeter, Jersey, Norwich and Southampton) and Ryanair (a wide range destinations, including Birmingham, Bournemouth, Bristol, Doncaster, Durham Tees Valley, Edinburgh, Leeds Bradford, Liverpool, London Gatwick, London Luton and London Stansted, Manchester, Newcastle and Nottingham).

Shannon International Airport: Situated in County Clare, 24km (15mi) from Limerick, Shannon airport handles transatlantic flights and flights from the UK. Aer Lingus flies from London Heathrow and some US airports, and Ryanair from many UK destinations, including Bournemouth, Bristol, Edinburgh, Glasgow, Liverpool, London Gatwick, London Stansted, Manchester and Nottingham.

Ferries: Irish Ferries sail from Holyhead (in Wales) to Dublin and Pembroke (Wales) to Rosslare, and offer a selection of combined rail and ferry services from locations across the UK. Stena Line operates ferry services from Fishguard (Wales) to Rosslare, Holyhead to Dun Laoghaire (near Dublin) and Dublin, and P&O Ferries sail between Liverpool and Dublin via the Isle of Man.

9

Communications

Communications in Ireland are modern and sophisticated with widespread use of mobile phones, although internet services aren't on a par with much of the rest of Europe. The telecommunications market was liberalised in the '90s and the state provider, Telecom Eireann, was privatised in 1999 and is now known as Eircom. It remains the principal provider of telephone services, although its competitors are increasing their market share. The country dialling code is 353 and Ireland has international direct dialling (IDD) to over 200 countries.

Fixed-line Telephones: There are a number of providers competing with Eircom, the main ones being BT Ireland, Perlico and Smart Telecom. Public telephone boxes can be found in all main centres and operate with prepaid phone cards, which can be purchased from post offices and newsagents.

Mobile Telephones: There's widespread use of mobile phones and the main providers are 3 Ireland, O2, Meteor and Vodafone. Ireland operates on the GSM 900/1800 network and Irish SIM cards are available.

Internet: Ireland lags behind the rest of Europe in internet use and those who do have access mainly use dial-up connections, although internet service providers are beginning to offer more broadband services. Eircom is the main provider, along with BT Ireland, Irish Broadband and Smart Telecom. There are a growing number of internet cafes, particularly in Dublin, although in rural areas they're hard to find.

Postal Services: Provided by An Post, the state postal service, which is one of Ireland's biggest employers and offers a letter and parcel service (including Swiftpost, which guarantees next day delivery to all parts of Ireland) and banking. Letters to European destinations take three to four days. Main post offices are open from 9.30am to 5.30pm, Mondays to Fridays, with shorter hours on Saturdays. Dublin's General Post Office is open 8am to 8pm, Mondays to Fridays.

General Information

Crime Rate

Ireland's crime rate is low, particularly the rate of serious and violent crime, although 'petty' crime such as burglary and car theft is a problem in some areas, particularly parts of Dublin. Hired cars and tourists are sometimes targeted, and bag-snatching and pick-pocketing are on the increase.

Medical Facilities

Medical facilities are generally excellent in Ireland, with highly skilled medical staff. Ireland has a national health scheme for residents paying social security and retirees who are EU citizens. However, high demand and a limited number of public hospitals and practitioners mean that there are often long waiting lists for non-urgent treatment. It's wise to take out private health insurance.

Pets

9

Ireland is part of the EU Pet Passport Scheme and so pets coming from qualifying countries don't need to be quarantined. However, they must be identifiable by microchip or tattoo, have an EU Pet Passport, be vaccinated against rabies and have a blood test to prove they're rabies free. All official paperwork must be issued by a government-authorised vet.

Visas & Permits

Visas: UK citizens don't need a visa (or even a passport) to enter Ireland, although most carriers require photographic identification. All EU citizens and nationals of some other countries, including Australia, Canada, New Zealand and the US, can visit Ireland for up to 90 days without a visa.

Residence Permits: EU citizens planning to stay for more than 90 days must apply for a residence permit from the Department of Justice and prove that they can support themselves without having to rely on the state. This includes showing that you have adequate funds and private health insurance, particularly if you plan to retire or won't be earning a living in Ireland. Permits are usually issued for five years or the duration of an employment contract.

Non-EU citizens must register with the local police (*gardai*) within three months of arrival, preferably as soon as they arrive. Residence is linked to confirmation of employment or permission to do business in the country. You're granted permission on an annual basis and given a certificate of registration known as a Green Book, which must be reviewed to obtain permission for renewal on an annual basis.

Work Permits: Unnecessary for EU nationals and difficult for other foreigners to obtain. Non-EU citizens must obtain a Green Card and are allowed to work only in occupations that have recognised skills shortages.

Reference

Further Reading

Living and Working in Ireland (includes Buying a Home in Ireland), Joe Laredo (Survival Books). Everything you need to know about living and working and buying a home in Ireland.

Useful Addresses

Department of Justice, Equality and Law Reform (Immigration and Citizenship Division), 13/14 Burgh Quay, Dublin 2, Ireland (☎ 01-616 7700, 🖥 www.justice.ie).

The Law Society of Ireland, Blackhall Place, Dublin 7, Ireland (☎ 01-672 4800, 🖥 www.lawsociety.ie).

The Irish Auctioneers' and Valuers' Institute (IAVI), 38 Merrion Square, Dublin 2, Ireland (☎ 01-661 1794, 🖥 www.iavi.ie). The IAVI represents the majority of estate agents (called auctioneers) in Ireland.

Irish Embassy (UK), 17 Grosvenor Place, London SW1X 7HR, UK (☎ 020-7235 2171).

Irish Embassy (US), 2234 Massachusetts Ave, NW, Washington, DC 20008, US (☎ 202-462 3939, 🖥 www.irelandemb.org).

Irish Tourist Board (UK), Nations House, 103 Wigmore Street, London W1U 1QS, UK (☎ 020-7518 0800, 🖥 www.ireland.ie).

Irish Tourist Board (US), 345 Park Ave., New York, NY 10154, US (☎ 212-418-0800, 🖥 www.ireland.ie).

9

Europe: ITALY

Background Information

Capital: Rome.
Population: 59m.
   Foreign Community: Italy has become a favoured destination for North African and, more recently, Eastern European immigrants. Many foreigners live in the major Italian cities, but there are also foreign communities in many resorts and rural areas, particularly in central and northern Italy, including some 50,000 Britons.
   Area: 301,302km^2 (116,342mi^2).
   Geography: Italy has a wide variety of landscapes and vegetation, dominated by its two major mountain ranges, the Alps and the Apennines (almost 80 per cent of the country is covered by hills and mountains). The Alps, which extend across northern Italy and include the Dolomite range in the east, have a number of peaks over 4,000m (13,000ft). The Apennines form the backbone of the Italian peninsula, and Corno Grande (2,912m/9,554ft) is the highest peak. Northern Italy is the site of the vast Po Valley and lakes Como, Garda and Maggiore. The Po is Italy's longest river, flowing from east to west across the plain of Lombardy into the Adriatic. Northern Italy has large areas of woodland and farmland, while the south is mostly scrubland. Italy's principal islands are Sicily (with its active volcano, Mount Etna, rising to 3,342m/10,965ft), the largest island in the Mediterranean, Sardinia, Elba, Capri and Ischia. Italy is shaped like a boot and has a long coastline of some 7,500km (4,660mi) and borders with Austria, France, Slovenia and Switzerland.
   Climate: Italy has a varied climate, influenced by the Mediterranean and Adriatic Seas. Summers are generally hot, with average summer temperatures in July and August of around 24C (75F). Winters are cold and dry in the Alps, damp in the Po Valley and mild on the Italian Riviera and in Sicily. Rainfall is moderate to low in most regions and is rare anywhere in summer; fog is common in the north in autumn.
   Language: The official language is Italian, although significant numbers of people speak German, French, Slovene, Ladin and numerous regional dialects. Around 300,000 Italians in the Trentino-South Tyrol region of northern Italy speak German as their first language and many identify themselves as ethnic Austrians. French (or a dialect of French) is spoken in the Aosta Valley in north-west Italy, Slovene is spoken near the border with Slovenia and around 700,000 Italians in the Dolomite mountains in the north-east speak Ladin. In southern Italy, there are significant numbers of Greek speakers and almost the entire population of the island of Sicily, around 5m people, speaks Sicilian. English is widely spoken in the major cities and tourist centres.
   Political Situation: Italy has long been one of the most politically unstable countries in the European Union (EU), although this appears to have had little effect on the country's economy. There were numerous changes of government after the Second World War, largely because Italy's system of proportional representation almost guaranteed fragmented and shaky coalition governments. After a referendum in 1993, there was a move away from proportional representation to a first-past-the-post voting system (as used in the UK and US), although initially this failed to make governments any more long-lived and proportional representation was reintroduced for the 2006 election. Italy is a parliamentary democracy with a President and Prime Minister. Elections between 1994 and 2001 resulted in a series of centre-left coalitions. In April 2001, the general election was won by media magnate Silvio Berlusconi, leader of the right-of-centre coalition, Casa delle Liberta (consisting of several political parties), who remained in power for five years, heading the longest-serving government in Italian history. In the 2006 elections, Berlusconi narrowly lost to Romano Prodi

9

of the centre-left Unione coalition (which comprises around 10 political parties). Italy is a founder member of the EU.

Finance

Currency

Italy's currency is the euro (€).
Exchange Rate: £1 = €1.48.
Exchange Controls: None.

Cost & Standard of Living

Until recently, Italy's economy had enjoyed a long period of strength and stability, but in the last few years it has been weakened by the country's lack of competitiveness. This is partly due to its adoption of the euro and the restrictions imposed by European Central Bank controls, and partly because of the country's inflexible labour laws. Italy has a high standard of living, but taxes are among the highest in the EU. There's a huge disparity between the cost and standard of living (and the level of unemployment) in the prosperous north and central regions of Italy, and the relatively poor south. The cost of living in the major cities is much the same as in cities in the UK, France and Germany, although Italy in general has a slightly lower cost of living than northern European countries. Luxury and quality goods are expensive, as are cars, but wine and spirits are inexpensive.

Taxation

Individuals resident in Italy for over 183 days in the tax year are taxed on their worldwide income and non-residents are taxed only on income from an Italian source.

Personal Effects: Personal effects (including motor vehicles) can be imported duty free from any country provided there's proof that the relevant taxes and import duties were paid in that country.

Income Tax: Income tax (*IRPEF*) is high in Italy (tax evasion is widespread – which is both a cause and an effect of high rates) and rates are progressive, from 23 per cent (over €26,000) to 43 per cent (over €100,000). Residents require a fiscal number (*codice fiscale*), which must be used in all communications with the tax authorities. Non-residents must file a tax return stating the details of their Italian property, as property is considered to provide an income, whether it's let or used as a private residence. The 'assumed' letting income is based on the cadastral value (*rendita catastale*).

Capital Gains Tax (CGT): CGT isn't payable by individuals if a property is a principal residence or has been owned for more than five years. Gains made by companies are subject to corporation tax at 33 per cent.

Wealth Tax: None.

Inheritance & Gift Tax: Inheritance and gift tax were abolished in 2001 for all direct and indirect relatives. For those not related to the deceased, a register tax applies and rates vary with circumstances.

Value Added Tax (VAT): The standard rate of VAT is 20 per cent and there are reduced rates of 10 and 4 per cent. VAT is payable on new properties and varies from 10 per cent to 20 per cent (for luxury property), although it's usually included in the purchase price.

9

Property

Restrictions on Foreign Ownership & Letting

There are no restrictions on either, though you must obtain a *codice fiscale*, a tax identification number, before you can buy property (see **Purchase Procedure** below).

Market

Italy has long had a lively property market, with a high and steady demand for second homes from Italians and foreigners, although – unlike Portugal and Spain, for example – Italy has few developments that are built solely for foreigners. The housing market has experienced strong growth since around 2002, but the rental market has been relatively static compared with those of other European countries. This is partly because of the high rate of Italian home ownership: over 80 per cent.

Property prices have risen steadily but not by the large amounts seen in some countries and, until recently, the country has been of little interest to those wanting a capital investment or looking for a buy-to-let property. That's gradually changing, however, particularly in Rome and Milan, where letting property short term to tourists and long term to local and foreign businessmen can be very profitable. Long-term rentals can be problematic, however, as there are strict tenancy and rent controls (which favour the tenant over the landlord), such as a standard minimum four-year contract with automatic renewal and limited rent increases at the end of each four-year period.

Property buyers have traditionally also been interested in the Italian Lakes, Tuscany, coastal areas, the islands and ski resorts. In many areas, there's a feeling that the countryside and coastline have been damaged by uncontrolled development. The increase in the number of second homes in Tuscany is a particular cause of concern, as modern properties are increasingly built close to historic towns. However, many inland towns and villages remain almost totally unspoiled. Some of best buys in Italy are old rural houses requiring renovation, but bear in mind that the bureaucracy involved in obtaining planning permission to renovate them can turn the process into a nightmare. In cities, people generally live in apartments – houses are rare and prohibitively expensive for most people. Despite high prices in many areas, Italian property is generally an excellent investment, particularly in cities and popular resorts.

Areas

Cities: The main cities of interest to foreign property buyers are Florence, Milan, Rome and Venice. Florence and Venice are popular tourist destinations, so holiday lets are in demand, although you should obviously check whether this exceeds supply. Rome's rental market attracts tourists and locals, while Milan is the country's commercial capital, with plenty of opportunity for long-term rentals to businessmen. Prices in the popular cities are very high and although potential rental yields have increased over the last couple of years, caution should be exercised because of rent controls (see above). Rental yields are around 5 per cent in most of the cities, Florence yielding slightly more.

Coastal Areas, Lakes & Islands: The northern Adriatic coast, the Italian lakes, the Italian Riviera (e.g. Portofino and San Remo) and the Amalfi coast (e.g. Positano and Sorrento) are very popular for holiday homes, as are Sardinia and Sicily. Property on the Italian Riviera is expensive, but still cheaper than the French Riviera.

9

Countryside: The most popular areas include Tuscany, Liguria, Umbria, Lombardy, Le Marche, Veneto and Piedmont. So many Britons have bought homes in Tuscany that the Chianti region has been dubbed 'Chiantishire'. Prices are high in central Tuscany, but reasonably priced homes can still be found in northern Tuscany (e.g. in Lunigiana, north of Lucca). Rising prices in Tuscany have led British and other foreign buyers to cast their nets wider and many have turned to Umbria, le Marche and Liguria for cheaper alternatives.

Ski Resorts: Italy has a wide choice of resorts for people seeking a winter holiday home, including the Alpine resorts (e.g. Bormio and Sestriere) and the Dolomites resorts (e.g. Cortina d'Ampezzo and Madonna di Campiglio). Winter holiday homes are a good investment and have reasonable letting potential, although they're expensive (see **Cost** below).

Building Standards

Building quality varies from excellent to poor. New buildings are generally very well constructed. The quality of renovations varies but is usually very good; check carefully before buying.

Cost

Property prices in Italy vary considerably and are generally high in cities and towns and relatively low in rural areas (except where high demand from foreign buyers has driven them up, e.g. in parts of Tuscany).

Cities: In Milan, you can buy a two-bedroom apartment for as little as €100,000, and in Venice a two-bedroom apartment costs around €400,000. In Florence, a three-bedroom apartment close to the city's main attractions costs around €500,000, while in Rome you can expect to pay around €700,000 for a two-bedroom apartment in the city and luxurious apartments cost upwards of €1m.

Coastal Areas, Lakes & Islands: Along the Adriatic Coast and in areas such as Abruzzo, Puglia, Sardinia and Sicily, property is generally far cheaper than in the north of Italy. In Abruzzo, a two-bedroom house in need of renovation costs as little as €25,000 and a three-bedroom house needing a little restoration costs around €125,000. For €600,000, you can buy a large farmhouse with land. In Puglia and on the islands, you can buy a substantial four-bedroom house for around €250,000. Two-bedroom apartments close to the shore of Lake Como or Lake Maggiore cost around €200,000.

Countryside: The most popular rural area is Tuscany and the most popular (and hence expensive) part of Tuscany is the north – in and around Florence, Pisa and Siena. If you look slightly outside these areas, you can still find reasonably priced properties. A two-bedroom apartment away from Florence and Siena can cost as little as €80,000, while a farmhouse requiring extensive restoration costs around €100,000. Two- and three-bedroom houses start at around €300,000, but some require restoration. These are just starting prices, however, and luxurious four- and five-bedroom properties range from €750,000 to several million. Many property experts are championing nearby Umbria and Le Marche (both to the south-east of Tuscany) as cheaper alternatives to the popular areas of Tuscany. In Umbria, you can still find bargains: a small village property (which may need some work) costs around €60,000, while farmhouses requiring renovation sell for around €200,000. A newer three-bedroom house costs around €100,000 and a larger detached property around €300,000. In Le Marche, a small country house in need of restoration is around €80,000 and a fully restored two-bedroom farmhouse costs around €300,000, while more luxurious properties sell for several million euros.

Ski Resorts: In a top resort such as Sestriere, you must pay from around €120,000 to €160,000 for a studio, from €160,000 to €180,000 for a one-bedroom apartment, and up to €300,000 for a two-bedroom apartment.

Local Mortgages

Mortgages are available from Italian banks, although they usually take a long time to be approved and you can generally obtain better terms and a larger loan from a foreign lender. Maximum loans from Italian banks are generally between 70 and 80 per cent of a property's purchase price. The usual term is between 10 and 20 years, depending on your circumstances. The British bank Barclays is currently offering mortgages through its Italian sister company, the sympathetically named Banca Woolwich, and usually lends up to 70 per cent but over a longer term (up to 30 years). **Most banks (including Barclays) won't finance the purchase of land or of properties that are uninhabitable at the time of signing the preliminary contract.** Monthly repayments in Italy must not be over 30 per cent of your gross income. Most lenders charge an arrangement fee of around 1 per cent, there's a mortgage tax of 1 per cent and a notary's fee of 0.25 per cent for registering the mortgage.

Property Taxes

A community tax (*imposta comunale sugli immobili/ICI*) is imposed on all owners of property or land in Italy, whether they're resident or non-resident. It's levied at between 0.4 to 0.7 per cent of a property's cadastral value (*valore catastale*), the actual rate being decided by the local municipality according to a property's size, location, class and category. *ICI* is paid in two instalments, in June and December.

Purchase Procedure

When buying a property in Italy, you must first obtain a *codice fiscale*, a tax identification number. An offer is made through an estate agent and a small holding deposit put down. Once the offer is formally accepted, both parties sign a preliminary contract (*compromesso di vendita*), which may be drawn up by the vendor, the estate agent or a lawyer. The preliminary contract can be hand-written or a standard printed document. On signing the preliminary contract, both parties are bound to the transaction. A deposit (*capara penitenziale*) of around 10 per cent (but possibly up to 30 per cent) is paid to a notary (*notaio*), which is forfeited if the buyer doesn't go through with the purchase (if the vendor reneges, he must pay the buyer double the deposit). **Note that the deposit should be described as *caparra penitenziale* and not as *caparra confirmatoria*, as the latter allows the vendor to take legal action to force a buyer to go through with a purchase.** The preliminary contract contains the essential terms of the sale, including the purchase price, the financing plan, the closing date, and any other conditions that must be fulfilled before completion.

The final stage of the buying process, which usually takes around eight weeks after the signing of the preliminary contract, is the signing of the deed of sale (*il rogito*), which transfers ownership to you. The deed of sale (*atto di compravendita* or *scrittura privata*) is drawn up by a notary and both parties and the estate agent must be present for the signing. The notary issues a certified copy of the deed of sale and registers the original document with the Land Registry (*Registro Immobiliare*). Registration is of paramount importance, as until a property is registered you aren't the legal owner. There are two kinds of deed in Italy: a private deed and a public instrument, which provides more protection but is more expensive. When a property is purchased by private deed and is subsequently found to have a charge against it, such as a mortgage, the notary isn't responsible. When buying by public instrument, you can sue the notary for professional misconduct. All properties in Italy are owned freehold.

It's important to deal only with a qualified and licensed estate agent, and to engage a local lawyer (*avvocato*) before signing anything or paying a deposit. A local surveyor (*geometra*) may also be necessary, particularly if you're buying an old property or a property with a large plot.

9

Your lawyer or surveyor will carry out the necessary searches regarding such matters as rights of way. Enquiries must be made to ensure that the vendor has a registered title and that there are no debts against a property (e.g. mortgages or taxes). It's also important to ensure that a property has the relevant building licences and conforms to local planning conditions and that any changes have been notified to the local town hall. If a property is owned by several members of a family, which is common in rural areas, **all** owners must give their consent before it can be sold. With regard to a rural property, it's important to ensure that there's a reliable water supply.

Fees

Fees to buy a property in Italy are high – usually between 10 and 20 per cent of the purchase price. Registration tax ranges from 0 to 10 per cent of the declared purchase price (*rendita catastale*), the rate depending on the age of the property, its use (principal or holiday home) and your residence status. Those buying a first and principal residence pay 3 per cent, second home buyers (including non-residents) 7 per cent. If you're buying a new property you don't pay registration tax, but you do pay VAT (see above). Residents buying their first home must also pay a fixed land registry tax or stamp duty (*imposta catastale*) of around €100, other buyers 1 per cent of the declared price. A notary's fees are generally between 2 and 4 per cent of the declared price, the higher percentage applying to cheaper properties. A surveyor's fee is usually around €750 but depends on circumstances and can be higher for a large property with an extensive plot. An estate agent's fee (and who pays it) varies considerably, although it's usually between 3 and 8 per cent and shared between the vendor and the buyer.

General Information

Getting There

Plenty of scheduled (including budget) airlines fly to airports all over Italy. Below are the main airports for areas popular with property buyers and a list of regular flights from the UK and Ireland.

Abruzzo International Airport (also known as Pescara Airport): Convenient for the Adriatic resorts. Ryanair flies to Abruzzo from London Stansted.

Ancona Airport: Ancona, north of Rome, is convenient for Umbria. Ryanair flies from London Stansted (daily) and Liverpool (three times per week).

Bari & Brindisi Airports: These are relatively small airports but they're convenient for coastal resorts in the east of the country. At present, there are only a few international flights to these airports but that's set to change as interest in the area grows from tourists and property buyers. Bari airport has a British Airways service from London Gatwick and Easyjet flies from London Stansted. Brindisi airport has a Ryanair flight from London Stansted.

Milan (Linate) Airport: This airport has good road links to the rest of the country – particularly the north and the Italian Alps but also the south. Airlines operating to Linate are Aer Lingus (Dublin), Alitalia and British Airways (London Heathrow) and Easyjet (London Gatwick).

Milan (Malpensa) International Airport: One of three international airports in the Milan area, Malpensa has excellent road and rail connections to the city. Aer Lingus, Alitalia and British Airways offer flights from Dublin and London Heathrow, and Easyjet flies from Bristol, Edinburgh and London Gatwick.

Milan (Orio al Serio) International Airport: This is the main airport in Milan for budget airlines and is served by Eirjet and First Choice (Dublin), Jet2 (Belfast, Edinburgh, Leeds

9

Bradford and Manchester), MyTravel Airways (Belfast, London Gatwick and Manchester) and Ryanair (a variety of UK airports).

Perugia (San Egidio) Airport: Ryanair flies to Perugia, in Umbria, from London Stansted.

Pisa (Galileo Galilei) International Airport: One of the main airports for Tuscany (the other is Florence, but there are more flights from Pisa and there are excellent transport links between Pisa airport and Florence). Airlines operating to Pisa from the UK and Ireland are British Airways and Easyjet (London Gatwick), Jet2 (Belfast, Edinburgh, Leeds/Bradford, Manchester and Newcastle), Ryanair (various destinations) and Thomsonfly (Coventry, Doncaster and Sheffield).

Rome (Leonardo da Vinci) International Airport: This is Italy's largest airport, which, along with Milan airport, is a hub for the Italian national airline, Alitalia. Aer Lingus flies from Cork and Dublin, Alitalia flies from London Heathrow (as well as from all other major airports in Italy), British Airways flies from London Gatwick and London Heathrow, and BA Connect operates services from Birmingham and Manchester.

Rome (Ciampino) Airport: 15km (24mi) south-west of central Rome, this is a useful alternative airport for the city. There's a variety of budget flights, operated mainly by Easyjet and Ryanair, who between them offer flights from most major European destinations.

Communications

Italy has a modern, efficient telecommunications system. Although telephone services were privatised in 1997, the national telephone company, Telecom Italia, is still responsible for providing the majority of landlines, although competitors have recently entered the market. Mobile phone use is widespread (Italy has one of the highest user rates in the world) and internet use is also high. The country dialling code is 39 and international direct dialling (IDD) is available from all parts of the country.

Fixed-line Telephones: Alternative providers to Telecom Italia include BT Italy, Infrostada, Tele2 and Tiscali. Even if you use one of these companies, Telecom Italia must provide the line and handsets. There are plenty of public phone boxes in all main towns and cities, the majority of which accept phone cards, available from newsagents.

Mobile Telephones: Mobiles are so popular with Italians that many people don't bother to have a landline. Italy has the GSM and the Universal Mobile Telecommunications System (UMTS) networks, the latter being more expensive but allowing you to transfer data via your phone. The major mobile phone service providers are H3G, Omnitel Vodafone, TIM (Telecom Italia Mobile) and Wind.

Internet: The internet is used by around half of Italy's population, although many still have dial-up connections. Broadband connections are gradually taking over and services being improved. Internet service providers (ISPs) include Infostrada, Italian Online, Jumpy, Libero, Tin.it (Telecom Italia's mobile service), Virgilio and Wind.

Postal Services: The country's postal service is operated by Poste Italiane, which provides a wide range of postal and financial products. Post offices are open from 8am to 6.30pm Mondays to Saturdays, and letters and cards to Europe take around six days.

General Information

9

Crime Rate

The crime rate in Italy varies considerably from region to region. Violent crime is rare, although muggings occur in resort areas, as do various scams directed at tourists. Burglary and petty crime exist in most areas and car crime is widespread, including 'car-jacking'. Motor scooter thieves are common in some cities. Although organised crime and gang warfare are rife in some areas, they have no discernible impact on the lives of most foreigners in Italy (particularly in rural areas).

Medical Facilities

Medical facilities in Italy vary from poor to excellent. Italy has a public health service, although it's over-stretched and under-funded and the quality of service varies considerably with the region. If you're working in Italy, you don't have to make direct social security contributions; your employer pays or, if you're self-employed, you pay through your taxes. EU citizens resident in Italy receive the same health benefits as Italians, but they must be working and paying taxes or be retired. Otherwise, you must take out comprehensive private health insurance. You're usually asked to pay in advance for any private non-urgent treatment. Emergency treatment for citizens of any country (irrespective of whether they have insurance) is free.

Pets

There's no quarantine period for pets in Italy, as it's a full member of the EU and is part of the EU Pet Passport Scheme. Pets coming from qualifying countries don't need to be quarantined. However, they must be identifiable by microchip or tattoo, have an EU Pet Passport, be vaccinated against rabies and have a blood test to prove they're rabies free. In addition to the EU Pet Passport, Italy requires that an animal has a general health certificate issued by a government-authorised vet in your home country and in both Italian and your own language. In Italy, dogs must wear a muzzle in public places if they aren't on a lead. Some local administrations have additional regulations regarding pets.

Visas & Permits

Visas: Visas aren't required by citizens of EEA countries or nationals of Australia, Canada, New Zealand or the US for visits of up to 90 days. Nationals of other countries should apply for a visa to their nearest Italian embassy or consulate.

Residence Permits: EU citizens planning to take up residence but not to work or set up a business must obtain a residence permit (*carta di sogiorno*), also known as permit of stay, within 90 days of arrival. Since 2006, applications can be made at post offices or municipal offices. Permits are valid for five years and renewable on application. Although it isn't compulsory to have a residence permit it you're working, it's recommended, as they're required for all kinds of transactions in Italy.

Non-EU citizens require residence permits. No longer than eight days after arrival, they must present their visa (if applicable) and application for residence at the nearest police station.

Work Permits: Work permits are unnecessary for EU nationals but necessary and difficult to obtain for non-EU citizens, who must apply through their Italian embassy or consulate. Legislation passed in 2002 increased restrictions on work permits for non-EU citizens. Employers must not only obtain a work permit on their behalf and provide proof that no EU citizen is available to do the job, but must also provide housing and guarantee the cost of return travel to the employee's country.

9

Reference

Further Reading

Buying a Home in Italy, David Hampshire (Survival Books). Everything you need to know about buying a home in Italy.

Living and Working in Italy, Graeme Chesters (Survival Books). Everything you need to know about living and working in Italy.

A Small Place in Italy, Eric Newby (Lonely Planet Publications).

Italia (Italian State Tourist Board). A downloadable 'booklet' with extensive information about all areas of Italy and daily life in the country (🖳 www.italiantouristboard.co.uk).

Italy Magazine, Poundbury Publishing, Middle Farm, Middle Farm Way, Poundbury, Dorset, DT1 3RS, UK (☎ 01305-262760, 🖳 www.italymag.co.uk). Monthly lifestyle and property magazine.

The Informer, BuroService Snc, Via dei Tigli 2, 20020 Arese (MI), Italy (☎ 02-935 81477, 🖳 www.theinformer.it). Monthly magazine for people living in Italy, also available online.

Useful Addresses

Italian Embassy (UK), 14 Three Kings Yard, Davies St, London W1K 4EH, UK (☎ 020-7312 2200, 🖳 www.embitaly.org.uk).

Italian Embassy (US), 3000 Whitehaven St, NW, Washington, DC 20008, US (☎ 202-328 5500, 🖳 www.ambwashingtondc.esteri.it).

Italian State Tourist Board (UK and Ireland), 1 Princes St, London W1B 2AY, UK (☎ 020-7408 1254, 🖳 www.italianstatetouristboard.co.uk).

Italian Government Tourist Board (US), 630 Fifth Avenue, Suite 1565, New York, NY 10111, US (☎ 212-245 5618, 🖳 www.italiantourism.com).

Useful Websites

British Embassies (🖳 www.britishembassy.gov.uk). Go to 'Italy' and then 'British Embassy, Rome, where you'll find details of region-by-region English-language publications; newspapers are listed under 'Services for Britons Overseas'.

Italia Mia (🖳 www.italiamia.com). A detailed guide to all things Italian.

Europe: LATVIA

Background Information

9

Capital: Riga.

Population: 2.3m.

Foreign Community: Around 60 per cent of the population are Latvian, around 30 per cent are Russian and there are small numbers of Belarusians, Ukrainians, Poles and Lithuanians. There are very few UK and US residents.

Area: 64,589 km^2 (24,938 mi^2).

Geography: Latvia is the second-largest of the three Baltic States, with Estonia to the north and Lithuania to the south. The Baltic Sea is to the west and Russia to the east.

Climate: Latvia has a temperate, maritime climate, with wet, moderate winters and mild or warm summers. Average annual rainfall is high, between 56 and 79cm, with heavy rainfall in August and September. Average temperatures in July are between 16C (61F) and 18C (64F). The coldest months are January and February, when the average temperature is around -4C (25F).

Language: The official language is Latvian, spoken by around 60 per cent of the population. Around 40 per cent also speak Russian. English and German are spoken in some areas and English is becoming increasingly used in the capital, Riga.

Political Situation: Good. Along with Estonia and Lithuania, Latvia was under Russian rule from 1940 until it gained independence in 1991, when the Soviet Union collapsed. A large number of people, mainly Russian, immigrated at the time. (The rights of the Russian population and the use of the Russian language in schools remain controversial, although a treaty confirming the border between Latvia and Russia was finally signed in 2007.) Since independence, Latvia has become less dependent on trade with Russia and, like its Baltic neighbours, is keen to promote economic and political ties with western Europe. Latvia's main trading partners are the UK, Germany, Sweden and Lithuania. It joined NATO and the EU in 2004. Latvia is a Republic and is ruled by a coalition, led by Prime Minister Aigars Kalvitis, leader of the People's Party.

Finance

Currency

Latvia's national currency is the lat, introduced in 1993 and abbreviated to LVL. The lat is divided into 100 santims and is pegged to the euro at the rate of 1 euro = LVL0.702804. Latvia plans to adopt the euro as its currency during 2008. Property can be purchased only in lats, but because the lat is pegged to the euro, currency fluctuations are usually limited.

Exchange Rate: UK£1 = LVL1.

Exchange Controls: None.

Cost & Standard of Living

Although the Latvian economy was badly affected by the Russian economic crisis of 1998, it recovered in 2000 and, like its Baltic neighbours, Latvia is currently experiencing remarkable and continued economic growth, the highest in the EU. The currency is stable and in 2005 real wages increased by more than 10 per cent, with predictions of even greater increases. Wages and the cost of living are still lower than the western European average. In 2006, the average monthly wage was LVL300 (£300).

9

Taxation

Latvia followed the example of its Baltic neighbours and introduced a flat rate of income tax in 1995.

Personal Effects: Can be imported without restriction, provided there's no intention to resell.

Income Tax: Residents are taxed at a flat rate of 25 per cent on worldwide income. Allowable deductions are very small. Non-residents' income earned in Latvia is also charged at 25 per cent, including profits from the sale of property in Latvia (see below).

Capital Gains Tax (CGT): Individuals aren't charged CGT on the sale of property if the property has been held for 12 months or more. If property is held for less than 12 months or it formed part of a business concern, it's considered as income and taxed at the flat rate of 25 per cent.

Wealth Tax: None.

Inheritance & Gift Tax: None.

Value Added Tax (VAT): 18 per cent. New property sold during construction or within a year of completion or renovation is subject to VAT, but resales are exempt.

Property

Restrictions on Foreign Ownership & Letting

Foreigners may purchase apartments without restriction, but if they wish to buy land (i.e. a house or a building plot), they must form a local company. A good local agent or lawyer can arrange this as part of the purchase procedure, but it costs an additional £500 and take around two weeks to arrange.

There are no restrictions on letting, but tax on rental income must be entered on your annual tax declaration and is taxed at the flat rate of 25 per cent.

Market

The Latvian property market is booming, thanks to the country's healthy economy and significant wage rises. Latvian banks offer generous mortgages (see **Local Mortgages** below) to local and foreign buyers, which has helped push up prices. Latvians are eager to leave crowded Soviet-era tower blocks in the capital, Riga, and move into modern apartments, which are being constructed as part of Riga's 12-year development plan, implemented by the city council in 2006 to bring the city up to western European standards. This means that the demand for new properties is set to increase dramatically, Latvians constituting a large part of the market. There's also a growing short- and long-term letting market, especially in Riga, which is attracting increasing numbers of tourists, foreign professionals and young Latvian professionals. But the growing ease with which Latvians can purchase their own property means that buying to let to the local market may not be a reliable long-term investment.

Areas

Riga and its suburbs are of particular interest to foreign and local buyers. Riga is the region's largest city and the main commercial and industrial port on the Baltic, with good transport connections. The Old City is a UNESCO World Heritage Site, famous for its Art Nouveau architecture, and is attracting growing numbers of tourists, particularly since budget airlines began flying to Riga in 2004. Foreign investors are buying renovated pre-Soviet era properties, as they offer the highest rental yields and good resale potential.

There's also buyer interest in coastal towns such as Liepaja.

9

Building Standards

New buildings are constructed to high standards, but there are a large number of older buildings in a poor state of repair thanks to Soviet era incompetence. It's wise to have a structural survey of an older property.

Cost

In the growing number of new developments in and around Riga, one-bedroom apartments start at as little as LVL29,000 (£29,000), but the price of new properties has been rising by around 30 per cent during the construction period. Prices vary according to accessibility to the commercial district and Old City. Properties in the centre of the Old City are far more expensive, two-bedroom apartments costing around LVL170,000 (£170,000).

A three-bedroom house in Liepaja costs around LVL100,000 (£100,000).

Local Mortgages

Mortgages are freely available to foreign nationals from Latvian banks and are offered at between 70 and 85 per cent of the value of the property, for up to 40 years. You can get a mortgage in euros, lats or US dollars and rates are between 3.5 and 4.5 per cent, depending on your circumstances.

Property Taxes

There's an annual property tax of 1.5 per cent of the cadastral value. This is determined by the local council and depends on where the property is situated.

Purchase Procedure

You sign a preliminary sale contract and pay a deposit of around 10 per cent, at which point the property is removed from the market while searches are made at the central Land Registry (known as the Land Book). On completion, you sign a contract of purchase (also called a notary act) in front of a notary and pay the balance.

Off-plan Purchases: You sign a preliminary contract and pay a non-refundable deposit of between 10 and 15 per cent, which is paid into an escrow account by the lawyer or notary who oversees the transaction. There are no stage payments during construction and the balance is paid and the final contract signed only when the property is completed.

9 Fees

The purchase price isn't usually negotiable and includes the estate agent's fees and VAT where applicable. Stamp duty (to register the property at the Land Registry or transfer the property to your name) is 2 per cent. A notary's fees are around 0.2 per cent of the purchase price and an estate agent's fees, if not included in the price, usually 5 per cent.

General Information

Getting There

Riga's busy international airport is around 7km (4.5mi) from the city and is served by a variety of airlines. There are flights from Dublin (Aer Lingus), London Stansted, Glasgow and Liverpool (Ryanair) and London Gatwick (British Airways). Baltic Air and Easyjet also fly from the UK.

Communications

Communications are generally good, an increasing number of service providers entering the market since its liberalisation in 2003. The country dialling code is 371. Latvia has international direct dialling (IDD), including from public telephones.

Fixed-line Telephones: Fixed-line telephone quality and coverage outside the major cities is variable. The monopoly on fixed line services ended in 2003, but the state provider, Lattelkom, still controls the infrastructure. Public telephones are operated by phone cards, available at tourist offices and kiosks.

Mobile Telephones: There's more competition in the mobile telephone sector and consequently in 2006 there were around 2m mobile users in Latvia, compared with around 700,000 fixed-line users. The Latvian networks use the GSM 900 and 1800 system.

Internet: Internet use is growing in Latvia but isn't as widespread as in neighbouring Estonia. Some 50 per cent of the population regularly use ADSL (provided by Lattelcom), but broadband isn't available in rural areas. Wi-fi is available in some hotels and public buildings in larger towns.

Postal Services: Operated by the state-owned JSC Latvijas Pasts. The service is reasonably good and post to western Europe usually takes around six days.

Crime Rate

Latvia is safe by western European standards, although there's a certain amount of street crime in Riga, such as bag snatching, pick-pocketing and a variety of scams against tourists. Riga also has one of the highest rates of car theft in the world.

Medical Facilities

Medical care is gradually improving, although there's still a significant lack of equipment and resources. A few private clinics have good medical supplies and modern equipment, but in general they aren't up to western European standards. Although a European Health Insurance Card (EHIC) is valid in Latvia (for visitors only), it doesn't cover you for repatriation and the authorities insist on private health insurance, proof of which you must present on arrival.

9

Pets

Latvia is now a full EU member so there's no quarantine system for pets, but they must be identifiable by microchip or tattoo, have an EU Pet Passport and be vaccinated against rabies.

Visas & Permits

Visas: Visas aren't required for EU citizens and nationals of several other countries, including Australia, Canada, Japan and the US. Other nationals should check with their nearest Latvian embassy; the London embassy has a list of nationalities requiring visas (🖳 www. am.gov.lv/en/london/consular-information/entry-visas). EU citizens have the right to live in Latvia for up to 90 days during a six-month period, provided they have a valid ticket and a passport or national identity card.

Residence Permits: EU citizens require a residence permit to remain in Latvia for more than 90 days. You should apply to the Latvian embassy in London, The Foreigners' Service Centre in Riga or the Office of Citizenship and Migration Affairs (OCMA), also in Riga. Application forms are downloadable from the OCMA website (🖳 www.ocma.gov.lv). You must include evidence of sufficient financial means or employment with your application. Residence permits are usually issued for five years.

Citizens of some other countries, including the US, Australia, Singapore, Japan and many South American countries (see above OCMA website for the full list), are also permitted to apply for residence permits, but on a more restricted basis and usually subject to their employment or business status.

Work Permits: Not required for EU citizens, but you must have a residence permit (see above); required by non-EU citizens.

Reference

Useful Addresses

Embassy of Latvia (UK), 45 Nottingham Place, London W1U 5LY, UK (☎ 020-7312 0040, 🖳 www.london.am.gov.lv).

Embassy of Latvia, 2306 Massachusetts Avenue, NW, Washington, DC 20008, US (☎ 202-328 2840, 🖳 www.latvia-usa.org).

Useful Website

Latvia Tourist Board (🖳 www.latviatourism.lv).

EUROPE: LITHUANIA

Background Information

9

Capital: Vilnius.

Population: 3.6m.

Foreign Community: The majority of the population (84 per cent) are Lithuanian, with small numbers of Poles and Russian. There are very few UK and US residents.

Area: 65,200 km^2 (25,173mi^2).

Geography: Lithuania is the largest and most southerly of the three Baltic States and shares borders with Latvia to the north, Belarus to the south-east and Poland to the south. It has a short Baltic Sea coastline, of 38km (24mi).

Climate: Lithuania's climate has maritime and continental influences, with wet, moderate winters and mild summers. Summer temperatures vary from 14C (57F) to 22C (72F), while winter temperatures range from -4C (24F) to 3C (37F). Average rainfall is 34.5cm (higher on the coast), much of it in July and August.

Language: The official language is Lithuanian, which is spoken by over 80 per cent of the population. Russian and Polish are also spoken and English is becoming increasingly common, especially in the capital, Vilnius.

Political Situation: Good, although since 1991 the country has had 14 governments. Along with Estonia and Latvia, Lithuania was under Russian rule from 1940 until it gained independence in 1990, although the last Russian troops didn't withdraw until 1993. Lithuania has since restructured its economy and forged closer ties with the West. Its main trading partners are Poland, Sweden and Germany, and the country joined NATO and the EU in 2004. Lithuania is a Republic and a parliamentary democracy, with a four-party minority coalition led by Gediminas Kirkilas, leader of the Social Democrats.

Finance

Currency

Lithuania's national currency is the litas, which was introduced in 1993 and is abbreviated to LTL. The litas is divided into 100 centas and was pegged to the euro in February 2002 at 1 euro = LTL3.4528. Lithuania planned to adopt the euro as its currency at the beginning of 2007, but failed to meet the EU's strict economic criteria and euro adoption now seems likely in 2009 or 2010.

Exchange Rate: £1 = LTL5.1267.
Exchange Controls: None.

Cost & Standard of Living

Lithuania was the Baltic state with the closest trading ties to Russia and its economy was therefore badly affected by the Russian economic crisis of 1998. However, thanks to increased trade with the West and growing domestic consumption, the economy began to recover in 2001 and unemployment and inflation have decreased steadily. Lithuania's currency is stable because it's pegged to the euro, and earnings and the cost of living are low by western European standards. In 2005, average monthly earnings were around LTL1,000 (£195), but they've since grown by an average of 9 per cent per year.

Taxation

9

Lithuania followed the example of its Baltic neighbours and introduced a flat rate of income tax in 1994, which was reduced in 2006.

Personal Effects: Can be imported without restriction, provided there's no intention to resell.
Income Tax: Residents are taxed on worldwide income excluding rental income at a flat rate of 27 per cent and this will be reduced to 24 per cent on 1st January 2008. Allowable deductions

are usually very low but under certain conditions you can deduct items such as pension contributions and the cost of personal computers. Rental income is taxed at 15 per cent.

Non-residents pay 27 per cent on Lithuanian income, except rental income, which is charged at 15 per cent.

Capital Gains Tax (CGT): Non-residents are charged CGT at 10 per cent. Residents who have owned a property for over three years are exempt from CGT on its sale.

Wealth Tax: None.

Inheritance & Gift Tax: Inheritance tax is applied if the property inherited is in Lithuania or the heir is resident in Lithuania. The rate is 5 per cent if the asset is valued at under LTL500,000 (£100,000), 10 per cent if over that amount. Transfers between close family members are exempt, as are assets valued at less than LTL10,000 (£2,000).

Value Added Tax (VAT): 18 per cent. There's a reduced rate of 9 per cent for heating and 5 per cent for transport. The sale of new property is subject to VAT at the standard rate, but properties over two years old are exempt, as are exports. For businesses, the threshold for VAT registration is a turnover of LTL100,000 (£20,000) per year.

Property

Restrictions on Foreign Ownership & Letting

There are no restrictions on foreign ownership, but until 2011 the acquisition of some agricultural land must be approved.

There are no restrictions on letting, but residents and non-residents must pay tax on rental income at 15 per cent.

Market

Thanks to Lithuania's rapid economic growth since independence, its property market is healthy, with plenty of potential for growth. There are fewer foreign owners than in Estonia and Latvia, and property prices are considerably lower than in the other Baltic States. In addition, Lithuanian banks are offering mortgages at low interest rates (see **Local Mortgages** below). On the other hand, Lithuanians prefer to buy rather then rent property (they have the highest level of home ownership in Europe at over 90 per cent), which makes the market less attractive to buy-to-let investors.

Areas

Lithuania's capital, Vilnius, is the focus for property buyers, as over 60 per cent of Lithuanians live there and it's the country's administrative and commercial centre. Its Old Town, dating back to the 14th century, is a UNESCO World Heritage site owing to its unique combination of Renaissance and Gothic architecture. Prices in the Old Town have been rising quickly and a lot of properties are being renovated. North of the Old Town is a new city centre, north of the Neris River, where prices are 10 per cent lower than in the Old Town, with old and new properties available. Just outside the city, Antakalnis and Zverynas are popular, expensive residential areas, and the suburbs of Fabijoniskes and Santariskes are currently seeing the highest level of development in Vilnius. The long-term rental market is sluggish, especially for larger properties, as Lithuanians generally prefer to buy their own property. The rental market in the

9

suburbs is more active than in the Old Town, especially for small apartments let to young Lithuanians who aren't yet able to afford to buy property. Vilnius is also a growing tourist destination, though smaller, cheaper properties tend to be easier to let to tourists than two- and three-bedroom properties.

Building Standards

Standards are generally high in new buildings, but it's wise to have a structural survey on old properties.

Cost

A two-bedroom apartment in Vilnius' Old Town costs around LTL600,000 (£120,000), while a luxury three-bedroom apartment outside the Old Town but within walking distance of all the sights costs around LTL675,000 (£135,000). In the suburbs of Fabijoniskes and Santariskes, new properties are selling quickly: apartments start at around LTL200,000 (£40,000).

Local Mortgages

Lithuania's mortgage market is in its infancy but growing fast. Locals can borrow up to 80 per cent of the value of a property, but foreigners are restricted to around 60 per cent for a first property, slightly more for a second purchase. The maximum term is 40 years. A mortgage can be in euros, litas or US dollars and interest rates are between 3 and 5 per cent, depending on your circumstances.

Property Taxes

There's an annual property tax of between 0.3 and 1 per cent of the value of a property (excluding the land it occupies), rates being set by local authorities and taxable values (which are usually lower than 'market' values) by the Lithuanian Real Estate Register. There a separate tax of 1.5 per cent on the value of your land.

Purchase Procedure

When buying property in Lithuania, you sign a preliminary sale agreement and pay a deposit of around 10 per cent. When all the necessary checks have been made, you sign a sale-purchase agreement in the presence of a notary, who must certify it. This agreement is binding on both vendor and buyer. The final stage is the payment of the balance and the signing by both parties of a 'transfer acceptance' document, which must also be certified by the notary before it's entered in the Real Property Register.

Off-plan Purchases: You sign a preliminary contract and pay a non-refundable deposit of between 10 and 15 per cent, which is paid into an escrow account by the lawyer or notary who oversees the transaction. As in the other Baltic States, there are no stage payments during construction; on completion, you sign a sale-purchase agreement and pay the balance in the presence of a notary. Your ownership is then registered in the Real Property Register.

9

Fees

There's no stamp duty or transfer tax in Lithuania, but the buyer must pay between 0.5 and 1 per cent of the value of the property to cover the notary's fees and the registration of the property. An estate agent's fees range from 3 to 7 per cent (the higher the purchase price the lower the percentage) but are normally paid by the vendor.

General Information

Getting There

Vilnius airport, around 7km (4.5mi) south of the city, handles over a million passengers per year and has flights from London Gatwick and Dublin (Air Baltic and FlyLAL).

Communications

Telecommunications has been Lithuania's fastest growing economic sector since the market was liberalised in 2003. Communications are reasonable and improving, but in some areas there's still a shortage of land lines. The country dialling code is 370. Lithuania has international direct dialling (IDD), but to make a call you must first dial 8 (the long-distance code), then 10 (the international code), then the country code and the number.

Fixed-line Telephones: There are four main telephone providers, but fixed-line telephones are still usually provided by Lithuanian Telecom (Lietuvos Telekomas, now known as TEO). There are landline connections to Latvia and Poland, and major international connections to Denmark, Sweden and Norway. Public telephones can be operated only by a TEO phone card, available in local shops and tourist centres.

Mobile Telephones: Perhaps because of the shortage and unreliability of land lines, mobile telephone use in Lithuania is high, at around 83 per cent of the population, the highest in the EU. There are four major mobile telephone service providers, Omnitel, Bité, GSM and Tele2, using the GSM 900/1800 system.

Internet: Internet use is relatively low, especially compared with internet-friendly Estonia, but the sector is growing rapidly. Sales of personal computers are growing, not least because the government recently introduced tax deductions for PC purchases! Broadband internet access is becoming more widely available, especially in the main cities, and smaller towns and villages are beginning to install access points.

Postal Services: Operated by the state-owned Lietuvos Pastas (Lithuanian Post). The service is reasonably good, post to western Europe usually taking around a week.

Crime Rate

9

Lithuania is a relatively safe country, although 'petty' crime such as pick-pocketing and car theft is becoming more common in Vilnius.

Medical Facilities

Medical care in Lithuania is gradually improving, although medical facilities are sometimes not up to western European standards. Lithuania has many highly trained medical staff, but hospitals and clinics suffer from a lack of equipment and resources. EU citizens can make use of a European Health Insurance Card (EHIC) when visiting, but as this doesn't cover you for anything other than emergency treatment, health insurance is advised.

Pets

Lithuania is a full EU member so there's no quarantine system for pets, but they must be identifiable by microchip or tattoo, have an EU Pet Passport and be vaccinated against rabies.

Visas & Permits

Visas: EU citizens have the right to stay in Lithuania for up to 90 days during a six-month period, provided they have a valid travel ticket and a passport or national identity card. Citizens of some other countries, including the Australia, Canada and the US, may stay in Lithuania for up to 90 days during a six-month period without a visa. There's a full list of qualifying countries on the Migration Department website (💻 www.migracija.lt/MDEN/visas.htm).

Residence Permits: For longer stays, EU citizens must obtain a European Community (EC) residence permit – apply to the Immigration Division of the Migration Department in Vilnius. EC residence permits are usually issued for up to five years, depending on employment or business circumstances. If you don't plan to work in Lithuania, you must show evidence that you can support yourself and your dependants when you apply. After five years in Lithuania, EU citizens may apply for an EC permanent residence permit.

Citizens of some other countries, including the Australia, Canada and the US, may stay in Lithuania for up to 90 days during a six-month period. A full list of qualifying countries can be found on the Migration Department website (💻 www.migracija.lt/MDEN/visas.htm). For longer periods, citizens of these countries are required to apply for a temporary residence permit. You should apply to the Lithuanian embassy in your home country. The permit is valid for one year and is usually linked to an employment contract or business activity.

Work Permits: Not required for EU citizens but required for non-EU citizens. Work permits are issued by the Central Labour Exchange. The application process can take up to two months and work permits are usually issued for up to two years.

Reference

Useful Addresses

Lithuanian Embassy (UK), 84 Gloucester Place, London W1U 6AU, UK (☎ 020-748 6401/4, ✉ chancery@lithuanianembassy.co.uk).

   Lithuanian Embassy (US), 4590 MacArthur Blvd., NW, Suite 200, Washington DC 20007, US (☎ 202-234 5860).

EUROPE: MALTA

9

Background Information

Capital: Valletta.
   Population: 405,000. The island has a high population density, particularly in the area surrounding Valletta, where two-thirds of the population lives.

Foreign Community: There are around 10,000 British residents in Malta and many more holiday homeowners, but relatively few residents from other countries.

Area: 316km^2 (122mi^2).

Geography: Malta is situated in the middle of the Mediterranean, 93km (58mi) south of Sicily and 290km (180mi) from North Africa (Libya). It consists of three main islands, Malta, Gozo and Comino, and the small uninhabited islands of Cominotto and Filfla. The island of Malta, by far the largest, is 27km long and 14.5km wide at its maximum and has a coastline of 137km (85mi), indented with natural harbours, sandy beaches and rocky coves. Most of Malta consists of an undulating limestone plateaux with no mountains, woodland, rivers or lakes. All available land is under cultivation.

Climate: Malta has hot, dry summers and mild, damp winters. The temperature ranges from 10 to 21C (50 to 70F) in January and 25 to 33C (77 to 91F) in July. Malta enjoys an average of eight hours' sunshine a day. Most rain (around 7.5cm) falls between October and March, with just 1cm in the other six months.

Language: Maltese. Most Maltese also speak English, which is an official language. Italian is widely understood too.

Political Situation: Malta has been politically highly stable in recent years. Its government is a parliamentary democracy, with a President and a Prime Minister. The current President is Edward Fenech Adami, who was Prime Minister until April 2004, when Lawrence Gonzi's centre-right Nationalist Party (PN) won the general election and he became Prime Minister. The main opposition party is the Malta Labour Party (MLP). The next election is in 2008. Malta is a member of the British Commonwealth and joined the European Union (EU) in May 2004. Since it joined the EU, Malta has had an increasing problem with illegal immigrants from North Africa and has appealed to the EU for help. It has experienced strong economic growth and low inflation in recent years but has had to change its status as an offshore financial centre to meet EU regulations. However, it still operates a favourable tax regime (see **Taxation** below) and the government encourages (through tax breaks) foreign retirees to live in Malta.

Finance

Currency

Malta's currency is the Malta lira (MTL), often referred to as the Maltese pound. It's divided into 100 cents. Malta is expected to adopt the euro in January 2008.

Exchange Rate: £1 = MTL0.62.

Exchange Controls: None. However, you must declare amounts in excess of MTL5,000 (£7,800) to Maltese customs on entering the country.

Cost & Standard of Living

Malta's cost of living is 10 to 15 per cent lower than in northern European countries. Food and essential services are reasonably priced, and imported 'luxury' goods are less expensive now that the country is a member of the EU. The standard of living is relatively high and the island has excellent services and infrastructure.

Taxation

Residents are taxed on their worldwide income. (Although there's no strict definition of residence, it's generally based on where an individual has a home and stays for six months in a year.) Malta operates a low flat rate of 15 per cent income tax under the terms of the Residents Scheme Regulations of 2004, although to qualify you must meet certain criteria (see **Income Tax** below). Non-residents are taxed only on their Maltese income.

Personal Effects: EU citizens are exempt from VAT and import duty on personal effects (including one car, provided they pay registration tax in Malta). Non-EU citizens may be required to pay VAT and import duties, but these are refunded to anyone who spends at least 200 days a year in Malta.

Income Tax: Malta has a PAYE income tax system and income tax rates range from 15 to 35 per cent. Earnings over MTL6,751 (£10,645) attract the top rate. Permanent residence permit holders who obtain a certificate from the Maltese Inland Revenue are taxed at a flat rate of 15 per cent on income earned and capital gains in Malta and any income brought into Malta; they aren't taxed on their global income. To qualify, you must own or lease a property in Malta, have worldwide capital of more than MTL154,000 (£243,000) or an annual income of MTL10,280 (£16,200) and remit at least MTL6,170 (£9,700) per annum to Malta.

Capital Gains Tax (CGT): For individuals, CGT is levied at 7 per cent on gains made through inheritance before to 1992. Any other gains are taxed at 12 per cent and must be included on your annual income tax declaration. Residents are exempt from tax on gains from the sale of a property if they've used it as a principal residence for at least three years.

Wealth Tax: None.

Inheritance & Gift Tax: Malta levies a transfer tax of 5 per cent on the value of a property at the time of death. If the recipient is the spouse, transfer tax is levied on half the property's value.

Value Added Tax (VAT): The standard rate of VAT is 18 per cent, with a reduced rate of 5 per cent for hotel and holiday accommodation, electricity, printed matter and confectionery. There's a zero rating on transport, food and pharmaceuticals, while financial services, health, education and the sale and leasing of property are VAT-exempt.

Property

Restrictions on Foreign Ownership & Letting

Restrictions on foreign property ownership have been eased since Malta became a full EU member in 2004, but some restrictions still apply. An Acquisition of Immovable Property (AIP) permit is required for all purchases by foreigners **except** in the following circumstances:

- if the buyer is an EU citizen and the property is a primary residence;

- if the buyer is an EU citizen who has been resident in Malta for more than five years;

- if the buyer (EU or non-EU citizen) is buying property in a 'Special Designated Area' (see **Areas** below).

In all other cases – including EU citizens buying a second property or non-EU citizens buying any property outside a Special Designated Area – an AIP permit must be applied for; it takes around two months to be granted (see **Purchase Procedure** below).

Any property for which an AIP permit is required must cost at least MTL39,720 (£62,631) in the case of an apartment or MTL66,200 (£104,385) in the case of a house and must be for the buyer's personal use, i.e. may not be let, unless it's in a Special Designated Area, it's a villa or house with a private pool or it has been issued with a licence (Superior or Comfort category) from the Ministry of Tourism.

9

Market

The property market received an enormous boost ahead of EU accession in 2004 and prices have continued to rise by around 12 per cent per year since, partly because purchasing regulations for non-resident EU citizens have been relaxed.

A wide range of properties is available, old and new, and renovated village homes and farmhouses are popular with foreigners. Old properties are usually full of charm, although they rarely have garages, which are much sought-after on tiny Malta. Modern properties are generally larger than the average in many other countries.

Areas

A number of luxury waterside developments have recently been built and have proved very popular with buyers. Some are what's known as 'Special Designated Areas', where non-resident foreigners (both EU and non-EU citizens) may buy and let without restriction (see **Restrictions on Foreign Ownership & Letting** above). These usually include facilities such as marinas.

There are numerous attractive areas to live or holiday in Malta, including inland villages and coastal areas. Valletta and neighbouring Sliema are the most sought-after areas, some luxurious houses enjoying magnificent seas view, although prices reflect this. St. Julian's, a suburb of Sliema, is popular and part of it, the Portomaso Marina area, is one of the Special Designated Areas; others are Tigné Point, which is halfway between Valetta and Sliema, St. Angelo Mansions, in Vittoriosa, a short drive from Valletta, and Tas-Sellum in the north of Malta. There's also a Special Designated Area on Gozo, Chambrai.

Rural villages on the main island such as Siggiewi and Zeebug enjoy a relaxed lifestyle; Gzira and Ta Xbiex are favourites because of their central position. Gozo is quieter, with a slower pace of life. Although Gozo's population has increased considerably in recent years, there's far less construction than on the main island. However, the supply of property is limited, as many Maltese buy holiday or weekend homes on Gozo and tend to keep them for many years.

Building Standards

Standards of construction are generally high, although the design of some new buildings, particularly apartment blocks, is unimaginative. Recent waterside developments have generally been of a high quality and style.

Cost

Property prices are lower than in northern Europe, although they've risen considerably since EU accession. This is partly due to strong local demand but also because of foreign interest. Prices for a two-bedroom apartment on the main island start at around MTL50,000 (£80,000), two- or three-bedroom townhouses in Valetta cost around MTL100,000 (£160,000) and larger, colonial-style city apartments start at around MTL110,000 (£175,000), while three-bedroom farmhouses cost from around MTL300,000 (£450,000).

In the Special Designated Areas, properties tend to be apartments and prices start at around MTL60,000 (£95,000) for a two-bedroom apartment in St. Julian's Bay with sea views, while a luxurious four-bedroom apartment costs between MTL320,000 (£500,000) and MTL630,000 (£1m).

9

Prices on Gozo are lower and in some new developments two-bedroom apartments cost as little as MTL35,000 (£55,000). A three-bedroom detached villa costs from MTL130,000 (£200,000) and a four-bedroom farmhouse around MTL160,000 (£250,000).

Local Mortgages

Mortgages are available from many Maltese banks and loans can be up to 90 per cent of the value of a property, depending on your income. Loans must be repaid before the borrower reaches 65.

Property Taxes

There are no property taxes in Malta.

Purchase Procedure

Once a price has been agreed, both parties sign a preliminary agreement or 'promise of sale' (*konvenju*) which binds vendor and purchaser to the sale, subject to good title and the issue of an AIP if appropriate (see **Restrictions on Foreign Ownership & Letting** above). A lawyer should draw up this agreement. A deposit of 10 per cent is paid and deposited with the public notary, usually in a trustee (escrow) account. The preliminary agreement is usually valid for three months (longer if both parties agree), during which time the notary undertakes searches to prove good title and submits an application for an AIP (if required), which takes around two months to be granted. The final purchase contract is signed once the AIP is received and the balance of the purchase price has been paid, including fees. The notary registers the new details and lodges the contract with the Land Registry. Contracts may be written in English.

Fees

Total fees are around 6.5 per cent of the purchase price. They include 5 per cent stamp duty (1 per cent payable on signing the preliminary agreement and the remaining 4 per cent when the final contract is signed), 1 per cent legal and notary's fee, search and registration fees of around MTL300 (£500) and a fee for an AIP permit, if required, of around MTL100 (£160). Estate agents' fees are usually paid by the vendor.

General Information

Getting There

Malta has only one airport, on the main island; to reach the other islands, you must fly to Malta and take a ferry. There are hourly ferry services between Malta and Gozo, and less frequent services to the smaller islands.

Malta International Airport: Malta airport is the only airport serving the islands. It's 10km (6mi) from Valetta and a variety of scheduled (including budget) airlines operates from various

European destinations, including the UK and Ireland. Air Malta is the national airline, with flights from Dublin and nine UK airports. British Airways subsidiary GB Airways flies from London Gatwick, BritishJET operates flights from around ten UK airports, Thomas Cook and Thomsonfly fly from Birmingham, London Gatwick and Manchester, and Ryanair from Dublin and London Luton.

Communications

Malta has a limited number of providers of fixed-line telephone, mobile and internet services. Despite recent liberalisation of the market, the former state operator Maltacom is still the main provider. Around 80 per cent of the population uses mobile phones, and during 2004 and 2005 the country saw a big increase in the number of homes going online. The country dialling code is 356 and Malta has international direct dialling (IDD) to all other countries.

Fixed-line Telephones: In 2006 Maltacom upgraded its network and it now offers a wide variety of services, including 'voice over internet protocol' (VOIP) using a simple prefix. This is available from private and public telephone boxes. There are public phone boxes all over the islands and most use phone cards, which are available from shops and post offices.

Mobile Telephones: Mobile phones are widely used on Malta, although there are only two major providers: Go Mobile, which is owned by Maltacom, and Vodafone Malta. Mobile phones operate on the GSM 900/100 network.

Internet: The internet is growing in popularity in Malta and there's increasing competition among internet service providers (ISPs), although the market is still dominated by Maltacom's internet subsidiary, Datastream. Other ISPs, including Bellnet, Camline, Euroweb and Maltanet, are obliged to offer their services through Datastream.

Postal Services: Services are provided by MaltaPost, which offers a wide variety of modern, efficient services. Main post offices are open from 8am to 3.30pm on Mondays to Fridays and some open on Saturday mornings (e.g. 8.15am to 12.30pm), while smaller branches only open in the mornings. Letters posted before 7pm should reach EU destinations (and some non-EU) the following working day.

Crime Rate

The crime rate in Malta is exceptionally low, particularly for violent crime. Crime against property is also rare but has increased in recent years. Theft from cars is a common problem and there's some petty crime against tourists.

Medical Facilities

Medical facilities and care are excellent. There's a major general hospital (St. Luke's) on the island of Malta (with mostly British-trained medical staff) and a number of 24-hour health centres across the island. Private hospitals generally offer a higher standard of service than public hospitals. Public healthcare is funded by the government through mandatory contributions and is free or low cost to those paying contributions. EU citizens visiting Malta should bring a European Health Insurance Card (EHIC) to obtain free treatment. Retired resident EU citizens (who have paid social security contributions in their home country) are entitled to free healthcare but must register with the health authorities. Other foreign residents who aren't paying into the social security system should have private health insurance.

9

Pets

Malta doesn't operate a quarantine system for pets coming from countries that are part of the Pet Travel Scheme. However, pets must be identifiable by a microchip or tattoo, have an EU Pet Passport and be vaccinated against rabies. Pets coming from any other country are subject to a six-month quarantine period. All official paperwork must be issued by a government-authorised vet.

Visas & Permits

Visas: Citizens of any EEA country and a number of other countries, including Australia, Canada, Japan and the US, may visit Malta for up to 90 days without a visa. Check with the Maltese embassy in your home country for a full list of countries.

Residence Permits: Citizens of the above countries planning to stay in Malta for more than 90 days must apply for a residence permit before the 90-day period has expired. Both EU and non-EU citizens must report to the Immigration Division at their local Police station and complete a form. You must show evidence that you're able to support yourself and have adequate health insurance. There are no minimum capital and income requirements unless you want to apply for a permanent residence permit under the Residents Scheme Regulations of 2004 and enjoy the 15 per cent flat tax rate (see **Income Tax** above).

Work Permits: EU citizens have the right to live and work in Malta but must still obtain a work permit, although this is a formality and the requirement is likely to be discontinued soon. (Until 2011, the government may impose employment restrictions on EU citizens in exceptional circumstances.) Work permits are difficult to obtain for non-EU citizens, and a Maltese employer must apply for the permit and prove that the vacancy cannot be filled by an EU citizen.

Reference

Further Reading

Malta Independent, Standard Publications, Standard House, Birkirkara Hill, St. Julian's, STJ09, Malta (☎ 21-345 888, 🖳 www.independent.com.mt).

Malta Today, MediaToday, Vjal ir-Rihan, San Gwann SGN 02, Malta (🖳 www.malta today.com.mt).

Times of Malta, Allied Newspapers, Strickland House, 341 St Paul Street, Valletta VLT 07, Malta (☎ 25-594 100, 🖳 www.timesofmalta.com.mt). English-language newspaper which has an online bookshop offering a range of books about all the islands.

Useful Addresses

Maltese High Commission (UK), Malta House, 36-38 Piccadilly, London W1J 0DP, UK (☎ 020-7292 4800, ✉ maltahighcommission.london@gov.mt).

Embassy of Malta (US), 2017 Connecticut Avenue NW, Washington DC 20008, US (☎ 202-462 3611, ✉ maltaembassy.washington@gov.mt).

Malta Tourism Authority (UK), Unit C, Park House, 14 Northfields, London SW18 1DD, UK (☎ 020- 8877 6990, 🖳 www.visitmalta.com). Downloadable brochures available.

9

British Residents' Association (Malta), PO Box 20, Mellieha MLH 01, Malta (☎ 21-577 420, 🖳 www.britishresidentsinmalta.org).

Europe: POLAND

Background Information

Capital: Warsaw.
Population: 38m.
Foreign Community: Very few foreigners or ethnic communities, more than 95 per cent of the population considering themselves Polish. Officially recognised minorities include Belarusians, Germans, Lithuanians and Ukrainians. There are very few British or American residents.
Area: 312,683km^2 (120,728mi^2).
Geography: Poland is in Central Europe and is bordered to the west by Germany, to the south by the Czech Republic and Slovakia, to the east by Ukraine and Belarus and to the north by the Baltic Sea and Lithuania. A large part of the country is lowland plain; the Carpathian mountain range forms its southern border. Several large rivers cross the plain, including the Vistula and the Oder. The country is fertile and contains more than 9,000 lakes, mainly in the north.
Climate: Poland has a temperate climate, with mild summers and cold, cloudy winters. Average annual rainfall is 6cm, with some of the highest rainfall in the summer months. Winter lasts from November to March and the coldest month is usually January, when average temperatures range between 1C (30F) in the north of the country and 7C (45F) in the south. Heavy snowfall is common in winter. The hottest month is July, with temperatures between 16C (61F) in the north and 29C (84F) in the south.
Language: The official language is Polish, spoken by more than 90 per cent of the population.
Political Situation: Good. Poland is now a multi-party democracy, which was established in 1991 after the country's communist regime was overthrown in 1989. The President is head of state, elected for a five-year term, and his Prime Minister is leader of the government and appoints a Council of Ministers. As well as central government there are parliaments with a considerable amount of autonomy in each of the 16 regions (*województwa*). The current President is Lech Kaczynski of the Law and Justice Party and his brother, Jaroslaw Kaczynski, is Prime Minister. Their party narrowly won the parliamentary election in September 2005. Poland is a member of the EU, NATO and the World Trade Organisation.

Finance

9

Poland's national currency is the zloty, abbreviated to PLN. It has a floating exchange rate and isn't pegged to the euro. When Poland joined the EU, it was due to adopt the euro in 2008, but recent budget deficits mean that the country has been unable to meet EU criteria for adopting the currency.
Exchange Rate: £1 = PLN5.7.
Exchange Controls: None, although funds in excess of the equivalent of £7,000 must be declared to Polish customs.

Cost & Standard of Living

The cost of living varies considerably between the main cities, where it's fairly expensive, and rural areas. In general, it's lower than the EU average, with salaries around a quarter below the EU average. In January 2007, the gross average monthly salary in the public sector was PLN3,028.08 (£530), but the teaching and medical professions are poorly paid in comparison with the private sector, where those in managerial positions earn similar salaries to expatriates. Poland is experiencing strong economic growth, but it has a high unemployment rate (14.9 per cent in early 2007).

Taxation

The Polish Finance Ministry has plans to reform and simplify the taxation system, making it more conducive to economic growth. Current rates are to be maintained until 2008 but new scales become effective in 2009. Residents are subject to tax on their worldwide income but non-residents pay tax only on income earned in Poland (including rental income) and this is usually taxed at a flat rate of 20 per cent.

Personal Effects: Can be imported without any restrictions, provided there's no intention to resell them.

Income Tax: Poland currently has a complicated income tax system. Tax at 19 per cent is deducted monthly until your annual income reaches PLN40,405 (£7,600), at which point the rate rises to 30 per cent; if your salary reaches PLN85,528 (£15,000), you pay tax at the top rate of 40 per cent.

Capital Gains Tax (CGT): Any gains from the sale of property sold within five years of purchase are subject to 19 per cent tax (taxed as ordinary income tax). Gains from the sale of other assets sold within six months of purchase are subject to 10 per cent CGT.

Wealth Tax: None.

Inheritance & Gift Tax: Inheritance and gift tax rates depend on the relationship of the beneficiary to the donor and range from 3 to 20 per cent.

Value Added Tax (VAT): The standard rate of VAT is 22 per cent, with a reduced rate of 7 per cent and a super-reduced rate of 3 per cent. Exemptions from VAT include financial services and education. Property sales and leases are subject to VAT at the standard rate.

Property

Restrictions on Foreign Ownership & Letting

EU citizens must apply for a permit to purchase a second home or to purchase agricultural land. These restrictions may be lifted by 2009. Check with your lawyer, as restrictions vary according to your circumstances. Non-EU citizens must apply for a permit to purchase any property. Permits are issued through the Ministry of Internal Affairs and you may purchase property before obtaining the permit, provided you have a 'promise of permit issue'.

There are no restrictions on letting, but rental income must be entered on your annual tax declaration.

9

Market

According to the Royal Institution of Chartered Surveyors (RICS) in the UK, the housing market in Poland has been growing at a rapid rate since EU accession in 2004. Economic problems during 2001 and 2002 affected growth but the market has since recovered. Demand has been fuelled by increasing numbers of foreign investors and the fact that housing supply is short and much of it (built during the '70s and '80s) is in a bad state of repair. The market is centred around the cities of Warsaw and Krakow. (Long-term lets are more common in Warsaw, as it's a financial and business centre; short-term holiday lets (weekend breaks) in Krakow.) Developments have been springing up there as well as in Gdansk and Poznan, appealing to local professionals. Consequently, Poland is primarily a capital investor's market and is particularly attractive for those interested in buy-to-let properties.

Areas

Poland's capital, Warsaw, is the country's main business and economic centre, and growing numbers of Poles are moving there from rural areas in search of higher-paid jobs. An emerging 'middle class', these young professionals want high-quality, long-term rented accommodation, making Warsaw an attractive buy-to-let location. It isn't an attractive city, however, and so attracts few tourists.

On the other hand, the old capital of Poland, Krakow, a medieval city, is considered one of the most beautiful in Europe and is a UNESCO World Heritage Site. It's therefore a popular short-break location, and a number of budget airlines fly there regularly from British and Irish airports (see **Getting There** below).

There has also been a significant amount of recent interest in the port city of Gdansk, which has good beaches and an attractive old town.

Building Standards

Standards are generally high in new buildings, but there are a number of older buildings which require considerable renovation.

Cost

Prices in Warsaw depend on the age of a property and access to the city centre. Properties in the city tend to be apartments, houses being more readily available in the suburbs. A new one-bedroom apartment in the city costs around PLN400,000 (£70,000); a new two- or three-bedroom apartment costs around PLN550,000 (£100,000). Apartments in historic buildings in the centre of the city are more expensive, starting at around PLN770,000 (£140,000). Houses on the outskirts of the city cost from around PLN580,000 (£100,000) to around PLN1.3m (£240,000), depending on size and location.

In Krakow prices are lower, one-bedroom apartments starting at around PLN300,000 (£55,000), and in Gdansk prices start as low as PLN220,000 (£38,000) for a new two-bedroom apartment.

Local Mortgages

Polish banks (including other European banks with branches or subsidiaries in Poland) provide mortgages for foreign nationals. Mortgages are available in euros, sterling, Swiss francs and US dollars, at varying exchange rates, for up to 80 per cent of the value of a property. You must be able to show evidence of a regular income, and mortgages are repayment only, for terms of up to 30 years depending on your age and circumstances.

Property Taxes

There's an annual property tax, whose rates are set by local authorities. Charges are usually negligible – between around PLN0.50 and PLN0.65 (a few pence) per m^2.

Purchase Procedure

It's important to deal with reputable English-speaking estate agents and lawyers who are familiar with the local property market. Contracts are in Polish, so ensure you have an accurate translation before you sign.

Once a price has been agreed, the vendor and the buyer sign a preliminary contract in the presence of a notary public and you pay a deposit of between 10 and 30 per cent. The notary checks title and that there are no outstanding mortgages or other charges on the property. Once he's satisfied, both parties sign a final contract, transferring the property to the buyer. The notary puts an official stamp on the contract and registers the change of title at the Property Registry. This final process can take up to three months and the whole purchase procedure usually takes around six months.

Off-plan Purchases: You put down a small holding deposit and make stage payments as construction progresses. The transfer of title is made on completion, once the final payment has been made.

Fees

Notaries' fees are normally around 1.5 per cent of the purchase price, and court fees, a lawyer's and a translator's fees add a further 3 per cent. Stamp duty is 2 per cent. An agent's fees are normally shared between buyer and vendor, the buyer paying between 1.5 and 3 per cent. All fees are subject to VAT at 22 per cent. VAT on new properties only is charged at 7 per cent (this may rise to 22 per cent in 2008).

General Information

Getting There

Gdansk Airport: Named after former President Lech Walesa, hero of the Gdansk 'uprising', the airport is around 10km (6mi) from the city centre. It's quite small but is used by an increasing number of budget airlines. Centralwings has flights from Dublin, Edinburgh and Shannon. Ryanair began flights from Dublin in May 2007 and also flies from London Stansted, and Wizz Air flies from Cork, Doncaster (from July 2007), Glasgow, Liverpool and London Luton.

Krakow (John Paul II) International Airport: 11km (7mi) to the west of the city, the airport handles a surprisingly wide range of scheduled (including budget) flights. Aer Lingus flies from Dublin and British Airways from London Gatwick. Easyjet is increasing its flights to Krakow in 2007 to include Belfast, Bristol, Liverpool, London Gatwick, London Luton and Newcastle, while Ryanair has flights from Dublin, Glasgow, Liverpool, London Stansted and Shannon.

9

Warsaw (Frederic Chopin) Airport: The country's largest airport. (A second airport is being built 40km/25mi to the north of city.) Aer Lingus flies from Cork and Dublin, British Airways from London Heathrow, Centralwings from Cork, Edinburgh, London Gatwick, London Stansted and Shannon, and the Polish national airline, LOT, flies from Dublin, London Heathrow and Manchester.

Communications

Telecommunications in Poland are currently undergoing a long overdue modernisation. The state-owned monopoly Telekomunikacja Polska S.A (TPSA) was privatised in 2003, allowing other operators into the market. However, TPSA is still the main provider of fixed-line services and infrastructure. Internet access isn't as common as in other EU countries, due mainly to high charges. Fax services are widely available and more frequently used than in some other countries. The country dialling code is 48. International direct dialling (IDD) is available to countries worldwide.

Fixed-line Telephones: There's a long waiting time for fixed-line telephones and, as a result, mobile telephone usage has increased considerably over the last few years. Public telephones are operated by phone cards, available at tourist offices and kiosks.

Mobile Telephones: 98 per cent of the Polish population uses mobile phones. The three main providers are Era (owned by Deutsche Telekom), Orange and Plus (partly owned by Vodafone). All operate on the GSM network.

Internet: The internet isn't widely used and access is expensive. However, usage is growing and over 80 per cent of Polish businesses have internet access.

Postal Services: The postal service, Poczta Polska, which is in the process of privatisation, has become increasingly efficient after much criticism. Letters to countries in western Europe usually take around five days.

Crime Rate

Poland has a low rate of violent crime, but petty crime, such as pick-pocketing and tourist scams, is common on road and rail journeys. There's also an increasing amount of car crime (both from and of cars), particularly in cities.

Medical Facilities

Medical care and facilities are adequate and private medical facilities are inexpensive and of a good standard. Medical staff are well qualified and some speak English. EU citizens visiting Poland can obtain free emergency treatment on production of a European Health Insurance Card (EHIC). Residents who are paying into the Polish social security system and retired EU citizens are entitled to free or low-cost healthcare. Other residents must have comprehensive medical insurance.

9

Pets

As Poland is now a full EU member, it operates the Pet Travel Scheme for pets coming from qualifying countries. This means that there's no quarantine system but pets must be identified by microchip or tattoo, have an EU Pet Passport and be vaccinated against rabies. All paperwork must be certified by a government-authorised vet.

Visas & Permits

Visas: Visas aren't required by EEA citizens and citizens of some other countries, including Australia, Canada, Japan and the US. Check with your nearest Polish Embassy if necessary. Visitors from the above countries must have a valid passport and sufficient funds to support themselves and must register either with the hotel they're staying at or the local police station.

Residence Permits: For stays of longer than 90 days, EU citizens must apply for a residence card and show evidence that they're employed (and making social security contributions) or can support themselves and have adequate health insurance. Permanent residence is granted after five years. For non-EU citizens, residence is linked to employment or business activity (see below) and granted for the duration of a contract up to a maximum of a year.

Work Permits: The government restricts permits for some EU citizens, depending on how Polish citizens are treated in the country concerned; British, Irish and Swedish citizens can work freely in Poland without a permit. Non-EU citizens require permits but they're difficult to obtain. Work permits are issued by regional governments and are granted only if an EU national isn't able to fill the post.

Reference

Useful Addresses

Polish Embassy (UK), 47 Portland Place, London W1N 3AG, UK (☎ 020-7291 3900, 🖳 www.londynkg.polemb.net).

Polish Embassy (US), 2640 16th Street, NW 20009, Washington DC, US (☎ 202-234 3800, 🖳 www.polandembassy.org).

Polish National Tourist Office (UK), Westgate House, West Gate, London W5 1YY, UK (☎ 0870-067 5010, 🖳 www.visitpoland.org).

Polish National Tourist Office (US), 5 Marine View Plaza, Hoboken, New Jersey 07030, US (☎ 201-420 9910, ✉ pntony@polandtour.org).

Polish Information and Foreign Investment Agency, Bagatela Street 12, 00585 Warsaw, Poland (☎ 22-334 9800, 🖳 www.paiz.gov.pl).

EUROPE: PORTUGAL

Background Information

Capital: Lisbon.

Population: 10.7m.

Foreign Community: Portugal has large expatriate communities from the UK, Germany and the Scandinavian countries, most living on the Algarve and in Lisbon. There's also a large Brazilian population and recent arrivals include East Europeans and Chinese.

Area: 92,000km^2 (32,225mi^2).

Geography: Portugal is in the extreme south-west of Europe, occupying around one-sixth of the Iberian peninsula, with an Atlantic coastline of over 800km (500mi). It has a huge variety of landscapes, including sandy beaches, rugged mountains, rolling hills, vast forests (over a

9

quarter of the country is forested) and flat grasslands. Portugal also owns Madeira (and its neighbouring island of Porto Santo) and the Azores in the Atlantic. Madeira, which is off the West African coast north of the Canary Islands and around 1,000km (620mi) south-west of Lisbon, is 56km (34mi) long and 21km (13mi) wide, and has a population of 300,000. Like the Azores, it has volcanic origins and is green and mountainous with few beaches. The Azores, north-west of Madeira and approximately 1,500km (960mi) west of Lisbon, comprise nine islands covering an area of 2,350km^2 (907mi^2), with a population of around 250,000.

Climate: Mainland Portugal is noted for its generally moderate climate, with mild winters and warm or hot summers, with the notable exception of the north-east, which has long, cold winters and hot summers. The Algarve has one of the best year-round climates in Europe, with hot summers tempered by cooling breezes from the Atlantic and mild or warm winters. Most of Portugal's rain falls in winter, with the heaviest rain in the north-west. Average temperatures in the Algarve are 12C (54F) in January and 24C (75F) in July/August, although temperatures may fall to 5C (41F) in winter and can be over 30C (86F) in summer. Lisbon and Oporto (*Porto* in Portuguese) are only a few degrees cooler than the Algarve for most of the year. Madeira is sub-tropical, with mild, wet winters and warm summers. The average temperature is around 16C (61F) in winter (January) and 22C (72F) in summer (July/August). The climate in the Azores, which is influenced by the Gulf Stream, is temperate, with generally mild winters and warm summers but the islands' location mean that they sometimes experience a wide variety of weather conditions in a short time. Average temperatures range from 14C (57F) in winter to 22C (71F) in summer.

Language: Portuguese. English is widely spoken in resort areas.

Political Situation: Since the bloodless revolution of 1974, which ended 50 years of dictatorship, Portugal has had a stable democracy. Its constitution of 1976 made it a democratic republic with a President and a Prime Minister. The President is elected for a five-year term and his Prime Minster chooses the Council of Ministers. Both national and regional governments are dominated by the Socialist Party, which won the last election (2005), making their leader, José Sócrates, the first Socialist Prime Minister to win an overall majority. The Social Democrat Party is the main opposition party and the next election is due in 2009. Portugal joined the EU in 1986, enhancing the country's stability and position in Europe, and bringing huge economic benefits. Madeira and the Azores have their own parliament, government and administrative apparatus.

Finance

Currency

Portugal's currency is the euro (€).
Exchange Rate: £1 = €1.48.
Exchange Controls: None.

Cost & Standard of Living

9

Portugal has a low cost of living in comparison with most other western European countries, although it has increased considerably since the country joined the EU and is no longer a cheap country to live in, although food and wine are inexpensive. EU entry improved Portugal's economy, bringing inflation and unemployment down, and Portugal has made considerable progress in raising its standard of living. Inflation is low and unemployment is around 7 per cent, but salaries are still low for a 'developed' EU country.

Taxation

Portugal's tax system has undergone extensive reorganisation in recent years in order to stamp out widespread tax evasion. Many residents hold savings in offshore accounts in the Azores and Madeira, although this is illegal. Tax rates are moderate in comparison with those of other EU countries. Residents (those spending more than 183 days per year in the country) are taxed on their worldwide income and non-residents only on income arising in Portugal.

Personal Effects: Household goods can be imported duty free provided prior ownership can be proven, but VAT and duty are payable on vehicles imported from outside the EU.

Income Tax: Portugal has a PAYE system, with progressive rates from 10.5 to 42 per cent. The highest tax rate was introduced in 2006 for those earning over €60,000. There are numerous tax credits. Freelance workers and sole owners of companies can opt for a simplified system under which they pay a flat rate of 20 per cent on sales (up to a ceiling of around €150,000) and 45 per cent on other income (up to a ceiling of around €100,000). Choosing this taxation system exempts them from keeping accounts but reduces allowable deductions. Non-residents pay tax at varying rates, between 15 and 25 per cent, for income received in Portugal (including rental income).

Capital Gains Tax (CGT): In general, CGT is levied at the same rates as personal income, although only 50 per cent of the gain from a property which is a primary residence are taxable. If the proceeds are reinvested in another residence in Portugal within two years of the sale, gains are exempt.

Wealth Tax: None.

Inheritance & Gift Tax: Inheritance tax, which is payable by the beneficiary and not the estate, is levied at between 4 and 50 per cent, depending on the relationship between the donor and the beneficiary.

Value Added Tax (VAT): The standard rate of VAT is 21 per cent, which is levied on most products, including new homes. There's a reduced rate of 12 per cent for some foodstuffs, restaurant bills and farming equipment, and a rate of 5 per cent on basic foodstuffs. Madeira and the Azores have VAT rates of 15.8 and 4 per cent.

Property

Restrictions on Foreign Ownership & Letting

There are no restrictions on foreign ownership, but foreign property owners need a tax card (*carão de contribuinte*) and a fiscal number (*número de indentificação fiscal/NIF*) – see **Purchase Procedure** below. There are no restrictions on letting.

Market

The Portuguese property market is healthy, although stable compared with many other popular European holiday locations, with prices rising at around 7 per cent per year. The market is particularly buoyant in properties on luxury developments (offering leisure and sports facilities) and in sheltered housing for retirees. Recently, there has been a high demand for properties in Lisbon and Oporto from locals wanting to move from rural areas, and prices in these cities have risen faster than average because of a shortage of housing. As a result of the overdevelopment which has spoiled parts of the Algarve, a planning law (*Plano Regional de Ordenamento do Território Algarve/PROTAL*) was introduced in 1993, which has stabilised construction rates and

9

increased prices. It has also meant that most new developments are tasteful and in harmony with their surroundings. Portugal also has a wealth of older rural properties, many requiring renovation.

Areas

The most popular areas among foreign buyers are the Algarve on the south coast, the Atlantic Coast and Lisbon (mainly from buy-to-let investors).

The Algarve extends from the Spanish border to Cape St Vincent in the west, although the main tourist area is between Faro and Lagos. Recent years have seen an increase in luxury golf, beach and recreational developments, such as Vale de Lobo and Quinta do Lago, both of which are close to Faro airport. Few Algarve towns have been spoilt by over-development (Albufeira, Quarteira and Vilamoura are notable examples), and there are still many unspoiled fishing villages, particularly east of Faro, an area largely ignored by tourists and less developed than the west end of the Algarve. Tavira is one of the few popular areas in the east; beyond Lagos in the west, Martinhal and Sagres are the main resorts.

Other coastal areas popular with foreign buyers include Cascais and Estoril west of Lisbon on the Atlantic coast, the Obidos lagoon (on the so-called Silver Coast) north of Lisbon, and the Costa Verde, north of Oporto.

Those seeking a peaceful life in completely unspoiled surroundings may wish to investigate central Portugal (e.g. Beira Litoral), which has recently been discovered by developers from Belgium and the Netherlands.

Madeira and the Azores have relatively small property markets, although demand is growing.

Building Standards

Standards are generally high, particularly in luxury developments, but the quality of renovations is variable.

Cost

Property prices in Portugal vary considerably according to location, size and quality. The most expensive property is on the Algarve, especially if it's close to a beach or golf course, and the cheapest is in rural areas, where plenty of properties need renovation and restoration and can be bought for a song. Apartments and townhouses in urban areas rarely have a reserved parking space or garage and those that do are priced accordingly.

Resale apartments on the Algarve cost from around €90,000 for a studio, from €120,000 for a one-bedroom and from €180,000 for a three-bedroom. Two-bedroom townhouses cost around €200,000 and two-bedroom detached villas from around €200,000. Three- and four-bedroom villas cost between €600,000 and €1m. It can be cheaper to build a villa than to buy a resale property. In inland areas, old cottages and houses on large plots in need of complete restoration can be purchased from around €50,000. However, you should expect to spend two or three times the purchase price on renovation.

In the last decade, the Algarve has seen a flood of luxury developments (mostly built by foreign, often British, developers) with a wide range of leisure and sports facilities, including golf courses. Prices can be high, e.g. €200,000 for a tiny studio or one-bedroom apartment, €350,000 for a two-bedroom apartment and from €500,000 for a three-bedroom apartment or townhouse. The price usually includes golf club membership and the use of all country club

9

facilities. Luxury developments generally have high annual maintenance fees, e.g. from around €2,000 for a studio apartment to over €4,500 for a three-bedroom villa.

Prices in other areas (apart from major cities and a few fashionable areas such as Cascais and Estoril) are generally lower than on the Algarve. On less developed parts of the Atlantic coast, prices are far lower, a three-bedroom villa costing around €200,000. Prices in Lisbon are around €200,000 for a two-bedroom apartment and around €300,000 for a larger apartment in an exclusive area. Lisbon is undergoing extensive regeneration, although its infrastructure isn't yet on a par with that of other major European capitals.

Local Mortgages

Mortgages are available from Portuguese and foreign banks, including Barclays Bank, which is well established in Portugal. Mortgages are usually up to 70 per cent of the value of a property for non-residents, but residents can obtain loans of between 80 and 90 per cent. Some lenders offer nothing but interest-only loans and it's difficult to obtain a mortgage on a rural property that needs extensive renovation. The mortgage term is usually between 25 and 30 years, and it must be repaid by the age of 75.

Property Taxes

Annual property or municipal tax (*imposto municipal sobre imóveis* or *IMI*) is between 0.2 and 0.8 per cent of a property's fiscal value (*valor matrical*) depending on a property's value and location and the standard of local services.

Purchase Procedure

Foreign property buyers must obtain a fiscal number (*número de indentificação fiscal/NIF*), which is a simple procedure that your lawyer can arrange. The buyer and the vendor sign a preliminary or promissory sale-purchase contract (*contrato de promessa de compra e venda*) in the presence of a notary public which contains the property details, price, completion date and date of possession. The deposit is agreed between the parties but is usually between 10 and 30 per cent of the purchase price, depending on the price and the date of completion. It's forfeited if the buyer fails to go through with the purchase, except in certain circumstances (e.g. you're unable to obtain a mortgage); if the vendor withdraws, he must pay the buyer double the deposit. A buyer must engage a lawyer (*advogado*) to check for outstanding debts such as a mortgage, charges or restrictive covenants. **When buying property in Portugal, you should deal only with a government-registered estate agent (*mediador autorizado*) and employ an English-speaking lawyer to protect your interests and carry out necessary searches.**

Completion is performed by the notary and is when the deed (*escritura de compra e venda*) is signed by both parties and the balance of the purchase price is paid. At this point, the notary's fee and the property transfer tax (see **Fees** below) are paid. The original deed is stored in the notary's office and a stamped certified copy is given to the buyer. Ownership is registered at the local Land Registry Office (Conservatória de Registo Predial) by you or your legal representative. Note that registration can take several months and you're advised to send a certified copy of the contract to the Land Registry Office as soon as possible (preferably the same day) to protect your ownership rights. Most properties in Portugal are owned freehold.

Off-plan Purchases: When buying off plan, you must pay a small holding deposit, e.g. €1,000, to reserve a property until a promissory contract is signed (usually around four weeks

9

later). At this point, you pay 30 per cent, and the remainder in four stage payments during construction.

Fees

The fees for buying a property in Portugal are usually between 7 and 10 per cent of the purchase price. Notary and registration fees are around 1.5 per cent and legal fees are usually between 1 and 2 per cent of the price. Property transfer tax (*imposto municipal sobre transmissoes* or *IMT*) is also payable and is calculated on a sliding scale, from 0 to 8 per cent of the declared value of the property (the 8 per cent rate applying only to the value of a property over around €265,000). VAT (at 21 per cent) is included in the price of new properties.

General Information

Getting There

Portugal's main airports are Faro, Lisbon and Oporto. The Azores and Madeira have airports offering limited international services (see below).

Faro Airport: Faro airport is 7km (4mi) west of the city and serves the whole of the Algarve. It handles a variety of scheduled (including budget) and charter flights. Scheduled services are operated by Aer Lingus (from Dublin and Cork), British Airways/GB Airways (from London Gatwick and London Heathrow), and TAP Portugal, the Portuguese national airline (from Dublin and London Heathrow). Budget and charter flights are offered by Easyjet (from eight UK airports), First Choice Airways (from 11 airports in the UK and Ireland), Flyglobespan (from the main Scottish airports), Monarch Airlines (scheduled and charter flights from Birmingham, Glasgow, London Gatwick, London Luton and Manchester) and Ryanair (from Dublin and Shannon).

Lisbon (Portelo) Airport: Unusually, the airport is situated in the heart of the city. It's Portugal's main international airport and the base for the national airline, TAP Portugal. An alternative site, 50km (30mi) north of Lisbon, has been mooted to replace it, but no decision had been made. Airlines serving Lisbon from the UK and Ireland are Aer Lingus (Dublin), Bmibaby (Birmingham), British Airways (London Heathrow), Easyjet (London Luton), Monarch (London Gatwick) and TAP Portugal (London Gatwick and London Heathrow).

Oporto: The airport is 10km (6mi) north of the centre of Oporto and is served by Ryanair (Dublin and London Stansted) and TAP Portugal (London Gatwick and London Heathrow).

Azores (João Paulo II) Airport: Sometimes known as Ponta Delgada, this is the main airport for the Azores and there are flights from Madeira, Lisbon and Oporto as well as to all the Azorian Islands. There's only one direct flight from London, which is operated by SATA International Airlines (the Azorian airline).

Funchal Airport: Madeira's only airport is served by First Choice Airways (Exeter, London Gatwick and Manchester), GB Airways (London Gatwick), TAP Portugal (London Gatwick and London Heathrow) and budget airlines Thomas Cook (from seven airports across the UK) and XL Airways (London Gatwick, Manchester and Newcastle).

9

Communications

Portugal Telecom was a monopoly until 1994 and was privatised in 2000. Despite this, it still has a dominant position in the Portuguese and Brazilian markets, enjoying a virtual monopoly, despite protests from the EU. Its service, however, is modern and efficient. Portugal has one of the highest percentages of mobile phone users in the world, and high speed-internet access is widespread. The country dialling code is 351.

Fixed-line Telephones: International direct dialling (IDD) is available to all countries, including from public phone boxes, which accept coins and phone cards. Cards are available from Portugal Telecom shops and post offices.

Mobile Telephones: There's a little more competition in the mobile phone market and usage is very high. There are three main network service providers, Optimus, TMN and Vodafone.

Internet: High-speed internet access (via ADSL) is widely available in Portugal and there are plenty of internet cafes and post offices offering internet access via the Netpost service. There are a growing number of wi-fi internet access points in airports, hotels and other public areas.

Postal Services: The Portuguese postal service, Correios de Portugal, is modern and efficient and offers a variety of services, including Netpost, an internet access service available in the majority of main post offices. Post offices are open from 9am to 6pm Mondays to Fridays, sometimes later and on Saturdays, and letters take around five days to reach European destinations and seven days to the rest of the world.

Crime Rate

Portugal has a low crime rate in western European terms, particularly for serious and violent crime, although as in most European countries crime has risen dramatically over the last decade, particularly petty and car crime.

Medical Facilities

Healthcare in Portugal has greatly improved in the last decade or so and since 2002 the national health service has been undergoing major reform to improve both facilities and services. There are many English-speaking doctors in resort areas and major cities, but hospital facilities are limited in some rural areas. Visitors who are residents of EU member states may use a European Health Insurance Card (EHIC) to obtain free or low-cost treatment. Residents who are receiving an EU state pension or are contributing to the social security scheme are entitled to free basic healthcare, although they may have to pay for non-essential medicines. Other residents need comprehensive private health insurance.

Pets

Portugal is part of the EU, so there's no quarantine system for pets, but they must be identifiable by microchip or tattoo, be vaccinated against rabies and have an EU Pet Passport. All paperwork must be issued by a government-authorised vet.

9

Visa & Permits

Visas: Visas aren't required for visits of up to 90 days by EU citizens and citizens of some other countries, including Australia, Canada, Japan and the US. Citizens of some non-EU countries need to obtain a visa from a Portuguese consulate in their home country before coming to Portugal to work, study or live. Non-EU nationals planning to reside permanently in Portugal must obtain a residence visa (*visto para residência*) before entering the country. Proof of income must be provided.

Residence Permits: EU citizens may stay longer than 90 days without formality provided they don't take up paid employment, although non-working residents must have sufficient income to maintain themselves. Those who take up paid employment require a temporary residence card (valid for up to a year) or a permanent residence card (valid for five years), as well as a fiscal number (see page 277) to identify themselves to the tax authorities. Applications for residence cards are made to the offices of the Portuguese Ministry of Internal Affairs.

Non-EU nationals planning to reside permanently in Portugal must obtain a residence visa (*visto para residência*) before entering the country. They must then apply to the Portuguese Ministry of Internal Affairs for a residence card – either temporary (valid for two years and renewable) or permanent (valid for five years). Proof of income is required for residence cards (and work permits). After receiving your residence card you must obtain a Portuguese (blue) identity card (*bilhete de indentidade*).

Work Permits: For employment contracts of between three months and one year, EU citizens require a temporary residence card and for longer periods a permanent residence card (see above). No work permit is required by citizens of the original 15 EU member countries (those who joined before May 2004) and citizens of Cyprus, Iceland, Liechtenstein, Malta, Norway and Switzerland. Citizens of the newer EU member countries have restricted rights of employment until May 2009.

Work permits are difficult to obtain by non-EU citizens. The employer must apply on your behalf and prove that the post cannot be filled by an EU citizen.

Reference

Further Reading

Anglo-Portuguese News (APN), Avda Sao Pedro 14-D, 2765 Monte Estoril, Portugal (☎ 214-661 431). Weekly English-language newspaper, including a property supplement.

Buying a Home in Portugal, David Hampshire (Survival Books). Everything you need to know about buying a home in Portugal.

Portugal Magazine, Merricks Media, Units 3 & 4, Riverside Court, Lower Bristol Road, Bath BA2 3DZ, UK (☎ 01225-786820, ✉ portugalmagazine@merricksmedia.co.uk). Bi-monthly magazine for those interested in Portugal and planning to live or buy property there.

The Portugal News, CP13, Lagoa 8401–901, Portugal (☎ 282-341 100, 💻 http://the-news.net). English-language newspaper, also available online.

The Resident Magazine, Fleet Street Publicidade e Publicações Unipessoal, Rua Visconde de Lagoa, Nº 2 e 3, 8400–329 Lagoa, Algarve, Portugal (☎ 282-342 936, 💻 http://portugalresident.com).

Useful Addresses

9

The Anglo-Portuguese Society, Canning House, 2 Belgrave Square, London SW1X 8PJ, UK (☎ 020-7245 9738).

The Association of Foreign Property Owners in Portugal, Apartado 728, 8501–917 Portimão, Algarve, Portugal (☎ 282-458 509, ✉ info@afpop.com).

Portuguese Embassy (UK), 11 Belgrave Square, London SW1X 8PP, UK (☎ 020-7235 5331, ✉ london@portembassy.co.uk).

Portuguese Embassy (US), 2125 Kalorama Rd., NW, Washington, DC 20008, US (☎ 202-328 8610, 🖥 www.portugal.org).

Portuguese National Tourist Office (UK), 11 Belgrave Square, London SW1X 8PP, UK (☎ 0845-355 1212, 🖥 www.visitportugal.com).

Portuguese National Tourist Office (US), 590 Fifth Avenue, New York, New York 10036, US (☎ 212-354 4403).

EUROPE: ROMANIA

Background Information

Capital: Bucharest.
Population: 22m.
    Foreign Community: Around 90 per cent of the population is Romanian. There are a number of ethnic Hungarians (6 per cent) and Germans (2.5 per cent), most in Transylvania. There are very few UK and US residents.
    Area: 237,500km^2 (91,700mi^2).
    Geography: Romania is in south-east Europe and is bordered by Hungary and Serbia to the south and west, Ukraine and Moldova to the north and east, and Bulgaria to the south. It has a small stretch of Black Sea coast in the south-east. The landscape is one-third mountains, one-third hills and one-third plains. The Danube River forms much of Romania's southern border and the Danube Delta, the lowest point in the country, flows into the Black Sea. The eastern, southern and western Carpathian mountain ranges run through the centre of the country, the highest point being 2,400m (7,875ft).
    Climate: Romania's climate is part temperate and part continental, mainly due to the Carpathian mountain ranges, which act as a weather barrier. The north has a temperate climate, with cold, cloudy winters with snow and fog, while the south enjoys a far milder climate. Average annual rainfall is 63cm, although some mountainous areas receive much more and coastal areas far less. In Bucharest, in the south-east, average temperatures range from -3C (27F) in January to 23C (73F) in July, although the temperature is unpredictable all year: from December to February, temperatures can fall to as low as -20C (4F) and in summer leap to 40C (104F).
    Language: The official language is Romanian, spoken by more than 90 per cent of the population, with Hungarian and German important minority languages.
    Political Situation: Reasonably stable. Romania returned to democracy in 1989, after the fall of the Communist regime. However, the country then experienced more than a decade of economic instability, with inflation reaching 300 per cent in the three years to 1992. Six years of left-wing government reduced that significantly but when a centre-right coalition took over in 1996, inflation was still running at nearly 60 per cent. However, the presidential and parliamentary elections of 2000 were a turning point for Romania, when economic reforms and the prospect of EU membership finally brought inflation down to a more manageable level (8.9 per cent in 2005). The economy is now showing healthy growth, there's low unemployment and far lower inflation.
    Romania is a semi-presidential democratic republic and power is shared between the President (currently Traian Băsecu, elected 2004) and the Prime Minister (currently Călin Popescu-Tăriceanu, also elected in 2004). The country has a multi-party system, making it almost impossible for one party to gain a majority and so a group of parties must form a coalition. The current government is a four-party coalition led by the National Liberal Party and the Social Democratic Party and also including the Conservative Party (known as the Humanists) and the Democratic Union of Hungarians in Romania. It's thought that the next election will take place in 2008. Romania joined NATO in 2004 and the EU on 1st January 2007.

9

Finance

Currency

Romania's national currency is the new leu (abbreviated as RON), divided into 100 bani. The new leu was adopted in 2005 and replaced the old leu (ROL), knocking several noughts off leu amounts (1 new leu is equal to 10,000 old leu). It has a floating exchange rate and isn't pegged to the euro. Romania is unlikely to adopt the euro before 2012.

Exchange Rate: £1 = RON4.95.

Exchange Controls: Yes, although in September 2006 the National Bank of Romania liberalised foreign currency transactions and their authorisation is no longer required. However, any payments abroad must still be accompanied by full documentation. Transactions between residents in Romania must be in local currency.

Cost & Standard of Living

Bucharest is one of the least expensive capitals in Europe, although some rents in the city are high (around €1,500 per month). Earnings, the other hand, are low (around €250 per month). But salaries in Bucharest are around three times the national average, and the cost of living outside the capital is extremely low. Since the economy has stabilised, there has been increased foreign investment in Romania, more than any other European country over the last few years. Major infrastructure improvements are planned and the Romanian government is working hard to make the country more attractive to foreign investors and to improve the country's business climate.

Taxation

Personal Effects: Can be imported without restriction, provided there's no intention to resell.

Income Tax: The Romanian tax system has been undergoing major reform in recent years and tax legislation in 2005 introduced a 16 per cent flat rate for individuals on most types of income (including rental income). From 2007, all residents are taxed on their worldwide income, although certain conditions may apply to foreign residents. Foreigners need to obtain a fiscal registration number from the tax authorities.

Capital Gains Tax (CGT): Capital gains are taxed as ordinary income at 16 per cent.

Wealth Tax: None.

Inheritance & Gift Tax: None.

Value Added Tax (VAT): The standard rate is 19 per cent, with a reduced rate of 9 per cent for printed material, medicines and hotel services. VAT exemptions include banking, educational, financial and medical services.

9 Property

Restrictions on Foreign Ownership & Letting

Foreigners (including, until 2014, EU citizens) may not buy land or a property with land privately but only through a Romanian registered company (see **Purchase Procedure** below).

There are no restrictions on letting, but rental income must be entered on your annual tax declaration.

Market

Despite the restriction on foreign ownership (see above) and problems with title (see **Purchase Procedure** below), Romania's property market, like that of many former Communist countries, has shown healthy growth over the last few years, as prospective EU membership and foreign investment have turned the economy around. Nevertheless, the property market is still 'emerging', and while that means that significant profits can be made, there are also more risks involved than in an established market. Romania is primarily a serious investor's market and is centred around Bucharest, where long-term lets to foreign businessmen are common, although some other areas are increasing in popularity. A growing number of international companies are doing business in Bucharest and buy-to-let properties aimed at the expatriate population usually achieve a high rental yield. Local young professionals, keen to escape the utilitarian housing of the Communist era, are eager buyers of modern apartments.

Areas

Investor interest is concentrated in Bucharest because of the rental possibilities. The north of the city has some of the most upmarket areas, popular with diplomatic staff and foreign businessmen. It boasts some beautiful 19th-century architecture, which provides relief from the uninspiring apartment blocks built in the Communist era – unlike the suburbs, which consist mainly of run-down apartments.

Romania has a few Black Sea coast resorts, notably Constanta and Mamaia, which have potential for holiday homes, although the summer season is limited to around four months and some of the resorts are unattractive.

The central Transylvanian region is becoming an increasingly popular tourist destination, partly thanks to its association with Count Dracula (a Dracula theme park is being built in the area) and its dramatic Carpathian mountain setting. The ski resort of Poiana Brasov is luxurious (it's popular with affluent Romanians) and claims to offer some of the best skiing in Europe.

Building Standards

Standards are generally high in new buildings, but apartment blocks built during the Communist era are often shoddily built and in a poor state of repair.

Cost

Most properties in Bucharest are apartments. A new, one-bedroom apartment in the city costs around RON230,000 (£50,000), while two-bedroom apartments start at RON340,000 (£70,000). Properties built before 1989 are far cheaper, with prices as low as RON100,000 (£20,000), although the quality of the building may leave much to be desired and renovation be required. Most properties in the north of the city (dubbed the Paris of the East), are villas, built in the 19th and early 20th centuries, and command far higher prices but often require expensive renovation. Prices start at around RON1.5m (£350,000) and rise to well over RON3m (£650,000).

9

Prices in the Black Sea resorts start at around RON200,000 (£40,000) for a new one-bedroom apartment and rise to around RON600,000 (£120,000) for a three-bedroom beachside apartment.

In the city of Brasov, in the central Transylvanian region, an off-plan two-bedroom apartment costs around RON230,000 (£50,000) and an off-plan two-bedroom villa around RON340,000 (£70,000). Traditional rural houses with good views of the Carpathian mountains are cheaper, and it's possible to find a four-bedroom villa for around RON300,000 (£60,000). Ski apartments in Poiana Brasov start at around RON135,000 (£30,000) and rise to around RON800,000 (£170,000).

Local Mortgages

Mortgages aren't currently available to non-Romanians, although this is set to change, with increasing interest in the property market from foreign investors and the country's recent EU accession.

Property Taxes

Property taxes are set by the local authority. There's a building tax, payable by all property owners, residents and non-residents. Rates for individuals range from 0.1 to 0.2 per cent of the value of the property, and for companies are between 0.5 and 1 per cent. In theory, land tax isn't payable by companies on land 'used to host buildings', but it is payable in certain circumstances at varying rates according to location and the use of the land; land outside urban areas is taxed at a fixed rate, but this is negligible. Individuals aren't permitted to buy land (see **Restrictions on Foreign Ownership & Letting** above).

Purchase Procedure

Before 1990, the majority of land in Romania was 'owned' by the state, but after the fall of the Communist regime a law was passed allowing the reclamation of land by its previous owners (or their descendants). However, many of those who had their property and land confiscated are still in the process of reclaiming it, so it's vital to find a local English-speaking lawyer familiar with this situation to help you ascertain legal title and avoid problems.

Non-Romanians aren't permitted to buy land or a house with land (this includes EU citizens, until 2014) and you must therefore set up a Romanian company, which buys the land. This is a fairly simple process and your lawyer can arrange it as part of the purchase procedure. It costs around RON1,500 (£300). **Many Romanians don't use a lawyer for buying and selling property, but it's vital for a foreigner to use a reputable English-speaking lawyer who's familiar with the procedures and possible problems with title.** The purchase contract (*contractul de vanzare-cumparare*) must be signed in the presence of a notary public, who endorses the contract and registers the new ownership with the Land Registry. Registration can take up to six months.

9

Fees

Notary fees and stamp duty amount to around 2 per cent of the purchase price. Legal fees can be anything from 2 to 10 per cent and an estate agent's fees are around 6 per cent, split equally between buyer and vendor. There's also a transfer tax (payable by the vendor), which varies according to the duration of ownership. If you've owned the property for less than three years, the charge is 3 per cent of its value up to RON200,000 (just over £40,000) and then a flat fee plus 2 per cent of the additional value. If you've owned the property for more than three years, the charge is only 2 per cent up to RON200,000 and a flat fee plus 1 per cent of the extra value. VAT on new apartments is charged at the standard rate of 19 per cent.

General Information

Getting There

Bucharest has two main airports: Băneasa, which is used by the budget airlines, and Otopeni, the largest airport in Romania, which is served by a variety of European and international airlines, and is the hub of the national airline, TAROM. The Black Sea resorts can be reached via an internal flight from Bucharest (around 35 minutes) or by road or rail (around four hours). The Transylvania region is also accessible by air from Bucharest (one hour) as well as by rail (eight hours). There's no airport at Brasov (the nearest city to the Poiana Brasov ski resort) but it can be reached by train in around two hours from Bucharest.

Băneasa (Aurel Vlaicu) International Airport: The airport is 10km (6mi) south of the city and in 2007 experienced a European low-cost airline 'invasion', although the only UK operator is Wizz Air, which flies from London Luton. This is set to change in 2007 and 2008, when it's thought that the number of low-cost operators flying to Bucharest will double. The majority of charter flights serving Bucharest use this airport.

Otopeni (Henri Coandă) International Airport: This is Bucharest's main airport and is north of the city. British Airways and TAROM have flights from London Heathrow.

Communications

Telecommunications in Romania are generally good in urban areas, but some rural areas have outdated or non-existent services. Romtelecom, the former state monopoly, is still the main provider, despite privatisation in 2003, and has been criticised for poor service and high call charges. Romania has a high rate of mobile phone use (98 per cent of the population) and internet use is increasing fast. The country code is 40 and international direct dialling (IDD) is available throughout the country.

Fixed-line Telephones: Romtelecom is the largest provider of fixed-line services (with a majority shareholding by OTE, the Greek telecommunications company; its main competitors are Astral Telecom and RDS.Tel. The majority of public phones accept only phone cards, which are widely available from post offices and kiosks.

Mobile Telephones: 98 per cent of the Romanian population use mobile phones. The two main mobile telephone providers are Orange (the largest operator) and Vodafone, while Cosmote Romania and Zapp mobile have a relatively small market share. All operate on the GSM network, and Orange and Vodafone also operate on the UMTS network.

Internet: There are around 15 internet service providers (ISPs) in Romania, some of which offer only dial-up and some both dial-up and high-speed (ADSL) connections. The largest are Romanian Cable Systems and Romanian Data Systems. There are plenty of internet cafes in Bucharest and all main towns, and the major hotels offer data ports with high-speed connections.

Postal Service: The Romanian postal service (Posta Romana) offers a variety of services, including an internet access service, PostNetAccess, at many of its major post offices. In 2005, it was announced that the Romanian postal service will be restructured and privatised by 2008.

9

The service is reasonably efficient, with post offices open from 7am to 7pm Mondays to Fridays and until 1pm on Saturdays, although some central post offices are open until 10pm. Letters to western Europe usually take around a week.

Crime Rate

Romania has low levels of serious and violent crime, but petty crime and tourist scams are rife, especially pick-pocketing on public transport. There's also a high level of institutional corruption, particularly in Bucharest.

Medical Facilities

Medical care and facilities aren't up to western European standards and medical supplies are limited outside the major cities. Romania introduced a social health insurance scheme in 1998 and all employed residents must contribute to the scheme. Visiting EU citizens can obtain free emergency treatment on production of a European Health Insurance Card (EHIC). Retired EU citizens are entitled to free or low-cost healthcare, although the system may not run efficiently yet because of Romania's recent membership of the EU. Other residents must have comprehensive medical insurance. Note, however, that Romania's first private hospital chain opened only in 2006 so private facilities are as yet embryonic.

Pets

As Romania is now a full EU member, it should operate the Pet Travel Scheme for pets coming from qualifying countries, although the procedures may take time to put into place. This means that there should be no quarantine period for pets from qualifying countries, but they must be identifiable by microchip or tattoo, have an EU Pet Passport and be vaccinated against rabies. All paperwork must be certified by a government-authorised vet.

Visas & Permits

Visas: Visas aren't required by EEA citizens and citizens of some other countries, including Australia, Canada, Japan and the US. Check with the nearest Romanian embassy about current visa requirements. Visitors must have a valid passport and sufficient funds to support themselves for stays of up to 90 days.

Residence Permits: For stays of longer than 90 days, EU citizens must apply for a registration certificate from the Romanian Authority for Aliens and, unless employed and therefore contributing to social security, show evidence that they can support themselves and have adequate health insurance. Permanent residence is granted after five years.

For non-EU citizens, residence is linked to employment or business activity and granted for the duration of an employment contract.

Work Permits: Work permits aren't required by EU citizens. For non-EU citizens they're required but difficult to obtain; as in the rest of the EU, they're granted only if an EU national isn't able to fill the post.

9

Reference

Useful Addresses

Romanian Embassy (UK), 4 Palace Green, London W8 4QD, UK (☎ 020-7937 9666, 🖳 www.londra.mae.ro).

Romanian Embassy (US), 1607, 23rd Street, NW 20008, Washington DC, US (☎ 202-332 4846, 🖳 www.roembus.org).

Romanian National Tourist Office (UK & Ireland), 22 New Cavendish Street, London W1M 7LH, UK (☎ 020-7224 3692, 🖳 www.romaniatourism.com).

Romanian National Tourist Office (US), 355 Lexington Avenue, 19th Floor, New York, NY 10017, US (☎ 212-545 8484, 🖳 www.romaniatourism.com).

EUROPE: SLOVAKIA

Background Information

Capital: Bratislava.
Population: 5m.
Foreign Community: The population is around 85 per cent Slovak and 10 per cent Hungarian. There are small communities of Roma and Ukrainians but very few UK or US residents.
Area: 48,845km^2 (18,860 mi^2).
Geography: Slovakia is a landlocked country, with the Czech Republic and Austria to the west, Poland to the north, Ukraine to the east and Hungary to the south. The landscape in northern and central areas is mountainous (the Carpathian mountain range runs across the north of country). The Tatra mountains, in particular the High Tatras, are a popular skiing destination, as well as the site of some of Slovakia's many beautiful lakes. The country's major river is the Danube, which runs along the south-west border with Austria and Hungary.
Climate: Slovakia has a temperate climate, with warm summers and cold, humid winters. Average rainfall is 4.8cm, much of it falling in summer. The coldest months are usually December and January, with average temperatures around -1C (30F), although in mountainous areas temperatures are often ten degrees lower. Heavy snowfall is common in winter, especially in the mountains, with around 130 days of snow at the highest points. The hottest months are July and August, with temperatures averaging 21C (70F), sometimes rising to 36C (97F).
Language: The official language is Slovak, spoken by some 84 per cent of the population. Hungarian is spoken by around 10 per cent and Roma and Ukrainian are minority languages. Many Slovaks understand German and Russian, and English is increasingly spoken, particularly in Bratislava.
Political Situation: Good. The former Czechoslovakia was under Communist control until 1989, and in 1993 the Czech Republic and Slovakia went their separate ways in an amicable split, sometimes known as the 'Velvet Divorce'. The two countries maintain close ties with each other and with many other eastern European countries. In 1998, much needed economic reforms were put into place and the country began a slow economic recovery. By 2002, Slovakia was achieving impressive levels of foreign investment and in 2004 the World Bank reported that the country had the world's most rapidly improving investment climate.

9

Slovakia is a parliamentary democratic republic, with a multi-party system. There's a President (currently Ivan Gašparoviè, elected in 2004) and a Prime Minister (currently Robert Fico, elected 2006), who is appointed by the President and must form a majority coalition government. The current coalition consists of Fico's centre-left Smer-SD party, the People's Party and the Slovak National Party. Slovakia joined the EU on 1st May 2004.

Finance

Currency

Slovakia's national currency is the koruna, introduced in June 1993 to replace the Czechoslovak koruna. It's abbreviated as SKK and is divided into 100 haliers. The currency joined the European Exchange Rate Mechanism II (ERM II) in 2005. Slovakia plans to adopt the euro on 1st January 2009.

Exchange Rate: £1 = SKK49.22.

Exchange Controls: There was extensive liberalisation of exchange controls when Slovakia joined the EU in 2004, although the Central Bank can intervene to control unacceptable swings in the exchange rate with major foreign currencies.

Cost & Standard of Living

Slovakia is experiencing strong economic growth, with low inflation (around 4 per cent) and the cost of living is considerably lower than in western Europe. Wages have been rising, thanks partly to foreign investment, particularly that of several foreign car manufacturers. In 2006, the average monthly wage was around SKK18,000 (£365). Nevertheless, according to recent press reports, Slovaks don't feel they earn reasonable salaries or have a high standard of living.

Taxation

Slovakia is one of several countries in eastern Europe to have introduced a flat rate of income tax, which has encouraged foreign investment and makes the country attractive to property buyers. The country's current economic success is also due in part to its lack of stamp duty and inheritance tax, and a favourable capital gains tax regime (see below). Slovakian tax residents are taxed on their worldwide income, non-residents only on income earned in Slovakia (such as rental income).

Personal Effects: Can be imported from any EU country without restriction or payment of duty.

Income Tax: Slovakia has a liberal tax system with a flat rate of 19 per cent on all income earned by residents, non-residents and companies.

Capital Gains Tax (CGT): Gains are considered as ordinary income and taxed at 19 per cent, but you're exempt if you've lived in a property for at least two years or have been the legal owner for at least five years.

Wealth Tax: None.

Inheritance & Gift Tax: None.

Value Added Tax (VAT): 19 per cent flat rate for companies with an annual turnover of more than SKK1.5m (£30,000). There's a reduced rate of 10 per cent on selected items, including medicines and medical equipment, and exports are exempt.

© Survival Books

© Survival Books

© Alan Smillie (www.shutterstock.com)

© dra_schwartz (www.istockphoto.com)

© Ushi Hering (www.shutterstock.com)

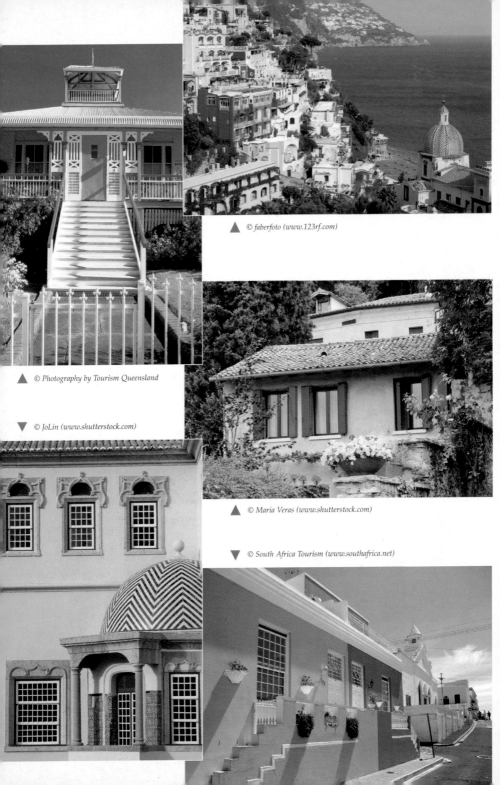

© faberfoto (www.123rf.com)

© Photography by Tourism Queensland

© JoLin (www.shutterstock.com)

© Maria Veras (www.shutterstock.com)

© South Africa Tourism (www.southafrica.net)

▲ © South Africa Tourism (www.southafrica.net)

▲ © Ales Liska (www.shutterstock.com)

▲ © New Zealand Tourism

▼ © Priyendu (www.bigstockphoto.com)

▼ © New Zealand Tourism

Property

Restrictions on Foreign Ownership & Letting

There are no restrictions on ownership or letting, but rental income must be entered on your annual tax declaration.

Market

Slovakia is one of Europe's emerging property markets, its favourable tax regime and impressive economic growth making it a tempting prospect for investors. It has a strategic position in central Europe, with good transport links to western Europe and the emerging eastern European markets. It's very close to Vienna (just 30 minutes via a new motorway) and many Viennese workers have been buying property in the Slovak capital and commuting across the border to work so that they can enjoy far lower property prices and favourable tax rates. Slovakia is also an attractive location for a second home, although so far it has mainly attracted those looking for capital investment. There's a shortage of good quality properties, however, so demand is outstripping supply – which is good news for buy-to-let investors, especially in Bratislava.

As in many of the other new EU member countries, property prices in Slovakia rose dramatically in anticipation of membership but have since stabilised. Slovakia and Slovenia probably have the best potential for growth and, according to analysts, Slovakia's economy and property market are at least the equal of those of the Baltic States (Estonia, Latvia and Lithuania).

Many properties in Bratislava are apartments, either new developments or uninspiring Communist-era blocks, although there are also attractive older houses. A similar mix of property is to be found in other parts of the country.

Areas

The focus of the market is Bratislava, but the Slovak mountains (the High Tatras) are also of interest, with good skiing in winter and spectacular hiking in summer. Property available there is limited, however, as there are building restrictions because the area is classified as a National Park.

Bratislava is the favourite location for foreign buyers, especially since the introduction of budget flights to the city in 2004 (see **Getting There**). It's also increasingly popular with tourists because of the attractive medieval Old Town and the city's position on the River Danube. Bratislava has a confusing array of districts but, in general, the closer you are to the Old Town, the more desirable (and more expensive) are the properties. The area has good rental potential, with plenty of foreign diplomatic staff and expatriate businessmen. Recently built properties are the most desirable, while older properties and those let to locals don't achieve such high rental returns.

Building Standards

Standards are usually high for new buildings, but many older buildings need extensive renovation and historic properties often need enormous investment to restore them to their former glory.

9

Cost

Prices in Bratislava start at around SKK3m (£60,000) for a two-bedroom apartment in need of renovation. For around SKK5m (£100,000) you can buy an older, characterful two-bedroom apartment close to the Old Town. A three-bedroom townhouse in the same area costs around SKK15m (£300,000) and a modern two-bedroom apartment in the city centre costs around SKK2.5m (£50,000). Attractive developments are being built along the Danube River, where one-bedroom apartments start at around SKK3m (£60,000) and are expected to have a high yield.

Properties in ski resorts range from SKK1.75m (£35,000) for a small apartment to around SKK7.5m (£150,000) for a large chalet.

Local Mortgages

Mortgages are available from European and some Slovakian banks at an interest rate of around 5 per cent. They're in korunas or euros and are usually up to around 70 per cent of the value of the property, although some banks offer up to 85 per cent. The period is up to 30 years, although the mortgage must be paid off before the borrower reaches 65. Banks charge an arrangement fee of between 0.3 and 1 per cent.

Property Taxes

There's a nominal annual property tax of around SKK1,500 (£30).

Purchase Procedure

Once a price is agreed, a preliminary sale agreement is signed and a deposit of 10 per cent paid. A lawyer must check title carefully and that the property is free of debts. As with other central and eastern European countries previously under Communist rule, title can be uncertain. If all is in order, the lawyer arranges certified translations of all paperwork because all contracts must be in Slovak. Once contracts are prepared and signed, the notary public registers the change of ownership at the Land Registry. The whole purchase procedure usually takes only around four weeks.

Off-plan Purchases: You sign a reservation contract and pay a non-refundable deposit of around 30 per cent. The remainder is paid at specified points during construction.

Fees

There's no stamp duty or property transfer tax in Slovakia, making purchase costs low in comparison with those of most other countries. Legal fees (including a notary's fees and translations) are usually a set price, around SKK20,000 (£400). It costs around SKK15,000 (£300) to register a property at the Land Registry. Properties less than five years old are subject to 19 per cent VAT if the vendor is VAT registered. An estate agent's fees are between 2 and 5 per cent but are paid by the vendor (although they're 'included' in the purchase price).

General Information

Getting There

Slovaki has two international airports (see below), but Bratislava is only two hours' drive from Vienna airport, which handles a wider range of international flights (thought mostly at higher prices).

Bratislava Airport: 9km (5.5mi) north-east of the city centre, this is Slovakia's main international airport and is served by two budget airlines: Ryanair (flights from Dublin and London Stansted) and SkyEurope (flights from Dublin, London Stansted and Manchester).

Poprad Airport: SkyEurope also has flights from London Stansted to Poprad airport, which is closer to the ski resorts in the High Tatra mountains.

Communications

Slovakian telecommunications have recently undergone extensive modernisation and privatisation, which has improved the quality of the telephone service and reduced the waiting time for lines. The main provider of fixed lines is T-Com, formerly the state-owned Slovak Telecom (majority owned by Deutsche Telekom). Mobile phone use is widespread, although private internet use isn't high. The country dialling code is 421 and international direct dialling (IDD) is available to most countries through three international exchanges.

Fixed-line Telephones: There's an extensive network of public telephones, particularly in Bratislava, some of which operate with coins and some with phone cards, available at newspaper kiosks. Not all public telephones allow calls to mobile phones or to foreign numbers.

Mobile Telephones: There are three main mobile telephone operators: O2 (run by the Spanish company Telefonica), Orange and T-Mobile (formerly Eurotel). All use the GSM 900/1800 system.

Internet: Internet use isn't widespread. Although around 90 per cent of businesses regularly use the internet, the percentage of private users is far lower (around 30 per cent) and internet cafes are few and far between, even in Bratislava.

Postal Services: Services, provided by Slovenska Posta, are usually efficient. Airmail to European destinations usually takes three or four days.

Crime Rate

Slovakia has a high rate of street crime, although this is usually non-violent, petty crime. There's widespread pick-pocketing and bag-snatching, particularly in popular tourist areas such as Bratislava Old Town and on public transport – thieves often work in pairs to distract their victims. Car crime is also rife, so it's recommended not to leave personal items in vehicles, even if they're locked.

9

Medical Facilities

Medical facilities in Slovakia underwent major changes in the '90s, dividing them into public and private. The quality and availability of medical services varies within the country, but there's a network of general hospitals, policlinics and medical centres. Employed residents contribute to a health insurance scheme, while visiting EU citizens can obtain free emergency treatment and free or low-cost medical treatment on production of a European Health Insurance Card (EHIC). Retired EU citizens are entitled to free or low-cost healthcare. Other residents and non-EU citizens must have comprehensive medical insurance.

Pets

As Slovakia is a full member of the EU, there's no quarantine system for pets, but they must be identifiable by microchip or tattoo, have an EU Pet Passport and be vaccinated against rabies. All paperwork must be certified by a government-authorised vet.

Visa & Permits

Visas: No visas are required for visits of up to 90 days by EEA citizens and citizens of certain other countries, such as Australia, Canada, Japan and the US. Contact your nearest Slovakian embassy to check.

Residence Permits: For stays of longer than 90 days, EU citizens must register with the local police department and be in possession of a passport or national identity card. EU citizens no longer need to apply for temporary residence permits, but must obtain permanent residence permits, which are granted for ten years, if planning to settle in Slovakia. If you don't plan to work, you must show evidence of sufficient income to support yourself.

Non-EU citizens are granted temporary residence permits for business or employment purposes for not more than two years, but these can be renewed on application. Applicants must be able to prove sufficient income to support themselves and, if relevant, that their employer is a resident and major investor in Slovakia.

Work Permits: Not required by EU citizens but required by non-EU citizens, along with a temporary residence permit (see above). Applications should be made via the Slovak embassy in your home country. Permits are granted by the labour authorities in Slovakia for one year initially but can be renewed for up to one year, depending on your employment situation.

Reference

Further Reading

The Slovak Spectator, Námestie SNP 30, PO Box 260, 810 00 Bratislava, Slovakia (☎ 2-5923 3300, 🖳 www.slovakspectator.sk). English-language weekly newspaper (also available online by subscription).

9 Useful Addresses

Embassy of Slovakia (UK), 25 Kensington Palace Gardens, London W8 4QY, UK (☎ 020-7313 6470, 🖳 http://dev.dracon.biz/embassy).

Embassy of Slovakia (US), 3523 International Court NW 20008, Washington DC, US (☎ 202-237 1054, 🖳 www.slovakembassy-us.org).

Slovakian Tourist Board (UK), 16 Frognal Parade, Finchley Road, London NW3 5HD, UK (☎ 020-7794 3263, 🖳 www.slovakiatourism.sk).

Tourist and Commercial Office of Slovakia (US), 10 East 40th Street, Suite 3606, New York, NY 10016, US (☎ 212-679 7045, ⌨ www.cometoslovakia.com).

Europe: SLOVENIA

Background Information

Capital: Ljubljana.
Population: 2m.
Foreign Community: Around 91 per cent of the population are Slovenian, communities from the former Yugoslavia comprising just over 6 per cent of the population. There are very few UK or US residents.
Area: 20,273km^2 (7,827mi^2).
Geography: Slovenia is in southern central Europe. It's an Alpine country, with a short Adriatic coastline in the south-west. Austria is to the north, Croatia to the south and east, Hungary to the north-east and Italy to the west. Its Alpine region stretches over much of the northern half of the country, adjacent to Austria and Italy, and contains the country's highest peak, Mount Triglav, at 2,864m (9,396ft), within a beautiful National Park. Around half of the country is forested and remnants of primeval forest remain – the largest in the southern Koèevje area. The Pannonian region in the east is fertile farmland, with extensive vineyards.
Climate: Slovenia has three climatic zones: the centre and north-west have long, cold Alpine winters and mild summers; the coastal region has a Mediterranean climate, with hot summers and mild winters; and the rest of the country has a continental climate, with cold winters and warm or hot summers. Average rainfall varies: it's around 100cm (39in) on the coast, but almost three times as much in the Alps. Average temperatures are -2C (28F) in January and 21C (70F) in July, although they can be around 10 degrees lower in mountain areas.
Language: The main official language is Slovenian, spoken by more than 90 per cent of the population. Hungarian and Italian are also official languages in areas close to the borders with those countries.
Political Situation: Very stable. Slovenia was part of Yugoslavia until it declared its independence in 1991 after a ten-day war. Slovenia made the transition from socialism to a market economy quickly and efficiently. It's the most prosperous of the ten countries that joined the EU in May 2004 and has achieved impressive economic growth, low inflation and low unemployment. It's a parliamentary democratic republic, with a President (currently Janez Drnovsek, elected in 2002), who has a largely ceremonial role, and a Prime Minister (currently Janez Jansa, elected in 2004), who heads a four-party coalition consisting of his own centre-right Slovenian Democratic Party, the New Slovenia Party, the People's Party and the Democratic Party of Pensioners. Slovenia is a member of NATO and joined the EU on 1st May 2004.

Finance

9

Currency

Slovakia adopted the euro (€) on 1st January 2007. It was the first of the ten countries which joined the EU in May 2004 to do so, having successfully met the criteria limiting public debt, budget deficit, interest rates and inflation.

Exchange Rate: £1 = €1.48.

Exchange Controls: Foreign transactions (by Slovenes or foreigners) must be carried out through an authorised commercial bank.

Cost & Standard of Living

Slovenia is one of the most affluent of the ten countries that joined the EU in 2004. Slovenes have high purchasing power but the cost of living is still well below that in western Europe. Rents in city centres average around €300 per month, and an average meal in a restaurant costs around €10. The minimum monthly wage is €522 and the average wage in Ljubljana is €800.

Taxation

Residents are taxed on their worldwide income and non-residents only on income earned in Slovenia. Compared with many of the country's neighbours, Slovenia imposes high taxes, and the country doesn't have the flat rate system that has been adopted by many countries in the region to boost foreign investment and the economy.

Personal Effects: Can be imported from any EU country without restriction or payment of duty.

Income Tax: There are three progressive rates: 16 per cent (up to €6,800), 27 per cent (up to €13,600) and 41 per cent (over €13,600). Rental income is also taxed at these rates. Income tax is paid throughout the year, in advance instalments.

Capital Gains Tax (CGT): For individuals, rates varying according to how long a property has been owned. CGT is levied at 20 per cent when the property has been owned for up to five years, 15 per cent between five and ten years, 10 per cent between 10 and 15 years, and 5 per cent between 15 and 20 years. You're exempt if you've owned a property for 20 years or more.

Wealth Tax: None.

Inheritance & Gift Tax: Rates depend on the relationship between donor and beneficiary, and the value of a property. Rates for spouses and children of the donor are between 5 and 14 per cent, for parents and siblings of the donor between 8 and 17 per cent, and others are taxed at rates between 12 and 39 per cent.

Value Added Tax (VAT): There's a standard rate of 20 per cent and a reduced rate of 8.5 per cent on selected items, including new buildings for residential purposes, agricultural products, food and pharmaceuticals. Exempt items include banking, financial and insurance services, and exports. Businesses with an annual turnover exceeding €25,000 must register for VAT.

Property

9 Restrictions on Foreign Ownership & Letting

Restrictions were removed for EU citizens when Slovenia became a full EU member in 2004, although the government retained a safeguard clause for up to seven years after accession allowing it to re-apply restrictions in certain circumstances – but it's unlikely you'd be subject to restrictions. Non-EU nationals must obtain permission from the Ministry of Justice, a process which takes around five months.

There are no restrictions on letting, but rental income must be included on your annual tax declaration.

Market

The Slovenian property market has only recently begun to take off, with around 15 per cent growth between 2004 and 2006. It's expected that this growth will continue, particularly since the country has recently adopted the euro and relaxed restrictions for EU property buyers (see above). Unlike the capitals of many of Slovenia's neighbours, however, Ljubljana isn't yet an attractive buy-to-let prospect because of a lack of development, the high price of property and the lack of local mortgages for foreigners (see **Local Mortgages** below). However, many other parts of the country have become popular with those looking for a second home with letting potential for tourists. The tourist industry is growing in many parts of Slovenia, particularly with people in search of good facilities for skiing and other outdoor pursuits. Indeed, Slovenia's beautiful Alpine landscape has been compared with Switzerland's.

Areas

Ljubljana has limited appeal because of its expensive property, despite the fact that it's an attractive city. The main areas of interest are the ski resorts in the north, close to the Austrian and Italian borders. These are popular all year, for skiing in winter and hiking, riding and other outdoor activities in summer. The most popular resort is Kranjska Gora, although areas around Lake Bled and Lake Bohinj are just as spectacular and less expensive. In the north-east, near the Austrian, Croatian and Hungarian borders, is the city of Maribor. It's known as Slovenia's second city and the surrounding area is popular for skiing as well as for its vineyards and thermal spas.

The short stretch of Adriatic coast has some attractive, Venetian-style towns such as Piran, but prices are high.

Building Standards

Standards are reasonable, although some older properties need extensive renovation.

Cost

One- and two-bedroom apartments in Kranjska Gora start at around €140,000, a three-bedroom chalet costs €230,000 and a four-bedroom house €410,000. A one-bedroom apartment close to Lake Bled costs around €170,000 and a three-bedroom chalet around €280,000. In Maribor, one-bedroom apartments start at €80,000 and three-bedroom apartments at €200,000.

In Ljubljana, two-bed apartments cost around €350,000 and luxury houses up to €1m.

9

Local Mortgages

Slovenian banks don't usually lend to non-resident foreigners, although this may change in the near future.

Property Taxes

There's an annual property tax of between 0.1 and 1 per cent of the value of a property, depending on what it's used for. There are generous exemptions for families and those who have carried out extensive renovation. There's also a variable land tax, set by local authorities.

Purchase Procedure

This is far simpler and quicker for EU citizens now that Slovenia is a full EU member, though non-EU citizens must still obtain permission (see **Restrictions on Foreign Ownership & Letting** above). Once a price is agreed, a preliminary contract is signed and a 10 per cent deposit paid. The buyer must then apply for a tax identification number (*EMSO*) which can be done through a lawyer. Searches are made at the Land Registry, which is a quick and efficient process in Slovenia and usually only takes two or three days. Slovenian law requires that all documents, including those from the Land Registry, insurance policies and sale contracts, must be translated by a court translator to ensure that all signatories are clear about what they're signing, so allow time and money for official translations. On completion, buyers and sellers must sign contracts in English and Slovenian. A new copy of the Land Registry entry is prepared and an official tax evaluation presented so that taxes can be collected on completion.

Fees

There's no stamp duty in Slovenia, but there's a property transfer tax of 2 per cent of the purchase price, usually paid by the vendor. Court administration fees are around €20. Lawyer's fees and translation costs are approximately €500. Estate agents' fees are controlled by law and cannot be more than 4 per cent of the property price and are usually split between the buyer and seller. VAT is charged on new buildings that will be used for residential purposes at 8.5 per cent; for any other use, the rate is 20 per cent.

General Information

Getting There

Slovenia's main airport, Brnik, is 26km (16mi) north of Ljubljana. It's served by scheduled (including budget) airlines, including the national airline, Adria Airways (flights to Birmingham, Dublin, London Gatwick and Manchester), and Easyjet, which flies from London Stansted. There's also an airport in Maribor, in the north-east, to which Ryanair flies from London Stansted.

9

Communications

Liberalisation of the telecommunications market in Slovenia began in 2001 to bring it into line with EU criteria but services still haven't been fully privatised, which has been criticized by the EU. The main operator is the former state-owned Telekom Slovenije (TS), whose service is of a reasonably high standard. Mobile phone use is very high and internet use is increasing. The country dialling code is 386 and international direct dialling (IDD) is available from private phones and public telephone boxes, which can be found in all central areas and post offices.

Fixed-line Telephones: In 2005, a second operator (Voliatel) entered the fixed-line market, finally bringing some competition, but the use of fixed lines has been decreasing in the last few years as mobile phone use increases. Most public phone boxes accept only phone cards, which can be bought from post offices and kiosks.

Mobile Telephones: Mobile phone use has increased rapidly in Slovenia, reaching around 95 per cent. There are three main operators: Mobitel (a subsidiary of TS), SI Mobil (partly owned by Vodafone) and Vega. All operate on the GSM 900/1800 network.

Internet: Around 90 per cent of businesses regularly use the internet and around 50 per cent of the population. The number of users continues to grow as costs fall. Internet cafes with wireless facilities are available in Ljubljana, although they're less common in other parts of the country.

Postal Services: Postal services are provided by Posta Slovenije and are usually efficient. Post offices are open from 7am to 7pm on weekdays and on Saturdays until 1pm, although the central post office in Ljubljana is open 24 hours. Airmail to European destinations usually takes three or four days.

Crime Rate

Slovenia has a low crime rate.

Medical Facilities

Since 1992, medical and healthcare facilities have come under the jurisdiction of the Health Insurance Institute of Slovenia (HIIS). The quality and availability of services is generally good and services are funded by compulsory social security contributions paid by employers and employees. Visiting EU citizens can obtain free emergency treatment and free or low-cost medical treatment on production of a European Health Insurance Card (EHIC), including treatment from a private doctor as long, provided he is contracted to the HIIS. Retired EU citizens are entitled to free or low-cost healthcare under reciprocal health agreements. Other residents and non-EU citizens must have comprehensive medical insurance.

Pets

As Slovenia is a full member of the EU, there's no quarantine for pets, but they must be identifiable by microchip or tattoo, have an EU Pet Passport and be vaccinated against rabies. All paperwork must be certified by a government-authorised vet.

Visa & Permits

9

Visas: Visas aren't required for visits of up to 90 days by EEA citizens and citizens of certain other countries, such as Australia, Canada and the US. Contact your nearest Slovenian embassy to check.

Residence Permits: For periods of longer than 90 days, EU citizens must register with the nearest administration unit of the Ministry of the Interior. They must then apply for a certificate of registered residence, which is linked to employment and business interests in Slovenia.

Anyone not employed in the country must show proof of income and adequate health insurance. After five years of uninterrupted residence, you may apply for a permanent residence permit.

Non-EU citizens are granted temporary residence permits for business or employment purposes, for a period of not more than one year, but the permits can be renewed on application, depending on circumstances. Applicants must be able to prove sufficient income and a permanent address. Applications should be made through the Slovenian embassy in your home country before arriving in Slovenia.

Work Permits: Not required by EU citizens but required by others, along with a temporary residence permit (see above). Slovenia has strict rules on the issuing of work permits to non-EU citizens. Applications should be made via the Slovenian embassy in your home country and, if granted by the labour authorities in Slovenia, permits are initially for one year. Permits can be renewed for up to a year, depending on your employment situation.

Reference

Useful Addresses

Embassy of Slovenia (UK), 10 Little College Street, London SW1P 3SH, UK (☎ 020-7222 5700, 🖳 www.gov.si/mzz-dkp/veleposlanistva/eng/london).

Embassy of Slovenia (US), 1525 New Hampshire Avenue NW 20036, Washington DC, US (☎ 202-667 5363, 🖳 www.gov.si/mzz-dkp/veleposlanistva/eng/washington).

Slovenian Tourist Office (UK), South Marlands, Itching Field, Horsham, West Sussex, R13 0NN, UK (☎ 0870-225 5305, 🖳 www.slovenia-tourism.si).

Slovenian Tourist Office (US), 2929 East Commercial Boulevard, Suite 201, Fort Lauderdale, FL 33308, US (☎ 954-491 0112, 🖳 www.slovenia-tourism.si).

EUROPE: **SPAIN**

Background Information

Capital: Madrid.
Population: 40m.
Foreign Community: Spain has a large expatriate community in its major cities and resorts, including many Americans, Britons, Germans, Scandinavians and other Europeans.
Area: 510,000km^2 (197,000mi^2).
Geography: The Spanish mainland is 805km (500mi) from north to south and 885km (550mi) from east to west, making it the second-largest country in western Europe (after France). The Balearic Islands off the east coast, comprising the islands of Majorca (*Mallorca*), Ibiza, Minorca (*Menorca*) and Formentera, cover an area of 5,014km^2 (1,936mi^2), while the Canary Islands, situated 97km (60mi) off the west coast of Africa, cover 7,272km^2 (2,808mi^2). Spain also has two North African enclaves, Ceuta and Melilla, administered by the provinces of Cadiz and Malaga respectively. The Pyrenees in the north form a natural barrier between Spain and France, while to the west is Portugal. To the east and south is the Mediterranean, although the extreme south-west is on the Atlantic Ocean. The southern tip of Spain is just 16km (10mi) from Africa, across the Strait of Gibraltar, a British territory claimed by Spain and a constant source of friction between Britain and Spain. Spain has 2,119km (1,317mi) of mainland coastline.

9

The country consists of a vast plain (the *meseta*) surrounded by mountains and is the highest country in Europe after Switzerland, with an average altitude of 650m (2,132ft) above sea level. The *meseta* covers an area of over 200,000km^2 (77,000mi^2), at altitudes of between 600 and 1,000m (2,000 and 3,300ft). Mountains fringe the coast on three sides, with the Cantabrian chain in the north (including the Picos de Europa), the Pénibetic chain in the south (including the Sierra Nevada) and a string of lower mountains throughout the regions of Catalonia and Valencia in the east. The highest peak on the mainland is the Pico de Mulhacén in the Sierra Nevada range (3,482m/11,423ft), the highest in Spain being Mount Teide (3,718m/12,198ft) on the Canary island of Tenerife.

Climate: Spain is the sunniest country in Europe and the climate (on the Costa Blanca) has been described by the World Health Organisation as among the healthiest in the world. Spain's Mediterranean coast, from the Costa Blanca to the Costa del Sol, enjoys an average of 320 days of sunshine per year. Mainland Spain has three climatic zones, Atlantic, continental and Mediterranean, in addition to which some areas, particularly the Balearic and Canary Islands, have distinct micro-climates. In coastal areas, there can be huge differences in the weather between the seafront and the mountains a few kilometres inland. On Majorca, rainfall varies from between 30 and 40cm (12 to 16in) in the south to over 1.2m (47in) in the north, and Minorca experiences strong winds in winter.

Language: Spanish, or more correctly Castilian (*castellano*), is the main language, although Basque (spoken by 2 per cent of the population), Catalan (17 per cent) and Galician (7 per cent) are also official languages in their respective regions. There are also a number of dialects, including *Mallorquin* (Mallorca), *Menorquin* (Minorca) and *Ibiçenco* (Ibiza). English is widely spoken in resort areas and the major cities.

Political Situation: Very good. The death of General Franco in 1975 heralded the end of 36 years of dictatorship. Spain became a parliamentary democracy in 1978 and now has, arguably, the most liberal constitution in western Europe. The country is a constitutional monarchy, with King Juan Carlos as head of state and the Prime Minister (currently José Luis Rodríguez Zapatero of the Socialist PSOE, elected 2004) as head of the government. The country has been a member of the European Union (EU) since 1986. The next parliamentary election is in March 2008.

Finance

Currency

Spain's currency is the euro (€).

Exchange Rate: £1 = €1.48.

Exchange Controls: None. However, the government requires notification of the movement of certain funds to limit money-laundering and tax evasion. Foreign currency transfers should be through a registered bank.

Cost & Standard of Living

9

Spain's standard of living has been increasing along with its economic prosperity, although its high inflation rate and lack of competitiveness against its main trading partners are areas for concern. In the last decade or so, inflation has brought the prices of many goods and services in Spain in line with those of most other European countries, although many things remain cheaper, including property and rents, food, alcohol, dining out and general entertainment. Except in the major cities, where the higher cost of living is generally offset by higher salaries, the cost of living is lower than that of many other European countries, particularly in rural and coastal areas.

Taxation

Tax laws which came into force on 1st January 2007 are designed, among other things, to combat tax evasion and prevent money-laundering. Personal taxation rates and thresholds have changed and the new laws also affect the rates of capital gains tax for residents and non-residents (see below). Residents in Spain pay tax on their worldwide income and non-residents on Spanish income, although non-residents living in another EU country can opt to be taxed in Spain on all their income under certain conditions. Individuals who have been sent by their company to work in Spain can choose to be taxed as a non-resident (subject to certain conditions) for the first six years of the assignment and are subject to a flat tax rate of 24 per cent.

Personal Effects: EU citizens planning to take up permanent or temporary residence in Spain are allowed to import furniture and personal effects free of duty and taxes, provided they were purchased tax-paid within the EU or have been owned for at least six months. Non-EU nationals must have owned and used them for at least six months to qualify for duty-free import. A vehicle owned and used for six months in another EU country can be imported into Spain tax and duty free. VAT (16 per cent) and duty (10 per cent) are payable on vehicles imported from outside the EU. A registration tax (*impuesto municipal sobre circulación de vehículos*) of 13 per cent of a vehicle's current market value is payable after six months.

Income Tax: From 2007, personal income tax is levied on a sliding scale from 24 per cent (on annual income up to €17,360) to 43 per cent (on annual income over €52,360). Non-resident property owners in Spain are liable for income tax at a flat rate of 24 per cent on income arising in Spain, including property rent. All property owners in Spain (residents and non-residents) must have a fiscal number (*número de identificación de extranjero/NIE*) – see **Purchase Procedure** below.

Capital Gains Tax (CGT): Capital gains tax (*impuesto sobre incremento de patrimonio*) is payable on the profit from sales of certain assets in Spain, including property. From 1st January 2007, the CGT rate for residents and non-residents is 18 per cent. In addition, non-resident sellers must pay a withholding tax of 3 per cent at the time of sale to cover any tax liabilities. An annual deduction (for inflation) of 11.11 per cent for properties owned before 1994 continued to apply until 20th January 2006. Since this date, sellers have had to pay CGT at 18 per cent on the portion of their profits generated after 20th January 2006. CGT isn't payable when you're a resident of Spain and sell your principal home, provided the proceeds are used to buy a new home in Spain within two years. Individuals over 65 are exempt from CGT, provided they've owned the property for over three years.

Wealth Tax: Residents and non-resident property owners in Spain are subject to a wealth tax (*impuesto extraordinario sobre el patrimonio*, known simply as *patrimonio*) on their worldwide assets. Residents may deduct around €110,000 as an individual allowance and an additional €150,000 if part of their assets is a principal residence. These deductions are per person, so married couples may each deduct the individual allowance and the allowance on their share of the principal residence. Assets worth up to €167,00 above these exemptions are taxed at between 0.2 and 2.5 per cent (the highest rate on assets above €10.7m). Wealth tax and income tax combined may not exceed 60 per cent of your total taxable income. Non-residents must pay wealth tax on the total value of their assets in Spain at the same rates as residents, but aren't entitled to any deductions.

Inheritance & Gift Tax: Inheritance tax (*impuesto sobre sucesiones y donaciones*), which is paid by the beneficiaries and not by the deceased's estate, depends on the relationship between the donor and the recipient, the amount inherited, and the wealth of the recipient, and varies from 0.2 to 34 per cent. There are allowances for close relatives.

9

Value Added Tax (VAT): The standard rate of VAT (*IVA*) is 16 per cent. There are reduced rates of 7 per cent (e.g. drinks other than alcohol, fuel, water, communications, medicines, transport, hotel accommodation, restaurant meals and theatre and cinema tickets) and 4 per cent (e.g. food and books). New property is subject to VAT at 7 per cent. Certain goods and services are exempt, including healthcare (e.g. doctors' and dentists' services), educational services, insurance and banking. VAT doesn't apply in the Canary Islands (where there's a similar tax, but at lower rates) or in the enclaves of Ceuta and Melilla.

Property

Restrictions on Foreign Ownership & Letting

There are no restrictions on foreign ownership or letting, but an 'imputed' letting tax is payable by some property owners (see **Property Taxes** below), irrespective of whether you let a property. Tax is payable on actual letting income at a flat rate of 24 per cent.

Market

The Spanish property market is well established, having 'emerged' more than 30 years ago, when foreigners first began buying second homes in the sun. Foreign buyers, particularly the British, but also Germans and Scandinavians, have had a huge impact on the Spanish market, enormous numbers of them buying second and retirement homes. More recently, the country has attracted younger families who want to live abroad permanently, Spain coming a close second to Australia among the most popular relocation spots. The market has had more than its fair share of boom but has never quite gone down as far as bust, although experts continue to predict a crash. The main boom was in the late '90s and, although the market stabilised into the new Millennium, prices were still increasing at between 15 and 20 per cent per year. Since around 2004, the market has slowed significantly and regional price differences have become more marked. In popular coastal areas, there's a problem of oversupply, particularly with new developments, although the rate of construction continues unabated.

Prices in the major cities have remained fairly stable, being less dependent on foreign buyers and the vagaries of the world economic climate, although Madrid and Barcelona have some of Europe's most expensive property. Nevertheless, those cities and their suburbs are seeing increasing interest from investors because of their rental demand, which, in Barcelona for example, can be all year.

Spain undoubtedly suffered in the '80s from a reputation for 'crooked' agents and developers and, more recently, it has had a bad press as a result of the 'Valencia Land Grab Law' and corruption scandals involving property and several local governments, notably in Marbella on the Costa del Sol. The country is becoming a safer place to buy, but it's still plagued by unregistered and inexperienced 'estate agents', red tape and a plethora of property-related taxes.

Areas

The most popular locations with foreign buyers continue to be the coastal areas and the Spanish islands. They're favourites with all types of buyers, not just those looking for a holiday home, but also retirees and, increasingly, younger families who want to start a new life abroad. The most popular areas include the following:

Balearic Islands: Ibiza is the third-largest of the three islands and is famous throughout Europe for its nightlife. Majorca is the largest and most popular island with tourists and has a large foreign population, primarily Britons and Germans, while Minorca is far quieter and less developed.

Canary Islands: Situated around 60 miles off the north-west coast of Africa and 700 miles from Spain, this official Spanish region is separated into two provinces: Las Palmas, in the east, which consists of the islands of Gran Canaria, Fuerteventura and Lanzarote; and Santa Cruz de Tenerife in the west, the greener of the two provinces, consisting of the islands of Tenerife, La Gomera, El Hierro and La Palma. The islands have a large foreign community and Tenerife and Gran Canaria are the most popular tourist islands; if you prefer something quieter, stay away from the traditional tourist spots and choose the north or west coasts of Tenerife, for example. The Canary Islands enjoy sun almost all year, so property there has good rental potential. However, property prices slowed significantly in 2006, so it isn't the place for those wishing to make a short-term capital investment.

Costa Blanca: Part of the Valencia region in the east of the country. The most popular locations for tourists and foreign residents are the coastal areas in the province of Alicante, although inland areas are proving increasingly popular as people tire of the *costas* and seek out the 'real Spain'.

Costa del Sol: Situated in the province of Malaga in the region of Andalusia and stretching across the south-west and south of the country from Gibraltar to Almería, the Costa del Sol remains eternally popular with holidaymakers, retirees and second-home owners, despite relentless construction. Many foreign buyers turned their attention inland some years ago, but properties with a sea view still command higher prices. The Costa del Sol is Europe's sunniest region during the winter, although if you want really hot weather and wish to swim in the sea during winter without freezing, the only choice is the Canaries.

Other Coastal Areas: Increasingly, other *costas* are proving popular. They're less developed and many retain their traditional charm, despite the relentless advance of developers, keen to install cranes and bulldozers on any untouched piece of land. They include the Costa de Almería, east of the Costa del Sol; the Costa Brava, close to Barcelona in the north-east, which has become a stylish holiday destination (as long as you avoid the traditional tourist spots such as Lloret de Mar) and attracts many affluent people from Barcelona as well as tourists from all over Europe, making the rental potential good, although the traditional holiday season is far shorter than on the south coasts; the Costa Cálida, between Almería and Alicante in the south-east, where prices have risen considerably in the last few years, despite the fact that vast swathes of the countryside are covered in plastic sheeting, which protects fruit and vegetables grown for export; the Costa Dorada, south of Barcelona; and the Costa de la Luz, west of Gibraltar on the Atlantic coast. The Costa de Almería and Costa Dorada are less developed and contain some beautiful old towns and good beaches.

Cities: The major cities, particularly Barcelona, Madrid and, more recently, Valencia, are also increasingly popular with foreigners, especially those who want a buy-to-let investment or a second home for short breaks.

Barcelona is one of Spain's most popular cities, thanks to its vibrant culture and efficient infrastructure. It's a favourite with tourists, particularly as a short-break destination. The most popular locations, particularly if you're interested in buy-to-let investment, are in the Old City (*Ciutat Vella*) and the Born district, both of which are close to the main tourist attractions. Barcelona's suburbs are a favourite with expatriates and locals who commute into the city. The most popular areas are Gràcia, San Cugat and the most prestigious part of the city, Sarrià, in the high area of Barcelona.

In Madrid, there are plenty of rental possibilities, both short term to tourists and long term to locals, expatriate businessmen and students. Property in the city centre often consists of older apartment blocks with no parking facilities; the suburbs, although more expensive, are therefore more popular and likely to provide a better rental yield. Chamartín and La Moraleja, north of the city, are the most sought-after areas.

9

Many buyers turned their attention to the city of Valencia when it was chosen to host the America's Cup in 2007. That aside, it's a cosmopolitan city, which is served by several budget airlines, and it has benefited from major improvements to its infrastructure thanks to the America's Cup.

Other Areas: Buyers are realising that there's much more to Spain than the Mediterranean coastal resorts and the islands, and regions such as Galicia, Asturias and Cantabria in the north and inland cities such as Seville and Granada have increasing numbers of enthusiasts. Prices are naturally lower in these areas, there's beautiful unspoiled countryside and, in the north of the country, a stunning, rugged coastline, an abundance of traditional houses rather than new developments and fewer foreign tourists.

Building Standards

Building standards vary enormously, from high to low. Care must be taken when buying property, whether new or old, and unless you're absolutely confident that it's sound you should have a survey.

Cost

Prices in Spain vary considerably with the region and town, as well as with the size and quality of the property. All types of property are available: new developments and resales, as well as country houses, small and large, for renovation. Resale properties are often good value in Spain, particularly in resort areas, where the majority of low- to medium-price apartments and townhouses are sold fully furnished. A Spanish government report on property prices in 2006 showed that central and northern Spain experienced the highest price rises in the country, while coastal areas lagged well behind.

Balearic Islands: Majorca commands the highest prices, although it's still possible to find a two-bedroom apartment in a popular tourist area for around €180,000 and small villas start at around €350,000. Less expensive properties can be found in Palma, the stylish capital of Majorca. Prices on Minorca are lower, as it's the quietest island. Apartments start at around €150,000 and larger villas at around €300,000. Ibiza's prices are similar to those on Majorca, reflecting the wealth of visitors to the island. The rental season on Ibiza is short but very lucrative, as demand is high from wealthy tourists and seasonal workers.

Canary Islands: Property in resort areas on Tenerife starts at around €150,000 for a one-bedroom apartment and you must pay around €400,000 for a four-bedroom duplex. In the quieter areas of Los Gigantes on the west coast, a two-bedroom apartment costs around €150,000, while a four-bedroom villa costs around €400,000. Property on Gran Canaria, the other popular tourist area, is around the same as on Tenerife.

Costa Blanca: Prices are generally lower than on the Costa del Sol and showed only a small increase in 2006. The northern half of the region (north of Alicante), where development is more restrained, is the most expensive, and prices start at around €150,000 for a two-bedroom apartment, while a three-bedroom villa with a private pool costs around €400,000. In the south of the Costa Blanca, prices are lower, but the area is far more developed and construction appears to be continuing unabated. In popular areas such as Benidorm and Torrevieja, a one-bedroom apartment costs from around €70,000 and villas start at around €150,000, depending on the number of bedrooms and size of plot. In areas inland of the Costa Blanca, it's still possible to buy very inexpensive properties, especially those in need of renovation, which cost as little as €40,000, although you must allow around twice as much to make them habitable.

Costa del Sol: This part of the coast is divided roughly into western, central and eastern areas. Prices are highest in the west, e.g. in Sotogrande, Estepona and Marbella, falling as you

9

head eastwards, through central areas such as Fuengirola and Torremolinos, past Malaga to the eastern end of the coast at Nerja. In exclusive Sotogrande, two-bedroom apartments start at around €400,000, many of the larger villas costing several million euros. In central areas, a two-bedroom apartment costs around €250,000 and a three-bedroom villa around €750,000, while in Nerja a three-bedroom villa costs around €600,000.

Other Coastal Areas: The Costa Cálida in Murcia is home to the exclusive La Manga Club resort, where prices for a two-bedroom apartment start at around €200,000, townhouses at €300,000 and villas at €450,000. Prices on the Costa Brava reflect the wealth of the people it attracts and even tiny apartments cost from €160,000, while villas start at around €400,000 and rise to more than €1m in some areas. On the Costa de Almería, new two-bedroom apartments cost around €90,000, three-bedroom townhouses around €120,000, while on the Costa Dorada new one-bedroom apartments start at around €190,000, two-bedroom apartments at €200,000 and three-bedroom resale villas at €240,000.

Cities: Madrid has some of the highest property prices in Spain, but they depend on the position and letting potential of the property. A two-bedroom apartment in the centre of the city costs around €300,000, while larger apartments and modest family homes cost at least €500,000. Houses in the fashionable suburbs of Madrid are very expensive, spacious family homes costing around €1m or more.

Although slightly less expensive than Madrid, Barcelona comes a close second. In the Old City, prices for small apartments start at around €200,000 and in the suburbs of Gràcia and San Cugat a three-bedroom apartment costs around €500,000, while a larger, family home is approaching €1m. But there's year-round rental potential – short-term tourist lets in the city centre, long-term lets to businessmen in the suburbs.

Prices in Valencia are increasing quickly (at around 15 per cent in 2006), but they're still only around half those of Madrid and Barcelona and, surprisingly, there's no shortage of supply. Prices for an apartment in the city start at around €100,000 and a three-bedroom house in the suburbs costs around €300,000.

Other Areas: In 2006, average price increases in Asturias (12.3 per cent), Cantabria (11.7 per cent) and Galicia (19.3 per cent) were among the highest in Spain. Prices are still comparatively low, however, a three-bedroom country house costing around €80,000, while a five-bedroom house can cost as little as €100,000.

Local Mortgages

Mortgages are freely available from Spanish banks for principal and second homes, up to a maximum of 80 per cent of the purchase price (70 per cent for non-residents). Many Spanish mortgages can now be repaid over 25 years, depending on the lender, but the mortgage must be repaid before you reach 75. Shop around, as there's a variety of financial institutions offering all kinds of mortgages, including foreign banks with Spanish branches. British bank Lloyds TSB offers mortgages on Spanish properties to non-residents only through its subsidiary company, Own Overseas. Applicants should be over 21 and UK residents and homeowners. Own Overseas offers three types of mortgage secured on Spanish properties: a variable rate mortgage, a fixed rate, which reverts to the variable rate after an agreed period, and a euro variable rate, which tracks the base rate of the European Central Bank.

9

Property Taxes

Property tax (*impuesto sobre bienes inmuebles/IBI*) in Spain is based on the fiscal value (*valor catastral*) of a property, which is assessed by the local authority and may be different from a property's actual or market value. **It's important to check the fiscal value of a property, as a number of taxes are linked to it, including income, wealth and inheritance tax.** In general, property tax rates in Spain are from 0.4 per cent to 1.1 per cent of the fiscal value according to whether your land is classed as urban (*urbana*) or agricultural (*rústicas*).

An 'imputed' letting tax at 2 per cent of the *valor catastral* is payable by non-residents on all Spanish property and by residents on second homes, even if they aren't letting the property. If you do let your property and make a non-resident tax declaration, this tax doesn't have to be paid.

Finally, there's an annual fee for rubbish collection and mains drainage (*basura y alcantarillado*), which depends on the size of the property and is charged by the local authority.

Purchase Procedure

All property buyers must have a foreigner's identification number (*número de identificación de extranjero/NIE*), obtainable from any national police station, and all transactions must be overseen by a notary (*notaio*). A notary is an independent representative of the Spanish government whose job it is to ensure that both parties understand what they're agreeing to, that any taxes due are paid and that the transfer of ownership is properly registered. He doesn't act for either buyer or vendor.

Once a buyer and vendor agree on a price, a reservation contract (*documento de reserva*) can be signed and a goodwill deposit paid to secure the property for a short period (usually around a month). Neither of these is mandatory and, if you withdraw for any reason, this deposit is forfeited. Once you're ready to go ahead with the purchase, you sign a purchase contract (*contrato privado de compraventa*) and pay a deposit, which is usually 10 per cent. This creates a legally binding agreement between you and the vendor; you cannot back out unless the vendor agrees. You should therefore ensure that the contract is a *contrato de arras*, which means that you may cancel, although you forfeit your deposit, and if the vendor cancels, he must pay you double the deposit. If there's any doubt whether you can complete the purchase within a specified time, you should include an option to purchase (*opción de compra*), which gives you the exclusive right to purchase within a specified time but releases you from your obligation to buy after that time, although you lose your deposit. **Ensure that you know precisely the terms under which a deposit will be repaid or forfeited before paying it and that it will be held in a separate bonded (escrow) account.**

Completion takes place when you sign the deed of sale (*escritura de compraventa*) in the notary's office and pay the balance (usually by banker's draft). The law requires that a notary checks the property register (not more than 48 hours before making the title deed) for any debts against a property or other restrictions which would 'inhibit' a sale. A copy of the *escritura* is usually available for your scrutiny before the official signing and, if you don't understand it, you should obtain an official translation. You can give a representative in Spain general power of attorney (*poder general*) so that he can sign a contract on your behalf. Even if you're present yourself for the signing, your lawyer should also be present to ensure that there aren't any last-minute changes that you haven't agreed to.

When the contract is signed, the notary will give you a certified copy (*primera copia*) of the deed. A notarised copy is lodged at the property registry office (*registro de la propiedad*) and the new owner's name is entered on the registry deed. You should ensure that the *escritura* is registered **immediately** after signing it, if necessary by registering it yourself. **Registering your ownership is the most important act of buying property in Spain, as until it's registered – even after you've signed the contract before a notary – charges can be levied against it or someone else can register it in their name.** Following registration, the original deed is returned to you, usually after a few months.

9

Buying property in Spain has been the subject of much adverse publicity, some commentators even going so far as to advise people not to buy in Spain at all. It should be noted, however, that most purchasers who have had problems didn't suffer so much from fraud, but from the insolvency of developers (or their own carelessness). Developers are now required to have financial guarantees and the legal situation has been tightened to prevent fraud, although the possibility must never be ignored. Nevertheless, it cannot be emphasised too strongly that anyone planning to buy (or sell) property in Spain (or anywhere else) must take expert, independent legal advice. One of the Spanish laws that property buyers should be particularly aware of is the law of subrogation, whereby property debts, including mortgages, local taxes and community charges, remain with a property and are inherited by the buyer. Checks must be carried out both before signing a preliminary contract and before signing the deed of sale. If you get into a dispute over a property deal, it can take many years for it to be resolved in the Spanish courts, and even then there's no guarantee that you'll receive satisfaction.

Off-plan Purchases: When buying a property off plan, take care when signing a reservation or option contract that it isn't a binding purchase contract. **It's also important to ensure that the developer is financially secure and that any money paid is protected if he goes bust.**

Fees

The fees payable when buying a property in Spain amount to around 10 per cent of the purchase price. They include a transfer tax (*impuesto de transmisiones patrimoniales*/ITP) on resale properties of between 6 and 7 per cent, depending on the regional government. There's no transfer tax on new properties, but 7 per cent VAT (*IVA*) is payable. Stamp duty of between 0.5 and 1 per cent (depending on location) is payable on the first sale of a property. Legal fees are usually around 1 to 2 per cent of the purchase price for an average property. The notary who officiates at a sale is paid a fixed fee based on a sliding scale, depending on the amount of land, the size of the building(s) and the price, which usually amounts to between 1 and 2 per cent of the declared value. The property registration fee is usually between 1 and 1.5 per cent of the declared value. A land tax (*plus valía*) on the increased land value since the last sale is also payable and should be paid by the vendor (but you should confirm this). Most fees are based on the declared purchase price of a property.

General Information

Getting There

Spain is easy to reach by air and sea, and boasts an enormous choice of charter and scheduled flights from a variety of European destinations.

There's no shortage of flights to all the main coastal areas and major cities. British Airways and the national airline, Iberia, are the major operators, but there are also plenty of budget airlines and charter operators, including Bmibaby, Easyjet, GB Airways and Ryanair. Routes are too numerous to list, but the airports for each region and the main airlines serving them from the UK and Ireland are detailed below.

Balearic Islands: Majorca airport (*Aeropuerto de Palma de Mallorca*) is 8km (5mi) east of Palma and during the summer is one of Europe's busiest airports. The main airlines serving Majorca are Bmibaby, British Airways, Easyjet, First Choice Airways, Flyglobespan, Jet2, Monarch Airlines, My Travel Airways, Thomsonfly and XL Airways.

Minorca airport is relatively small and is served by Easyjet (Bristol, Liverpool, London Gatwick, and Newcastle), Flyglobespan (Edinburgh and Glasgow), GB Airways (London Gatwick) and Monarch Airlines (London Luton and Manchester).

The smallest island, Ibiza, has the least flights and they're generally seasonal. The main airlines are Bmibaby (from Cardiff and East Midlands), Easyjet (from across the UK),

Flyglobespan (Edinburgh and Glasgow), Jet2 (Belfast, Leeds and Manchester) and Monarch Airlines (Birmingham, London Luton and Manchester).

Canary Islands: The most popular of the Canary Islands, Tenerife, has two airports. Tenerife North (known as Los Rodeos), 11km (7mi) from Santa Cruz de Tenerife, is within easy reach of many popular resorts and is used mainly by budget and charter airlines and for connecting flights within Spain. It's served by GB Airways, Ryanair and Thomsonfly. Tenerife South airport (known as Reina Sofia) is approximately 10km (6mi) from the popular resorts of Los Cristianos and Las Americas, and is mainly a tourist airport. Airlines include Aer Lingus, First Choice Airways (flights across the UK), GB Airways, Jet2, Monarch Airlines, Thomas Cook Airways and Thomsonfly.

Gran Canaria has an international airport on the east of the island, around 25km (15mi) from most of the popular tourist resorts. It has two terminals and is served by a number of charter and scheduled airlines, including Aer Lingus, Excel Airways, First Choice Airways, GB Airways, Monarch Airlines and Thomsonfly.

Costa Blanca: Alicante International airport is 9km (5.5mi) from the town and is the main airport serving the Costa Blanca and Murcia. 80 per cent of its passenger traffic is international and a new terminal is being built (expected completion 2009) to cope with increasing numbers of passengers. It's served by a variety of airlines, including Aer Lingus, Easyjet, Flyglobespan, Jet2, Monarch Airlines, My Travel Airways, Ryanair and Thomsonfly.

Costa del Sol: Malaga International airport is the main airport serving the Costa del Sol. It's 8km (5mi) south-west of Malaga, close to all the popular tourist resorts. It has connections to over 60 countries and two terminals, with a third is under construction (expected completion 2008). Airlines serving Malaga include Aer Lingus, Bmibaby, Easyjet, Flybe, Flyglobespan, GB Airways, Jet2, Monarch Airlines, Ryanair and Thomsonfly.

Other Costas: The Costa Almería has an international airport, around 10km (6mi) east of the city of Almeria, served by Aer Lingus (Dublin), Easyjet (London Gatwick and Stansted), Jet2 (Leeds/Bradford and Newcastle), Monarch Airlines (London Luton and Manchester) and Ryanair (Dublin and London Stansted).

Murcia airport, 27km (17mi) south of the city, serves the Costa Cálida (although many travellers use Alicante airport because it has a wider choice of flights). It's a small airport, used mainly by charter and low-cost airlines, including Bmibaby (Birmingham and Cardiff), Easyjet (Bristol and London Gatwick), Flyglobespan (Aberdeen and Edinburgh), Jet2 (regional UK airports), Monarch (Birmingham and London Gatwick) and Ryanair (Irish and UK airports).

The Costa Brava and Costa Dorada are both served by Barcelona international airport (see below).

Cities: Barcelona (El Prat) airport is Spain's second-largest, 10km (6mi) from the city centre. It's currently undergoing considerable expansion, and a new terminal will open in 2009. Airlines flying to Barcelona include Aer Lingus (Cork and Dublin), Bmibaby (Birmingham), British Airways (London Gatwick and Heathrow), BA Connect (Birmingham), Easyjet (Bristol, Liverpool, London Gatwick, Heathrow, Luton and Stansted and Newcastle), Flyglobespan (Aberdeen, Edinburgh and Glasgow), Iberia (London Heathrow), Monarch Airlines (Manchester) and Thomsonfly (Coventry and Cardiff).

Madrid Barajas International Airport, north-east of the city centre, is the largest airport in Spain and the hub of the national airline, Iberia, used by more than 45m passengers in 2006. Easyjet flies into Terminal One from Bristol, Edinburgh, Liverpool, London Luton and Gatwick, as does Ryanair from Dublin, East Midlands and Shannon airports. Aer Lingus (Cork and Dublin), British Airways (London Gatwick and Heathrow) and Iberia (London Heathrow) fly to Terminal Four. There are seasonal flights with Iberworld from a wide variety of UK regional airports.

Valencia airport is 9km (5.5mi) west of Valencia and is the main airport for business travellers to Valencia. It was recently expanded to handle the increased traffic for the America's Cup 2007. An increasing number of budget airlines are operating to Valencia, including Easyjet (Bristol, London Gatwick and Stansted), Jet2 (various UK regional airports) and Ryanair (Dublin, East Midlands and London Stansted).

9

Northern Spain: Locations in northern Spain are accessible from Bilbao airport or the ferry ports of Bilbao and Santander. Bilbao airport is close to the French border in the Basque country and is served by a number of European airlines, including Aer Lingus (Dublin), Easyjet (London Stansted) and Iberia (London Heathrow).

There are ferry services from Portsmouth to Bilbao and from Plymouth to Santander. The port of Bilbao is 15km (9mi) west of the city centre, while the port of Santander is in the autonomous community of Cantabria, on the north coast of Spain, and is well positioned for Asturias to the west and the Basque country to the east.

Communications

Communications in Spain are highly developed, with a large number of telephone landlines and extensive mobile and internet use. The former state monopoly, Telefonica, continues to provide the majority of services, controls much of the infrastructure and must still install lines. It's often criticised for slowness and poor customer service. It can take weeks, sometimes months, to have a telephone and internet connection installed, especially in remote areas. Telefonica's main competitors are Euskaltel, which offers services in the north of Spain (the Basque country), Jazztel and ONO. All offer fixed-line, mobile and internet services. The country dialling code is 34 and international direct dialling (IDD) is available worldwide.

Fixed-line Telephones: Public telephone boxes (*cabinas*) are plentiful and accept coins and phone cards, which are available from tobacconists'. In main cities and coastal areas, there are also phone cabins (usually combined with an internet services) from which you can make international calls at reasonable rates.

Mobile Telephones: There's widespread use of mobile phones in Spain and they operate on GSM and UMTS networks. There are four main mobile phone providers: Movistar (Telefonica), Orange España, Vodafone España and Yoigo.

Internet: Internet services in Spain are sophisticated, with a wide range of dial-up and high-speed (ADSL) access providers. There's plenty of competition among providers, who offer a range of packages. There are internet cafes in all major towns and cities.

Postal Services: The Spanish postal service, known as Correos, has improved dramatically in recent years but is still somewhat unpredictable, particularly in remote areas. Post offices are usually open from 9am to 2pm, Mondays to Fridays, and on Saturday mornings, although some post offices in popular tourist areas open for longer hours. Letters to European destinations usually take around three to four days but more from some areas. Central post offices have more frequent collections.

Crime Rate

Spain's crime rate is among the lowest in Europe, although, like most European countries, it has increased dramatically over the last decade. Violent crime is rare, although muggings and burglaries have increased in resort areas. Petty crime, such as handbag snatching, pick-pocketing and theft from vehicles, is widespread throughout Spain. You should **never** leave anything on display in your car, including your stereo, which should be removed when parking in cities and resorts. Burglary has become an increasing problem, particularly for holiday homeowners. It's necessary to take comprehensive measures to make your property as thief-proof as possible and not to leave valuables or money lying around (a home safe is recommended).

9

Medical Facilities

Medical facilities in Spain vary but are generally excellent, particularly in resort areas and major cities, although they can be limited in rural areas. There are English-speaking Spanish and foreign doctors and dentists in resort areas and major cities. Spain has a national health service, funded by mandatory social security contributions. If you're an EU citizen visiting Spain, you must produce a European Health Insurance Card (EHIC) to qualify for free or low-cost treatment under reciprocal EU agreements. Retired EU citizens resident in Spain are also covered by reciprocal health agreements, but on arrival they must complete the appropriate forms and provide evidence of social security contributions in their home country to obtain a social security card. If you aren't covered by the public health service, private health insurance is essential; it's recommended in any case if you want the widest choice of practitioners and the best treatment without having to wait.

Pets

Spain is part of the EU and therefore doesn't operate a quarantine system for pets coming from 'qualifying countries'. However, they must be identifiable by a microchip or tattoo, have an EU Pet Passport and be vaccinated against rabies. All official paperwork must be issued by a government-authorised vet.

Visas & Permits

Visas: Visas aren't required for visits of up to 90 days by citizens of EEA countries or a number of other countries, including Australia, Canada and the US. Check with a Spanish embassy or consulate. Citizens of non-exempt countries must obtain visas before arriving in Spain.

Residence Permits: Residence cards are no longer required by EU citizens who wish to stay in Spain longer than 90 days. However, they must still register in person at a national police station, where their details are entered in the central registry of foreigners (*registro central de extranjeros*). Registration formalities are completed on the spot as long as you can present a valid passport or national identity card. It's recommended to carry some form of photographic identification in case you're asked to produce it.

Non-EU citizens require a residence card and, if necessary, a work permit (see below), to live and work in Spain. Check with a Spanish embassy about requirements before arriving in Spain.

Work Permits: Not required for EU citizens but required for non-EU citizens. Applications must be made to the Ministry of Labour and Social Affairs and work permits are usually valid for five years, depending on the type of employment. Permits are renewable, depending on your employment situation.

Reference

Further Reading

Buying a Home in Spain, David Hampshire (Survival Books). Everything you need to know about buying a home in Spain.

Costa Blanca News, C/Alicante 9, Polígono Industrial La Cala, Finestrat, Alicante, Spain (☎ 96-585 5286, 🖳 www.costablanca-news.com). Weekly English-language regional newspaper. Also available online.

9

Costa del Sol News, C/Las Moriscas Local 10, Avda Juan Lusi Peralta, 29629 Benalmádena Pueblo, Malaga, Spain (☎ 95-244 8730, 💻 www.costadelsolnews.es). Weekly English-language regional newspaper. Also available online.

Earning Money from your Spanish Home, Joanna Styles (Survival Books). How to make your Spanish home pay its way.

Island Connections (💻 www.ic-web.com). Fortnightly English-language newspaper issued in the Canary Islands, also available online.

Living and Working in Spain, David Hampshire (Survival Books). Everything you need to know about living and working in Spain.

Living Spain, Albany Publishing, R&J Offices, New Cut East, Ipswich, Suffolk IP3 0EA, UK (☎ 01234-710 992, 💻 www.livingspain.co.uk). Bi-monthly Spanish lifestyle and property magazine.

Making a Living in Spain, Anne Hall (Survival Books). Everything you need to know about making a living in Spain.

Spain Magazine, The Media Company Publications, 21 Royal Circus, Edinburgh EH3 6TL, UK (☎ 0131-226 7766, 💻 www.spainmagazine-co.uk). Monthly Spanish lifestyle magazine.

Spanish Magazine (now part of **Homes Worldwide Magazine**), Merricks Media, Units 3 & 4, Riverside Court, Lower Bristol Road, Bath BA2 3DZ, UK (☎ 01225-786 800, 💻 www.merricksmedia.co.uk).

Sur in English, Diario Sur, Avda. Doctor Marañón, 48, 29009 Málaga, Spain (☎ 95-264 9741, 💻 www.surinenglish.com). Free weekly newspaper available in southern Spain. Also available online.

You and the Law in Spain, David Searl (Santana Books).

Useful Addresses

Spanish Embassy (UK), 39 Chesham Place, London SW1X 8SB, UK (☎ 020-7235 5555, ✉ mbespuk@mail.mae.es).

Spanish Embassy (US), 2375 Pennsylvania Ave, NW, Washington, DC 20037, US (☎ 202-452 0100, ✉ embespus@mail.mae.es).

Turespaña (Spanish National Tourist Office, UK and Ireland), PO Box 4009, London W1A 6NB UK (☎ 020-7486 807, 💻 www.tourspain.co.uk).

Turespaña (Spanish National Tourist Office, US), Brickell Avenue 1395, 33133 Miami, US (☎ 305-358 1992, 💻 www.okspain.org).

Useful Websites

Spanish Property Insight (💻 www.spanishpropertyinsight.com). Excellent website offering independent advice about all aspects of the Spanish property market and Spanish property purchase procedure.

Spain For Visitors (💻 www.spainforvisitors.com). Useful general information about visiting Spain and Spanish life.

9 EUROPE: SWITZERLAND

Background Information

Capital: Berne.
Population: 7.5m.

Foreign Community: Switzerland has a lot of foreign residents – around 20 per cent of the total population, and higher in cities such as Geneva. There are large numbers of expatriates from France, Germany, Italy, Portugal, Spain and the former Yugoslavia, and a significant number from the UK and the US.

Area: 41,288km^2 (16,100mi^2).

Geography: Switzerland is in the central Alpine region of Europe and has borders with five countries: Italy to the south, Austria and Liechtenstein to the east, Germany to the north and France to the west. Switzerland is Europe's highest country and the Alps, which are mainly in the centre of the country, reach altitudes of over 4,000m (around 13,000ft), the highest point being the Dufour Peak of the Monte Rosa (4,634m/15,203ft) and the lowest Lake Maggiore (193m/633ft above sea level). The Swiss Alps are the source of the Rhine and Rhône rivers and are crossed by the St Gotthard, Grimsel, Furka and Oberalp passes.

Climate: It's difficult to generalise about the Swiss climate, as it varies considerably from region to region (probably no country in Europe has such diverse weather patterns in such a small area). The Alps, which extend from east to west, form a major weather division between the north and south of the country, and separate weather forecasts are usually given for each area. The climate north of the Alps is continental, with hot summers and cold winters, although prolonged periods when the temperature is below freezing are rare during the daytime (unless you live on top of a mountain). South of the Alps in Ticino, a mild Mediterranean climate prevails and even in winter it's significantly warmer there than elsewhere in Switzerland. Spring and autumn are usually mild and fine in most areas, although it can be dull and wet in some regions.

Language: Switzerland has three official languages: German, French and Italian. Rhaeto-Romanic (Romansch), which is spoken by around 60,000 people in the canton of Graubünden, is a national but not an official language. English is widely spoken in Switzerland.

Political Situation: Switzerland is the most politically stable and democratic country in the world. The Swiss constitution is unique in that it's a confederation of 26 cantons, all of which enjoy considerable autonomy, and there are three levels of government: federal, cantonal and communal. The most unusual aspect of Switzerland's government is that it allows its people direct or representative democracy, with all important decisions made by the cantons and the people themselves through referenda. The country is governed by the Swiss Federal Council, which is elected annually and consists of seven members, headed by a President, who undertakes official duties but isn't head of state or government and has no more power than other members of the Federal Council. The federal government is run by the four main parties: the conservative Liberal Democratic Party, the centre-right Christian Democratic Party, the populist Swiss People's Party and the left-wing Social Democratic Party. The next federal election is due in October 2007. The Swiss voted against joining the European Economic Area (EEA) in 1992, as it was seen by many as the first step to joining the EU. There's a division between, on the one hand, German and Italian speakers, who mostly oppose membership of the EU, and on the other French speakers, who are largely in favour. Despite this, Switzerland's main trading partners are EU countries and it has a number of bilateral agreements with the EU, which means that the country's laws are gradually changing to align it with the EU.

Finance

Currency

Switzerland's currency is the Swiss franc (SFr). Historically, the Swiss franc has been a strong currency and since 2003 its exchange rate with the euro has been stable and any currency fluctuations are linked to those of the euro.

Exchange Rate: £1 = SFr2.40.

9

Exchange Controls: None and you aren't obliged to register foreign loans or capital received from abroad, although an anti-money laundering law obliges banks and other financial institutions to investigate clients involved in 'suspicious' transactions. There are no distinctions between resident and non-resident accounts.

Cost & Standard of Living

Switzerland has one of the highest costs of living in the world, but also has one of the highest standards of living, the highest GDP per head and the highest per capita spending power. Geneva and Zurich are among the most expensive cities in the world. Switzerland's economy has become even healthier in recent years, but salary differences between the highest and the lowest paid are widening. The average monthly salary in Zurich is around SFr6,000 (£2,500).

Taxation

Everyone (whether Swiss or foreign) is subject to Swiss income tax if they're resident in Switzerland for over 90 days and aren't involved in an economic activity, or resident for over 30 days while involved in an economic activity. Non-residents are liable to pay Swiss income tax only on income from property and business activities in Switzerland.

Personal Effects: No duty is payable on personal effects (including a car) that have been used and owned for at least six months, although they should be imported within three months of taking up residence or buying a holiday home. However, an inventory must be provided, along with any required entry permits, full identification and copies of purchase contracts or rental agreements.

Income Tax: Income tax is levied by the federal government (direct federal tax) and by cantons and communities. In 2007, the maximum federal income tax rate was 11.5 per cent. Maximum canton tax rates are up to 30 per cent (they're often much lower) and there's a maximum rate of 40 per cent for federal, cantonal and communal taxes combined. Non-working residents, e.g. retirees, can arrange to pay a lump sum in some cantons, which is often negotiated individually and is called a 'fiscal deal'. Applicants must have a net worth of not less than SFr2m (£835,000) and mustn't undertake any economic activity.

Capital Gains Tax (CGT): No capital gains is tax levied at federal level, and cantons differ in their treatment of capital gains, although they're usually taxed as general income. Capital gains tax on property depends on the amount of profit and the length of ownership.

Wealth Tax: Wealth tax is levied on residents and non-residents by all cantons (there's no federal wealth tax). The rate is progressive and depends on the canton and community where you live, but in most cases it's around 1.5 per cent of your assets above a certain level.

Inheritance & Gift Tax: Inheritance and gift taxes aren't levied by the federal government, but by all cantons except Schwyz (which levies neither tax) and Lucerne (which doesn't have a gift tax). Non-residents are liable for inheritance tax only if the donor was a Swiss resident at the time of death or the property is situated in Switzerland. A number of cantons don't levy this tax if the beneficiary is a spouse or direct descendent. Inheritance tax, which may be as low as 4 or 5 per cent, varies depending on the canton and the relationship of the beneficiary to the deceased.

Value Added Tax (VAT): The standard rate of VAT is 7.6 per cent and there are reduced rates of 3.6 per cent on hotel accommodation and 2.4 per cent on food and drink, medicines, books, newspapers and water.

Church Tax: If you're a member of one of the state-recognised religions (Catholic or Protestant), you must pay a church tax (*Kirchensteuer/impôt du culte*) based on your salary, your community and your religion, which can be anything between 0 and 2.3 per cent. It's levied to cover church expenses and varies from canton to canton.

Property

Restrictions on Foreign Ownership & Letting

Restrictions have been relaxed for EEA citizens resident in Switzerland but some remain; they depend on the type of residence permit held. Those with a C permit (permanent residence) can buy property without restriction, while those with a B permit (temporary annual residence) must obtain permission from their local canton authorities. In addition, US citizens who live and work in the country are exempt from restrictions if they plan to use a property as a primary residence, and citizens of any country who become permanent residents and make a tax arrangement with the local authorities are likewise exempt. Most tourist areas (i.e. ski resorts) limit non-EEA citizens to a single property and authorisation must be given by the canton concerned.

Restrictions on non-resident foreign ownership have also recently been relaxed and further relaxation is under discussion in Parliament, although no laws have yet been approved to that effect. Currently, a complex authorisation process must be undergone, though this varies considerably from canton to canton. Non-resident foreigners (including EU citizens), must be financially independent and may buy one property only, which is restricted to 200m^2 (2,200ft^2) of living area (non-living areas may be any size). All cantons have an annual quota of authorisations. The annual quota for second homes sold to non-resident foreigners is around 1,400 for the whole of Switzerland, the majority in the cantons of Grisons, Ticino, Valais and Vaud. In general, there are fewer opportunities to buy in German-speaking cantons than in French-speaking cantons. No quotas are set for Basle City, Geneva or Zurich and it's generally impossible for non-residents to buy property in the major cities. Elsewhere, in recent years quotas haven't been filled because of the recession, high property prices and resale restrictions. Since 1997, non-Swiss nationals have been permitted to purchase property for business purposes, which has encouraged some investors, but you aren't permitted to buy a property in the name of a foreign company, although joint-ownership is allowed.

There are also restrictions on property sales to prevent property speculation; these also vary with the canton. For example, in the canton of Valais, foreigners may sell within a year to a Swiss national but aren't allowed to sell to another foreigner for ten years. In Ticino, there's a three- to five-year restriction on resales. **Before committing yourself to a property, check the resale rules carefully, as they're currently undergoing significant change.**

Regarding letting, a foreign owner must occupy a Swiss property for a minimum of three weeks a year and rentals must be shorter than a year (they're typically for up to 11 months).

Market

Until recently, the Swiss property market was virtually non-existent because of the high cost of property and restrictions on foreign ownership (see above). The property market has been stimulated by the gradual lifting of restrictions and low interest rates, and some foreign investors are showing an interest, although the Swiss market has a long way to develop. Many Swiss homes are built for rental, as home ownership among the Swiss is low (only around 35 per cent). The main investment interest is in the ski resorts, where properties are usually new apartments and chalets, although investors shouldn't expect to make rapid gains. **Buying in Switzerland should be seen as a long-term commitment, as restrictions on sales (see above) and high prices often make it difficult to sell a property quickly.**

9

Areas

Switzerland is synonymous with skiing and some of the most popular ski resorts are in cantons where property buying restrictions have been relaxed. Despite this, restrictions vary even from village to village within a canton. In general, the French- and Italian-speaking cantons are more accommodating than the German-speaking ones. In the famous resort of Verbier, which is within the canton of Valais, it's fairly easy for a foreigner to buy property, while in neighbouring resorts, such as Crans-Montana, Saas-Fee and Zermatt, it's more difficult. The canton of Vaud in the west is home to the lakeside town of Montreux and Villars, only a short drive from Geneva airport and boasting its own golf course. Ownership rules in Vaud are more liberal, but prices are higher. Ticino, which is an Italian-speaking canton in the southern Alps with beautiful lakeside towns, also has relatively liberal rules.

Building Standards

Swiss building standards and the quality of materials, fixtures and fittings used are among the highest in the world.

Cost

Swiss property is among the most expensive in the world. In the exclusive resort of Verbier (in the Valais canton), prices start at around SFr1.2m (£500,000) for a two-bedroom apartment.

Prices are lower in Saas-Fee in the same canton, where a three-bedroom chalet costs around SFr600,000 (£250,000).

Villars, in the canton of Vaud, is slightly more expensive than Saas-Fee. Two-bedroom apartments there cost around SFr700,000 (£300,000) and three-bedroom chalets around SFr1m (£400,000). In the Ticino region, a two-bedroom apartment costs from SFr650,000 (£270,000).

Local Mortgages

Swiss mortgages are available from local banks (in Swiss francs only). Banks lend between 60 and 80 per cent of the purchase price, offering low interest rates compared with the rest of Europe, although rates may be higher for non-residents. A mortgage in Switzerland is usually split between a first mortgage (60 to 65 per cent of the price) and a second mortgage (10 to 15 per cent), repayable at different interest rates. The first mortgage is never normally repaid, as you pay only the interest, while the second mortgage is repaid over 10 to 20 years. You must provide proof of income (which can include rental income) and loans are usually over between 30 and 35 years but must be repaid before the borrower reaches 70.

9

Property Taxes

Some cantons charge an annual property tax based on the value of a property determined by the tax authorities. Rates are between 0.2 and 0.3 per cent of the value, depending on the location of the property.

Purchase Procedure

The process of buying a property in Switzerland is among the most efficient and secure in the world. However, you must obtain authorisation to purchase from both the cantonal authorities and the Federal Department of Justice and Police (see **Restrictions on Foreign Ownership & Letting** above). Property sales in Switzerland are handled by a public notary (*Notar/notariat*), who acts for both the vendor and the buyer. Contracts are written in the local language (French, German or Italian) and a certified translation is provided if necessary. A 10 per cent deposit is paid when the preliminary contract is signed. The purchase contract is always contingent on the buyer obtaining a mortgage (if necessary). On completion of the purchase and registration of ownership, legal fees and a transfer tax (*Übertragungssteuer/impôt sur les transferts*) amounting to around 5 per cent of the purchase price are payable to the notary. The title deed must be registered at the local land registry (which takes just a few days) and the Central Land Registry in Bern.

Fees

Fees vary from canton to canton but usually total around 5 per cent of the purchase price and include transfer tax, notary's fees and land registry fees. VAT at 7.6 per cent is included in the price of new properties.

General Information

Getting There

Switzerland's main airports are Basel-Mulhouse, Geneva and Zurich.

Basel-Mulhouse: One of the few airports in the world which is operated by two countries, France and Switzerland. It's technically on French soil, but is conveniently close to the French, German and Swiss borders. British Airways operates flights from London Heathrow, Easyjet flies from Liverpool, London Luton and Stansted, and Swiss European Airlines flies from London City and Manchester.

Geneva International Airport: Situated 5km (3mi) from the city, with its northern limit on the Swiss-French border, the airport can be easily reached from both countries, and there are good transport connections (bus, rail and road) from the airport. The airport is served by a large number of European airlines, both 'regular' and budget, including Aer Lingus (Dublin), Bmibaby (Birmingham, Cardiff, Manchester and Nottingham), British Airways (London Gatwick and Heathrow) and Easyjet from a number of regional UK airports as well as London Gatwick, Luton and Stansted, and Edinburgh and Glasgow. Flybe has flights from Birmingham, Exeter and Southampton, while Flyglobespan flies from Edinburgh.

Zurich International Airport: Switzerland's largest international airport, with excellent transport connections (particularly rail) to many parts of Switzerland. Airlines operating from Zurich include Aer Lingus (Dublin), British Airways (London City, Gatwick and Heathrow), Easyjet (London Luton) and Swiss International Airlines (London Heathrow).

9

Communications

Switzerland enjoys excellent domestic and international communications services. Mobile and internet use is widespread and services are efficient and sophisticated. Until 1998, the Swiss fixed telephone market was dominated by the state provider, Telecom PTT, now called Swisscom, which continues to fight the government's efforts to open the market further and so still enjoys the largest market share for fixed, mobile and internet services. The country dialling code is 41 and international direct dialling (IDD) is available worldwide.

Fixed-line Telephones: International calls are less expensive with a prepaid calling card, which can be used from any kind of telephone, including mobile phones and public phone boxes. Public phone boxes are hard to find in Switzerland, however, because of the popularity of mobiles, but they're still found in post offices, airports and railways stations. Most accept only phone cards, which you can buy from post offices or Swisscom shops.

Mobile Telephones: A very high percentage of the Swiss population uses mobile phones and there are three main providers and a number of smaller ones, offering good rates. The big players are Orange, Sunrise and Swisscom, which has the best network coverage in the country but charges the highest rates. All three operate on the GSM network and Swiss SIM cards are available to use in your own mobile phone.

Internet: Internet access is widespread in Switzerland and there's a wide range of internet service providers (ISPs) offering dial-up and broadband connections. Internet cafes are common, particularly in the cities, and many shops and call centres have terminals for use by their customers.

Postal Services: Swiss Post offers an efficient and modern postal service, available in English, French, German and Italian, as well as financial services and online shopping. Post offices are open from 7.30am to 6pm Mondays to Fridays, and 7.30 to 11am on Saturdays, although post offices in city centres have longer opening hours. Letters sent within Switzerland often arrive on the same day and those to Europe usually take two or three days.

Crime Rate

The crime rate in Switzerland is among the lowest in the world. Crimes against property (e.g. homes and cars) are particularly low and violent crime is rare. There's some pick-pocketing and bag snatching in popular tourist areas, airports and railway stations.

Medical Facilities

Medical facilities in Switzerland are among the best in the world, although also some of the most expensive. Private health insurance is compulsory and anyone who stays in Switzerland for more than three months must take out at least basic health insurance – you may be asked for proof of cover. You must arrange this yourself, even if you're employed, as your employer doesn't do it for you. A number of companies offer health insurance, so shop around for the best prices. You don't need to arrange insurance if you're in Switzerland working for an international company or you're a diplomat. EU citizens visiting Switzerland may use a European Health Insurance Card (EHIC), although you may have to pay in full for treatment and claim a refund.

9 Pets

There's generally no quarantine for animals in Switzerland. All dogs and cats over five months old must have an international health certificate stating that they've been vaccinated against rabies. You must have an official letter stating that your pet was in good health before the vaccination, which must be dated at least 30 days and not more than one year before entering Switzerland. Certificates are accepted in English, French, German and Italian. Dogs and cats under five months of age may be imported from many countries without a vaccination but require a veterinary attestation of their age and good health. Once in Switzerland, pets must be registered with the authorities within 14 days of arrival and in some cantons a dog licence is required. Contact the local cantonal veterinary office for advice.

Visas & Permits

Visas: No visas are required by citizens of EU countries and citizens of some other countries, including members of the European Free Trade Association (Iceland, Liechtenstein and Norway), Australia, Canada and the US, who may stay in Switzerland for up to three months, provided they have a valid passport or national identity card.

Residence Permits: If you intend to stay in Switzerland for more than three months, you must register with the local authority within eight days of entering the country. Residence permits are required and are closely linked to employment. They're difficult to obtain by the non-employed (euphemistically called 'leisured foreigners' by the Swiss authorities) and permits are normally issued only to those over 60 (i.e. pensioners) or people of independent means – particularly the **very** rich (and famous). You're required to furnish proof that you have sufficient assets or income to live in Switzerland (usually a statement from your bank) and to have sufficient health insurance. There are a variety of residence permits, but the main ones are Type B (valid for five years for EU/EFTA nationals and one year for others) and Type C (a settlement permit, usually granted after five to ten years' residence to EU/EFTA citizens and ten years to other nationals). The Type B permit is linked to employment and is initially granted if you can show that you have an employment contract for at least a year, after which it's extended for up to five years, as long as the employment continues.

Work Permits: Each canton has an annual work permit quota. Citizens of EU/EFTA countries benefit from bilateral agreements between the EU and Switzerland and have the same rights to jobs as Swiss nationals. If you're a citizen of one of the original 15 member countries of the EU, Cyprus or Malta, you no longer require a work permit but must obtain a residence permit. Citizens of other EU countries require work permits until 30th April 2011. For contracts of between three months and a year, you receive a residence and work permit for the duration of the contract. No residence or work permits are required for seasonal jobs lasting up to three months.

Work permits are required by citizens of all other countries, but they're difficult to obtain and the labour authorities give preference to highly qualified people.

Reference

Further Reading

Living and Working in Switzerland, David Hampshire (Survival Books). Everything you need to know about living and working in Switzerland.

George Mikes Introduces Switzerland, Raffael Ganz (Andre Deutsch).

The Perpetual Tourist, Paul N. Bilton (Bergli Books).

Switzerland for Beginners, George Mikes (Andre Deutsch).

Ticking Along With The Swiss, Dianne Dicks (Bergli Books, Rümelinplatz 19, CH 4001, Basle, Switzerland (☎ 61-373 2777, 🖳 www.bergli.ch).

Hello Basel, Hello Bern and Hello Zurich (three separate magazines), Network Relocation Ltd (🖳 www.network-relocation.com). English-language magazines for expatriates living in these three cities.

9

Swiss News, Köschenrütistr. 109, 8052 Zürich, Switzerland (☎ 44-306 4700, 💻 www. swissnews.ch). Monthly English-language newspaper with Swiss news and events.

Useful Addresses

The British Residents' Association of Switzerland (BRA), Case Postale 55, Au Bret, CH-1617, Remaufens, Switzerland (☎ 021-728 6255, 💻 www.britishresidents.ch).
   Swiss Embassy (UK), 16-18 Montagu Place, London W1H 2BQ, UK (☎ 020-7616 6000, 💻 www.eda.admin.ch/london).
   Swiss Embassy (US), 2900 Cathedral Ave, NW, Washington, DC 20008, US (☎ 202-745 7900, 💻 www.eda.admin.ch/washington).
   Switzerland Tourism (UK), Switzerland Travel Centre, 1st floor, 30 Bedford Street, London WC2E 9ED, UK (☎ 0800-100 20030, ✉ info.uk@switzerland.com).
Switzerland Tourism (US), Switzerland Tourism, Swiss Center, 608 Fifth Avenue, New York, NY 10020–2303, US (☎ 212-757 5944, ✉ info.usa@switzerlandtourism.com).

Useful Websites

The Federation of Anglo-Swiss Clubs (FASC, 💻 www.angloswissclubs.ch).
Swiss Info (💻 www.swissinfo.org). Switzerland's news and information platform.
Swiss Style (💻 www.swissstyle.com). Business, financial, health and legal issues.
Swiss Tourism (💻 www.myswitzerland.com).
Swiss World (💻 www.swissworld.org). Information portal about the country.

EUROPE: TURKEY

Background Information

Capital: Ankara.
Population: 70m.
   Foreign Community: Turkey doesn't have a large expatriate population, although in recent years the country has become popular for holiday homes with western Europeans, and the foreign community is growing.
   Area: 774,815km^2 (299,179mi^2).
   Geography: Turkey is in the south-east extremity of Europe and some 95 per cent of the country is technically in Asia. The European part is west of the Bosporus, linking the Sea of Marmara to the Black Sea. Istanbul, on the west bank of the Bosporus, is Turkey's largest city, with a population of around 5.5m. The capital, Ankara, is in the middle of the Anatolian peninsula, a large part of which is mountainous. Turkey has borders (which were established only in 1923) with Armenia, Bulgaria, Georgia, Greece, Iran, Iraq and Syria, and some 8,000km (around 5,000mi) of coastline – around half on the Mediterranean and Aegean Seas and half on the Black Sea. Many parts of Turkey lie on a major seismic fault line and the country is liable to earthquakes and tremors, particularly in the east. In 1991, an earthquake east of Istanbul, measuring more than 7 on the Richter Scale, killed 18,000 people.
   Climate: Turkey is a huge country with a variety of climates, ranging from temperate in the Black Sea region to continental in the centre and Mediterranean on the south coast. The Aegean, Marmara and Mediterranean coasts have a typical Mediterranean climate, with hot

9

summers (over 300 days of sunshine a year), mild winters and low rainfall. The Black Sea coast has a temperate climate, with warm summers, mild winters and fairly high rainfall. Anatolia's climate is generally cold in winter (with snow in the east) and hot in summer (mild in the east), most rain falling in winter in the south-east (which also has relatively mild winters). The average maximum temperature in the popular holiday town of Antalya on the Mediterranean coast ranges from 10C (50F) in January to around 28C (82F) in July and August. Average daytime January and July temperatures in the major cities are: Ankara 0/23C (32/73F), Istanbul 5/23C (41/73F) and Izmir 9/28C (48/82F).

Language: The main language is Turkish, spoken by some 86 per cent of the population, most of the remainder speaking Kurdish (11 per cent) and Arabic (2 per cent). Some English is spoken in tourist areas and main cities, and many Turks speak German as a result of having worked in Germany.

Political Situation: Despite a volatile political history, Turkey began a new era of civilian rule in 1983, since when it has been relatively stable. However, Turkey has a poor record of maintaining democracy, which it's striving to improve in order to achieve EU accession, although many experts believe the country won't meet EU requirements until around 2015. Turkey is also plagued by internal unrest (e.g. from the Kurds, who are seeking their own state, and Islamic militants) and has poor relations with some of its neighbours. It has a poor human rights record, tainted in particular by its brutal treatment of the Kurds. Turkey has historically had poor relations with Greece, which were exacerbated by Turkey's military occupation of northern Cyprus in 1974. The country began EU membership negotiations in 2005, but talks were suspended in 2006 over border disputes between the Republic of Cyprus and the Turkish-controlled northern sector of the island.

The country is a parliamentary democracy with a President and a Prime Minister, the latter heading a Council of Ministers. The President is currently Ahmet Necdet Sezer, who was elected in 2000 for a seven-year term. The Prime Minister is Recep Tayyip Erdogan, of the conservative Islamic party, the AKP, elected in 2003 for a four-year term, when his party won an absolute majority. The military traditionally has a powerful influence on government, although it's gradually being reduced, in compliance with EU demands. Turkey is a founding member of the United Nations and the Organisation for Economic Cooperation & Development (OECD).

Finance

Currency

Turkey's currency is the new Turkish lira (*Yeni Türk Lirasi*/YTL). The currency changed from the old Turkish lira on 1st January 2005.

Exchange Rate: £1 = YTL2.73.

Exchange Controls: The Central Bank of Turkey regulates exchange controls and the Treasury authorises only certain banks to process foreign exchange transactions. Property buyers must provide proof that funds were imported from abroad.

Interest Rate: Interest rates are high (a base rate of around 14 per cent in early summer 2007, although housing loans could be over 20 per cent), but in February 2007 Turkey introduced a new mortgage law, which it's hoped will stabilise the mortgage market and bring rates down.

9

Cost & Standard of Living

Turkey has traditionally suffered from persistent high inflation, partly due to its reluctance to allow privatisation and foreign investment. Matters begin to improve in the '80s and '90s, but the resulting economic growth was accompanied by serious recessions and financial crises, the last in 2001. However, following reforms initiated since 2001, inflation and unemployment have dropped dramatically and there has been increased confidence from investors as government controls on foreign trade have been gradually reduced. There's a considerable income gap between households and regions in Turkey, and salaries are low in comparison with those of western Europe. The minimum gross monthly wage in January 2007 was YTL562 (£245). Turkey still has a low standard of living and cost of living, though basic foodstuffs and other necessities are inexpensive. On the other hand, luxuries and imported items (including cars) are expensive.

Taxation

Personal Effects: Personal effects and household goods (including a car) may be imported duty-free by permanent residents, provided they aren't intended for commercial use. You may have to prove residence, with details of your address or a purchase or rental contract. Non-residents may have to pay import duty on certain items.

Income Tax: Income, including salaries, rent and interest, is taxed at progressive rates between 15 and 35 per cent, although since 1st January 2007 rental income (from residential property only) has been subject to an exemption of YTL2,300 (£800). Rental income above this amount must be declared at your local tax office. If you're employed, there's a PAYE system.

Capital Gains Tax (CGT): For properties purchased (i.e. registered) before 1st January 2007, CGT is levied if the property is sold within four years. For those purchased after this date, the tax is due if the property is sold within five years. CGT is charged at income tax rates (see above), but the first YTL6,400 (£2,300) of any gain is exempt.

Wealth Tax: None.

Inheritance & Gift Tax: Inheritance (succession) tax is payable by the beneficiary. It's levied at between 1 and 30 per cent, depending on the relationship between the beneficiary and the donor or deceased. There are generous exemptions for direct family members. When property is inherited, there's a charge of 0.9 per cent of the value of the property to transfer it to the name of the beneficiary at the land registry office.

Value Added Tax (VAT): The standard rate of VAT (*KDV*) is 18 per cent, with reduced rates of 8 and 1 per cent. New properties are liable for VAT at 18 per cent (1 per cent for an area of less than 150m^2). Property rental payments are also subject to VAT at 18 per cent.

Other Taxes: A 'special consumption tax' (*SCP*), which is effectively a green tax and payable on goods which affect the environment, security and health, and certain luxury items, is levied at varying rates.

Property

Restrictions on Foreign Ownership & Letting

9

Restrictions on foreign ownership were relaxed in 2007 and, in general, citizens of countries in which Turks can buy freely are entitled to buy without restriction in Turkey; these include most EU countries but not Belgium, Cyprus, the Czech Republic or Slovakia. Check with a Turkish embassy to see if your country has a reciprocal agreement with Turkey. If not, you're limited to 30ha (74 acres) of land. Foreigners aren't permitted to buy property in certain villages or military areas.

There are no restrictions on letting, but rental income above YTL2,300 (£800) is taxed (see **Income Tax** above).

Market

Until recently, Turkey had a small but rapidly growing market for holiday homes, mostly on the Aegean and Mediterranean coasts. Since 2006, however, when restrictions on foreigners buying property were lifted, the market has taken off significantly – mainly with second home buyers, but also with retirees. Investor confidence was boosted in 2005 by the instigation of negotiations for Turkey's EU membership and by an increase in the number of budget flights to Turkey in 2006, and a number of global corporations are looking to invest in Turkish property following an enormous investment by the ruler of Dubai. A number of 'holiday village' developments are being built to meet this demand, with a variety of sports and leisure facilities, including swimming pools, tennis and volleyball courts, football pitches, children's play areas and shops. But Turkey also appeals to people looking for something 'different' – it's a largely unspoiled country, rich in culture and history.

Areas

Turkish properties of most interest to foreigners are new apartments and villas, mainly in the coastal resorts. There's plenty of available inland property, but much of it requires extensive renovation. The most popular locations for foreign buyers are on the Aegean and Mediterranean coasts, particularly around the towns of Antalya, Bodrum (opposite the Greek island of Kos), Kusadasi and Marmaris. Turkey also has a number of winter sports resorts on the Anatolian peninsula, although facilities aren't as extensive as in European ski resorts. The cities, mainly Ankara and Istanbul, are also attracting increased interest, especially from investors wanting buy-to-let properties.

Antalya, on the southern Mediterranean coast, is one of Turkey's main tourist centres, and Bodrum and Kusadasi are other popular spots. Marmaris, a resort in the south-west, is also popular, particularly with those who enjoy sailing. The Bodrum peninsula in the far south is less hectic and spoiled than Kusadasi, on the west coast (around 90km south of Izmir), and retains much of its original charm, including a beautiful harbour and castle. However, the area is rapidly developing and there's a danger of property oversupply for people considering a capital investment.

For potential buy-to-let investors, Ankara has plenty of students and some tourists, but Istanbul is the favourite city destination as it's the country's main commercial and business centre as well as a popular tourist location, with a far higher demand for rental properties than Ankara. The city has benefited from major infrastructure improvements and re-building since the 1999 earthquake east of the city. Istanbul's property market saw considerable growth in 2005 and 2006.

Building Standards

Building standards in Turkey are variable and, although some properties are outstanding, the quality of construction is generally poor. But the situation is improving, especially with new properties. Particular care has been taken with properties built since 1999, which are reinforced against earthquakes.

9

Cost

Turkish property prices are low, despite the fact that the new Turkish lira is proving to be strong against the major currencies. Two-bedroom apartments on the Mediterranean coast cost from around YTL220,000 (£85,000) and three-bedroom villas from YTL375,000 (£135,000). Prices are higher in more exclusive areas. Istanbul's prices are far lower than in many European capitals: a new three-bedroom apartment in the city costs around YTL460,000 (£170,000). The quality of construction, however, varies and it's important to shop around.

Local Mortgages

Turkish banks have traditionally been unwilling to lend to foreigners, but in 2007 the Turkish government passed a new mortgage law, allowing lenders more freedom in their mortgage offers, to include variable-rate mortgages and loans for up to 30 years. Some foreign banks offer loans on Turkish properties, including HSBC.

Property Taxes

An annual property tax is levied on the estimated market value of land and buildings, at rates varying from 0.1 to 0.3 per cent (depending on the location of the property and how it's used). The tax is doubled if the property is in a large city. Some local councils add a surcharge for the protection of historical and cultural structures. In addition, there's a local tax for what's known as 'environmental cleaning'. These taxes are usually payable in two instalments, in May and November. Both resident and non-resident property owners must also pay an environmental services tax (EST), which is included in water charges (marginally higher in the cities than elsewhere).

Purchase Procedure

When the vendor and buyer agree a price and, if applicable, permission to purchase has been obtained (see **Restrictions on Foreign Ownership & Letting** above), a preliminary contract is signed and a deposit of 10 per cent paid. You should engage a lawyer to carry out the normal checks and draw up a notarised contract. **Note that lawyers' checks usually take from four to six months.** Both parties must then apply to the Land Registry office (TAPU) to transfer the title to your name. The deed is signed at the Land Registry office and the balance, plus any outstanding taxes, duties and the registration fee, paid. You receive a copy of the deed on the same day and the original is sent to Ankara to be registered.

There are two major precautions you must take when buying property in Turkey: to have your property checked by a surveyor for earthquake risk and to protect yourself against title irregularities, which are common. In view of Turkey's earthquake risk, it's essential to check the level of risk in the area where you're planning to buy and to employ a surveyor to check a property and assess its potential to withstand tremors. Buildings constructed after the last major earthquake should comply with new standards, and many other buildings have been reinforced, but you should obtain professional advice before committing yourself. **Earthquake insurance is a legal requirement for all Turkish property owners (see Fees below).**

Although the property purchase procedure in Turkey is straightforward, extreme care must be exercised because more than half of existing properties are believed to have some kind of title irregularity. Although it isn't required by law, the assistance of an English-speaking lawyer, familiar with common problems and the purchase procedure in Turkey, is essential. Always have any contract translated by an official translator into a language you're fluent in and ensure that you sign notarised copies of contracts in Turkish and your own language.

9

Fees

Fees are usually between 7 and 9 per cent of the declared purchase price. Stamp duty is levied at 1.5 per cent, split equally between vendor and buyer except when one party is a Turkish resident and the other isn't, in which case the Turkish resident normally pays the full amount. There's also a title deed charge (sometimes called a sale-and-acquisition levy) of 1.5 per cent each (vendor and buyer), which is collected before the transfer of ownership at the Land Registry. A notary's fees are usually around 1 per cent, and legal fees between 1.5 and 2 per cent (plus a fee for the official translation of the contract). If you're buying through an agent, his fee is around 3 per cent and this is normally split between vendor and buyer. **Earthquake insurance is a legal requirement for all Turkish property owners and the cost depends on the size and location of the property.**

General Information

Getting There

A number of charter and scheduled airlines fly to Turkish airports, although the country isn't as well served by scheduled airlines as many other popular holiday destinations. Charter flights to coastal tourist spots generally operate only between May and October, and fly to Antalya, Bodrum-Milas and Dalaman airports.

Ankara airport has only a few international flights and is mainly a domestic airport, despite being the capital city. British Airways operates a flight from London Heathrow.

Turkey's major international airport is Ataturk International in Istanbul, 15km (9mi) south-west of the city. British Airways and Turkish Airlines are the main operators, with flights from London Heathrow and Stansted respectively. Easyjet began a service to Istanbul in 2006, but flights go to Istanbul's other airport, Sabiha Gökçen International, which is on the Asian side of the city, 45km (28mi) east of the European centre of Istanbul, although it has excellent transport connections.

Communications

Telecommunications in Turkey have recently undergone extensive modernisation and expansion to bring them up to western European standards. All residential areas have an efficient, direct dialling system, which is ranked sixth in the world in terms of efficiency. The majority of services are provided by Turk Telecom, the former state provider, which was privatised and sold to Saudi Arabia's Oger Telecom in 2005. Mobile phone and internet use are fairly widespread and growing rapidly, and both are also dominated by Turk Telecom. The country dialling code is 90 and international direct dialling (IDD) is available worldwide.

Fixed-line Telephones: Public telephone boxes are common; they're operated by Turk Telecom and have pictorial instructions to help users. Most use phone cards, which you can buy at post offices, shops and hotels.

Mobile Telephones: Mobile phones are used by around 70 per cent of the population and operate on the GSM 900 and 1800 networks. There are currently three main providers, Avea, Telsim and Turkcell (the largest provider).

Internet: Internet use is growing rapidly in Turkey, with a mixture of dial-up and ADSL services. Internet cafes are common in the larger cities and the use of wireless access is growing. Turk Telecom is the main provider through its subsidiary, TTnet, which offers ADSL.

9

Postal Services: Services are provided by the state service, PTT, and are fairly reliable and efficient. Post offices are open between 9am and 5pm on weekdays, although larger and central post offices open from 8am to midnight. Letters to Europe take around a week to arrive.

Crime Rate

Serious crime is rare in Turkey, but during the last five years or so petty crime has increased considerably, particularly bag-snatching and pick-pocketing in cities. In 2004, Turkey's rate for violent and property-related crime rose by around 10 per cent (15 per cent in Istanbul), so you're advised to take precautions. In 2003, there was a serious Al-Qaeda attack on the British Consulate and HSBC bank in Istanbul, which killed 30 people and wounded hundreds.

Medical Facilities

The quality of Turkey's medical facilities varies enormously, but the new private hospitals in Ankara and Istanbul have excellent facilities and well trained staff. Public hospitals sometimes lack equipment and expertise, and those with serious conditions may need to be transferred to other hospitals for treatment. All working residents pay into a national health insurance scheme, but those who aren't working (including retirees) must have comprehensive private health insurance. EU citizens visiting Turkey **aren't** entitled to use a European Health Insurance Card (EHIC), so make sure your insurance covers all eventualities.

Pets

There's no quarantine system in Turkey, but your pet requires a certificate (issued not more than ten days before the date of import) stating that it's in good health and has been vaccinated against rabies not more than six months and not less than 15 days before departure. You don't need authorisation from the Turkish embassy or consulate provided you accompany your pet. Each person may import only one pet.

Visas & Permits

Visas: Citizens of most countries (EU and non-EU) require a visa to enter Turkey but a three-month multiple-entry visa can be obtained at the border (for around £10) if your passport is valid for at least six months on entry. Holders of a British National Overseas (BNO) or British Protected Persons (BPP) passport must obtain a visa **before** arriving in Turkey.

Residence Permits: If you have a valid visa, you don't need a residence permit for stays of up to 90 days. If you wish to stay longer, you should apply to the Turkish embassy in your home country **before** departure for a residence visa and you must register at the nearest police station on arrival in Turkey. Failure to do so can result in a fine, which increases considerably the longer you overstay your welcome! Retirees must have sufficient income to maintain themselves and comprehensive health insurance.

Work Permits: Work permits are difficult to obtain and applications must be for a position that cannot be filled by a Turkish national. You should apply to the nearest Turkish embassy with a letter from your prospective employer. If your application is approved, you'll be granted a visa (if applicable) and residence and work permits for the period of your employment. You employer must submit details of your employment to the Ministry of Labour and Social Security.

9

Reference

Further Reading

The Turkish Daily News, Karum Is Merkezi, 21/443, Kat 6 Gaziosmanpasa, Ankara, Turkey (☎ 312-468 9178, 🖳 www.turkishdailynews.com.tr). The main English-language newspaper in Turkey, with political economic and international news. Also available online.

Useful Addresses

Turkish Embassy (UK), 43 Belgrave Square, London SW1X 8PA, UK (☎ 020-7393 0202, 🖳 www.turkishembassylondon.org).

Turkish Embassy (Economic Counsellor), 43 Belgrave Square, London SW1X 8PA, UK (☎ 020-7235 2743, 🖳 www.turkisheconomy.org.uk). Excellent information about Turkey's economy, buying property and entry regulations.

Turkish Embassy (US), 2525 Massachusetts Ave, NW, Washington, DC 20008, US (☎ 202-612 6700, 🖳 www.turkishembassy.org).

Turkish Culture and Tourism Office (UK), 4th Floor, 29-30 St. James's Street, London SW1A 1HB, UK (☎ 020-7839 7778, 🖳 www.gototurkey.co.uk).

Turkish Culture and Tourism Office (USA), 821 United Nations Plaza, New York, NY 10017, US (☎ 212-687 2194/5/6, 🖳 www.tourismturkey.org).

Turkish Office of Information (UK), 1st Floor, 170-173 Piccadilly, London W1V 9DD, UK (☎ 020-7734 8681).

Turkish Information Office (US), 821 United Nations Plaza, New York, NY 10017, US (☎ 212-687 2194).

Europe: UNITED KINGDOM

Background Information

Capital: London.

Population: 60.5m.

Foreign Community: The UK's population is around 92 per cent British. There are also resident foreigners from all over the world, mainly in the major cities. Almost 2 per cent of the population is Indian, 1.5 per cent Pakistani and 2.8 per cent other nationalities, including African, Asian, Bangladeshi, Caribbean and Chinese nationals.

Area: 244,820km^2 (94,525mi^2).

Geography: The UK (officially The United Kingdom of Great Britain and Northern Ireland) is made up of England, Northern Ireland, Scotland and Wales. It's in north-west Europe and is surrounded by water: the English Channel is to the south, between the UK and France, the Irish Sea and Atlantic Ocean is to the west, the North Atlantic is to the north, and the North Sea is to the east. Northern Ireland has a land border with the Republic of Ireland (Eire) and England is linked to France by the Channel Tunnel. The UK's geography is varied: much of England consists of lowland, but there's mountainous terrain in the north-west (the Cumbrian mountains in the Lake District) and the north (the Pennines and the Peak District). Northern Ireland is mostly hilly and contains the largest lake in the UK, Lough Neagh. Scotland has a

9

variety of terrains, with lowlands in the south and east, and highlands in the north and west, including Ben Nevis, which is the highest mountain in the UK, at 1,344m (4,406ft) – barely a hill by many other countries' standards. There are also several hundred islands off the west and north coasts of Scotland, the best known being the Hebrides, the Orkney Islands and the Shetland Islands. Wales is mostly mountainous, the highest peak being Mount Snowdon, at 1,085m (3,560ft).

Climate: The climate varies considerably across the UK and is unpredictable, although it's generally temperate, with mild, wet weather brought by prevailing south-west winds. The south-east of England has the highest summer temperatures (up to 32C/90F – occasionally higher), due to its proximity to the European mainland. Winter temperatures there sometimes fall to -4C (25F) but freezing weather is the exception rather than the rule. Snow sometimes falls in the UK in winter and early spring, although usually only on higher ground. Northern Ireland has a temperate maritime climate, which is wet for much of the year, although the west of the region receives more rain than the east. Scotland's climate is temperate, oceanic and very changeable, with temperatures lower than the rest of the UK. In winter, average temperatures are around 6C (43F), in summer 18C (64F). Western Scotland is usually warmer than the east due to the moderating influence of Atlantic Ocean currents, while the western highlands are the wettest place in the country, with annual rainfall often exceeding 300cm (120in). Wales has a similar climate to England: wet and mild.

Language: There's no official language in the UK, but the dominant language is English. A form of Gaelic is spoken by around 60,000 people in Scotland, and around 25 per cent of the Welsh population speaks Welsh. Immigrants from Commonwealth countries speak a variety of other languages (the UK has the largest number of Bengali, Gujarati, Hindi, Punjabi and Urdu speakers outside Asia).

Political Situation: High. Since the economic problems and industrial strife of the '70s, the UK has become one of the most stable and economically prosperous countries in the world, particularly during the last decade or so. Margaret Thatcher, who led the Conservative Party in the '80s, began the economic recovery of the country, although her critics accuse her of increasing social divisions. Despite a serious economic recession in the early '90s, the election of Tony Blair's 'New' Labour government in 1997 in effect continued Margaret Thatcher's policy of reducing public ownership and enforcing stringent economic measures. In 2007, Blair stepped down in favour of Gordon Brown, and the next parliamentary election must take place on or before 2010. The UK's economy is one of the strongest in Europe, enjoying low rates of inflation, interest and unemployment, despite the fact that the country hasn't adopted the euro due to strong pressure from the electorate.

The UK is a parliamentary democracy, with the monarch, Queen Elizabeth II, as head of state. Scotland and Wales have devolved governments, following referenda in 1999. The Scottish Parliament has responsibility for most aspects of domestic, economic and social policy, whereas the Welsh Assembly doesn't have the power to make primary legislation but may make secondary legislation and 'fast-track' primary legislation via the English Parliament in Westminster. Although devolved government was established in Northern Ireland in 1998, it's currently suspended due to a lack agreement over power-sharing between political parties.

The UK has been a member of the EU since 1973, although much of the electorate opposes European integration.

9 Currency

The UK's currency is the pound sterling (£).
Exchange Rate: £1 = €1.48/US$2.
Exchange Controls: None.

Cost & Standard of Living

The UK has a high standard of living, the south of the country generally more prosperous than the north, although it varies from area to area. The cost of living in the UK is also very high, particularly in the main cities such as London (although people working in London usually receive an extra salary allowance). Accommodation, food and transport costs are all high, although high salaries compensate. The hourly minimum wage is £5.52 (from October 2007, increased annually).

Taxation

UK taxation is low by European standards, but the enforcement of tax law is strict and the government has recently introduced further measures to combat tax evasion. The tax treatment of individuals is complicated and depends on whether you're 'resident', 'ordinarily resident' or 'domiciled' in the UK. There are three direct taxes: income tax, inheritance tax and capital gains tax.

Personal Effects: Household goods purchased within the EU can be imported duty free and don't need to be retained for a minimum period. However, goods (including vehicles) purchased outside the EU must have been owned for at least six months and cannot be sold for 12 months after importation.

Income Tax: The UK operates a PAYE system, but the self-employed and those with other income must declare their earnings independently. All income is taxed progressively, with rates starting at 10 per cent (on the first £2,230), moving to 22 per cent for amounts up to £34,600 and 40 per cent for amounts over that. Certain personal allowances are deductible from taxable income (depending on your circumstances) and parents may claim tax-free child benefits.

Capital Gains Tax (CGT): CGT for individuals is taxed as ordinary income (see rates above). Gains on the sale of a principal residence are exempt. On other assets, including second homes, the first £9,200 is exempt (this is a per person exemption, for spouses and civil partners) and there's a system of taper relief which reduces the amount of tax payable, depending on how long an asset has been held.

Wealth Tax: None.

Inheritance & Gift Tax: Applied to the value of any inheritance (including property) and gifts made in the seven years before the death of the donor. Inheritance and gifts in excess of £300,000 are subject to tax at 40 per cent.

Value Added Tax (VAT): The standard rate of VAT is 17.5 per cent, with a reduced rate of 5 per cent for domestic fuel and the installation of energy-saving materials, and a 0 rate for private housing, most food, public transport and children's clothes.

Other Taxes: The government is currently levying a variety of 'green taxes', including levies taxes on vehicle fuels and air travel, to address environmental issues. There are tax allowances for people who buy energy-saving items, and stamp duty (see **Fees** below) isn't charged on new homes that have zero carbon emissions.

Property

9

Restrictions on Foreign Ownership & Letting

There are no restrictions on foreign ownership or letting, but rental income must be declared on your tax return.

Market

The UK property market has been buoyant for around a decade and the Office of National Statistics (ONS) reported in April 2007 that UK house prices have risen by 204 per cent since 1997. Many experts have been predicting for some time that a house-price crash is imminent, but in early 2007 two major UK building societies reported price rises of 10 per cent over the previous 12 months. There have been concerns that UK interest rate rises combined with problems in the US housing market could adversely affect the market, but no such effect has so far occurred. Analysts point to the lack of housing supply in the UK as the main reason that prices remain high. The Royal Institute of Chartered Surveys (RICS) reported that in 2006, the highest price rises were in London and the south-east, and the price gap between London and the rest of the country was the largest ever recorded, the strong financial services sector in London taking property prices out of the reach of all but the wealthiest people. Growth slowed at the end of 2006 but in early 2007 the London property market regained its momentum, although the highest percentage rises were in Northern Ireland and Scotland.

Areas

The UK has something for everyone: thriving cities and attractive rural and coastal areas. London and the south-east are favourite areas with buyers looking for jobs or a good investment but also the most expensive. Prices are highest in the London Borough of Kensington and Chelsea, and there has recently been considerable interest (particularly from investors) in East London, where prices are comparatively low but investment in the 2012 Olympics could mean significant capital gains over the next five to ten years. Many formerly run-down areas of London close to more expensive areas are undergoing 'gentrification', and the area around Ashford in Kent, where the new Eurostar station opens in 2007, are increasing in popularity. Parts of the north and north-west of England, close to cities undergoing extensive regeneration such as Bradford, Liverpool and Leeds, are also proving popular. In Scotland, cities are also the most popular with buyers, especially Aberdeen, Dundee, Edinburgh and Glasgow. In Northern Ireland, Lisburn, almost in the centre of the province, is one of the most popular and expensive areas, while Craigavon and Armagh saw annual price increases of around 50 per cent in 2006.

Building Standards

Building standards are generally high, although some old buildings are in a poor state of repair and renovation is expensive.

Cost

Average prices in Greater London vary considerably. In Kensington and Chelsea (the most expensive borough), even a small flat costs around £700,000, while a terraced house costs around £1m and a detached house at least £1.75m, sometimes much more. In Hackney in East London (the cheapest), on the other hand, a two-bedroom flat costs around £245,000 and a semi-detached house around £450,000.

One of the south-east's most desirable areas is the county of Surrey, thanks to a combination of beautiful countryside and what's perceived to be easy commuting to London.

The average price for a small flat in Surrey is around £225,000 and for a detached house around £600,000; top-of-the-range properties cost well over £1m. Prices in Kent are considerably lower, a small flat costing around £150,000, a semi-detached house around £240,000 and a detached house around £400,000.

Property in cities in the north of England is even more affordable, with average prices in Bradford, Leeds and Liverpool around £120,000 for a small flat, £150,000 for a semi-detached house and £300,000 for a detached house. Scottish cities are also relatively inexpensive, with prices in Edinburgh among the highest at an average of around £200,000, Aberdeen coming second (£150,000) and Glasgow third (£140,000). In Northern Ireland, a flat costs around £150,000, a semi-detached house around £200,000 and a detached house £350,000.

Local Mortgages

The mortgage market in the UK is extremely competitive and sophisticated, with banks and building societies offering a huge variety of mortgages. You can choose, for example, among a repayment loan, an endowment mortgage, an individual savings account (ISA) mortgage and a pension mortgage. Interest rates are either fixed or variable, and because competition is so fierce it pays to shop around for the best deal. Loans are usually around 80 per cent of the value of a property and granted over 25 to 30 years, depending on the lender.

Property Taxes

An annual council tax is charged by local authorities to cover all local services and facilities. Rates vary considerably across the country. Each business and residential property is allocated a tax band based on the value of the property. In 2006, the average annual tax was just over £1,000 and there are various reductions, depending on your personal circumstances. You can check the council tax valuation of a property in England or Wales by contacting the Valuation Office Agency (VOA), which has offices around the country (their locations are given on 💻 www.voa.gov.uk). Properties in Scotland are dealt with by Scottish Assessors (💻 www. saa.gov.uk). Leaseholders (see **Purchase Procedure** below) must pay 'ground rent', which may be nominal (known as a 'peppercorn' rent) and a share of expenses relating to the maintenance of communal parts of the building, e.g. the roof; check whether there's a fund to cover these and what major items are in need of repair or maintenance.

Purchase Procedure

Most property in the UK is sold freehold, although there's also a system of leasehold for apartments (flats), by which buyers buy a lease; when the lease expires, the property reverts to the principal owner, i.e. the freeholder. Provided at least 60 years remain on a lease, you should be able to obtain a mortgage (as most lenders insist that at least 20 years remains at the end of the mortgage term), although you should consider possible resale problems if the lease is near to expiry.

When buying property in England, Wales or Northern Ireland, you make an offer subject to a satisfactory survey and contract. Either side can amend or withdraw from a sale at any time before the exchange of contracts, when the sale becomes legally binding. This often leads to the unsavoury practice of gazumping, where the vendor accepts a higher offer before exchange and you're left with no property and no redress. Note, however, that even if you aren't gazumped, a sale can fall through for the most trivial reason or because someone higher up the

9

purchase 'chain' pulls out, causing all the sales lower down the chain to fall through. In Scotland, neither side can pull out once an offer has been made and accepted.

Once the vendor has accepted your offer, you may be asked to pay a small deposit (to the estate agent, if the property is being sold through one, as is normal). This isn't usually more than £500 and shows that you're serious about proceeding with the purchase, although it has no legal significance and is repayable if the sale doesn't go through. Contracts are prepared by the vendor's solicitor and sent to the buyer's solicitor. Title is checked and if the buyer needs to obtain a mortgage, the contract will be subject to a satisfactory valuation by the lender. In addition, from 1st June 2007, all vendors must by law provide buyers with a Home Information Pack (HIP), which should be prepared by the agent marketing the property **before** it goes on the market. A HIP must contain an Energy Performance Certificate, details of searches and evidence of title, and may contain certain other documents, e.g. a Home Condition Report. HIPs are controversial and the requirement for them may be amended or scrapped; for more information on HIPs go to ▣ www.homeinformationpack.co.uk.

Once the purchase deed is drafted by the buyer's solicitor and he has made his searches, you must pay a more substantial deposit (usually 10 per cent), which is sent along with the purchase deed and any queries back to the vendor's solicitor. The exchange of contracts and completion (usually a month after exchange) can take place when the buyer's solicitor is happy that all the necessary checks have been made and the results are satisfactory. The whole process usually takes between two and three months – unless the vendor withdraws from the sale.

Fees

The fees for buying property in the UK are among the lowest in the world. There are various fees for obtaining a mortgage, including a valuation fee (for the lender's valuation), indemnity insurance and a mortgage arrangement or acceptance fee. A survey is optional, but it's wise to have an independent structural survey, which is common practice when buying an older property. Stamp duty land tax (SDLT), which is in effect a property transfer tax, is levied in progressive bands, depending on the value of the property. Properties up to a value of £125,000 are exempt, those valued between £125,000 and £250,000 attract a charge of 1 per cent, those between £250,000 and £500,000 a charge of 3 per cent and those valued at over £500,000 4 per cent. There are small land registration fees and charges for local authority searches, which are usually included in the solicitor's fees. You can use a solicitor or a licensed conveyancer to prepare the contracts; their fees vary and are often negotiable. Whichever you choose, you should check what his fee includes (e.g. stamp duty, searches, land registration fees and VAT), particularly if you've negotiated a flat fee. You should also check what their charges might be if the sale falls through. If it does, you'll probably still have to pay for the mortgage valuation and survey. An estate agent's fees are usually between 1 and 2 per cent, but are negotiable and normally paid by the vendor.

General Information

9

Getting There

There's a wide choice of transport to and from the UK, with international and domestic airports around the country, extensive rail services within the country and to Europe (via the Channel Tunnel), and ferry services to European destinations from ports all over the UK.

Air: London alone has five international airports, although three of them are a considerable distance from the capital. The largest and busiest is London Heathrow, around 24km (15mi) west of central London, which is the hub of British Airways, the national airline, and handles a vast selection of charter and scheduled flights, though few budget services, which mostly operate into Gatwick, Luton and (especially) Stansted. The second-largest is London Gatwick, which is in Crawley in West Sussex, around 45km (28mi) south of London, and the others London Luton, 48km (30mi) north of London, London Stansted, in Essex around 48km (30mi) north-east of London, and London City, a small airport in the Docklands area of East London designed to serve the financial district but offering some international services. All London airports have good road and rail connections.

All the UK's other large cities have international airports and there are also a number of smaller international airports around the country.

Rail: As well as having a comprehensive (though not always efficient) intercity and local rail network, the UK is connected to France and Belgium by the Channel Tunnel. Eurostar services to London Waterloo station (London St. Pancras from November 2007) operate from Avignon, Brussels, Lille and Paris. (Non-EU citizens travelling to the UK by Eurostar must complete a landing card at check-in, which should be presented to the immigration authorities on arrival – see **Visas & Permits** below).

Ferry: There are ferry services to the UK from a range of European ports. Dover, Plymouth and Portsmouth in the south of England are among the busiest ports, with ferry services to France and Spain. There are also ferries to Newcastle in the north-east from Belgium, Holland and Scandinavia, and to Liverpool in the north-west and Holyhead and Fishguard in Wales from the Republic of Ireland.

Communications

Communications in the UK are highly sophisticated and regulated. The main fixed-line provider is the former state-owned British Telecom (BT), which still provides the majority of services, despite full privatisation of the telecommunications industry. There's widespread use of mobile phones and the internet. The country dialling code is 44 and international direct dialling (IDD) is available worldwide.

Fixed-line Telephones: Public phone boxes are plentiful, especially in towns and cities, and may use cash, credit cards or phone cards, which are available from most newsagents. BT's two main competitors are NTL (Virgin Media) and Telewest, but their share of the market is only a fraction of BT's.

Mobile Telephones: The UK has more mobile phones than people, and the network covers most areas. The main operators are O2, Orange, T-Mobile, 3 Telecommunications, Virgin Mobile and Vodafone. Minor operators include MobileWorld and Tesco Mobile. All the main operators operate on the GSM and GPRS networks, and some offer 'High-Speed Downlink Packet Access' (HSDPA), which provides internet access via your mobile phone.

Internet: Internet use is widespread, an increasing number of private users installing high-speed (ADSL) connections. The main internet service providers are BT, AOL and NTL. Internet cafes are common in the larger towns and cities, and the use of wi-fi technology is growing.

Postal Services: Services are provided by Royal Mail and are generally reliable and efficient, with daily collections from and deliveries to all but the most remote areas of the country. Post offices are usually open between 9am and 5pm on weekdays, although opening hours vary across the country and small offices are threatened with closure. Services also vary from one post office to another, but many provide banking facilities and a variety of other services. Letters to western Europe take around three days, to non-European destinations around a week.

9

Crime Rate

The crime rate in the UK varies significantly from area to area but overall it has increased considerably in recent years, particularly in inner cities, which are the worst areas for violent crimes and burglary. Drug-related violent crime is an increasing problem and car crime is widespread.

Medical Facilities

Medical facilities and services are generally excellent, although over-stretched and under-funded in many areas. Employees and retirees are covered by the National Health Service (NHS) through mandatory social security contributions. All visitors are entitled to free emergency treatment and all permanent residents to full NHS care.

Pets

Animals imported into the UK from 'qualifying countries', i.e. those that are part of the European Pet Passport scheme (listed on the website of the Department for Food & Rural Affairs, 🖥 www.defra.gov.uk/animalh/index.htm), must be microchipped and have a veterinary certificate of vaccination against certain diseases, including rabies, and a blood test report which proves that they have the required antibodies against rabies following vaccination. Animals without the necessary documents or imported from non-qualifying countries must spend six months in quarantine on arrival.

Visas & Permits

Visas: EEA nationals and citizens of some other countries, including Australia, Canada, Japan and the US, don't require a visa to enter the UK. Visitors may remain for up to six months.

Residence Permits: EEA citizens have the right to live in the UK, as long as they have a job or sufficient funds to support themselves without relying on the state. There's no requirement for a residence permit or any kind of registration certificate, but if you wish to obtain one for identification purposes and to confirm your right to live and work in the UK, you may apply to the Border and Immigration Agency. Registration certificates are valid indefinitely. Note that citizens of the states that joined the EU in May 2004 and January 2007 (except Cyprus and Malta) have restricted rights if they wish to work in the UK (see **Work Permits** below).

Nationals of most non-EEA countries require a visa, a residence permit and a work permit (see below) to remain permanently in the UK. These must be obtained before arrival, via a British embassy or consulate. Non-EEA retirees and 'people of independent means' must be able to prove that they're able to support and accommodate themselves and their dependants indefinitely without working or recourse to public funds.

Work Permits: No work permits are required for EEA citizens, but citizens of the states that joined the EU in May 2004 and January 2007 (except Cyprus and Malta) have restricted rights for one year: they must join the Worker Registration Scheme if planning to work for longer than a month, and Bulgarian and Romanian nationals who wish to work in the UK must obtain permission to do so before starting work.

9

Non-EU citizens must obtain a visa, residence permit and work permit before arriving in the UK (see above). Work permits must be applied for by a UK employer.

Reference

Further Reading

Buy, Sell and Move House, Which? Publications, Castlemead, Gascoyne Way, Hertford, SG14 1LH, UK (☎ 01903-828557, 🖳 www.which.co.uk).

Buying or Renting a Home in London, David Hampshire and Sue Harris (Survival Books). Everything you need to know about London's property market.

Buying, Selling and Letting Property (UK), David Hampshire (Survival Books). Everything you need to know about the UK property market.

Living and Working in Britain, David Hampshire (Survival Books). Everything you need to know about living and working in the UK.

Living and Working in London, Joe Laredo (Survival Books). Everything you need to know about living and working in London.

Renting and Letting, Which? Publications (details as above).

UK Housing Review, Council of Mortgage Lenders, Bush House, North West Wing, Aldwych, London WC2B 4PJ, UK (☎ 0845-373 6771, 🖳 www.cml.org.uk).

Useful Addresses

The Association of Relocation Professionals, PO Box 189, Diss, IP22 1PE, UK (☎ 0870-073 7475, 🖳 www.relocationagents.com).

The British Association of Removers (BAR), Tangent House, 62 Exchange Road, Watford, Herts, UK (☎ 01923-699480, 🖳 www.bar.co.uk).

British Embassy (US), 3100 Massachusetts Ave, NW, Washington, DC 20008, US (☎ 900-990 8472 – premium rate number, 🖳 www.britainusa.com).

National Association of Estate Agents (NAEA), Arbon House, 21 Jury Street, Warwick CV34 4EH, UK (☎ 01926-496800, 🖳 www.naea.co.uk).

Visit Britain (Tourist Authority), Thames Tower, Black's Road, Hammersmith, London W6 9EL, UK (☎ 020-8846 9000, 🖳 www.visitbritain.com).

Useful Websites

Border and Immigration Agency (🖳 www.ind.homeoffice.gov.uk). The Border and Immigration Agency is part of the Home Office, with responsibility for managing immigration control in the UK. Its website contains extensive information on the immigration system and obtaining permission to stay in the UK as an EEA or non-EEA citizen.

UK Government (🖳 www.direct.gov.co.uk). An excellent government website with a wide variety of information about all aspects of life in the UK. In the 'Home and Community' section, there's extensive advice about buying, selling and letting a home.

9

Africa: MOROCCO

Background Information

Capital: Rabat.
Population: 32m.
Foreign Community: The majority of the population is of Arab, Berber or mixed Arab-Berber descent. There's a very small Jewish community and around 100,000 foreign residents, most of them French or Spanish. There are few UK or US residents.
Area: 446,550km^2 (172,414mi^2).
Geography: Known officially as the Kingdom of Morocco, the country is in the north-west corner of Africa, with Atlantic and Mediterranean coastlines. Algeria is to the east, Western Sahara to the south, mainland Spain to the north (across the Strait of Gibraltar), and the Spanish enclaves of Ceuta and Melilla within Morocco's territory. The country is dominated by two mountain ranges: the Atlas mountains, which are the country's backbone, rising from the Mediterranean in the north-east to a height of 4,175m (13,697ft) in the south-west; and the Rif mountains, which border the Mediterranean from the north-west to the north-east. The Atlas mountains insulate the country from the Sahara desert and provide water for the land to their west, which, along with an extensive fertile plain close to the Atlantic coast, provides most of the country's food. South and east of the Atlas Mountains is mostly uninhabited desert.
Climate: Morocco's climate is broadly Mediterranean, although it's extreme in the interior, particularly from June to September, when temperatures of 38C (100F) and above are normal. Coastal towns don't suffer from such intense heat and temperatures are a pleasant 25C (77F) in summer and 15C (59F) in winter (November to May). There's often heavy rain in winter, with an average annual total of 31mm (1.2in).
Language: The official language is Arabic, with Berber dialects spoken by around 12m people, mainly in rural areas. French is the unofficial second language and the primary language of business, government and diplomacy. English is rapidly becoming the third language for the country's educated youth, mainly as a result of the 2002 education reforms, which led to English being taught in all public schools.
Political Situation: Good. Morocco has been a constitutional monarchy since 1972. The country has an elected parliament, although the last election, in 2002, was considered Morocco's first free and fair election and the King (Mohammed VI since 1999), as head of state, has extensive executive powers and can dissolve government or deploy the military as he sees fit. King Mohammed is seen as a moderniser and has initiated political and economic changes, including the massive Vision 2010 strategy, which aims to improve the country's infrastructure and boost tourism and foreign investment. The constitution guarantees a multi-party system and the major political parties are the Union Socialiste des Forces Populaires (USFP) and the conservative Istiqlal party. The main opposition is the Parti de la Justice et du Développement (PJD). Driss Jettou, who isn't a member of any political party, heads a governing coalition made up of six parties. The next election is due in late 2007. Morocco is a member of the Arab League and the Organisation of the Islamic Conference and is a non-NATO ally of the US.

9

Finance

Currency

Morocco's currency is the Moroccan dirham (MAD), consisting of 100 centimes.

Exchange Rate: £1 = MAD16.47.

Exchange Controls: Foreign exchange is controlled by the Foreign Exchange Office (Office de Changes) and it's strictly forbidden to import or export dirham. However, non-residents may freely exchange foreign currency at authorised banks in Morocco, although all exchange records should be kept.

Cost & Standard of Living

Morocco's cost of living is far lower than that of most European countries, although it's rising fast as increased foreign investment pushes up prices. The main cities are rather more expensive than rural areas. The standard of living for most Moroccans is low, many living in poverty. King Mohammed VI has promised to address the problem of poverty and the wide wealth gap between ordinary Moroccans and the country's affluent class. Unemployment is around 10 per cent and the minimum monthly wage is MAD2,010 (£125).

Taxation

Residents (defined as people who stay in the country for over 183 days per year) pay tax on worldwide income. Non-residents pay tax only on Moroccan income.

Personal Effects: Furniture and personal effects can be imported without duty, but you must have a residence permit which has been certified by a Moroccan embassy or consulate in your home country. Cars can be imported only for three months duty free; if they aren't exported within that period, you become liable for high import duties.

Income Tax: Morocco has a PAYE system and income tax rates are progressive, up to 44 per cent.

Capital Gains Tax (CGT): CGT is levied at 20 per cent if a property is sold within five years and 10 per cent if it's sold after six to ten years; there's no CGT after ten years' ownership.

Wealth Tax: None.

Inheritance & Gift Tax: Family members are exempt from inheritance tax but you should draw up a Moroccan will to dispose of your assets.

Value Added Tax (VAT): 20 per cent VAT is levied on most transactions. There are reduced rates of 14 per cent (construction and passenger transport), 10 per cent (catering and hotel accommodation, banking and leasing) and 7 per cent (goods for general consumption and motor vehicles). Exempt items include basic foodstuffs, books and newspapers. Non-residents must appoint a VAT representative in Morocco.

Property

Restrictions on Foreign Ownership & Letting

Foreigners aren't permitted to buy agricultural land. There are no restrictions on letting, but rental income is taxed at ordinary income tax rates (see above).

Market

The Moroccan property market has only recently begun to attract foreign investors. Previously, a few rich and famous foreigners bought large, traditional houses (called riads) at modest prices, but Morocco didn't attract 'normal' buyers. The market received a kick-start in 2001, when King Mohammed VI announced a major plan to improve the country's infrastructure, attract foreign investment and boost tourist numbers to 10m per year by 2010. Called 'Vision 2010', the project has a budget of US$billions, and the construction of several beach developments on the Atlantic and Mediterranean coasts is well under way. As a result, Morocco has been attracting a lot more interest from foreign buyers, particularly investors.

Areas

Marrakech, in the foothills of the Atlas mountains in the south-west, has long been a favourite destination for tourists. It's exotic and unspoiled, with a beautiful historic Old Town (*medina*). Buyers who want the authentic feel of Morocco find it there. Marrakech is best known for traditional houses (*riads*), set around beautiful courtyards. Many *riads* have been renovated, mainly by foreigners (particularly French, but also British and Italian), and prices have risen considerably over the last few years. Marrakech also has some luxurious modern villas, mostly French-owned, which command prices of several million euros.

Tangier, on the northern tip of Morocco, is also attracting increased interest, partly due to its lively, cosmopolitan atmosphere but also to a planned tunnel under the Strait of Gibraltar, linking Gibraltar and Tangier, which is due to begin construction in 2008 – though no one yet knows how long it will take to complete!

Other areas attracting considerable investor interest are the new resorts being built on the Atlantic coast. One of the most popular of these, particularly with second homeowners, is Essaouira, a picturesque old fishing town.

There's also increased interest in the Mediterranean coast, notably the luxurious resort being built at Saidia and due to include golf courses, an enormous marina, a water park and a commercial centre.

Building Standards

Standards are variable, particularly in older properties. The standard of new construction is generally high, but it's recommended to have a structural survey.

Cost

Prices of traditional properties in Marrakech vary considerably according to how much renovation is required. They start at around MAD4m (£250,000) for a small, basic, renovated *riad*, while a large one with several bedrooms costs from around MAD5.75m (£350,000) and prices rise to well over MAD11m (£700,000) for the best.

Prices in Tangier are around 25 per cent lower than similar properties a few kilometres away in Spain. Two-bedroom apartments cost around MAD825,000 (£50,000) and three-bedroom villas are around MAD1.6m (£100,000).

Properties on the Atlantic coast in and around Essaouira are relatively inexpensive and a two-bedroom apartment close to the beach costs around MAD400,000 (£25,000), while a large villa is around MAD2.75m (£170,000).

The Mediterranean coast is more expensive and properties in luxury beach developments start at around MAD2m (£120,000) for a two-bedroom apartment, while a three-bedroom villa costs over MAD3m (£200,000).

9

Local Mortgages

Local lenders offer mortgages up to 70 per cent of the purchase price or approved valuation. Mortgages can be obtained in euros, sterling or US dollars. Mortgages are usually for 15 years and must be paid off before retirement age. You must provide proof of income.

Property Taxes

Three annual taxes are payable after the first five years of ownership, but you qualify for a 75 per cent discount if a property is a permanent or holiday home. Property tax is levied according to the assessed value of a property, which may be below its market value. The first MAD3,000 is exempt and then rates rise progressively from 10 per cent (on the next MAD3,000) to 30 per cent (on the value above MAD60,000). Rates may vary slightly with the local authority. There's also a tax of 13.5 per cent of the assessed rental value of your property, and a rubbish collection tax of 10 per cent of the same value.

Purchase Procedure

The purchase procedure is relatively straightforward, although **it's advisable to exercise extreme caution where there are or may be multiple owners**. Some older properties don't have title deeds and may therefore have multiple owners. Sometimes there's an *adoul*, which is a scroll on which an official scribe has documented ownership of the property, but it may date back hundreds of years. Moroccan inheritance law states that anyone with a claim on a property must agree to its sale, but this requirement is often almost impossible to comply with and, if you discover that there are multiple owners and/or no deed, it's often better to abandon the purchase. In any case, it's vital to employ a lawyer who is familiar with Moroccan property law. If a property doesn't have a deed, it's sometimes possible to obtain legal title after a sale. The notary can arrange this and the charge is an extra 1 per cent of the value of the property, but you're then assured that the property is legally yours.

The sale is overseen by a public notary (*notaire*) but it's wise to appoint a lawyer who is fluent in your language and understands Moroccan property purchase procedure. You should also employ a translator to help with negotiations (usually in Arabic, although some vendors and developers will negotiate in French or Spanish). Once you've found a property and agreed a purchase price, a preliminary agreement is drawn up, a deposit of between 10 and 15 per cent paid (30 per cent for off-plan properties) and a completion date decided. Your lawyer will then make the necessary checks. Payment must be made in Moroccan dirhams, which aren't available outside Morocco, so you need to open a sterling or euro bank account in Morocco and transfer the required amount to convert into dirhams. You should inspect the property before completion and ensure that it's empty and in exactly the same state as when you agreed to buy it. Once all is in order, the balance is paid and the notary registers the property in your name.

Fees

9

Purchase fees in Morocco are around 8 per cent. An estate agent's fees are around 5 per cent but usually shared between the buyer and the vendor. The notary's fee is around 1 per cent (plus VAT), legal fees are around 1 per cent, transfer tax is 2.5 per cent and the property registration fee is 1 per cent (plus VAT). In addition, VAT is payable on new properties and off-plan purchases, but not on resale properties and land.

General Information

Getting There

There are four main airports in Morocco: Casablanca, Marrakech, Fez and Tangier.

Casablanca (Mohammed V) International Airport: Morocco's major airport and the hub of the national airline, Royal Air Maroc, handles flights from Canada, a number of European cities and the US. GB Airways, a subsidiary of British Airways, and Royal Air Maroc operate services from London Heathrow. A second terminal, which is expected to double passenger capacity to 10m per year, is due to be completed in 2007.

Marrakech (Menara) International Airport: Marrakech airport is far smaller and mainly serves European destinations. GB Airways offers flights from London Gatwick and London Heathrow, Easyjet and Atlas Blue (a subsidiary of Royal Air Maroc) offer London Gatwick services, and Ryanair and Thomsonfly operate flights from London Luton and Manchester.

Fez (Saïss) Airport: The even smaller airport at Fez has flights from UK and other European destinations. GB Airways operates a London Heathrow service, Easyjet started a London Gatwick service in September 2007 and Ryanair flies from London Luton.

Tangier (Ibn Batouta) International Airport: Tangier airport serves a small number of European destinations and has a Royal Air Maroc service from London Heathrow.

Ferries: Many people travel to Morocco by ferry, mainly from Spain. The Spanish port of Algeciras is the main departure point, with sailings to Ceuta (journey time 40 minutes) and Tangier (two hours). There's also a ferry connection between the smaller Spanish port of Tarifa and Tangier, taking around 35 minutes.

Communications

Communications in Morocco are fairly sophisticated and the three main telecoms providers – Maroc Telecom (IAM), the state-owned telecoms company and main provider, Meditel and Wana – offer fixed-line and mobile phone services. Mobile phone and internet use is widespread, although access to internet facilities isn't as good in rural areas. The country dialling code is 212 and international direct dialling (IDD) is available worldwide.

Fixed-line Telephones: International calls are fairly expensive for subscribers, but pre-paid phone cards significantly cut the cost. Public phones can be found in most city centres and there are also private telephone offices (*téléboutiques* or *télékiosques*).

Mobile Telephones: Services are provided by the three main operators (see above) and operate on the GSM network. Pre-paid phone cards are available from Maroc Telecom shops and SIM cards (*carte Jawal*) obtainable.

Internet: Internet use is widespread in Morocco and is provided by Maroc Telecom under the brand name of Menara. There are plenty of internet cafes in the cities and main towns, often close to *télékiosque* shops. Connection is faster in the north of the country.

Postal Services: Postal services are generally efficient, although unreliable. The service is provided by Poste Maroc. Airmail to Europe takes around a week. Most major city post offices have a *post restante* service where post can be sent for your collection. Post offices are open from 8.30am to midday and 2.30 to 6.30pm on weekdays, and from 8.30am to 2pm on Saturdays.

9

Crime Rate

Morocco's crime rate is low, although it's increasing in urban and popular tourist areas. Petty crime such as passport theft, pick-pocketing and bag snatching is on the increase, as is crime (and aggressive begging) near cash machines. Credit card fraud and scams such as substituting inferior goods for those that were chosen and paid for are common; always check before leaving a shop. There's also a significant danger of terrorism in Morocco, where there were suicide bombings (in Casablanca) in 2007.

Medical Facilities

Medical facilities and treatment for routine health problems are widely available, but emergency and specialised care are limited and few medical staff speak good English. Serious medical problems often require air evacuation. Many doctors and hospitals require immediate payment in cash for treatment, irrespective of whether you have travel insurance. Morocco has a public health system which employees contribute to, but visitors and foreign residents are advised to take out comprehensive private health insurance.

Pets

To avoid quarantine, pets entering Morocco require a health certificate from a government-authorised vet in your home country, certifying that they're free from disease and have had the necessary vaccinations (including rabies), not more than six months before travel. The certificate must be taken to your nearest Moroccan embassy or consulate to be stamped and certified.

Visas & Permits

Visas: Visas aren't required by citizens of most EU countries or Australia, Japan, New Zealand and the US for visits of up to 90 days.

Residence Permits: If you wish to stay longer, you must apply for a registration permit from the Directorate General for National Security, locally represented by the foreign registration department at police stations. Apply immediately on arrival in Morocco if your intention is to remain in the country because the application process takes time. Once issued, a residence permit is valid for ten years.

Work Permits: All foreign nationals must obtain a work permit before starting work. The work permit must be applied for by your employer, who has to prove that the post cannot be filled by a Moroccan. The application process can be lengthy.

Reference

Further Reading

9

Morocco Today, Val Fleurie, BP 6048, CP 90006, Tangier, Morocco (☎ 61-505 555, ⌨ www.moroccotoday.net). English-language newspaper, also available online.

The North Africa Journal, PO Box 1001, Concord, Massachusetts, MA 10742, US (☎ 978-371 2511, ⌨ www.northafricajournal.com). English-language journal containing economic and political analysis of North African markets, including Morocco.

Tingis, University of New England, Department of English, 11 Hills Beach Road, Biddeford, ME 04005, US (☎ 207-602 2614, ☐ www.tingismagazine.com). Moroccan-American online cultural magazine.

Useful Addresses

Moroccan Embassy (UK), 49 Queen's Gate Gardens, London SW7 5NE, UK (☎ 020-7581 5001, ☐ www.morocco-uk.com).
Moroccan Embassy (US), 1601 21st Street, NW, Washington DC 20009, US (☎ 202-462 7979, ☐ www.moroccanconsulate.com).
Moroccan National Tourist Office (UK), 205 Regent Street, London W1R 7DE, UK (☎ 020-7437 0073, ☐ www.tourism-in-morocco.com).

AFRICA: SOUTH AFRICA

Background Information

Capital: Pretoria.
Population: 44m.
Foreign Community: South Africa has some 6m residents of European origin, including over 500,000 Britons. After the Second World War, it was one of the most popular countries for migrants from Europe, particularly the UK, France, Germany and Holland. It's an extremely cosmopolitan country, and although the bulk of post-war immigrants have come from Europe, many African-Americans have migrated to South Africa since the end of apartheid. On the other hand, recent years have seen a net outflow of qualified workers, those leaving (including a high number of professionals) outnumbering new arrivals by around two to one.
Area: 1,228,376km^2 (471,444mi^2).
Geography: South Africa is the second-largest country in southern Africa (five times the size of the UK) and occupies the southernmost region of the African continent. It's an ancient land comprising two zones: the interior and the coastal fringe, which is separated from the interior by the Fringing Escarpment, a major communications barrier. The coastline is almost 2,900km (1,800mi) long and borders the Atlantic Ocean in the south-west and the Indian Ocean (which is much warmer than the Atlantic) in the south and east. South Africa is one of the world's most beautiful countries and contains a wealth of breathtaking natural features. It has a wide variety of landscapes, including majestic mountains reaching over 2,500m (8,000ft), numerous lakes and rivers, vast plains, huge tracts of dense forest and jungle, and many magnificent game parks and reserves.
Climate: South Africa's climate is temperate and (on the Kwazulu-Natal coast) sub-tropical, the southern coast (around Cape Town) enjoying an almost Mediterranean climate, recognised as one of the best in the world. As in Australia and New Zealand, the seasons in South Africa are opposite to those in the northern hemisphere, which makes the country a popular choice for a (northern) winter holiday home with Europeans and North Americans. Coastal regions enjoy a warmer climate than inland regions, the summer heat tempered by balmy sea breezes. The coolest months are June to September (winter), which is also the rainy season.
Language: The main languages are English and Afrikaans, although South Africa has 11 official languages. The major African languages are Xhosa and Zulu. Over 60 per cent of the population speaks English.

9

Political Situation: Currently good but with an uncertain future. Apartheid officially ended in 1991 and a government of National Unity was established after the 1994 general election, with Nelson Mandela (of the African National Congress/ANC) as President. Mandela retired in 1999, leaving his successor, Thabo Mbeki, with many social and economic problems, including high unemployment and widespread AIDS. In the 2004 general election, Mbeki was re-elected as President for a second five-year term. The ANC won 70 per cent of the vote and its nearest rival was the Democratic Alliance. The ANC now controls eight of the nine provinces in South Africa (KwaZulu Natal is the exception). While South Africa's democracy seems stable, there are sporadic outbreaks of civil unrest and crime is a major problem (see **Crime Rate** below). However, the South African government encourages foreign investment, particularly from the UK and the US, which are among the country's main trading partners.

Finance

Currency

South Africa's currency is the rand (R), consisting of 100 cents; it's also the currency of the Common Monetary Area of Lesotho, Namibia, South Africa and Swaziland.

Exchange Rate: £1 = R14.05.

Exchange Controls: None for imports, but there are controls on the export of foreign currency. For full details of exchange controls, check the website of the South African Reserve Bank (🖳 www.reservebank.co.za) or any commercial bank in South Africa.

Cost & Standard of Living

The cost of living in South Africa is lower than most that of western European countries but higher than North America's. Locally produced food and alcohol are inexpensive, but imported goods are expensive, including motor vehicles (although there are concessions for migrants). Johannesburg is rated as one of the least expensive major cities in the world. There's no minimum wage in South Africa, although the Ministry of Labour can determine wages in a particular sector. Although South Africa is considered a third-world country, it offers luxury accommodation, goods and amenities at a fraction of the cost in most developed countries. Property is a particular bargain by international standards.

Taxation

Since 2002, South African residents – for tax purposes, those who have stayed in the country for more than 91 days per year during the current and preceding five tax years – have been subject to tax on their worldwide income and any capital gains. Non-residents are taxed only on income from South Africa and capital gains on property.

Personal Effects: Immigrants can bring in household goods and possessions without restriction but must pay a deposit equivalent to the duty payable on the goods. This deposit is refunded when you leave the country permanently or become a resident. Migrants may import a motor vehicle (that has been owned for at least a year) but must obtain permission from the South African Bureau for Standards (🖳 www.sabs.co.za); however import duties and VAT can amount to 70 per cent of a vehicle's value!

9

Income Tax: South Africa has a PAYE system. If your income from employment is less than R60,000 (£4,300) per year, you don't need to file a tax return. Anyone receiving an income from other sources must make provisional payments every six months. Tax rates for individuals are progressive, with six rates, ranging from 18 per cent on income up to R100,000 (£7,150) to 40 per cent on income over R400,000 (£28,500). There are rebates for all individuals, depending on circumstances. Employees must contribute the equivalent of 1 per cent of gross income to the Unemployment Insurance Fund; the same amount is contributed by their employers.

Capital Gains Tax (CGT): CGT is levied at 25 per cent on gains from property sales, although gains of less than R1.5m (£107,000) on the sale of a primary residence are exempt and there's an exemption of R12,500 (£900) on the sale of non-primary residences.

Wealth Tax: None.

Inheritance & Gift Tax: A 'donations' tax of 20 per cent is levied on gifts over the value of R50,000 (£3,600) and an estate tax, also of 20 per cent, on inheritances valued at over R2.5m (£180,000), except when left to a surviving spouse.

Value Added Tax (VAT): VAT is levied at 14 per cent on goods and services, with the exception of basic foodstuffs.

Property

Restrictions on Foreign Ownership & Letting

There are currently no restrictions on foreign ownership, although in 2006 the Pretoria government announced that it was considering restrictions for foreigners because of concerns that foreign property buyers were pushing up prices and making property unaffordable for South Africans. No decision has yet been taken.

There are no restrictions on letting.

Market

The past few years have seen a booming property market for second and permanent homes in South Africa, prompted by the relatively stable political climate and low prices. The market has been fuelled by strong demand from overseas buyers, particularly Britons and Germans. South Africa is due to host the 2010 football World Cup, which has further boosted its attractiveness to investors. As a result, property prices have risen considerably, although they're still low by European standards. The last few years have seen rises of between 20 and 30 per cent per year – the biggest increases being in Cape Town – but annual growth is starting to level off, although it's still around 10 per cent, a level likely to be maintained until the World Cup. Despite these increases, property in South Africa is still excellent value, and favourable exchange rates mean even better value for those buying in major currencies.

South Africa offers a wide choice of property, including superb examples of colonial architecture (e.g. Dutch 'gable' houses), thatched cottages and 19th-century homesteads. New marina and golf apartment and townhouse developments are also attracting foreign buyers. Many larger homes have luxury features such as swimming pools, jacuzzis, saunas, tennis courts, landscaped gardens, barbecue patios ... and extensive security. Many older homes (including most detached properties) have self-contained apartments, which were originally designed as servants' quarters. In many areas, it's normal for foreigners (and wealthy locals) to live in gated communities, with schools and other facilities within the gates. Most property is sold freehold, although it can also be leasehold, sectional title (mostly in the case of condominiums) or 'share block'.

9

Areas

The most popular provinces with foreign buyers are the Western and Eastern Capes, followed by Kwazulu-Natal. The coastal areas around Cape Town on the Western Cape, Port Elizabeth, Port Alfred and East London on the Eastern Cape, and Durban in Kwazulu-Natal are the most sought-after areas – none more so than the so-called Garden Route, which stretches along the south coast from Hermanus in the Western Cape to Port Elizabeth in the Eastern Cape.

Cape Town is perennially popular with buyers. It's one of the world's most attractive cities and is noted for its beautiful surrounding countryside and magnificent coastline. There are numerous prestigious residential areas, including the area south of the city, known as the Gardens suburb, and the Waterfront area north of the city, as well as the southern suburbs of Claremont, Constantia, Observatory and Kenilworth.

The nearby towns of Somerset West, Stellenbosch and Hout Bay on the Atlantic coast are also popular, as are Fish Hoek and Simon's Town on the Indian Ocean, which, although not as attractive, are cheaper than the Central and Western Cape areas. Knysna on the Western Cape (between Cape Town and Port Elizabeth) has become a prime retirement area and Port Alfred is becoming increasingly popular.

Wealthy Gauteng is popular, although expensive because it's the main commercial centre of the country and close to Johannesburg. Prices are lower than in Cape Town, however.

The Northern Cape, which runs north of Cape Town to the Botswana and Namibia borders, appeals mainly to those looking for tranquility.

Building Standards

Standards are variable but generally high.

Cost

Average prices along the Garden Route are around R1.9m (£135,000). You can still buy a three-bedroom house with sea views for under R1.4m (£100,000) and five-bedroom properties with extensive gardens cost around R2.8m (£200,000). In the popular southern suburbs of Cape Town, few apartments are available and many properties are large, luxurious villas which start at around R2m (£150,000) for a three-bedroom property and rise to around R5m (£360,000) for four or five bedrooms and up to R25m (£1.75m) for top-range properties.

In Gauteng, a two-bedroom house starts at R1.5m (£110,000) and a three-bedroom house costs around R3.5m (£250,000).

On the coast of Kwazulu-Natal, a three-bedroom house costs around R1.5m (£110,000), while a more substantial family home costs around R3m (£220,000), although a similar property in a beachside location starts at around R4.5m (£320,000).

Local Mortgages

9

Mortgages (called bonds in South Africa) of up to 90 or even 100 per cent over 20 years are available to residents, although interest rates are high. Mortgages of up to 50 per cent of the purchase price are available to non-residents, although if you've consistently brought funds into the country over a number of years, you may borrow (in theory) up to 100 per cent. There's usually an 'initiation' fee of between 1 and 1.5 per cent, a registration fee of 1 per cent and an inspection fee of 0.2 per cent. There are no non-status (or self-certification) mortgages in South

Africa, so all mortgage applications must be backed up by proof of income. Many buyers find it's cheaper to obtain a mortgage abroad.

Property Taxes

Most South African property owners must pay municipal taxes (rates) for services and refuse collection, which are based on the estimated market value of their property. Some rural properties are exempt, although there are government plans to include them. Rates are around 1 per cent but vary according to the size of the property and other factors. Municipalities may levy different rates for different types of property.

Purchase Procedure

Buying property in South Africa is usually trouble free and the country has a highly efficient system of land registration. Most properties are sold freehold through an estate agent. Agents must be qualified and registered with the Estate Agents' Board. Offers must be made in writing and, when an offer is accepted, a deposit of 10 per cent is normally paid to the seller's estate agent, which is held in the agent's trust (escrow) account. A deposit isn't compulsory but is a sign of good faith. It's usual to have a survey (inspection), which should include checks for damp and termites. An agreement of sale is drawn up by the agent and should contain all the details of the sale, including the particulars and obligations of the buyer and the vendor. The buyer can appoint a lawyer to carry out the necessary checks and register the new ownership at the Registrar of Deeds office, although most procedures can be done (cheaper) by a licensed conveyancer, who is required to register the transfer of ownership. The deed is held by the buyer's bank when there's a mortgage. The whole purchase procedure usually takes between two and three months.

Fees

The tariffs for legal fees, conveyancing costs and transfer duty are set by the government. Transfer duty is high, although the first R500,000 (£36,000) is exempt. Property valued at between R500,000 and R1m (£72,000) is subject to 5 per cent duty (on the amount over R500,000), and property valued at over R1m to a fixed amount of R25,000 (£1,800) plus 8 per cent of the value exceeding R1m. Transfer duty isn't payable on new properties, whose price includes VAT (at 14 per cent). Conveyancing costs (payable to the seller's lawyer) are variable and are usually between 1 and 2 per cent of the purchase price. Other fees total around 1 per cent, depending on whether or not you use a lawyer. An estate agent's fees are around 7.5 per cent and also attract VAT.

9 General Information

Getting There

South Africa's three major international airports are Cape Town, Durban and Johannesburg.
Johannesburg (OR Tambo International) Airport: The largest airport in South Africa (and the busiest in the whole of Africa) is 24km (15mi) north-east of the city. (In 2006 it was officially

named after Oliver Tambo, former President of the African National Congress.) It handles regular flights from the UK and other European destinations (with British Airways, South African Airways and Virgin Atlantic).

Cape Town Airport: The country's second-largest airport and a major entry point for tourists visiting South Africa, Cape Town also handles regular flights from the UK and other European destinations (with British Airways, South African Airways and Virgin Atlantic).

Durban Airport: The smallest of the three airports has a limited number of flights, but in 2006 work began on a new airport at La Mercy, 30km (19mi) north of the city. It will replace the existing airport and should be operational by 2010, in time for the football World Cup.

Communications

South Africa boasts an outstanding telecommunications infrastructure, and telecommunications is the fastest growing industry in the country. It has the most developed communications network in Africa, including the latest fixed-line, wireless and mobile technology. The market is dominated by Telekom SA, the country's only licensed provider of fixed lines. Mobile and internet use is becoming more widespread as other operators enter the market. The country dialling code is 27 and there's international direct dialling (IDD) across the world.

Fixed-line Telephones: Costs are relatively high due to the virtual monopoly of Telekom SA, but a second operator is due to enter the market in 2007. Public telephones use either coins or phone-cards, which can be bought from post offices, stationers and cafes.

Mobile Telephones: Mobile phones are used by over 70 per cent of the population, the introduction of mobile internet technology having led to a marked increase in usage. The main mobile phone operators are Call C, MTN South Africa, Telekom SA, Virgin Mobile and Vodacom.

Internet: Despite the fact that there are more than 200 internet service providers (ISPs) in the country, Telekom SA has created an expensive operating environment, making the market difficult for other operators, but it's finally facing more competition. Many subscribers still use dial-up services. Internet cafes can be found in the main towns and cities.

Postal Services: Services are provided by the South African Post Office (SAPO), which also offers banking services. Post offices are open from 8am to 4.30pm on weekdays and from 8am to 12pm on Saturdays. An independent postal service called PostNet South Africa offers a range of postal and business services to small and medium-size businesses. Letters to European destinations take around a week.

Crime Rate

The crime rate is very high in some cities and urban areas, particularly crimes against property and robbery (including mugging). South Africa's murder rate is the highest in the world but is distorted by the high level of inter-tribal fighting; most murders occur in the townships and in areas away from tourists and foreign residents. The South African authorities give high priority to protecting tourists, with dedicated tourist police deployed in the main towns. Most 'white' areas, where most foreigners buy property, including the popular resorts in the Eastern and Western Capes, are relatively crime-free. Many foreigners live in gated communities or install extensive security systems (including barbed wire and high walls) or employ security guards. Wherever you are in South Africa, it's necessary to take precautions to protect yourself and your property and it's best to avoid high-crime areas. Carjacking is rife in some cities (such as Johannesburg), where it can be dangerous to stop a car at night, even at a red light! Johannesburg is considered a particularly dangerous place, especially the business district, despite efforts by the authorities to control crime. Passport

9

theft is common in South Africa, especially at airports on arrival and departure, so always carry photocopies of your passport with you.

Medical Facilities

Public health facilities in South Africa are under-funded, inefficient and over-used. In some rural areas, public facilities are extremely basic. The state contributes only around 40 per cent of healthcare expenditure, so residents must pay towards their treatment, depending on earnings. There are no reciprocal health agreements, so visitors must also pay for treatment.

In contrast, the private medical sector is growing and attracts highly qualified professionals, with excellent facilities. Comprehensive private health insurance is essential for visitors and residents, including cover for evacuation in case of an emergency.

South Africa has high levels of HIV/AIDS, malaria and multi-drug resistant tuberculosis.

Pets

South Africa operates a limited quarantine period of 14 days for dogs arriving from some countries, but there's no quarantine for cats. Regulations are subject to change, so always check well in advance before travelling, either with a South African embassy or consulate or with the Department of Agriculture Veterinary Services (💻 www.nda.agric.za/vetweb).

All dogs and cats must be micro-chipped for identification and vaccinated against rabies not less than 30 days and not more than a year before arrival. All pets must have an import permit and a health clearance certificate, completed by a government-authorised vet in your home country within ten days of travel. Puppies and kittens less than three months old don't require a rabies vaccination.

Visas & Permits

Visas: Visas aren't required by citizens of most EU countries and some other countries, such as Australia, Japan, New Zealand and the US. Visas are required by citizens of most African, Asian, eastern European and South American countries, and must be obtained before arrival in South Africa. However, all visitors require a visitor's permit, which is granted on arrival and valid for three months.

Residence Permits: Temporary residence permits are granted to those who have short-term employment (over three months but less than a year), those who are studying and those who have close relatives in South Africa (but not residents). In all cases, you must provide evidence that you can support yourself and have comprehensive medical insurance for the period of the permit. You aren't allowed to work part-time to subsidise your studies.

Permanent residence permits are issued to close relatives of a South African citizen or permanent resident; retirees (who must provide evidence that they have a net worth of not less than R12m/£85,700 and the right to a pension of R20,000/£1,400 per month); financially independent people who have a minimum net worth of R20m (£140,000) and pay an upfront fee of R100,000 (£7,000) to the Department of Home Affairs; entrepreneurs who wish to establish a business (investing R2.5m/£180,000 and employing at least five South African citizens); and those who have permanent employment in the country. All applications for permanent residence permits incur a fee of R1,520 (£250).

Work Permits: Work permits are required by any foreigner wishing to work in South Africa for any period. Employers must produce evidence that the position cannot be filled by a South African, except in the following circumstances:

- your employment is within the quota for a specific work category, such as electrical and civil engineers;

- you have 'exceptional' skills, such as a researcher or an academic;

- you're one of several workers on a corporate work permit, which allows companies to employ a number of foreign workers (approval must still be granted by the Department of Labour);

- you're on an internal company transfer, in which case you may not work in South Africa for more than two years.

Reference

Further Reading

Buying a Home in South Africa, Graeme Chesters (Survival Books). Everything you need to know about buying a home in South Africa.
Live and Work in South Africa, Avril Harper (Grant Dawson).
Footprint South Africa Handbook, Sebastian Ballard (Footprint Handbooks).
Lonely Planet: South Africa, Lesotho and Swaziland (Lonely Planet Publications).
Emigrate South Africa, Outbound Media and Exhibitions, 1 Commercial Road, Eastbourne, East Sussex, BN21 3XQ, UK (☎ 01323-726040, 🖳 www.emigrate2.co.uk). Extensive emigration information about a selection of countries, including South Africa.

Useful Addresses

South African High Commission (UK), South Africa House, Trafalgar Square, London WC2N 5DP, UK (☎ 020-7925 8900, 🖳 www.southafricahouse.com).
South African Embassy (US), 3051 Massachusetts Ave., NW, Washington, DC 20008, US (☎ 202-232 4400, 🖳 www.saembassy.org).
South African Tourism (UK), 6 Alt Grove, Wimbledon, London SW19 4DZ, UK (☎ 020-8971 9350, 🖳 www.southafrica.net).
South African Tourism (US), 500 5th Avenue, 20th Floor, Suite 2040, New York NY 10110, US (☎ 212-730 2929, 🖳 www.southafrica.net).

Useful Websites

Institute of Estate Agents South Africa (🖳 www.ieasa.org.za).
South Africa Online (🖳 www.southafrica.co.za).
South African Government (🖳 www.gov.za).
South African Government, Department of Home Affairs (🖳 www.home-affairs.gov.za).
South African Government, Department of Labour (🖳 www.labour.gov.za).

9

NORTH AMERICA: CANADA

Background Information

Capital: Ottawa.
Population: 32m.
Foreign Community: Canada has the highest per capita immigration rate in the world, according to its federal government. As a result of the large number of immigrants, it's a cosmopolitan country, and Montreal, Toronto and Vancouver are among the most multicultural cities in the world. Over 30 per cent of Canada's population is of British origin and 30 per cent is of French origin, and the country also has large German, Dutch and Ukrainian communities. There has been a large influx of Asian immigrants in the last 15 years, particularly from Hong Kong. Most of Canada's new immigrants come from Asia, Africa and Latin America.
Area: 9,976,185km^2 (3,852,106 mi^2).
Geography: Canada is the largest country in the world, with an area equal to that of Europe (40 times that of the UK and 18 times that of France) and a coastline of 250,000km (155,000mi) – equivalent to six times the earth's circumference. Sparsely populated, Canada has huge areas of wilderness, including mountains, forests (one third of the country), tundra, prairies and polar desert in the north and west. Almost 8 per cent of the country consists of fresh water, including four of the world's largest lakes (Huron, Superior, Great Bear and Great Slave).

In the east are the maritime provinces of Newfoundland, Nova Scotia, New Brunswick and Prince Edward Island, and the predominantly French-speaking province of Quebec. The central province of Ontario borders the Great Lakes, extending north across the Canadian Shield (a vast rocky 'plain' covering much of the north of the country) to Hudson Bay. Further west are the prairie provinces of Manitoba, Saskatchewan and Alberta, with fertile farmlands in the south and lake-strewn forests on the sub-arctic wastelands of the north. South-western Alberta contains a substantial part of the Rocky Mountains, with peaks rising to over 4,000m (13,120ft). The westernmost province, British Columbia, is mountainous and comprises forests, lakes and sheltered valleys with rich farmland. The vast, largely unpopulated, northern areas include the Yukon Territory bordering Alaska and the extensive Northwest Territories.
Climate: The Canadian climate is noted for its extremes of heat and cold, which are more pronounced inland than on the coast. Regional climates vary enormously. The Pacific coast (e.g. Vancouver) is warm and fairly dry in summer and mild, cloudy and wet in winter. Inland conditions are more extreme, depending on the altitude. The region from the Great Lakes to the Rocky Mountains experiences cold winters and warm summers with low rainfall. The southern areas of central Canada are humid, with hot summers and cold winters, and rain throughout the year, while the Atlantic regions have a humid but temperate climate. The northern regions, comprising some 40 per cent of the country's area, experience arctic conditions, with temperatures below freezing for most of the year and falling as low as -40C (-40F) in winter. Average daily temperatures are around 21C (69F) in summer (July) in Montreal and Toronto, falling to between -7 and -10C (20 to 14F) in winter (January). In Vancouver, average temperatures are around 17C (63F) in July and 2.5C (36F) in January.
Language: Canada has two official languages, English and French (spoken mostly in Quebec), which enjoy equal status. English is spoken by some 60 per cent of the population and French by 25 per cent; around 15 per cent are fluent in both languages. Chinese is Canada's third most widely spoken language due to the large number of Asian immigrants.
Political Situation: Canada's system of government is based on the British parliamentary model and it's one of the most politically stable countries in the world, although tensions have been running high for some years between Quebec and the rest of Canada. This is because of the agitation of the provincial separatist Parti Québécois (PQ) for independence, although support for the PQ has waned recently. Canada is a constitutional monarchy, with Queen

Elizabeth II as Head of State, represented by her Governor General in Canada. The country has two tiers of government, federal and provincial, ten provinces enjoying considerable autonomy. The main political parties at federal level are the Conservative Party, Liberal Party, the Bloc Québécois (only in Quebec Province) and the New Democratic Party (NDP). Michaelle Jean has been Governor General since September 2005 and Stephen Harper, leader of the Conservative Party, was elected Prime Minister in February 2006. Canada is a member of the North American Free Trade Association (NAFTA) – with the US and Mexico – as well as NATO and the British Commonwealth.

Finance

Currency

Canada's currency is the Canadian dollar (C$), consisting of 100 cents.
Exchange Rate: £1 = C$2.15.
Exchange Controls: None.

Cost & Standard of Living

Canada is one of the world's wealthiest nations and enjoys a high standard of living. The Canadian economy is very healthy and has had steady growth over the last decade, with low unemployment. Canada has a low cost of living (lower than most western European countries), with low inflation and high salaries. Minimum wages vary with the province but average between C$7 and C$8.50 per hour. The quality of life in Canada has been rated the highest in the world by the United Nations.

Taxation

Residents in Canada must pay federal and provincial income tax and the combined rates are high, reflecting the high level of government healthcare and university education subsidies. Anybody resident in Canada for more than 183 days per year is considered a resident for tax purposes and taxed on their worldwide income. Those who work in Canada for shorter periods are usually considered non-residents and taxed only on Canadian income.

Personal Effects: Personal effects can be imported duty free but must have been owned and used before entry and must be retained for a minimum of one year. A detailed list of all items to be imported must be provided.

Income Tax: Federal income tax rates range from 15.5 per cent on earnings up to C$37,178 to 29 per cent on earnings above C$120,887. Provincial income tax rates vary considerably and are applied by each province, although collected by the federal government. British Columbia and Ontario have some of the lowest rates, while Labrador and Newfoundland, Manitoba and New Brunswick have some of the highest.

Capital Gains Tax (CGT): CGT is levied on the sale or purchase of any asset excluding your principal residence. 50 per cent of any gains are included in your taxable income. The lifetime capital gains ceiling was raised to C$750,000 in 2007. Non-resident property owners must also pay CGT on the sale of property in Canada.

Inheritance & Gift Tax: None, although beneficiaries may be required to pay income tax on a bequest.

9

Value Added Tax (VAT): A goods and services tax (GST) of 6 per cent and a harmonised sales tax (HST) of 14 per cent are levied by the federal government on most goods and services. Some provinces also apply a provincial sales tax (PST) on retail sales, but three (New Brunswick, Newfoundland and Labrador and Nova Scotia) have subsumed their PST within HST. Sales tax isn't included in advertised prices but is added when you pay for goods. Property sales are generally taxable at the above rates, but in some circumstances they're exempt, such as re-sales by a private person (not a builder). If you're selling a property, you're required to collect GST/HST on behalf of the government, unless you're a non-resident.

Property

Restrictions on Foreign Ownership & Letting

There are no restrictions on foreign ownership in British Columbia, New Brunswick, Newfoundland, Nova Scotia, Ontario or Quebec, provided you spend less than six months per year in Canada. In Banff, Alberta, which is in a National Park, only businesses and employees of the park can own property, which they must do through renewable 42-year leasehold agreements. There are no restrictions on letting in Canada, but rental income is taxable at 25 per cent.

Market

Canada's property market is mature and well regulated and has been flourishing for many years. It has remained healthy despite the serious problems experienced by the US market. Experts believe this is in part due to Canada's less high-risk lending practices, which caused overheating and a near crash in the US market. Prices in Canada peaked in 2005 and the country now enjoys sustained, if less dramatic, growth. Throughout the country, price increases averaged around 10 per cent in 2006, although there are significant regional differences, Alberta and British Columbia currently experiencing something of a boom.

There's a huge variety of property for sale in Canada, from apartments (condominiums) to large detached properties with substantial plots. Condominiums usually have communal garages and sports facilities. The property market in British Columbia has been boosted by the fact that it's hosting the 2010 Winter Olympics.

Areas

Western provinces, especially Alberta and British Columbia, are currently more popular with homebuyers than those in the east. With British Columbia due to host the 2010 Winter Olympics, interest has increased in the area around the ski resort of Whistler and also in Vancouver, which has long been a favourite location for people buying property in Canada. The major cities of Montreal and Toronto remain popular, while people after a holiday home for winter skiing and/or summer 'wilderness' holidays often choose the popular ski resorts, such as Banff, Jasper, Lake Louise, Okanagan Valley, Whistler and various resorts in Quebec. Like 75 per cent of the Canadian population, most permanent Canadian residents live just north of the US border, where they're close to the main cities and can enjoy the most pleasant weather.

9

Building Standards

Building standards are generally high. Buildings have efficient insulation due to the extremely cold winters in most of the country.

Cost

The average price across the country in early 2007 was C$311,000 (£137,000). In popular areas of British Columbia, such as Whistler, prices for a one-bedroom apartment start at around C$260,000 (£120,000). A two-bedroom townhouse costs around C$450,000 (£210,000), while a luxurious four-bedroom house costs over C$1m (£470,000). In Vancouver, the highest price rises have been for condominiums, a two-bedroom property costing around C$400,000 (£185,000), a detached bungalow around C$750,000 (£350,000) and a large, two-storey house around C$830,000 (£385,000).

The other popular province is Alberta, whose urban areas inlcude Calgary and Edmonton and which also boasts the ski resort of Banff in the National Park. Property prices in new developments in Alberta start at around C$450,000 (£210,000), upmarket houses costing around C$850,000 (£400,000).

City properties in Montreal and Toronto tend to be apartments, for which demand outstrips supply. Prices in Montreal start at around C$270,000 (£125,000) for a one-bedroom apartment, while duplex and triplex properties cost around C$650,000 (£300,000). Toronto prices tend to be a little higher, two-bedroom apartments starting around C$400,000 (£185,000).

In Newfoundland, two enormous new developments are aimed at the winter sports market. One is situated beside a coast lake and includes a variety of luxury amenities. Two-bedroom apartments there start at C$360,000 (£165,000) and luxurious ski chalets cost from C$650,000 (£300,000). Similar ski properties in Lake Tremblant in Quebec are less expensive: around C$280,000 (£130,000) for an apartment and C$1.4m (£650,000) for a large luxury chalet.

Local Mortgages

Mortgages of up to a maximum of 80 per cent of the purchase price (65 per cent for non-residents) are available from local banks and other financial institutions. The term is traditionally for 25 to 30 years, although shorter terms are available. New residents in Canada may find it difficult to obtain a mortgage because you must provide proof of a perfect credit record (preferably in Canada) to secure one.

Property Taxes

Property taxes are levied by local municipalities and vary considerably. Each of Canada's ten provinces decides its own property transfer tax rates. People living in apartments also pay monthly community fees.

9

Purchase Procedure

Buying a home in Canada is generally very safe and there are few traps for the unwary, as it's a highly regulated market However, it's wise to engage a buyer's broker, who acts solely for you and works in your best interests. You should also use the services of a qualified appraiser to obtain an accurate valuation of a property. It's important to have a structural survey before buying a resale home, which should include a termite inspection, particularly for homes located near water.

The majority of estate agents use the Multiple Listing Service (MLS), which can narrow your search for a property. The purchase procedure and regulations differ according to the province. In some areas, there aren't any restrictions on foreign ownership (see above) and each province has different restrictions on land ownership. Once you've found a property, a small goodwill deposit is usually paid, although this is refunded if you cannot continue with the sale for any reason. An independent realtor or buyer's agent will draft an Offer to Purchase, which may have certain conditions and is accompanied by a 10 per cent deposit. Once this is signed by buyer and vendor, the sale can proceed and title checks be made. Once all is in order, the balance is paid, along with taxes, and title transferred to the new owner.

Fees

The fees associated with buying a home in Canada include those for an appraisal, survey, lawyer, land transfer tax, title registration and a compliance certificate. Legal fees are usually 0.75 to 1 per cent and land transfer tax is from 0.5 to 2 per cent of the purchase price. New houses are subject to GST and in some provinces PST is also levied (see **Value Added Tax** on page 350).

General Information

Getting There

Canada's main airports are, in order of popularity, Toronto (Ontario), Vancouver (British Columbia), Montreal (Quebec), Calgary and Edmonton (Alberta), Ottawa (Ontario), Winnipeg (Manitoba) and Halifax (Nova Scotia).

Toronto (Pearson) Airport: The busiest airport in the country is around 27km (17mi) west of the city centre, with excellent road connections. It has three terminals and handles a vast range of flights from the US, Europe and other destinations. It's the hub for the national airline, Air Canada, which flies from Dublin, London Heathrow, Manchester and Shannon airports. British Airways has a flight from London Heathrow and Zoom Airlines has flights from a large selection of UK airports.

Vancouver International Airport: Located on Sea Island around 15km (9mi) from the city of Vancouver, it has flights from Asia, Australasia, the Caribbean, Europe and the US. Air Canada and British Airways have flights from London Heathrow and Flyglobespan flies from Glasgow, London Gatwick and Manchester. My Travel and Thomas Cook operate some seasonal flights from UK airports, while Zoom Airlines has flights from around six UK airports.

Montreal International Airport: Located 20km (12mi) from the city, this airport serves the French-speaking province of Quebec. The airport handles flights from Africa, Asia, the Caribbean, Central and South America, Europe and the US. Airlines operating into Montreal include Air Canada and British Airways (London Heathrow), Thomas Cook Airlines and Zoom Airlines (European and UK destinations).

9

Communications

Canada has modern and efficient communications. Bell Canada was the government-owned monopoly until deregulation of the industry in the mid-'80s. There's no longer a single national telephone provider, and each of the ten provinces has its own provider and regulations. Many providers offer telephone, mobile and internet services in a single package of 'bundle'. There's widespread use of mobile phones and domestic internet services. The country dialling code is 1 and international direct dialling (IDD) is available worldwide.

Fixed-line Telephones: International calls are very expensive but you can cut costs by using a pre-paid international calling card. These cards can be used from any kind of telephone, including public telephone boxes, although these are reducing in number in Canada as mobile phone use rises.

Mobile Telephones: Mobile usage is rising quickly in Canada, many subscribers using mobile phones in preference to fixed lines and many households having several mobile phones. The main providers are Aliant (New Brunswick, Newfoundland and Labrador, and Nova Scotia), Bell Mobility and Rogers/Fido-Microcell (Ontario and Quebec), Telus Mobility (Alberta, British Columbia, Ontario and Quebec), Sprint Canada (Ontario and Quebec), Sasktel (Saskatchewan) and Virgin Mobile (Ontario). There are two systems, CDMA and GSM, which operate on the 800, 850 and 1900 frequencies. If you bring a mobile phone from your home country, check with your provider whether you can use it in Canada.

Internet: Canada has dial-up, high-speed ADSL and cable internet connections, although only dial-up is generally available outside the major cities. The largest national internet service provider is Bell Sympatico, which owns a significant amount of infrastructure, but there's an enormous variety of providers in each province. Internet cafes and wi-fi areas can be found in all main towns and cities.

Postal Services: Postal services are provided by Canada Post, which offers a variety of bilingual services throughout the country. Post offices are open from 9am to 6pm on weekdays, and some shops offer basic postal services. Letters and parcels take around a week to reach Europe.

Crime Rate

The crime rate in Canada is low. Canada has strict gun control laws and a low murder rate, which is similar to that of most western European countries.

Medical Facilities

Medical facilities are generally excellent. Healthcare is financed by mandatory public health insurance contributions by employees. Nearly all Canadian workers and their employers must contribute to the federal employment insurance (EI) fund. Many employers also provide supplementary healthcare, and most businesses offer dental plans. If you aren't contributing to the national health insurance scheme, treatment is very expensive and private health insurance is vital.

9

Pets

Pet imports are regulated by the Canadian Food Inspection Agency. All animals are subject to a veterinary inspection at the port of entry. Some (e.g. birds) are required to undergo a period of quarantine. Otherwise, domestic pets can enter Canada for long or short stays without a rabies vaccination or a quarantine period as long as they're imported from rabies-free countries (e.g. the UK). Pets from countries with rabies must have a rabies vaccination, issued at least a month before their importation. Detailed pet import information is available on the website of the Canadian government's Food Inspection Agency (🖥 www.inspection.ga.ca).

Visas & Permits

Visa: Citizens of many countries, including Australia, some Caribbean countries, most EU countries and residents of the US (including foreigners in possession of a Green Card), don't require a visa to visit Canada. You may stay for up to six months of the year, but if you wish to remain longer, you must leave Canada and re-enter or apply to the Immigration Services well in advance. Check with a Canadian embassy about the requirements before travelling.

Residence Permits: Canada has annual immigration quotas, but these are among the most generous in the world. It operates a points system, with preference given to those with special skills that are in demand, those wishing to start a business, those with family ties, and refugees. Being bi-lingual (English/French) is an advantage if you wish to immigrate to find work. It's very difficult to retire to Canada unless you're sponsored by a close family member, who has to demonstrate that he can support you for up to ten years. Most of the provinces have separate immigration quotas. Quebec has specific immigration regulations which must be met once you've been approved by the federal government; more information is available on the Quebec Immigration website (🖥 www.immigration-quebec.gouv.qc.ca).

Work Permits: Work permits are linked to residence permits (see above) and Canada's immigration quotas, based on certain skills. To work in Canada, you must have a job offer and the employer who sponsors you must be able to prove that a Canadian isn't available to fill the post.

Reference

Further Reading

Living and Working in Canada, edited by Graeme Chesters (Survival Books). Everything you need to know about living and working in Canada.

Canadian Immigration Made Easy, Tariq Nadeem (Self Help Publishers).

Emigrate Canada, Outbound Media and Exhibitions, 1 Commercial Road, Eastbourne, East Sussex, BN21 3XQ, UK (☎ 01323-726040, 🖥 www.emigrate2.co.uk). Extensive emigration information about a selection of countries, including Canada. Also available online.

Getting Into Canada, Benjamin A. Kranc & Elena Constantin (How To Books).

Getting a Job in Canada, Valerie Gerrard (How To Books).

A Newcomer's Introduction to Canada (Canadian Ministry of Employment and Immigration). Also downloadable via the Citizen and Immigration Canada website (see below).

9

Useful Addresses

Canadian High Commission (UK), Macdonald House, 38 Grosvenor Street, London W1K 4AA, UK (☎ 020-7258 6506, 🖥 www.canada.org.uk).

Canadian High Commission (US), 501 Pennsylvania Ave., NW, Washington, DC 20001-2114, US (☎ 202-682 1740, 🖥 www.canadianembassy.org).

Canadian Real Estate Association, 200 Catherine Street, 6th Floor, Ottawa, ON KP2 2K9, Canada (☎ 613-237 7111, 🖥 www.crea.ca).

Visit Canada Centre, PO Box 5396, Northampton, NN1 2FA, UK (☎ 0870-161 5151, ✉ visitcanada@dial.pipex.com). ·

Useful Website

Canada Revenue Agency (🖥 www.cra-arc.ca).
Citizenship and Immigration Canada (🖥 www.cic.gc.ca).

NORTH AMERICA: THE CARIBBEAN

Background Information

The Caribbean Sea contains two major island chains: the Greater Antilles (which account for nearly 90 per cent of the region's land area) and the Lesser Antilles (which are made up of the Leeward Islands in the north and the Windward Islands in the south). (Bermuda is included in this section, although it isn't strictly in the Caribbean, lying to the north-east, in the Atlantic Ocean.) The Caribbean islands extend almost 4,000km (2,500mi) in a wide arc from the Bahamas, 100km (60mi) off the east coast of Florida, to Trinidad, 24km (15mi) off the coast of Venezuela. Most of the major islands are independent countries, although they retain close ties with their former rulers, and some remain colonies or dependent territories of the UK, France, the Netherlands or the US. The Caribbean islands which attract the most foreign property buyers are the following:

Island(s)	Area	Population
Antigua & Barbuda	442km^2/179mi^2	69,000
Bahamas	13,938km^2/5,382mi^2	304,000
Barbados	430km^2/166mi^2	274,000
Bermuda	53km^2/20mi^2	69,000
Cayman Islands	259km^2/100mi^2	53,000
Dominica	748km^2/289mi^2	72,000
Guadeloupe	1,710km^2/66mi^2	453,000
Jamaica	10,990km^2/4,243mi^2	2.7m
Martinique	1,100km^2/425mi^2	399,000
Montserrat	102km^2/39mi^2	5,000

9

Puerto Rico	8,897km²/3,435mi²	4m
St. Christopher (St. Kitts) & Nevis	360km²/139mi²	45,000
St. Lucia	622km²/240mi²	160,000
St. Vincent & the Grenadines	388km²/150mi²	118,000
Trinidad & Tobago	5,130km²/1,981mi²	1.3m
Turks & Caicos Islands	430km²/166mi²	32,000
British Virgin Islands	153km²/59mi²	27,000
US Virgin Islands	340km²/130mi²	117,000

Population: The majority of the 'native' inhabitants of the Caribbean are of African descent, their ancestors having been shipped there as slaves and servants. Some islands also have a large Indian population, whose forebears were brought to the Caribbean as labourers by the British. The population of many islands swells considerably in the winter, when many visitors stay for the whole season.

Foreign Community: There's a significant foreign community on most Caribbean islands, mainly British and American retirees and expatriate workers engaged in financial services and tourism. Many foreigners spend up to half the year in the Caribbean.

Geography: The Caribbean islands comprise a total land area of 234,000km² (90,350mi²) and, with the exception of the Bahamas and Bermuda, lie between latitude 10° north and the Tropic of Cancer (23°27' north). They're made up of literally thousands of tropical islands and cays (the Bahamas alone comprise some 700), the vast majority of which are tiny and uninhabited. The islands are noted for their dazzling white sandy beaches (some of the finest in the world) and fine coral reefs, warm clear seas, lush vegetation and exotic flora and fauna (rainforests, tropical plants and flowers), mountains, rivers and waterfalls, and cloudless blue skies. The area lies on the mostly oceanic tectonic plate known as the Caribbean Plate. Some islands have active volcanoes, including Guadeloupe, Martinique, St. Vincent and Montserrat, which was devastated in 1997 when its Soufriere Hills volcano erupted, spewing ash and lava over half the island and burying the capital, Plymouth.

Climate: The Caribbean islands enjoy a tropical or (in the northern Bahamas and Bermuda) sub-tropical climate, which is one of the healthiest in the world, with 3,000 hours (some 300 days) of sunshine a year. However, the climate differs considerably between the islands, as a result of their varying topography. On most islands, daytime temperatures rarely drop below 16C (61F) or rise above 32C (90F), and the average annual temperature is around 25C (77F). In winter, the weather is usually pleasant, with temperatures between around 18 and 25C (64 to 77F). The difference between the highest and lowest average temperatures varies throughout the year by just 3C (5.5F) in the southern Antilles and 6C (11F) in the Bahamas. (During the northern hemisphere's winter, the Caribbean is the world's cruise centre.) Average sea temperatures range from around 28C (82F) in the warmest months to 25C (77F) in the coolest (in the sub-tropical Bahamas the temperature is a few degrees lower, cooler again around Bermuda).

Many islands experience high humidity, particularly in summer, although the heat is tempered by cooling trade winds. Annual rainfall varies considerably but on most islands is between 1m and 1.5m (39 to 59in), with the wettest months between May and November and the driest from December to April, although some islands see rainfall throughout the year. The region is susceptible to violent storms and hurricanes between June and November, and most islands experience severe tropical storms around every ten years (hurricanes less frequently).

9

Language: The official language is English (American English), French, Dutch or Spanish, depending on the island's former (or current) colonial allegiance. On the majority of islands, the official language is English, while many also have their own colloquial languages, such as Creole and Papiamento, the *patois* spoken in the former British possessions.

Political Situation: The political situation varies according to the island but is generally good to excellent. Many islands are colonies or dependent territories (by choice) and are thus as stable as their 'parent' countries. Most ex-British colonies have a system of government based on the British parliamentary model. Some governments have been involved in corruption scandals in recent years, although this is the exception. Many Caribbean countries are members of the Caribbean Community (CARICOM), formed in 1973. In 2001, the original treaty was revised and the CARICOM Single Market and Economy (CSME) was established and came into effect in 2006. Members of the CSME will all eventually have a common passport, harmonisation of economic and fiscal polices and a single currency.

Finance

Currency

The formation of the CSME (see above) means that all Caribbean islands will eventually have a single currency. At present, the economy of the Caribbean is closely tied to the economy of the US, and some of the island's currencies are linked to the US$ at a fixed exchange rate. Eight islands – Anguilla, Antigua & Barbuda, Dominica, Grenada, Montserrat, St. Kitts & Nevis, St. Lucia, and St. Vincent – are members of the Organisation of Eastern Caribbean States (OECS) and share a currency, the Eastern Caribbean dollar (EC$). US$ banknotes are widely accepted (the US$ is the *de facto* currency in the Caribbean) and the US$ is the official currency of some islands. Many islands are popular tax havens, particularly the Bahamas and the Cayman Islands.

Exchange Controls: These vary from island to island – many have none, but some do, including Antigua, the Bahamas, Barbados and Montserrat. Membership of the CSME (see above) means that controls may be lifted, although policy is in the process of formulation. In some islands, the export of local currency is subject to restrictions and may be prohibited. Some islands require foreign currency to be declared on entry and exit, and only imported currency can be exported. Always check with the relevant embassy or consulate or the country's Central Bank.

Interest Rate: Rates vary from island to island but are usually much higher than in Europe and the US. Each island's Central Bank sets regulatory controls, although lenders are given a certain amount of freedom to decide their own rates. Rates for US$ loans are usually lower (around 6 per cent), but these are only available to overseas residents and must be repaid in US$.

Cost & Standard of Living

The cost of food and essential services is reasonably low on most islands, although some islands are becoming more expensive, such as Bermuda and the Cayman Islands. Imported goods (including most consumer durables) are expensive. Cars, clothing and appliances are expensive, while items such as jewellery, perfumes and alcohol are generally inexpensive. The cost of living is similar to that in most western European countries but higher than in the US and Canada, although favourable income tax rates on most islands mean that earnings are also higher.

9

Taxation

One of the great attractions of the Caribbean islands is their favourable tax regime and the area is well known for its 'tax haven' status. However, the introduction of the CARICOM Single Market and Economy (CSME) in 2006 means that member countries are working towards (among other things) tax harmonisation, and tax rates may change. Always check the latest rates with a tax adviser.

Personal Effects: Personal effects can be freely imported, although duty is payable (at high rates) on some large items, such as motor vehicles. In some cases, items of high value, such as photographic equipment, portable computers, electronics apparatus and sports equipment, must be declared.

Income Tax: There's no income tax on many Caribbean islands; where there is, it's relatively low or there's a fairly high threshold before you become liable for taxation. Retired foreign nationals may be exempt from paying income tax on income earned abroad. On the other hand, tax on rental income on some islands is high.

Capital Gains Tax (CGT): Most Caribbean islands have no capital gains tax. A notable exception is the Dominican Republic, where new laws in 2006 introduced a CGT rate of 30 per cent for non-residents.

Wealth Tax: None on most islands, but in 2006 the Dominican Republic introduced a wealth tax of 1 per cent (flat rate) on a property's market value. This is in addition to property tax (see page 361).

Inheritance & Gift Tax: None on most islands.

Value Added Tax (VAT): Not all islands have a value added or sales tax, although this is beginning to change as more become part of the CSME (see above) and seek a uniform tax scheme among Caribbean countries. Those which are implementing a sales tax are setting it at 15 per cent and it's thought that the entire Caribbean region will have VAT or sales tax by 2010. The main source of income for most Caribbean governments is import duty, which is levied on most imported goods. Some islands have other taxes, such as a tax on hotel bills, although these are now being integrated into the sales tax.

Property

Restrictions on Foreign Ownership & Letting

Official government permission is usually required for foreigners to buy land or property, and regulations differ from island to island. The following restrictions apply to foreign buyers on the main islands:

- **Antigua & Barbuda** – Buyers must obtain a licence, known as a Non-Citizen Land Holding Licence, which can take up to six months to process, costs 5 per cent of the value of the property and is specific to the property.

- **Bahamas** – Non-residents must register their purchase with the Foreign Investments Board and a permit is required if the property is over five years old or if you plan to let it. Foreigners must also register their investment with the Exchange Control Department at the Central Bank of the Bahamas, to ensure eventual repatriation of funds, should this be necessary.

- **Barbados** – The island has few restrictions but non-residents must obtain permission from the Central Bank. This is a formality, but failure to do so voids your purchase.

- **Dominican Republic** – Although there aren't any restrictions on foreign ownership of property, there's a history of fraud by estate agents and little protection for buyers, so extreme vigilance is necessary. You should also be aware that higher prices are charged to foreigners, particularly those who speak only English.

- **British Virgin Islands** – All foreigners and non-residents must obtain a 'Non-Belonger Land Holding Licence' (NBLHL) before purchase. The NBLHL is only granted for a specific property and takes between 12 and 24 months to obtain. If you plan to let the property, you must have this added to your NBLHL, but permission to let isn't always granted. Applications must be accompanied by financial, character and police references.

There are letting restrictions on some other Caribbean islands and you should check these carefully before committing yourself; on some islands you must obtain permission. Most developers provide a management and letting service.

Market

There are a lot of Caribbean islands, making it difficult to generalise about the region's property market, although there's a buoyant market in luxury homes on most islands, with high prices on some. Many experts believed that the recent downturn in the US property market would have a knock-on effect on the Caribbean, but it has remained stable. Beachfront properties are in particularly high demand. Recently, some developers have begun to build developments in gated communities on some of the less well known islands. Although prices may seem attractive, crime levels might be high, making it dangerous to leave your gated community. On most of the islands, rental yields are low to moderate and predominantly seasonal.

Areas

The most buoyant markets in the Caribbean have traditionally been on islands in the Lesser Antilles, such as the Bahamas, Barbados and the British Virgin Islands (BVI), but property there is expensive. More recently, Antigua and Barbuda have begun to attract more interest, along with some less well known islands, where new developments are being built. The information below covers the most popular islands and those whose market has shown substantial growth in recent years.

Antigua & Barbuda: These have long been popular with buyers who don't need to budget. Most foreigners want a beachfront property, although they rarely become available. Jolly Harbour beach on the west coast has attracted a lot of recent interest, but prices are high. However, new developments close to the capital, St. John's, are more affordable. This has combined with more competitively priced air travel to keep the island's property market healthy.

Bahamas: Easy access to the US (the Bahamas is a short flight from South Florida) has made the Bahamas popular with American tourists and homebuyers. Nassau, the capital and commercial centre, and the Family Islands (also known as the Out Islands) are the most popular areas. The ten Family Islands are popular with the rich and famous because of their isolation and natural beauty.

Barbados: One of the most famous Caribbean islands and long popular with tourists, Barbados has hosted a number of high-profile sporting events, including the 2007 Cricket World Cup. This has increased interest in its property market. The west coast is the most popular, with both foreign residents and tourists, but the south coast is growing in popularity, as it has a more traditional feel and property prices are lower.

9

British Virgin Islands (BVI): This group of islands is among the most expensive in the Caribbean. It's popular with millionaires, and the BVI government is keen to keep it that way. They carefully control development and there's plenty of demand for properties, even those costing several million dollars. The island of Virgin Gorda has seen much of the islands' development, although it's very high quality and expensive.

Dominican Republic: There has been increased interest in the Dominican Republic in recent years, mainly because of the construction of high-profile luxury beach developments. They're on the north-east and south-east coasts, including Cap Cana on the latter, which has been developed by Donald Trump and includes several five-star hotels, golf courses and luxury homes.

Building Standards

There's usually a huge difference between what estate agents sometimes call a 'local property', which is likely to be poorly constructed and in need of substantial renovation, and the high-end property built for the tourist industry, foreign market and affluent locals. These tend to be luxurious detached homes or new developments, the latter usually providing a wide range of amenities, e.g. restaurants, bars, shops, tennis courts, swimming pools, water sports facilities, private beaches, boat docks and on-site management offices. Homes are usually built in the local style, employing local materials (e.g. wood) whenever possible.

Cost

Homes on most islands are expensive, the result of the scarcity of land and because most building materials, fixtures and fittings must be imported. On the most popular islands, apartments start at around US$300,000 and detached villas at US$700,000, although cheaper property is available on some islands. Prices have risen considerably over the last decade and beachfront properties are prohibitively expensive on many islands. Most new developments comprise luxury condominiums (apartments) or luxury detached homes. Prices are usually quoted in US$.

- **Antigua** – In the Jolly Harbour area, a two-bedroom apartment is around US$300,000 and a four-bedroom villa around US$700,000.

- **Bahamas** – Even a small beachfront property starts at around US$800,000, while anything larger costs from around US$1.5m upwards.

- **Barbados** – In Bridgetown, prices vary with the district. The exclusive St. James area has properties starting at around US$900,000, while larger properties are around US$5m.

- **Dominican Republic** – A small house costs from around US$300,000, while larger villas are around US$1.5m.

- **British Virgin Islands** – These have the highest house prices in the Caribbean, and beachfront properties start at well over US$5m, while larger properties are around the US$10m mark. If you don't want (or cannot afford) a property on the beach, a small house starts at around US$700,000.

9

Local Mortgages

Mortgages are available from local banks on most islands and are usually available in US$, sterling or euros. Maximum loans are usually 70 per cent on second homes, with repayment over a maximum of 20 years. A small duty may be imposed on mortgages. Lenders generally insist that properties are insured for their full value and borrowers may also require life insurance.

Property Taxes

Property taxes are levied on most islands and are based on the market or rentable value. On some islands, property taxes are the only form of tax **and** they're fairly low.

- **Antigua & Barbuda** – There's a non-resident property tax of 14 per cent, except in northern and central parts of the capital, St. John's, where the rate is only 5 per cent.

- **Bahamas** – For residents, rates are 1 per cent of the market value of a property between US$250,000 and US$500,000, and 1.5 per cent of the market value above US$500,000. Non-residents pay 1 per cent of the market value up to US$500,000, 2 per cent over that amount.

- **Barbados** – There's an annual tax on the improved value of a property. Rates are low and range from 0.1 per cent to 0.75 per cent (the latter rate on properties valued at over US$172,840).

- **Dominican Republic** – The island has a property tax based on the assessed value, levied on properties with a value over US$146,413 at 1 per cent.

- **British Virgin Islands** – There's a tax of US$50 on land up to half an acre, up to 1 acre is charged at US$150 and each additional acre is US$50. In addition, a house tax is levied at a flat rate of 1.5 per cent on the assessed annual rental value.

Purchase Procedure

Purchase procedures vary throughout the Caribbean and you're recommended to obtain local professional advice. On most islands, procedures are based on the British model and there's an efficient and safe legal system, meaning that problems are rare. It's impossible to generalise, but the information below provides some guidance about the procedures on the most popular islands.

- **Antigua & Barbuda** – Once you have your Non-Citizen Land Holding Licence (see **Restrictions on Foreign Ownership & Letting** above), the process is similar to the British system. You should arrange a survey and a local lawyer should carry out title searches. Property transfers must be registered at the local Lands Office.

- **Bahamas** – The Bahamas property industry is well regulated for the protection of buyers and sellers. A local lawyer carries out title searches and gives what's called a professional opinion on the safety of title. This is in effect title insurance, as lawyers are liable if there proves to be a problem with title.

9

- **Barbados** – Once you have permission to buy (see above), a contract is drawn up and a 10 per cent deposit is paid, which is held in an escrow account until completion. A local lawyer must search the title deed and once all is in order the vendor pays the balance and any taxes. Transfer of ownership must be recorded in the Land Registry.

- **Dominican Republic** – The buying process is similar to that in many other Spanish-speaking countries: a notary oversees the drawing up and signing of a sale contract and the paying of taxes. A 10 per cent deposit is required to reserve the property and a local lawyer carries out title searches. Once these are satisfactory, the balance is paid and transfer of title registered in the Title Registry Office under the supervision of the notary.

- **British Virgin Islands** – Strict regulations are in place to prevent property speculation. Buyers pay a 10 per cent deposit on signing a Sale and Purchase agreement, which usually has a conditional clause so that the buyer can withdraw if the NBLHL (see above) isn't granted. The deposit is held in an escrow account until completion, when transfer of ownership is recorded in the BVI Land Registry.

Fees

Most of the popular countries have high buying costs, which include the issue of necessary licences. Estate agents' fees are high, usually between 5 and 10 per cent, and legal (conveyance) fees are usually 2.5 to 3 per cent of the sale price.

- **Antigua & Barbuda** – Transaction costs include 5 per cent Non-Citizen Land Holding Licence fees; stamp duty, which is paid by both buyer and vendor (2.5 and 7.5 per cent respectively); legal fees of between 1 and 2 per cent; and estate agents' fees of between 5 and 7 per cent, paid by the vendor.

- **Bahamas** – Fees include stamp duty, which is between 2 and 10 per cent, estate agents' fees of between 6 and 15 per cent, and legal fees of between 0.5 and 2.5 per cent. Buyers must also pay for a Certificate of Registration, which costs between US$50 and US$100, and a Home Owner Resident Card, which costs US$500.

- **Barbados** – Fees comprise a transfer tax of 10 per cent, stamp duty of 1 per cent, estate agents' fees of 5 per cent (paid by the buyer) and legal fees of between 1.5 and 2 per cent.

- **Dominican Republic** – Fees are relatively low: the buyer pays a 3 per cent transfer tax, around 1 per cent in legal fees and a 1.3 per cent stamp duty. The vendor pays estate agents' fees, which are 5 per cent.

- **British Virgin Islands** – Transaction costs are stamp duty of 12 per cent, legal fees of 2 per cent and fees for the application and issue of a Non-Belonger Land Holding Licence, which amount to around US$1,000. Estate agents' fees are paid by the seller and are between 6 and 8 per cent.

9 General Information

Getting There

All the major Caribbean islands have airports, but not all have direct services from Canada, Europe, South American or the US. The airports serving the most popular destinations are as follows.

Antigua & Barbuda: The main airport is VC Bird International Airport, on Antigua, 8km (5mi) north-east of St. John's, the capital. There are direct flights from Canadian, UK and US airports with Caribbean airline LIAT, Air Canada, American Airlines, BMI, British Airways, First Choice Airways and Virgin Atlantic Airways. Barbuda is linked by inter-island flights.

Bahamas: The Bahamas have two airports, but the main one is Lynden Pindling International airport, west of New Providence Island, close to the capital, Nassau. The airport receives a huge number of flights, due to its proximity to the US, and it's the hub of the national airline, Bahamasair. Among other airlines that operate direct flights to the Bahamas are Air Canada, American Airlines, British Airways, Continental Airlines, Delta Airlines, First Choice Airways and United Airlines.

Barbados: Grantley Adams International Airport is a major gateway to the Eastern Caribbean islands. It operates direct services from Africa, Canada, Europe, South America and the US, and it was recently renovated to deal with increased passenger numbers for the 2007 Cricket World Cup. The airport is served by major airlines such as Air Canada, American Airlines, British Airways, Delta Airways, First Choice Airways, Monarch Airlines, Virgin Atlantic and XL Airways.

Dominican Republic: The republic is served by two international airports, Las Americas and La Isabela. Las Americas is the larger, with two terminals, one completed in 2006. La Isabela, recently built north of the city centre, handles mostly domestic and charter flights.

Grenada: Point Salines International Airport is 8km (5mi) north of the capital, St. George's. There are direct flights with Air Canada, American Airlines, British Airways, Virgin Airlines and XL Airways.

St. Lucia: There are two airports on St. Lucia, the larger being Hewanorra International Airport. George FL Charles airport mainly handles domestic and inter-island flights. There are direct flights to Hewanorra from a wide variety of European and US destinations, with Air Canada, American Airlines, British Airways, Delta Airlines, Virgin Atlantic Airways and XL Airways.

British Virgin Islands: There are no direct flights to the BVI from outside the Caribbean. Passengers must fly to another Caribbean airport and take a connecting flight to Terrence B. Lettsome Airport, on Beef Island.

Communications

Communications are generally good on the more popular islands, but not on the more remote ones. Cable and Wireless used to have a monopoly on services to much of the Caribbean, but recent years have seen increased competition, mainly from Digicel, which is based on Jamaica and offers mobile and internet services to many Caribbean countries. Each island has its own area code, which must be used after the US code (1) and there's international direct dialling (IDD) from most islands to many countries.

Fixed-line Telephones: Cable and Wireless remains the main fixed line provider in many Caribbean countries, although on Bermuda it provides only international services; local services are provided by the local Bermuda Telephone Company. Prepaid phone cards are available from hotels and other tourist venues, and can be used in any telephone. There are public telephone boxes on most Caribbean islands, although many accept only prepaid phone cards.

Mobile Telephones: Mobile phone coverage was until recently concentrated on the major islands, but it has been expanded to cover the majority of smaller islands too. The main providers are Cable and Wireless, Digicel and Nokia. Mobile phones don't operate on the GMS network but on the TDMA (Time Division Multiple Access) digital network, and you must ensure that your phone is compatible or hire a local one.

Internet: Internet penetration in the Caribbean is low compared with many countries, mainly due to the high cost of personal computers and broadband access. Barbados and Jamaica have the most users – around 50 per cent of the population. The main providers are Cable and Wireless and Digicel. Internet cafes are found in popular tourist locations.

9

Postal Services: Services vary from island to island, but the service from the major islands is usually good. Post offices are generally open from 8am to around 5pm, but times vary with the island. Post to Canada and the US usually takes between one and two weeks, to Europe two to three weeks.

Crime Rate

The crime rate is low on most islands, although crime has risen considerably on many in recent years. Passport theft and pick-pocketing are common, particularly in tourist areas. Violent and serious crime rates are relatively low but increasing in some areas. Certain areas of some islands are to be avoided, particularly at night. Organised crime, such as drug trafficking and money laundering, is a problem on some islands. Check the latest travel advice.

Medical Facilities

Medical facilities are good on most islands, although some facilities aren't available on the smaller islands. Private international health insurance is highly recommended, as the best hospitals are often private and it may be necessary to be evacuated to the US or a neighbouring country in the case of serious health problems (which must be covered by your insurance).

Pets

Regulations vary from island to island. There's no quarantine for pets on most islands, but usually your pet must have an animal import certificate, be microchipped and have had a rabies vaccine at least six months before entry. Check with the veterinary authority of the island concerned.

Visas & Permits

Visas: Entry and visa requirements vary from island to island. Visas aren't usually required by citizens of most Commonwealth countries, the EU and some other countries, but you must check. For most islands, your passport must be valid for six months. Some islands only allow you to stay for one month, after which you must apply for an extension from the relevant Immigration Department. **US Citizens should note that from January 2007, those travelling by air to and from the Caribbean are required to have a valid passport to re-enter the US (which wasn't previously required).**

Residence Permits: Obtaining permission to reside is usually a formality, provided you have adequate means of financial support and own a property (or have made an investment) worth above a certain amount, e.g. US$500,000 on the Bahamas. In most cases, a temporary (e.g. annual) or permanent residence certificate must be obtained, for which fees are high, e.g. up to US$5,000 on the Bahamas. On some islands, the fee for a residence certificate is based on the value of your property. Note that some islands also levy high fees for those wishing to become tax residents. Citizenship based on investment is available on some islands, but many islands protect their own citizens and workforce by insisting on high levels of regular investment.

Work Permits: These are usually difficult and expensive to obtain unless you plan to start a business and create employment, when there are minimum levels of investment. Many islands protect their own citizens and workforce by making work permits difficult for foreigners

9

to obtain. Employers must usually sponsor a foreign employee and show that there isn't a similarly qualified local resident available to fill the position.

Reference

Further Reading

Antigua Property Paper, Astra House, St. Mary's Street, Box 845, St. John's, Antigua (☎ 268-562 5050, 💻 www.antiguapropertypaper.com).

Antigua Sun, Sun Printing & Publishing, 15 Pavilion Drive, Coolidge, Box W263, St. John's, Antigua (☎ 268-480 5960, 💻 www.antiguasun.com).

Baedeker Caribbean (AA/Baedeker).

Bermuda Sun, PO Box HM 1241, Hamilton, HMFX, Bermuda (☎ 441-295 3902, 💻 www.bermudasun.bm).

Maverick Guide to Bermuda, Catherine Harriot (Pelican Publishing/Maverick Guide Series).

Nassau Guardian, 4 Cater Street, Oakes Field, PO Box N-301, NP Bahamas (☎ 242-302 2300, 💻 www.thenassauguardian.com). Leading Bahamas newspaper.

Useful Addresses

High Commission for Antigua and Barbuda (UK), 2nd Floor, 45 Crawford Place, London W1H 4LP, UK (☎ 020-7258 0070, 💻 www.antigua-barbuda.com).

The High Commission of the Commonwealth of the Bahamas (UK), Bahamas House, 10 Chesterfield Street, London W1X 8AH, UK (☎ 020-7408 4488, ✉ information @bahamashclondon.net).

Embassy of The Commonwealth of The Bahamas (US), 2220 Massachusetts Ave, NW Washington, DC 20008, US (☎ 202-319 2660, ✉ bahemb@ad.co).

The High Commission for Barbados (UK), 1 Great Russell Street, London WC1B 3JY, UK (☎ 020-7631 4975, 💻 www.foreign.gov.bb).

Embassy of Barbados (US), 2144 Wyoming Avenue, NW, Washington, DC 20008, US (☎ 202-939 9200, ✉ washington@foreign.gov.bb).

Office of the High Commission of the Commonwealth of Dominica (UK), 1 Collingham Gardens, London SW5 0HW, UK (☎ 020-7370 5194/5, 💻 www.dominica.co.uk).

Embassy of the Dominican Republic (UK), 139 Inverness Terrace, Bayswater, London W2 6JF, UK (☎ 020-7727 3693, 💻 www.dominicanembassy.org).

Embassy of the Dominican Republic (US), 1715 22nd Street, NW, Washington DC 2008, US (☎ 202-332 6280, 💻 www.domrep.org).

High Commission for Grenada (UK), The Chapel, Archel Road, West Kensington, London W14 9QH, UK (☎ 020-7385 4277, ✉ grenada@high-commission.demon.co.uk).

Grenada Board of Tourism, 11 Blades Court, 121 Deodar Road, London SW15 2NU, UK (☎ 020-8877 4516, 💻 www.grenadagrenadines.com).

Embassy of Grenada (US), 1701 New Hampshire Ave, NW, Washington, DC 20009, US (☎ 202-265 2561, 💻 www.grenadaembassyusa.org).

Jamaican High Commission (UK), 1-2 Prince Consort, London SW7 2BZ, UK (☎ 020-7823 9911, 💻 http://jhcuk.org).

Embassy of Jamaica (US), 1520 New Hampshire Ave, NW, Washington, DC 20036, US (☎ 202-452 0660, 💻 www.embassyofjamaica.org).

9

Embassy of St. Kitts and Nevis (UK), 2nd Floor, 10 Kensington Court, London W8 5DL, UK (☎ 020-7937 9718, 🖥 www.stkittsnevis.org).

St. Lucia High Commission (UK), 1 Collingham Gardens, London SW5 0HW, UK (☎ 020-7370 7123, ✉ hcslu@btconnect.com).

Embassy of St. Vincent and the Grenadines (UK), 10 Kensington Court, London W8 5DL, UK (☎ 020-7565 2874, ✉ info@svghighcom.co.uk).

High Commission of the Republic of Trinidad and Tobago (UK), 42 Belgrave Square, London SW1X 8NT, UK (☎ 020-7245 9351, 🖥 www.immigration.gov.tt).

Embassy of the Republic of Trinidad and Tobago (US), 1708 Massachusetts Ave, NW, Washington, DC 20036, US (☎ 202-467 6490, ✉ embttgo@erols.com).

Representative Office of the British Virgin Islands (UK), 15 Upper Grosvenor Street, London W1K 7PJ, UK (☎ 020-7355 9570, 🖥 www.bvi.org.uk).

(Note that there's no BVI representation in the US.)

Useful Websites

British Virgin Islands (🖥 www.bvi.gov.vg). Government website.

British Virgin Islands Tourist Board (🖥 www.bvitourism.com).

Caribbean Net News (🖥 www.caribbeannetnews.com). Useful portal for news and background information about the Caribbean.

Caribbean Guide (🖥 www.caribbean-guide.info). Background information about the Caribbean.

Caribbean Newspapers (🖥 www.caribbeannewspaper.com). Details of and links to all local newspapers in the region.

NORTH AMERICA: UNITED STATES

Background Information

Capital: Washington DC.

Population: 301.1m.

Foreign Community: The original nation of immigrants, the US has an extremely cosmopolitan population, particularly in the major cities, although only some 7.5 per cent of the current population is foreign-born.

Area: 9,399,300km^2 (3,615,125mi^2).

Geography: The US consists of 48 contiguous states on the mainland of North America, plus Alaska and Hawaii, and it's the third-largest country in the world, after Canada and China. It measures around 4,023km (2,500mi) from east to west (from the Atlantic to the Pacific coasts) and stretches some 1,931km (1,200mi) from north to south, from the Canadian border (mostly along the 49th parallel) to the Gulf of Mexico. Alaska, which joined the Union as the 49th (and largest) state in 1959, is north-west of Canada and is separated from Russia by the Bering Strait. Hawaii joined the Union in 1960 as the 50th state and comprises a group of islands in the mid-Pacific Ocean, some 4,023km (2,500mi) south-west of continental America. The US also administers over 2,000 islands, islets, cays and atolls in the Pacific and Caribbean, including American Samoa, Guam, Puerto Rico and the US Virgin Islands.

The contiguous states consist broadly of the highland region of Appalachia in the east, the Rocky Mountains in the west and the Great Plains in the centre. The highest point in the US is

9

Mount McKinley (6,193m/20,320ft) in Alaska and the lowest Death Valley in California (86m/282ft below sea level).

Climate: Because of its vast size and varied topography, ranging from sub-tropical forests to permanent glaciers, and from deserts to swamplands, America's climate varies enormously. The range of weather in the contiguous states is similar to that experienced in Europe (from northern Finland to southern Spain). In winter, it's cold or freezing everywhere except in the southern states; the coldest areas include the Plains, the Midwest and the Northeast, where temperatures can remain well below freezing for weeks. A long, hot summer is normal throughout America, except in northern New England, Oregon and Washington State.

Language: English (American English, of course) is the official language, although it isn't the primary language of some 15 per cent of Americans. Spanish is the most widely spoken other language, spoken by some 30m people.

Political Situation: The US is one of the world's most politically stable countries. The Constitution lays down the division of power, which is split between the executive (the President), the legislature (Congress) and the judiciary. Power is also split between federal, state and local governments. Each state has a semi-autonomous government, headed by a governor elected every four years. There's no system of proportional representation in America and elections are based on a 'winner takes all' system. This usually results in a very stable government, as coalition governments are unknown. American politics is dominated by just two parties, the Democrats and the Republicans, which fill every seat in Congress and provide most state governors and other posts at state and local government level. President George W. Bush (Republican Party) has been President since 2001, but since the 2006 mid-term election the Democratic Party has held a majority of seats in both the House of Representatives and the Senate for the first time since 1994. The next presidential and legislative elections will be held in November 2008.

Finance

Currency

The American currency is the US dollar (US$), which is one of the world's major currencies.
Exchange Rate: £1 = US$2.
Exchange Controls: None.

Cost & Standard of Living

The US enjoys one of the highest standards and lowest costs of living in the world, although it varies considerably between states and regions, and between cities and rural areas. The cost of 'luxury' imported goods is lower than in almost any other country. Cars are also inexpensive, costing up to 50 per cent less than in some European countries, and fuel is much cheaper than in Europe.

9

Taxation

All US citizens and resident foreigners pay federal tax on their worldwide income, irrespective of its source. Foreigners who are present in the US for 183 days or more are regarded as residents for tax purposes. Taxes are levied at federal, state and local level. Federal taxes are principally income tax and social security, which are collected via a PAYE system. Most states and some local authorities impose an additional income tax and rates vary considerably from state to state, although guidelines are set by the federal government. States that don't impose income tax include Alaska, Florida, Nevada, New Hampshire, South Dakota, Tennessee, Texas, Washington and Wyoming. The highest rate of state income tax is in Vermont.

Non-residents are generally taxed only on income from sources in the US, but non-resident homeowners must file an annual tax return, even if they think they're exempt from tax. Tax on rental income earned by non-residents is levied at 30 per cent, although mortgage interest and other expenses can be offset against income.

Personal Effects: When you enter America to take up permanent or temporary residence, you can usually import your belongings duty and tax free. Any duty or tax payable depends on your country of origin, where you purchased the goods, how long you've owned them, and whether duty or tax has been paid in another country. Personal effects owned and used for at least one year before importation are usually exempt from import duty.

Income Tax: Federal income tax rates are in six bands from 10 to 35 per cent. State and local taxes are at various rates.

Capital Gains Tax (CGT): Capital gains are included in gross income but the maximum rate for long-term gains is 20 per cent and rates are being reduced for taxpayers in the 10 and 15 per cent income tax brackets. Once every two years, US taxpayers may exclude up to $250,000 ($500,000 for married taxpayers filing jointly) of gains derived from the sale of a principal residence. The residence must have been owned and used for at least two of the five years preceding the sale. When a non-resident sells a property, he must report any gain on a non-resident's tax return (form 1040NR), and the buyer is usually required to withhold 10 per cent of the purchase price as security against unpaid taxes.

Wealth Tax: None.

Inheritance & Gift Tax: Estate tax and gift tax are paid by the donor (or his estate) at between 18 and 46 per cent and aren't usually payable if the beneficiary is a spouse or a registered charity or the proceeds are used for educational or medical expenses. An Estate Tax Return (form 706) must be filed when an estate worth over US$2m is inherited. Residents receive a credit against estate taxes worth US$780,000, which is indexed annually for inflation. In addition to federal estate tax, some 20 states also impose estate taxes. Non-residents are liable for estate tax only on property in the US and are entitled to an exemption of the first US$60,000.

Residents can give US$12,000 to any individual during any calendar year without incurring gift tax; a couple can agree to treat gifts to individuals as joint gifts and exclude up to US$24,000 a year. If a gift exceeds these amounts, you should declare it on a Gift Tax Return (form 709).

Value Added Tax (VAT): There's no system of VAT in the US, but most states and many municipalities levy a sales tax, which varies between 4 per cent (Alabama) and 7.25 per cent (California). The relevant sales tax must usually be added to advertised or displayed prices.

Other Taxes: Some states and local authorities impose a variety of other taxes for goods and services. Some impose a sales tax on letting income, and certain counties in some states (e.g. Florida) levy other taxes on letting income, such as a tourist development tax, resort tax, tourist impact tax or a convention development tax.

9 Property

Restrictions on Foreign Ownership & Letting

There are no restrictions on foreign ownership, although most foreigners may remain in the US for only 90 days without a visa (see **Visas & Permits** below). For this reason, most developers (e.g. in Florida) provide management and letting services for foreign owners.

There are restrictions on letting in some states and communities. Known as zoning regulations, they determine the length of time that properties can be let. In some areas, short-term rentals (generally less than 28 or 30 days, but in some cases less than six months) are prohibited, although if this is so you should be notified before buying. Restrictions can vary within a state. For example, in Florida there are four counties, all of which have different regulations regarding short-term letting (known as 'zoning' restrictions); in some you cannot let for less than a month. **If you plan to invest in a buy-to-let property, or just want to let your property occasionally to cover costs, obtain detailed information about any restrictions before committing yourself.**

Rental income earned by non-residents is taxable in the US and in some states (e.g. Florida) you must also charge a sales tax on short-term rentals, payable to the state, and pay various local taxes (see **Other Taxes** above).

Market

Until recently, the US property market was vast and flourishing. Between 2001 and 2005, it enjoyed unprecedented growth, prices in many areas rising astronomically due to confidence in the US economy and low interest rates. In addition, limited housing stock and the American public's insatiable desire to become homeowners and/or investors meant that it was a seller's market. Foreigners were also snapping up holiday homes, particularly in what's known as the American 'sunbelt', which stretches from California in the west to Florida in the east. In 2005, the Florida market in particular was seriously affected by Hurricane Katrina, and the following year the National Association of Realtors (NAR) reported falling sales, as prices became unaffordable and mortgage debt increased with rising interest rates. By early 2007, over 2m people had defaulted on their mortgages. Some economists were concerned that this could spur a recession, as more than 25 lenders declared bankruptcy, with significant losses. In most areas, sales have dropped significantly, turning the US property market into a buyer's market, many sellers reducing prices and developers offering a variety of incentives to would-be buyers. The demand for holiday homes from non-resident foreigners remains fairly strong, if a little more cautious than in the past, but investors remain wary.

The variety of property in the US is huge and includes golf and country club developments, ski chalets, marina and waterfront homes with private moorings, city 'brownstones' and a vast range of unique properties. Developments may consist of individual plots (e.g. 'ranches' or villas for what are known as one-family homes) and/or townhouse/condominium complexes with communal swimming pools, saunas, heated spas, squash and tennis courts, golf courses, health clubs or fitness centres, and picnic and barbecue areas. Residential communities (some specifically aimed at retirees) are common in many states and usually have comprehensive fitness, recreational and social facilities (many free to residents). American homes are generally bigger, more luxurious and better equipped than homes in other developed countries, particularly in rural areas.

Areas

Every American state has a particular appeal – for holiday homeowners as for permanent residents – and many are ideal locations for summer and winter holiday homes. Traditionally, the most popular US destinations for foreigners have been California, Florida and New York, although buyers are now spreading their wings to a variety of other parts of the country. Although many Europeans, particularly the British, still think of Florida as the only American state worth buying a holiday home in, many other states offer excellent year-round weather and aren't as congested as Florida.

9

Nevertheless, Florida remains among the most popular states, especially the areas around Clearwater, Orlando, Sarasota, St Petersburg and Tampa Bay, although some of these were affected by Hurricane Katrina in 2005, which has reduced buyer's enthusiasm – not least because of the enormous insurance premiums and increased property taxes that home owners are now obliged to pay. Elsewhere, Las Vegas (Nevada) has been increasingly popular with investors, while the mountain states of Arizona, Colorado, Idaho, Montana, New Mexico, Utah and Wyoming are attracting growing numbers of holiday home buyers, particularly winter sports enthusiasts. Other popular areas are Phoenix (Arizona), Georgia, North and South Carolina, Louisiana, Tennessee, Texas, Washington (e.g. Seattle), Virginia and West Virginia. Cities such as New York, San Francisco and Washington DC have traditionally been popular; the US market downturn has affected some more than others. New York has remained a strong market, with a constant demand for quality properties, while San Francisco and Washington DC have suffered a significant slump, due in part to higher mortgage interest rates. A large number of (usually free) property catalogues, magazines and newspapers is published in all states.

Building Standards

Building standards are strictly controlled (and therefore high) and high-quality fixtures and fittings are usually standard. American property generally provides excellent value with regard to size and quality of construction and fixtures and fittings.

Cost

Property prices in America have traditionally remained fairly stable, but between 2001 and 2005, the market experienced meteoric price rises. The most pronounced were in California, which saw rises of more than 80 per cent between 2002 and 2005. In 2007, however, prices experienced a severe downturn, which means that buyers can find bargains. Popular areas are Los Angeles, Orange County, the San Francisco Bay Area and Ventura County, where average house prices are US$650,000; prices are significantly lower in less popular areas.

The market in Florida, the favourite location for British home buyers, saw around 40 per cent growth in 2005 and 2006, but in 2007 prices began to drop, leading to an oversupply of apartments, which has affected the buy-to-let market as well as sales. In addition, home owners have faced increased insurance costs and property taxes and some are being forced to sell. If you aren't relying on rental returns and simply want a holiday home, prices are reasonable, particularly when compared with the UK's. The most popular areas for tourists and home buyers are Orlando, Miami, Sarasota and Tampa, where average house prices are around US$240,000. Southern and central Florida have become more expensive in recent years, particularly around Disney World and on the southern Gulf coast, and you generally need to look north of Tampa to find the best value. Although most foreigners buy new homes – which come with a wide range of high-quality fixtures and fittings installed as standard and in popular resort areas can be bought 'turn-key furnished', i.e. ready to occupy – resale homes are often better value.

New York City experienced impressive price rises until 2006, when, in line with the rest of the US, the market began to show signs of a downturn, but it has held its own better than most areas. Prices in Manhattan and upmarket suburban areas (e.g. the Hamptons on Long Island) have always been among the highest in the country, a one-bedroom apartment costing around US$750,000 and a four-bedroom house in an exclusive area over US$4m. Other popular cities, such San Francisco and Washington DC, have seen a major slowdown in price rises since

2006, and the average house price in San Francisco is US$740,000, in Washington US$430,000.

Prices in other areas vary tremendously and the current fluctuating market means that average prices are constantly changing. You can keep up to date with latest prices by checking the monthly reports published by the National Association of Realtors (NAR, 🖳 www. realtor.org), which also provides a comparison of prices in particular areas and states and has plenty of useful links.

Local Mortgages

The US mortgage market went through a crisis in 2007, when millions of homeowners defaulted on their mortgages and sent around two dozen mortgage lenders into bankruptcy. Worst affected was the 'sub-prime lending market' (loans higher than the average rate), but all lending practices were revised as a result. Many lenders had been offering over 100 per cent mortgages, but these are now less widely available and non-resident foreigners are usually required to contribute between 20 and 35 per cent of the purchase price. Check the terms of any mortgage carefully, exercising caution over any adjustable-rate mortgage (ARM), which means that repayments may start at a low level and then rise considerably after a given period. Mortgages are available from a number of sources, including savings and loan associations (which provide over half of all US mortgages), commercial banks, mortgage bankers, insurance companies, builders and developers, and government agencies.

Property Taxes

Tax is levied annually on property in all states to help pay for local services, such as primary and secondary education, police and fire services, libraries, public transport, waste disposal, highways and road safety, and social services. As property prices rose steeply during the recent boom, so did property taxes, which are based on the assessed value of a property. Predictably, although the value of property has since dropped dramatically, taxes are still based on the high average values of the last five years, making them an increasing burden for many homeowners. In 2006, some states cut property taxes or granted generous rebates to those in need, but some added the shortfall to other areas (such as sales tax). Tax rates are expressed as an amount per US$100 or US$1,000 (the latter known as the 'millage' rate) of the assessed market value of a property (e.g. US$15 per US$1,000). As taxes are fixed by communities, rates vary considerably, but in 2007 the most expensive state was New Jersey (US$5,000 per annum on an average property), followed by Connecticut and New Hampshire (around US$4,000), New York, Rhode Island and Vermont (US$3,000), and Alaska, California and Maryland (over US$2,000).

Purchase Procedure

An offer is made through a realtor and an initial 'good faith' deposit (also known as 'earnest money'), e.g. US$1,000 to US$5,000, is paid to show that you're a serious buyer. If you withdraw, the vendor keeps the deposit. A contract is then drafted (**be aware that in the US, the buyer accepts the property in the condition it's in at the time the sale contract is signed**). In California and some other states, your deposit and all other funds must be placed with a neutral third party, the 'escrow agent', who is usually selected by the buyer's realtor (but is subject to approval by all parties). He's responsible for compiling and checking

9

documents and ensuring that the transaction can 'close' within the period specified in the purchase contract.

Once the contract is signed, a closing date is set, which is usually 30 days after the signing. All obligations (searches made and the necessary finance obtained, etc.) must be completed by then. If you withdraw from a purchase, you lose your deposit or can be forced to go through with the sale, so don't sign a contract without taking legal advice. Contracts usually contain a number of conditions (riders or contingencies) that must be met before they become valid and binding, e.g. satisfactory house and termite inspections and your ability to obtain a mortgage (if necessary) by a certain date. Conditions may vary from region to region and state to state. Some, such as a termite inspection, may be required by law, while others (e.g. a house inspection or survey) may be insisted upon by your realtor or lender. The contract must list anything included in the price, such as furniture, fittings and extras, and should specify who pays the fees associated with the purchase (see below). Standard contracts can usually be tailored to individual requirements. Once the deal closes, the escrow agent records the deed and pays the funds to the appropriate parties.

From a legal viewpoint, America is one of the safest countries in the world in which to buy a home. However, as when buying property in any country, you should never pay any money or sign anything without first taking legal advice and you should take the usual precautions regarding deposits and obtaining proper title. Owner's title insurance (to protect against a potential claim on the title by a third party) is mandatory in some states and is usually required by lenders. In many states, hiring a lawyer for a property transaction is standard practice, although it isn't always necessary when a state (such as California) has mandatory escrow procedures and title insurance. Before hiring a lawyer, compare the fees charged by other practices and make sure that he's experienced in property transactions.

Most experts believe that you should always have a home inspection (survey) on a resale property, and a termite inspection is almost mandatory on an older home, as America has numerous varieties of wood-boring insect. Make sure that all local taxes and water/sewerage bills have been paid by the previous owner, as these charges usually come with the property (and if unpaid are passed on to subsequent owners). You're afforded extra protection if you buy from a licensed and registered realtor, rather than an estate agent, as realtors are bound by a strict code of ethics. You must **never** sign anything pertaining to the purchase of property in the US without going there and checking that the developer and land actually exist (they've been known not to!). As in most countries, there are crooks who prey on 'greenhorn' foreigners.

Fees

You should allow around 5 per cent of the purchase price for 'closing' or 'settlement' costs, although fees vary with the state. Costs may include a lender's appraisal (valuation) fee, legal fees, title search fees, title insurance, recording fees, a survey or home inspection, homeowner's insurance and mortgage tax. Many people use a buyer's broker or agent, which doesn't usually cost any more than buying direct from a vendor. Before you engage an agent, however, make sure you know who will pay his fees, which are normally around 6 per cent and split between the buyer and seller.

9 General Information

Getting There

The US Department of Homeland Security (DHS) has declared an 'orange' (i.e. high) 'terror alert status' for all international and domestic flights in the US. To find out what this means in practice, go to the website of the DHS (💻 www.dhs.gov), which has detailed definitions, as well as information about travel security and immigration procedures.

There are over 60 international airports in the US but the main airports serving areas most popular with tourists and foreign homebuyers are as follows:

California: The major airports on the west coast are Los Angeles and San Francisco International Airports. Los Angeles airport is around 27km (16mi) south-west of the city. It's the second-busiest airport in the US and handles flights from around 70 foreign destinations (in Asia, Europe and Latin America) and 90 domestic destinations. It's a major hub of United Airlines.

San Francisco airport is 21km (13mi) from the city and a major gateway to America from Asia, Australia and Europe. Like Los Angeles, it's a major hub of United Airlines, and from summer 2007 it will also become the hub of Virgin American. Freeway 101 provides access to surrounding areas, though it can be horrendously busy.

Florida: Miami International Airport, 14km (9mi) north-west of Miami, is South Florida's main airport for international flights from cities throughout the Americas and Europe. Some low-cost and domestic carriers use Fort-Lauderdale Hollywood International Airport and Palm Beach International Airport.

New York: The major airport for passenger traffic into the US, John F. Kennedy International Airport is 19km (12mi) south-east of New York City. Other international airports in the New York City area are Newark and La Guardia.

East Coast: Other major East Coast airports include Logan International (Boston) and Washington Dulles International, which serves the Washington DC metropolitan area.

Communications

The US has a vast, highly sophisticated and technologically advanced communications system. The market is dominated by the world-famous American Telephone and Telegraph Company (better known as AT&T). Mobile and internet use are widespread and growing fast, whilst landline use is falling. The country dialling code is 1 and international direct dialling (IDD) is available worldwide.

Fixed-line Telephones: Former government-owned AT&T was broken up in 1984 and its local exchange services split into seven regional holding companies, although it continued to operate long-distance services. The break-up led to competition from a variety of other operators, mainly BellSouth, MCI, Qwest, Sprint and Verizon. (In 2005, AT&T was bought by SBC Communications but kept its famous name as part of the deal.) In 2006, cable companies began offering 'triple-play' packages, combining telephone with entertainment services. Long-distance calls are surprisingly inexpensive, but local call charges have risen dramatically in recent years. Public phone boxes (pay phones) are widely available, and pre-paid phone cards can be bought from most shops and used for international calls.

Mobile Telephones: Known as cell phones in the US, mobile phone services are dominated by AT&T Mobility, Sprint Nextel, T-Mobile and Verizon Wireless. All operators except Verizon use the GSM and GPRS networks and have facilities for internet access.

Internet: Some subscribers in the US are still using dial-up services, but high-speed broadband services are provided by a number of cable TV providers. The leader in the internet market is Verizon, with BellSouth, Earthlink DSL, Qwest and SBC Yahoo fighting for a share of the market. Internet cafes are widespread, particularly in towns and cities.

Postal Services: The United States Postal Service (USPS) has a vast network of main post offices and community post offices across the country. International letters and parcels take between around four and seven days, depending on the destination.

9

Crime Rate

One of the major drawbacks of living in the US is the high crime rate, particularly violent crime. Violent crime rates in many areas having been dropping significantly since 2001, although rates remain high in cities such as Los Angeles and New York. The crime rate varies considerably with the state, county and city, town or neighbourhood, and it's important to check crime statistics and avoid high crime areas. If you come from a country with a relatively low crime rate, e.g. anywhere in western Europe, it's important to alter your thinking and behaviour accordingly. Avoid the 'ghetto' areas of inner cities day and night, be extremely careful where you go at night and always use a taxi rather than walk. In addition, since 11th September 2001, the US is considered a high risk for further terrorist attacks.

Medical Facilities

Healthcare in the US is among the best in the world, provided you can afford it! **There's no free treatment for visitors who fall ill in America and comprehensive health insurance is essential for visitors and residents.** Moreover, the health insurance cover required when visiting most other countries is totally inadequate in America, where the recommended minimum cover is around US$500,000 per accident or sickness. Health insurance in America is **very** expensive, a typical policy for a family of four costing thousands of dollars a year (around US$2,000 per month is typical). The average American family spends around 15 per cent of its income on healthcare!

Pets

All animals and birds imported into America must meet health and customs requirements (as must pets taken out of America and returned). Pets, particularly cats and dogs, must be examined at the port of entry for signs of disease that can be transmitted to humans. Dogs must be vaccinated against rabies at least 30 days before entry; exceptions include puppies less than three months old and dogs originating from or having been located for at least six months in areas designated by the Public Health Service as being rabies-free. Vaccination against rabies isn't required for cats. Birds must be quarantined upon arrival for at least 30 days in a facility operated by the US Centers for Disease Control and Prevention (CDC). In general, the CDC doesn't require health certificates for pets entering the US. However, some states and airlines require them, so contact the state, county or municipal authorities for local restrictions on importing pets. For example, cats and dogs imported into Hawaii face quarantine of 130 days. More information is available on the CDC website (💻 www.cdc.gov).

Visas & Permits

Visas: Citizens of Andorra, Australia, Austria, Belgium Brunei, Denmark, Finland, France, Germany, Iceland, Ireland, Italy, Japan, Liechtenstein, Luxembourg, Monaco, the Netherlands, New Zealand, Norway, Portugal, San Marino, Singapore, Slovenia, Spain, Sweden, Switzerland, and the UK don't need a visa provided they have a valid, machine readable passport and a valid onward or return ticket, they're travelling on business or for pleasure or are in transit, and they don't plan to stay in the US for more than 90 days. (This is known as the Visa Waiver Program.)

Citizens of the above countries who plan to study, work or remain more than 90 days in the US and citizens of any other country visiting the US for any reason must obtain a Non-Immigrant Visa from a US embassy or consulate before travelling. **Those on the Visa Waiver Program will be refused entry if an immigration official has reason to believe that they're going to study, work or stay longer than 90 days in the US.**

Rule changes implemented after the terrorist attacks of September 11th 2001 have made visa applications subject to greater scrutiny and restriction. If you need a visa, it's wise to apply well in advance of the date of departure. Those entering the US are often subject to detailed questions about the purpose and length of their visit; if in doubt about these, immigration officials simply refuse entry.

Residence Permits: Anyone wishing to live permanently in the US (whether intending to work or not) must obtain an Immigrant Visa. An application must be made to a US embassy before travel and, if accepted, you're processed for a Permanent Residence Card (PRC – often referred to as a Green Card) on arrival. There are essentially three categories of person eligible for residence: close relatives of US citizens or other legal residents; those with skills or professions in demand; and those selected for the Diversity Immigrant Program, which grants PRCs by lottery to citizens of countries with low rates of immigration to the US. Preference is given to anyone who will create jobs for at least ten (unrelated) people and has a minimum of US$1m to invest in a new enterprise. Residence permits aren't issued to retirees (unless they're **very** rich!).

Work Permits: Work permits as such don't exist in the US. In order to work (legally), you must obtain an Immigrant Visa and a PRC (Green Card) – see above. It's therefore difficult to work in the US unless you qualify for a PRC by virtue of having skills or professions in demand or through birthright, relationship, or investment, although there's an annual quota of 105,000 for 'employment-based' Immigrant Visas, which are sometimes given to non-skilled workers; applicants may need approval from the Department of Labour.

Reference

Further Reading

Buying a Home in Florida, David Hampshire (Survival Books). Everything you need to know about buying a home in Florida.

Buying or Renting a Home in New York, Graeme Chesters and Bev Laflamme (Survival Books). Everything you need to know about buying and renting property in New York.

Emigrate America, Outbound Media and Exhibitions, 1 Commercial Road, Eastbourne, East Sussex, BN21 3XQ, UK (☎ 01323-726040, 💻 www.emigrate2.co.uk). Extensive emigration information about a selection of countries, including the US.

Essentially America, Phoenix International Publishing, PO Box 615, Horsham, West Sussex RH13 5WF, UK (☎ 01403-276609, 💻 www.essentiallyamerica.com). The UK's leading consumer magazine about travel and lifestyle in the US, published quarterly. The website has downloadable guides about specific areas in the US.

Florida Travel and Lifestyles Magazine (☎ 888-248 5711, 💻 www.floridatravelusa.com). Travel and lifestyle magazine.

Florida Trend, Trend Magazines, 490 First Ave South, St Petersburg, Florida 33701, US (☎ 727-821 5800, 💻 www.floridatrend.com). Business magazine.

Life in America's Small Cities, Kevin Heubusch (Prometheus Books).

9

Living and Working in America, David Hampshire (Survival Books). Everything you need to know about living and working in America.

Welcome to New York, Roberta Seret (American Welcome Services Press).

Useful Addresses

American Association of Retired Persons (AARP), 601 East Street, NW, Washington, DC 20049, US (☎ 800-687 2277, 🖳 www.aarp.org).

American Embassy (UK), 24 Grosvenor Square, London W1A 1AE, UK (☎ 020-7499 9000, 🖳 www.usembassy.org.uk).

California Association of Realtors (CAR), 525 South Virgil, Los Angeles, California CA 90020, US (☎ 213-739 8200, 🖳 www.car.org).

Department of Housing and Urban Development, 451 7th Street, SW, Washington, DC 20410, US (☎ 202-708 1112, 🖳 www.hud.gov).

Florida Association of Realtors, 7025 Augusta National Drive, Orlando, FL 32872-5025, US (☎ 407-438 1400, 🖳 www.floridarealtors.org).

Florida Brits Group, Stanhope House, 18 Grange Close, Skelton, York YO3 6YR, UK (☎ 01904-471800, 🖳 http://floridabritsgroup.com).

Manhattan Association of Realtors, 350 5th Avenue, New York, NY 10118, US (☎ 212-594 2233, 🖳 www.manrealtor.com)

National Association of Realtors (NAR), 430 North Michigan Avenue, Chicago, Illinois 60611, US (☎ 800-874 6500, 🖳 www.realtor.org).

Useful Websites

Internal Revenue Service (🖳 www.irs.gov). US Tax Office. The publications section has a Tax Guide for Aliens (No. 519).

See America (🖳 www.seeamerica.org). Travel and tourist information for all areas of the US.

US Government (🖳 www.usa.gov).

US Government, Department of Homeland Security (🖳 www.dhs.gov).

Visit USA Association (🖳 www.vistusa.org.uk). Tourist information and downloadable brochures.

CENTRAL AMERICA: COSTA RICA

Background Information

9

Capital: San José.

Population: 4.2m.

Foreign Community: Only around 1 per cent of the population is indigenous. The vast majority of Costa Ricans (94 per cent) are mestizos – people of mixed indigenous and European (mostly German, Italian and Polish) ancestry. There's also a reasonably large expatriate community, from Canada, Germany, the Netherlands, the UK and the US.

Area: 51,032km^2 (19,652mi^2).

Geography: Costa Rica is in Central America and is a narrow strip of land (isthmus), with Nicaragua to the north and Panama to the south-east. Its eastern coastline (around 200km/124mi long) borders the Caribbean Sea, the western (1,000km/620mi long) the Pacific Ocean. Costa Rica includes a number of islands off its coast, the largest of which is Calero Island, with an area of 151km^2 (58mi^2). The mainland is split into two from north to south by the volcanic Central Mountain range, which surrounds the capital, San José, and extends south into Panama. In between the mountains is the Central Valley, which contains several active volcanoes, the highest of which is Irazú, at 3,431m (11,257 ft). There are 26 National Parks, all of which are protected under conservation laws and ecotourism policies.

Climate: Costa Rica's climate is tropical. It's hot and humid in the coastal lowlands and more temperate in the interior highlands. Summer (between December and May) is the dry season and winter (June to November) is the wet season, the Caribbean coast being far wetter than the Pacific coast. Temperatures in San José are pleasant because of its altitude and average 15 to 26C (59-79F), whereas the coasts are far hotter, with temperatures averaging 21 to 33C (70-91F). From December to April, Costa Rica experiences strong trade winds from the north-east. The El Niño phenomenon has a significant effect on the country's weather patterns.

Language: The official language is Spanish, with English also spoken in tourist areas.

Political Situation: Politically, Costa Rica is fairly stable. It's a democracy in which executive power is held by a President, who is elected for a four-year term. Until recently, Costa Rica had a reputation as one of the least corrupt Latin American countries, but in 2004 three former Costa Rican presidents were investigated on corruption charges. Two main parties have, until recently, dominated Costa Rican Politics, the National Liberation Party (PLN) and Social Christian Unity Party (PUSC). However, the 2006 election saw the emergence of new parties, including the Citizens' Action Party (PAC) and the Libertarian Movement (ML). The most recent election saw the PLN regain power and the PAC become the official opposition party. The PLN's candidate was former president Dr Oscar Arias Sanchez, who was elected President after the closest-fought election in Costa Rican history. Costa Rica is a member of the UN and has no national army, which was abolished in 1949.

Finance

Currency

Costa Rica's currency is the Costa Rican colón (CRC), which consists of 100 centimos and is named after Christopher Columbus (Cristóbal Colón in Spanish). The colón is pegged to the US Dollar at a rate of US$1 = CRC517.
Exchange Rate: £1 = CRC1,030.
Exchange Controls: None.

Cost & Standard of Living

Costa Rica enjoys a high standard of living compared with most Latin American countries, and the country's GDP per capita is the highest in Central America. The economy is fairly stable and depends heavily on tourism and agriculture. Inflation is high and the cost of living is the highest in the region, although it's still far cheaper than western Europe and the US. Costs obviously depend on your lifestyle, but a couple can well comfortably on the equivalent of US$1,200 per month and in luxury for US$2,000. Imported luxury goods are expensive (e.g. most cars attract

9

an import duty of 33 per cent). Housing is more expensive the closer you are to San José, but living too far from the city may be impractical due to the lack of infrastructure. Monthly minimum wages for professionals are CRC285,635 (US$550) and for blue collar workers and domestic employees the minimum monthly wage is CRC72,586 (US$140).

Taxation

Costa Rican tax law is currently being reformed, particularly income tax and VAT, and there's likely to be a move towards a form of worldwide income taxation for residents. Currently, Costa Rica taxes only income earned within the country.

Personal Effects: Personal effects can be imported duty free, but they must have been owned and used before entry and cannot be resold. Customs may insist on a list of all the items to be imported.

Income Tax: Individuals, irrespective of their tax residence status, are liable for income tax on their Costa Rican income, at progressive rates from 10 to 25 per cent. Income up to CRC215,600 (US$417) is exempt, and 10 per cent is payable for amounts between CRC215,600 and CRC324,100 (US$624). Amounts over that are taxed at 20 per cent. Self employed professionals also pay progressive rates, but they're slightly different: earnings up to CRC958,000 (US$1,840) are exempt and then there are progressive rates up to 25 per cent for earnings over CRC4,785,000 (US$9,200).

Capital Gains Tax (CGT): Capital gains are taxed as ordinary income. Property sales aren't subject to CGT, unless you regularly buy and sell property.

Inheritance & Gift Tax: None, but large gifts and inheritances may be scrutinised and, if they appear to be a means of evading tax, may be subject to a 'substitute' tax.

Wealth Tax: None.

Value Added Tax (VAT): A sales tax of 13 per cent applies to most transactions, with a reduced rate of 5 per cent for some items, such as household electricity. Exempt items include books, educational supplies, food and medicine. There's no sales tax on property.

Property

Restrictions on Foreign Ownership & Letting

The purchase of land and property is considered a right in Costa Rica, irrespective of whether you're a resident. Consequently, restrictions are few and apply equally to Costa Ricans and foreigners. The main restriction applies to the Maritime Zone, which runs 200m inland from the shoreline, where the first 50m from the shore is considered public property and nothing may be built on it, while the remaining 150m can be leased for private use through the local municipality. Leases are granted for periods of between 5 and 20 years and are registered in the Public Registry; an annual fee must be paid. Foreigners cannot hold a lease unless they've lived in Costa Rica for over five years. **As a result of the above regulations, beachfront property in Costa Rica is untitled.**

There are no restrictions on letting, but rental income is taxed (at ordinary income tax rates – see above).

9

Market

The property market in Costa Rica has been booming for several years. Buyers are mainly from the US and tend to be buy-to-let investors or baby boomers looking for a retirement home. In the US, the country is marketed as a prime retirement spot, with good healthcare, a relatively low cost of living and affordable housing. UK buyers, particularly those nearing retirement, are also beginning to show interest in Costa Rica. With the introduction of direct flights from the UK and the US and considerable inward investment in the country, the market looks set to maintain its growth. Many properties are part of new luxury resort developments close to a beach, or ranch-style properties in the countryside. Some areas are beginning to suffer from over-development, particularly Guanacaste province on the northern Pacific coast, which has been transformed over the past three years.

Areas

Costa Rica is made up of seven provinces: Alajuela, Cartag, Guanacaste, Heredia, Limon, Puntarenas and San José. The most developed area is Guanacaste in the north, which consisted of unadulterated jungle and cattle ranches until 1997, when it was bought by a Costa Rican developer. The largest project there is Peninsula Papagayo, a luxurious 2,300-acre development which includes luxury homes, hotels, a marina and three golf courses. Prices have risen four-fold over the last three years.

Costa Rica's Central Valley area is popular because of its temperate climate and easy access to the capital, San José. A number of small towns within a short drive of the capital are favourites with expatriate retirees, and provinces such as Heredia and Alajuela to the north of San José and Cartago to the east are particularly popular with US retirees. These areas have seen 25 per cent annual price increases since 2003.

The coast close to the Panama border is also popular with foreign buyers: previously the haunts of surfers and backpackers, Jaco Beach and Hermoso have seen considerable recent development and prices have rise dramatically since 2005.

Building Standards

Standards of construction are generally high, especially for new buildings. Costa Rica has fairly strict building codes, but the codes aren't always enforced, particularly in rural areas. Ensure that the developer is using a reputable builder.

Cost

Property prices are often quoted in US dollars rather than Costa Rican colones. A three-bedroom apartment close to the beach on the northern Pacific coast costs around US$300,000, a three-bedroom house around US$600,000 and luxury five-bedroom villas start at around US$850,000, rising to US$ several million. Rental yields here are high, at around 15 per cent per annum. In the Central Valley area, a small house costs around US$450,000, while a larger, luxurious house costs from around US$900,000. In and around San José, prices depend on location, but a small apartment can be had in most areas for around US$150,000, a two-bedroom house for around US$400,000 and a larger house around US$600,000. Rental yields are also fairly high in San José, ranging from 6 to 12 per cent per annum, depending on the property. Coastal properties near the Panama border, in areas such as Jaco Beach, start at around US$200,000 for a small apartment and rise to around US$600,000 for a large house.

9

Local Mortgages

Local mortgages aren't easy to obtain unless you're a resident of Costa Rica. This is beginning to change and several US lenders are entering the mortgage market, offering US$ mortgages, which attract a lower interest rate, based on the New York prime rate plus around 2 per cent, although the exact rate depends on the lender. Local lenders will finance up to 80 per cent of the appraised value, depending on your residence status. Interest rates also vary with status but are often 2 to 4 per cent above the US prime rate (the rate offered to the most credit-worthy customers). Loan terms can be up to 30 years, depending on your circumstances.

Property Taxes

There's a national property tax (*Impuesto sobre bienes inmuebles*) levied on the cadastral value of the property. The cadastral value is usually lower than the actual value and is assessed by the tax authorities. Local authorities also levy annual property taxes at a flat rate of 0.25 per cent.

Purchase Procedure

Once you've chosen a property, you must pay a deposit into an escrow account and the buyer and vendor sign an option to buy/sell. Engage an independent lawyer, who should check that the property is registered in the Public Registry (*Registro Nacional*), a process which can now be done online. This check will reveal whether there are any charges on the property and details of the owners. All titled properties have what's known as a *Folio Real*, which is a unique number which identifies the province, the property itself and the number of legal owners. **Unless a property has this number, clean title cannot be obtained**. Thorough checks of title deeds by an independent lawyer are vital. Some properties in Costa Rica aren't recorded on the Public Registry because they've been owned by families for centuries. **The only way you can obtain legal title is if the property is registered in the Public Registry and can be legally transferred to you. It's wise to avoid any transaction where ownership is unclear. Title insurance is recommended.**

A notary public must then prepare the Transfer Deed (*Escritura de Traspaso*), which will contain all the details of the sale and, once signed, is recorded at the Public Registry and registered in the name of the new owner. Costa Rica operates a 'first in time, first in right' system, which means it's vital for the new owner to be registered immediately.

Fees

The fees associated with buying a home in Costa Rica are around 8 per cent but all except mortgage registration fees are normally shared between the buyer and the vendor. Transfer taxes are 1.5 per cent and documentary stamps, which must be affixed to the deed, cost a further 0.5 per cent. Notaries' fees are set by law and are 1.25 per cent. If you have to register a mortgage, the charge is 0.6 per cent of the mortgage value. An estate agent's fees are between 2.5 and 5 per cent.

General Information

Getting There

Costa Rica has four airports: one in Liberia, in Guanacaste Province (the main tourist airport), one in Limon, offering only a domestic service, and two in San José, the capital. Liberia International Airport is the main airport for tourists visiting the Pacific coast and is mainly served by North American airlines, primarily Continental Airlines and Delta Airlines. First Choice Airways offers a service from London Gatwick. San José's Santamaria International airport is Costa Rica's main international airport, with around 3m passengers a year, mainly tourists from Canada, Europe and the US. It's served by a number of American and European airlines. British Airways offers a service from London Heathrow, via Puerto Rico.

Communications

Although Costa Rica's telecommunications systems are quite modern, it's the least liberalised market in Latin America and the state provider, Grupo ICE (Instituto Costarricense de Electricidad) and its subsidiary, RACSA, are the only providers of fixed-line telephones, mobile phones and internet services. Non-residents cannot buy fixed or mobile phones and residents are subject to long waits for the installation of services. Mobile phone and internet use is fairly widespread. The country dialling code is 506. International direct dialling (IDD) is available to most countries.

Fixed-line Telephones: International calls are fairly expensive, but you can call using an internet phone service at some internet cafes or by using a calling card (*tarjeta telefonica*), which is available from pharmacies and kiosks. Most public telephones also use calling cards (those using coins are few and far between).

Mobile Telephones: The only provider of mobile phones is the state provider, Grupo ICE (see above), which uses the GSM 1800 network. Note that local SIM cards aren't available. Check with your mobile phone provider regarding the cost of using your phone in Costa Rica before travelling.

Internet: Internet use is fairly widespread, particularly in business. RACSA is the only authorised provider of internet services. There are plenty of internet cafes in tourist areas and most hotels have facilities for lap-top connection to the internet.

Postal Services: Operated by Correos de Costa Rica, the service is fairly efficient. Letters to US destinations take around five days and to European destinations between 10 and 15 days. There are post offices in most main towns, but service is slow and unreliable. The main post office at San José offers a more reliable service and is open from 7.30am to 5pm, Mondays to Fridays, with a limited service on Saturdays.

Crime Rate

The crime rate is generally fairly low in Costa Rica, although there has been an increase in crimes against tourists in the past few years. This is mainly the theft of personal belongings, passports and travel documents, although there has also been an increase in violent crime against tourists, including muggings and robberies – even in daylight on busy streets. Car theft is common.

9

Medical Facilities

Medical care and facilities are of a high standard and Costa Rica's health system is one of the best in Latin America. Many of the medical staff speak English, as they've been trained in the UK or the US. Private healthcare is available at low cost (compared with the US, for example) and is of a high standard. However, there are no reciprocal health agreements and only emergency medical treatment is available without charge to visitors, so comprehensive private health insurance is recommended. Costa Rica's public healthcare system provides low-cost healthcare through the social security service, known as Caja Costarricense de Seguro Social (CCSS). Foreign residents can also join the CCSS by paying a monthly fee, which is based on a percentage of income. Alternatively, inexpensive health insurance is available from the state monopoly, Instituto de Seguro Nacional (INS). **There's an increasing risk of dengue fever and malaria in Costa Rica.**

Pets

Pets entering Costa Rica aren't subject to quarantine provided that they meet certain requirements. Your pet must be identified by a microchip and have had a rabies vaccine not more than one year and at least 30 days before departure. An import permit isn't required if a pet travels with its owner.

Visas & Permits

Visas: Citizens of many countries, including Australia, Canada, most EU countries and the US, don't require a visa to visit Costa Rica for up to 90 days.

Residence Permits: If you wish to stay longer, you must obtain a temporary residence permit, which is usually granted for employment contracts and study purposes. Permanent residence permits are granted to retirees (who must have an income from outside Costa Rica of at least US$600 per month), those without a job but with a proven income of at least US$1,000 per month, investors who plan to invest at least US$200,000 in a project in the country and those who are sponsored by a family member who is a Costa Rican citizen. Check with a Costa Rican embassy before travelling.

Work Permits: Work permits are required for all nationalities and must be applied for via your employer. Work permits are usually issued for six months and renewed for a further six months. Permits are issued mainly to highly trained professionals and must be approved by the Immigration and Labour Department.

Reference

9 Further Reading

The Golden Door to Retirement and Living in Costa Rica, Christopher Howard (Costa Rica Books).

Living Abroad in Costa Rica, Erin Van Rheenen (Avalon Travel Publishing).

The Tico Times, Apartado 4632-1000, San José, Costa Rica (☎ 258-1558, 🖳 www. ticotimes.net). Daily and weekly English-language newspaper, also available online.

Useful Addresses

Embassy of Costa Rica (UK), 14 Lancaster Gate, London W2 3LH, UK (☎ 020-7706 8844, ✉ costaricanembassy@btconnect.com).

Embassy of Costa Rica (US), 2114 S Street, NW, Washington DC 20008, US (☎ 202-234 2945, 💻 www.costarica-embassy.org).

Costa Rica Real Estate Brokers Board, Apartado 1006-2100 Guadalupe, Costa Rica (☎ 283-0191, 💻 www.camaracbr.or.cr).

Useful Website

Costa Rica Tourism Board (💻 www.visitcostarica.com).

CENTRAL AMERICA: MEXICO

Background Information

Capital: Mexico City, often called Mexico DF (*Distrito Federal*) by Mexicans.

Population: 103m.

Foreign Community: The Mexican population consists mainly of people with Spanish or European descent who have settled in Mexico since the 16th century and mestizos (those of mixed European and indigenous ancestry). There's a large foreign community, mainly retired North Americans living in coastal areas.

Area: $1,964,375km^2$ ($758,449mi^2$), of which more than $5,000km^2$ ($1,930mi^2$) are islands.

Geography: Mexico lies in North and Central America, with the US to the north (the border is over 3,200km/2,000mi long), Belize and Guatemala to the south, the Pacific Ocean to the west and the Gulf of Mexico to the east. It's a mountainous country, crossed from north to south by two mountain ranges, the Sierra Madre Oriental and the Sierra Madre Occidental, which are an extension of the Rocky Mountains. The Sierra Nevada mountain range (also known as the Trans-Mexican Volcanic Belt) runs east to west. Central and southern Mexico, which are home to the majority of the population, are an earthquake zone. Much of the country is arid or semi-arid and the north contains the vast empty plains of the Mesa Central. In the south-east is the low-lying Yucatan peninsula, popular with tourists and retirees.

Climate: Mexico's climate varies with altitude and latitude. The Tropic of Cancer divides the country into temperate and tropical zones, with tropical conditions in the lowlands and temperate or cold conditions in the mountains, some of which are snow-capped for most of the year. There's very little rainfall in the north, while central areas (including the capital) have a rainy season from June to September, but are dry for the rest of the year. Southern areas have an annual average temperature of around 26C (79F), with little variation throughout the year. Parts of north Mexico have cold winters.

Language: The official language is Spanish and there are at least 62 indigenous languages. English is widely spoken.

Political Situation: Mexico is a Federal Republic with a President who is head of state and is elected for one six-year term. There was a major change in Mexican politics in late 2000, when Vicente Fox, leader of the right-of-centre Alliance for Change party, was elected President, ending an uninterrupted 70-year hold on power by the Institutional Revolutionary Party (PRI). The 2006 elections were bitterly fought and Felipe Calderón, of the same party as

9

Fox, won the election by a margin of less than 1 per cent, beating candidates from the left-of-centre PRD party and the PRI. There was considerable dispute over the result, but Calderón finally took office in December 2006. The new President has similar priorities to Vicente Fox, tackling drug-related violence, poverty and attempting fiscal reforms. The next election will be in 2012. Mexico is a member of the United Nations, the World Trade Organisation (WTO) and the Organisation for Economic Co-operation and Development (OECD).

Finance

Currency

Mexico's currency is the Mexican peso (MXN), consisting of 100 centavos, but prices are often quoted in US$.
Exchange Rate: £1 = MXN21.4.
Exchange Controls: None but funds over MXN100,000 (£5,000) must be declared on entry into Mexico.
Interest Rate: Interest rates in Mexico are volatile.

Cost & Standard of Living

The cost of living in Mexico is far lower than in the US, which is one of the reasons why large numbers of Americans retire there. However, the standard of living is very low for much of the population and wealth is very unevenly distributed. Mexico has three minimum wages, depending on the district, but the average daily wage is around MXN50 (just over £2.00), with minimum annual salaries of around US$1,500. Local goods and produce are cheap but imported goods are expensive.

Taxation

Residents pay tax on their worldwide income and foreigners are considered tax resident when they spend over 183 days per year in the country and establish a home there. Non-residents are taxed only on their Mexican income; non-residents who let property must pay 25 per cent tax on the income and no deductions are permitted.
Personal Effects: Those with an FM-3 permit (see **Visas & Permits** below) may import household effects duty free only for the duration of their permit and cannot import a car. Those with an FM-2 permit may import effects, including a car, duty free indefinitely but must present their permit and an inventory (in Spanish) which has been certified by a Mexican consulate.
Income Tax: Mexico has a PAYE system. The top tax rate is being reduced by 1 per cent per year and in 2007 was 28 per cent. Rates are progressive and start at 3 per cent for earnings up to MXN5,953 (£283) and increase in four bands up to 28 per cent on income over MXN103,218 (£490).
Capital Gains Tax (CGT): Principal residences are exempt from CGT and residents of Mexico are exempt on the sale of a second home if they can prove that they've been resident for at least two years. CGT can be levied in one of two ways: either the buyer of a property withholds 25 per cent of the purchase price (no deductions can be claimed) and pays it to the tax authorities or the vendor pays tax at the top rate (currently 28 per cent) on the gain after deductions. Non-resident vendors must appoint a representative, resident in Mexico, to arrange

payment of CGT after the sale and notify the notary of any deductions to which they're entitled. A tax return must be submitted within 15 days of the sale.

Wealth Tax: None.

Inheritance & Gift Tax: There's no inheritance or gift tax for residents of Mexico who inherit property, but non-residents are taxed at 20 per cent on the assessed value of inherited property.

Value Added Tax (VAT): VAT applies to most transactions at the standard rate of 15 per cent. There's a reduced rate of 10 per cent for supplies to residents of a frontier zone. VAT exemptions include the construction of houses, certain financial and insurance services, and teaching and medical services.

Property

Restrictions on Foreign Ownership & Letting

In a restricted zone (within 50km of a coastline or 100km of a border), all foreigners must apply for a permit to buy from the Foreign Secretary's office. This is a formality (costing US$150!) and you'll be asked to sign a Calvo Clause, which states that you won't appeal to foreign jurisdiction regarding your property transaction. You must also set up a bank trust called a *fideicomiso* (see **Purchase Procedure** below).

There are no restrictions on letting, but rental income earned by non-residents is subject to 25 per cent tax and no deductions are allowed.

Market

The Mexican property market is extremely buoyant and hasn't been affected by the downturn in the US market. Foreign property investors are mainly Americans looking for holiday or retirement homes, although Mexico is becoming increasingly attractive to Canadian and European retirees. In popular cities and coastal areas, prices have been rising significantly, although it's still possible to find inexpensive property and land. High-profile investors have recently entered the Mexican property market (Donald Trump built the Trump Ocean Resort in Baja, prompting other investors to follow his lead). The new President, Felipe Calderón, supports the expansion of the housing market and is keen to encourage foreign investment and tourism.

Areas

Popular areas with foreign buyers include Acapulco on the Pacific coast, Guadalajara and much of the Yucatan Peninsula.

Acapulco is probably the best known beach resort. It's close to the Sierra Madre mountain range, has plenty of beautiful beaches and welcomes over 3m tourists per year, so there's plenty of rental potential.

Further north along the Pacific coast, in the province of Guadalajara, are a number of popular resorts, many around Baya de Banderas, Mexico's largest natural bay. They include Cabo del Sol, which has one of the best golf courses in Latin America, Lake Chapala, which has a huge expatriate American community, Puerto Vallarta and Tenochtitlan. These areas have a warm climate all year and plenty of leisure facilities. Puerto Vallarta in particular has seen huge

9

development and has been transformed from a small fishing village into a world-class resort, but it manages to retain its relaxed atmosphere and traditional feel.

The Yucatan Peninsula is famous for its natural beauty and is quieter than the Guadalajara resorts, for this reason attracting a number of retirees. Cancun is the Yucatan's (and Mexico's) most popular resort. At the lower end of the market, resorts in Baja California Sur, particularly Los Cabos at the southern tip of the peninsula, are experiencing a property boom, although homes are still inexpensive in comparison with Cancun.

Building Standards

Standards are variable but generally high in modern properties, although there are no official construction standards. A structural survey on any type of property is advisable and, if you're buying close to the coast or in areas with lots of volcanic rock, it's wise to have a soil survey.

Cost

In Acapulco, apartments (condominiums) close to the beach start at around US$150,000 (£76,000) for one- and two-bedroom units and rise to around US$300,000 (£152,000) for large units. Large villas with a pool start at around US$500,000 (£255,000); luxurious villas cost up to US$1m (£508,000).

In and around the Puerto Vallarta region, apartments start at around US$170,000 (£86,000) and rise to as much as US$1m (£510,000) for a large, luxurious unit. Beachfront villas start at around US$1m and can cost several million. Property in this area is considered a good investment, as prices are rising faster than in Acapulco or Cancun.

Prices in the Yucatan Peninsula are lower (including in Cancun), although they're rising fast. You can still find a small three-bedroom house close to the beach for around US$180,000 (£92,000) and a four-bedroom house for around US$250,000 (£127,000). A house with eight bedrooms costs around US$500,000 (£255,000) and a ten-room hotel costs US$1m (£510,000). In Cancun, properties are mainly apartments and you can buy a two-bedroom apartment close to a golf course for around US$100,000 (£51,000). In the Los Cabos resort of Baja California Sur, you can buy a one-bedroom apartment close to the beach for around US$80,000 (£41,000).

Local Mortgages

Until recently, it was impossible for a foreigner to obtain a mortgage in Mexico, but this is slowly changing and several US lenders have entered the market. Canadians and Americans are eligible for mortgages and, in some circumstances, so are other foreigners with permanent residence status who can prove their income history in Mexico. Loans are up to 80 per cent of the value of a property, over terms of between 10 and 30 years. Loans can be in US$ or Mexican pesos. If you aren't a US or Canadian citizen, however, it may be easier to take out a loan in your home country.

9

Property Taxes

There's an annual property tax called *impuesto predial*, which ranges from 0.275 to 1.35 per cent, depending on where your property is; each state has a different tax rate.

Purchase Procedure

The notary public is an important part of the property purchase procedure in Mexico, as he's required by law to make a full title search for the benefit of the buyer. The notary will guide you through the buying process, but as he's a government official, working of behalf of the government, you should also employ the services of an independent lawyer to protect your interests. If you're buying from a developer, he should check that all the necessary permits are in place, but it's wise to have your lawyer double-check.

The most important thing for your lawyer to check is whether the land that your property is on isn't *ejido* **land.** This means agricultural land controlled by collectives of landowners, where in some cases vendors don't have full title to the land. In theory, you can buy the land, but the sale requires agreement from the whole community of owners – a long and uncertain procedure. Sometimes developers buy a large plot of *ejido* land to redevelop and the land is usually re-registered for private ownership, but you (or your lawyer) should check that it has been. Many experts advise you to take out title insurance on **any** property you buy in Mexico.

If everything is in order and a price is agreed between the vendor and the buyer, you enter into a written agreement to buy/sell (*convenio de compra/venta*) and pay a deposit of between 5 and 10 per cent. At this point, if you're buying property in a restricted zone (within 50km of a coastline or 100km of a border), you must apply for a permit to buy from the Foreign Secretary's office (see **Restrictions on Foreign Ownership & Letting** above) and set up a bank trust (*fideicomiso*). The bank holds the trust deed for the owner, who becomes the trustee and retains all ownership rights, usually for a period of 50 years, and this is renewable. The bank will check ownership and that there are no charges on the property.

The signing of the deed and the transfer of ownership are done in the notary's office. At this point the balance is paid, along with the notary's and lawyer's fees (see below). The property is then registered in your name at the Land Registry (Registro Publico de la Propriedad).

Fees

Total fees are around 9 per cent of the purchase price and include an acquisition (transfer) tax of 2 per cent, the notary's fees of 1.5 per cent and a Land Registry registration fee of 1.3 per cent. If you need to set up a bank trust (see **Purchase Procedure** above), this costs between US$350 and US$700, and the Foreign Secretary's office permit a further US$150. A lawyer's fees are negotiable, but are usually around 1 per cent. Estate agents' fees are between 3 and 6 per cent, usually paid by the vendor.

General Information

Getting There

The quickest way to travel to and from Mexico (even from the US) is by air. The main tourist airports are Acapulco, Cancun, Los Cabos, Mexico City and Puerto Vallarta.

Acapulco Airport: Officially known as General Juan N. Alvarez International Airport, it's 26km (16mi) from the centre of Acapulco. It's the largest airport on the southern Pacific coast and is used mainly by tourists. Most international flights are from Canadian and US destinations. Only Thomsonfly operates scheduled services direct from the UK (Birmingham and

9

Manchester), although there are some charter flights. There are frequent domestic flights to Acapulco from the capital, Mexico City (see below).

Cancun International Airport: The second-busiest airport in the country, after Mexico City, is on the Caribbean coast of the Yucatan Peninsula. There's a vast choice of flights from US, Canadian and European destinations. UK destinations include Glasgow, London Gatwick and Manchester (First Choice Airways) and Belfast and Birmingham (My Travel Airways, Thomas Cook Airlines and Thomsonfly).

Los Cabos International Airport: Close to the US border, this airport handles mainly American tourists.

Mexico City International Airport: Mexico's and Latin America's largest and busiest airport, with flights from over 100 destinations worldwide, mainly in Canada, Latin America and the US, as well as domestic destinations. British Airways operates a service from London Heathrow.

Puerto Vallarta: Officially called Licenciado Gustavo Diaz Ordaz International Airport, it's on the Pacific coast and handles national and international flights, many from the US, although First Choice Airways operates from London Gatwick and Manchester all year round and Thomsonfly will introduce services from the same airports in mid-2008.

Communications

Communications in Mexico are of a reasonable standard and are largely controlled by Telefonos de Mexico, commonly known as Telmex. This former state-owned monopoly was privatised in 1991, although it still operates a quasi-monopoly, as its few competitors must use Telemex lines and infrastructure. Mobile phone and internet use is growing fast, although Mexico lags behind many countries. The country dialling code is 52 and international direct dialling (IDD) is available to around 50 countries, although international calls from fixed-line phones are expensive.

Fixed-line Telephones: The main provider is Telmex and its service is considered poor, although it has improved considerably in the last 15 or 20 years. Other providers are AT&T and Axtel (Telmex's main competitor). Public phone boxes accept pre-paid calling cards, which are widely available from newsagents' and supermarkets.

Mobile Telephones: Mexico's main provider is Telcel, owned by America Movil and operating on the GSM network. Other providers include Spain's Movistar and IUSA Cell. Call charges are high and it's recommended to buy a Mexican SIM card to use in your mobile phone.

Internet: Internet use has increased dramatically over the last few years, high-speed ADSL connections are available in most towns and cities and there's wi-fi access in many areas of Mexico City. There are a number of internet cafes in the major cities, particularly Mexico City.

Postal Services: Provided by Servicio Postal Mexicano, services can be slow and unreliable, and many people prefer to use courier services. Letters to Canada and the US usually take around a week, while those to European destinations can take up to two weeks. Post offices are open from 9.30am to 5pm from Mondays to Fridays, some also opening on Saturdays.

9

Crime Rate

Street crime in Mexico is on the increase, particularly in urban areas and especially in Mexico City. Petty crime in popular tourist areas and on public transport and in hotels, particularly at night, is common. In Mexico City, crime is a serious problem and foreigners should avoid travelling alone on public transport, particularly at night. There's also an increasing number of opportunist, short-term kidnappings in the capital.

Medical Facilities

Medical facilities are reasonable in most major cities, although not up to North American or western European standards. Public hospitals are under-staffed and under-funded, and serious medical problems often require air evacuation. Many hospitals won't deal directly with medical insurance companies but ask you to pay on the spot for treatment and claim a refund from the company later. There's a public health system which employees contribute to directly through their salaries, but visitors and foreign residents are advised to take out private health insurance.

Pets

Pets entering Mexico don't have to go into quarantine but they do require a current vaccination certificate (including rabies, hepatitis and leptospirosis), as well as a health certificate from a government-authorised vet in your home country, certifying that your pet is free from disease. This must be issued no more than 72 hours before importing your pet.

Visas & Permits

Visas: Visas aren't required by citizens of most EU countries and some other countries, including Australia, Japan, New Zealand and the US, for visits of up to 90 days. Check with a Mexican embassy or consulate before travelling. All visitors require a tourist card (known as an *FMT*), which can be obtained on entry into Mexico. It's wise to keep your tourist card safe, as you may be asked to produce it.

Residence Permits: If you want to stay in Mexico for longer than 90 days, you must obtain either a permit, the type depending on your circumstances, as follows:

- **Non-Immigrant Permit (FM-3)** – for people who intend to visit Mexico for a specific purpose and then depart, e.g. tourism, business dealings, study or a journalistic, artistic or sporting project;

- **Immigrant Permit (FM-2)** – for people who wish to live in Mexico, short or long term. The permit must be renewed annually for four years, after which you can apply for permanent residence.

- **Retiree Immigration Permit** – allows you to live in Mexico if you're over 50 and aren't earning an income in Mexico but have sufficient income from abroad to live on. This must be renewed annually in the same way as an FM-2.

- **Work Permits:** Foreigners may not work without a Non-Immigrant or Immigrant Permit (see above), and preference is given to those who can fill posts for which there's a lack of local expertise.

Reference

9

Further Reading

Choose Mexico for Retirement, John Howells and Don Merwin (Globe Pequot).
Live Better South of the Border in Mexico, Mike Nelson (Fulcrum).

Living Abroad in Mexico, Ken Luboff (Avalon Travel Publishing).
The Plain Truth About Living in Mexico, Doug Bower and Cynthia M. Bower (Universal Publishers).

Useful Addresses

Mexican Embassy (UK), 42 Hertford Street, London W1J 7JR, UK (☎ 020-7499 8586, 🖳 www.sre.gob.mx/reinounido).
    Mexican Embassy (US), 1911 Pennsylvania Avenue, NW, Washington DC 20006, US (☎ 202-728 1600, 🖳 http://portal.sre.gob.mx/usa).

Useful Websites

Go2 Mexico (🖳 www.go2mexico.com). Good Mexico travel and tourism guide.
Mexican Tourist Office (🖳 www.visitmexico.com).
Mexico Connect (🖳 www.mexconnect.com). Website for foreigners living in Mexico.
Mexpatriate (🖳 www.mexpatriate.net). Interesting expatriate website with good links.
Mexperience (🖳 www.mexperience.com). Comprehensive information about travel, lifestyle, living and working in Mexico.

CENTRAL AMERICA: PANAMA

Background Information

Capital: Panama City.
Population: 3.2m.
    Foreign Community: Panama's population is a mixture of people of Afro-Caribbean, Arab, Asian, Indian, Italian and Spanish descent. There are a growing numbers of UK and US residents.
    Area: 77,381km^2 (29,762mi^2).
    Geography: Panama is a long, narrow country in the middle of Central America. Costa Rica is to the west, Colombia to the east, the Caribbean to the north and the Pacific to the south. Panama has over 1,600km (1,000mi) of coastline and around 1,600 islands. It's divided by the Panama Canal, one of the world's busiest shipping lanes, which is sometimes referred to as the 'Eighth Wonder of the World'. Much of the country is mountainous, with a central spine of mountain ranges fringed by coastal plains. The eastern region of Darién, which is adjacent to Colombia, is dominated by dense tropical rain forest, while Chiriqui province in the west, bordering Costa Rica, includes the main fertile agricultural areas.
    Climate: Panama has a subtropical climate, with mild temperatures all year. Average temperatures are around 24C (75F) during the day and 16C (60F) at night. The wet season is from April to December, when thunderstorms and heavy rain are common.
    Language: The official language is Spanish. English is understood by most professional and business people and is widely spoken in tourist areas.
    Political Situation: Good. Since the overthrow of the military leader General Noriega in 1989, Panama has become a stable democracy with a directly elected President, who serves one five-year term, and a legislative assembly. The current President is Martin Torrijos, leader

9

of the Partido Revolucionario Democrático (PRD), who took office in 2004. The next election will be in 2009. Panama is a member of the United Nations and the World Bank.

Finance

Currency

Panama's currency is the balboa (PAB), which is exists only in coins, with no banknotes. The US$ is also legal currency and the two currencies are worth the same.

Exchange Rate: £1 = PAB2.

Exchange Controls: None.

Interest Rate: Interest rates aren't fixed by the government and so fluctuate according to a variety of economic factors. Rates offered by banks depend on the lender but have fallen dramatically over the last 20 years.

Cost & Standard of Living

Panama has a low cost of living compared to western Europe and the US, and a high standard of living, making it one of the best places to live in Latin America. Prices are around two thirds of those in the US, and utilities and locally produced goods are particularly good value. Imported goods, however, can be expensive.

Taxation

Panama introduced a series of tax reforms in 2005, with amendments in 2007, which closed tax loopholes and addressed the large deficit in the Social Security Fund. Individuals are liable for tax on any type of income earned in Panama. Tax residence applies if you spend more than 180 days per year in the country or, under certain circumstances, own property there.

Personal Effects: Residents, including holders of a retirement visa (see **Residence Permits** below), may import belongings and household goods duty free. Those who hold a retirement visa may import a new car every two years.

Income Tax: The first PAB/US$9,000 is exempt and then there are five bands, from 16.5 to 27 per cent.

Capital Gains Tax (CGT): CGT is levied on property transfers in Panama according to a complicated system based on the cadastral value and the number of years' ownership. Those liable may pay 5 per cent or 2 per cent CGT; those who choose the higher rate can avoid the 2 per cent RETT payable on transfer (see **Fees** below). You should obtain specialist advice to ascertain your liability.

Inheritance &Gift Tax: There's no inheritance tax, but property that's gifted is subject to tax at varying rates, depending on the relationship between donor and beneficiary.

Wealth Tax: None.

Value Added Tax (VAT): There's a 5 per cent sales tax on most transactions. A rate of 10 per cent applies to alcoholic drinks and 15 per cent to tobacco products. Exempt items include books, food, fuel and medicine. Panama also levies an excise tax of 5 per cent on some products and services, including cars, motorcycles, insurance premiums and air fares.

9

Property

Restrictions on Foreign Ownership & Letting

Foreigners may not purchase property within 10km (6mi) of a national border or on an island. There are strict regulations (applicable to all buyers) regarding property renovation, which must be carried out quickly and in sympathy with the country's renovation programme.

There are no restrictions on letting, but income tax must be paid on any rental income and VAT at 5 per cent is payable on monthly rental income over PAB/US$3,000.

Market

Panama has had a fairly buoyant property market for some years, but since 2003 it has been booming, thanks to increased interest from foreign buyers, particularly Americans. Property values across the country have risen by an average of around 25 per cent per annum over the last three years. Retirees are especially attracted by the mild climate, the low cost of living and the beautiful coastline. Panama City is popular with both foreigners and locals. Rental yields in beach locations are the country's highest (between 8 and 15 per cent), while Panama City rental yields are around 10 per cent.

There's a wide variety of property available, including traditional stilt-houses built on the water, luxury beach properties, skyscraper apartments and colonial buildings.

Areas

Foreign retirees have traditionally headed for the western province of Chiriqui, close to the border with Costa Rica. It's a scenic, mountainous area including the popular Bocas de Toro archipelago in the Bay of Chiriqui and the towns of Boquete and Volcan. It's a seven-hour drive from Panama City and an increasing number of developments are being constructed along the route.

The coast west of Panama City is popular with foreign buyers and there are a number of beach property developments along the coastal road, the best known being Coronado, Playa Blanca and Santa Clara.

Panama City itself is popular too and offers a choice of skyscrapers, luxury apartments annexed to a yacht club (with a casino and private beach) and colonial properties in the historic Old Town (*Casco Viejo*).

Building Standards

Standards are variable but generally high in new properties.

9

Cost

Prices in Panama have risen considerably in recent years, but they're still low when compared with other popular beach holiday and retirement locations. A two-bedroom house in the popular Chiriqui area costs around PAB/US$200,000, while a larger, luxurious home costs around

PAB/US$400,000. Beach properties west of Panama City start at around PAB/US$100,000 for a one-bedroom apartment, rising to around PAB/US$350,000 for a three-bedroom house and PAB/US$700,000 for a five-bedroom house. In Panama City, a small apartment costs around PAB/US$150,000, a three-bedroom house around PAB/US$400,000 and a five-bedroom home around PAB/US$700,000. A two-bedroom renovated apartment in the Old Town costs around PAB/US$300,000. Cheaper properties in need of renovation are also available, but regulations are strict (see **Restrictions on Foreign Ownership & Letting** above).

Local Mortgages

Mortgages are available to foreigners from a number of local banks. Most offer between 70 and 80 per cent of the value of a property. Interest rates and mortgage terms vary considerably with the bank. Buyers who plan to live in their property and who can show a regular income are offered better terms than those who plan to use the property as a capital investment. **You cannot obtain a mortgage on a Possession Rights property (see Purchase Procedure below).**

Property Taxes

Property tax (*impuesto de inmuebles*) is payable annually on the assessed value of a property plus any improvements. Homes valued at under PAB/US$30,000 are exempt, those valued at between PAB/US$30,000 and PAB/US$75,000 are taxed at 1.75 per cent and those valued at over PAB/US$75,000 at 2.10 per cent.

Purchase Procedure

Not all property in Panama has legal title. In some cases, you may be able to purchase only 'possession rights' (see below), so always use the services of an experienced lawyer to verify the status of your chosen property. Some Panamanian estate agents have been known to put a mark-up (of as much as 100 per cent) on property prices without the knowledge of the vendor, pocketing the difference in addition to their commission. Always ask to talk to the owner directly and check the selling price; if the agent is reluctant to arrange this, the purchase is best avoided. **All contracts and legal documents must be written in Spanish. Contracts in English carry no legal weight in Panama.**

Titled Properties: If the property you plan to buy has legal title, it should be recorded at the Public Registry Office (Registro Publico) and your lawyer will be able to make all the usual checks and searches. Buyer and vendor usually enter into a 'promise to purchase' agreement and a small goodwill deposit is paid by the buyer while the lawyer carries out the necessary searches and any financing is arranged. Once everything is in order, a purchase and sale agreement is signed and the change of ownership registered at the Public Registry Office. Final payment isn't made to the vendor until the transfer of ownership has been registered, although often both parties enter into an agreement whereby the funds are deposited with a lawyer in an escrow account pending registration.

Possession Rights Properties: Many beachfront properties and properties on the islands are owned by the national or local government and don't have title deeds. You cannot own these outright but will be granted only 'possession rights' (*derecho possessorio*) for a certain period. **If you decide on such a property, you should exercise extreme caution and use the services of an experienced and independent local lawyer.** He should ensure that your

9

possession rights are issued by the correct authorities and that there's a full description of your rights under the agreement.

The purchase procedure for possession rights property is similar to that for titled property, but checks and searches are more difficult to make as contracts aren't lodged in a central registry. Buyers sign a 'promise to purchase' contract and make a small goodwill deposit to secure the property. You lawyer should check that the owner has a valid Certificate of Rights of Possession issued by a competent government authority and that it contains a description of the property and boundary details. There should also be a survey document which is stamped and certified by a licensed surveyor. If everything is in order, the purchase and sale agreement is signed and the balance paid once the Certificate of Rights of Possession has been transferred to the buyer's name. Contracts relating to the purchase of possession rights property cannot be registered at the Public Registry but should still be authenticated by a public notary.

Fees

Fees for property purchase are low, a lawyer's and notary's fees amounting to around 2 per cent of the purchase price, real estate transfer tax (RETT) 2 per cent and an estate agent's fee between 3 and 5 per cent, the last two being paid by the seller.

General Information

Getting There

Panama's strategic location between North and South America means that it's easy to reach from both by air, but there are few direct flights from Europe. Panama's main airport is Tocumen International Airport, 24km (15mi) from Panama City. In 2006, it underwent major expansion to deal with increased passenger numbers. American Airlines, Copa Airlines (the national airline) and Delta Airlines offer a range of flights from US airports, including Atlanta, Houston, Miami and Washington. Only one European airline, Iberia, flies to Tocumen (from Madrid). **If you travel via the US, you must have a machine-readable passport or a valid US Non-Immigrant Visa, which must be obtained before travelling.**

Communications

Panama has one of the most advanced telecommunications systems in Latin America and the cost of telephone calls to Europe and the US has fallen considerably since 49 per cent of the national telecommunications monopoly, INTEL, was bought by UK-based Cable and Wireless in 1997. Mobile phones are used by around 75 per cent of the population and internet use is becoming widespread. The country dialling code is 507 (there are no area codes in Panama) and international direct dialling (IDD) is available worldwide.

Fixed-line Telephones: Around five operators compete with Cable and Wireless to provide fixed-line services. Prepaid telephone cards are popular for making international calls and can be bought from many shops and kiosks and used with any type of telephone. The most popular card is the ClaroCOM. There are public phones throughout the country in Cable and Wireless offices, which are open every day from 7.30am to 10pm.

9

Mobile Telephones: The two main providers are Cable and Wireless and Movistar (owned by Spanish telecommunications giant Telefonica). Both operate on the GSM network and local SIM cards are available.

Internet: High-speed connection is available throughout the country and there are around ten internet service providers (ISPs). There are internet cafes in all the main towns and in Panama City.

Postal Services: Panama's post office (Dirección General de Correos y Telegrafos) is reasonably efficient, and post to the US usually takes around a week, although it's advisable to post items in Panama City and courier services are recommended for urgent or valuable mail. Post offices are open from 7am to 6pm on weekdays and 7am to 5pm on Saturdays.

Crime Rate

There's a fairly high level of street crime in Panama, particularly in Panama City and especially in the Old Town, which is popular with tourists. You shouldn't carry large sums of cash and should always beware of pickpockets on public transport and busy shopping and tourist areas. It's advisable to only use registered taxi companies and not to travel alone, particularly at night. There are also, occasionally, more serious incidents in some parts of Panama City, usually connected with organised crime.

Medical Facilities

Medical facilities are generally good, with highly trained medical staff. Panama City has some good private hospitals, where treatment is reasonably priced, although outside the capital facilities can be limited. Many of the country's doctors trained in the US and bi-lingual doctors are common in all Panama City hospitals. The Hospital Nacional in Panama City is one of the best in Central America and provides treatment under several international health insurance policies, although many expatriates prefer to travel to the US for specialist medical treatment. Comprehensive private medical insurance is recommended even for foreign residents who have a retirement visa, which entitles them to discounts on medical treatment and medicines.

Pets

Pets require a Health and Vaccination Certificate issued by a government-authorised vet in your home country, declaring that your pet has had mandatory vaccinations (including rabies) and is in good health. You must take the certificate to a Panamanian embassy to be certified. On arrival in Panama, your pet must be examined by the Panamanian veterinary authorities and is usually subject to 30 days' home quarantine.

Visas & Permits

9

Visas: Visas aren't required by citizens of the EEA for visits of up to 90 days. Citizens of Australia, Canada, the Caribbean and the US are issued with 'tourist cards', which can be used for visits of up to 30 days (extendable to 90 days). Citizens of other countries should check entry requirements with a Panamanian embassy or consulate.

Residence Permits: If you plan to stay longer than 90 days or wish to live permanently in Panama, you need an Immigration Visa, which can be obtained via a Panamanian embassy or consulate in your home country or on arrival, through the National Directorate of Immigration and Naturalisation (💻 www.migracion.gob.pa). There are several kinds of visa, depending on your circumstances. The Retirement Visa (*Pensionado Visa*) is issued to those who can prove they have an assured minimum income of US$500 per month, plus US$100 for each dependent, and entitles you to a number of benefits. An Investor Visa is granted if you invest in agriculture or forestry in Panama. Other types of visa are granted if you can prove you can support yourself financially, either as a retiree or non-retired person with minimum assets of US$200,000.

Work Permits: Work permits must be obtained by any non-Panamanian who wishes to work in the country. Permits are issued by the Ministry for Labour and Social Welfare (within government quotas) and your employer is required to prove that there isn't a Panamanian citizen who could fill the job. You must provide a certificate of your qualifications and professional experience, which must be certified by a Panama consul. Work permits must be renewed annually.

Reference

Further Reading

Choose Panama...the Perfect Retirement Haven, William Hutchings (Authorhouse).
Living and Investing in Panama, Christopher Howard (Costa Rica Books).
Lonely Planet Panama, Regis St. Louis (Lonely Planet Publications).

Useful Addresses

Consulate of Panama in London, Panama House, 40 Hertford Street, London W1J 7SH, UK (☎ 020-7409 2255, 💻 www.panaconsul.com).
 Embassy of Panama (US), 2862 McGill Terrace, NW, Washington, DC 20008, US (☎ 202-438 1407, 💻 www.embassyofpanama.org).

Useful Websites

Explore Panama (💻 www.explorepanama.com). Comprehensive information about life in Panama.
 Panama Guide (💻 www.panama-guide.com). Extensive information and news about Panama, in English.
 Panama Info (💻 www.panamainfo.com). Extensive information about business, living, retiring and tourism in Panama.
 Retire Panama (💻 www.retirepanama.com). The website of the Retiree Association of Panama.
 Visit Panama (💻 www.visitpanama.com). Panama's official tourist website.

9

ASIA: MALAYSIA

Background Information

Capital: Kuala Lumpur (Putrajaya is the administrative capital).
Population: 26m.

Foreign Community: Around 65 per cent of the population is Malay, around 25 per cent Chinese and just over 7 per cent Indian. There are around 60,000 expatriates in Malaysia, the majority British.
Area: 329,758km^2 (127,317mi^2).

Geography: Malaysia is in south-east Asia and has two distinct parts, separated by the South China Sea. The majority of the country is in what's known as Peninsular Malaysia (or West Malaysia), with Thailand to the north and Singapore and Indonesia to the south. The remainder of the country, which consists of the two states of Sabah and Sarawak along with the federal territory of Labuan, are in East Malaysia, on the north and west coasts of the island of Borneo and bordering Brunei and Indonesia. The Strait of Malacca, which lies between Peninsular Malaysia and Sumatra, is one of the world's most important shipping lanes. The two parts of the country share a similar landscape, of coastal plains rising to forested hills and mountains. The west coast of Peninsular Malaysia consists of mangrove swamps and mudflats, although some coastal plains have been cleared and cultivated. The east coast consists of beaches backed by dense jungle. There are three major islands off the west coast (Langkawi, Pangkor and Penang) and five off the east coast (Kapas, Perhentian, Rawa, Redang and Tioman). The highest peak in the country is Mount Kinabalu at 4,095m^2 (13,435ft).

Climate: The climate is tropical, i.e. hot and humid, with humidity generally between 80 to 90 per cent, except in the highlands, where it's lower. The main rainy season is from October to February in East Malaysia, with the heaviest rains in Sabah and Sarawak. August is the wettest month in West Malaysia. Rainfall in both parts of the country depends on the prevailing monsoon winds. In Kuala Lumpur, the average temperature is 27C (81F) all year.

Language: Malay is the official language and other languages spoken include Chinese, Iban and Tamil. English is widely spoken.

Political Situation: Good. Since Malaysia became independent from British rule in 1957, it has been governed by a multi-party coalition known as Barisan Nacional (BN). The country is a federal constitutional monarchy, with the King as Head of State. The King has a largely ceremonial role and the position is rotated every five years between the nine hereditary state rulers. Sultan Mizan Zainal Abidin became Malaysia's 13th King in December 2006. Malaysia's system of government is closely modelled on that of the UK. The coalition government is made up of the United Malays Organisation (UMNO), the Malaysian Chinese Association (MCA), the Malaysian Indian Congress (MIC) and a series of smaller parties. In 2003, Malaysia's longest-serving Prime Minister, Mahathir Mohamad, retired and Abdullah Ahmad began a five-year term in March 2004. He's considered a moderniser who intends to stamp out corruption and poverty. Malaysia is a member of the Commonwealth, the UN and the Association of Southeast Asian Nations (ASEAN).

Finance

9

Currency

Malaysia's currency is the Malaysian ringgit (abbreviated to MYR but often referred to as RM), which is divided into 100 sen. Until 2005, it was pegged to the US dollar, but it's now allowed to float against several major currencies, although Malaysia's central bank, the Bank Negara Malaysia (BNM) intervenes if necessary to maintain its stability.

Exchange Rate: £1 = MYR6.84.

Exchange Controls: Non-residents may import only MYR1,000 (£150) and export the equivalent in foreign currency or travellers' cheques. Residents may import only MYR1,000 but may export the equivalent of up to MYR10,000 (£1,500) in foreign currency and travellers' cheques. You may apply to the BNM to exceed these limits in certain circumstances, but approval can be a long process and you must have written approval before attempting to import or export the funds. All travellers, irrespective of the amount they import or export, are required to complete a Traveller's Declaration Form (TDF) at immigration on arrival and departure. Customs officers are authorised to search you and any vehicles and luggage on arrival and departure. For further information, contact Customs Headquarters in Putrajaya (see **Useful Addresses** below).

Cost & Standard of Living

Malaysia's standard of living is the highest in south-east Asia after Singapore's. The country's economy has been transformed by a move away from an agricultural economy towards high-tech manufacturing, with Malaysia currently one of the world's largest producers of microchips. Unemployment, inflation and the cost of living are low, although life in cities such as Kuala Lumpur is naturally more expensive, mainly due to high accommodation costs. There's enormous economic disparity in Malaysia – between the high earners and those who live in extreme poverty. There's no legal minimum wage, but the Malaysian Trades Union Congress has been pushing for one for many years.

Taxation

You're taxed only on income earned in Malaysia. Income earned outside the country (by residents and non-residents) isn't taxable. You're considered a tax resident if you stay in the country for more than 182 days per year.

Personal Effects: Furniture and personal effects which are more than six months old can be imported duty free into Malaysia if you're planning to live or work in the country. Documentary evidence of the age of the items may be required. You may import a car for up to three months, but it's subject to import duty of between 100 and 300 per cent and it must be re-exported at the end of this period unless you applied for an Approval Permit from the Ministry of International Trade and Industry before shipping the car, which must not be more than five years old.

Income Tax: Malaysia uses the PAYE system. Residents are charged on all income earned in Malaysia at progressive rates up to 28 per cent (on earnings over MYR25,000). Rental income for non-residents is taxed at 28 per cent; income-generating expenses are deductible but depreciation isn't.

Capital Gains Tax: None.

Wealth Tax: None.

Inheritance & Gift Tax: None.

Value Added Tax (VAT): VAT is known as sales tax and is levied at a standard rate of 10 per cent, but 15 per cent on beer, cigarettes and wine, and 5 per cent on advertising, insurance and entertainment. Exempt items include basic medical equipment and certain foods.

Property

Restrictions on Foreign Ownership & Letting

Restrictions on foreign ownership were relaxed in 2005. Foreigners may now buy up to two residential properties (either two condominiums or one condominium and one terraced house or semi-detached house), which must have a minimum value of MYR250,000 (£40,000), and must have the approval of the Foreign Investment Committee, although this is a formality and is usually arranged by your lawyer as part of the purchase procedure (see below).

There are no restrictions on letting, but rental income is subject to 28 per cent tax (see **Income Tax** above).

Market

The Malaysian property market has been strong since the early to mid-'90s, when it saw annual growth of up to 26 per cent. The Asian Financial Crisis of the late '90s hit the market hard, prices falling by as much as 40 per cent in Kuala Lumpur. The market has since recovered, and prices have been rising steadily since 2000. The rental market is small, as around 85 per cent of housing is owner-occupied, although in Kuala Lumpur there's demand for rental properties from expatriates and yields are reasonable. The relaxing of restrictions on foreign ownership (see above) and the abolition of capital gains tax in April 2007 further encouraged foreign investment in property.

Areas

The property market is concentrated into two distinct sectors: Kuala Lumpur, where many expatriates live and where there's a strong demand for luxury properties, and the resorts and islands, which are popular with people retiring to Malaysia under a government programme called 'Malaysia, My Second Home' (see **Visas & Permits** below).

Kuala Lumpur, in particular Kuala Lumpur city centre (known as KLCC), is the most popular area for property investors. Strong economic growth has seen a huge rise in demand for high-quality property to buy or rent. Kuala Lumpur is thriving – full of gleaming new skyscrapers such as the Petronas Twin Towers (until recently the world's tallest building) – and annual rental yields are around 8 per cent. Retirees and foreign residents sometimes prefer to buy on the islands off the west coast, the most popular being Langkawi and Penang, and at beach locations such as Cherating in Pahang province and Johor, south from Pahang on the west coast. Some retirees also buy in the cooler Cameron Highlands, also in Pahang province.

9

Building Standards

Standards are generally high in new buildings, but the climate takes its toll quite quickly and regular maintenance is required. A structural survey is advisable on all properties.

Cost

Prices in Kuala Lumpur rose by around 7 per cent in 2006. One-bedroom condominiums in KLCC cost from MYR600,000 (£90,000), while luxurious three-bedroom apartments cost around MYR1.5m (£220,000). On the popular islands, such as Penang, a three-bedroom beachfront apartment costs around MYR550,000 (£75,000), while a new three-bedroom house costs around MYR1.5m (£220,000). Prices in Johor and the Cameron Highlands are considerably lower, around MYR250,000 (£40,000) for a two-bedroom apartment.

Local Mortgages

Mortgages are available from local banks for as much as 90 per cent of the purchase price, over a period of up to 30 years. Some banks, including the HSBC in Malaysia, offer Islamic mortgages, which are also available to non-Muslims. This method of financing is based on Islamic principles, meaning that interest cannot be charged by the lender in the normal way. It's sometimes called a 'deferred payment sale' and you enter into a buy-and-sell agreement with a bank rather than a home loan arrangement. You put down the deposit in the usual way, the bank buys the house on your behalf and you buy it back from the bank with agreed monthly payments.

Property Tax

There's a local property tax called an assessment tax, which is based on the annual rental value of a property, as assessed by the local authority. The rate is 6 per cent and it's payable in two instalments.

Purchase Procedure

The property purchase procedure is similar to the UK's. However, it isn't exactly the same and caution should be exercised. It's wise to use the services of an independent property lawyer to protect your interests. All foreigners wishing to invest in property must have their purchase approved by the Foreign Investment Committee (see **Restrictions on Foreign Ownership & Letting** above). Once this has been done, a provisional agreement called a letter of offer/acceptance is signed and a 3 per cent deposit paid, with an additional 7 per cent payable within 14 days of signing. The binding contract is known as a sale and purchase agreement, which is stamped by the Stamp Office once stamp duty is paid. All properties are sold freehold and have what's known as a strata title deed. Completion and final payment must take place within three months and the transfer must be registered at the Land Office Registry.

   Caution should be exercised when buying a new property in an unfinished development. You should ensure that the developer has a valid licence and an advertising and sales permit. You should also check that you're protected in case the developer goes out of business.

9

Fees

Total costs are between 3.5 and 7 per cent, depending on the value of a property. A lawyer's fees, which are between 0.4 and 1 per cent, also depend on the value of the property: the higher the value, the lower the fee (as a percentage). An estate agent's fees are between 2 and 2.75 per cent and are usually paid by the vendor. Stamp duty on transfer of title is at 1 per cent on the first MYR100,000, 2 per cent between MYR100,000 and 500,000 and 3 per cent over MYR500,000.

General Information

Getting There

Malaysia has five international airports: Kota Kinabalu (8km/5mi from the city of Kota Kinabalu, the capital of Sabah in East Malaysia and a popular tourist destination), Kuala Lumpur, Kuching (in Sarawak in East Malaysia and recently renovated), Penang (16km/10mi south of Georgetown, the capital of one of the most popular islands in Malaysia), and Senai (near Johor in West Malaysia and serving the southern states), but only Kuala Lumpur handles flights from Europe and the US; for all other airports you must fly via KL.

Kuala Lumpur International Airport: The largest and most important airport in the country is around 60km (38mi) south of the city. It's one of Asia's major airports and the principal hub for Air Asia and Malaysian Airlines, the national airline, which operates frequent direct flights from a vast number of worldwide destinations including London Heathrow. There are also regular flights from KL airport to all major cities within West and East Malaysia, and domestic air travel is cheap.

Communications

Malaysia has a sophisticated communications network. Mobile phone penetration is around 75 per cent and internet and email are widely used, particularly in Kuala Lumpur, Penang and Johor. The main telecommunications provider is Telekom Malaysia Berhard (TM), which has a monopoly on the fixed-line network and a considerable market share of the mobile phone market. The country code is 60 and international direct dialling (IDD) is available to most countries.

Fixed-line Telephones: TM is the only provider and offers prepaid calling cards called iTalk which allow callers to make national and international calls at economical rates. Public phone boxes also use prepaid phone cards, but if you're making an international call, you must use a dedicated box.

Mobile Telephones: There are three main providers: Celcom, DiGi and Maxis, which all use the GSM 900 and 1800 systems. Malaysian SIM cards are available.

Internet: Internet use is widespread in the major cities, particularly Kuala Lumpur, Johor and Penang, although rural areas are less well served. Services are provided by TM Net, a subsidiary of TM, which offers broadband services. TM Net has recently been joined by NasionCom, a new provider in the telecommunications market, which offers broadband internet services, along with a package of other services. There are plenty of internet cafes, particularly in Kuala Lumpur.

Postal Services: Pos Malaysia provides reliable and economical postal services worldwide. Letters to Europe take around ten days. Post offices are open Mondays to Saturdays from 8am to 5pm.

9

Crime Rate

The violent crime rate is fairly low in Malaysia, but 'petty' crime such as pick-pocketing, burglary and car theft is common. Credit card fraud and scams against tourists are rife, the latter including the spiking of drinks and gambling scams.

Medical Facilities

Medical services are good in Malaysia and there's an extensive network of public and private hospitals. There has been an increase in the number of private specialist hospitals and clinics in recent years, as the Malaysian Government is promoting the country as a 'health tourism' destination. Malaysia has a government health insurance scheme and public hospitals are heavily subsidised. However, visitors and residents are advised to take out comprehensive health insurance (as do most Malaysians who can afford it) and check with their doctor before travelling to the country, as malaria is present in some parts of East Malaysia.

Pets

Quarantine requirements in Malaysia depend on which country your pet is travelling from. Animals from Australia, Brunei, Ireland, Japan, New Zealand, Singapore, Sweden and the UK (known as 'scheduled' countries) don't need to be quarantined, but those from other ('non-scheduled') countries do. If your pet is arriving from a scheduled country, it avoids quarantine but must still have an import permit, which must be submitted to the Malaysian veterinary authorities before travel, showing details of vaccinations, and a health certificate issued by a government-authorised vet not more than seven days before arrival, confirming that it's free of disease.

Visas & Permits

Malaysia encourages employment of foreigners who are skilled professionals – see the Malaysian Government Immigration website (🖳 www.imi.gov.my) – but certain visas and permits are required.

Visas: Visas aren't required by EU citizens or citizens of certain other countries, including Australia, Canada and the US, for visits of up to 90 days. Check with a Malaysian embassy or consulate for a full list of countries. However, anyone travelling to Malaysia must have a valid return ticket and will be issued with a Social Visit Pass at the point of entry to the country.

Residence & Work Permits: For visits of longer than 90 days or if you plan to take up paid employment, you must obtain a pass, the nature of which depends on your circumstances, as follows:

- **Employment Pass** – required if you're taking up a work contract of at least two years and will have a monthly income of at least MYR3,000 (£450); can be applied for before leaving your home country or once you're in Malaysia;

- **Visit Pass** – for employment of less than two years.

- **'Malaysia, My Second Home' (MM2H)** – a long-term Social Visit Pass which allows you to stay for an initial period of between five and ten years (you're granted a multiple entry visa if applicable) and is renewable. However, it doesn't entitle you to permanent residence or allow you to work. You must fulfil certain criteria to be granted this pass: if you're younger than 50, you must:

  - open an account with the sum of MYR300,000 (£45,000); after a year, you may withdraw up to MYR240,000 (£35,000) for approved expenses (e.g. house purchase, education or medical fees);

9

– maintain a minimum balance of MYR60,000 (£9,000) throughout your stay in Malaysia;

If you're 50 or older, you must:

– open an account with the sum of MYR150,000 (£22,000) or show proof of a monthly offshore, government-approved income, such as a pension, of at least MYR10,000 (£1,500); after a year, you may withdraw up to MYR90,000 (£13,000) for approved expenses (as above);

– maintain a minimum balance of MYR60,000 (£9,000) throughout your stay in Malaysia.

Other passes are issued for family members of those with an employment pass, those married to a Malaysian citizen, students and retirees (or semi-retirees who wish to live long-term in Malaysia).

Reference

Further Reading

Living and Working in the Far East, Graeme Chesters (Survival Books). Everything you need to know about living and working in the Far East.

House Buyers' Guide Book, Malaysian National House Buyers' Association, 31, Level 3, Jalan Barat, Off Jalan Imbi, 55100 Kuala Lumpur, Malaysia (☎ 3-2142 2225, 🖳 www.hba.org.my).

The New Straits Times, Balai Berita, 31 Jalan Riong, 59100 Kuala Lumpur, Malaysia (☎ 3-2282 3131, 🖳 www.nstp.com.my). English-language daily newspaper and umbrella organisation for the *Business Times* and *Malay Mail*.

Useful Addresses

The Board of Valuers, Appraisers and Estate Agents Malaysia, Suite 3B-10-3A, Level 10, Block 3B, Plaza Sentral, Jalan Stesen Sentral 5, Kuala Lumpur Sentral, 50470 Kuala Lumpur, Malaysia (☎ 3-2273 7839, 🖳 www.lppeh.gov.my).

Department of Currency Exchange Control, Bank Negara Malaysia, Jalan Dato' Onn, 50480 Kuala Lumpur, Malaysia (☎ 3-291 0772, 🖳 www.bnm.gov.my).

Embassy of Malaysia (UK), 45 Belgrave Square, London SW1 8QT, UK (☎ 020-7235 8033, ✉ mwlondon@btinternet.com).

Embassy of Malaysia (US), 3516 International Count, NW, Washington DC 20008, US (☎ 202-572 9700, 🖳 www.kln.gov.my/perwakilan/Washington).

Immigration Department, Block 1 (North), Level 4, Damansara Town Centre, 50550 Kuala Lumpur, Malaysia (☎ 3-8880 1000, 🖳 www.imi.gov.my).

Malaysia Tourism Promotion Board (UK), 57 Trafalgar Square, London WC2N 5DU, UK (☎ 020-7930 7932, ✉ mtpb.london@tourism.gov.my).

Malaysia Tourism Promotion Board (US), 120 East, 56th Street, Suite 810, New York, NY 10022, US (☎ 212-745 1114, ✉ mtpb.ny@tourism.gov.my).

Malaysian National House Buyers' Association, 31, Level 3, Jalan Barat, Off Jalan Imbi, 55100 Kuala Lumpur, Malaysia (☎ 3-2142 2225, 🖳 www.hba.org.my).

9

Useful Websites

Foreign Investment Committee (🖳 www.epu.jpm.my).
Malaysia, My Second Home Programme (🖳 www.mm2h.gov.my).
Malaysiakini (🖳 www.malaysiakini.com). English-language online newspaper.
Ministry of Agriculture, Department of Veterinary Services (🖳 http://agrolink.moa.my).
The Star (🖳 http://thestar.com.my). English-language daily online newspaper.

ASIA: THAILAND

Background Information

Capital: Bangkok.
Population: 65m.
   Foreign Community: The majority of the population (75 per cent) is Thai, the biggest foreign community being Chinese (14 per cent), with a small percentage of Malay nationals. There's a small British and American expatriate community.
   Area: 513,115km^2 (195,512mi^2).
   Geography: Thailand is in south-east Asia, with Burma to the west and north, Laos to the north and east, and Cambodia to the east. Southern Thailand consists of a long peninsula, with the Indian Ocean to the west and the South China Sea and the Gulf of Thailand to the east. To the south lies Malaysia. Thailand has several distinct geographical regions. The north of the country is mountainous, its highest point being Doi Inthanon, at 2,576m (8,451ft). To the north-east is the Khorat Plateau, which is bordered to the east by the Mekong River. The centre of the country is mainly flat and dominated by the Chao Phraya river valley, which runs into the Gulf of Thailand. In the south of the country, there's a narrow land bridge, known as the Kra Isthmus, which connects the Malay Peninsula to the mainland of Asia. Thailand has hundreds of islands dotted around its coast, the most famous of which is Phuket, Thailand's largest island and a popular property-buying location with foreigners.
   Climate: Thailand's climate is tropical and is characterised by monsoons. It has three distinct seasons: a wet (monsoon) season from June to October, a cool, dry season from November to February, and a hot season from March to May. Average temperatures are usually around 32C (90F), the period from March to May averaging around 36C (96F), with high humidity. The southern isthmus (Kra Isthmus) is always hot and humid. The north and north-east of the country is generally cooler than the capital, Bangkok, in the winter, but hotter in summer. Average rainfall in central Thailand is around 11cm (4.3in) and the wettest months are, naturally, June to October, when the monsoon season brings rainfall of up to 30cm (11.8in) in one month; average monthly rainfall from May to October is around 20cm (8in). In the north and north-eastern regions, it's slightly lower at around 16cm (6in) per month. Widespread flooding in the north and centre of the country is usual at this time, particularly in September and October, the height of the monsoon season.
   Language: The official language is Thai, with English the second language of educated Thais. There are many ethnic and regional dialects.
   Political Situation: Uncertain, following a bloodless military coup against the Thai civilian government in September 2006. Thailand is a constitutional monarchy, with a much-revered and long-serving King, Bhumibol Adulyadeh, who came to the throne in 1946 and is the world's longest-reigning monarch. In 2002, the Thai Rak Thai Party, headed by Prime Minister Thaksin Shinawatra, formed the first government in Thai history to complete a four-year term. But after corruption allegations, an election was called in 2006, boycotted by the opposition. Thaksin was

9

re-elected but allegations continued, leading to the September coup, and in May 2007 the Thai Rak Thai Party was dissolved for breaching electoral rules. The UK's Trade and Investment department reports that the situation in Bangkok and elsewhere in Thailand is calm, and business continues much as it always has. An interim Prime Minister, Surayud Chulanont, a well respected army veteran, was appointed in October 2006 but martial law remains in effect throughout the country. As a result of the coup, an election is scheduled for late 2007. Thailand is a member of the United Nations (UN).

Finance

Currency

Thailand's currency is the baht (THB), consisting of 100 satang. Until the Asian financial crisis of 1997, the baht was pegged to the US dollar at a rate of US$1 = THB25. Following the crisis, the baht was floated and halved in value. Its value has now recovered considerably, and in 2007 it reached a rate of around US$1 = THB32.

Exchange Rate: £1 = THB65.01.

Exchange Controls: In theory, most foreign currency transactions are regulated by, and require the permission of, the Bank of Thailand. However, regulations have been relaxed considerably in recent years and only foreign currency transactions of relatively high values need Central Bank approval. All other transactions can be processed by commercial banks.

Cost & Standard of Living

The cost of living is generally low in Thailand, although there are huge variations between the capital, Bangkok, and rural areas. An average monthly salary in Bangkok is around THB35,000 (£550) and rented accommodation usually costs around between THB3,000 and THB 10,000 (£46 and £155) per month, depending on size and style. On the other hand, food and dining in restaurants are inexpensive by European standards, as are imported goods, particularly cars.

Taxation

Tax residents are defined as individuals who spend more than 180 days per year in Thailand and they may be taxed on income from foreign sources brought into Thailand. Non-residents pay tax only on income from sources in Thailand.

Personal Effects: May be imported duty free provided you have a valid visa and work permit for at least one year (see **Visas & Permits** below). Imported cars are heavily taxed and require approval from the Ministry of Commerce before arrival.

Income Tax: Income up to THB100,000 (£1,550) is exempt and there are subsequently four progressive rates, from 10 per cent between THB100,000 and THB500,000 (£1,550 to £7,700) up to 37 per cent for income over THB4m (£61,500).

Capital Gains Tax (CGT): Capital gains are taxed as ordinary income, at the rates detailed above.

Wealth Tax: None.

Inheritance & Gift Tax: None.

Value Added Tax (VAT): The standard rate is 10 per cent. There's no VAT on exports, and businesses with a turnover of less than THB1.2m (£18,500) are exempt.

9

Property

Restrictions on Foreign Ownership & Letting

Foreigners cannot buy land in their own name but they can lease land for up to 30 years at a time. Many take on three 30-year renewable leases, which give them effective ownership, but the lease must be registered with the Land Office to be valid. Foreigners can also own an apartment in a registered building, provided there isn't more than 49 per cent foreign ownership in the development as a whole. They can also enter into a partnership with Thai nationals in a majority Thai-owned company. **Asking a Thai national to buy on your behalf is very risky, as the foreign 'owner' has no rights to the property, even following divorce from or the death of a partner in whose name the property was bought.** Funds used to purchase a property must be shown to have been brought into Thailand and recorded by a Thai bank on a Dor Tor 3 Form.

There are no restrictions on letting, but tax of between 10 and 30 per cent is payable on rental income.

Market

Although the 2004 tsunami didn't affect the property market, the military coup of 2006 did. Following the Asian economic crisis of 1997, the Thai property market recovered well thanks to strong economic growth. Prices rose by more than 50 per cent between 1999 and 2006, with particularly high rises in the three years to 2006 (especially in Bangkok). However, the military junta which now controls Thailand has introduced several policies which are having a negative effect on the economy, such as tighter restrictions on the foreign ownership of companies and capital controls by the Central Bank. Many experts feel that unless economic and political stability is restored to Thailand, the economy and the housing market will suffer long-term damage. Ironically, before the coup, the market was beginning to open up to a wider selection of property buyers, with Thai banks offering attractive loan facilities and the Thai Land Code being changed to allow foreigners to own land, subject to certain restrictions (see **Restrictions on Foreign Ownership & Letting** above).

Foreign buyers tend to favour apartments or condominiums, especially in beach resorts and the islands in the south of the country. Bangkok is also popular and all areas promise good rental possibilities as a result of Thailand's growing tourist market. Many properties offer guaranteed rental schemes.

Areas

There are several areas popular with foreign buyers: Bangkok, Chiang Mai (Thailand's second city, located 700km/435mi north of Bangkok), Hua Hin (on the west coast of the Gulf of Thailand), Koh Samui (a popular holiday island in the south) Krabi (a popular holiday destination on the south-west coast) and Phuket, Thailand's favourite tourist spot.

Bangkok: The property market began to take off in the capital in 2003 and the favourite area with foreign buyers is the central business district, where it's quite easy to let property to expatriate businessmen and diplomatic staff. The Sukumvit area is modern, with plenty of shops and restaurants, while the Sathorn Road area is home to embassies and financial institutions. Most properties are high-rise apartments, condominiums or townhouses, often with luxury facilities.

9

Chiang Mai: A favourite with expatriates, Chiang Mai is the cultural capital of Thailand, set in the attractive, mountainous north. It's a fast-developing business centre and has several international schools and state-of-the-art hospitals. Housing is inexpensive compared with Bangkok, people working in the city usually opting for centrally located luxury apartments, while families sometimes prefer larger suburban houses with land. City apartments have reasonable letting potential and the new Bangkok to China highway, which runs via Chiang Mai, means that transport connections with the capital are excellent.

Hua Hin: This is the oldest Thai beach resort and is a popular holiday home location for wealthy Thais. Property here is cheaper and the market less developed than in some coastal areas.

Koh Samui: The third-largest Thai island, after Phuket and Koh Chang, 700km (435mi) south of Bangkok. It's a popular tourist destination and therefore a good location for short-term rentals, although the property market is already fairly developed, with prices to match.

Krabi: The capital of Krabi Province, the area has over 130 islands and plenty of beautiful countryside and beaches. It's less developed, quieter and more relaxed than Phuket but is becoming increasingly popular with tourists. Resorts and developments are beginning to appear, but the authorities are keen not to over-develop and there are building restrictions.

Phuket: Thailand's largest and most famous island, attracting around 3m tourists a year. Tourism was severely affected by the 2004 tsunami, but not for long, and in 2005, tourists began to return. Phuket is popular with tourists, residents and, increasingly, retirees. Developments specifically aimed at the over-50s are being built in beach locations. Property varies tremendously, from basic beachfront apartments to luxury condominiums, bungalows and houses. The more expensive homes attract foreigners from many countries, including Australia, China and the UK.

Building Standards

Standards are generally high, but some developers and builders take advantage of absent foreigner owners and cut corners.

Cost

Prices in the more desirable areas of Bangkok, such as Sukhumvit, start at around THB12m (£185,000) for a two-bedroom apartment, and luxurious four-bedroom apartments are priced at around THB35m (£540,000). Prices in the suburbs are slightly lower, but you should ensure that transport connections to the city are adequate.

In Chiang Mai, prices are far lower and properties in the suburbs are often large houses with land. A two-bedroom apartment in the city costs around THB5m (£80,000), a three-bedroom house in the suburbs around THB2m (£30,000). Four-bedroom houses with land cost around THB5m (£80,000).

In Hua Hin, prices for apartments start at around THB1.5m (£25,000), although a three-bedroom beachfront apartment can cost as much as THB7.5m (£120,000). A three-bedroom house costs around THB2.5m (£40,000), while a six-bedroom house costs around THB5m (£80,000).

In Koh Samui, which is more popular, more developed and hence more expensive than Hua Hin, a two-bedroom apartment costs around THB8m (£125,000) and a three-bedroom, beachfront house around THB30m (£460,000).

In Krabi, townhouses cost around THB3m (£50,000), while a three-bedroom new house costs around THB6m (£95,000).

In Phuket, a small townhouse close to the beach costs from THB9m (£150,000), while a luxurious three-bedroom villa is around THB15m (£240,000).

9

Local Mortgages

It's difficult if not impossible for foreigners to obtain a local mortgage. In the last few years, the Bangkok Bank and the HSBC in Bangkok have begun to offer financing of around 70 per cent of property values, although, depending on your circumstances, the loan may be as low as 50 per cent and conditions change frequently and apparently arbitrarily. For an HSBC loan, borrowers must currently be Thai nationals or expatriates with an Alien Certificate or Certificate of Residence (see **Visas & Permits** below), living and working in Thailand. Your minimum gross income must be THB360,000 (around £5,500) and the loan must be paid off before the borrower reaches 65.

Property Taxes

There are two kinds of property tax in Thailand: house and land tax and local development tax. House and land tax is 12.5 per cent of the assessed annual letting value of the property. Local development tax is imposed on anyone who owns land or unoccupied buildings; rates vary with the local authority.

Purchase Procedure

Establishing title is often problematic, as many properties have disputed ownership and building isn't allowed on certain types of land. The best type of land title, although rare, is called *chanott ti din*, which gives you incontestable possession of land. Most title is known as *nor sor sam* or *nor sor sam kor*, which gives clear ownership, although boundaries may be uncertain. Any other title should be avoided, as it cannot be legally sold or transferred. Beware of unlicensed developers offering title, which is illegal and, finally, ensure that every single document is reliably translated into a language you understand. Your embassy can usually arrange this. **Laws concerning foreign property ownership in Thailand are complicated and subject to change. You should obtain up-to-date advice from an independent legal professional before committing yourself to a purchase.**

In general, there are restrictions on the purchase of land (see above) and therefore the purchase procedure varies according to whether a property has land or not. Foreigners are allowed to own the freehold of property without land – usually apartments in registered blocks – or property built on leased land. The purchase procedure for apartments is relatively straightforward and the buyer usually pays a 10 per cent deposit while the purchase contract is prepared. After title checks and payment of the balance, completion can take place (usually between 30 and 60 days later). The necessary identification and foreign exchange documents must then be sent to the vendor's solicitor to prepare the application for transfer of title.

The purchase of property with land is more complicated. Until 2006, foreigners circumvented laws prohibiting foreign ownership by purchasing via a Thai company. Although this is still possible, the Land Department is making checks on Thai companies with foreign shareholders. All shareholders must prove their financial interest in the company; without this proof, the transfer of land to a company with foreign ownership will be blocked. A legitimate partnership is allowed. Another way of purchasing land and property as a foreigner is to buy on a leasehold basis. Many people buy retirement or holiday homes on three 30-year leases, but the lease **must** be registered with the Land Department or it becomes void after three years. More risky options include marrying a Thai national (all property reverts to them in the case of divorce or death) and asking a Thai national to purchase on your behalf (you have no rights in the property whatsoever).

9

Fees

Fees are high. Transfer tax is 2 per cent of the assessed value, stamp duty is 0.5 per cent and there's a 'specific business tax' of 3 per cent of the declared amount, which is imposed on the sale of immovable property in lieu of VAT. There's a further municipal tax, which is 10 per cent of the specific business tax amount, and the government charges withholding tax of 1 per cent. An estate agent's commission is between 3 and 5 per cent but is usually paid by the vendor.

General Information

Getting There

Until 2006, Bangkok's main international airport was Don Mueang International, but this was closed to make way for Suvarnabhumi Airport, which is also known as Bangkok International Airport. Despite objections from the authorities and various airlines, Don Mueang was re-opened in March 2007 as a second international airport.

Bangkok (Suvarnabhumi) International Airport: 25km (15mi) east of the city in the Bang Phli district, the country's main airport is the hub of Bangkok Airways, Thai Air Asia and Thai International Airways and an important base for China Airlines and a number of other Asian airlines. British Airways, Qantas and Thai International Airways operate flights from London Heathrow, and there are connecting flights to all the popular tourist areas of Thailand. Thai International Airways offers a range of flights from other European cities as well as destinations across Asia and the US.

Communications

Thailand has an extensive telephone network throughout the country, dominated by the state-owned Telephone Organisation of Thailand (TOT). After the 2006 military coup, Prime Minister Surayud Chulanont announced plans to merge TOT with CAT Telecom, the international arm of TOT, which owns and operates the country's international telecommunications infrastructure. TOT, in association with the True Corporation, operates the domestic telephone network in Bangkok, while other provinces are served by another arm of TOT, in association with TT&T. Only around half the Thai population owns a mobile phone, but ownership is growing quickly as a result of a price war in the fixed telephone and mobile phone markets. Broadband access is available in major towns but not in smaller towns and rural areas, and the majority of internet users still rely on dial-up services. The country code is 66 and international direct dialling (IDD) is available to more than 80 countries.

Fixed-line Telephones: The standard tariffs for international calls are high but pre-paid calling cards, which work out cheaper, are available.

Mobile Telephones: Use is fairly widespread, if lower than in many countries. There are several mobile phone providers; Advanced Info Service (AIS), which is the largest operator, DTAC and True Move (formerly Orange) are the market leaders. Other companies, such as Hutch, CAT and TOT Mobile, have a smaller share of the market. All services operate on the GSM 900 or 1800 networks and SIM cards are available.

Internet: Internet use isn't as widespread as in some countries but it began to grow substantially in 2005 with the advent of broadband facilities. Business use of the internet is common, although e-commerce isn't yet fully developed. There are currently around 20 internet service providers (ISPs), the main provider being TOT, which provides nationwide dial-up

9

access via a local rate number. Pre-paid dial-up internet packages can be bought at local supermarkets and there's no shortage of internet cafes in main towns and cities.

Postal Services: Reliable, efficient and reasonably cheap services are offered by the Post and Telegraph Department (PTD) in Thailand. Post offices are open from 8am to 4.30pm on weekdays, and the main Post Office in Bangkok is open until 6pm Mondays to Fridays and until 1pm at weekends. Postal services to European destinations take around a week but international courier services offer next-day delivery to many worldwide destinations.

Crime Rate

Thailand has a high incidence of opportunist crime against tourists, including passport theft, the drugging of drinks in bars and sexual offences against men and women. Beware of approaches by 'friendly' strangers. There's also a high risk of terrorism throughout the country and the UK Foreign Office advises against all but essential travel to the most southerly provinces of the country, where there's continued civil unrest, most recently in the form of bombings (February 2007).

Medical Facilities

Thailand has a well established healthcare system, with a network of state and private facilities, although they aren't always up to western European standards, particularly in the islands. There's a mandatory health insurance scheme for employees but some doctor and hospital consultations must be paid for. There are no reciprocal health agreements and you're advised to obtain comprehensive private medical insurance.

Cases of Avian Flu and Dengue Fever have been reported in Thailand. In addition, there's a significant rate of HIV infection and AIDS as a result of Bangkok's thriving sex industry. HIV is common among prostitutes of both sexes.

Pets

There's no quarantine system for domestic pets provided they meet certain requirements. On arrival at Bangkok airport, you must complete application forms (Ror 7 and Kor Sor Kor 102) for authorisation to import a pet. You may be required to pay import duty, unless you're importing a pet for six months or less. All pets must be identified by a microchip and have a health certificate signed by a government-authorised vet in your home country. The pet must have been resident in your home country for at least six months before departure and vaccinated against rabies at least 15 days before your departure for Thailand. More information is available from the Bangkok Airport Customs Office (🖥 www.customs.go.th).

Visas & Permits

Visas: Citizens of many countries, including Australia, Canada, Ireland, Japan, the UK and the US, can visit Thailand as tourists for up to 60 days without obtaining a visa in advance; they're issued with a tourist visa at the airport on arrival. Others must apply to their nearest Royal Thai embassy for a visa before travelling. Citizens of some (mainly African) countries must produce a valid international health certificate showing that they don't have Yellow Fever at the port of entry.

If you wish to stay longer than is permitted on a tourist visa or intend to work, you must obtain an extension to your tourist visa, known as a non-immigrant visa, from an Immigration Bureau in Thailand. This can be done at a Royal Thai Embassy in your home country or an Immigration Bureau in Thailand. There are a variety of non-immigrant visas, depending on your reason for being in the country, including a Type B (for business and investment purposes), which may be for single entry and a stay of up to 90 days or for multiple entry over a three-year period, each visit not exceeding 90 days; and a Type O-A (long-stay) visa for those over 50 who wish to stay for up to a year without working. **Overstaying your visa period is considered a serious matter by the authorities and you can be held in detention until a fine is paid.**

Residence Permits: An Alien Certificate or Certificate of Residence is issued only in specific circumstances once you've been in the country for at least three consecutive years on a Non-Immigrant visa. You'll be subject to a police check and must reveal details of your financial assets and connection to the country, as well as be able to speak and understand the Thai language.

Work Permits: A work permit is required by any foreigner who wishes to work in Thailand and is linked to the Non-Immigrant visa (see above), which you must have before you can apply for a work permit. You require a letter from your prospective employer confirming your appointment and requesting a work permit. You must provide details of relevant qualifications and your visa. You may work only for the company that originally applied for your work permit. If you wish to leave Thailand, you must obtain a Re-Entry Permit from the Immigration Bureau or your visa and work permit become invalid on your return.

Reference

Further Reading

Living and Working in the Far East, Graeme Chesters (Survival Books). Everything you need to know about living and working in the Far East.

Retiring in Thailand (Paiboon Publishing, 🖳 www.retiringinthailand.com).

How to Buy Land and Build a House in Thailand, Philip Bryce (Paiboon Publishing, 🖳 www.buildingthailand.com).

Bangkok Post, The Post Publishing Company, Bangkok Post Building, 136 Na Ranong Road, Long Toey, Bangkok 10110, Thailand (☎ 2-240 3700, 🖳 www.bangkokpost.co.th). English-language newspaper, also available online.

The Nation, 44 Moo, 10 Bang Na-Trat KM 4.5, Bang Na District, Bangkok 10230, Thailand (☎ 2-325 5555, 🖳 www.nationmultimedia.com). English-language newspaper, also available online.

Useful Addresses

Immigration Bureau, Soi Suan Plu, South Sathorn Road, Bangkok 10120, Thailand (☎ 2-287 3101, 🖳 www.police.go.th/thaiimb).

Royal Thai Embassy (UK), 29-30 Queen's Gate, London SW7 5JB, UK (☎ 020-7589 2944, 🖳 www.thaiembassyuk.org.uk).

Royal Thai Embassy (US), 1024 Wisconsin Avenue, NW, Washington DC 20007, US (☎ 202-944 3600, 🖳 thaiembdc.org).

Tourism Authority Thailand (UK and Ireland), 3rd Floor, Brook House, 98/99 Jermyn Street, London SW1 6EE, UK (☎ 020-7925 2511, 🖳 www.tourismthailand.org).

9

Tourism Authority Thailand (US), 61 Broadway, Suite 2810, New York, NY 10006, US
(☎ 212-269 2597, 💻 www.tourismthailand.org).

Useful Websites

Thai Government, Ministry of Foreign Affairs (💻 www.mfa.go.th).
Thai Board of Investment/BOI (💻 www.boi.go.th).

MIDDLE EAST: UNITED ARAB EMIRATES

Background Information

Capital: Abu Dhabi.
Population: 4.4m.
   Foreign Community: The United Arab Emirates (UAE) has a very large foreign community:
over 75 per cent of its population is foreign workers, mainly from South Asia, the majority of
whom work in the oil industry; around 5 per cent comprises affluent expatriates, mainly
American, Australian, British and Japanese.
   Area: 83,600km^2 (32,278mi^2).
   Geography: The UAE is on the south-east tip of the Arabian Peninsula, near the mouth of
the Arabian Gulf and bordering the Gulf of Oman. Qatar lies to the north-west, Saudi Arabia to
the west and south, and Oman to the east. The country consists of seven autonomous states
or sheikdoms, which are the Emirates: Abu Dhabi, Dubai, Ajman, Fujairah, Ras al Khaimah,
Sharjah and Umm al Quwain. In the south and west of the country, around four-fifths of the
terrain is desert, with the occasional oasis. In the north, the Hajar Mountain range extends south
into Oman. The east is rich fertile plain and the country has more than 700km (434mi) of
coastline, 600km (373mi) of which are along the Arabian Gulf and 100km (62mi) border the Gulf
of Oman. There are over 100 islands off the Arabian Gulf coast.
   Climate: The climate is dry in desert areas and sub-tropical in the east, i.e. warm and sunny
in winter, hot and humid in summer. The Indian Ocean has a strong influence on the weather
and means that the high summer temperatures are accompanied by high humidity in coastal
areas. The most pleasant months are November to February, when temperatures average 24C
(75F) during the day and fall to around 15C (59F) at night. By March, temperatures rise to
around 30C (86F) during the day, although humidity is still low. June to September is the hottest
time, with temperatures of 40C (104F) and higher and 100 per cent humidity. Most of the
average annual rainfall, which is low at 6.5cm (2.5in), comes in short, sharp bursts between
December and March.
   Language: Arabic is the official language. Other languages quite widely spoken include
English, Hindi and Urdu.
   Political Situation: Good, although the UAE had no elected political body until December
2006, when it held its first election. The country is governed by a Supreme Council of Rulers,
made up of seven Emirs, each representing an Emirate of the UAE. The Emirs appoint the
President, Vice-President, Prime Minister and Council of Ministers. From the inception of the
1971 Constitution, the country's was Sheikh Zayed bin Sultan Al Nahyan (ruler of Abu Dhabi),
who is credited with, among other things, directing oil industry revenues into infrastructure,
education and health. On his death in 2004, his son, Khalifa bin Zayed Al Nahayan, was elected
President. After the 2006 election (in which less than 1 per cent of the population was permitted
to vote, according to unspecified criteria), half the Supreme Council was (for the first time)

9

elected. It's expected that the next election will be in 2010, when all members of the Supreme Council will be elected and voting rights will be extended. The UAE is one of the most liberal countries in the Gulf region, and foreign cultures and religious beliefs other than Islam are generally tolerated. The UAE is a member of the Arab League, the Organisation of the Islamic Conference (OIC) and the United Nations (UN).

Finance

Currency

The currency of the UAE is the dirham (its official currency code is AED, but it's commonly abbreviated to Dh), consisting of 100 fils. The dirham is pegged to the US dollar at a rate of US$1 = Dh3.671.
Exchange Rates: £1 = Dh7.35.
Exchange Controls: None.

Cost & Standard of Living

The UAE generally enjoys a high standard of living thanks to its oil wealth and recent diversification into construction and property development, which has softened the impact of oil price fluctuations. Dubai is enjoying a construction boom, billions of dollars being pumped into showpiece developments (including the world's tallest building), while its business and tourist sectors are growing rapidly. The cost of living in Dubai in particular has increased considerably since around 2002, housing costs (i.e. rent) accounting for around 50 per cent of monthly expenses. The cost of living in Abu Dhabi isn't as high as Dubai's, although it's catching up fast. Personal taxation in the UAE is non-existent, which balances the high living costs in the main cities.

Taxation

A large proportion of government revenue comes from the oil industry and therefore taxation of all kinds is low or non-existent, making it an attractive location for expatriates.
Personal Effects: There's no customs duty on used personal effects that are brought into Dubai, but customs officials have absolute control over the entry of certain items. Cars may be imported but duty is payable at 5 per cent on an official valuation. Once imported, a car must be registered with the Dubai Traffic Police, who issue local registration (licence) plates. In general, the UAE has a liberal free trade policy and low import taxes.
Income Tax: None.
Capital Gains Tax (CGT): None.
Wealth Tax: None.
Inheritance & Gift Tax: None, but independent advice should be obtained concerning local inheritance law, which is part of Sharia law and distributes any assets in a specific manner. For example, beneficiaries include parents and siblings, if still alive, and daughters inherit only half as much as sons. Non-UAE nationals and non-Moslems should draft a will detailing their heirs, which should be notarised by the Sharia Court.
Value Added Tax (VAT): None, but individual Emirates may charge taxes on certain products, such as alcohol and cigarettes, and on services provided by the hospitality industry.

9

Property

Restrictions on Foreign Ownership & Letting

There's no law in the UAE defining freehold and you should exercise extreme caution with land and property ownership issues in all of the Emirates, including Dubai. Land registry procedures aren't fully established and ownership rights are difficult, if not impossible, for foreigners to obtain. This is beginning to change, particularly in Dubai, where the government has now established land ownership policies; In March 2007, it became possible for foreigners to register property transfers with the Dubai Land Department through one major developer, and it's expected that this will be extended to other developers in the near future. Nevertheless, extreme caution must be still be exercised, as the legal position is still unclear. **It's vital to obtain independent legal advice, even if you're offered property on a 'freehold' basis.** According to the Dubai Real Estate Law, only citizens of the UAE and other Gulf Co-operation Council (GCC) countries (Bahrain, Kuwait, Oman, Qatar and Saudi Arabia) may own freehold land and property in any part of Dubai. Foreigners are limited to areas approved by the ruler of Dubai. In Al Ain, a large city in Abu Dhabi, foreigners can buy property on a 99-year leasehold basis only and in other Emirates rules vary considerably, so always obtain legal advice.

There are no restrictions on letting, and no tax is payable on rental income.

Market

A foreign property market didn't exist in the UAE until 2002, when the ruler of Dubai announced that foreign residents in the UAE would be permitted to buy freehold property within designated areas of Dubai only. Before this, foreign residents had to rent property and many still do. Although the law didn't come into effect until 2006, the market in Dubai started to boom immediately after the 2002 announcement and some developments sold out within 24 hours. Between 2002 and 2005, many foreigners bought into the off-plan Dubai market, despite uncertainties over legal transfer of title (see **Purchase Procedure** below), and the value of some developments has risen by as much as 60 per cent between the initial deposit and completion. Some investors 'flipped' their properties several times (see **Short-Term Investment & Flipping** on page 92) and some areas of property market became overheated as a result. By late 2005 and early 2006, there was a significant drop in off-plan sales and many experts were expressing concerns about over-supply. The market appears to be stabilising in 2007 and the majority of property is still sold off-plan.

When Dubai announced that it was relaxing property ownership laws, the other Emirates followed suit, although not on the same scale. Neighbouring Abu Dhabi, the richest of the Emirates, has a less mature property market than Dubai. Laws were relaxed in 2005 and at the end of 2006 the government announced massive investment in Abu Dhabi's infrastructure. By 2007, it was estimated that US$270bn worth of property development projects were under way. Nevertheless, there isn't the same demand for properties in Abu Dhabi as there is in Dubai, so property is more affordable, but foreigners can buy only on a 99-year leasehold basis.

If you're considering a buy-to-let investment in Dubai or Abu Dhabi, caution should be exercised, as rents have been capped in both cities by the Department of Social Services and Commercial Buildings (known as the Khalifa Committee).

In the other Emirates, the property market is relatively small, although the most northern of the Emirates, Ras al Khaimah, is beginning to offer modest, environmentally friendly developments, and developers in Umm Al Quwain have begun to build a large marina.

9

Laws governing legal property ownership by foreigners in the UAE are complicated and constantly changing, particularly in Dubai. Before making any investment, check the latest situation with an independent legal professional.

Areas

Foreigners may buy property only in designated areas and almost all of these are in the shiny new developments of Dubai and Abu Dhabi, whose size and grandeur come as a surprise to some people.

In Dubai, the areas where foreigners are permitted to buy have become known as New Dubai, where many (often ambitious) developments are still under construction, including those on the so-called Palm Islands (Deira, Jebel Ali and Jumeirah) – the three largest man-made islands in the world, which can be seen from outer space. More huge developments are on the horizon, including the World Islands, a series of 300 islands in the shape of the map of the world around 5km (3mi) off the Dubai coast, due to be completed in 2008, where properties will be part of a luxurious complex including a marina, sports facilities and shopping malls; Dubailand, an enormous tourism and entertainment complex which will consist of five themed zones and is expected to be completed in 2015; and Burj Dubai (Dubai Tower), consisting of luxury freehold apartments in both modern and traditional style built around the tallest building in the world, a tower of 700m (3,000ft), whose expected completion date is 2009. Another popular area in Dubai is the Dubai Marina, the world's largest man-made marina and waterfront development, which boasts over 200 high-rise buildings housing a variety of one-, two- and three-bedroom apartments in a 'city-within-a-city' development. More modest developments include International City, 9km (5.5mi) from Dubai International Airport, which has relatively low-price properties with country-themed architecture and is due for completion in 2007, and The Meadows, popular with expatriates and consisting of three- to seven-bedroom properties with extensive amenities within easy reach of the city. Central (downtown) Dubai contains mainly new apartments, some built in traditional architectural styles.

In Abu Dhabi, some of the most popular developments are in beachfront locations. The capital city is situated on the Arabian Gulf and waterfront developments here are expected to command high prices. As in Dubai, gleaming new developments are the main type of property available, and one of the most prestigious is the 83-storey Sky Tower, the capital's tallest building, in the heart of the city, which offers one-, two-, three- and four-bedroom luxury apartments. Other similar developments are planned, with myriad leisure facilities, parks and gardens.

The smaller Emirates of Ras al Khaimah and Umm al Quwain, relative newcomers to the property market, have both begun constructing property developments, including a massive indoor ski village in the former and a luxury villa and townhouse development, including boutique hotels and facilities for yachts, in the latter.

Building Standards

Standards are generally high. However, concerns have been raised about the quality of some developments in Dubai, where in the rush to meet the 'demands' of the property boom standards have sometimes been compromised.

9

Cost

In Dubai, apartment prices have risen by as much as 100 per cent over the last four years, with the average price for a studio apartment now around Dh554,000 (£75,000), for a three-bedroom apartment around Dh2.4m (£330,000), while a three-bedroom villa costs from around Dh2.1m (£290,000), sometimes much more.

In the Dubai Marina development, where properties are mainly apartments, a luxury studio apartment costs around Dh450,000 (£61,000) and a two-bedroom apartment around Dh1m (£130,000). Palm Islands properties, although not yet completed, have already begun to change hands. Luxury five-bedroom villas start at around Dh12m (£1.6m) and three-bedroom waterfront apartments cost around Dh2.5m (£340,000). One-bedroom apartments in the Burj Dubai development (expected completion 2009) start at around Dh930,000 (£125,000) and two-bedroom apartments are around Dh1.4m (£185,000). In Dubai's International City, prices are lower: one-bedroom apartments start at around Dh295,000 (£40,000), while two-bedroom apartments cost around Dh745,000 (£100,000). Three- and four-bedroom houses in the Meadows developments are Dh 3-4m (£410,000-540,000).

Two-bedroom apartments in the prestigious Sky Tower in central Abu Dhabi cost around Dh2m (£270,000), and luxurious waterfront properties start at over Dh7m (around £1m).

Local Mortgages

Mortgages are offered mainly by home finance companies, which are usually linked to a developer (all UAE developers are government approved). Around 85 per cent of the mortgage market is controlled by these lenders, and interest rates are normally around 7.5 per cent. Finance companies offer either a purchase and re-sale contract (known as a *murabaha*), whereby the lender buys the property and resells it to the buyer on a deferred basis, or a leasing arrangement (*ijarah*), whereby the lender buys the property and lets it to the buyer at a certain rate over a certain period, at the end of which ownership is transferred to the buyer. Some international banks (including the HSBC) and local banks have negotiated agreements with certain developers and lend up to 60 per cent of a property's value to residents and non-residents, but these loans are available only on a few developments.

Property Taxes

There's a 5 per cent residential tax, based on the rental value of your property, and municipal taxes are levied in most Emirates, at varying rates.

Purchase Procedure

Most purchases are transacted in the office of the developer, who issues sale and transfer agreements. This means that the procedure is largely unregulated, although all UAE developers are government approved so there should be no 'cowboys', and the system is currently under review to meet the demands of foreign investors. Land or property can be purchased in the name of a company, but the company must be 100 per cent owned by a national of the UAE. In Dubai (but not the other Emirates), property can now be registered with the Land Department and foreign purchasers are granted a Land Certificate (but see **Restrictions on Foreign Ownership & Letting** above). Some developers require a small non-refundable holding deposit as evidence of your serious intention to buy. Most off-plan properties require an additional 10 or 15 per cent deposit on signing of the purchase document.

Fees

In Dubai, there's a Land Registry fee of 2 per cent of the purchase price, and a fee may be payable to the developer, but there are no fee limits or guidelines, so always check before committing yourself. There's no stamp duty, although it's thought that Dubai may introduce it in the near future. No fees are payable in the other Emirates.

General Information

Getting There

There are six international airports in the UAE, the two principal airports being in Abu Dhabi and Dubai. The main airlines serving these airports are Eithad Airways (the UAE national airline), Emirates Airlines (Dubai's national airline) and Gulf Air, although a host of foreign airlines also operate services.

Abu Dhabi International Airport: The airport is 35km (22mi) from the city and is the hub of Eithad Airways. British Airways operates a route from London Heathrow, Eithad Airways flies from Dublin, London Heathrow and Manchester, and a number of other airlines operate from Europe, the Middle East and the US.

Dubai International Airport: Around 5km (3mi) south-east of the city, this is the busiest airport in the UAE. All the world's leading airlines operate scheduled services to Dubai, including Aer Lingus (Dublin), British Airways (London Heathrow), Emirates Airlines (flights to European, UK and US destinations) and Virgin Atlantic (London Heathrow). The Dubai government has also announced the construction of a massive new airport south of Dubai, called Dubai World Central International Airport (also known as Jebel Ali Airport City), which will be part of a residential and commercial complex, due for completion in 2010.

Communications

Telecommunications in the UAE are sophisticated and efficient. The main telecommunications provider is the Emirates Telecommunications Corporation (known as ETISALAT), which has upgraded the entire system with digital technology in recent years. Mobile penetration is high, particularly in Abu Dhabi and Dubai, which together account for around 75 per cent of mobile use in the UAE. Internet use isn't as high as in some other countries (around 50 per cent), although it's growing fast and the government is promoting Dubai as an e-commerce centre. The country dialling code is 971 and international direct dialling (IDD) is available to more than 150 countries.

Fixed-line Telephones: Fixed-line penetration has reduced dramatically (to around 30 per cent of the population) as mobile penetration has increased and owing to a lack of competition. ETISALAT has been the sole provider of telecommunications services in the UAE since 1976. In 2007, one competitor, Du (also known as the Emirates International Telecommunications Company/EITC), entered the market. Calls within each Emirate are free, and ETISALAT offers pre-paid phone cards, which can be used on any kind of phone, including public call boxes. Directory enquiries in English are available by dialling 180.

Mobile Telephones: There's around 75 per cent mobile phone penetration in the UAE and it's growing rapidly. The main operators are ETISALAT and Du, both of which operate on the GSM network but are in the process of moving to the 3G network, to enable use of internet services on mobile phones. Local SIM cards are available.

9

Internet: The main provider of internet services in the UAE is eCompany (a subsidiary of ETISALAT). Sahm Net has recently entered the market and Du began offering internet services in February 2007. Services are both dial-up and broadband. ETISALAT has been criticised for censorship, as it routinely blocks hundreds of websites that don't conform to religious and political 'norms'. There are very few internet cafes.

Postal Services: Modern and efficient services are provided by Emirates Post (EmPost) and post offices are open from 8am to 1pm and 4pm to 7pm, Sundays to Thursdays. Postal services to European destinations take between three and eight days. EmPost's courier service offers next-day delivery.

Crime Rate

The UAE is a very safe country, where crime is rare. Women, children and the family are held in high regard. On the other hand, there's a danger of terrorism, particularly against 'Western' interests, and the UK Foreign Office advises vigilance in public places.

Medical Facilities

Healthcare facilities are excellent – on a par with those in western Europe. In particular, the massive Healthcare City project will turn Dubai into a centre for specialised healthcare, medical education and research. However, there are no reciprocal health agreements with any other countries and medical care must be paid for at the time of treatment. Comprehensive health insurance is therefore essential.

Pets

Pets don't need to undergo quarantine when coming to the UAE, provided they meet certain requirements. They must be at least four months old and for domestic (not commercial) use, have been microchipped and vaccinated against rabies at least 30 days and not more than a year before travelling and have full vaccination records and a health certificate signed by a government-authorised vet from your home country. You must also have an Animal Import Permit issued by the Ministry of Agriculture and Fisheries in the UAE, which has recently adopted an online payment system so that import permits can be obtained in advance. Pets are examined on entry and any pet not complying with the regulations is quarantined or returned to the country of origin. More information is available from The British Veterinary Centre in Abu Dhabi (🖳 www.britvet.com).

Visas & Permits

Visas: Citizens of most EEA countries and some other countries, including Australia, Canada, Japan and the US (check with a UAE embassy or consulate regarding other countries), don't require a visa to visit the UAE as tourists or on business for 30 days, and this period can be extended on request to up to 90 days. However, all visitors must have a return ticket and a passport valid for a minimum of three months (tourists) or six months (employment or business) from the date of entry. Other nationals may obtain a visa through sponsorship by an individual or company resident in the UAE or through a hotel or travel agency.

Residence Permits: These are generally linked to employment, as all non-UAE citizens resident in the country must be sponsored by an employer, who is responsible for you throughout your stay and must ensure that you leave the country at the end of your contract. Your employer will obtain a residence visa on your behalf, and the Ministry of Labour and Social Affairs must give its approval before a visa is issued by the Immigration Department of the Emirate concerned. If you're coming to the UAE with your family, you should apply for a family visa, but you must be earning more than Dh4,000 (£550) per month. Residence visas are normally issued for three years and to obtain one you must take a medical test and obtain a health card. In Dubai, the government also issues residence visas to freehold property owners and their immediate families. **If you overstay your visa period, fines are levied and, in certain cases, legal action may be taken against you.**

Work Permits: These are linked to residence visas (see above).

Reference

Further Reading

Living and Working in the Gulf States and Saudi Arabia, Robert Hughes & Graeme Chesters (Survival Books). Everything you need to know about living and working in the Gulf States.

Abu Dhabi Explorer: The Complete Residents' Guide: Living and Working for Expats (Explorer Publishing).

Dubai Explorer: The Complete Residents' Guide: Living and Working for Expats (Explorer Publishing).

Gulf News, Al Nisr Publishing, Abu Dhabi, UAE (☎ 2-634 3744, 💻 www.gulfnews.com). Daily English-language print and online newspaper.

Khaleej Times, Head Office, PO Box 11243, Dubai, UAE (☎ 4-338 3535, 💻 www. khaleejtimes.com). Daily English-language print and online newspaper.

What's On, Motivate Publishing, 5th Floor, Building 8, Dubai Media City, UAE (☎ 4-390 3550, 💻 www.whatsonlive.com). Magazine covering social and cultural events within the UAE.

Useful Addresses

Embassy of the United Arab Emirates (UK), 30 Princes Gate, London SW7 1PT, UK (☎ 020-7581 1281, 💻 www.uaeembassyuk.net).

Embassy of the United Arab Emirates (US), 3522 International Court, Suite 400, Washington DC 2008, US (☎ 202-243 2400, 💻 www.uae-embassy.org).

Useful Websites

Ten Real Estate (💻 http://realestate.theemiratesnetwork.com). Extensive property information for all the Emirates and property-related news.

UAE Interact (💻 www.uaeinteract.com). News and information about the United Arab Emirates.

United Arab Emirates Government (💻 www.government.ae). Links to all government websites and information about residence and business.

United Arab Emirates, Ministry of the Interior, Naturalisation and Residency Administration (💻 www.dnrd.gov.ae).

9

Australasia: AUSTRALIA

Background Information

Capital: Canberra.

Population: 20.6m.

Foreign Community: Australia is largely a nation of migrants, mostly descended from European settlers who arrived during the 19th and 20th centuries. The country launched an ambitious immigration programme after the Second World War, when hundreds of thousands of Europeans – in particular Britons – began a new life in Australia. It's still the most popular destination for those wishing to relocate from the UK and the Australian government operates a controlled immigration system, which encourages young, highly qualified foreigners to settle there. It's an extremely cosmopolitan country and in addition to immigrants from the UK and other European countries, many now come from Asia.

Area: 7,682,300km^2 (2,966,368mi^2).

Geography: Australia is the world's largest island, with an area almost equal to the continental US and a coastline of 36,755km (22,827mi). It consists of six states (New South Wales, Queensland, South Australia, Tasmania, Victoria and Western Australia), two mainland territories (the Australian Capital Territory and the Northern Territory) and other minor territories. On its western coast is the Indian Ocean and on its east the Coral and Tasman seas of the South Pacific Ocean. The Great Barrier Reef, the world's largest coral reef, 2,000km (1,250mi) long, lies just off the north-east coast. The country is around 25 times the size of the British Isles and almost twice the combined area of India and Pakistan. The average elevation in Australia is less than 300m (984ft), compared with a worldwide average of around 700m (2,297ft). The highest point is Mount Kosciusko (2,228m/7,310ft), which is in the Australian Alps in the south-east of the country. Australia is one of the oldest and driest land masses in the world, with vast, uninhabitable arid and semi-desert areas. But Australia is a land of great contrasts, with rain forests and vast plains in the north, desert in the centre, fertile croplands in the east, south and south-west, and snowfields in the south-east.

Climate: Australia's climate ranges from tropical in the northern 40 per cent of the country (above the Tropic of Capricorn) to temperate in much of the rest. It's less subject to climatic extremes than other regions of comparable size because it's surrounded by oceans and has no high mountain ranges. Clear skies and low rainfall are characteristic of the weather in most of the continent. Coastal regions generally enjoy an excellent year-round climate, with no state capital averaging less than 5.5 hours of sunshine per day. Australia's seasons are the opposite of those in the northern hemisphere, i.e. summer is from December to February and winter from June to August. In mid-summer (January), average temperatures range from 29C (84F) in the north to 17C (63F) in the south, and in mid-winter (July), from 25C (77F) in the north to 8C (46F) in the south. Average annual rainfall is 46.5cm (18in), although rainfall varies considerably according to the region, from less than 15cm (6in) in the centre to over 2m (79in) in parts of the tropics and western Tasmania. The wettest cities are Darwin, Sydney, Brisbane and Perth. Adelaide, Canberra, Hobart and Melbourne receive around half the rainfall of Sydney. The northern (tropical) region experiences heavy rainfall and oppressive temperatures between November and March.

Language: English is the national language, although there are regional variations in pronunciation and phraseology. Around 80 per cent of the population speaks English as a first language, a small percentage speaking Chinese languages and Italian. Many first- and second-generation migrants are bilingual.

Political Situation: Australia's system of government is based on the British parliamentary model and is very stable. The government is a federation, but within the framework of a constitutional monarchy. The Queen (who is represented by the Governor-General in Australia)

9

is Head of State and under the 1901 Australian Constitution political authority is distributed between the federal government and the six States (the Territories have separate, self-governing arrangements). Three main parties dominate the Australian political arena: the centre-right Liberal Party, the conservative National Party of Australia and the social democratic Australian Labor Party, which traditionally represents the working class. John Howard, leader of the Liberal Party, is currently Australian Prime Minister (elected 2004) and the next elections are due in late 2007 or early 2008. Australia is a member of the British Commonwealth, although many Australians are in favour of the country becoming a republic.

Finance

Currency

Australia's currency is the Australian dollar (A$), consisting of 100 cents.
Exchange Rates: £1 = A$2.40.
Exchange Controls: None, although there are certain restrictions on investments made by non-residents. Movements of A$10,000 (or the foreign currency equivalent) or more in cash in or out of the country must be reported to the tax authorities. Tough anti-money laundering laws came into force in 2007.

Cost & Standard of Living

Australia has a strong Western-style economy, which encourages overseas investment and boosts consumer confidence. There has been partial deregulation of the labour market and privatisation of state-owned industries in an effort to increase competitiveness. The standard of living is high and Australian cities rate highly in terms of quality of life, according to *The Economist* worldwide quality of life index. In January 2007, unemployment was 4.6 per cent and the average monthly wage is around A$4,500. Living costs vary from state to state and even within states, and much depends on where you live and your lifestyle. Overall, the cost of living is similar to that of most northern European countries. Prices are low for essentials such as food, drink and clothes, but manufactured goods are generally expensive because many are imported. Car prices are around 25 per cent higher than in most western European countries and up to twice those in the US (imported cars are particularly expensive).

Taxation

Individuals resident in Australia are taxed on their worldwide income, but residents working overseas for more than 91 days are exempt from Australian tax on foreign earnings (if those earnings are taxed at source abroad). Non-residents are taxed only on income earned in Australia and are exempt from the Medicare tax (see below). Tax residence usually applies if you spend more than half the tax year in Australia. In 2005, the government announced a four-year temporary exemption for 'first-time temporary residents' on their foreign source income. Anyone who plans to earn money in Australia, irrespective of nationality, must have a Tax File Number (TFN), which identifies them to the tax authorities.
Personal Effects: Personal effects can be imported duty free provided they've been owned for more than a year. Immigrants can import a car, but duty and sales tax are payable on its value. Rates depend on the type of vehicle, the date of importation and whether it's subject to

9

luxury car tax (LCT). It's wise to contact a customs office before preparing to import a vehicle, as rates are subject to change.

Income Tax: Australia has a PAYG (pay as you go) scheme with four tax bands. The basic rate is 15 per cent on income of A$6,000 to A$25,000, rising to 45 per cent on income above A$150,000. In addition, residents must pay a 1.5 per cent levy to fund Medicare, a universal health programme which provides free basic medical and hospital care. Those with taxable income over A$50,000 have to pay a Medicare surcharge of 1 per cent. Non-residents are taxed at different rates, starting at 29 per cent (income up to A$25,000) and increasing in stages to 45 per cent (over A$150,000). Non-residents don't pay the Medicare levy.

Capital Gains Tax (CGT): Capital gains are taxed at ordinary income tax rates (see above) and there's no CGT on profits from the sale of a taxpayer's principal residence. Capital gains made by residents are taxed in the tax year in which they were realised.

Inheritance & Gift Tax: None, but you may be liable to capital gains tax on any gains from the sale of inherited property, although if the property was the donor's principal residence, CGT may be waived.

Value Added Tax (VAT): Australia has a goods and service tax (GST), which is levied at a flat rate of 10 per cent on most goods and services. Basic food items and certain medical aids are exempt.

Property

Restrictions on Foreign Ownership & Letting

Any foreigner **not** resident in Australia and temporary residents (with a visa period of less than 12 months) must obtain approval to purchase, in accordance with the country's foreign investment policy. The process normally takes around 30 days but in some cases up to 90 days. You can exchange contracts before obtaining approval but you must have a conditional clause inserted in case approval isn't given. **This protects the buyer but, more importantly, if you sign a contract without this condition, you may be forced to resell the property.** Those with temporary residence status may buy a property only as a principal residence and it must be sold when their visa expires and they leave Australia. Approval depends on your current visa status and the nature of the property you wish to buy. You cannot get round this regulation by buying through an Australian company. If you need approval to buy, any contract signed **must** include a conditional clause to that effect. More information is available on the FIRB website (www.firb.gov.au).

There are no restrictions on letting but any rental income earned by non-residents is taxed at 29 per cent.

Market

9

Australia has a flourishing property market and around 80 per cent of Australians own their own homes, one of the highest rates in the world. The market has recently enjoyed a boom, which accelerated ahead of the 2000 Olympic Games in Sydney. Despite variations across the country, prices have shown considerable growth since as long ago as the early '90s. Recent interest rate rises have attempted to stop the market overheating, and previously popular areas have begun to see a downturn (see below), while new, sometimes unlikely, areas have shown considerable growth. Some people cannot afford to buy their own homes, so there's a significant rental market.

Australia has a huge choice of homes in different architectural styles, including apartments, townhouses and a wide range of standard and individually designed, detached homes. Apartments (called 'units' or 'home units') are common in inner cities and coastal areas, and townhouses are common in the suburbs of the major cities. Outside the major cities, most people have a home built to a standard (or their own) design on an individual plot. Waterfront homes are in short supply and are considered a sound investment.

Areas

Australia is a highly urbanised society, over 70 per cent of the population living in the main cities, i.e. Adelaide, Brisbane, Darwin, Hobart, Melbourne, Perth and Sydney, all situated on the coast but each with a distinct character and attractions. Only some 15 per cent of Australians live in rural areas. According to a 2006 report by the Real Estate Institute of Australia (REIA), Western Australia is still booming (with annual price rises of more than 30 per cent in the last quarter of 2006), while New South Wales has slumped, with falling prices. However, New South Wales (and Sydney in particular) continues to be popular with high earners, who haven't felt the effect of the rise in interest rates, while people on lower incomes are being priced out of the market – Sydney has a booming rental market for those who cannot afford to buy their own home. Melbourne is also experiencing a downturn, although, like Sydney, it's still enjoying buoyant prices in some suburbs and the top end of the market continues to flourish. Melbourne is consistently popular as a relocation and investment spot, particularly because it's considered one of the most attractive areas by many foreigners. Perth has recently become very popular, with high price rises, despite the fact that it's geographically isolated, the only large city on the west coast. Although it doesn't have the charisma of Melbourne or Sydney, Perth is becoming increasingly popular with families relocating to Australia, waterside properties being the most popular buys.

Building Standards

Standards are generally high, though construction varies from brick to brick veneer (a timber inner frame lined with plasterboard), weatherboard and fibre cement – in descending order of quality and durability.

Cost

Property prices vary considerably throughout the country and in the various suburbs of the major cities. Unsurprisingly, the further you are from a town or city, the lower the price of land and property.

In Adelaide, South Australia, prices rose by around 5 per cent in 2006 and the average house price is around A$300,000, although some suburbs are more expensive than others.

Brisbane, Queensland, saw price rises of around 7 per cent in 2006 and the average house price is currently around A$400,000. Brisbane is becoming more popular with families relocating to Australia and, while prices in some coastal areas have fallen, suburbs within easy commuting distance of the centre have seen price rises.

Darwin, in the Northern Territory, has an average house price of around A$350,000 and has seen some of the strongest demand and fastest price rises in the country, some apartment blocks selling out before construction has started. Waterfront properties and those close to golf courses command the highest prices.

9

Until recently, Hobart, in Tasmania, enjoyed far lower prices than the rest of Australia, but investors from the mainland have begun to push prices up. The average price is around A$250,000, the inner suburbs being the most popular.

Melbourne, in Victoria has an average house price of A$350,000, and prices have remained stable for some time. The eastern suburbs are more popular and have seen higher price growth.

Prices in Perth, Western Australia, are generally lower than those in the east of the country, although the last year has seen a dramatic rise in property prices of up to around 35 per cent. The strongest growth has been in the least expensive suburbs and average house prices are around A$400,000. Some of Perth's most popular areas are Dalkeith and around the coastal town of Mandurah, which has good road links, although there's a great deal of construction.

Sydney, the largest and most cosmopolitan city in Australia, has some of the highest prices in the country. It experienced a temporary setback at the end of 2006, but experts say that it's now back in fashion, with average house prices around A$600,000. There's a shortage of good quality property on the market in Sydney.

Local Mortgages

The Australian mortgage market is well developed and sophisticated, with mortgages available from a large number of banks and building societies. They're usually for a maximum of 75 or 80 per cent of a property's value, although 100 per cent loans are sometimes available. The maximum term is 30 years, although the repayment period is usually between 15 and 25 years. Variable- and fixed-rate loans are available. Many developers offer fixed-term loans, which may or may not offer more favourable interest rates and terms than a mortgage.

Property Taxes

Property taxes vary considerably with the municipality and are the only form of taxation collected by local governments. There have been large increases (more than 40 per cent) in recent years.

Purchase Procedure

All foreign nationals, unless they have permanent resident status or meet another exemption, need to seek prior approval from the Foreign Investment Review Board (FIRB) before buying any property or land (see **Restrictions on Foreign Ownership** above).

Property is sold either by private contract or by auction and, once an offer is made, the property remains on the market until all offers have been considered. At this point, there's no obligation on either side. An offer can contain the conditions of sale and isn't legally binding until a contract is signed. Once your offer is accepted, there's usually a 'cooling off' period of around five days. A 10 per cent deposit ensures that the property is taken off the market.

Conveyancing is done by a qualified conveyancing agent or a solicitor. The Australian government has a National Electronic Conveyancing System (NECS), which means that professionals can make searches and register new owners electronically, speeding up the process for buyers and sellers. The sale is completed once the balance has been paid, along with any taxes due, and new ownership is registered with the NECS. Once it's registered with the national body, the information is passed to the state Land Registry. Most land and property in Australia is owned freehold, the only exception being land in the Australian Capital Territory (ACT) and Canberra, which is sold on a 99-year lease.

9

Off-plan Purchases: In the case of off-plan purchases, your deposit secures the property and there are no stage payments, simply the balance on completion. The estate agent prepares a contract which includes the terms and conditions of the sale and the completion date.

Fees

Fees usually total 4 to 5 per cent of the purchase price. The main fees are stamp duty, land tax and legal fees. Stamp duty varies with the state and is normally between 1 and 2 per cent. It's lowest in New South Wales and highest in the Northern Territory and Victoria. Some states waive or reduce stamp duty for first-time buyers and there are certain other concessions, depending on your circumstances. Legal and conveyancing fees are usually 1 to 2 per cent of the purchase price, but costs may be based on the work involved. Land transfer registration is imposed by each state and may be a flat or variable fee.

General Information

Getting There

Australia has a vast network of international and domestic airports all over the country, including at least one international airport in each state capital. The main international airports are Brisbane, Melbourne, Perth and Sydney.

Brisbane International Airport: Situated 13km (8mi) from the city centre, the airport is convenient for the Gold Coast and northern New South Wales. It has an international and a domestic terminal and is served by around 40 airlines via scheduled flights, mainly from Asian destinations, although there are flights from US and European destinations. The airport has efficient onward transport connections.

Melbourne (Tullamarine) International Airport: Situated 24km (15mi) north-west of the city, this is an important airport for the inhabitants of Victoria and South Australia. It handles international and domestic flights to Asian, European and US destinations, and is second in terms of passenger traffic to Sydney airport. There are fast toll roads and excellent bus services to and from the airport.

Perth Airport: This is the major commercial airport serving Western Australia but is small by international standards. It handles international and domestic flights from many Asian, African, European and Pacific destinations.

Sydney (Kingsford Smith) International Airport: Situated in the Sydney suburb of Mascot, this is Australia's largest and busiest airport, with around 30m passengers in 2006. It's the major hub for the national airline, Qantas, and is served by airlines from around the world. There are underground airport rail links connecting the airport with the city.

Communications

9

Telecommunications in Australia are sophisticated, efficient and well regulated. Providers tend to offer a package of services to customers, which include fixed telephone lines, mobile phones and internet services. The market is dominated by Telstra (Telecom Australia), which is part government-owned and part market-controlled.

The country code is 61 and international direct dialling (IDD) is available worldwide. The Australian communications market was privatised in 1997 and more than 20 operators have since entered the market.

Fixed-line Telephones: The main operators in the fixed line market (apart from Telstra) are AAPT (owned by Telecom New Zealand), Optus (owned by Singapore Telecommunications), Powertel, Primus Telecom, Soul and Vodafone. There's an extensive network of public telephone boxes throughout the country, which accept coins or prepaid phone cards, available from post offices and newsagents. 'Crediphones' accept most major credit cards. You can make long-distance calls from public telephone boxes.

Mobile Telephones: There's almost 100 per cent mobile phone coverage in Australia and around 20m subscribers. The main operators are Optus Mobile, Telstra Mobile, 3 Telecommunications, Virgin Mobile and Vodafone. All operate on the GSM network (apart from 3 Telecommunications), and Optus, Telstra and Vodafone offer internet access from phones. Australian SIM cards are available.

Internet: The internet first appeared in Australia in 1989 and by 1995 dial-up access was available across the country, although it was too expensive for personal use. In recent years, access has become far more widespread and sophisticated, and more operators are entering the market, offering faster connections and lower prices. The main internet service providers (ISPs) are Internode, iNet and Telstra. Telstra alone began offering high-speed (broadband) access at the beginning of 2007. Rural areas have less choice of ISP, connection speeds are usually slower and prices higher. There are plenty of internet cafes in main towns and cities across the country.

Postal Services: These are operated by Australia Post through post offices or, in rural areas, post agencies. Post offices and agencies are usually open Mondays to Fridays from 9am to 5pm; post offices in larger cities are sometimes open later and on Saturdays. Although domestic postal services have been criticised for unreliability and slow delivery, the international postal service is efficient and a letter usually takes five to ten days to reach Asia, Europe or the US.

Crime Rate

Violent crime in Australia is rare and the crime rate has fallen since 2000. However, burglary and car crime are common in the major cities.

Medical Facilities

Medical facilities are excellent. Australia has a compulsory contributory national health scheme called Medicare, which pays for 85 per cent of medical costs (known as the 'scheduled fee') and provides free hospital treatment. Australia has reciprocal health agreements giving restricted access to Medicare for visitors from nine countries: Ireland, Italy, Finland, Malta, the Netherlands, New Zealand, Norway, Sweden and the UK. Private health insurance is necessary for non-residents and retirees who aren't covered by Medicare. The private sector provides high quality healthcare.

9 Pets

Australia has strict quarantine laws to protect its unique wildlife and livestock. Quarantine length depends on which country the animal has been imported from. Pets from the Republic of Ireland and the UK must spend 30 days in quarantine on arrival in Australia. To import a pet (e.g. a cat or dog) you must obtain an import permit from the Australian Quarantine and Inspection Service (AQIS), GPO Box 858, Canberra ACT 2601, Australia (☎ 1800-020504 or 02-6272 3933, 🖥 www.aqis.gov.au).

Visas & Permits

Visas: Anyone wishing to visit Australia for any purpose requires a visa, which must be obtained before travelling. The only exception is New Zealand citizens, who may obtain a 'special category visa' on arrival. Regulations are constantly changing and it's wise to check the latest rules with an immigration consultant or Australian embassy. There are a variety of visa types, depending on the purpose of your visit, and you must ensure you have the correct one, without which you'll be refused permission to travel to Australia. There are four main categories of visa: visitor, student, temporary residence and migration. Multiple-entry visas are issued to those who need to visit frequently over a long period, such as businessmen.

Citizens of some countries may apply online for an electronic travel authority (ETA, 🖥 www.eta.immi.gov.au). You must apply for an ETA from outside Australia, and a visa is issued after being checked electronically by airlines and government agencies, thereby avoiding a visit to an embassy or consulate. If you wish to extend your visa, you must re-apply.

Residence Permits: Australia has an annual immigrant quota and immigration is decided on a points system, points being earned by age (or lack of it), skills and other factors, with preference given to those with special skills that are in demand and those wishing to start a business. Temporary residence is usually linked to employment (an individual must be sponsored by an employer) and is granted only for certain categories of skilled worker and professional, for contracts lasting between three months and four years. It must be shown that the post cannot be filled by an existing resident. There are, however, other ways of qualifying for Australian residence, including social and cultural reasons and 'international relations'.

Retirees who wish to live permanently in Australia must obtain an 'Investment Retirement Visa', for which they must be aged 55 or over and transfer at least A$800,000 or, if they have an annual pension or income of over A$50,000, at least A$200,000. They must also have comprehensive private medical cover, as this visa doesn't allow you access to Medicare. A visa is initially for four years, but unlimited two-year extensions are usually granted provided all the above requirements continue to be met.

Permanent residence gives you similar rights to an Australian citizen (although there are certain returning restrictions). More information can be found on the website of the Department of Immigration and Citizenship (🖥 www.immi.gov.au).

Work Permits: These are linked to visas and residence permits under the points system mentioned above. The Employer Nomination scheme allows Australian employers to nominate personnel for migration if they're unable to fill the post from the Australian labour market. An individual who has set up a business in the country while on a temporary business visa may apply for permanent residence under the Established Business in Australia system.

Reference

Further Reading

Buying a Home in Australia and New Zealand, Graeme Chesters (Survival Books). Everything you need to know about buying a home in Australia and New Zealand.

Living and Working in Australia, David Hampshire (Survival Books). Everything you need to know about living and working in Australia.

Australian Times, Blue Sky Publications Limited, 17 Heathmans Road, Parsons Green, London SW6 4TJ, UK (☎ 0845-456 4910, 🖥 www.australiantimes.co.uk).

Australian Outlook, Consyl Publishing, 13 London Road, Bexhill-on-Sea, East Sussex T39 3JR, UK (☎ 01424-223111, 🖥 www.consylpublishing.co.uk). Monthly publication with up-to-date information about all aspects of Australian life and migration policies.

9

Travel Australia and New Zealand, Consyl Publishing (as above). Leading newspaper with travel and visa information for visitors to Australia and New Zealand.

The Australian, GPO Box 4245 Sydney, NSW 2010, Australia (☎ 02-9288 3000, 🖳 www. theaustralian.news.com.au). Australia's national daily newspaper, available in print and online.

Useful Addresses

Australian Embassy (US), 1601 Massachusetts Ave., NW, Washington, DC 20036, US (☎ 202-797 3000, 🖳 www.usa.embassy.gov.au).

Australian High Commission (UK), Australia House, Strand, London WC2B 4LA, UK (☎ 020-7379 4334, 🖳 www.uk.embassy.gov.au).

Australian Tourist Commission (UK), Australia Centre, Australia House, 6th Floor, Melbourne Place, Strand, London WC2B 4LG, UK (☎ 020-7438 4601, 🖳 www.australia.com).

Australian Tourist Commission (US), 6100 Center Drive, Suite 1150, Los Angeles CA 90045, US (☎ 310-695 3200, 🖳 www.australia.com).

Foreign Investment Review Board, Department of the Treasury, Langton Crescent, Parkes, ACT 2600, Australia (☎ 02-6263 3795, 🖳 www.firb.gov.au). Provides information for non-residents and retirees about buying property in Australia.

Useful Websites

Australian Government (🖳 www.australia.gov.au). Excellent government website with extensive information on all aspects of life in Australia, including laws, regulations and news.

Australian Local Government (🖳 www.gov.au). Access to information and the services of the Australian state, territory and local governments.

Australian Government, Department of Foreign Affairs & Trade (🖳 www.dfat.gov.au). Excellent information and links for foreigners and investors.

Australian Government, Department of Immigration & Citizenship (🖳 www. immi.gov.au). Information on immigration requirements.

Real Estate Institute of Australia (🖳 www.reiaustralia.com.au). Latest information about the property market and links to all state Real Estate Institutes.

Reserve Bank of Australia (🖳 www.rba.gov.au).

Workingin.com (🖳 www.workingin-australia.com). Extensive information about working in Australia, visas, jobs and businesses.

AUSTRALASIA: NEW ZEALAND

Background Information

9

Capital: Wellington.
Population: 4.1m.

Foreign Community: New Zealand is largely a nation of immigrants (around 70 per cent of the population is of European descent) and a cosmopolitan country, although less so than Australia. The bulk of immigrants still come from the UK and most of the remainder from a few other European countries, although recent years have seen increasing numbers of Asian and South African immigrants. The indigenous Maori make up around 10 per cent of the population (some 400,000) and Polynesians (mostly from Fiji, Samoa and Tonga) 4.5 per cent. Auckland has the largest concentration of Polynesians in the world.

Area: 268,680km^2 (103,737mi^2).

Geography: New Zealand is in the South Pacific, some 2,200km (1,370mi) east of Australia. The country is almost 1,600km (994mi) long and 420km (260mi) wide at its widest point. It comprises two main islands, called North Island and South Island, which differ considerably in geography, vegetation and character. New Zealand also has a number of outlying islands, including the Stewart and Chatham Islands, and territories in the Pacific such as the Kermadec Islands and Kiribati. It's a mountainous country, with some three-quarters of the land over 200m (650ft) and over half forested. The highest peak is Mount Cook (3,764m/12,349ft) in South Island's Southern Alps, which divide the wet rain forest on the west coast from the dry pasture on the east coast. New Zealand is one of the world's most beautiful and unspoiled countries, some 30 per cent consisting of protected conservation sites. The country is noted for its wealth of volcanoes, geysers, glaciers, fjords, rivers and lush vegetation. The South Island in particular has an abundance of unspoiled mountain scenery and a thriving skiing industry.

Climate: Most of New Zealand has a temperate oceanic climate (except the far north, which is sub-tropical) and four distinct seasons that are opposite to those in the northern hemisphere. Summers (December to February) are warm or hot, winters (June to August) are cool or cold, temperatures sometimes dropping below freezing during the day on the east coast and snow not uncommon in Christchurch (South Island). The northern part of South Island generally has New Zealand's mildest weather and the most sunshine (an average of around 6.5 hours a day). Average rainfall in North Island is 135cm (53in) per year, while in South Island it varies considerably between the east and west coasts; it's very high (usually torrential) on the west coast, where many areas receive over 5m (195in) of rain per year. The eastern coasts of both islands are much drier, e.g. Auckland has rain on around 12 days a month in winter and six days a month in summer, while Christchurch has rain on around six days a month all year. New Zealand's major cities suffer from strong winds, Wellington vying with Chicago for the title 'Windy City'. New Zealand's temperatures are usually moderate (except in the mountains), averaging 23C (73F) in summer and 14C (57F) in winter in Auckland, 22C (72F) and 11C (52F) in Christchurch, 19C (66F) and 11C (52F) in Dunedin, and 20C (68F) and 14C (57F) in Wellington.

Language: English and Maori are the official languages, and most official signs and forms are bi-lingual.

Political Situation: Excellent. New Zealand is a parliamentary democracy modelled on the British system. Like Australia, New Zealand is a member of the British Commonwealth and Queen Elizabeth II is head of state, represented by the Governor General Anand Satyanand (since 2006). New Zealand has a multi-party system, with eight parties currently represented in Parliament. Since 1996, neither of the two main parties (the Labour Party, which is centre-left, and the National Party, which is centre-right) has been able to govern without the support of other parties in coalition. The current Prime Minister is Helen Clark of the Labour Party, who was first elected in 1999 and is now serving her third term. The leader of the Opposition is John Key of the National Party. The next election will be in 2008.

Finance

9

Currency

New Zealand's currency is the New Zealand dollar (NZ$), consisting of 100 cents.

Exchange Rates: £1 = NZ$2.67.

Exchange Controls: None, but the monitoring of foreign exchange transactions has increased since 1997. Financial institutions are required to verify the identity of customers and keep records. Anyone carrying more than NZ$10,000 in cash in or out of the country must report it to customs.

Cost & Standard of Living

New Zealand enjoys a high standard of living (the tenth-highest in the world according to a recent survey, and superior to Australia's). The cost of living is reasonable and food and essential goods and services are inexpensive. Imported goods such as motor vehicles and electrical goods are expensive, although prices have fallen in real terms in recent years. The average weekly salary is around NZ$1,000 (£375). Many New Zealanders own second homes (known as a *bach* or a *crib*) in the country or on the coast.

Taxation

Individuals are considered tax resident if they've lived in the country for over 183 days in a year or have a permanent home in New Zealand. Residents are taxed on their worldwide income. Non-residents pay tax only on income in New Zealand, unless the income is exempt under a double-taxation agreement.

Personal Effects: If you're intending to take up residence in New Zealand, you can import goods owned for 12 months (including a car) without payment of duty, subject to certain restrictions. Note that New Zealand has strict laws to protect its agricultural industries from pests and diseases: all personal effects including household goods and unaccompanied luggage require clearance by customs and the Ministry of Agriculture and Forestry, and it's worth employing a reputable and experienced customs agent to guide you through the process.

Income Tax: New Zealand has a PAYE system and income tax rates are 19.5 per cent (on income up to NZ$38,000), 33 per cent (NZ$38,000 to NZ$60,000) and 39 per cent (over NZ$60,000). In addition, employees pay an earners' levy (at a flat rate of 1.3 per cent) to cover the cost of non-work-related injuries.

Capital Gains Tax (CGT): None.

Wealth Tax: None.

Inheritance & Gift Tax: There's no inheritance tax. Gifts above NZ$27,000 in any year are taxed on a graduated scale up to 25 per cent (on gifts exceeding NZ$72,000).

Value Added Tax (VAT): New Zealand has a goods and services tax (GST) of 12.5 per cent. It's usually included in the advertised price rather than added when you pay (as in the US). There are various exemptions, including residential property, financial services and rented accommodation.

Property

9

Restrictions on Foreign Ownership & Letting

There are no restrictions for foreigners who are permanent residents or whose application for permanent residence is being processed (see **Residence Permits** below), and the Overseas Investment Act, 2005 relaxed restrictions for 'non-sensitive' land (mainly in urban areas). Non-resident foreigners can buy property and land of less than five hectares (12 acres) in non-sensitive areas without restriction, provided it isn't in or adjoining 'sensitive' land (including reserves, specified islands and historic or heritage land or lakes). If it's adjoining sensitive land, foreigners are permitted to buy only up to one acre without restriction; if it's adjoining the seafront, the limit is half an acre. Above these limits, permission is required from the Overseas Investment Office (OIO), formerly the Overseas Investment Board.

There are no restrictions on letting, but tax must be paid on rental income.

Market

New Zealand has a thriving property market, and some 75 per cent of families own their own homes. The Real Estate Institute of New Zealand (REINZ) reported in 2006 that the average house price had doubled since 1996. There's concern that many first-time buyers cannot afford to buy a home, but the New Zealand Institute of Economic Research believes that prices will stabilise between now and 2009 due to higher interest rates and higher prices for some imported goods.

The most common type of home in New Zealand is a single-storey detached house built on a plot known as a section – traditionally a quarter of an acre and dubbed 'the quarter-acre paradise' (although plots are now often smaller, as many sections have been split by developers). Apartments (usually called units) and townhouses are common in cities but rare elsewhere. Most homes are constructed of wood and brick, and there's a limited variety of architectural styles.

Areas

The most popular areas are the major cities: Auckland (North Island), Christchurch (South Island) and Wellington (the capital, at the southern tip of North Island). Auckland is the country's largest city and received substantial investment ahead of the 2003 America's Cup yachting competition. It has an attractive waterfront, with luxury apartments.

Popular regions for second homes are the Coromandel Peninsula and the Bay of Islands in the extreme north of North Island, and the Southern Alps, the Glaciers, Mount Cook and Milford Sound in South Island. The most popular areas for retirement homes in North Island include the Coromandel Peninsula, the Bay of Islands, the Bay of Plenty and the Kapati Coast (north of Wellington); in South Island, the northern Marlborough region (e.g. Blenheim, Nelson and Picton) is popular, as is Banks Peninsula, south of Christchurch.

Building Standards

Standards are generally high, although corrugated iron roofs and weatherboard (wooden) exterior walls are used on cheaper houses, which (paradoxically) don't always stand up well to the weather.

9

Cost

The average house price in New Zealand at the beginning of 2007 was around NZ$363,000 (£136,000). There are regional variations and the cities have seen the largest recent price growth, particularly Christchurch. Average prices in North Island towns are NZ$350,000 (£131,000), the most expensive area being the eastern suburbs of Auckland, with an average price of NZ$700,000 (£262,000). In Wellington, average prices are NZ$350,000 (£131,000), the most expensive part being east Wellington, at NZ$450,000 (£168,000). South Island towns are generally less expensive, with average house prices around NZ$300,000 (£112,000). The most expensive suburbs of Christchurch are by the coast, where the average price is NZ$450,000 (£168,000). Apartments are often more expensive than houses and townhouses, as they're invariably located in inner cities (inner city living has become fashionable in recent years), whereas most houses are in suburbs or the country. Advertised prices are usually up to 10 per cent above a property's 'market' value (i.e. the price you should expect to pay).

Local Mortgages

Mortgages of up to 80 per cent (95 per cent for New Zealand citizens and permanent residents) are available from all major banks and building societies. If you're a temporary resident with a work permit you typically have to fund at least 20 per cent and sometimes up to 50 per cent of the price, depending on the lender. Repayment mortgages are known as table mortgages. The maximum repayment term is 25 years.

Property Taxes

Property taxes (residential rates), which usually include water charges, are levied by local authorities according to the size of a property. The annual bill for an average family house is between NZ$1,000 (£375) and NZ$2,000 (£750); the average in Auckland is NZ$1,142 (£428). In some areas, there are additional fees for certain services, e.g. refuse collection and water.

Purchase Procedure

You can buy property by public auction or via a private contract. Before you make an offer on a property, obtain a copy of the relevant Land Information Memorandum (LIM) from the local council, which provides information about the property's 'zoning' (e.g. whether it's in a residential or industrial area), boundaries and building permissions. It costs around NZ$300 (£110). You can use the information in an LIM to negotiate the price. Your offer can also be conditional on identified faults being corrected by the seller. Conveyancing and searches can be done by a licensed conveyancer or a solicitor. New Zealand's land registry system is currently in the process of becoming electronic and by July 2008 the process should be complete. Known as Landonline (🖥 www.landonline.govt.nz), it provides all professionals with access to New Zealand's land registry and should speed up searches and new ownership registration. Once a price is agreed, a deposit of 10 per cent is payable and a binding contract is signed. The deposit is usually non-refundable, but most contracts include a clause requiring its return if the title to the property isn't clear or the land is subject to government requisition (compulsory purchase). The sale is usually completed within around three weeks.

It isn't wise to sign a contract before taking legal advice and confirming that the title is clear, as this commits you to the purchase. Many estate agents try to get purchasers to sign as soon as a sale is agreed. If you feel obliged to sign a contract before the conveyance checks are complete, you should ask your lawyer to insert a clause in the contract to the effect that it's is null and void if any problems arise.

Fees

Fees are low because there's no stamp duty. A lawyer's fees are usually between NZ$1,000 (£375) and NZ$2,000 (£750), a building inspection report costs around NZ$500 (£190), the optional LIM (see above) is around NZ$300 (£110) and the land transfer registration fee is NZ$150 (£55). Banks levy a mortgage processing fee of 1 per cent of the mortgage amount. An estate agent's fees are between 3 and 4 per cent plus goods and services tax and are normally paid by the vendor.

General Information

Getting There

New Zealand has two international airports, Auckland in North Island and Christchurch in South Island. (Wellington's airport is comparatively small and its short runway means that it cannot handle international flights, although it's a major domestic airport.) Many flights from the UK and Europe are operated by Qantas and British Airways and are routed via the US and Australia, some via Hong Kong.

Auckland International Airport: Auckland is the larger airport and is 21km (13mi) south of the city. It's the hub of the national airline, Air New Zealand, which operates direct flights from London Heathrow, as well as flights from Australia and Asia.

Christchurch International Airport: Christchurch airport is 12km (7.5mi) north-west of the city and mainly serves Australian and Asian destinations. It's about to undergo major renovation and some rebuilding, which is due to be completed in 2009.

Communications

The telecommunications market in New Zealand was privatised in 1990, although the former state-owned Telecom New Zealand, which has been severely criticised for high prices and poor service, still dominates the fixed-line market. Mobile use is widespread, as is internet use, but there's a shortage of lines suitable for broadband access. The country dialling code is 64 and international direct dialling (IDD) is available worldwide.

Fixed-line Telephones: Telecom New Zealand's main competitors in the fixed-line market are Ihug (a subsidiary of Vodaphone) and Vodafone New Zealand. There are public phone boxes in most towns and cities, which mostly accept credit cards and phone cards (available from newsagents); very few accept coins.

Mobile Telephones: Mobile penetration is over 90 per cent and the market is dominated by the same operators as the fixed-line market – Telecom New Zealand, TelstrarClear and Vodafone. Vodafone and TelstraClear operate on the GSM network and offer internet access via mobile phones; Telecom NZ operates on the 'Code Division Multiple Access' (CDMA) system.

Internet: Broadband access is limited, mainly due to inefficiency on the part of Telecom New Zealand. But the internet market is developing and a number of internet service providers (ISPs) began operating in 2005 and 2006. The main ISPs are Ihug (Vodafone), TelstraClear, and Xtra (Telecom New Zealand). There are internet cafes in the main towns and cities.

Postal Services: Postal services are provided by New Zealand Post, and letters take around five days to reach western Europe and two weeks to reach the US. Post offices are open Mondays to Fridays from 9am to 5pm.

9

Crime Rate

New Zealand is a safe country with a low rate of violent and serious crime. However, as in most other developed countries, crime has risen over the last decade, and pick-pocketing and other petty crime occurs in urban areas. There has also been an increase in car theft and theft from hotel rooms in tourist areas.

Medical Facilities

New Zealand has a high-quality national health system for residents, although there are long waiting lists for non-urgent hospital treatment. The state scheme doesn't pay for visits to a doctor (the cost of a consultation is between NZ$35 and NZ$50/£13-19), prescriptions (although they're subsidised), optometrists (opticians) or dental treatment for those over 18. Over 30 per cent of New Zealanders have supplementary private health insurance, which is highly recommended since it pays for the above treatment and private hospital care. Reciprocal agreements cover visitors from many countries, including the UK, and medical treatment for injuries sustained in accidents is provided free for all visitors.

Pets

The regulations for importing animals into New Zealand are rigorous and include vaccinations and veterinary checks. An import permit is required and most pets are subject to a quarantine period. The exceptions are animals from Australia, Hawaii, Norway, Sweden and the UK, which aren't subject to quarantine but must undergo veterinary checks. If your animal needs to be quarantined, you must contact the Ministry of Agriculture and Forestry in advance to book space in an approved quarantine facility (💻 www.biosecurity.govt.nz).

Visas & Permits

Visas: Citizens of many countries (check with a New Zealand embassy or consulate) don't require a visa to visit New Zealand for up to three months. Australian and British citizens and residents can visit for up to six months without a visa.

Residence Permits: New Zealand has an immigration quota system. Immigration is based on a points system, with priority given to those with skills that are in demand and those wishing to start a business. If you wish to become a resident, you must be 'sponsored' by a close family member who is already a resident, be part of the 'Work to Residence' scheme, be a 'skilled worker' or invest over NZ$2m in New Zealand. The Work to Residence scheme allows you temporary residence (usually for nine months) while the authorities assess your suitability for permanent residence – i.e. the extent to which you integrate with and contribute to Kiwi society. Temporary residence is also granted to those working for a relocation company and those with a job offer from a New Zealand company. Immigration New Zealand has further information on its website (💻 www.immigration.govt.nz).

Work Permits: Work permits (and residence permits) are issued by the immigration authorities to 'skilled migrant workers' under the Work to Residence scheme (see above).

9

Reference

Further Reading

Buying a Home in Australia and New Zealand, Graeme Chesters (Survival Books). Everything you need to know about buying a home in Australia and New Zealand.

Living and Working in New Zealand, Graeme Chesters (Survival Books). Everything you need to know about living and working in New Zealand.

Emigrate, Outbound Media and Exhibitions, 1 Commercial Road, Eastbourne, East Sussex, BN21 3XQ, UK (☎ 01323-726040, ⌨ www.emigrate2.co.uk). Extensive emigration information about a selection of countries, including New Zealand.

New Zealand Outlook, Consyl Publishing, 13 London Road, Bexhill-on-Sea, East Sussex T39 3JR, UK (☎ 01424-223111, ⌨ www.consylpublishing.co.uk). Monthly publication with up-to-date information about all aspects of life in New Zealand and migration policies.

Travel Australia and New Zealand, Consyl Publishing 13 London Road, Bexhill-on-Sea, East Sussex T39 3JR, UK (☎ 01424-223111, ⌨ www.consylpublishing.co.uk). Leading newspaper, with travel and visa information for visitors to Australia and New Zealand.

New Zealand News Ltd, Quadrant House, 250 Kennington Lane, London SE11 5RD, UK (☎ 0845-270 7902, ⌨ www.nznewsuk.co.uk). Excellent source of information for New Zealand expatriates in the UK and those wishing to migrate to New Zealand. Print and online version available (updated daily).

Background Information

Harcourts Real Estate, (Head Office) 7-9 Alpers Avenue, PO Box 99-549, Newmarket, Auckland, New Zealand (☎ 09-520 5569, ⌨ www.harcourts.co.nz). New Zealand's largest estate agency. Publishes *Blue Book* guides to the property market in the major areas of New Zealand.

Land Information New Zealand (LINZ), 160 Lambton Quay, PO Box 5501, Wellington, New Zealand (☎ 04-460 0110, ⌨ www.linz.govt.nz).

Ministry of Agriculture and Forestry, 25 The Terrace, PO Box 2526, Wellington, New Zealand (☎ 04-894 0100, ⌨ www.maf.govt.nz/quarantine).

New Zealand High Commission (UK), New Zealand House, 80 Haymarket, London SW1Y 4TQ, UK (☎ 020-7930 8422, ⌨ www.nzembassy.com).

New Zealand Embassy (US), 37 Observatory Circle, NW, Washington, DC 20008, US (☎ 202-328 4800, ⌨ www.nzemb.com).

Overseas Investment Office, Land Information New Zealand, 160 Lambton Quay, Private Box 501, Wellington, New Zealand (☎ 04-462 4490, ⌨ www.linz.govt.nz).

Real Estate Institute New Zealand (REINZ), PO Box 1247, Wellington, New Zealand (☎ 04-472 8942, ⌨ www.reinz.org.nz).

Tourism New Zealand (UK), New Zealand House, Haymarket, London SW1Y 4TQ, UK (☎ 020-7930 1662, ⌨ www.newzealand.com).

Tourism New Zealand (US), Suite 2510, 222 East 41st Street, New York, NY 10017, US (☎ 212-661 7088, ⌨ www.newzealand.com).

9

Useful Websites

Immigration New Zealand (⌨ http://immigration.govt.nz). Excellent government website with extensive information about migration to New Zealand.

Emigrate2 (⌨ http://www.emigrate2.com). Good information about a number of countries, including New Zealand.

9

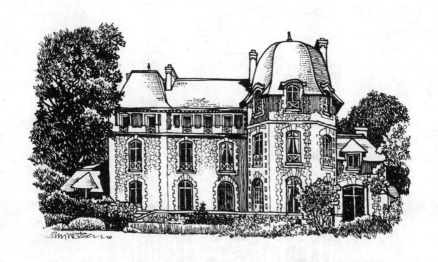

INDEX

SURVIVAL BOOKS

Survival Books was established in 1987 and by the mid-'90s was the leading publisher of books for people planning to live, work, buy property or retire abroad.

From the outset, our philosophy has been to provide the most comprehensive and up-to-date information available. Our titles routinely contain up to twice as much information as rival books and are updated frequently. All our books contain colour photographs and some are printed in two colours or full colour throughout. They also contain original cartoons, illustrations and maps.

Survival Books are written by people with first-hand experience of the countries and the people they describe, and therefore provide invaluable insights that cannot be obtained from official publications or websites, and information that is more reliable and objective than that provided by the majority of unofficial sites.

Survival Books are designed to be easy – and interesting – to read. They contain a comprehensive list of contents and index and extensive appendices, including useful addresses, further reading, useful websites and glossaries to help you obtain additional information as well as metric conversion tables and other useful reference material.

Our primary goal is to provide you with the essential information necessary for a trouble-free life or property purchase and to save you time, trouble and money.

We believe our books are the best – they are certainly the best-selling. But don't take our word for it – read what reviewers and readers have said about Survival Books at the front of this book.

To see our current list of titles, visit our website: **www.survivalbooks.net**

CULTURE WISE SERIES
The Essential Guides to Culture, Customs & Business Etiquette

Our **Culture Wise** series of guides is essential reading for anyone who want to understand how a country really 'works'. Whether you're planning to stay for a few days or a lifetime, these guides will help you quickly find you feet and settle into your new surroundings.

Culture Wise guides reduce the anxiety factor in adapting to a foreign culture; explain how to behave in everyday situations in order to avoid cultural and social gaffes; help you get along with your neighbours, make friends and establish lasting business relationships; and enhance your understanding of a country and its people.

People often underestimate the extent of the cultural isolation they can face abroad, particularly in a country with a different language. At first glance, many countries seem an 'easy' option, often with millions of visitors from all corners of the globe and well-established expatriate communities. But, sooner or later, newcomers find that most countries are indeed 'foreign' and many come unstuck as a result.

Culture Wise guides will enable you to quickly adapt to the local way of life and feel at home, and – just as importantly – avoid the worst effects of culture shock.

Culture Wise – the wise way to travel

To see our current list of titles, visit our website: **www.survivalbooks.net**

LIVING AND WORKING SERIES

O ur ***Living and Working*** guides are essential reading for anyone planning to spend a period abroad, whether it's an extended holiday or permanent migration, and are packed with priceless information designed to help you avoid costly mistakes and save you both time and money.

Living and Working guides are the most comprehensive and up-to-date source of practical information available about everyday life abroad. They aren't, however, simply a catalogue of dry facts and figures, but are written in a highly readable style - entertaining, practical and occasionally humorous.

Our aim is to provide you with the comprehensive practical information necessary for a trouble free life. You may have visited a country as a tourist, but living and working there is a different matter altogether; adjusting to a different environment and culture and making a home in any foreign country can be a traumatic and stressful experience. You need to adapt to new customs and traditions, discover the local way of doing things (such as finding a home, paying bills and obtaining insurance) and learn all over again how to overcome the everyday obstacles of life.

All these subjects and many, many more are covered in depth in our *Living and Working* guides – don't leave home without them!

To see our current list of titles, visit our website: **www.survivalbooks.net**

BUYING A HOME SERIES

B uying a home abroad is not only a major financial transaction but also a potentially life-changing experience; it's therefore essential to get it right. Our *Buying a Home* guides are required reading for anyone planning to purchase property abroad and are packed with vital information to guide you through the property jungle and help you avoid disasters that can turn a dream home into a nightmare.

The purpose of our *Buying a Home* guides is to enable you to choose the most favourable location and the most appropriate property for your requirements, and to reduce your risk of making an expensive mistake by making informed decisions and calculated judgements rather than uneducated and hopeful guesses. Most importantly, they will help you save money and will repay your investment many times over.

Buying a Home guides are the most comprehensive and up-to-date source of information available about buying property abroad – whether you're seeking a detached house or an apartment, a holiday or a permanent home (or an investment property), these books will prove invaluable.

To see our current list of titles, visit our website: **www.survivalbooks.net**

OTHER SURVIVAL BOOKS

A New Life Abroad: The most comprehensive book available for anyone planning to live, work or retire abroad, containing surveys of over 50 countries.

The Best Places to Buy a Home in France/Spain: Unique guides to where to buy property in France and Spain, containing regional profiles and market reports.

Buying, Selling and Letting Property: The best source of information about buying, selling and letting property in the UK.

Earning Money From Your Home: Essential guides to earning income from property in France and Spain, including short- and long-term letting.

Foreigners in France/Spain: Triumphs & Disasters: Real-life experiences of people who have emigrated to France and Spain, recounted in their own words.

Investing in Property Abroad: Essential reading for anyone planning to buy property abroad, containing surveys of over 30 countries.

Making a Living: Comprehensive guides to self-employment and starting a business in France and Spain.

Renovating & Maintaining Your French Home: The ultimate guide to renovating and maintaining your dream home in France.

Retiring in France/Spain: Everything a prospective retiree needs to know about the two most popular international retirement destinations.

Running Gîtes and B&Bs in France: An essential book for anyone planning to invest in a gîte or bed & breakfast business in France.

Rural Living in France: An invaluable book for anyone seeking the 'good life' in France, containing a wealth of practical information about all aspects of country life.

Shooting Caterpillars in Spain: The hilarious and compelling story of two innocents abroad in the depths of Andalusia in the late '80s.

Wild Thyme in Ibiza: A fragrant account of how a three-month visit to the enchanted island of Ibiza in the mid-'60s turned into a 20-year sojourn.

To see our current list of titles, visit our website: **www.survivalbooks.net**